lonely planet

Scotland

**Orkney &
Shetland**
p397

**Northern Highlands
& Islands**
p347

**Northeast
Scotland**
p210

**Inverness & the
Central Highlands**
p293

**Southern
Highlands &
Islands**
p241

**Central
Scotland**
p177

Edinburgh
p48

Glasgow
p106

**Southern
Scotland**
p140

D1424279

C016714385

Contents

HIGHLAND HORSE, SHETLAND P416

EDINBURGH P48

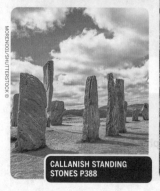

CALLANISH STANDING STONES P388

Contents

ON THE ROAD

LOCH LUBNAIG P252

Contents

UNDERSTAND

Scotland Today	430
History	432
The Scottish Larder	440
Scottish Culture	446
Natural Scotland	452

PUFFINS, LUNGA P288

MACALLAN WHISKY P238

Welcome to Scotland

Scotland has many treasures crammed into its compact territory – big skies, ancient architecture, spectacular wildlife, superb seafood and hospitable, down-to-earth people.

Outdoor Adventure

Scotland harbours some of the largest wilderness areas left in Western Europe. In this wildlife haven you can see golden eagles soar above the lochs and mountains of the northern Highlands, spot otters tumbling in the kelp along the shores of the Outer Hebrides, and watch minke whales breach off the coast of Mull. Scotland's also an adventure playground: you can tramp the tundra plateaus of the Cairngorms, balance along tightrope ridges strung between the peaks of the Cuillin, sea kayak among the seal-haunted isles of the Outer Hebrides, and take a speedboat ride into the white water of the Corryvreckan whirlpool.

Turbulent History

Scotland is a land with a rich, multilayered history, a place where every corner of the landscape is steeped in the past – a deserted croft on an island shore, a moor that was once a battlefield, a cave that sheltered Bonnie Prince Charlie. Hundreds of castles, from the plain but forbidding tower houses of Hermitage and Smailholm to the elaborate machicolated fortresses of Caerlaverock and Craigmillar, testify to the country's often turbulent past. And battles that played a pivotal part in the building of a nation are remembered and brought to life at sites such as Bannockburn and Culloden.

A Taste of Scotland

Visitors have discovered that Scotland's restaurants have shaken off their old reputation for deep-fried food and unsmiling service and can now compete with the best in Europe. A new-found respect for top-quality local produce means that you can feast on fresh seafood mere hours after it was caught, beef and venison that was raised just a few miles away from your table, and vegetables that were grown in your hotel's own organic garden. Top it all off with a dram of single-malt whisky – rich, complex and evocative, it's the true flavour of Scotland.

The Culture

Be it the poetry of Robert Burns, the crime fiction of Ian Rankin or the songs of Emeli Sandé, Scotland's cultural exports are appreciated around the world every bit as much as whisky, tweed and tartan. But you can't beat reading Burns' poems in the village where he was born, enjoying an Inspector Rebus novel in Rankin's own Edinburgh, or catching the latest Scottish bands at a music festival. And museums such as Glasgow's Kelvingrove, Dundee's Discovery Point and Aberdeen's Maritime Museum celebrate the influence of Scottish artists, engineers, explorers, writers and inventors in shaping the modern world.

Why I Love Scotland

By Neil Wilson, Writer

It's the weather. Yes, seriously. We get four proper seasons here (sometimes all of them in one day) and that means that you get to enjoy the same landscapes over and over again in a range of different garbs – August hills clad in purple heather, native woodlands gilded with autumn colours, snow-patched winter mountains, and Hebridean machair sprinkled with a confetti of spring wildflowers. The unpredictability of the weather means that even the wettest day can be suddenly transformed by parting clouds and slanting shafts of golden light. Sheer magic.

For more about our writers, see p480

Above: The Trossachs (p248)

Scotland

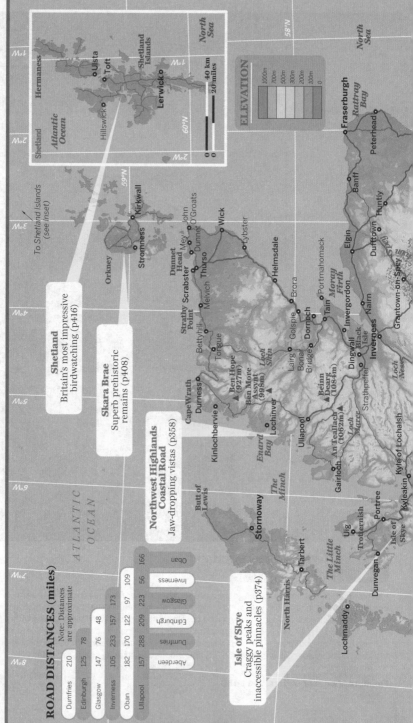

ROAD DISTANCES (miles)

Note: Distances are approximate

	Dumfries	Edinburgh	Glasgow	Inverness	Oban	Ullapool
Dumfries	210					
Edinburgh	125	78				
Glasgow	147	76	48			
Inverness	105	233	157	173		
Oban	182	170	122	97	109	
Ullapool	157	288	209	223	56	166
	Aberdeen	Dumfries	Edinburgh	Glasgow	Inverness	Oban

Shetland
Britain's most impressive birdwatching (p416)

Skara Brae
Superb prehistoric remains (p408)

Northwest Highlands
Coastal Road
Jaw-dropping vistas (p358)

Isle of Skye
Craggy peaks and inaccessible pinnacles (p374)

ELEVATION

1000m
700m
500m
300m
200m
100m
0

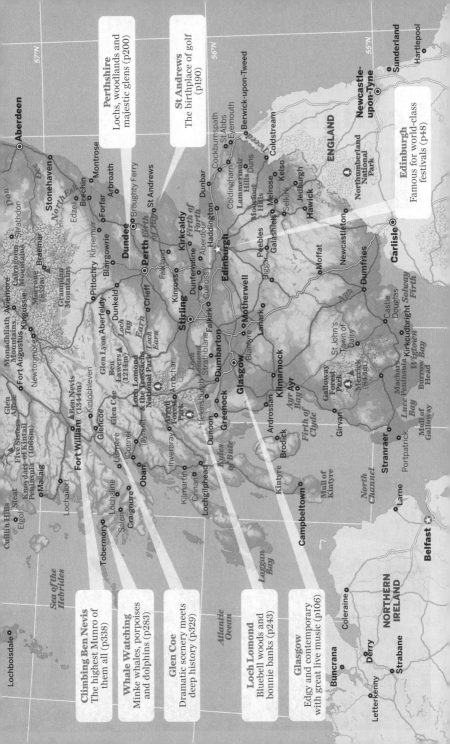

Perthshire
Lochs, woodlands and majestic glens (p200)

St Andrews
The birthplace of golf (p190)

Edinburgh
Famous for world-class festivals (p48)

Climbing Ben Nevis
The highest Munro of them all (p338)

Whale Watching
Minke whales, porpoises and dolphins (p283)

Glen Coe
Dramatic scenery meets deep history (p329)

Loch Lomond
Bluebell woods and bonnie banks (p243)

Glasgow
Edgy and contemporary with great live music (p106)

Scotland's
Top 16

Isle of Skye

1 In a country famous for stunning scenery, the Isle of Skye (p374) takes top prize. From the craggy peaks of the Cuillins and the bizarre pinnacles of the Old Man of Storr (p383; pictured) and the Quiraing to the spectacular sea cliffs of Neist Point, there's a photo opportunity awaiting you at almost every turn. Walkers can share the landscape with red deer and golden eagles, and refuel at the end of the day in convivial pubs and top seafood restaurants.

Edinburgh

2 Scotland's capital may be famous for its festivals, but there's much more to the city than that. Edinburgh (p48) is a place of many moods: visit out of season to see the Old Town silhouetted against a blue spring sky and a yellow haze of daffodils, or on a chill December morning with the fog snagging the spires of the Royal Mile, rain on the cobblestones and a warm glow beckoning from the window of a pub.

WESTEND61 GMBH/ALAMY ©

JOHN BRACEGIRDLE /ALAMY ©

Loch Lomond

3 Despite being less than an hour's drive from the bustle and sprawl of Glasgow, the bonnie banks and braes of Loch Lomond (p243) – immortalised in the words of one of Scotland's best-known songs – comprise one of the most scenic parts of the country. At the heart of Scotland's first national park, the loch begins as a broad, island-peppered lake in the south, its shores clothed in bluebell woods, narrowing in the north to a fjord-like trench ringed by 900m-high mountains.

Climbing Ben Nevis

4 The allure of Britain's highest peak is strong – around 100,000 people a year set off up the summit trail, though not all make it to the top. Nevertheless, the highest Munro of them all is within reach of anyone who's reasonably fit. Treat Ben Nevis (p338) with respect and your reward (weather permitting) will be a truly magnificent view and a great sense of achievement. Real walking enthusiasts can warm up by hiking the 96-mile West Highland Way first.

Marine Wildlife Watching

5 Scotland is one of the best places in Europe for seeing marine wildlife. In the high season (July and August) many cruise operators on the west coast can almost guarantee sightings of minke whales and porpoises, and the Moray Firth is famous for its resident population of bottlenose dolphins (pictured). Basking sharks – at up to 12m, the biggest fish to be found in British waters – are another common sighting. Tobermory (p243) and Easdale (near Oban) are top departure points.

Walking the West Highland Way

6 The best way to really get inside Scotland's landscapes is to walk them. Despite the wind, midges and drizzle, walking here is a pleasure, with numerous short- and long-distance trails, hills and mountains begging to be tramped. Top of the wish-list for many hikers is the 96-mile West Highland Way (p34) from Milngavie (near Glasgow) to Fort William, a challenging weeklong walk through some of the country's finest scenery, finishing in the shadow of its highest peak, Ben Nevis.

Glasgow

7 Scotland's biggest city (p106) lacks Edinburgh's classical beauty, but it more than makes up for it with a barrelful of things to do and a warmth and energy that leave every visitor impressed. Edgy and contemporary, it's a great spot to browse art galleries and museums, and to discover the works of local hero Charles Rennie Mackintosh. Add what is perhaps Britain's best pub culture and one of the world's best live-music scenes, and the only thing to do is live it.

Northwest Highlands

8 The Highlands abound in breathtaking views, but the far northwest is where things become truly awe-inspiring. The coastal road that runs between Durness and Kyle of Lochalsh offers jaw-dropping scenes at every turn: the rugged mountains of Assynt (p347), the desolate beauty of Torridon and the remote cliffs of Cape Wrath. These and the nooks of warm Highland hospitality found in the region's classic rural pubs make this an unforgettable corner of the country. Eilean Donan Castle (p373)

Golf

9 Scotland invented the game of golf and is still revered as its spiritual home by hackers and champions alike. Links courses are the classic experience here – bumpy coastal affairs where the rough is heather and machair and the main enemy is the wind, which can make a disaster of a promising round in an instant. St Andrews (pictured; p190), the historic Fife university town, is golf's headquarters, and an irresistible destination for anyone who loves the sport.

Perthshire – Big Tree Country

10 Blue-grey lochs shimmer, reflecting the changing moods of the weather; venerable trees, centuries old, tower amid riverside forests; majestic glens scythe their way into remote wildernesses; and salmon leap upriver to the place of their birth. In Perthshire (p320), the heart of Scotland, picturesque towns bloom with flowers, distilleries emit tempting malty odours and sheep graze in impossibly green meadows. There's a feeling of the bounty of nature that no other place in Scotland can replicate. The Queen's View (p325), Loch Tummel

Glen Coe

11 Scotland's most famous glen (p329) combines those two essential qualities of the Highlands landscape: dramatic scenery and deep history. The peace and beauty of this valley today belie the fact that it was the scene of a ruthless 17th-century massacre, when the local MacDonalds were murdered by soldiers of the Campbell clan. Some of the glen's finest walks – to the Lost Valley, for example – follow the routes used by clanspeople trying to flee their attackers, and where many perished in the snow. The Lost Valley (p329)

Whisky

12 Scotland's national drink – from the Gaelic *uisge bagh,* meaning 'water of life' – has been distilled here for more than 500 years. More than 100 distilleries are still in operation, producing hundreds of varieties of single malt, with new ones opening every year. Learning to distinguish the smoky, peaty whiskies of Islay (p262) from, say, the flowery, sherried malts of Speyside has become a hugely popular pastime. Many distilleries offer guided tours, rounded off with a tasting session, and ticking off the local varieties is a great way to explore the whisky-making regions.

Ardbeg distillery (p263)

Birdwatching in Shetland

13 Sparsely populated, and with large areas of wild land, Scotland is an important sanctuary for all sorts of wildlife. Amazing birdwatching is on offer throughout the country, but the seabird cities of the Shetland Islands take first prize for spectacle. From their first arrival in late spring to the raucous feeding frenzies of high summer, the vast colonies of gannets, guillemots, puffins (pictured) and kittiwakes at Hermaness (p426), Noss and Sumburgh Head provide one of British birdwatching's most impressive experiences.

Island Hopping

14 Much of the unique character of western and northern Scotland is down to its expansive vistas of sea and islands – there are almost 800 islands off Scotland's coast, of which almost 100 are inhabited. A network of ferry services links these islands to the mainland and each other, providing a fascinating way to explore. It's possible to hop all the way from Arran or Bute to the Outer Hebrides, touching the mainland only at Kintyre and Oban (pictured).

Castles

15 Desolate stone fortresses looming in the mist, majestic strongholds such as Stirling Castle (pictured; p178) towering over historic towns, or luxurious palaces built on expansive grounds by lairds more concerned with pampering than with defence: Scotland has a full range of castles that reflect its turbulent history and its tense relations with its southern neighbour. Most castles have a story (or 10) to tell of plots, intrigues, imprisonments and treachery – as well as a ghost rumoured to stalk their halls.

Skara Brae

16 When visiting ancient sites it can be difficult to bridge the gulf of years or sense a connection with the people that built them, but Scotland's superb prehistoric remains have an immediate impact. Few places offer a better glimpse of everyday Stone Age life than Skara Brae (p408) in Orkney, with its carefully constructed fireplaces, beds, cupboards and water cisterns. Buried in coastal sand dunes for centuries, it can feel as though the inhabitants have just slipped out to go fishing and could return at any moment.

15

16

Need to Know

For more information, see Survival Guide (p455)

Currency
Pound sterling (£)

Language
English, Gaelic and Lallans

Visas
Generally not needed for stays of up to six months. The UK is not a member of the Schengen Area.

Money
ATMs widely available; credit cards widely accepted, though not in all restaurants or B&Bs.

Mobile Phones
The UK uses the GSM 900/1800 network. Local SIM cards can be used in unlocked phones.

Time
Greenwich Mean Time

Driving
In Scotland, drive on the left.

When to Go

Cool to mild summers, cold winters

Lerwick
GO mid-May–mid-July

Stornoway
GO May–Sep

Inverness
GO May–Sep

Fort William
GO May–Sep

Edinburgh
GO year-round

High Season
(Jul & Aug)

➡ Accommodation prices 10% to 20% higher (book ahead if possible).

➡ Warmest time of year, but often wet.

➡ Midges at their worst in Highlands and islands.

Shoulder
(May, Jun & Sep)

➡ Wildflowers and rhododendrons bloom in May and June.

➡ Statistically, the best chance of dry weather, minus midges.

➡ June evenings have daylight till 11pm.

Low Season
(Oct–Apr)

➡ Rural attractions and accommodation often closed.

➡ Snow on the hills November to March.

➡ Gets dark at 4pm in December.

➡ Can be very cold and wet from November to March.

Useful Websites

Lonely Planet (lonelyplanet.com/scotland) Destination information, hotel bookings, traveller forum and more.

VisitScotland (www.visitscotland.com) Official tourism site; booking services.

Internet Guide to Scotland (www.scotland-info.co.uk) Best online tourist guide to Scotland.

Traveline (www.travelinescotland.com) Up-to-date public-transport timetables.

ScotlandsPeople (www.scotlandspeople.gov.uk) Official genealogical website that lets you search the indexes to old parish registers and statutory registers, as well as census returns, on a pay-per-view basis.

Important Numbers

Country code	☎44
International access code	☎00
Emergencies	☎112 or ☎999
Police (non-emergencies)	☎101

Exchange Rates

Australia	A$1	£0.57
Canada	C$1	£0.59
Euro zone	€1	£0.89
Japan	¥100	£0.69
New Zealand	NZ$1	£0.53
USA	US$1	£0.78

For current exchange rates, see www.xe.com.

Daily Costs

Budget: Less than £40

➡ Dorm bed: £13–25

➡ Wild camping: free

➡ Takeaway fish and chips: £4–7

Midrange: £40–130

➡ Double room at midrange B&B: £60–100

➡ Bar lunch: £12

➡ Dinner at midrange restaurant: £30

➡ Car hire per day: £36

➡ Petrol costs per mile: around 15p

Top End: More than £130

➡ Double room at high-end hotel: £130–250

➡ Dinner at high-end restaurant: £40–60

➡ One-way flight to islands: £65–130

Opening Hours

Hours may vary throughout the year; in rural areas many places have shorter hours from around October to April. In the Highlands and islands Sunday opening is restricted.

Banks 9.30am–4pm Monday to Friday, some to 1pm Saturday.

Post offices 9am–6pm Monday to Friday, to 12.30pm Saturday.

Nightclubs 9pm–1am Thursday to Saturday.

Pubs 11am–11pm Monday to Thursday, to 1am Friday and Saturday, 12.30pm–11pm Sunday; lunch noon–2.30pm, dinner 6pm–9pm daily.

Shops 9am–5.30pm Monday to Saturday, often 11am–5pm Sunday.

Restaurants Lunch noon–2.30pm, dinner 6pm–9pm.

Arriving in Scotland

Edinburgh Airport Bus 100 runs from the airport to Waverley Bridge (one way/return £4.50/7.50, 30 minutes), every 10 minutes from 4am to midnight and every 30 minutes through the night. Trams run from the airport to the city centre (one way/return £6/8.50, 33 minutes, every six to eight minutes from 6am to midnight). An airport taxi to the city centre costs around £20 and takes 20 to 30 minutes.

Glasgow Airport Bus 500 runs every 10 or 15 minutes (half-hourly or hourly late at night, 24 hours a day) from Glasgow Airport to Buchanan bus station (single/return £8/12, 25 minutes). A taxi costs around £25.

Getting Around

Transport in Scotland can be expensive compared to the rest of Europe; bus and rail services are sparse in the more remote parts of the country. For up-to-date timetables, visit Traveline Scotland (www.travelinescotland.com).

Car Useful for travelling at your own pace, or for visiting regions with minimal public transport. Cars can be hired in cities and major towns. Drive on the left.

Train Relatively expensive, with extensive coverage and frequent departures in central Scotland, but only a few lines in the northern Highlands and southern Scotland.

Bus Cheaper and slower than trains, but useful for more remote regions that aren't serviced by rail.

Boat A network of car ferries links the mainland to the islands of western and northern Scotland.

For much more on **getting around**, see p465

First Time Scotland

For more information, see Survival Guide (p455)

Checklist

➡ Make sure your passport is valid for at least six months past your arrival date.

➡ Make all necessary bookings (for accommodation, events and travel).

➡ Check airline baggage restrictions.

➡ Inform your debit-/credit-card company of your travels.

➡ Arrange appropriate travel insurance.

➡ Check if you can use your mobile (cell) phone.

What to Pack

➡ Passport

➡ Driving licence

➡ Good walking shoes or boots

➡ Waterproof jacket

➡ Camera

➡ UK electrical adapter

➡ Insect repellent

➡ Binoculars

➡ Hangover cure (all that whisky, you know)

Top Tips for Your Trip

➡ Quality rather than quantity should be your goal: instead of a hair-raising race to see everything, pick a handful of destinations and give yourself time to linger. The most memorable experiences in Scotland are often the ones where you're doing very little.

➡ If you're driving, get off the main roads when you can. Some of the country's most stunning scenery is best enjoyed on secondary or tertiary roads that wind their narrow way through standout photo ops.

➡ Make the effort to greet the locals. The best experiences of Scotland are to be had courtesy of the Scots themselves, whose helpfulness, friendliness and fun has not been exaggerated.

➡ Be prepared for midges – tiny biting flies that can make life a misery in summer in the Highlands. Bring along insect repellent, antihistamine cream and long-sleeved shirts and trousers.

What to Wear

Scotland is a fairly casual destination and you can wear pretty much whatever you like all the time. For fancy dinners, smart casual is all that's required. No restaurant will insist on jackets or ties, nor will any theatre or concert hall.

Summer days can be warm but rarely hot, so you'll always want something around your legs and shoulders when the inevitable cool sets in.

In the end, the factor that will determine your outfits the most is the weather, which also means that a light, waterproof jacket should always be close at hand.

Sleeping

Book in advance, especially in summer, at weekends, and on islands (where options are often limited). Book at least two months ahead for July and August.

B&Bs Small, family-run houses that are generally good value. More luxurious versions resemble boutique hotels.

Hotels Range from half-a-dozen rooms above a pub to restored country houses and castles, with a commensurate variety of rates.

Hostels A good choice of institutional and independent hostels, many housed in historic buildings.

Money

➡ The British currency is the pound sterling (£), with 100 pence (p) to a pound. 'Quid' is the slang term for pound.

➡ Three Scottish banks issue their own banknotes, meaning there's quite a variety of different notes in circulation. They are legal currency in England, too, but you'll sometimes run into problems changing them. They are also harder to exchange once you get outside the UK.

➡ Euros are accepted in Scotland only at some major tourist attractions and a few upmarket hotels – it's always better to use sterling.

Bargaining

A bit of mild haggling is acceptable at flea markets and antique shops, but everywhere else you're expected to pay the advertised price.

Tipping

Hotels One pound per bag is standard; gratuities for cleaning staff are completely at your discretion.

Pubs Not expected unless table service is provided, then £1 for a round of drinks.

Restaurants For decent service 10%; up to 15% at more expensive places. Check to see if service has been added to the bill already (most likely for large groups).

Taxis Fares are generally rounded up to the nearest pound.

A pub in Edinburgh (p48)

Etiquette

Although largely informal in their everyday dealings, the Scots do observe some rules of etiquette.

Greetings Shake hands with men, women and children when meeting for the first time and when saying goodbye. Scots expect a firm handshake with eye contact.

Conversation Generally friendly but often reserved, the Scots avoid conversations that might embarrass.

Language The Scots speak English with an accent that varies in strength – in places such as Glasgow and Aberdeen it can often be indecipherable. Oddly, native Gaelic speakers often have the most easily understood accent when speaking English.

Table service In general, cafes have table service, but pubs do not. In some pubs, you should order food at the bar (after noting your table number); others will have food waiters to take your order.

Buying your round at the pub Like the English, Welsh and Irish, Scots generally take it in turns to buy a round of drinks for the whole group, and everyone is expected to take part. The next round should always be bought before the previous round is finished. In pubs, you are expected to pay for drinks when you order them.

Eating

You'll have plenty of choice for eating (p440) in Scotland. It's wise to book ahead for midrange restaurants, especially at weekends. Top-end restaurants should be booked at least a couple of weeks in advance.

Cafes Open during daytime (rarely after 6pm), cafes are good for a casual breakfast or lunch, or simply a cup of coffee.

Pubs Most of Scotland's pubs serve reasonably priced meals, and many can compete with restaurants on quality.

Restaurants Scotland's restaurants range from cheap and cheerful to Michelin starred, and they cover every cuisine you can imagine.

What's New

Dundee Waterfront

The redevelopment of Dundee's waterfront continues, graced by a stunning new building – opened in September 2018 – that is home to an outpost of London's Victoria & Albert Museum. (p212)

Northeast 250

The success of the North Coast 500 has seen the launch of another scenic driving route, this time linking the spectacular coastline of Aberdeenshire and Moray with the Cairngorms National Park and Royal Deeside. (p240)

Newport

The restaurant established by the 2016 winner of the UK TV series *Masterchef,* Jamie Scott, serves superb Scottish cuisine in a stunning setting overlooking the Firth of Tay. Book well in advance... (p210)

Mackintosh at the Willow

Launched in 2018 to celebrate Mackintosh's 150th anniversary, this elaborate recreation of his famous Sauchiehall St tearoom in the original premises is a major project that includes a visitor exhibition. (p110)

Great Trossachs Path

This newly designated 30-mile walking trail links Callander to Loch Lomond, with the chance to overnight in new camping pods at Loch Katrine. (p243)

A'Challtain

This sustainable fish restaurant is at the heart of a rejuvenation of Glasgow's Barras market area, which has brought new life to the weekend scene here without altering its traditional character. (p127)

Arran Art Trail

This initiative brings together some of Arran's many creatives, providing visitors with a series of studios, galleries and workshops to investigate. (p272)

Lindores Abbey Distillery

New distilleries are popping up like mushrooms across the country. The one that's got whisky aficionados most excited is Lindores Abbey in Fife, built on the site of the earliest recorded reference to whisky (1494). (p188)

Falls of Shin

A smart new visitor centre with a likeable community-run cafe has opened at this classic Highland locale near Lairg, long famous as a place to spot salmon leaping up the waterfalls. (p352)

New Waverley

This modern development linking Edinburgh's Old Town with Waverley train station opened in 2018 with a new public square, a gaggle of hotels, and restored railway arches housing quirky shops and bars (http://newwaverley.com).

For more recommendations and reviews, see **lonelyplanet.com/ scotland**

If You Like...

Castles

The clash and conflict of Scotland's colourful history has left a legacy of military strongholds scattered across the country, from the border castles raised against English incursions to the island fortresses that controlled the seaways for the Lords of the Isles.

Edinburgh Castle The biggest, the most popular and the Scottish capital's reason for being. (p51)

Stirling Castle Perched on a volcanic crag at the top of the town, this historic royal fortress and palace has the lot. (p178)

Craigievar Castle The epitome of the Scottish Baronial style, all towers and turrets. (p236)

Culzean Castle Enormous, palatial 18th-century mansion in a romantic coastal setting. (p162)

Eilean Donan The perfect lochside location just by the main road to Skye makes this the Highlands' most photographed castle. (p347)

Hermitage Castle Bleak and desolate borderland fortress speaking of a turbulent relationship with England. (p162)

Wild Beaches

Nothing clears a whisky hangover like a walk along a wind-whipped shoreline, and Scotland is blessed with a profusion of wild beaches. The west coast in particular has many fine stretches of blinding-white sands and turquoise waters that could pass for the Caribbean if not for the weather.

Kiloran Bay A perfect curve of deep golden sand – the ideal vantage point for stunning sunsets. (p269)

Sandwood Bay A sea stack, a ghost story and 2 miles of windblown sand – who could ask for more? (p361)

Bosta A beautiful and remote cove filled with white sand beside a reconstructed Iron Age house. (p388)

Durness A series of pristine sandy coves and duney headlands surrounds this northwestern village. (p360)

Scousburgh Sands Shetland's finest beach is a top spot for birdwatching as well as a bracing walk. (p424)

Orkney's Northern Islands Most have spectacular stretches of white sand with seabirds galore and seals lazing on the rocks. (p413)

Good Food

Scotland's chefs have an enviable range of quality meat, game, seafood and vegetables at their disposal. The country has shaken off its once dismal culinary reputation as the land of deep-fried Mars Bars and now boasts countless regional specialities, farmers markets, artisan cheesemakers, smokeries and microbreweries.

Ondine Sustainably sourced seafood at one of Edinburgh's finest restaurants. (p82)

Café 1 International menu based on quality Scottish produce at this Inverness bistro. (p299)

Café Fish Perched on the Tobermory waterfront, serving fresh seafood and shellfish straight off the boat. (p285)

Monachyle Mhor Utterly romantic location deep in the Trossachs and wonderful food with sound sustainable principles. (p252)

Peat Inn One of Scotland's most acclaimed restaurants sits in a hamlet amid the peaceful Fife countryside. (p196)

Gamba In the top rank of Glasgow's seafood restaurants, serving sustainably sourced fish from Scotland and beyond. (p125)

Outdoor Adventures

Scotland is one of Europe's finest outdoor-adventure playgrounds. The rugged mountain terrain and convoluted coastline of the Highlands and islands offer unlimited opportunities for hiking, mountain biking, surfing and snowboarding.

Fort William The self-styled Outdoor Capital of the UK, a centre for hiking, climbing, mountain biking, winter sports... (p333)

Shetland A top coastline for sea kayaking, with an abundance of bird and sea life to observe at close quarters. (p416)

7stanes Mountain-biking trails for all abilities in the forests of southern Scotland. (p172)

Cairngorms Winter skiing and summer hill walking amid the epic beauty of this high, sub-arctic plateau. (p309)

Thurso Right up the top of Scotland, this is an unlikely surfing hotspot, but the waves are pretty good. (p357)

River Tay Perhaps the finest salmon-fishing river in Europe, and famous for white-water rafting, too. (p321)

Live Music & Festivals

Scotland's festival calendar is a crowded one, with music festivals springing up in the most unlikely corners. The ones that have stood the test of time are full of character, with superb settings and a smaller, more convivial scale than monster gigs like Glastonbury and Reading.

Groove Loch Ness Perhaps the most scenic festival site in the country, held in June with Loch Ness as a backdrop. (p305)

Top: Craigievar Castle (p236)

Bottom: Mountain biking at Nevis Range (p337)

Arran Folk Festival June sees the fiddles pulled out all over this scenic island. (p271)

King Tut's Wah Wah Hut Nightly live music at a legendary venue, one of many great places in Glasgow. (p131)

Orkney Folk Festival Stromness vibrates to the wail of the fiddle in this good-natured, late-partying island festival. (p410)

Hebridean Celtic Festival A feast of folk, rock and Celtic music held in the grounds of Stornoway's Lews Castle. (p386)

Rural Museums

Every bit as interesting and worthy of study as the 'big picture' history – especially if you're investigating your Scottish ancestry – the history of rural communities is preserved in a wide range of fascinating museums, often in original farm buildings and historic houses.

Arnol Blackhouse Preserved in peat smoke since its last inhabitant left in the 1960s. (p388)

Highland Folk Museum Fascinating outdoor museum in Newtonmore populated with real historic buildings reassembled here on site. (p315)

Scottish Crannog Centre Head back to the Bronze Age in this excellent archaeological reconstruction of a fortified loch house at Kenmore. (p327)

Tain Through Time Entertaining local museum with a comprehensive display on Scottish history and Tain's silversmithing tradition. (p351)

Stromness Museum Delightful museum covering the Orkney fishing industry, the world wars and local marine wildlife. (p409)

Pubs

No visit to Scotland is complete without a night in a traditional Scottish hostelry, supping real ales, sipping whisky and tapping your toes to traditional music. The choice of pubs is huge, but in our opinion the old ones are the best.

Drover's Inn A classic Highland hostelry in Inverarnan with kilted staff, candlelight and a stuffed bear. (p246)

Sandy Bell's A stalwart of the Edinburgh folk scene, with real ale and live trad music. (p93)

Glenelg Inn The beer garden here *is* actually a garden – with sensational views across the water to Skye. (p374)

Horse Shoe All real ales and polished brass, this is Glasgow's best traditional pub. (p129)

Stein Inn A lochside pub in Skye with fine ales, fresh seafood and a view to die for. (p383)

Shopping

Scotland offers countless opportunities for shoppers to indulge in retail therapy, from designer frocks and shoes in city malls to local art, handmade pottery and traditional textiles in Highland and island workshops.

Glasgow A shopper's paradise, with everything from designer boutiques to secondhand records. (p134)

Edinburgh Boasts Harvey Nicks, malls, cashmere, tartan and quirky little gift shops. (p48)

Wigtown An amazing array of secondhand and specialist bookshops cluster around the square. (p140)

Isle of Skye Every second cottage on Skye seems to be home to a workshop or artist's studio. (p374)

Classic Walks

Scotland's wild, dramatic scenery and varied landscape has made hiking a hugely popular pastime. There's something for all levels of fitness and enthusiasm, but the really keen will want to tick off some (or all) of the classic walks.

West Highland Way Everyone wants to do the WHW, the granddaddy of Scottish long-distance walks. (p34)

Glen Affric to Shiel Bridge A classic two-day cross-country hike, with a night in a remote hostel. (p302)

Southern Upland Way Crosses Southern Scotland's hills from coast to coast; longer and harder than the WHW. (p150)

Ben Lawers One of central Scotland's classic hill walks, with super views over Loch Tay. (p253)

Fife Coastal Path Seascapes and cliff tops galore on this picturesque route right around the 'Kingdom'. (p190)

Hidden Gems

For those who enjoy exploring off the beaten track, Scotland is littered with hidden corners, remote road-ends and quiet cul-de-sacs where you can feel as if you are discovering the place for the first time.

Falls of Clyde Normally associated with shipbuilding, the River Clyde reveals the bucolic side of its character further upstream. (p156)

Old Man of Hoy (p411)

Glen Clova The loveliest of the Angus glens lies on the quiet side of Cairngorms National Park. (p319)

Benmore Botanic Garden Tucked in the Cowal peninsula, this Victorian garden is a riot of colour in spring and early summer. (p254)

Scotland's Secret Bunker It's back to the Cold War in this nuclear hideout hidden in the middle of rural Fife. (p198)

Cape Wrath A boat-minibus combo grinds you through a missile range to this spectacular headland at Britain's northwestern tip. (p363)

Natural Wonders

Scotland's stunning landscapes harbour many awe-inspiring natural features, including spectacular sea stacks and rock formations, thundering waterfalls, impressive gorges and swirling tidal whirlpools.

Old Man of Hoy The spectacular west coast of Orkney's Hoy includes Britain's tallest sea stack. (p411)

Corryvreckan Whirlpool One of the world's three most powerful tidal whirlpools, squeezed between Jura and Scarba. (p267)

Falls of Measach A trembling suspension bridge provides a scary viewpoint for one of Scotland's most impressive waterfalls. (p368)

Quiraing This jumble of pinnacles and landslip blocks in northern Skye is one of the country's weirdest landscapes. (p383)

Fingal's Cave Accessible only by boat, this columnar sea cave inspired Mendelssohn's *Hebrides Overture*. (p288)

Islands

Scotland has almost 800 islands scattered around its coastline. While the vast majority of visitors stick to the larger, better-known ones such as Arran, Skye and Mull, it's often the smaller, lesser-known islands that provide the real highlights.

Iona Beautiful, peaceful and of huge historic and cultural importance, Iona is the jewel of the Hebrides. (p243)

Eigg The most intriguing of the Small Isles, with its miniature mountain, massacre cave and singing sands. (p345)

Jura Wild and untamed, with more deer than people, and a dangerous whirlpool. (p241)

Isle of May This mile-long island erupts to the clamour of hordes of puffins in spring and summer. (p197)

Month by Month

January

The nation shakes off its Hogmanay hangover and gets back to work, but only until Burns Night comes along. It's still cold and dark, but the skiing can be good.

✗ Burns Night

Suppers all over the country (and the world for that matter) are held on 25 January to celebrate the anniversary of national poet Robert Burns, with much eating of haggis, drinking of whisky and reciting of poetry.

✿ Celtic Connections

Glasgow hosts the world's largest winter music festival, a celebration of Celtic music, dance and culture, with participants arriving from all over the globe. Held mid- to late January. (p120)

✿ Up Helly Aa

Half of Shetland dresses up with horned helmets and battleaxes in this spectacular re-enactment of a Viking fire festival, with a torchlit procession leading the burning of a full-size Viking longship. Held in Lerwick on the last Tuesday in January. (p419)

February

The coldest month of the year is usually the best for hill walking, ice-climbing and skiing. The days are getting longer now, and snowdrops begin to bloom.

☆ Six Nations Rugby Tournament

Scotland, England, Wales, Ireland, France and Italy battle it out in this prestigious tournament, held February to March. Home games are played at Murrayfield, Edinburgh. See www.sixnationsrugby.com.

✦ Fort William Mountain Festival

The UK's Outdoor Capital celebrates the peak of the winter season with ski and snowboard workshops, talks by famous climbers, kids' events, and a festival of mountaineering films. See www.mountainfestival. co.uk.

April

The bluebell woods on the shores of Loch Lomond come into flower and ospreys arrive at their Loch Garten nests. Weather is improving, though heavy showers are still common.

☆ Rugby Sevens

A series of weekend, seven-a-side rugby tournaments held in various towns throughout the Borders region in April and May, kicking off with Melrose in early April. Fast and furious rugby (sevens was invented here), crowded pubs and great craic. (p144)

✿ Shetland Folk Festival

The end of April sees this engagingly eccentric music festival, with performances of traditional music from around the world staged everywhere from Lerwick pubs to remote island village halls. (p418)

May

Wildflowers on the Hebridean machair, hawthorn hedges in bloom and cherry blossom in city parks – Scottish weather is often at its best in May.

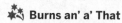 **Burns an' a' That**

Ayrshire towns are the venues for performances of poetry and music, children's events, art exhibitions and more in celebration of the Scottish bard. (p160)

Spirit of Speyside

Based in the Moray town of Dufftown, this festival of whisky, food and music involves five days of distillery tours, knocking back the 'water of life', cooking, art and outdoor activities. Held late April to early May. (p238)

June

Argyllshire is ablaze with pink rhododendron blooms as the long summer evenings stretch on till 11pm. Border towns are strung with bunting to mark gala days and Common Ridings.

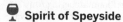 **Common Ridings**

Following the age-old tradition that commemorates the ancient conflict with England, horsemen and -women ride the old boundaries of common lands, along with parades, marching bands and street parties. Held in various Border towns; the Jedburgh event (www.jethartcallants festival.com) is one of the biggest and best.

West End Festival

June is Glasgow's equivalent of Edinburgh's August festival season, when the city hosts several major events, the most important of which is the West End Festival, the city's biggest music and arts event. (p120)

July

School holidays begin, as does the busiest time of year for resort towns. It's high season for Shetland birdwatchers.

Hebridean Celtic Festival

The gardens of Lews Castle in Stornoway provide the scenic setting for this four-day blast of folk, rock and Celtic music. (p386)

August

It's festival time in Edinburgh (www. edinburghfestivalcity.com) and the city is crammed with visitors. On the west coast, this is the peak month for sighting minke whales and basking sharks.

Edinburgh Festival Fringe

The biggest festival of the performing arts anywhere in the world. Takes place over 3½ weeks in August, the last two weeks overlapping with the first two of the Edinburgh International Festival. (p75)

Edinburgh International Festival

The world's top musicians and performers congregate in Edinburgh for three weeks of diverse and inspirational music, opera, theatre and dance. Takes place over the three weeks ending on the first Saturday in September. The program is usually available from April. (p75)

October

Autumn brings a blaze of colour to the forests of Highland Perthshire and the Trossachs, as the tourist season winds down and thoughts turn to log fires and malt whiskies in country-house hotels.

Enchanted Forest

Crowds gather in the Explorers Garden at Pitlochry to experience this spectacular sound-and-light show. Events occasionally spill into November. (p323)

December

Darkness falls mid-afternoon as the shortest day of the year approaches. The cold and wet weather is relieved by Christmas and New Year festivities.

Hogmanay

Christmas celebrations in Edinburgh (www.edin burghschristmas.com) culminate in a huge street party on Hogmanay (31 December). The fishing town of Stonehaven echoes an ancient, pre-Christian tradition with its procession of fireball-swinging locals who parade to the harbour and fling their blazing orbs into the sea (www.stonhaven fireballs.co.uk). (p76)

Itineraries

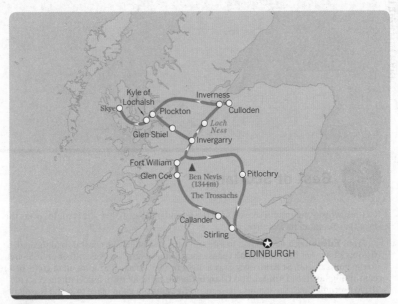

 A Highland Fling

This tour takes in Scotland's scenic and historical highlights.

No trip to Scotland would be complete without a visit to **Edinburgh**, and even if your Scottish trip lasts only a week, the capital is worth two days of your time. On day three, head northwest to **Stirling** to see Scotland's other great castle, then on to the **Trossachs** for your first taste of Highland scenery (overnight in **Callander**).

Day four starts with a scenic drive north via **Glen Coe** and **Fort William**, then along the Great Glen to **Loch Ness** in time for an afternoon visiting Urquhart Castle and the Loch Ness Centre & Exhibition. An evening cruise on Loch Ness rounds off the day; spend the night in **Inverness**.

On day five visit **Culloden Battlefield**, then drive west via Achnasheen and **Plockton** to **Kyle of Lochalsh** and cross the bridge to the **Isle of Skye**. Devote day six to Dunvegan Castle and the Trotternish peninsula.

Spend your last day taking the long drive back south – the scenic route goes via **Glen Shiel**, **Invergarry**, Spean Bridge (pause at the Commando Monument), Laggan and then south on the A9 to Edinburgh, with a stop in **Pitlochry**.

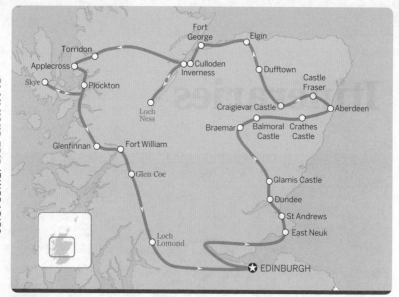

Best of Scotland

2 WEEKS

Castles, whisky, mountain scenery and the legendary Isle of Skye – this route covers the best that Scotland has to offer.

From **Edinburgh** head north to Fife and turn east along the coastal road through the fishing villages of the **East Neuk** (pause for a seafood lunch at Anstruther or St Monans) to the home of golf, **St Andrews**. Stay a night or two – heck, play a round of golf – before continuing north to **Dundee** and **Glamis Castle**, with its royal associations. A scenic drive north through the mountains leads to **Braemar**, a good place to spend the night.

A feast of castles lies ahead as you make your way east along Royal Deeside – take your time and visit (at the very least) the royal residence of **Balmoral Castle** and the fairy-tale **Crathes Castle** on your way to the granite city of **Aberdeen**. Plan to overnight here.

Now strike west again along the A944, visiting **Castle Fraser** and **Craigievar Castle** before heading north to **Dufftown** and Aberlour in the heart of Speyside. Base yourself here for at least a day while you explore the local whisky distilleries – there are some good places to eat, plus the Quaich whisky bar at the nearby Craigellachie Hotel.

Head northwest to **Elgin** and its magnificent ruined cathedral, then west on the A96, visiting **Fort George** and **Culloden** on the way to Inverness (you'll probably need a stopover in Nairn). **Inverness** itself is worth a night or two – there are some excellent hotels and restaurants, and the opportunity for a side trip to **Loch Ness** (Drumnadrochit for monster spotters; Dores Inn for foodies).

Now for a glorious drive from Inverness to **Torridon** via Kinlochewe through stunning mountain scenery; try to spend a night at the Torridon hotel. Then head south via **Applecross** and the pretty village of **Plockton** to Kyle of Lochalsh and the bridge to **Skye**.

Spend two days exploring Scotland's most famous island before taking the ferry from Armadale to Mallaig, and follow the Road to the Isles in reverse, stopping to visit **Glenfinnan**, where Bonnie Prince Charlie raised his Highland army in 1745. Overnight at **Fort William**, and drive back to Edinburgh via the scenic road through **Glen Coe** and along the bonnie banks of **Loch Lomond**.

Top: Callanish Standing
Stones (p388)

Bottom: Glamis Castle
(p219)

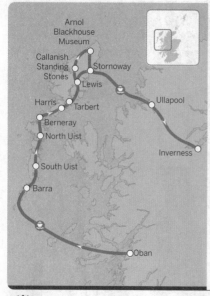

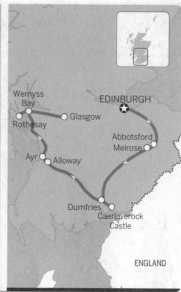

PLAN YOUR TRIP ITINERARIES

 Island Hopscotch
1 WEEK

 Border Raid
5 DAYS

This route is usually done by car, but it also makes a brilliant cycling tour (270 miles, including the 60 miles from Ullapool to Inverness train station, making both start and finish accessible by rail).

From **Oban** it's a five-hour ferry crossing to **Barra**; plan to spend the night here and book ahead. On day two, after a visit to Kisimul Castle and a tour around the island, take the ferry to **South Uist**. Walk the wild beaches of the west coast, sample the local seafood and perhaps go fishing on the island's trout lochs. Continue through Benbecula and **North Uist**, prime birdwatching country.

Overnight at Lochmaddy on North Uist (if you're camping or hostelling, a night at **Berneray** is a must) before taking the ferry to **Harris**, whose west coast has spectacular beaches. The road continues north from **Tarbert**, where you'll find good hotels, through rugged hills to **Lewis**. Loop west via the **Callanish Standing Stones** and **Arnol Blackhouse museum**. Spend your final night in **Stornoway** (eat at Digby Chick), then take the ferry to **Ullapool** for a scenic drive to **Inverness**.

Southern Scotland is often overlooked by visitors, but fans of Robert Burns and Sir Walter Scott will find much to enjoy here.

From **Edinburgh** your first objective should be a visit to Sir Walter Scott's former home at **Abbotsford**, followed by the beautiful Border abbeys of **Melrose** and nearby Dryburgh; Melrose is a charming place to stay the night, with a choice of good hotels.

Next morning head west along the A708 to Moffat, passing through glorious scenery around St Mary's Loch. Continue to **Dumfries**, where you'll visit the first of several sights related to Scotland's national poet Robert Burns, and make a short side trip to see spectacular **Caerlaverock Castle**.

Take the A76 northwest towards Ayr, and spend the rest of day three in **Alloway** visiting the birthplace of Robert Burns (and other Burns-related sites); nearby **Ayr** has plenty of accommodation options.

North now to **Wemyss Bay** and the ferry to **Rothesay** on the Isle of Bute, where you can visit stunning Mount Stuart, one of Scotland's most impressive stately homes. Spend the night on the island, then return to the mainland and head east to **Glasgow**.

Plan Your Trip

Outdoor Activities

Scotland is a brilliant place for outdoor recreation and has something to offer everyone, from those who enjoy a short stroll to full-on adrenalin junkies. Although hiking, golf, fishing and cycling are the most popular activities, there is an astonishing variety of other things to do.

Walking

Scotland's wild, dramatic scenery and varied landscape have made walking a hugely popular pastime for locals and tourists alike. There really is something for everyone, from after-breakfast strolls to the popular sport of Munro bagging.

Planning

For gentle walks along clearly defined tracks, the most planning you'll need to do is to take a look at the weather forecast and decide how many layers to wear. Highland hikers should be properly equipped and cautious, as the weather can become vicious at any time of year. After rain, peaty soil can become boggy, so always wear stout shoes or boots and carry extra food and drink – many unsuspecting walkers have had to survive an unplanned night in the open. Don't depend on mobile (cell) phones (although carrying one with you is a good idea, and can be a lifesaver if you can get a signal). Leave a note with your route and expected time of return on the dashboard of your car.

The best time of year for hill walking is usually May to September, although snow can fall on the highest summits even in midsummer. Winter walking on the higher

Best Experiences

➡ Hiking the West Highland Way
➡ Climbing Ben Nevis
➡ Cycle touring the Outer Hebrides
➡ Mountain biking the 7Stanes Trails
➡ Sea kayaking in Shetland

Essential Walking Gear

☐ Good waterproofs
☐ Spare warm clothing
☐ Map and compass
☐ Mobile (cell) phone (but don't rely on it)
☐ First-aid kit
☐ Head torch
☐ Whistle (for emergencies)
☐ Spare food and drink

Safety Checklist

☐ Check the weather forecast before you go
☐ Let someone know your plans
☐ Set your pace and objective to suit the slowest member of your party

hills of Scotland requires the use of an ice axe and crampons and is for experienced mountaineers only.

Access & Rights of Way

There is a tradition of relatively free access to open country in Scotland, a custom that was enshrined in law in the 2003 Land Reform (Scotland) Bill, popularly known as 'the right to roam'. The Scottish Outdoor Access Code (www.outdooraccess-scotland.scot) states that everyone has the right to be on most land and inland waters, providing they act responsibly.

You should avoid areas where you might disrupt or disturb wildlife, lambing (generally mid-April to the end of May), grouse shooting (from 12 August to the third week in October) or deer stalking (1 July to 15 February, but the peak period is August to October). You can get up-to-date information on deer stalking in various areas through the Heading for the Scottish Hills (www.outdooraccess-scotland.scot/hftsh) service.

Local authorities aren't required to list and map rights of way, so they're not shown on Ordnance Survey (OS) maps of Scotland, as they are in England and Wales. However, the Scottish Rights of Way & Access Society (www.scotways.com) keeps records of these routes, provides and maintains signposting, and publicises routes in its guidebook, *Scottish Hill Tracks*.

You are free to pitch a tent almost anywhere that doesn't cause inconvenience to others or damage to property, as long as you stay no longer than two or three nights in any one spot, take all litter away with you, and keep well away from houses and roads. (Note that this right does not extend to the use of motorised vehicles to reach camping spots.)

Long-Distance Footpaths

Scotland has no fewer than 26 official long-distance footpaths (ie waymarked trails), which are all described on the website www.scotlandsgreattrails.org.uk. Each trail also has its own dedicated website, and at least one print guidebook such as those published by Cicerone (www.cicerone.co.uk) and Rucksack Readers (www.rucsacs.com).

West Highland Way

This classic hike – the country's most popular long-distance trail – stretches for 96 miles through some of Scotland's most spectacular scenery, from Milngavie (mull-*guy*), on the northwestern fringes of Glasgow, to Fort William.

The route begins in the Lowlands, but the greater part of the trail is among the mountains, lochs and fast-flowing rivers of the western Highlands. After following the eastern shore of Loch Lomond and passing Crianlarich and Tyndrum, the route crosses the vast wilderness of Rannoch Moor and reaches Fort William via Glen

---

TOP 10 SHORT WALKS

Quiraing (p383; Isle of Skye) One to two hours; bizarre rock pinnacles.

Steall Meadows (p336; Glen Nevis) One to two hours; waterfall beneath Ben Nevis.

Lost Valley (p329; Glen Coe) Three hours; impressive mountain scenery.

Conic Hill (p243; Loch Lomond) Two hours; views over Loch Lomond.

Loch an Eilein (p309; Aviemore) One hour; lovely lochan (small loch) amid Scots pines.

Linn of Quoich (www.nts.org.uk; Braemar) One hour; rocky gorge and waterfall.

Plodda Falls (p302; Cannich) One hour; dizzying viewpoint above waterfall.

Duncansby Head (p356; John O'Groats) One hour; spectacular sea stacks.

Stac Pollaidh (p364; Coigach) Two to four hours; ascent of miniature mountain.

Old Man of Hoy (p411; Orkney) Three hours; Britain's tallest sea stack.

Top: A hiker on the West Highland Way (p34)

Bottom: Canoeing on Loch Lubnaig (p252)

ILIAS KOUROUDIS/SHUTTERSTOCK ©

Nevis, in the shadow of Britain's highest peak, Ben Nevis.

The path is easy to follow, making use of old drove roads (along which Highland cattle were once driven to Lowland markets), an old military road (built by troops to help subdue the Highlands in the 18th century) and disused railway lines.

Best done from south to north, the walk takes about six or seven days. Many people round it off with an ascent of Ben Nevis. You need to be properly equipped, with good boots, waterproofs, maps, a compass, and food and drink, for the northern part of the walk. Midge repellent is also essential.

It's possible to do just a day's hike along part of the trail. For example, the Loch Lomond Water Bus allows you to walk the section from Rowardennan to Inversnaid, returning to your starting point by boat.

The West Highland Way Official Guide, by Bob Aitken and Roger Smith, is the most comprehensive guidebook, while the Harvey map *West Highland Way* covers the entire route in a single waterproof sheet.

Accommodation shouldn't be too difficult to find, though between Bridge of Orchy and Kinlochleven it's limited. At peak times (May, July and August), book accommodation in advance. There are some youth hostels and bunkhouses on

BEATING THE MIDGES

Forget Nessie. The Highlands have a real monster in their midst: a voracious, bloodsucking female fully 2mm long, known as *Culicoides impunctatus* – the Highland midge. (The male midge is an innocent vegetarian.) The bane of campers and as much a symbol of Scotland as the kilt or the thistle, they can drive sane folk to distraction as they descend in swarms of biting misery. Though mostly vegetarian too, the female midge needs a dose of blood in order to lay her eggs. And like it or not, if you're in the Highlands in summer, you've just volunteered as a donor.

The midge season lasts from late May to early September, with June to August being the worst months. Climate change has seen warmer, damper springs and summers that seem to suit the midges just fine – in recent years they've increased both in numbers and in range. They're at their worst in the morning and evening, especially in calm, overcast weather; strong winds and strong sunshine help keep them away.

You can get an idea of how bad they are going to be in your area by checking the midge forecast (www.smidgeup.com/midge-forecast; only operates during midge season).

Be Prepared!

Cover up by wearing long trousers and long-sleeved shirts, and (if the midges are really bad) a head net (available in most outdoor shops) worn over a brimmed hat. Also be sure to use a repellent.

Many kinds of repellents have been formulated over the decades, some based on natural ingredients such as citronella and bog myrtle, but until recently there was only one that worked reliably – DEET, which is a nasty, industrial chemical that smells bad, stings your eyes and seems to be capable of melting plastic. A repellent called Saltidin claims to be both effective and pleasant to use (marketed under the brand name Smidge).

However, there's another substance that has shot to prominence since 2005 despite not being marketed as an insect repellent. Avon's 'Skin So Soft' moisturiser spray is so effective that it is regularly used as a midge repellent by professionals including the Royal Marines, forestry workers and water engineers, as well as thousands of outdoor enthusiasts. You can find it in most outdoor stores in the west of Scotland. Not only does it keep the midges away, it claims to leave your skin feeling 'velvety soft'.

or near the path, and it's possible to camp in some parts. A list of accommodation is available from tourist offices.

For more information, see www.west highlandway.org.

Speyside Way

This long-distance footpath follows the course of the River Spey, one of Scotland's most famous salmon-fishing rivers. It starts at Buckie and first follows the coast to Spey Bay, east of Elgin, then runs inland along the river to Aviemore in the Cairngorms (with branches to Tomintoul and Dufftown). There are plans to extend the trail to Newtonmore.

The 66-mile route has been dubbed the 'Whisky Trail' as it passes near a number of distilleries, including Glenlivet and Glenfiddich (p238), which are open to the public. If you stop at them all, the walk may take considerably longer than the usual three or four days! The first 11 miles from Buckie to Fochabers makes a good day hike (allow four to five hours).

The Speyside Way, a guidebook by Jacquetta Megarry and Jim Strachan, describes the trail in detail. Check out the route at www.speysideway.org.

Munro Bagging

At the end of the 19th century an eager hill walker, Sir Hugh Munro, published a list of Scottish mountains measuring over 3000ft (914m) in height – he couldn't have realised that in time his name would be used to describe all Scottish mountains over 3000ft, and that keen hill walkers would set themselves the target of reaching the summit of (or bagging) all of Scotland's 282 Munros.

To the uninitiated it may seem odd that Munro baggers see venturing into mist, cloud and driving rain as time well spent. However, for those who can add one or more ticks to their list, the vagaries of the weather are part of the enjoyment, at least in retrospect. Munro bagging is, of course, more than merely ticking off a list – it takes you to some of the wildest and most beautiful corners of Scotland.

Once you've bagged all the Munros you can move on to the Corbetts – hills over 2500ft (700m), with a drop of at least 500ft (150m) on all sides – and the Donalds, lowland hills over 2000ft (610m). And for connoisseurs of the diminutive,

there are the McPhies: 'eminences in excess of 300ft (90m)' on the island of Colonsay.

Further Information

Every tourist office has leaflets (free or for a nominal charge) of suggested walks that take in local points of interest. Lonely Planet's *Walking in Scotland* is a comprehensive resource, covering short walks and long-distance paths; its *Walking in Britain* guide covers Scottish walks, too. For general advice, VisitScotland's **Walking in Scotland** (http://walking.visitscotland.com) website describes numerous routes in various parts of the country, and also offers safety tips and other useful information. **WalkHighlands** (www.walkhighlands.co.uk) is an online database of more than 2000 walks complete with maps and detailed descriptions.

Golf

A round in the home of golf isn't about nostalgia: the sport is part of Scotland's fabric. Playing here is a unique experience; you're almost guaranteed heart-stopping scenery and a friendly atmosphere whatever the weather. Scotland's tradition of public courses means that outstanding golf is usually accompanied by sociable moments and warm hospitality.

History

The first known mention of golf is from 1457, when James II banned it to prevent archery, crucial for military reasons, from being ignored as an activity.

The oldest club is the Honourable Company of Edinburgh Golfers (1744), based at Muirfield. In 1754 the Royal and Ancient Golf Club of St Andrews, which became the game's governing body, was born.

Modern golf really evolved in the late 19th and early 20th centuries. Legendary figures such as James Braid and Old Tom Morris designed courses across Britain; the latter was a founding figure of the Open Championship and won it four times.

Scotland is also very much at the forefront of international professional golf,

SIX OF THE BEST GOLF COURSES

St Andrews (p191) The public Old Course is the game's spiritual home, and you can't help but be awed by the history and atmosphere here. The 17th – the Road Hole – is famous for its blind drive, nasty bunker and seriously sloping green. Several other courses for all abilities make this Scotland's premium golfing destination.

Turnberry (p162) Now owned by Donald Trump, Turnberry's Ailsa is one of Scotland's most prestigious links courses, with spectacular views of Ailsa Craig offshore.

Royal Dornoch (p353) Up north, the sumptuous championship course rewards the journey with picture-perfect links scenery and a quieter pace to things.

Machrihanish Dunes (p262) On the Kintyre peninsula, this Old Tom Morris–designed course is one of Scotland's most scenic. There's no easing into your round here; strike long and clean on the first or you'll be on the beach – literally.

Gleneagles (p206) Three brilliant courses and a five-star hotel with truly excellent service make this legendary Perthshire destination a great choice for golfing breaks.

Muirfield (☏01620-842123; www.muirfield.org.uk; Duncur Rd, Muirfield, Gullane) Handy for Edinburgh, this private course on land reclaimed from the sea allocates some public tee times. It's one of Scotland's more traditional – and many would say outrageously sexist – institutions, and hit the headlines in 2017 when it finally allowed women to join its ranks.

with high-profile events such as the 2018 Open at Carnoustie, the 2019 Solheim Cup at Gleneagles and the 2021 Open at St Andrews.

Where to Play

With more golf courses per capita than any other country, Scotland has a bewildering choice. A selection of world golf's most iconic courses offers some of the sport's most famous holes, with deep, challenging bunkers where you might only get out backwards, if at all. But there's also great pleasure to be had on simpler, local fairways eked out by small Highland or island communities, where you'll have to improvise shots over the sheep or deer nibbling at the green.

Links Courses

Links, the seaside courses where modern golf was born, present unique challenges with their undulating fairways, unforgiving rough, vertical bunkers and enormous greens that can resemble the Scottish Highlands in miniature. They're usually wholly treeless, with gorse, heather and machair making up the vegetation. But that's not to say that they're easy. Far from it.

On sandy uncultivable ground between the fields and the sea and largely un-

planned, they follow the contours of the landscape. Exposed and unprotected, they are at the mercy of wind and weather: on a sunny day you can post flattering scores, but a healthy sea breeze means that approaches into scarily angled greens need meticulous execution. It pays to listen to locals.

Further Information

When to Play

Summer is most enjoyable – long daylight hours mean you can tee off at 6am or 7pm. Courses are busy in these months, though; a good compromise is to play in May or September.

Resources

VisitScotland (www.visitscotland.com/golf) Useful information, including on discount golf passes. Publishes *Golf in Scotland,* a free annual brochure listing courses, costs and accommodation information.

Scotland Golf (www.scottishgolfcourses.com) Good for investigating courses to play.

Costs

A round at an unfashionable rural course may cost as little as £10. Showpiece courses charge green fees of £160 to £250 in high season. It's more economical in winter, it's often cheaper midweek, and 'twilight' rates (teeing off after 4pm or so) can save you up to 50% at some clubs.

Cycling

Cycling is an excellent way to explore Scotland. There are hundreds of miles of forest trails and quiet minor roads, and dedicated cycle routes along canal towpaths and disued railway tracks. Depending on your energy and enthusiasm, you can take a leisurely trip through idyllic glens, stopping at pubs along the way, or head off on a long and arduous road tour.

The network of signposted cycle routes maintained by Sustrans (www.sustrans.org.uk) makes a good introduction. Much of the network is on minor roads or cycle lanes, but there are long stretches of surfaced, traffic-free trails between Callander and Killin, between Oban and Ballachulish, on Royal Deeside, and along the Union and Forth & Clyde canals between Glasgow and Edinburgh.

But it's the minor roads of the Northwest Highlands, the Outer Hebrides, Orkney and Shetland that are the real attraction for cycle tourers, offering hundreds of miles of peaceful pedalling through breathtaking landscapes.

The classic Scottish cycle tour is a trip around the islands of the west coast, from Islay and Jura north via Mull, Coll and Tiree to Skye and the Outer Hebrides (bikes travel for free on Calmac car ferries).

Further Information

Many regional tourist offices have information on local cycling routes and places to hire bikes. They also stock cycling guides and books. Other resources include the following:

VisitScotland (www.visitscotland.com/see -do/active) Publishes a useful free brochure, *Active Scotland,* and has a website with more information.

Sustrans (www.sustrans.org.uk) For up-to-date, detailed information on Scotland's cycle-route network.

Cycling UK (www.cyclinguk.org) A membership organisation offering comprehensive information about cycling in Britain.

Mountain Biking

A combination of challenging, rugged terrain, a network of old drove roads, military roads and stalkers' paths, and legislation that enshrines free access to the countryside has earned Scotland a reputation as one of the world's top mountain-biking destinations. Fort William has hosted the UCI Mountain Bike World Championships every year since 2007.

Scotland offers everything from custom-built forest trails with berms, jumps and skinnies to world-class downhill courses such as those at Laggan Wolftrax and Nevis Range. But perhaps the country's greatest appeal is its almost unlimited potential for adventurous, off-road riding. Areas such as the Galloway hills, the Angus Glens, the Cairngorms, Lochaber, Skye and most of the Northwest Highlands have large roadless regions where you can explore to your heart's content.

Top trails include Glen Feshie, Glenlivet and Rothiemurchus Forest in the Cairngorms, Spean Bridge to Kinlochleven via the Lairig Leacach and Loch Eilde Mor, and the stretch of the West Highland Way between Bridge of Orchy and Kinlochleven. The 37-mile loop from Sligachan on Skye (south through Glen Sligachan to Camasunary, over to Kilmarie, and back north via Strath Mor) was voted by *Mountain Bike Rider* magazine as the best off-road trail in Britain. Check out the Where to Ride link on www.dmbins.com.

But the ultimate off-road experience is a coast-to-coast ride. There's no set route and no waymarking, so it's as much a planning and navigational challenge as a physical one. A coast-to-coast trip can be as short as the 36 miles from Ullapool to Bonar Bridge via Glen Achall and Glen Einig, or as long as the 250 miles from Aberdeen to Ardnamurchan.

The most popular coast-to-coast route, though, is from Fort William to Montrose (starting and finishing at a railway station) via Fort Augustus, Aviemore, Tomintoul, Ballater and Edzell, taking in the Corrieyairack Pass, the Ryvoan Pass, Glen Builg, Glen Tanar and Glen Esk (195 miles). You can camp wild along the way or book accommodation at B&Bs and hostels, or join a guided expedition with an organisation such as Wilderness Scotland (p40).

Top Five MTB Trail Centres

7stanes (www.7stanesmountainbiking.com) Series of seven forest-trail centres strung across the Southern Uplands, with fantastic trails for all skill levels from beginner to expert.

Nevis Range (www.nevisrange.co.uk/bike) Ski resort offering summer sport in the form of a world-championship downhill course, and a 3.7-mile red-grade cross-country trail from the top station of the gondola.

Witch's Trails (www.nevisrange.co.uk/bike) Has 22 miles of forest road and single track in the shadow of Ben Nevis. Hosts the annual cross-country world championships and the annual 10 Under the Ben endurance event.

Laggan Wolftrax (http://scotland.forestry.gov.uk/visit/laggan-wolftrax) Forest centre near Newtonmore with everything from novice trails and a bike park to hard cross-country and a challenging black route with drop-offs, boulder fields and rock slabs.

Highland Wildcat (www.highlandwildcat.com) The hills above Golspie harbour have the biggest single-track descent in the country (390m drop over 4 miles, from the top of Ben Bhraggie almost to sea level). Plenty for beginners and families, too.

Fishing

Fishing – coarse, sea and game – is enormously popular in Scotland; its lochs and rivers are filled with salmon, sea trout, brown trout and Arctic char. Fly-fishing in particular is a joy – it's a tricky but rewarding form of angling, closer to an art form than a sport.

Fishing rights to most inland waters are privately owned and you must obtain a permit to fish in them – these are usually readily available from the local fishing-tackle shop or hotel, which are also great sources of advice and local knowledge. Permits cost from around £5 to £20 per day, but salmon fishing on some rivers – notably the Tweed, Dee, Tay and Spey – can be much more expensive (up to £150 a day).

For wild brown trout the close season is early October to mid-March. The close season for salmon and sea trout varies between districts; it's generally from mid-October to mid-January.

FishPal (www.fishpal.com/scotland) provides a good introduction, with links for booking fishing on various rivers and lochs.

Canoeing & Kayaking

Scotland's islands, sea lochs and indented coastline provide some of the finest sea kayaking in the world. There are sheltered lochs and inlets ideal for beginners, long and exciting coastal and island tours, and gnarly tidal passages that will challenge even the most expert paddler, all amid spectacular scenery and wildlife – encounters with seals, dolphins and even whales are relatively common.

The inland lochs and rivers offer excellent Canadian and white-water canoeing. Lochs Lomond, Awe and Maree all have uninhabited islands where canoeists can set up camp, while a study of the map will suggest plenty of cross-country expeditions involving only minor portages. Classic routes include Fort William to Inverness along the Great Glen; Glen Affric; Loch Shiel; and Loch Veyatie–Fionn Loch–Loch Sionascaig in Assynt.

There are dozens of companies offering sea kayaking and canoeing courses and guided holidays. Recommended options include the following:

Arran Adventure Company (p270)

NorWest Sea Kayaking (p362)

Rockhopper Sea Kayaking (p341)

Sea Kayak Shetland (p425)

Whitewave Outdoor Centre (p376)

Wilderness Scotland (☑01479-420020; www.wildernessscotland.com)

Further Information

Scottish Canoe Association (www.canoescotland.org) Publishes coastal navigation sheets and organises tours, including ones for beginners.

The Northern Isles (by Tom Smith and Chris Jex) A detailed guide to sea kayaking the waters around Orkney and Shetland.

The Outer Hebrides (by Mike Sullivan, Robert Emmott and Tim Pickering) A detailed guide to sea kayaking around the Western Isles.

Scottish Sea Kayak Trail (www.scottishseakayaktrail.com; by Simon Willis) Covers the Scottish west coast from the Isle of Gigha to the Summer Isles.

Top: Cyclist in the highlands

Bottom: St Andrews Old Course (p191)

CSTRINGER/SHUTTERSTOCK ©

Snow Sports

There are five ski centres in Scotland, offering downhill skiing and snow-boarding:

Cairngorm Mountain (p313) (1097m) Has almost 30 runs spread over an extensive area.

Glencoe Mountain Resort (p329) (1108m) Has only five tows and two chairlifts.

Glenshee Ski Resort (p319) (920m) Situated on the A93 between Perth and Braemar; offers Scotland's largest network of lifts and widest range of runs.

Lecht 2090 (p316) (793m) The smallest and most remote centre, on the A939 between Ballater and Grantown-on-Spey.

Nevis Range (p337) (1221m) Near Fort William; offers the highest ski runs, the grandest setting and some of the best off-piste potential in Scotland.

The high season is from January to April, but it's sometimes possible to ski from as early as November to as late as May; con-

---

ALTERNATIVE ACTIVITIES

Horse Riding

VisitScotland publishes the *Riding in Scotland* (http://riding.visitscotland.com) brochure, which lists riding centres around Scotland. The Trekking & Riding Society of Scotland (www.ridinginscotland.com) can provide information on horse-riding courses and approved riding centres.

Yachting

The west coast of Scotland, with its myriad islands, superb scenery and challenging winds and tides, is widely acknowledged to be one of the finest yachting areas in the world. Beginners can take a Royal Yachting Association (www.rya.org.uk) training course in yachting or dinghy sailing at many schools around the coast.

Surfing

Even with a wetsuit you definitely have to be hardy to enjoy surfing in Scottish waters. That said, the country does have some of the best surfing breaks in Europe; the north and west coasts, particularly around Thurso and in the Outer Hebrides, have outstanding, world-class surf. For more information, contact Hebridean Surf (www.hebrideansurf.co.uk).

Scuba-Diving

It may lack coral reefs and warm waters, but Scotland offers some of the most spectacular and challenging scuba diving in Europe. There are spectacular drop-offs, challenging drift dives, and fascinating wildlife, ranging from colourful jewel anemones and soft corals to giant conger eels, monkfish and inquisitive seals. There are also hundreds of fascinating shipwrecks. For more information, contact the Scottish Sub Aqua Club (www.scotsac.com).

Rock Climbing

Scotland has a long history of rock climbing and mountaineering, with many of the classic routes on Ben Nevis and Glen Coe having been pioneered in the 19th century.

Scottish Rock volumes 1 and 2, by Gary Latter, and the Scottish Mountaineering Club's *Scottish Rock Climbs* are excellent guidebooks that cover the whole country.

Mountaineering Council of Scotland (www.mountaineering.scot) General background and information.

Scottish Mountaineering Club (www.smc.org.uk) Publisher of climbing guidebooks.

UK Climbing (www.ukclimbing.com) Discussion forums and databases of crags and routes.

versely, the fickleness of Scottish weather means it's also possible for resorts to close temporarily in season due to high winds or lack of snow.

VisitScotland's *Ski Scotland* brochure is useful and includes a list of accommodation options. General information, and weather and snow reports, can be obtained from Ski Scotland (www.ski-scotland.com) and Winterhighland (www.winterhighland.info).

Whale Watching

Scotland has cashed in on the abundance of minke whales off its coast by embracing whale watching. There are now dozens of operators around the coast offering whale-watching boat trips lasting from a couple of hours to all day; some have whale-sighting success rates of 95% in summer.

The best places to base yourself for whale watching include Oban, the Isle of Mull, Skye and the Outer Hebrides. Orkney and Shetland offer the best chance of spotting orcas (killer whales), while the Moray Firth has a resident population of bottlenose dolphins. Seals, porpoises and dolphins can be seen year-round, but minke whales are most commonly spotted from June to August, with August the peak month for sightings.

The Hebridean Whale & Dolphin Trust (https://hwdt.org) has lots of information on the species found in Scottish waters, and how to identify them. A booklet entitled *Is It a Whale?* is available from tourist offices and bookshops, and provides tips on identifying the various marine mammals that you're likely to see.

The Scottish Marine Wildlife Watching Code (www.snh.scot/marinecode) provides guidance on best practice and legal considerations.

Outfits operating whale-watching cruises include the following:

➡ Sea Life Surveys (p284)
➡ Seafari Adventures (p280)
➡ Aquaxplore (p379)
➡ Gairloch Marine Cruises (p368)
➡ Hebridean Whale Cruises (p368)
➡ Arisaig Marine (p341)
➡ Hebridean Adventures (p386)

Birdwatching

Scotland is the best place in the British Isles (and in some cases, the only place) to spot bird species such as the golden eagle, white-tailed eagle, osprey, corncrake, capercaillie, crested tit, Scottish crossbill and ptarmigan. The country's coast and islands also provide some of Europe's most important seabird nesting grounds.

There are more than 100 ornithologically important nature reserves managed by Scottish Natural Heritage (www.nnr.scot), the Royal Society for the Protection of Birds (www.rspb.org.uk) and the Scottish Wildlife Trust (www.swt.org.uk).

Further information can be obtained from the Scottish Ornithologists Club (www.the-soc.org.uk).

Regions at a Glance

Which regions of Scotland you choose to visit will naturally depend on how much time you have, and whether you've been here before. First-time visitors will want to squeeze in as many highlights as possible, so they could try following the well-trodden route through Edinburgh, the Trossachs, Pitlochry, Inverness, Loch Ness and the Isle of Skye.

It takes considerably more time to explore the further-flung corners of the country, but the ruined abbeys and castles of the Borders, the jaw-dropping scenery of the northwest Highlands and the gorgeous white-sand beaches of the Outer Hebrides are less crowded and ultimately more rewarding. The long journey to Orkney or Shetland means that you'll want to devote more than just a day or two to these regions.

Edinburgh

Culture
History
Food

Festival City

The Scottish capital is a city of high culture where, each summer, the world's biggest arts festival rises rave reviews.

Edinburgh Castle

Perched on a brooding black crag overlooking the city centre, Edinburgh Castle has played a pivotal role in Scottish history. The growth of the city from its medieval origins and the parallel development of Scottish nationhood is documented in its excellent museums.

Dining Out

Edinburgh has more restaurants per head of population than any other city in the UK. Eating out is commonplace, not just for special occasions, and the eateries range from stylish but inexpensive bistros and cafes to gourmet restaurants with Michelin stars.

p48

Glasgow

Culture
Music
Style

Kelvingrove Art Gallery & Museum

Glasgow's mercantile, industrial and academic history has left the city with a wonderful legacy of museums and art galleries, dominated by the grand Kelvingrove, boasting a bewildering variety of exhibits.

King Tut's Wah Wah Hut

Glasgow is the star of Scotland's live-music scene, with legendary venues like King Tut's Wah Wah Hut staging gigs that range from local start-ups to top international acts.

Charles Rennie Mackintosh

With Charles Rennie Mackintosh's iconic buildings, the centre's grand Victorian architecture, the fashion boutiques of the Italian Centre and design exhibitions at the Lighthouse, Glasgow is Scotland's most stylish city.

p106

Southern Scotland

Historic Buildings
Architecture
Activities

Great Abbeys

Ruined abbeys dot Scotland's southern border. The Gothic ruins of Melrose, Jedburgh, Dryburgh and Sweetheart and the martial towers of Hermitage Castle, Caerlaverock Castle and Smailholm are testimony to a turbulent past.

Dumfries House

This region is rich in Adam-designed mansions such as Culzean Castle, Paxton House, Floors Castle and Mellerstain House, but Dumfries House takes top place.

Mountain Biking

The hills of the Southern Uplands can't compete with the Highlands for scenery, but Galloway and Arran are prime hill-walking country, and the 7stanes trails offer some of the UK's best and most challenging mountain biking.

p140

Central Scotland

Activities
Coastal Scenery
Castles

St Andrews

Scotland is the home of golf, and the Old Course at St Andrews is on every golfer's wishlist. The game has been played here for more than 600 years; the Royal & Ancient Golf Club, the game's governing body, was founded in 1754.

East Neuk of Fife

The scenic coastline of the East Neuk of Fife is dotted with picturesque harbours and quaint fishing villages, their history recounted in the excellent Scottish Fisheries Museum in Anstruther.

Stirling Castle

Some say that Stirling has the finest castle in the country, but the region has plenty of others worth visiting, including Castle Campbell, Kellie Castle and Doune Castle.

p177

Northeast Scotland

Culture
Castles
History

Speyside Distilleries

Don't leave Scotland without visiting a whisky distillery; the Speyside region, around Dufftown in Moray, is the epicentre of the industry. More than 50 distilleries open during the Spirit of Speyside festival; many open year-round.

Scottish Baronial Style

Aberdeenshire and Moray have the greatest concentration of Scottish Baronial castles in the country, from the turreted splendour of Craigievar and Fyvie to the elegance of Crathes and Balmoral.

Pictish Stones

The Picts carved mysterious stones (dating from the 7th and 8th centuries) that can be seen in places such as Aberlemno and St Vigeans Museum (near Arbroath).

p210

Southern Highlands & Islands

Nature
Geography
Food

Whales & Eagles

See some of Scotland's most spectacular wildlife, from magnificent white-tailed sea eagles in Mull to majestic minke whales and basking sharks cruising the west coast.

Island-Hopping

Island-hopping is one of the best ways to explore the western seaboard, and the cluster of islands here – Islay, Jura, Mull, Iona, and the gorgeous beaches of Colonsay, Coll and Tiree – provide a brilliant introduction.

Harvest of the Sea

Whether you dine at a top restaurant in Oban or Tobermory, or eat with your fingers on the harbourside, the rich harvest of the sea is one of the region's biggest drawcards.

p241

Inverness & the Central Highlands

Activities
Royalty
Legends

Hiking & Skiing

The Highland towns of Aviemore and Fort William offer outdoor adventure galore. Be it climbing, walking, biking or skiing, there's something for everyone.

Royal Deeside

The valley of the River Dee between Ballater and Braemar has been associated with the royal family since Queen Victoria acquired her holiday home, Balmoral Castle.

The Loch Ness Monster

Scotland's most iconic legend, the Loch Ness monster, lurks in here. You might not spot Nessie, but the magnificent scenery of the Great Glen makes a visit worthwhile, as does Culloden battlefield, the undoing of another Scottish legend, Bonnie Prince Charlie.

p293

Northern Highlands & Islands

Scenery
Activities
History

Mountains & Beaches

From the peaks of Assynt and Torridon to the pinnacles of the Cuillin Hills, and the beaches of the Outer Hebrides, the big skies and lonely landscapes of this area is the very essence of Scotland.

Adventure Sports

The northwest's vast spaces make one huge adventure playground for hikers, mountain bikers, climbers and kayakers, and provide the chance to see some of the UK's most spectacular wildlife.

The Clearances

The abandoned rural communities of the north teach much about the Clearances, especially Arnol Blackhouse. Prehistoric remains include the famous standing stones of Callanish.

p347

Orkney & Shetland

History
Wildlife
Music

Skara Brae

These islands have a fascinating Viking heritage and unique prehistoric villages, tombs and stone circles. Skara Brae is northern Europe's best-preserved prehistoric village; Maeshowe is one of Britain's finest Neolithic tombs.

Birdwatching

Shetland is a birdwatcher's paradise, its cliffs teeming in summer with gannets, fulmars, kittiwakes, razorbills and puffins, and Europe's largest colony of Arctic terns. Hermaness on Unst is Scotland's northernmost inhabited island.

Folk Festivals

The pubs of Kirkwall, Stromness and Lerwick are fertile ground for exploring the traditional-music scene. Both Orkney and Shetland host annual folk-music festivals.

p397

On the Road

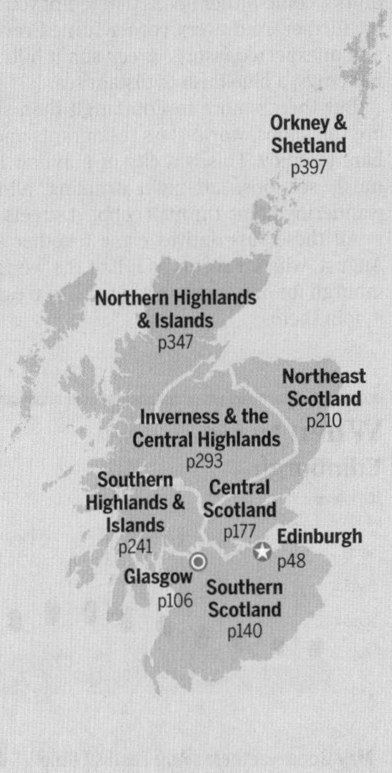

Orkney &
Shetland
p397

Northern Highlands
& Islands
p347

Northeast
Scotland
p210

Inverness & the
Central Highlands
p293

Southern
Highlands &
Islands
p241

Central
Scotland
p177

Edinburgh
p48

Glasgow
p106

Southern
Scotland
p140

Edinburgh

POP 513,210

Best Places to Eat

➡ Kitchin (p89)

➡ Gardener's Cottage (p83)

➡ Ondine (p82)

➡ Timberyard (p88)

➡ Contini (p84)

➡ Aizle (p89)

Best Places to Stay

➡ Witchery by the Castle (p77)

➡ Pilrig House (p81)

➡ Sheridan Guest House (p81)

➡ Southside Guest House (p80)

➡ Two Hillside Crescent (p77)

➡ 14 Hart Street (p77)

Why Go?

Edinburgh is a city that begs to be explored. From the vaults and wynds (narrow lanes) that riddle the Old Town to the urban villages of Stockbridge and Cramond, it's filled with quirky, come-hither nooks that tempt you to walk just a little bit further. And every corner turned reveals sudden views and unexpected vistas – green sunlit hills, a glimpse of rust-red crags, a blue flash of distant sea.

But there's more to Edinburgh than sightseeing – there are top shops, world-class restaurants and a bacchanalia of bars to enjoy. This is a city of pub crawls and impromptu music sessions, late-night drinking, all-night parties and wandering home through cobbled streets at dawn.

All these superlatives come together at festival time in August, when it seems as if half the world descends on Edinburgh for one enormous party. If you can possibly manage it, join them.

When to Go
Edinburgh

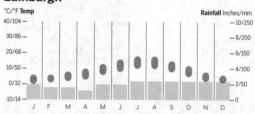

| **May** Good weather (usually), flowers and cherry blossom everywhere and (gasp!) no crowds. | **Aug** Festival time! Edinburgh is crowded and mad but irresistible. | **Dec** Christmas decorations, cosy pubs with open fires, ice skating in Princes Street Gardens. |

Edinburgh Highlights

1 **Edinburgh Castle** (p51) Taking in the views from the battlements.

2 **Royal Yacht Britannia** (p70) Nosing around the Queen's private quarters.

3 **Arthur's Seat** (p63) Climbing to the summit of the city's miniature mountain.

4 **Sandy Bell's** (p93) Listening to live Scottish folk music.

5 **Castle Terrace** (p88) Enjoying the finest of Scottish cuisine.

6 **Real Mary King's Close** (p58) Exploring Edinburgh's subterranean history in these haunted vaults.

7 **Rosslyn Chapel** (p101) Trying to decipher the Da Vinci Code at this mysterious chapel.

History

Edinburgh owes its existence to the Castle Rock, the glacier-worn stump of a long-extinct volcano that provided a near-perfect defensive position guarding the coastal route from northeast England into central Scotland.

In the 7th century the Castle Rock was called Dun Eiden (meaning 'Fort on the Hill Slope'). When it was captured by invaders from the kingdom of Northumbria in north-east England in 638, they took the existing Gaelic name 'Eiden' and tacked it onto their own Old English word for fort, 'burh', to create the name Edinburgh.

Originally a purely defensive site, Edinburgh began to expand in the 12th century when King David I held court at the castle and founded the abbey at Holyrood. The royal court came to prefer Edinburgh to Dunfermline and, as parliament followed the king, Edinburgh became Scotland's capital. The city's first effective town wall was constructed around 1450, enclosing the Old Town as far east as Netherbow and south to the Grassmarket. This overcrowded area – by then the most populous town in Scotland – became a medieval Manhattan, forcing its densely packed inhabitants to build upwards instead of outwards, creating tenements five and six storeys high.

The capital played an important role in the Reformation (1560–1690), led by the Calvinist firebrand John Knox. Mary, Queen of Scots, held court in the Palace of Holyroodhouse for six brief years, but when her son James VI acceded to the English throne in 1603 he moved his court to London. The Act of Union in 1707 further reduced Edinburgh's importance, but its cultural and intellectual life flourished.

In the second half of the 18th century a planned new town was created across the valley to the north of the Old Town. During the Scottish Enlightenment (c 1740–1830), Edinburgh became known as 'a hotbed of genius', inhabited by leading scientists and philosophers such as David Hume and Adam Smith.

In the 19th century the population quadrupled to 400,000, not much less than today's population, and the Old Town's tenements were taken over by refugees from the Highland Clearances and the Irish famines. A new ring of crescents and circuses was built to the north of New Town, and grey Victorian terraces spread south of the Old Town.

In the 1920s the city's borders expanded again to encompass Leith in the north, Cramond in the west and the Pentland Hills to the south. Following WWII the city's cultural life blossomed, stimulated by the Edinburgh International Festival and its fellow traveller, the Fringe, both held for the first time in 1947 and now recognised as world-class arts festivals.

Edinburgh entered a new era following the 1997 referendum vote in favour of a devolved Scottish parliament, which first convened in 1999 in a controversial modern building at the foot of the Royal Mile. The 2014 independence referendum saw Scots vote to remain part of the United Kingdom.

◉ Sights

Edinburgh's main attractions are concentrated in the city centre – on and around the Old Town's Royal Mile between the castle and Holyrood, and in the New Town. A major exception is the Royal Yacht *Britannia*, which is in the redeveloped docklands district of Leith, 2 miles northeast of the centre.

If you tire of sightseeing, good areas for aimless wandering include the posh suburbs of Stockbridge and Morningside, the pretty riverside village of Cramond and the winding footpaths of Calton Hill and Arthur's Seat.

◉ Old Town

Edinburgh's Old Town stretches along a ridge between the castle and Holyrood, and tumbles southward down Victoria St and West Bow to the broad expanse of the Grassmarket and the mossy stones of Greyfriars Kirkyard. It's cleft along its spine by the cobbled ravine of the Royal Mile.

Half the fun is just exploring this medieval maze, but the Old Town is also home to the city's most important historical sights – Edinburgh Castle, St Giles Cathedral, the Real Mary King's Close and Greyfriars Kirkyard, along with the Museum of Edinburgh and the National Museum of Scotland.

Until the founding of the New Town in the 18th century, old Edinburgh was an overcrowded, unsanitary hive of humanity squeezed between the boggy ground of the Nor' Loch (North Loch, now drained and occupied by Princes Street Gardens) to the north and the city walls to the south and east. The only way for the town to expand was upwards, and the five- and six-storey tenements that were raised along the Royal Mile in the 16th and 17th centuries were the skyscrapers of their day, remarked upon with wonder by visiting writers such as Daniel Defoe. All classes of society, from beggars to magistrates, lived cheek by jowl in these urban ant nests, the wealthy occupying the middle floors – high enough to be above the noise and stink of the streets, but not so high that climbing the stairs would be too tiring – while the poor squeezed into attics, basements, cellars and vaults amid rats, rubbish and raw sewage.

The renovated Old Town tenements still support a thriving city-centre community, and today the street level is crammed with cafes, restaurants, bars, backpacker hostels and tacky souvenir shops.

◉ Royal Mile

★ Edinburgh Castle CASTLE
(Map p58; ☏ 0131-225 9846; www.edinburgh castle.gov.uk; Castle Esplanade; adult/child £18.50/11.50, audio guide £3.50/£1.50; ⊙ 9.30am-6pm Apr-Sep, to 5pm Oct-Mar, last entry 1hr before closing; ☐ 23, 27, 41, 42, 67) Edinburgh Castle has played a pivotal role in Scottish history, both as a royal residence – King Malcolm Canmore (r 1058–93) and Queen Margaret first made their home here in the 11th century – and as a military stronghold. The castle last saw military action in 1745; from then until the 1920s it served as the British army's main base in Scotland. Today it is one of Scotland's most atmospheric and popular tourist attractions.

The brooding, black crags of Castle Rock, rising above the western end of Princes St, are the very reason for Edinburgh's existence. This rocky hill was the most easily defended hilltop on the invasion route between England and central Scotland, a route followed by countless armies from the Roman legions of the 1st and 2nd centuries AD to the Jacobite troops of Bonnie Prince Charlie in 1745.

The **Entrance Gateway**, flanked by statues of Robert the Bruce and William Wallace, opens to a cobbled lane that leads up beneath the 16th-century **Portcullis Gate** to the cannons ranged along the Argyle and Mills Mount Batteries. The battlements here have great views over the New Town to the Firth of Forth.

At the far end of Mills Mount Battery is the famous **One O'Clock Gun**, where crowds gather to watch a gleaming WWII 25-pounder fire an ear-splitting time signal at exactly 1pm (every day except Sundays, Christmas Day and Good Friday).

South of Mills Mount, the road curls up leftwards through **Foog's Gate** to the highest part of Castle Rock, crowned by the tiny, Romanesque **St Margaret's Chapel**, the oldest surviving building in Edinburgh. It was probably built by David I or Alexander I in memory of their mother, Queen Margaret, sometime around 1130 (she was canonised in 1250). Beside the chapel stands **Mons Meg**, a giant 15th-century siege gun built at Mons (in what is now Belgium) in 1449.

EDINBURGH IN...

Two Days
A two-day trip to Edinburgh should start at **Edinburgh Castle**, followed by a stroll down the Royal Mile to the **Scottish Parliament Building** (p61) and the **Palace of Holyroodhouse** (p61). You can work up an appetite by climbing **Arthur's Seat** (p63), then satisfy your hunger with dinner at **Ondine** (p82) or **Castle Terrace** (p88). On day two spend the morning in the **National Museum of Scotland** (p63), then catch the bus to Leith for a visit to the **Royal Yacht Britannia** (p70). In the evening, have dinner at one of Leith's many excellent restaurants, or scare yourself silly on a guided ghost tour.

Four Days
Two more days will give you time for a morning stroll around the **Royal Botanic Garden** (p70), followed by a trip to the enigmatic and beautiful Rosslyn Chapel, or a relaxing afternoon visit to the seaside village of **Cramond** (p71); bring binoculars (for birdwatching and yacht-spotting) and a book (to read in the sun). Dinner at **Aizle** (p89) or **Gardener's Cottage** (p83) could be before or after your sunset walk to the summit of Calton Hill. On day four head out to the pretty harbour village of Queensferry, nestled beneath the Forth Bridges, and take a cruise to Inchcolm Island.

Edinburgh

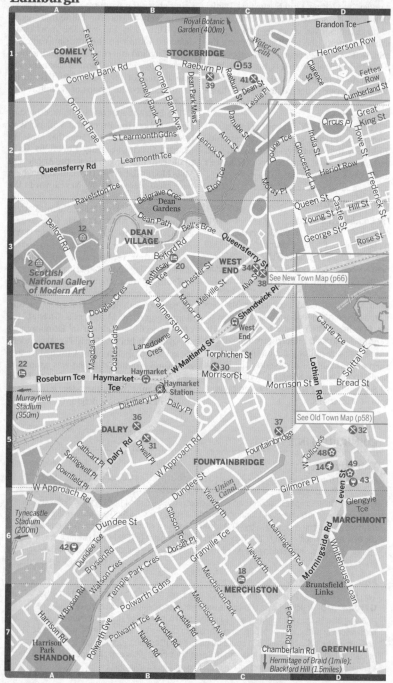

Royal Botanic Garden (400m)

Water of Leith

Brandon Tce

Henderson Row

COMELY BANK

STOCKBRIDGE

Fettes Ave

Comely Bank Rd

Comely Bank St

Comely Bank Ave

Dean Park Mews

Raeburn Pl

53

39

41

Dean St

Leslie Pl

Raeburn St

Clarence St

Fettes Row

Cumberland St

Orchard Brae

S Learmonth Gdns

Learmonth Tce

Danube St

Ann St

Lennox St

Circus Pl

India St

Howe St

Great King St

Queensferry Rd

Ravelston Tce

Belgrave Cres

Dean Gardens

Eton Tce

Doune Tce

Gloucester La

Heriot Row

Queen St

Castle St

Hill St

Young St

Frederick St

Belford Rd

12

DEAN VILLAGE

Dean Path

Bell's Brae

Belford Rd

Moray Pl

George St

Rose St

2

Scottish National Gallery of Modern Art

Douglas Cres

Rothesay Tce

20

Chester St

Melville St

Manor Pl

WEST END

34

38

Alva St

Queensferry St

See New Town Map (p66)

COATES

22

Roseburn Tce

Magdala Cres

Coates Gdns

Lansdowne Cres

Palmerston Pl

W Maitland St

Shandwick Pl

West End

Torphichen St

Castle Tce

Spittal St

Haymarket Tce

Haymarket Tce

Haymarket Station

30

Morrison St

Morrison St

Lothian Rd

Bread St

Murrayfield Stadium (950m)

Distillery La

Dalry Pl

See Old Town Map (p58)

DALRY

36

31

Dalry Rd

Orwell Pl

37

Fountainbridge

32

Cathcart Pl

Springwell Pl

Downfield Pl

W Approach Rd

FOUNTAINBRIDGE

Tollcross

48

14

49

Leven St

43

Tynecastle Stadium (200m)

W Approach Rd

Dundee St

Dundee Tce

Bryson Rd

Gibson Tce

Dundee St

Viewforth

Union Canal

Gilmore Pl

Leamington Tce

Glengyle Tce

MARCHMONT

Morningside Rd

42

W Bryson Rd

Watson Cres

Temple Park Cres

Polwarth Gdns

Dorset Pl

Granville Tce

Viewforth

18

MERCHISTON

Merchiston Park

Bruntsfield Links

Whitehouse Loan

Harrison Rd

SHANDON

Harrison Park

Polwarth Gve

Polwarth Tce

W Castle Rd

Napier Rd

E Castle Rd

Merchiston Ave

Forbes Rd

Chamberlain Rd

GREENHILL

Hermitage of Braid (1mile); Blackford Hill (1.5miles)

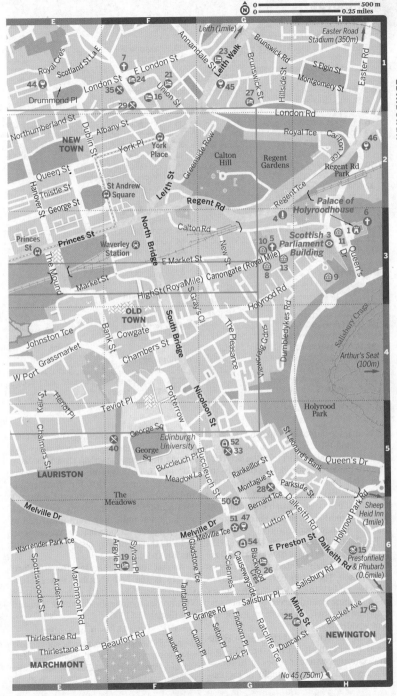

Edinburgh

The main group of buildings on the summit of Castle Rock is ranged around Crown Sq, dominated by the shrine of the **Scottish National War Memorial**. Opposite is the Great Hall, built for James IV (r 1488–1513) as a ceremonial hall and used as a meeting place for the Scottish parliament until 1639. Its most remarkable feature is the original, 16th-century hammerbeam roof.

The **Castle Vaults** beneath the Great Hall (entered via the **Prisons of War Exhibition**) were used variously as storerooms, bakeries and a prison. The vaults have been renovated to resemble 18th- and early 19th-century prisons, where graffiti carved by French and American prisoners can be seen on the ancient wooden doors.

On the eastern side of the square is the **Royal Palace**, built during the 15th and 16th centuries, where a series of historical tableaux leads to the highlight of the castle: a strongroom housing the **Honours of Scotland** (the Scottish crown jewels), among the oldest surviving crown jewels in Europe. Locked away in a chest following the Act of Union in 1707, the crown (made in 1540 from the gold of Robert the Bruce's 14th-century coronet), sword and sceptre lay forgotten until they were unearthed at the instigation of novelist Sir Walter Scott in 1818. Also on display here is the Stone of Destiny (p65).

Among the neighbouring **Royal Apartments** is the bed chamber where Mary, Queen of Scots, gave birth to her son James VI, who was to unite the crowns of Scotland and England in 1603.

➔ National War Museum of Scotland

(Map p58; www.nms.ac.uk/national-war-museum; with Edinburgh Castle free; ⊙9.45am-5.45pm Apr-Oct, to 4.45pm Nov-Mar; 🚍23, 27, 41, 42) At the western end of Edinburgh Castle (p51), to the left of the castle tearooms, a road leads down to the National War Museum of Scotland, which brings Scotland's military history vividly to life. The exhibits have been personalised by telling the stories of the original owners of the objects on display, making it easier to empathise with the experiences of war than any dry display of dusty weaponry ever could.

Scotch Whisky Experience MUSEUM
(Map p58; www.scotchwhiskyexperience.co.uk; 354 Castlehill; adult/child from £15.50/7.50; ⏰10am-6pm Apr-Jul, to 5pm Aug-Mar; 🚌23, 27, 41, 42) A former school houses this multimedia centre that takes you through the making of whisky, from barley to bottle, in a series of exhibits, demonstrations and talks that combine sight, sound and smell, including the world's largest collection of malt whiskies (3384 bottles!). The pricier tours include extensive whisky tastings and samples of Scottish cuisine. There's also a restaurant (p82) that serves traditional Scottish dishes with, where possible, a dash of whisky thrown in.

**Camera Obscura &
World of Illusions** MUSEUM
(Map p58; www.camera-obscura.co.uk; Castlehill; adult/child £15.50/11.50; ⏰9am-10pm Jul & Aug, 9.30am-8pm Apr-Jun, Sep & Oct, 10am-7pm Nov-Mar; 🚌23, 27, 41, 42, 67) Edinburgh's camera obscura is a curious 19th-century device – in constant use since 1853 – that uses lenses and mirrors to throw a live image of the city onto a large horizontal screen. The accompanying commentary is entertaining and the whole experience has a quirky charm, complemented by an intriguing exhibition dedicated to illusions of all kinds. Stairs lead up through various displays to the **Outlook Tower**, which offers great views over the city.

Gladstone's Land HISTORIC BUILDING
(NTS; Map p58; ☎0131-226 5856; www.nts.org.uk/visit/places/gladstones-land; 477 Lawnmarket; adult/child £10/5; ⏰by prebooked guided tour; 🚌23, 27, 41, 42, 67) One of Edinburgh's most prominent 17th-century merchants was Thomas Gledstanes, who in 1617 purchased the tenement later known as Gladstone's Land. It contains fine painted ceilings, walls and beams, and some splendid furniture from the 17th and 18th centuries. The guided tours (phone to book) provide a wealth of anecdotes and a detailed history.

Writers' Museum MUSEUM
(Map p58; ☎0131-529 4901; www.edinburghmuseums.org.uk; Lady Stair's Close; ⏰10am-5pm; 🚌23, 27, 41, 42) **FREE** Tucked down a close between the Royal Mile and the Mound you'll find Lady Stair's House (1622), home to this museum that contains manuscripts and memorabilia belonging to three of Scotland's most famous writers: Robert Burns, Sir Walter Scott and Robert Louis Stevenson.

St Giles Cathedral CHURCH
(Map p58; www.stgilescathedral.org.uk; High St; ⏰9am-7pm Mon-Fri, to 5pm Sat, 1-5pm Sun Apr-Oct, 9am-5pm Mon-Sat, 1-5pm Sun Nov-Mar; 🚌23, 27, 41, 42) **FREE** The great grey bulk of St Giles Cathedral dates largely from the 15th century, but much of it was restored in the 19th century. One of the most interesting corners of the kirk is the **Thistle Chapel**, built in 1911 for the Knights of the Most Ancient & Most Noble Order of the Thistle. The elaborately carved Gothic-style stalls have canopies topped with the helms and arms of the 16 knights – look out for the bagpipe-playing angel amid the vaulting.

Properly called the High Kirk of Edinburgh (it was only a true cathedral – the seat of a bishop – from 1633 to 1638 and from 1661 to 1689), the church was named after the patron saint of cripples and beggars. The interior lacks grandeur but is rich in history: a Norman-style church was built here in 1126 but was destroyed by English invaders in 1385 (the only substantial remains are the central piers that support the tower). St Giles was at the heart of the Scottish Reformation, and John Knox served as minister here from 1559 to 1572.

There are several ornate monuments in the church, including the tombs of **James Graham, Marquis of Montrose**, who led Charles I's forces in Scotland and was hanged in 1650 at the Mercat Cross; and his opponent, Covenanter (an adherent of the Scottish Presbyterian Church) **Archibald Campbell, Marquis of Argyll**, who was decapitated in 1661 after the restoration of Charles II. There's also a bronze memorial to author **Robert Louis Stevenson**, and a copy of the National Covenant of 1638.

By the side of the street, outside the western door of St Giles, is the **Heart of Midlothian** (Map p58; High St; 🚌23, 27, 41, 42), set into the cobblestone paving. This marks the site of the Tolbooth. Built in the 15th century and demolished in the early 19th century, the Tolbooth served variously as a meeting

Royal Mile

A GRAND DAY OUT

Planning your own procession along the Royal Mile involves some tough decisions – it would be impossible to see everything in a single day, so it's wise to decide in advance what you don't want to miss and shape your visit around that. Remember to leave time for lunch, for exploring some of the Mile's countless side alleys and, during festival time, for enjoying the street theatre that is bound to be happening in High St.

The most pleasant way to reach the Castle Esplanade at the start of the Royal Mile is to hike up the zigzag path from the footbridge behind the Ross Bandstand in Princes Street Gardens (in springtime you'll be knee-deep in daffodils). Starting at **Edinburgh Castle** ❶ means that the rest of your walk is downhill. For a superb view up and down the length of the Mile, climb the **Camera Obscura's Outlook Tower** ❷ before visiting **Gladstone's Land** ❸ and **St Giles Cathedral** ❹.

CLAUDIO DIVIZIA / SHUTTERSTOCK ©

ROYAL VISITS TO THE ROYAL MILE

1561: Mary, Queen of Scots arrives from France and holds an audience with John Knox.
1745: Bonnie Prince Charlie fails to capture Edinburgh Castle, and instead sets up court in Holyroodhouse.
2004: Queen Elizabeth II officially opens the Scottish Parliament building.

Edinburgh Castle
If you're pushed for time, visit the Great Hall, the Honours of Scotland and the Prisons of War exhibit. Head for the Half Moon Battery for a photo looking down the length of the Royal Mile.

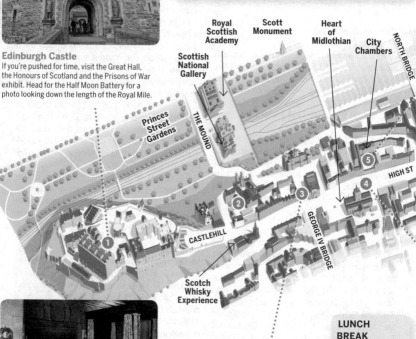

Gladstone's Land
The 1st floor houses a faithful recreation of how a wealthy Edinburgh merchant lived in the 17th century. Check out the beautiful Painted Bedchamber, with its ornately decorated walls and wooden ceilings.

DE AGOSTINI / W BUSS / GETTY IMAGES ©

LUNCH BREAK

Burger and a beer at **Holyrood 9A**; steak and chips at **Maxie's Bistro**; slap-up seafood at **Ondine**.

If history's your thing, you'll want to add **Real Mary King's Close** ❺, **John Knox House** ❻ and the **Museum of Edinburgh** ❼ to your must-see list.

At the foot of the mile, choose between modern and ancient seats of power – the **Scottish Parliament** ❽ or the **Palace of Holyroodhouse** ❾. Round off the day with an evening ascent of Arthur's Seat or, slightly less strenuously, Calton Hill. Both make great sunset viewpoints.

TAKING YOUR TIME

Minimum time needed for each attraction:
» **Edinburgh Castle**: two hours
» **Gladstone's Land**: 45 minutes
» **St Giles Cathedral**: 30 minutes
» **Real Mary King's Close**: one hour (tour)
» **Scottish Parliament**: one hour (tour)
» **Palace of Holyroodhouse**: one hour

Real Mary King's Close
The guided tour is heavy on ghost stories, but a highlight is standing in an original 17th-century room with tufts of horsehair poking from the crumbling plaster, and breathing in the ancient scent of stone, dust and history.

Canongate Kirk

CANONGATE

ST MARY'S ST

SOUTH BRIDGE

Tron Kirk

Our Dynamic Earth

Scottish Parliament
Don't have time for the guided tour? Pick up a 'Discover the Scottish Parliament Building' leaflet from reception and take a self-guided tour of the exterior, then hike up to Salisbury Crags for a great view of the complex.

Palace of Holyroodhouse
Find the secret staircase joining Mary, Queen of Scots' bedchamber with that of her husband, Lord Darnley, who restrained the queen while his henchmen stabbed to death her secretary (and possible lover), David Rizzio.

St Giles Cathedral
Look out for the Burne-Jones stained-glass window (1873) at the west end, showing the crossing of the River Jordan, and the bronze memorial to Robert Louis Stevenson in the Moray Aisle.

PHOTOPROF130 / SHUTTERSTOCK ©

HEARTLAND ARTS / SHUTTERSTOCK ©

DAVID IONUT / SHUTTERSTOCK ©

Old Town

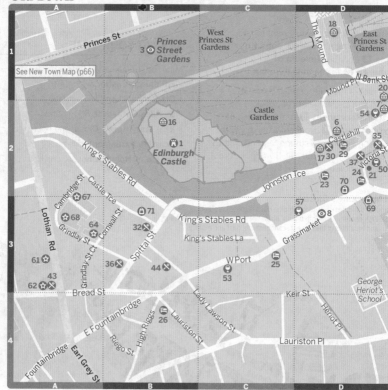

place for parliament, the town council and the General Assembly of the Reformed Kirk, before becoming law courts and, finally, a notorious prison and place of execution. Passers-by traditionally spit on the heart for luck (don't stand downwind!).

At the other end of St Giles is the **Mercat Cross** (Map p58; 📟35), a 19th-century copy of the 1365 original, where merchants and traders met to transact business and royal proclamations were read.

⭐**Real Mary King's Close** HISTORIC BUILDING (Map p58; 📞0131-225 0672; www.realmary kingsclose.com; 2 Warriston's Close; adult/child £15.50/9.50; ⏱10am-9pm Apr-Oct, 9am-5.30pm Mon-Thu, 9.30am-9pm Fri & Sat, to 6.30pm Sun Nov, 10am-5pm Sun-Thu, to 9pm Fri & Sat Dec-Mar; 📟23, 27, 41, 42) Edinburgh's 18th-century City Chambers were built over the sealed-off remains of Mary King's Close, and the lower levels of this medieval Old Town alley have

survived almost unchanged amid the foundations for 250 years. Now open to the public, this spooky, subterranean labyrinth gives a fascinating insight into the everyday life of 17th-century Edinburgh. Costumed characters lead tours through a 16th-century townhouse and the plague-stricken home of a 17th-century gravedigger. Advance booking recommended.

The scripted tour, complete with ghostly tales and gruesome tableaux, can seem a little naff, milking the scary and scatological aspects of the close's history for all they're worth. But there are also things of genuine interest to see: there's something about the crumbling 17th-century **tenement room** that makes the hair rise on the back of your neck, with tufts of horsehair poking from collapsing lath-and-plaster walls that bear the ghost of a pattern, and the ancient smell of stone and dust thick in your nostrils.

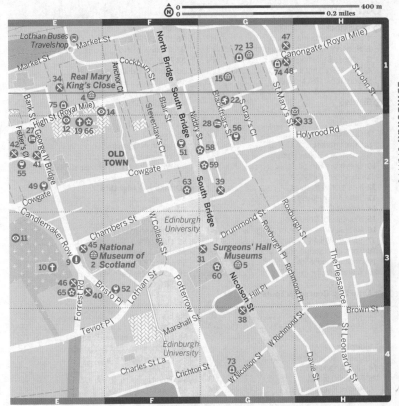

In one of the former bedrooms off the close, a psychic once claimed to have been approached by the ghost of a little girl called Annie. It's hard to tell what's more frightening – the story of the ghostly child, or the bizarre heap of tiny dolls and teddies left by sympathetic visitors.

Museum of Childhood MUSEUM

(Map p58; ☎0131-529 4142; www.edinburgh museums.org.uk; 42 High St; ☺10am-5pm Mon & Thu-Sat, noon-5pm Sun; 🚌300) **FREE** Halfway down the Royal Mile is 'the noisiest museum in the world'. Often filled with the chatter of excited children, it covers serious issues related to childhood – health, education, upbringing etc – but also has an enormous collection of toys, dolls, games and books, recordings of school lessons from the 1930s to modern times, and film of children playing street games in 1950s Edinburgh.

John Knox House HISTORIC BUILDING

(Map p58; www.tracscotland.org/scottish-story telling-centre/john-knox-house-step-inside-history; 43-45 High St; adult/child £5/1; ☺10am-6pm Mon-Sat year-round, plus 10am-6pm Sun Jul & Aug; 🚌35) The Royal Mile narrows at the foot of High St beside the jutting facade of John Knox House. This is the oldest surviving tenement in Edinburgh, dating from around 1490. John Knox, an influential church reformer and leader of the Protestant Reformation in Scotland, is thought to have lived here from 1561 to 1572. The labyrinthine interior has some beautiful painted-timber ceilings and an interesting display on Knox's life and work.

People's Story MUSEUM

(Map p52; www.edinburghmuseums.org.uk; 163 Canongate; ☺10am-5pm Wed-Sat, noon-5pm Sun; 🚌300) **FREE** One of the surviving symbols of the Canongate district's former independence is the **Canongate Tolbooth**. Built in 1591, it served successively as a collection

Old Town

point for tolls (taxes), a council house, a courtroom and a jail. With picturesque turrets and a projecting clock, it's an interesting example of 16th-century architecture. It now houses a fascinating museum called the People's Story, which covers the life, work and pastimes of ordinary Edinburgh folk from the 18th century to today.

Museum of Edinburgh   MUSEUM
(Map p52; ☎ 0131-529 4143; www.edinburgh museums.org.uk; 142 Canongate; ⊙ 10am-5pm Mon & Thu-Sat, noon-5pm Sun; ☐ 300) FREE You can't miss the colourful facade of Huntly House, brightly painted in red and yellow ochre, opposite the Tolbooth clock on the Royal Mile. Built in 1570, it houses a museum covering Edinburgh from prehistory to the present. Exhibits of national importance include an original copy of the National Covenant of 1638, but the big crowd-pleaser is the dog collar and feeding bowl that once belonged to Greyfriars Bobby (p63), the city's most famous canine citizen.

Canongate Kirkyard CHURCH
(Map p52; www.canongatekirk.org.uk; Canongate; ☉dawn-dusk; 🚌300) The attractive curved gable of the Canongate Kirk, built in 1688, overlooks a kirkyard that contains the graves of several famous people, including economist Adam Smith, author of *The Wealth of Nations;* Agnes Maclehose (the 'Clarinda' of Robert Burns' love poems); and poet Robert Fergusson (1750–74; there's a statue of him on the street outside the church). An information board just inside the gate lists notable graves and their locations.

Fergusson was much admired by Robert Burns, who paid for his gravestone and penned the epitaph – take a look at the inscription on the back.

◉ Holyrood & Arthur's Seat

★**Scottish Parliament**
Building NOTABLE BUILDING
(Map p52; ☎0131-348 5200; www.parliament.scot; Horse Wynd; ☉9am-6.30pm Tue-Thu, 10am-5pm Mon, Fri & Sat in session, 10am-5pm Tue-Thu in recess; 👶; 🚌6, 300) **FREE** The Scottish Parliament Building, on the site of a former brewery and designed by Catalan architect Enric Miralles (1955–2000), was opened by the Queen in October 2004. The ground plan of the complex is said to represent a 'flower of democracy rooted in Scottish soil' (best seen looking down from Salisbury Crags). Free, one-hour tours (advance bookings recommended) include visits to the Debating Chamber, a committee room, the Garden Lobby and the office of a member of parliament (MSP).

Miralles believed that a building could be a work of art. However, this weird concrete confection at the foot of Salisbury Crags initially left the good people of Edinburgh scratching their heads in confusion. What does it all mean? The strange forms of the exterior are each symbolic in some way, from the oddly shaped windows on the western wall (inspired by the silhouette of *The Reverend Robert Walker Skating on Duddingston Loch,* one of Scotland's most famous paintings) to the asymmetrical panels on the main facade (representing a curtain being drawn aside – a symbol of open government).

The **Main Hall**, inside the public entrance, has a low, triple-arched ceiling of polished concrete, like a cave, or cellar, or castle vault. It is a dimly lit space, the starting point for a metaphorical journey from this relative darkness up to the **Debating Chamber** (sitting directly above the Main Hall), which is, in contrast, a palace of light – the light of democracy. This magnificent chamber is the centrepiece of the parliament, designed not to glorify but to humble the politicians who sit within it. The windows face Calton Hill, allowing parliamentarians to look up to its monuments (reminders of the Scottish Enlightenment), while the massive, pointed oak beams of the roof are suspended by steel threads above the MSPs' heads like so many Damoclean swords.

The public areas of the building – the Main Hall, where there is an exhibition, shop and cafe, and the public gallery in the Debating Chamber – are open to visitors (free tickets are needed for the public gallery – see the website for details). If you want to see the parliament in session, check the website to see when it will be sitting – business days are normally Tuesday to Thursday year-round.

★**Palace of Holyroodhouse** PALACE
(Map p52; ☎0303-123 7306; www.royalcollection.org.uk/visit/palace-of-holyroodhouse; Canongate, Royal Mile; adult/child incl audio guide £14/8.10; ☉9.30am-6pm, last entry 4.30pm Apr-Oct, to 4.30pm, last entry 3.15pm Nov-Mar; 🚌6, 300) This palace is the royal family's official residence in Scotland but is more famous as the 16th-century home of the ill-fated Mary, Queen of Scots. The highlight of the tour is **Mary's Bedchamber**, home to the unfortunate queen from 1561 to 1567. It was here that her jealous second husband, Lord Darnley, restrained the pregnant queen while his henchmen murdered her secretary – and favourite – David Rizzio. A plaque in the neighbouring room marks the spot where Rizzio bled to death.

The palace developed from a guesthouse attached to Holyrood Abbey that was extended by James IV in 1501. The oldest surviving part of the building, the northwestern tower, was built in 1529 as a royal apartment for James V and his wife, Mary of Guise. Mary, Queen of Scots, spent six turbulent years here, during which time she debated with John Knox, married both her second and third husbands, and witnessed Rizzio's murder.

The self-guided audio tour leads you through a series of impressive royal apartments, culminating in the **Great Gallery**. The gallery's 89 portraits of Scottish kings were commissioned by Charles II and supposedly record his unbroken lineage from Scota, the Egyptian pharaoh's daughter who discovered the infant Moses in a reed basket on the banks of the Nile. The tour continues to the oldest part of the palace, which contains Mary's Bedchamber, connected by a secret stairway to her husband's bedroom, and ends with the ruins of Holyrood Abbey.

The palace is closed during royal visits; check the website for dates.

➡ **Holyrood Abbey**

(Map p52; www.historicenvironment.scot/visit-a -place/places/holyrood-abbey; Canongate; with Palace of Holyroodhouse free; ⊘ 9.30am-6pm, last entry 4.30pm Apr-Oct, to 4.30pm, last entry 3.15pm Nov-Mar; 🚌 6, 300) David I founded this abbey in the shadow of Salisbury Crags in 1128. It was probably named after a fragment of the True Cross (*rood* is an old Scots word for cross), said to have been brought to Scotland by David's mother, St Margaret. Most of the ruins date from the 12th and 13th centuries, although a doorway in the far-southeastern corner has survived from the original Norman church. Admission is included in the cost of a Palace of Holyroodhouse (p61) ticket.

➡ **Queen's Gallery**

(Map p52; www.royalcollection.org.uk/visit/the-queens-gallery-palace-of-holyroodhouse; Horse Wynd; adult/child £7/3.50, with Holyroodhouse £17.50/10; ⊘ 9.30am-6pm, last entry 4.30pm Apr-Oct, to 4.30pm, last entry 3.15pm Nov-Mar; 🚌 6, 300) This stunning modern gallery, which occupies the shell of a former church and school, is a showcase for exhibitions of art from the Royal Collections. The exhibitions

THE RESURRECTION MEN

In 1505 Edinburgh's newly founded Royal College of Surgeons was officially allocated the corpse of one executed criminal per year for the purposes of dissection. But this was not nearly enough to satisfy the curiosity of the city's anatomists, and in the following centuries an illegal trade in dead bodies emerged, which reached its culmination in the early 19th century when the anatomy classes of famous surgeons such as Professor Robert Knox drew audiences of up to 500.

The readiest supply of corpses was to be found in the city's graveyards, especially Greyfriars. Grave robbers – who came to be known as 'resurrection men' – plundered newly buried coffins and sold the cadavers to the anatomists, who turned a blind eye to the source of their research material.

This gruesome trade led to a series of countermeasures, including the mort-safe – a metal cage that was placed over a coffin until the corpse had begun to decompose; you can see examples in **Greyfriars Kirkyard** (Map p58; www.greyfriarskirk.com; Greyfriars Pl; ⊘ 10.30am-4.30pm Mon-Fri, 11am-2pm Sat Apr-Oct, 11am-3pm Thu Nov-Mar; 🚌 2, 23, 27, 41, 42, 67) and on level five of the National Museum of Scotland. Watchtowers, where a sexton, or relatives of the deceased, would keep watch over new graves, survive in St Cuthbert's and Duddingston kirkyards.

The notorious William Burke and William Hare, who kept a lodging house in Tanner's Close at the western end of the Grassmarket, took the body-snatching business a step further. When an elderly lodger died without paying his rent, Burke and Hare stole his body from the coffin and sold it to the famous Professor Knox. Seeing a lucrative business opportunity, they figured that rather than waiting for someone else to die, they could create their own supply of fresh cadavers by resorting to murder.

Burke and Hare preyed on the poor and weak of Edinburgh's Grassmarket, luring them back to Hare's lodging house, plying them with drink and then suffocating them. Between December 1827 and October 1828, they murdered at least 16 people and sold their bodies to Professor Knox. When the law finally caught up with them, Hare turned king's evidence and testified against Burke.

Burke was hanged outside St Giles Cathedral in January 1829 and, in an ironic twist, his body was given to the anatomy school for public dissection. His skeleton, and a wallet made from his flayed skin, are still on display in the Surgeons' Hall Museums.

It was as a result of the Burke and Hare case that the *Anatomy Act* 1832 – regulating the supply of cadavers for dissection, and still in force today – was passed.

change every six months or so; for current details, check the website.

★ **Arthur's Seat** VIEWPOINT
(Holyrood Park; 🚌6, 300) The rocky peak of Arthur's Seat (251m), carved by ice sheets from the deeply eroded stump of a long-extinct volcano, is a distinctive feature of Edinburgh's skyline. The view from the summit is well worth the walk, extending from the Forth bridges in the west to the distant conical hill of North Berwick Law in the east, with the Ochil Hills and the Highlands on the northwestern horizon. You can hike from Holyrood to the summit in around 45 minutes.

Our Dynamic Earth MUSEUM
(Map p52; www.dynamicearth.co.uk; Holyrood Rd; adult/child £15.50/9.75; ⊙10am-5.30pm Easter-Oct, to 6pm Jul & Aug, 10am-5.30pm Wed-Sun Nov-Easter; 🚼; 🚌6, 300) Housed in a modern-istic white marquee, Our Dynamic Earth is an interactive, multimedia journey of discovery through Earth's history from the Big Bang to the present day. Hugely popular with kids of all ages, it's a slick extrava-ganza of whiz-bang special effects and 3D movies cleverly designed to fire up young minds with curiosity about all things geo-logical and environmental. Its true purpose, of course, is to disgorge you into a gift shop where you can buy toy dinosaurs and souve-nir T-shirts.

⊙ South of the Royal Mile

★ **National Museum of Scotland** MUSEUM
(Map p58; 📞0300-123 6789; www.nms.ac.uk/national-museum-of-scotland; Chambers St; ⊙10am-5pm; 🚼; 🚌45, 300) **FREE** Elegant Chambers St is dominated by the long facade of the National Museum of Scotland. Its extensive collections are spread between two buildings: one modern, one Victorian – the golden stone and striking architecture of the new building (1998) make it one of the city's most distinctive landmarks. The museum's five floors trace the history of Scotland from geological beginnings to the 1990s, with many imaginative and stimu-lating exhibits. Audio guides are available in several languages. Fees apply for special exhibitions.

The modern building connects with the original Victorian museum, dating from 1861, the stolid, grey exterior of which gives way to a beautifully bright and airy, glass-

roofed exhibition hall. The old building houses an eclectic collection covering natu-ral history, archaeology, design and fashion, science and technology, and the decorative arts of ancient Egypt, the Islamic world, China, Japan, Korea and the West.

★ **Surgeons' Hall Museums** MUSEUM
(Map p58; 📞0131-527 1711; www.museum.rcsed. ac.uk; Nicolson St; adult/child £7/4; ⊙10am-5pm; 🚌3, 5, 7, 8, 14, 30, 31, 33) Housed in a grand Ionic temple designed by William Playfair in 1832, these three fascinating museums were originally established as teaching col-lections. The **History of Surgery Muse-um** provides a look at surgery in Scotland from the 15th century to the present day. Highlights include the exhibit on murder-ers Burke and Hare, which includes Burke's death mask and a pocketbook made from his skin, and a display on Dr Joseph Bell, who was the inspiration for the character of Sherlock Holmes.

The adjacent **Dental Collection**, with its wince-inducing extraction tools, covers the history of dentistry, while the **Pathol-ogy Museum** houses a gruesome but com-pelling 19th-century collection of diseased organs and massive tumours pickled in formaldehyde.

Greyfriars Kirkyard CEMETERY
(Map p58; www.greyfriarskirk.com; Candlemaker Row; ⊙24hr; 🚌2, 23, 27, 41, 42, 67) Greyfriars Kirkyard is one of Edinburgh's most evoc-ative cemeteries, a peaceful green oasis dotted with elaborate monuments. Many famous Edinburgh names are buried here, including poet Allan Ramsay (1686–1758); architect William Adam (1689–1748); and William Smellie (1740–95), editor of the first edition of the *Encyclopaedia Britannica*. If you want to experience the graveyard at its scariest – inside a burial vault, in the dark, at night – go on a City of the Dead (p73) guided tour.

A more recent addition to the graveyard's reputation is the idea that it is the resting place of JK Rowling's famous villain Vold-emort. Rowling is said to have been in-spired to create the dark lord by the grave of 19th-century gentleman Thomas Riddell, who died in 1806 aged 72.

Greyfriars Bobby Statue MONUMENT
(Map p58; cnr George IV Bridge & Candlemaker Row; 🚌23, 27, 41, 42, 45, 67) Probably the most pop-ular photo opportunity in Edinburgh, the

life-size statue of Greyfriars Bobby, a Skye terrier who captured the hearts of the British public in the late 19th century, stands outside Greyfriars Kirkyard (p63). From 1858 to 1872 the wee dog maintained a vigil over the grave of his master, an Edinburgh police officer. The story was immortalised in a novel by Eleanor Atkinson in 1912, and in 1961 was made into a movie by – who else? – Walt Disney.

The statue is always surrounded by crowds of visitors taking photos of themselves posing beside the little dog. Bobby's own grave, marked by a small, pink-granite stone, is just inside the entrance to Greyfriars Kirkyard, behind the monument, and you can see his original collar and bowl in the Museum of Edinburgh (p60).

Grassmarket   STREET
(Map p58; 🗖 2) The site of a cattle market from the 15th century until the start of the 20th century, the Grassmarket has always been a focal point of the Old Town. It was once the city's main place of execution, and over 100 martyred Covenanters are commemorated by a monument at the eastern end, where the gallows used to stand. The notorious murderers Burke and Hare (p62) operated from a now-vanished close off the western end.

Nowadays the broad, open square, lined by tall tenements and dominated by the looming castle, has many lively pubs and restaurants, including the **White Hart Inn** (Map p58; 📞 0131-226 2806; www.whitehart-edinburgh.co.uk; 34 Grassmarket; ⊗ 11am-midnight Sun-Thu, to 1am Fri & Sat; 🗖 2), which was once patronised by Robert Burns. Claiming to be the city's oldest pub in continuous use (since 1516), it also hosted William Wordsworth in 1803. **Cowgate** – the long, dark ravine leading eastwards from the Grassmarket – was once the road along which cattle were driven from the pastures around Arthur's Seat to the safety of the city walls. Today it is the heart of Edinburgh's nightlife, with around two dozen clubs and bars within five minutes' walk of each other.

◉ New Town

Edinburgh's New Town lies north of the Old, on a ridge running parallel to the Royal Mile and separated from it by the valley of Princes Street Gardens. Its regular grid of elegant, Georgian terraces is a complete contrast to the chaotic tangle of tenements and wynds that characterises the Old Town, and is the world's most complete and unspoilt example of Georgian architecture and town planning.

Apart from the streetscape, the main sights are the art galleries and gardens on Princes St, and the Scottish National Portrait Gallery (p68) near St Andrew Sq, all within walking distance of each other.

◉ Princes Street

Princes St is one of the world's most spectacular shopping streets. Built up on the north side only, it catches the sun in summer and allows expansive views across Princes Street Gardens to the castle and the crowded skyline of the Old Town.

★Princes Street Gardens   GARDENS
(Map p58; Princes St; ⊗ dawn-dusk; 🗖 Princes St) **FREE** These beautiful gardens lie in a valley that was once occupied by the Nor' Loch (North Loch), a boggy depression that was drained in the early 19th century. At the gate beside The Mound is the **Floral Clock**, a working clock laid out in flowers; it was first created in 1903 and the design changes every year.

In the middle of the western part of the gardens is the **Ross Bandstand**, a venue for open-air concerts in summer and at Hogmanay (p76), and the stage for the famous fireworks concert during the Edinburgh International Festival (p75) (there are plans to replace the bandstand with a modern pavilion).

The gardens are split in the middle by **The Mound** – around two million cartloads of earth that were dug out from foundations during the construction of the New Town and dumped here to provide a road link across the valley to the Old Town. The road was completed in 1830.

Scott Monument   MONUMENT
(Map p66; www.edinburghmuseums.org.uk; East Princes Street Gardens; £5; ⊗ 10am-7pm Apr-Sep, to 4pm Oct-Mar; 🗖 Princes St) The eastern half of Princes Street Gardens is dominated by the massive Gothic spire of the Scott Monument, built by public subscription in memory of novelist Sir Walter Scott after his death in 1832. The exterior is decorated with 64 carvings of characters from his novels; inside you can see an exhibition on Scott's life, and climb the 287 steps to the top for a superb view of the city.

Scottish National Gallery   GALLERY
(Map p58; ☎0131-624 6200; www.national
galleries.org; The Mound; ☉10am-5pm Fri-Wed, to
7pmThu; ☐all PrincesStbuses, ☐Princes St) FREE
Designed by William Playfair, this imposing
classical building with its Ionic porticoes
dates from 1850. Its octagonal rooms, lit by
skylights, have been restored to their original Victorian decor of deep-green carpets
and dark-red walls. The gallery houses an
important collection of European art from
the Renaissance to the post-Impressionism
era, with works by Verrocchio (Leonardo da
Vinci's teacher), Tintoretto, Titian, Holbein,
Rubens, Van Dyck, Vermeer, El Greco,
Poussin, Rembrandt, Gainsborough, Turner,
Constable, Monet, Pissarro, Gauguin and
Cézanne.

The upstairs galleries (14 to 18) house
portraits by Allan Ramsay and Sir Henry
Raeburn, and a clutch of **Impressionist
paintings**, including Monet's *Poplars on the
River Epto,* Van Gogh's colourful *Orchard In
Blossom* and Gauguin's hallucinatory *Vision
of the Sermon.* But the painting that really
catches your eye is the gorgeous portrait
Lady Agnew of Lochnaw by John Singer
Sargent.

The basement galleries dedicated to
Scottish art include glowing portraits by
Allan Ramsay and Sir Henry Raeburn, rural
scenes by Sir David Wilkie and Impressionis-
tic landscapes by William MacTaggart. Look
out for Sir George Harvey's hugely entertaining *A Schule Skailin'* (A School Empty-
ing) – a stern *dominie* (teacher) looks on as
the boys stampede for the classroom door,
one reaching for a confiscated spinning top.
Kids will love the fantasy paintings of Sir
Joseph Noel Paton in room B5; the incredibly detailed canvases are crammed with
hundreds of tiny fairies, goblins and elves.

Recent research has suggested that the
iconic 1790s painting of *Reverend Robert
Walker Skating on Duddingston Loch,* historically attributed to Sir Henry Raeburn,
may in fact be the work of French artist
Henri-Pierre Danloux.

Each January the gallery exhibits its
collection of Turner watercolours, be-
queathed by Henry Vaughan in 1900.
Antonio Canova's white marble sculpture,
The Three Graces, is owned jointly with
London's Victoria & Albert Museum; when
not in London it can be seen in room 10.
There's a charge for some special exhibitions.

THE STONE OF DESTINY

On St Andrew's Day 1996 a block of sandstone – 26.5 inches by 16.5 inches by 11 inches
in size, with rusted iron hoops at either end – was installed with much pomp and circum-
stance in Edinburgh Castle. For the previous 700 years it had lain in London, beneath the
Coronation Chair in Westminster Abbey. Almost all English, and later British, monarchs
from Edward II in 1307 to Elizabeth II in 1953 have parked their backsides firmly over this
stone during their coronation ceremony.

The legendary Stone of Destiny – said to have originated in the Holy Land, and on
which Scottish kings placed their feet (not their bums; the English got that bit wrong)
during their coronation – was stolen from Scone Abbey near Perth by Edward I of England in 1296. It was taken to London and there it remained for seven centuries – except
for a brief removal to Gloucester during WWII air raids, and a three-month sojourn in
Scotland after it was stolen by Scottish Nationalist students on Christmas in 1950 – as
an enduring symbol of Scotland's subjugation by England.

The Stone of Destiny returned to the political limelight in 1996, when the then Scottish
Secretary and Conservative Party MP Michael Forsyth arranged for the return of the
sandstone block to Scotland. A blatant attempt to boost the flagging popularity of the
Conservative Party in Scotland prior to a general election, Forsyth's publicity stunt failed
miserably. The Scots said thanks very much for the stone and then, in May 1997, voted
every Conservative MP in Scotland into oblivion.

Many people, however, believe Edward I was fobbed off with a shoddy imitation in
1296 and that the true Stone of Destiny remains safely hidden somewhere in Scotland.
This is not impossible – some descriptions of the original stone state that it was made
of black marble and decorated with elaborate carvings. Interested parties should read
Scotland's Stone of Destiny by Nick Aitchinson, which details the history and cultural
significance of Scotland's most famous lump of rock.

New Town

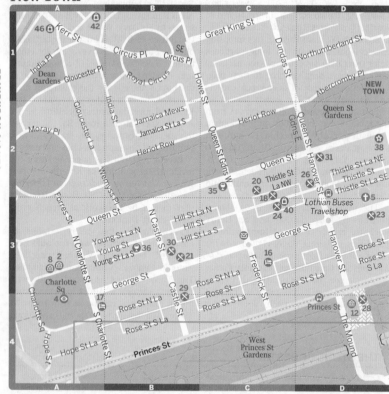

Royal Scottish Academy — GALLERY

(Map p66; ☎0131-225 6671; www.royalscottish
academy.org; The Mound; ⊙10am-5pm Mon-Sat,
noon-5pm Sun; 🚌Princes St) **FREE** This Greek
Doric temple, with its northern pediment
crowned by a seated figure of Queen Victoria,
is the home of the Royal Scottish Academy.
Designed by William Playfair and built between 1823 and 1836, it was originally called
the Royal Institution; the RSA took over the
building in 1910. The galleries display a collection of paintings, sculptures and architectural
drawings by academy members dating from
1831, and they host temporary exhibitions
throughout the year (fees for these vary).

The RSA and the Scottish National Gallery
(p65) are linked via an underground mall –
the Weston Link – that gives them twice the
temporary exhibition space of the Prado in
Madrid and three times that of the Royal
Academy in London, as well as housing cloak-
rooms, a lecture theatre and a restaurant.

⊙ George Street & Charlotte Square

Until the 1990s George St – the major axis
of the New Town – was the centre of Edinburgh's financial industry and Scotland's
equivalent of Wall St. Today the big financial
firms have moved to premises in the modern
Exchange office district west of Lothian Rd,
and George St's former banks and offices
house upmarket shops, pubs and restaurants.

At the western end of George St is **Charlotte Sq** (Map p66; 🚌19, 36, 37, 41, 47), the architectural jewel of the New Town, designed by
Robert Adam shortly before his death in 1791.
The northern side of the square is Adam's
masterpiece and one of the finest examples
of Georgian architecture anywhere. **Bute
House** (Map p66; 6 Charlotte Sq; 🚌19, 36, 37, 41,
47), in the centre at No 6, is the official residence of Scotland's first minister, the equivalent of London's 10 Downing St.

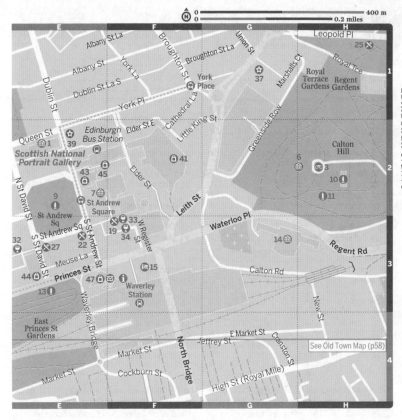

Georgian House   HISTORIC BUILDING
(NTS; Map p66; www.nts.org.uk; 7 Charlotte Sq; adult/child £8/6; ⊙10am-5pm Apr-Oct, 11am-4pm Mar & Nov, 11am-4pm Thu-Sun 1-16 Dec; 🚌19, 36, 37, 41, 47) The National Trust for Scotland's Georgian House has been beautifully restored and furnished to show how Edinburgh's wealthy elite lived at the end of the 18th century. The walls are decorated with paintings by Allan Ramsay, Sir Henry Raeburn and Sir Joshua Reynolds, and there's a fully equipped 18th-century kitchen complete with china closet and wine cellar.

⊙ St Andrew Square & Around

Not as architecturally distinguished as its sister Charlotte Sq (p66) at the opposite end of George St, St Andrew Sq is dominated by the fluted column of the Melville Monument (Map p66; 🚇St Andrew Sq), commemorating Henry Dundas, 1st Viscount Melville

(1742–1811). Dundas was the most powerful Scottish politician of his time, often referred to when alive as 'Harry IX, the Uncrowned King of Scotland'. The impressive Palladian mansion of **Dundas House** (Map p66; 🚇St Andrew Sq), built between 1772 and 1774 on the eastern side of the square, was built for Sir Laurence Dundas (1712–81; no relation to Viscount Melville). It has been the head office of the Royal Bank of Scotland since 1825 and has a spectacular domed banking hall dating from 1857 (you can nip inside for a look).

The square has seen some major changes since the central garden was opened to the public in 2008, with several upmarket restaurants now ranged along the south side, and the Edinburgh Grand luxury apartment complex on the east, housed in a gorgeous 1940s art deco building.

A short distance along George St is the **Church of St Andrew & St George** (Map

New Town

p66; www.stagw.org.uk; 13-17 George St; ☺10am-3pm Mon-Fri, 11am-2pm Sat; ☒10, 11, 12, 16, 22) **FREE**, built in 1784 with an unusual oval nave. It was the scene of the Disruption of 1843, when 451 dissenting ministers left the Church of Scotland to form the Free Church.

★**Scottish National
Portrait Gallery**   GALLERY
(Map p66; ☑0131-624 6200; www.nationalgalleries.org; 1 Queen St; ☺10am-5pm; ♿; ☒all York Pl buses, ☒St Andrew Sq) **FREE** The Venetian Gothic palace of the Scottish National Portrait Gallery is one of the city's top attractions. Its galleries illustrate Scottish history through paintings, photographs and sculptures, putting faces to famous names from Scotland's past and present, from Robert Burns, Mary, Queen of Scots, and Bonnie Prince Charlie to actor Sean Connery, comedian Billy Connolly and poet Jackie Kay. There's an admission fee for special exhibitions.

The gallery's interior is decorated in Arts and Crafts style, and nowhere more splendidly than in the **Great Hall**. Above the Gothic colonnade a processional frieze painted by William Hole in 1898 serves as a 'visual encyclopedia' of famous Scots, shown in chronological order from Calgacus (the chieftain who led the Caledonian tribes into battle against the Romans) to writer and philosopher Thomas Carlyle (1795–1881). The murals on the 1st-floor balcony depict scenes from Scottish history, while the ceiling is painted with the constellations of the night sky.

The gallery's selection of 'trails' leaflets adds a bit of background information while leading you around the various exhibits; the Hidden Histories trail is particularly interesting.

Mansfield Place Church   CHURCH
(Map p52; www.mansfieldtraquair.org.uk; Mansfield Pl; ☺1-4pm 2nd Sun of month Jan-Nov, plus 11am-1pm most days Aug; ☒8) **FREE** In complete contrast to the austerity of most of Edinburgh's religious buildings, this 19th-century, neo-Romanesque church at the foot of Broughton St contains a remarkable series of Renaissance-style frescos

painted in the 1890s by Irish-born artist Phoebe Anna Traquair (1852–1936). The murals have been restored and are on view to the public; check the website for current open days.

◉ Calton Hill

Calton Hill (Map p66; ▢1, 4, 5, 15, 34, 45) (100m), rising dramatically above the eastern end of Princes St, is Edinburgh's acropolis, its summit scattered with grandiose memorials dating mostly from the first half of the 19th century. It is also one of the best viewpoints in the city, with a panorama that takes in the castle, Holyrood, Arthur's Seat, the Firth of Forth, the New Town and the full length of Princes St.

On the southern side of the hill, on Regent Rd, is the modernist facade of **St Andrew's House** (Map p66; ▢1, 4, 5, 15, 34, 45), built between 1936 and 1939 and housing the civil servants of the Westminster government's Scottish Office until they were moved to the new Scottish Executive building in Leith in 1996.

Just beyond St Andrew's House, and on the opposite side of the road, is the imposing **Royal High School** building, dating from 1829 and modelled on the Temple of Theseus in Athens. Former pupils include Robert Adam, Alexander Graham Bell and Sir Walter Scott. It now stands empty. To its east, on the other side of Regent Rd, is the 1830 **Burns Monument** (Map p52; ▢4, 5, 34), a Greek-style memorial to Robert Burns.

You can reach the summit of Calton Hill via the road beside the Royal High School or by the stairs at the eastern end of Waterloo Pl. The largest structure on the summit is the **National Monument** (Map p66; ▢1, 4, 5, 15, 34, 45), an overambitious attempt to replicate the Parthenon in Athens and intended to honour Scotland's dead in the Napoleonic Wars. Construction – paid for by public subscription – began in 1822, but funds ran dry when only 12 columns had been completed.

Looking a bit like an upturned telescope – the similarity is intentional – and offering superb views, the **Nelson Monument** (Map p66; www.edinburghmuseums.org.uk; £5; ⊙10am-7pm Mon-Sat, noon-5pm Sun Apr-Sep, 10am-4pm Mon-Sat Oct-Mar; ▢1, 4, 5, 15, 34, 45) was built to commemorate Admiral Lord Nelson's victory at Trafalgar in 1805.

The design of the **City Observatory** (Map p66; ☎0131-556 1264; www.collective gallery.net; ⊙10am-5pm Tue-Sun Apr-Jul & Sep,

to 4pm Oct-Mar, to 6pm daily Aug; ▢1, 4, 5, 15, 34, 45) **FREE**, built in 1818, was based on the ancient Greek Temple of the Winds in Athens. Its original function was to provide a precise, astronomical timekeeping service for marine navigators, but smoke from Waverley train station forced the astronomers to move to Blackford Hill in the south of Edinburgh in 1895. The observatory has been redeveloped as a stunning space for contemporary visual art, and it is now open to the public for the first time in its history.

◉ West End & Dean Village

★ Scottish National Gallery of Modern Art
GALLERY

(Map p52; ☎0131-624 6200; www.national galleries.org; 75 Belford Rd; ⊙10am-5pm; ▢13) **FREE** Edinburgh's gallery of modern art is split between two impressive neoclassical buildings (p70) surrounded by landscaped grounds some 500m west of Dean Village. As well as showcasing a stunning collection of paintings by the popular, post-Impressionist Scottish Colourists – in *Reflections, Balloch,* Leslie Hunter pulls off the improbable trick of making Scotland look like the south of France – the gallery is the starting point for a walk along the Water of Leith. Fees apply for some exhibitions.

The main collection, known as **Modern One**, concentrates on 20th-century art, with various European movements represented by the likes of Matisse, Picasso, Kirchner, Magritte, Miró, Mondrian and Giacometti. American and English artists are also represented, but most space is given to Scottish painters – from the Scottish Colourists of the early 20th century to contemporary artists such as Peter Howson and Ken Currie.

There's an excellent **cafe** (Map p52; www. heritageportfolio.co.uk/cafes; mains £5-7; ⊙9am-4.30pm Mon-Fri, 10am-4.30pm Sat & Sun; 🛜♿; ▢13) downstairs, and the surrounding park features sculptures by Henry Moore, Rachel Whiteread and Barbara Hepworth, among others, as well as a 'landform artwork' by Charles Jencks, and the **Pig Rock Bothy**, a rustic timber event and exhibition space created in 2014 as part of the Bothy Project (www.thebothyproject.org).

A footpath and stairs at the rear of the gallery lead down to the **Water of Leith Walkway**, which you can follow along the river for 4 miles to Leith.

**Scottish National Gallery of
Modern Art – Modern Two**   GALLERY
(Map p52; www.nationalgalleries.org; Belford Rd; ⊙10am-5pm; 🚌13) **FREE** Directly across Belford Rd from Modern One (p69), another neoclassical mansion (formerly an orphanage) houses its annexe, Modern Two, which is home to a large collection of sculpture and graphic art created by Edinburgh-born artist Sir Eduardo Paolozzi. One of the 1st-floor rooms houses a recreation of Paolozzi's studio, while the rest of the building stages temporary exhibitions of modern art.

◉ Leith

Leith's history as Edinburgh's port is evident in its waterfront setting, with old warehouses converted into luxury flats, and a lush crop of trendy bars and restaurants along the river. The area was given an additional boost in the late 1990s when the Scottish Executive (a government department) moved to a new building on Leith docks.

The waterfront area is good for strolling, but the main attractions are Ocean Terminal (p95), a shopping and leisure complex, and the former Royal Yacht Britannia, which is moored alongside.

★**Royal Yacht Britannia**   SHIP
(www.royalyachtbritannia.co.uk; Ocean Terminal; adult/child incl audio guide £16/8.50; ⊙9.30am-6pm Apr-Sep, to 5.30pm Oct, 10am-5pm Nov-Mar, last entry 1½hr before closing; **P**; 🚌11, 22, 34, 36, 200, 300) Built on Clydeside, the former Royal Yacht Britannia was the British royal family's floating holiday home during their foreign travels from the time of her launch in 1953 until her decommissioning in 1997, and is now permanently moored in front of Ocean Terminal (p95). The tour, which you take at your own pace with an audio guide (available in 30 languages), lifts the curtain on the everyday lives of the royals, and gives an intriguing insight into the Queen's private tastes.

Britannia is a monument to 1950s decor, and the accommodation reveals Her Majesty's preference for simple, unfussy surroundings. There was nothing simple or unfussy, however, about the running of the ship. When the Queen travelled, with her went 45 members of the royal household, five tonnes of luggage and a Rolls-Royce that was carefully squeezed into a specially built garage on the deck. The ship's company consisted of an admiral, 20 officers and a 220-strong crew.

The decks (of Burmese teak) were scrubbed daily, but all work near the royal accommodation was carried out in complete silence and had to be finished by 8am. A thermometer was kept in the Queen's bathroom to make sure the water was the correct temperature, and when the ship was in harbour one crew member was charged with ensuring that the angle of the gangway never exceeded 12 degrees. Note the mahogany windbreak that was added to the balcony deck in front of the bridge: it was put there to stop wayward breezes from blowing up skirts and inadvertently revealing the royal underwear.

Britannia was joined in 2010 by the 1930s racing yacht Bloodhound, which was owned by the Queen in the 1960s. Bloodhound is moored alongside Britannia (except in July and August, when she is away cruising) as part of an exhibition about the royal family's love of all things nautical.

The Majestic Tour (p74) bus runs from Waverley Bridge to Britannia during the ship's opening times.

◉ Greater Edinburgh

★**Royal Botanic Garden**   GARDENS
(✆0131-248 2909; www.rbge.org.uk; Arboretum Pl; ⊙10am-6pm Mar-Sep, to 5pm Feb & Oct, to 4pm Nov-Jan; 🚌8, 23, 27) **FREE** Edinburgh's Royal Botanic Garden is the second-oldest institution of its kind in Britain (after Oxford), and one of the most respected in the world. Founded near Holyrood in 1670 and moved to its present location in 1823, its 70 beautifully landscaped acres include splendid **Victorian glasshouses** (admission £6.50), colourful swaths of rhododendrons and azaleas, and a world-famous rock garden. There's a second entrance to the gardens at 20a Inverleith Row.

The **John Hope Gateway** visitor centre is housed in a striking, environmentally friendly building overlooking the main entrance on Arboretum Pl, and has exhibitions on biodiversity, climate change and sustainable development, as well as displays of rare plants from the institution's collection and a specially created biodiversity garden.

Edinburgh Zoo   ZOO
(✆0131-334 9171; www.edinburghzoo.org.uk; 134 Corstorphine Rd; adult/child £19.50/9.95; ⊙10am-6pm Apr-Sep, to 5pm Oct & Mar, to 4pm Nov-Feb; ♿; 🚌12, 26, 31) Opened in 1913, Edinburgh Zoo is one of the world's leading conserva-

tion zoos. Edinburgh's captive breeding program has helped save many endangered species, including Siberian tigers, pygmy hippos and red pandas. The main attractions are the two **giant pandas**, Tian Tian and Yang Guang, who arrived in December 2011, and the **penguin parade** (the zoo's penguins go for a walk every day at 2.15pm). The zoo is 2.5 miles west of the city centre.

Cramond AREA

(📖41) With its moored yachts, stately swans and whitewashed houses spilling down the hillside at the mouth of the River Almond, Cramond is the most picturesque corner of Edinburgh. It is also rich in history. The Romans built a fort here in the 2nd century AD, but recent archaeological excavations have revealed evidence of a Bronze Age settlement dating from 8500 BC, the oldest known settlement site in Scotland. It's 5 miles northwest of the city centre.

Originally a mill village, Cramond has a historic 17th-century church and a 15th-century tower house, as well as some rather unimpressive Roman remains, but most people come to enjoy the walks along the river to the ruined mills and to stroll along the seafront. On the riverside, opposite the cottage on the far bank, is the **Maltings** (www.cramondheritage.org.uk; Riverside, Cramond; ☺2-5pm Sat & Sun Apr-Sep, daily during Edinburgh Festival; 📖41) , which hosts an interesting exhibition on Cramond's history.

Gilmerton Cove HISTORIC SITE

(📞07914 829177; www.gilmertoncove.org.uk; 16 Drum St; adult/child £7.50/4; ☺tours 11am-3pm Mon-Fri, noon-3pm Sat & Sun Apr-Sep, noon Mon-Fri, noon & 2pm Sat & Sun Oct-Mar) While ghost tours of Edinburgh's underground vaults and haunted graveyards have become a mainstream attraction, Gilmerton Cove remains an off-the-beaten-track gem. Hidden in the southern suburbs, the mysterious 'cove' is a series of subterranean caverns hacked out of the rock, their origin and function unknown. Advance bookings essential through **Rosslyn Tours** (📞07914 829177; www.rosslyntours.co.uk).

🏃 Activities

Edinburgh has plenty of places to perk up your sagging muscles with a spot of healthy exercise. Football and rugby fans can shout themselves hoarse at one of the city's three major stadiums, and golfers can take their pick from around 90 courses within easy reach of the city.

EDINBURGH FOR CHILDREN

Edinburgh has plentiful attractions for children, and most things to see and do are child-friendly. During the Edinburgh and Fringe Festivals there's lots of street theatre for kids, and in December there's a Ferris wheel and fairground rides in Princes Street Gardens and an ice rink in St Andrew Sq.

There are good, safe playgrounds in most Edinburgh parks, including Princes Street Gardens West, Inverleith Park (opposite the Royal Botanic Garden), George V Park (New Town), the Meadows and Bruntsfield Links.

Some more ideas for outdoor activities include exploring the Royal Botanic Garden, going to see the animals at Edinburgh Zoo, visiting the statue of Greyfriars Bobby (p63), and feeding the swans and playing on the beach at Cramond.

If it's raining, you can visit the Discovery Centre, a hands-on activity zone on level 3 of the National Museum of Scotland (p63), play on the flumes at the **Royal Commonwealth Pool** (Map p52; 📞0131-667 7211; www.edinburghleisure.co.uk/venues; 21 Dalkeith Rd; adult/family £6/15; ☺5.30am-9.30pm Mon-Fri, to 5pm Sat, 8am-5pm Sun; 🚻; 🚌2, 14, 30, 33), try out the earthquake simulator at Our Dynamic Earth (p63), or take a tour of the haunted Real Mary King's Close (p58).

Need to Know

Resources Edinburgh for Under Fives (www.efuf.co.uk) has a useful website and guidebook. *The List* (www.list.co.uk/kids) events guide has a kids' section.

Public Transport Up to two children under five may travel free when accompanied by a fare-paying adult. Children five to 15 pay half the adult fare.

Walking

Edinburgh is lucky to have several good walking areas within the city boundary, including Arthur's Seat (p63), Calton Hill (p69), **Blackford Hill** (Charterhall Rd; 🚌24, 38, 41), **Hermitage of Braid** (www.fohb.org; 🚌5, 11, 15, 16), **Corstorphine Hill** (www.corstorphinehill.org.uk; Clermiston Rd N; 🅿; 🚌26) and the coast and river at Cramond (p71). The **Pentland Hills** (www.pentlandhills.org) `FREE`, which rise to over 500m, stretch southwest from the city for over 15 miles, offering excellent high- and low-level walking.

You can follow the **Water of Leith Walkway** (www.waterofleith.org.uk/walkway) from the city centre to Balerno (8 miles), and continue across the Pentlands to Silverburn (6.5 miles) or Carlops (8 miles), and return to Edinburgh by bus. Another good walk is along the **Union Canal towpath**, which begins in Fountainbridge and runs all the way to Falkirk (31 miles). You can return to Edinburgh by bus at Ratho (8.5 miles) or Broxburn (12 miles), and by bus or train from Linlithgow (21 miles).

The **Scottish Rights of Way & Access Society** (☎0131-558 1222; www.scotways.com) provides information and advice on walking trails and rights of way in Scotland.

Cycling

Edinburgh and its surroundings offer many excellent opportunities for cycling (see http://citycyclingedinburgh.info and www.cycling-edinburgh.org.uk). The main off-road routes from the city centre out to the countryside follow the **Union Canal towpath** and then the **Water of Leith Walkway** from Tollcross southwest to Balerno

---

UNDERGROUND EDINBURGH

As Edinburgh expanded in the late 18th and early 19th centuries, many old tenements were demolished and new bridges were built to link the Old Town to the newly built areas to its north and south. South Bridge (built between 1785 and 1788) and George IV Bridge (built between 1829 and 1834) lead south from the Royal Mile over the deep valley of Cowgate, but so many buildings have been constructed around them that you can hardly tell they're bridges – George IV Bridge has a total of nine arches, but only two are visible; South Bridge has no fewer than 18 hidden arches.

These **subterranean vaults** were originally used as storerooms, workshops and drinking dens. But as Edinburgh's population swelled in the early 19th century with an influx of penniless Highlanders cleared from their lands, and Irish refugees from the potato famine, the dark, dripping chambers were given over to slum accommodation and abandoned to poverty, filth and crime.

The vaults were eventually cleared in the late 19th century, then lay forgotten until 1994, when the **South Bridge vaults** were opened to guided tours. Certain chambers are said to be haunted, and one particular vault was investigated by paranormal researchers in 2001.

Nevertheless, the most ghoulish aspect of Edinburgh's hidden history dates from much earlier – from the plague that struck the city in 1645. Legend has it that the disease-ridden inhabitants of **Mary King's Close** (a lane on the northern side of the Royal Mile, on the site of the City Chambers – you can still see its blocked-off northern end from Cockburn St) were walled up in their houses and left to perish. When the lifeless bodies were eventually cleared from the houses, they were so stiff that workers had to hack off limbs to get them through the small doorways and up the narrow, twisting stairs.

From that day on, the close was said to be haunted by the spirits of the plague victims. The few people who were prepared to live there reported seeing apparitions of severed heads and limbs, and the largely abandoned close fell into ruin. When the Royal Exchange (now the City Chambers) was constructed between 1753 and 1761, it was built over the lower levels of Mary King's Close, which were left intact and sealed off beneath the building.

Interest in the close revived in the 20th century when Edinburgh's city council began to allow occasional guided tours to enter. Visitors have reported many supernatural experiences – the most famous ghost is 'Annie', a little girl whose sad tale has prompted people to leave gifts of dolls in a corner of one of the rooms. In 2003 the close was opened to the public as the Real Mary King's Close (p58).

(7.5 miles) on the edge of the Pentland Hills, and the **Innocent Railway Cycle Path** from the southern side of Arthur's Seat eastwards to Musselburgh (5 miles) and on to Ormiston and Pencaitland.

There are several routes through the **Pentland Hills** that are suitable for mountain bikes. For details ask at any bike shop or check out the Pentland Hills Regional Park website. The Spokes *Edinburgh Cycle Map* (www.spokes.org.uk; available from cycle shops) shows all the city's cycle routes.

Bikes can be hired from **Biketrax** (Map p52; ☑ 0131-228 6633; www.biketrax.co.uk; 11-13 Lochrin Pl; per day from £20; ☺ 9.30am-6pm Mon-Fri, to 5.30pm Sat, noon-5pm Sun, longer hours Apr-Sep; ☐ all Tollcross buses) and **Cycle Scotland** (Map p58; ☑ 0131-556 5560; www.cyclescotland.co.uk; 29 Blackfriars St; tour per person £35, rental per day £25-35; ☺ 10am-6pm Mon-Sat; ☐ 300).

Golf

There are 19 golf courses in Edinburgh itself, and another 70 within 20 miles of the city, including some of the most famous links courses in the world – Muirfield, Gullane and St Andrews. For details of other courses in and around Edinburgh, check out www.scottishgolfcourses.com.

Scenic golf courses in Edinburgh include **Braid Hills Public Golf Course** (☑ 0131-447 6666; www.edinburghleisure.co.uk/venues/braid-hills-golf-course; Braid Hills Approach; green fees weekday/weekend £25.30/26.50), a challenging course to the south of the city centre, and **Duddingston Golf Course** (☑ 0131-661 7688; www.duddingstongolfclub.co.uk; Duddingston Rd W; green fees £35-55), set picturesquely at the foot of Arthur's Seat.

Tours

Edinburgh has a wealth of walking tours that allow you to explore the city by theme, as well as a number of hop-on, hop-off bus tours that run between the city's top sights.

Walking Tours

There are plenty of organised walks around Edinburgh, many of them related to ghosts, murders and witches.

City of the Dead Tours WALKING
(www.cityofthedeadtours.com; adult/concession £11/9; ☺ 9pm Easter-Oct, 8.30pm Nov-Easter) This nightly tour of Greyfriars Kirkyard is probably the scariest of Edinburgh's 'ghost' tours. Many people have reported encounters with the 'Mackenzie Poltergeist', the ghost of a 17th-century judge who persecuted the Covenanters and now haunts their former prison in a corner of the kirkyard. Not suitable for children under 12.

Cadies & Witchery Tours WALKING
(Map p58; ☑ 0131-225 6745; www.witcherytours.com; 84 West Bow; adult/child £10/7.50; ☺ 7pm year-round, plus 9pm Apr-Sep; ☐ 2) The becloaked and pasty-faced Adam Lyal (deceased) leads a 'Murder & Mystery' tour of the Old Town's darker corners. These tours are famous for their 'jumper-ooters' – costumed actors who 'jump oot' when you least expect it.

Mercat Tours WALKING
(Map p58; ☑ 0131-225 5445; www.mercattours.com; Mercat Cross; adult/child £13/8; ☐ 35) Mercat offers a wide range of fascinating history walks and 'Ghosts & Ghouls' tours, but its most famous is a visit to the hidden, haunted underground vaults beneath South Bridge. Tours depart from the Mercat Cross (p58).

Edinburgh Literary Pub Tour WALKING
(www.edinburghliterarypubtour.co.uk; adult/student £14/10; ☺ 7.30pm daily May-Sep, limited days Oct-Apr) An enlightening two-hour trawl through Edinburgh's literary history – and its associated howffs (pubs) – in the entertaining company of Messrs Clart and McBrain. One of the city's best walking tours.

Rebus Tours WALKING
(☑ 0131-553 7473; www.rebustours.com; per person £15; ☺ noon Sat) A two-hour guided tour of the 'hidden Edinburgh' frequented by novelist Ian Rankin's fictional detective, John Rebus. Not recommended for children under 10.

Trainspotting Tours WALKING
(www.leithwalks.co.uk; per person £7.50, minimum charge £15) A tour of locations from Irvine Welsh's notorious 1993 novel *Trainspotting*, and the 1996 film of the book, delivered with wit and enthusiasm. Not suitable for kids.

Invisible (Edinburgh) WALKING
(☑ 07500-773709; www.invisible-cities.org; per person £10) A new venture that trains homeless people as tour guides to explore a different side of the city. Tour themes include Crime & Punishment (includes Burke and Hare p62) and Powerful Women (from Maggie Dickson to JK Rowling). Must be booked in advance; check website for times.

Boat Tours

3 Bridges Tour
BOATING

(https://edinburghtour.com/3-bridges-tour; adult/child £22/11; ☺ Apr-Oct) This half-day tour begins with a bus trip from Waverley Bridge in Edinburgh to South Queensferry, where you board a boat for a tour beneath the three bridges that span the Firth of Forth – the bridges date from 1890 to 2017 – and then go to spot seals at Inchcolm Island (p104) (with the option of going ashore to visit the abbey ruins).

Bus Tours

Open-topped buses leave from Waverley Bridge, outside the main train station, and offer hop-on, hop-off tours of the main sights, taking in New Town, the Grassmarket and the Royal Mile. They're a good way to get your bearings, although with a bus map and a Day Saver bus ticket you could do much the same thing (but without the commentary).

City Sightseeing (www.edinburghtour.com; adult/child £15/7.50; ☺ daily year-round except 25 Dec) has bright-red, open-top buses depart every 20 minutes from Waverley Bridge.

Majestic Tour (www.edinburghtour.com; adult/child £15/7.50; ☺ daily year-round except 25 Dec) has hop-on, hop-off tour departing every 15 to 20 minutes from Waverley Bridge to the Royal Yacht *Britannia* at Ocean Terminal via the New Town, Royal Botanic Garden and Newhaven, returning via Leith Walk, Holyrood and the Royal Mile.

⭐ Festivals & Events

Edinburgh hosts an amazing number of festivals throughout the year, notably the Edinburgh International Festival, the Edinburgh Festival Fringe and the Military Tattoo. Hogmanay, Scotland's New Year's celebration, is also a peak party time.

April

Edinburgh International Science Festival
FESTIVAL

(☑ 0844-557 2686; www.sciencefestival.co.uk) First held in 1987, the two-week science festival hosts a wide range of events, including talks, lectures, exhibitions, demonstrations, guided tours and interactive experiments designed to stimulate, inspire and challenge. From dinosaurs to ghosts to alien life forms, there's something to interest everyone.

Beltane
CULTURAL

(https://beltane.org; tickets £10-13) A pagan fire festival that marks the end of winter and the rebirth of spring, Beltane was resurrected in modern form in 1988 and is now celebrated annually on the summit of Calton Hill. The spectacular rituals involve lots of fire, drumming, body paint and sexual innuendo (well, it's a fertility rite, after all).

Held annually on the night of 30 April into the early hours (around 1am) of 1 May.

May

Imaginate Festival
PERFORMING ARTS

(☑ 0131-225 8050; www.imaginate.org.uk; late May-early Jun) Britain's biggest festival of performing arts for children, Imaginate is a week-long event suitable for kids aged three to 12. Groups from around the world perform classic tales like *Hansel and Gretel* as well as new material written especially for a young audience.

June

Edinburgh International Film Festival
FILM

(☑ 0131-623 8030; www.edfilmfest.org.uk) One of the original Edinburgh Festival trinity, having first been staged in 1947 along with the International Festival and the Fringe, the two-week June film festival is a major international event, serving as a showcase for new British and European films, and staging the European premieres of one or two Hollywood blockbusters.

Royal Highland Show
FAIR

(☑ 0131-335 6200; www.royalhighlandshow.org; Royal Highland Centre, Ingliston; late Jun; ☺ adult/child £29/free) Scotland's hugely popular national agricultural show is a four-day feast of all things rural, with everything from show jumping and tractor driving to sheep shearing and falconry. Countless pens are filled with coiffed show cattle and pedicured prize ewes. The show is held over a long weekend (Thursday to Sunday).

July

Scottish Real Ale Festival
BEER

(www.sraf.camra.org.uk; Corn Exchange, Chesser Ave; late Jun or early Jul) A celebration of the fermented and yeasty, Scotland's biggest beer fest gives you the opportunity to sample a wide range of traditionally brewed beers from Scotland and around the world. Froth-topped bliss. Held over a long weekend.

FESTIVAL CITY

August in Edinburgh sees a frenzy of festivals, with several world-class events running at the same time.

Edinburgh Festival Fringe

When the first Edinburgh Festival was held in 1947, eight theatre companies didn't make it onto the main program. Undeterred, they grouped together and held their own mini-festival – on the fringe – and an Edinburgh institution was born. Today the **Edinburgh Festival Fringe** (☑ 0131-226 0026; www.edfringe.com; ☺ Aug) is the biggest festival of the performing arts anywhere in the world.

Since 1990 the Fringe has been dominated by stand-up comedy, but the sheer variety of shows on offer is staggering – everything from chainsaw juggling and performance poetry to Tibetan yak-milk gargling. So how do you decide what to see? There are daily reviews in the *Scotsman* newspaper – one good *Scotsman* review and a show sells out in hours – but the best recommendation is word of mouth. If you have the time, go to at least one unknown show – it may be crap, but at least you'll have your obligatory 'worst show I ever saw' story.

The big names play at megavenues organised by big agencies such as Assembly (www.assemblyfestival.com) and the Gilded Balloon (www.gildedballoon.co.uk), and charge megaprices (£15 to £20 a ticket and up, with some famous comedians notoriously charging more than £30), but there are plenty of good shows in the £5 to £15 range and, best of all, lots of free stuff – check out www.freefestival.co.uk and www.freefringe.org.uk.

The Fringe takes place over 3½ weeks, the last two weeks overlapping with the first two of the Edinburgh International Festival.

For bookings and information, head to the **Edinburgh Festival Fringe Office** (180 High St; ☺ noon-3pm Mon-Sat mid-Jun–mid-Jul, 10am-6pm daily mid-Jul–1 Aug, 9am-9pm daily Aug; ☐ all South Bridge buses).

Edinburgh International Festival

First held in 1947 to mark a return to peace after the ordeal of WWII, the **Edinburgh International Festival** (☑ 0131-473 2000; www.eif.co.uk; ☺ Aug) is festooned with superlatives – the oldest, the biggest, the most famous, the best in the world. The original was a modest affair, but today hundreds of the world's top musicians and performers congregate in Edinburgh for three weeks of diverse and inspirational music, opera, theatre and dance.

The festival takes place over the three weeks ending on the first Saturday in September; the program is usually available from April. Tickets for popular events – especially music and opera – sell out quickly, so it's best to book as far in advance as possible. You can buy tickets in person at the **Hub** (☑ 0131-473 2015; www.thehub-edinburgh.com; Castlehill; ☺ ticket centre 10am-5pm Mon-Fri; ☎; ☐ 23, 27, 41, 42), by phone or online.

Edinburgh Military Tattoo

August in Edinburgh kicks off with the **Edinburgh Military Tattoo** (☑ 0131-225 1188; www.edintattoo.co.uk; ☺ Aug), a spectacular display of military marching bands, massed pipes and drums, acrobats, cheerleaders and motorcycle display teams, all played out in front of the magnificent backdrop of the floodlit castle. Each show traditionally finishes with a lone piper, dramatically lit, playing a lament on the battlements. The Tattoo takes place over the first three weeks of August (from a Friday to a Saturday); there's one show at 9pm Monday to Friday and two (at 7.30pm and 10.30pm) on Saturday, but no performance on Sunday.

Edinburgh International Book Festival

Held in a little village of marquees in the middle of Charlotte Sq, the **Edinburgh International Book Festival** (☑ 0845 373 5888; www.edbookfest.co.uk; ☺ Aug) is a fun fortnight of talks, readings, debates, lectures, book signings and meet-the-author events, with a cafe-bar and tented bookshop thrown in. The festival usually coincides with the first two weeks of the Edinburgh International Festival.

Edinburgh International Jazz & Blues Festival
MUSIC

(☎ 0131-473 2000; www.edinburghjazzfestival.com; ◷ Jul) Held annually since 1978, the Jazz & Blues Festival pulls in top talent from all over the world. It runs for nine days, beginning on a Friday, a week before the Fringe (p75) and Tattoo (p75) begin. The first weekend sees a carnival parade on Princes St and an afternoon of free, open-air music in Princes Street Gardens.

Edinburgh Food Festival
FOOD & DRINK

(www.edfoodfest.com; ◷ Jul) This four-day festival, based in George Square Gardens, precedes the opening of the Edinburgh Fringe (p75) with a packed program of talks, cookery demonstrations, tastings, food stalls and entertainment.

August

The Edinburgh International Festival, the Edinburgh Festival Fringe, the Edinburgh International Book Festival and the Military Tattoo are all held around the same time in August (p75).

December

Edinburgh's Hogmanay is the biggest winter festival in Europe.

Edinburgh's Christmas
CHRISTMAS

(☎ 0131-510 0395; www.edinburghschristmas.com; ◷ late Nov-early Jan) First held in 2000, the Christmas bash includes a big street parade, Christmas markets, a fairground and Ferris wheel, and a circular open-air ice rink in St Andrew Sq.

🛏 Sleeping

Edinburgh offers a wide range of accommodation options, from moderately priced guesthouses set in lovely Victorian villas and Georgian town houses to expensive and stylish boutique hotels. There are also plenty of chain hotels, and a few truly exceptional hotels housed in magnificent historic buildings. At the budget end of the range, there is no shortage of youth hostels and independent backpacker hostels, which often have inexpensive double and twin rooms.

🛏 Old Town

Safestay Edinburgh
HOSTEL £

(Map p58; ☎ 0131-524 1989; www.safestay.com; 50 Blackfriars St; dm £34-40, tw £139; @ 🛜; 📶 300) A big, modern hostel, with a convivial cafe where you can buy breakfast, and mod cons such as keycard access and charging stations for mobile phones, MP3 players and laptops. Lockers in every room, a huge bar and a central location just off the Royal Mile make this a favourite among the young, party-mad crowd – don't expect a quiet night!

Castle Rock Hostel
HOSTEL £

(Map p58; ☎ 0131-225 9666; www.scotlands-top-hostels.com; 15 Johnston Tce; dm £15-19, d £55; @ 🛜; 📶 2) With its bright, spacious, mixed or female-only dorms, superb views and friendly staff, the 200-bed Castle Rock has lots to like. It has a great location – the only way to get closer to the castle would be to pitch a tent on the esplanade – a games room, a reading lounge and big-screen video nights. No under-18s.

Kickass Hostel
HOSTEL ££

(Map p58; ☎ 0131-226 6351; https://kickass hostels.co.uk; 2 West Port; dm £20-25, tw £74; @ 🛜; 📶 2) Great value and great location (the castle is just five minutes away) are

---

EDINBURGH'S HOGMANAY

Edinburgh's Hogmanay (☎ 0131-510 0395; www.edinburghshogmanay.com; street-party tickets £21; ◷ 30 Dec-1 Jan) is the biggest winter festival in Europe, with events including a torchlit procession, a huge street party and the famous 'Loony Dook', a chilly sea-swimming event on New Year's Day. To get into the main party area in the city centre after 8pm on 31 December you'll need a ticket – book well in advance.

Traditionally, the New Year has always been a more important celebration for Scots than Christmas. In towns, cities and villages all over the country, people fill the streets at midnight on 31 December to wish each other a Guid New Year and, yes, to knock back a dram or six to keep the cold at bay.

In 1993 Edinburgh's city council had the excellent idea of spicing up Hogmanay by organising some events, laying on some live music in Princes St and issuing an open invitation to the rest of the world. Most of them turned up, or so it seemed, and had such a good time that they told all their pals and came back again the next year.

the main attractions here, but the colourful decor, cheap cafe-bar and helpful staff are bonuses. Bunks have free lockers, bedside lights and phone-charging stations, too.

★ Witchery by the Castle   B&B £££
(Map p58; ☑ 0131-225 5613; www.thewitchery.com; Castlehill; ste from £345; [P]; [🖵] 23, 27, 41, 42) Set in a 16th-century Old Town house in the shadow of Edinburgh Castle, the Witchery's nine lavish Gothic suites are extravagantly furnished with antiques, oak panelling, tapestries, open fires, four-poster beds and roll-top baths, and supplied with flowers, chocolates and complimentary champagne. Overwhelmingly popular – you'll have to book several months in advance to be sure of getting a room.

Radisson Collection
Royal Mile Hotel   BOUTIQUE HOTEL £££
(Map p58; ☑ 0131-220 6666; www.radisson collection.com/en/royalmile-hotel-edinburgh; 1 George IV Bridge; r from £310; [🛜][❄]; [🖵] 23, 27, 41, 42) This style icon in the heart of the medieval Old Town is a bold statement of a hotel – modernist architecture, colourful designer decor, impeccably mannered staff (some dressed in designer kilts) and, most importantly, very comfortable bedrooms and bathrooms with lots of nice little touches, from fresh milk in the minibar to plush bathrobes.

Grassmarket Hotel   HOTEL £££
(Map p58; ☑ 0131-220 2299; www.grassmarket hotel.co.uk; 94-96 Grassmarket; s/d/tr from £144/167/248; [🛜]; [🖵] 2) An endearingly quirky hotel set in a historic Grassmarket tenement in the heart of the Old Town, this place has bedroom walls plastered with front pages from the *Dandy* (a DC Thomson comic published in Dundee) and coffee stations supplied with iconically Scottish Tunnock's teacakes and Irn-Bru. Some bargain rates available direct through the website.

🛏 Holyrood & Arthur's Seat

★ Prestonfield   BOUTIQUE HOTEL £££
(☑ 0131-668 3346; www.prestonfield.com; Priest-field Rd; r/ste from £335/425; [P][🛜][❄]) If the blond wood and brushed steel of modern boutique hotels leave you cold, then this is the place for you. A 17th-century mansion set in 8 hectares of parkland (complete with peacocks and Highland cattle), Preston-field is draped in damask and packed with antiques – look out for original tapestries,

17th-century embossed-leather panels and £500-a-roll hand-painted wallpaper.

The sumptuous bedrooms are supplied with all the mod cons, including Bose sound systems and internet-enabled plasma-screen TVs. The hotel is southeast of the city centre, east of Dalkeith Rd.

🛏 New Town

Code Pod Hostel   HOSTEL £
(Map p66; ☑ 0131-659 9883; www.codehostel. com; 50 Rose St N Lane; dm from £25, d £99; [🛜]; [🚇] Princes St) This upmarket hostel, bang in the middle of the New Town, combines cute designer decor with innovative sleeping pods that offer more privacy than bunks (four to six people per dorm, each with en suite shower room). There's also a luxurious double apartment called the Penthouse, complete with kitchenette and roof terrace.

★ Two Hillside Crescent   B&B ££
(Map p52; ☑ 0131-556 4871; www.twohillside crescent.com; 2 Hillside Cres; r from £115; [@][🛜]; [🖵] 19, 26, 44) Five spacious and individually decorated bedrooms grace this gorgeous Georgian town house – it's worth splashing out for the 'superior' room with twin floor-to-ceiling windows overlooking the gardens. Guests take breakfast around a large communal table in a stylishly modern dining room – smoked salmon and scrambled eggs is on the menu – and your hosts could not be more helpful.

★ 14 Hart Street   B&B ££
(Map p52; ☑ 07795 203414; http://14hartstreet. co.uk; 14 Hart St; s/d £115/125; [🛜]; [🖵] 8) Centrally located and child friendly, 14 Hart Street is steeped in Georgian elegance and old Edinburgh charm. Run by a retired couple, the B&B boasts three generous bedrooms, all en suite, and a sumptuous dining room where guests can enjoy breakfast at a time of their choosing. Indulgent extras include whisky decanters and shortbread in every room.

Broughton Townhouse   GUESTHOUSE ££
(Map p52; ☑ 0131-558 9792; https://broughton -hotel.com; 37 Broughton Pl; s/d/f from £80/120/150; [P][🛜]; [🖵] 8) This five-bedroom Georgian guesthouse combines great value with a great location, on a relatively quiet street a few minutes' walk from the restaurants and nightlife of Broughton St and Edinburgh's gay village, and just 10 minutes' walk from Princes St.

Ramsay's B&B

B&B ££

(Map p52; ☑0131-557 5917; www.ramsays bedandbreakfastedinburgh.com; 25 East London St; r from £100; ☎; ☐8) The four bright and fresh bedrooms in this tastefully decorated Georgian town house make a great base for exploring the New Town, with the vibrant bar and restaurant scene of Broughton's gay village just around the corner. Breakfasts are freshly prepared, with kippers on the menu as well as the usual options.

★Principal

BOUTIQUE HOTEL £££

(Map p66; ☑0131-341 4932; www.phcompany. com/principal/edinburgh-charlotte-square; 38 Charlotte Sq; r from £245; P☎; ☐all Princes St buses) Arriving in this modern makeover of a classic Georgian New Town establishment (formerly the Roxburghe Hotel) feels like being welcomed into a country-house party. Service is friendly and attentive without being intrusive, and the atmosphere is informal; in the bedrooms, designer decor meets traditional tweed, and breakfast is served in a lovely glass-roofed garden courtyard.

Balmoral Hotel

HOTEL £££

(Map p66; ☑0131-556 2414; http://balmoral hotel.grandluxuryhotels.com; 1 Princes St; r from £295; P☎☀; ☐all Princes St buses) The sumptuous Balmoral – a prominent landmark at the eastern end of Princes St – offers some of the best accommodation in Edinburgh, including suites with 18th-century decor, marble bathrooms and stunning sunset views of Princes St and the Scott Monument (p64). There's also a spa and gym with 20m pool in the basement.

West End & Dean Village

★Dunstane Houses

BOUTIQUE HOTEL £££

(Map p52; ☑0131-337 6169; https://thedunstane. com; 4 West Coates; r from £179, ste £425; P☎; ☐12, 26, 31, 100) Dunstane House and its companion, Hampton House, are large Victorian villas dating from the 1860s but totally refurbished in 2017. Gorgeous modern styling complements the many original features, including period fireplaces, stained-glass windows and ornate cornices. The rooms are individually decorated with designer fabrics and wallpapers, while the luxury suites have four-poster beds, chaise longues and roll-top copper baths.

🏃 City Walk
Old Town Alleys

START CASTLE ESPLANADE
END COCKBURN ST
LENGTH 1 MILE; ONE TO TWO HOURS

This walk explores the alleys and side streets around the Royal Mile, and involves a bit of climbing up and down steep stairs.

Begin on the ❶ **Castle Esplanade**, which provides a grandstand view south over the Grassmarket; the prominent quadrangular building with all the turrets is George Heriot's School. Head towards Castlehill and the start of the Royal Mile.

The 17th-century house on the right is known as ❷ **Cannonball House** because of the iron ball lodged in the wall (look between, and slightly below, the two largest windows on the wall facing the castle). The ball was not fired in anger but marks the gravitation height to which water would flow naturally from the city's first piped water supply.

The low, rectangular building across the street (now a touristy tartan-weaving mill) was originally the reservoir that held the Old Town's water supply. On its western wall is the ❸ **Witches Well**, where a bronze fountain commemorates around 4000 people (mostly women) who were executed between 1479 and 1722 on suspicion of witchcraft.

Go past the reservoir and turn left down Ramsay Lane. Take a look at ❹ **Ramsay Garden** – one of Edinburgh's most desirable addresses – where late-19th-century apartments were built around the octagonal Ramsay Lodge, once home to poet Allan Ramsay. The cobbled street continues around to the right below student residences to the towers of the ❺ **New College**, home to Edinburgh University's Faculty of Divinity. Nip into the courtyard to see the statue of John Knox (a firebrand preacher who led the Protestant Reformation in Scotland, and was instrumental in the creation of the Church of Scotland in 1560).

Just past New College, turn right and climb the stairs into Milne's Court, a student residence belonging to Edinburgh University. Exit into Lawnmarket, cross the street (bearing slightly left) and duck

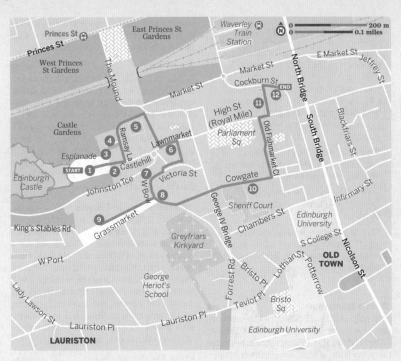

into **6 Riddell's Court**, a restored Old Town close at No 322–8. You'll find yourself in a small courtyard, but the house in front of you (built in 1590) was originally the edge of the street (the building you just walked under was added in 1726 – look for the date inscribed on the doorway on the right). The arch with the inscription *Vivendo discimus* (We live and learn) leads into the original 16th-century courtyard.

Go back into the street, turn right and right again down Fisher's Close, which leads to the delightful Victoria Tce, strung above the cobbled curve of shop-lined Victoria St. Wander right, enjoying the view – **7 Maxie's Bistro** (p82), at the far end of the terrace, is a great place to stop for a drink – then descend the stairs at the foot of Upper Bow and continue downhill to the Grassmarket. At the eastern end, outside Maggie Dickson's pub, is the **8 Covenanters Monument**, which marks the site of the gallows where more than 100 Covenanters were martyred in the 17th century.

If you're feeling peckish, the Grassmarket has several good places to eat and a couple of good pubs – poet Robert Burns once stayed at the **9 White Hart Inn** (p64). Head east along the gloomy defile of the Cowgate, passing under the arch of George IV Bridge – the buildings to your right are the new law courts, while high up to the left you can see the complex of buildings behind Parliament Sq. Past the courts, on the right, is **10 Tailors Hall** (built 1621, extended 1757), now a hotel and bar but formerly the meeting place of the Companie of Tailzeours (Tailors' Guild).

Turn left and climb steeply up Old Fishmarket Close, a typical cobbled Old Town wynd, and emerge once more onto the Royal Mile. Across the street and slightly downhill is **11 Anchor Close**, named for a tavern that once stood there. It hosted the Crochallan Fencibles, an 18th-century drinking club that provided its patrons with an agreeable blend of intellectual debate and intoxicating liquor. The club was founded by William Smellie, editor of the 1st edition of the *Encyclopedia Britannica;* Burns was its best-known member.

Go down Anchor Close to finish the walk on **12 Cockburn St**, one of the city's coolest shopping streets, lined with record shops and clothing boutiques. The street was cut through Old Town tenements in the 1850s to provide an easy route between Waverley station and the Royal Mile.

BOOKING SERVICES

If you arrive in Edinburgh without a place to stay, the Edinburgh tourist office (p98) booking service will try to find a room to suit you (and will charge a £5 fee if successful). If you have the time, pick up the tourist office's accommodation brochure and ring around yourself.

VisitScotland (www.visitscotland. com/edinburgh) Wide range of options from the official website.

Lonely Planet (www.lonelyplanet. com/hotels) Recommendations and bookings.

This Is Edinburgh (www.edinburgh. org) Promotional website with wide range of accommodation and weekend-break offers.

★**B+B Edinburgh**   HOTEL **£££**
(Map p52; ☑ 0131-225 5084; www.bb-edinburgh. com; 3 Rothesay Tce; d/ste from £120/190; 🛜; 🚇 West End) Built in 1883 as a grand home for the proprietor of the *Scotsman* newspaper, this Victorian extravaganza of carved oak, parquet floors, stained glass and elaborate fireplaces was given a designer makeover to create a striking contemporary hotel. Rooms on the 2nd floor are the most spacious, but the smaller top-floor rooms enjoy the finest views.

🛏 South Edinburgh

Argyle Backpackers   HOSTEL **£**
(Map p52; ☑ 0131-667 9991; www.argyle-back packers.co.uk; 14 Argyle Pl; dm/tw from £15/54; @🛜; 🚇41) The Argyle, spread across three adjacent terrace houses, is a quiet and re-laxed hostel offering triple, double and twin rooms as well as four- to six-bed dorms (mixed or female only). There's a comfort-able TV lounge, an attractive little conserv-atory and a pleasant walled garden at the back where you can sit outside in summer.

Sherwood Guest House   B&B **££**
(Map p52; ☑ 0131-667 1200; www.sherwood -edinburgh.com; 42 Minto St; s/d from £75/90; P🛜; 🚇all Newington buses) One of the most attractive guesthouses on Minto St's B&B strip, the Sherwood is a refurbished Geor-gian terrace house decked out with hanging baskets and shrubs. Inside are six en suite rooms that combine period features with modern fabrics and neutral colours.

No 45   B&B **££**
(☑ 0131-667 3536; www.edinburghbedbreakfast. com; 45 Gilmour Rd; d/tr £130/160; 🛜; 🚇all New-ington buses) A peaceful setting, a large gar-den and friendly owners contribute to the appeal of this Victorian terrace house, which overlooks the local bowling green. The decor is a blend of 19th and 20th century, with bold Victorian reds, pine floors and a period fireplace in the lounge, and a 1930s vibe in the three spacious bedrooms.

★**Southside Guest House**   B&B **£££**
(Map p52; ☑ 0131-668 4422; www.southsideguest house.co.uk; 8 Newington Rd; s/d from £100/140; 🛜; 🚇all Newington buses) Though set in a typical Victorian terrace, the Southside tran-scends the traditional guesthouse category and feels more like a modern boutique hotel. Its eight stylish rooms, featuring the clever use of bold colours and modern furniture, ooze interior design. Breakfast is an event, with Buck's Fizz (cava mixed with orange juice) on offer to ease the hangover.

Albyn Townhouse   B&B **£££**
(Map p52; ☑ 0131-229 6459; https://albyntown house.co.uk; 16 Hartington Gardens; s/d from £101/154; P🛜; 🚇11, 15, 16, 23, 36, 45) Set in a refurbished Victorian town house tucked away at the end of a quiet cul-de-sac in the fashionable Bruntsfield district, this B&B is a real home-away-from-home. Designer-ish decor doesn't detract from the welcoming atmosphere, and the owners (plus their charming dog) are only too pleased to offer advice on where to go and what to see.

94DR   BOUTIQUE HOTEL **£££**
(Map p52; ☑ 0131-662 9265; www.94dr.com; 94 Dalkeith Rd; r from £130; P; 🚇2, 14, 30, 33) This peaceful and elegant guesthouse is a sensi-tively restored Victorian town house with six individually designed bedrooms with views towards either Salisbury Crags or the Pentland Hills. Little extras include compli-mentary bicycles, a well-equipped honesty bar, seriously impressive breakfasts cooked by the chef-owner, and a lovely conservatory and garden.

Knight Residence   APARTMENT **£££**
(Map p58; ☑ 0131-622 8120; www.theknight residence.co.uk; 12 Lauriston St; 1/2/3-bedroom apt from £130/160/240; P🛜; 🚇2) Works by

contemporary artists adorn these modern studio, and one-, two- and three-bedroom apartments (available by the night; the three-bedroom options sleep up to seven), each with fully equipped kitchen and comfortable lounge with cable TV, DVD and stereo. It has a good central location in a quiet street only a few minutes' walk from the Grassmarket.

🛏 Leith

Edinburgh Central SYHA   HOSTEL £
(SYHA; Map p52; ✈ 0131-524 2090; www.syha. org.uk; 9 Haddington Pl; dm/tw £23/61; @ 📶; 🖵 all Leith Walk buses) This modern, purpose-built hostel, off Leith Walk about a half-mile north of Waverley train station, is a big (300 bed), flashy, five-star establishment with its own cafe-bistro as well as a self-catering kitchen, smart and comfortable eight-bed dorms and private rooms, and mod cons including keycard entry and plasma-screen TVs.

★Sheridan Guest House   B&B ££
(✈ 0131-554 4107; www.sheridanedinburgh.com; 1 Bonnington Tce; s/d from £85/95; P 📶; 🖵 11) Flowerpots filled with colourful blooms line the steps of this little haven hidden away north of the New Town. The eight bedrooms (all en suite) blend crisp colours with contemporary furniture, stylish lighting and colourful paintings, which complement the house's clean-cut Georgian lines. The breakfast menu adds omelettes, pancakes with maple syrup, and scrambled eggs with smoked salmon to the usual offerings.

Millers 64   B&B ££
(✈ 0131-454 3666; www.millers64.com; 64 Pilrig St; r £90-180; 📶; 🖵 11) Luxury textiles, colourful cushions, stylish bathrooms and fresh flowers added to a warm Edinburgh welcome make this Victorian town house a highly desirable address. There are just two bedrooms (and a minimum three-night stay during festival periods), so book well in advance.

Sandaig Guest House   B&B ££
(✈ 0131-554 7357; www.sandaigguesthouse. co.uk; 5 East Hermitage Pl, Leith Links; s/d/f from £100/110/150; 📶; 🖵 21, 25) From the welcoming glass of sherry to the cheerful goodbye wave, the owner of the Sandaig knows a thing or two about hospitality. Numerous details make staying here a pleasure, from the boldly coloured decor to the crisp cotton sheets, big fluffy towels and refreshing power showers, and a breakfast menu that includes porridge with cream and maple syrup.

★Pilrig House   APARTMENT £££
(✈ 0131-554 4794; www.pilrighouse.com; 30 Pilrig House Close; ☉ per week £945-1470; P 📶; 🖵 36) 🡒 Pilrig is a gorgeous 17th-century town house that was once home to Robert Louis Stevenson's grandfather (it gets a mention in his novel *Kidnapped*). Set at the end of a quiet cul-de-sac overlooking a peaceful park, the house offers two luxurious self-catering apartments with fully equipped kitchens and private parking. Seven-night minimum stay May to August.

🍴 Eating

Eating out in Edinburgh has changed beyond all recognition since the 1990s. Back then, sophisticated dining meant a visit to the Aberdeen Angus Steak House for a prawn cocktail, steak (well done) and chips, and Black Forest gateau. Today, Edinburgh has more restaurants per head of population than any other UK city, including a handful of places with Michelin stars.

🍴 Old Town

★Mums   CAFE £
(Map p58; ✈ 0131-260 9806; www.monstermash cafe.co.uk; 4a Forrest Rd; mains £9-12; ☉ 9am-10pm Mon-Sat, 10am-10pm Sun; 📶 🖔; 🖵 2, 23, 27, 41, 42, 300) 🡒 This nostalgia-fuelled cafe serves up classic British comfort food that wouldn't look out of place on a 1950s menu – bacon and eggs, bangers and mash, shepherd's pie, fish and chips. But there's a twist – the food is all top-quality nosh freshly prepared from local produce. There's also a good selection of bottled craft beers and Scottish-brewed cider.

★Brew Lab   CAFE £
(Map p58; ✈ 0131-662 8963; www.brewlabcoffee. co.uk; 6-8 S College St; mains £4-5; ☉ 8am-6pm Mon, to 8pm Tue-Fri, 9am-8pm Sat & Sun; 📶; 🖵 all South Bridge buses) 🡒 Students with iPads lolling in armchairs, sipping carefully crafted espressos amid artfully distressed brick and plaster, recycled school-gym flooring, old workshop benches and lab stools... this is coffee-nerd heaven. There's good food, too, with hearty soups and crusty baguette sandwiches. In summer, try the refreshing cold-brew coffee.

Scott's Kitchen
SCOTTISH, CAFE £

(Map p58; ☑ 0131-322 6868; https://scotts
kitchen.co.uk; 4-6 Victoria Tce; mains £8-10;
☺ 9am-6pm; [P][🛜][📶]; [🚌] 23, 27, 41, 42, 67) Green
tile, brown leather and arched Georgian
windows lend an elegant feel to this modern cafe, which combines fine Scottish produce with great value. Fill up on a breakfast
(served till 11.45am) of eggs Benedict, bacon
baps or porridge with honey, banana and
almonds, or linger over a lunch of Cullen
skink (smoked-haddock soup), venison casserole, or haggis.

Union of Genius
CAFE £

(Map p58; ☑ 0131-226 4436; www.unionofgenius.
com; 8 Forrest Rd; mains £4-7; ☺ 10am-4pm Mon-
Fri, noon-4pm Sat; [🚌] 2, 23, 27, 41, 42, 45) This
petite, buzzing cafe located in the heart
of Edinburgh's studentland celebrates the
humble bowl of soup. Focusing on fresh,
seasonal ingredients, imaginative recipes
and big flavours, soups might include beetroot and pink pepper, Caribbean chicken
and coconut, and mulligatawny. There's also
a soup van parked up at nearby George Sq.

★ Cannonball Restaurant
SCOTTISH ££

(Map p58; ☑ 0131-225 1550; www.contini.com/
cannonball; 356 Castlehill; mains £15-25; ☺ noon-
3pm & 5.30-10pm Tue-Sat; [🛜][📶]; [🚌] 23, 27, 41,
42) The historic Cannonball House next
to Edinburgh Castle's esplanade has been
transformed into a sophisticated restaurant
(and whisky bar) where the Contini family
work their Italian magic on Scottish classics
to produce dishes such as haggis balls with
spiced pickled turnip and whisky marmalade, and lobster with wild garlic and lemon
butter.

Mother India's Cafe
INDIAN ££

(Map p58; ☑ 0131-524 9801; www.motherindia.
co.uk; 3-5 Infirmary St; dishes £4-6; ☺ noon-2pm
& 5-10.30pm Mon-Wed, noon-11pm Thu-Sun; [🛜][📶];
[🚌] all South Bridge buses) A simple concept pioneered in Glasgow has captured hearts and
minds – and stomachs – here in Edinburgh:
Indian food served in tapas-size portions, so
that you can sample a greater variety of deliciously different dishes without busting a
gut. Hugely popular, so book a table to avoid
disappointment.

Devil's Advocate
PUB FOOD ££

(Map p58; ☑ 0131-225 4465; http://devils
advocateedinburgh.co.uk; 9 Advocates Close; mains
£10-23; ☺ food served noon-3pm & 5-10pm; [🛜];
[🚌] 6, 23, 27, 41, 42) No trip to Edinburgh is

complete without exploring the narrow
closes (alleys) that lead off the Royal Mile.
Lucky you if your explorations lead to this
cosy split-level pub-restaurant set in a converted Victorian pump house, with a menu
of top-quality pub grub – the barbecue ribs
are among the best in town. It gets rammed
on weekends, so book ahead.

Maxie's Bistro
BISTRO ££

(Map p58; ☑ 0131-226 7770; www.maxiesbistro.
com; 5b Johnston Tce; mains £11-25; ☺ noon-11pm;
[🛜][📶]; [🚌] 23, 27, 41, 42) This candlelit bistro,
with its cushion-lined nooks set amid stone
walls and wooden beams, is a pleasant setting for a cosy dinner, but at summer lunchtimes people queue for the tables on the
terrace overlooking Victoria St. The food is
dependable, ranging from pasta, steak and
stir-fries to seafood platters and daily specials. Best to book, especially in summer.

Amber
SCOTTISH ££

(Map p58; ☑ 0131-477 8477; www.scotchwhisky
experience.co.uk/restaurant; 354 Castlehill; mains
£12-25; ☺ noon-8.30pm Sun-Thu, to 9pm Fri & Sat;
[🛜][📶]; [🚌] 23, 27, 41, 42) You've got to love a place
where the waiter greets you with the words,
'I'll be your whisky adviser for this evening'.
Located in the Scotch Whisky Experience
(p55), this whisky-themed restaurant manages to avoid the tourist clichés and creates
genuinely interesting and flavoursome dishes using top Scottish produce, with a suggested whisky pairing for each dish.

★ Grain Store
SCOTTISH £££

(Map p58; ☑ 0131-225 7635; www.grainstore
-restaurant.co.uk; 30 Victoria St; mains £18-32;
☺ noon-2.30pm & 6-9.45pm Mon-Sat, noon-
2.30pm & 6-9.30pm Sun; [🚌] 2, 23, 27, 41, 42) An
atmospheric upstairs dining room on picturesque Victoria St, the Grain Store has a
well-earned reputation for serving the finest Scottish produce, perfectly prepared in
dishes such as Orkney scallops with pump-
kin, chestnut and pancetta, and braised
venison shoulder with brambles, salsify
and kale. The three-course lunch for £16 is
good value.

★ Ondine
SEAFOOD £££

(Map p58; ☑ 0131-226 1888; www.ondine
restaurant.co.uk; 2 George IV Bridge; mains £18-
38, 2-/3-course lunch £19/24; ☺ noon-3pm &
5.30-10pm Mon-Sat; [🛜]; [🚌] 23, 27, 41, 42) Ondine
is one of Edinburgh's finest seafood restaurants, with a menu based on sustainably sourced fish. Take a seat at the curved

Oyster Bar and tuck into oysters Kilpatrick, smoked-haddock chowder, lobster thermidor, a roast-shellfish platter or just good old haddock and chips (with minted pea purée, just to keep things posh).

White Horse Oyster & Seafood Bar
SEAFOOD £££
(Map p58; ☑ 0131-629 5300; www.whitehorse oysterbar.co.uk; 266 Canongate; mains £16-29; ☺ noon-10pm; ☐ 6, 300) One of Edinburgh's oldest pubs was transformed in 2017 into this intriguing seafood restaurant. The decor is bare stone and wood-panelling in shades of slate grey and brown, providing a dark canvas on which white platters of colourful shellfish and crustaceans shine all the more brightly. The menu also includes small plates (£8 to £12) to accompany a glass of wine.

Tower
SCOTTISH £££
(Map p58; ☑ 0131-225 3003; www.tower-restau rant.com; National Museum of Scotland, Chambers St; mains £22-34, 2-course lunch & pre-theatre menu £20; ☺ 10am-10pm Sun-Thu, to 10.30pm Fri & Sat; ☐ 45, 300) Chic and sleek, with a great view of the castle, Tower is perched in a turret atop the National Museum of Scotland (p63) building. A star-studded guest list of celebrities has enjoyed its menu of quality Scottish food, simply prepared – try half a dozen oysters followed by a 28-day salt-aged rib-eye steak. Afternoon tea (£26) is served from 2pm to 6pm.

Wedgwood
SCOTTISH £££
(Map p58; ☑ 0131-558 8737; www.wedgwood therestaurant.co.uk; 267 Canongate; mains £18-28, 2-/3-course lunch £16/20; ☺ noon-3pm & 6-10pm; ☐ 35) ✔ Fine food without the fuss is the motto at this friendly, unpretentious restaurant. Scottish produce is served with inventive flair in dishes such as beef tartare with soy, shaved egg, scurvy grass and bone-marrow crumb, or spiced monkfish with charred aubergine, pickled chilli and preserved lemon; the menu includes foraged wild salad leaves collected by the chef.

✗ Holyrood & Arthur's Seat
★ Rhubarb
SCOTTISH £££
(☑ 0131-225 1333; www.prestonfield.com/dine/ rhubarb; Prestonfield, Priestfield Rd; mains £26-40; ☺ noon-2pm & 6-10pm Mon-Sat, 12.30-3pm & 6-10pm Sun; ☐℗) Set in the splendid 17th-century Prestonfield hotel (p77), Rhubarb is a feast for the eyes as well as the taste

buds. The over-the-top decor of rich reds set off with black and gold and the sensuous surfaces that make you want to touch everything – damask, brocade, marble, gilded leather – are matched by the intense flavours and rich textures of the modern Scottish cuisine.

Take your postprandial coffee and brandy upstairs to the sumptuous fireside sofas in the Tapestry and Leather rooms. A two-course lunch menu is available for £27.

✗ New Town
★ Urban Angel
CAFE £
(Map p66; ☑ 0131-225 6215; www.urban-angel. co.uk; 121 Hanover St; mains £7-11; ☺ 8am-5pm Mon-Fri, 9am-5pm Sat & Sun; ☐♿; ☐ 23, 27) ✔ A wholesome deli that puts the emphasis on Fairtrade, organic and locally sourced produce, Urban Angel is also a delightfully informal cafe-bistro that serves all-day brunch (porridge with honey, French toast, eggs Benedict), mix-and-match salads, and a wide range of light, snacky meals.

Broughton Deli
CAFE £
(Map p52; ☑ 0131-558 7111; www.broughton-deli. co.uk; 7 Barony St; mains £7-11; ☺ 8am-6pm Mon-Fri, 9am-6pm Sat, 10am-5pm Sun; ☐☐♿; ☐ 8) Mismatched cafe tables and chairs in a bright back room behind the deli counter provide an attractive setting for brunch just off the main drag of the New Town's bohemian Broughton St. Brunch is served till 2pm weekdays or 3pm at weekends; choose from American-style pancakes, vegan burritos, and poached eggs on toast with avocado.

Social Bite
CAFE £
(Map p66; ☑ 0131-220 8206; http://social-bite. co.uk; 131 Rose St; mains £4-9; ☺ 7am-3pm Mon-Fri; ☐; ☐ all Princes St buses) ✔ Describing its mission as 'good food for a good cause', this cafe is a social enterprise set up to support the homeless (25% of employees are from a homeless background). The food – from freshly prepared sandwiches to hot lunches including Jamaican chicken, and haggis – is delicious, and you can donate a 'suspended item' to be claimed later by a homeless person.

★ Gardener's Cottage
SCOTTISH ££
(Map p66; ☑ 0131-558 1221; www.thegardeners cottage.co; 1 Royal Terrace Gardens, London Rd; 4-course lunch £21, 7-course dinner £50; ☺ noon-2pm & 5-10pm Mon-Fri, 10am-2pm & 5-10pm Sat

& Sun; all London Rd buses) This country cottage in the heart of the city, bedecked with flowers and fairy lights, offers one of Edinburgh's most interesting dining experiences – two tiny rooms with communal tables made of salvaged timber, and a set menu based on fresh local produce (most of the vegetables and fruit are from its own organic garden). Bookings essential; brunch served at weekends.

★ Contini
ITALIAN ££

(Map p66; 0131-225 1550; www.contini.com/contini-george-street; 103 George St; mains £14-18; 8am-10pm Mon-Fri, 10am-10.30pm Sat, 11am-8pm Sun; all Princes St buses) A palatial Georgian banking hall enlivened by fuchsia-pink banners and lampshades is home to this lively, family-friendly Italian bar and restaurant, where the emphasis is on fresh, authentic ingredients (produce imported weekly from Milan; homemade bread and pasta) and the uncomplicated enjoyment of food.

★ Dishoom
INDIAN ££

(Map p66; 0131-202 6406; www.dishoom.com/edinburgh; 3a St Andrew Sq; 8am-11pm Mon-Wed, to midnight Thu & Fri, 9am-midnight Sat, 9am-11pm Sun; ; St Andrew Sq) Dishoom is a new addition to Edinburgh's dining scene and the minichain's first opening outside London. Inspired by the Irani cafes of Bombay, this is exquisite Indian street food served in upmarket surroundings; the breakfasts, including the signature bacon naan, are legendary. Hugely popular – book well ahead, or be prepared to queue for a table.

Dome
SCOTTISH ££

(Map p66; 0131-624 8624; www.thedomeedinburgh.com; 14 George St; mains £15-28; 10am-late; St Andrew Sq) Housed in the magnificent neoclassical former headquarters of the Commercial Bank, with a lofty glass-domed

---

TOP FIVE VEGETARIAN RESTAURANTS

David Bann (Map p58; 0131-556 5888; www.davidbann.com; 56-58 St Mary's St; mains £12-14; noon-10pm Mon-Fri, 11am-10pm Sat & Sun; ; 300) If you want to convince a carnivorous friend that cuisine à la veg can be as tasty and inventive as a meat-muncher's menu, take them to David Bann's stylish restaurant – dishes such as puy lentil shepherd's pie, and risotto of braised leek and roasted red pepper are guaranteed to win converts.

Henderson's (Map p66; 0131-225 2131; www.hendersonsofedinburgh.co.uk; 94 Hanover St; mains £7-14; 8.30am-8.45pm Mon-Thu, to 9.15pm Fri & Sat, 10.30am-4pm Sun; ; 23, 27) Established in 1962, Henderson's is the grandmother of Edinburgh's vegetarian restaurants. The food is mostly organic and guaranteed GM-free, and special dietary requirements can be catered for. Trays and counter service lend something of a 1970s canteen feel to the place (in a good, nostalgic way), and the daily salads and hot dishes are as popular as ever.

Right around the corner on Thistle St is Henderson's Vegan, a 100% vegan bistro.

Kalpna (Map p52; 0131-667 9890; www.kalpnarestaurant.com; 2-3 St Patrick Sq; mains £8-13; noon-2pm & 5.30-10.30pm; ; all Newington buses) A long-standing Edinburgh favourite, Kalpna is one of the best Indian restaurants in the country, vegetarian or otherwise. The cuisine is mostly Gujarati, with a smattering of dishes from other parts of India. The all-you-can-eat lunch buffet (£8.50) is superb value.

Forest Café (Map p52; 0131-229 4922; http://blog.theforest.org.uk/cafe; 141 Lauriston Pl; mains £3-6; 10am-11pm; ; all Tollcross buses) A chilled-out, colourful and comfortably scuffed-around-the-edges antidote to squeaky-clean espresso bars, this volunteer-run, not-for-profit art space and cafe serves up humongous helpings of hearty vegetarian and vegan fodder, ranging from nachos to falafel wraps.

Mosque Kitchen (Map p58; www.mosquekitchen.com; 31 Nicolson Sq; mains £5-9; 11.30am-10pm, closed 12.50-1.50pm Fri; ; all South Bridge buses) Expect shared tables and disposable plates, but this is the place to go for cheap, authentic and delicious homemade curries, kebabs, pakoras and naan bread, all washed down with lassi or mango juice. Caters to Edinburgh's Central Mosque but welcomes all – local students have taken to it big time. No alcohol.

ceiling, pillared arches and mosaic-tiled floor, the Grill Room at the Dome is one of the city's most impressive dining rooms. The menu is solidly modern Scottish, with great steaks, seafood and venison. Reservations strongly recommended.

Ivy on the Square BRITISH ££
(Map p66; ☑0131-526 4777; https://theivy edinburgh.com; 6 St Andrew Sq; mains £13-19; ☺8am-midnight Mon-Sat, 9am-10.30pm Sun; ☎; ◪St Andrew Sq) The first Scottish outpost of London's famous celebrity haunt, the Ivy in Covent Garden, this classy but informal brasserie serves up traditional British dishes, from eggs Benedict for brunch through afternoon tea to the Ivy's classic dinner of shepherd's pie or steak, egg and chips.

Time 4 Thai THAI ££
(Map p66; ☑0131-225 8822; http://time4thai. co.uk; 45 N Castle St; mains £12-20; ☺noon-2.30pm & 5-11pm Mon-Thu, noon-11.30pm Fri & Sat, 1-11pm Sun; ◪; ◪24, 29, 42) Stylish modern decor, smartly dressed staff and designer tableware put this place a cut above your average Thai restaurant. The menu matches the elegance of the surroundings, with authentic recipes and intense flavours perfectly presented. The three-course lunch at £11.80 is great value.

Bon Vivant BISTRO ££
(Map p66; ☑0131-225 3275; http://bonvivant edinburgh.co.uk; 55 Thistle St; mains £13-17; ☺noon-10pm; ☎; ◪23, 27) Candlelight reflected in the warm glow of polished wood makes for an intimate atmosphere in this New Town favourite. The food is superb value for this part of town, offering a range of tapas-style 'bites' as well as standard main courses, with a changing menu of seasonal, locally sourced dishes such as cod fillet with bacon and mussel cream.

Scottish Cafe & Restaurant SCOTTISH ££
(Map p66; ☑0131-225 1550; www.contini.com/ scottish-cafe-and-restaurant; The Mound; mains £10-15; ☺9am-5pm Mon-Wed, Fri & Sat, to 7pm Thu, 10am-5pm Sun; ☎◪; ◪Princes St) ✿ This appealing modern restaurant (part of the Scottish National Gallery (p65) complex) has picture windows providing a view along Princes Street Gardens (p64). Try traditional Scottish dishes such as Cullen skink and leek-and-potato soup, or seasonal, sustainably sourced produce including smoked salmon and trout, free-range chicken and pork.

L'Escargot Bleu FRENCH ££
(Map p52; ☑0131-557 1600; www.lescargotbleu. co.uk; 56 Broughton St; mains £16-24; ☺noon-2.30pm & 5.30-10pm Mon-Thu, noon-3pm & 5.30-10.30pm Fri & Sat; ◪; ◪8) As with its sister restaurant, **L'Escargot Blanc** (Map p52; ☑0131-226 1890; www.lescargotblanc.co.uk; 17 Queensferry St; mains £15-25; ☺noon-2.30pm & 5.30-10pm Mon-Thu, noon-3pm & 5.30-10.30pm Fri & Sat; ◪; ◪19, 36, 37, 41, 47) ✿, this cute little bistro is as Gallic as garlic but makes fine use of quality Scottish produce – the French-speaking staff will lead you knowledgeably through a menu that includes authentic Savoyard *tartiflette*, steak tartare, and Basque-style mussels. Two-course lunch/early-bird menu £12.90/14.90.

Fishers in the City SEAFOOD ££
(Map p66; ☑0131-225 5109; www.fishers bistros.co.uk; 58 Thistle St; mains £16-23; ☺noon-10.30pm; ☎◪; ◪24, 29, 42) ✿ This more sophisticated city-centre branch of the famous Fishers Bistro (p89) in Leith, with granite-topped tables, split-level dining area and nautical theme, specialises in superior Scottish seafood – the knowledgeable staff serve up plump and succulent oysters, meltingly sweet scallops, and sea bass that's been grilled to perfection.

Café Royal Oyster Bar SEAFOOD £££
(Map p66; ☑0131-556 1884; www.caferoyal edinburgh.co.uk; 17a W Register St; mains £17-38; ☺noon-2.30pm & 5.30-9.30pm Mon-Fri, noon-9.30pm Sat & Sun; ◪St Andrew Sq) Pass through the revolving doors on the corner of West Register St and you're transported back to Victorian times – a palace of glinting mahogany, polished brass, marble floors, stained glass, Doulton tiles, gilded cornices and starched table linen so thick it creaks when you fold it. The menu is mostly classic seafood, from oysters on ice to Scottish lobster thermidor.

Cafe St Honore FRENCH £££
(Map p66; ☑0131-226 2211; www.cafesthonore. com; 34 Thistle St Lane NW; mains £16-25; ☺noon-2pm & 6-10pm; ◪Princes St) With candlelight glowing against old polished wood and reflected from antique mirrors, this intimate French restaurant is the ideal place for a romantic dinner. Service is discreet, the menu is sumptuous and the wine list is long. You can get a two-course dinner for £14.50, and a three-course set dinner for £25.50.

CLAUDIO DIVIZIA/SHUTTERSTOCK ©

1. Scottish Parliament Building (p61)
Officially opened by the Queen in 2004, this is a spectacular and idiosyncratic example of modern architecture.

2. Royal Yacht Britannia (p70)
Built in Glasgow, the yacht was the Royal Family's holiday home during their foreign travels from 1953 to 1997.

3. Edinburgh Castle (p51)
Once used as a royal residence, a prison and an army base, the castle now houses the Scottish crown jewels.

4. Rosslyn Chapel (p101)
This 15th-century chapel, which featured in Dan Brown's *The Da Vinci Code*, is a marvel of stonemasonry.

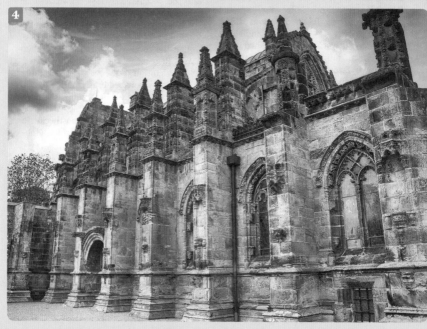

✕ West End & Dean Village

Cafe Milk CAFE £

(Map p52; ☑ 0131-629 6022; www.cafemilk.co.uk; 232 Morrison St; mains £6-9; ⏱ 7.30am-4pm Mon-Fri, 8am-4pm Sat, 8am-3pm Sun; 🛜 ⚡; 🚇 Haymarket) 🍴 This is fast food with a conscience – natural, nutritious, locally sourced and freshly prepared, from organic porridge to courgette, lemon and feta fritters, and North Indian dhal with rice or flatbread. Take away, or sit in and soak up the retro vibe amid old Formica tables, battered school benches, enamel plates and junk-shop cutlery stacked in golden-syrup tins.

★Kanpai Sushi JAPANESE ££

(Map p58; ☑ 0131-228 1602; www.kanpaisushi. co.uk; 8-10 Grindlay St; mains £9-15, sushi per piece £4-10; ⏱ noon-2.30pm & 5-10.30pm Tue-Sat; 🚌 all Lothian Rd buses) What is arguably Edinburgh's best sushi restaurant impresses with its minimalist interior, fresh, top-quality fish and elegantly presented dishes – the squid tempura comes in a delicate woven basket, while the sashimi combo is presented as a flower arrangement in an ice-filled stoneware bowl. Bookings recommended.

Shebeen SOUTH AFRICAN ££

(Map p58; ☑ 0131-629 0261; www.shebeenbar. co.uk; 8 Morrison St; mains £12-27; ⏱ 5-10pm Sun-Thu, noon-10pm Fri & Sat; 🚌 all Tollcross buses) This snugly rustic restaurant takes pride in an extremely meaty menu, which begins with Fanagalo – a sharing platter of ribs, *boerowors* (South African sausage), *frikedelle* (meatballs), pork belly and chicken wings served in a wooden pail (literally a bucket of meat!) – and moves on to a burger topped with beef brisket, and some of the finest steaks in the city.

Maison Bleue at Home FUSION ££

(Map p52; ☑ 0131-220 0773; www.home-restaurant.co.uk; 7-8 Queensferry St; mains £15-32; ⏱ noon-3pm & 5-10pm; 🚌 19, 36, 37, 47) Light, bright and modern, Home mixes social purpose with quality food. The globe-spanning menu includes steaks, tagines, gumbo and posh mac 'n' cheese. Diners can pay meals forward (to be claimed by homeless people), and 100% of profits go to charity.

★Timberyard SCOTTISH £££

(Map p58; ☑ 0131-221 1222; www.timberyard.co; 10 Lady Lawson St; 4-course lunch or dinner £55; ⏱ noon-2pm & 5.30-9.30pm Tue-Sat; 🛜 ♿; 🚌 2, 300) 🍴 Ancient, worn floorboards, cast-iron pillars, exposed joists, and tables made from slabs of old mahogany create a rustic, retro atmosphere in this slow-food restaurant where the accent is on locally sourced produce from artisan growers and foragers. Typical dishes include seared scallop with leek, fennel and cured egg yolk, and roast quail with salsify and thyme.

★Castle Terrace SCOTTISH £££

(Map p58; ☑ 0131-229 1222; www.castleterrace restaurant.com; 33-35 Castle Tce; 3-course lunch/dinner £33/70; ⏱ noon-2.15pm & 6.30-10pm Tue-Sat; 🚇2) 🍴 It was little more than a year after opening in 2010 that Castle Terrace was awarded a Michelin star under chef-patron Dominic Jack (the star was lost in 2015). The menu is seasonal and applies honed Parisian skills to the finest of local produce, be it Ayrshire pork, Aberdeenshire lamb or Newhaven crab – even the cheese in the sauces is Scottish.

✕ Stockbridge

Scran & Scallie GASTROPUB ££

(Map p52; ☑ 0131-332 6281; https://scranand scallie.com; 1 Comely Bank Rd; mains £12-20; ⏱ noon-10pm Mon-Fri, 8.30am-10pm Sat & Sun; 🛜 ♿ 🐕; 🚌 24, 29, 42) Established by the Michelin-starred team responsible for Kitchin and Castle Terrace, this laid-back gastropub adds a modern chef's touch to old-time dishes such as chicken-liver parfait, sausage and mash, and steak pie. There are also quality versions of classic pub grub such as burgers, seafood pie, and fish and chips, and veggie options that include a beetroot-and-lentil burger.

Taisteal INTERNATIONAL ££

(Map p52; ☑ 0131-332 9977; www.taisteal.co.uk; 1-3 Raeburn Pl; mains £14-19; ⏱ noon-2.30pm & 6-9.30pm Tue-Sat; 🚌 24, 29, 36, 42) 🍴 *Taisteal* is the Gaelic word for 'travel', so it's no surprise that the menu in this convivial bistro is a fusion of Scottish produce with influences and flavours from around the world – rabbit and pancetta ballotine with rabbit haggis and wild-garlic gnocchi is a typical concoction. There's also a three-course lunch for £16, and a five-course tasting menu for £35.

✕ South Edinburgh

Söderberg (The Meadows) CAFE £

(Map p52; ☑ 0131-228 5876; www.soderberg.uk; 27 Simpson Loan; mains £6-10; ⏱ 7.30am-7pm Mon-

Fri, 9am-7pm Sat & Sun; ☑ 🖶; ⧉ 23, 27, 45, 47, 300) This Swedish-style coffee house produces its own home-baked pastries and breads, which form the basis of lunchtime sandwiches with fillings such as roast beef with beetroot and caper salad, and roast butternut squash with sunblush tomato pesto. Breakfast (served till noon) can be a basket of breads with conserves and cheeses, or yoghurt with granola and fruit.

⭐**Aizle** SCOTTISH **££**

(Map p52; ☑ 0131-662 9349; http://aizle.co.uk; 107-109 St Leonard's St; 5-course dinner £55; ⧖ 5-9pm Wed-Sat; 🕾; ⧉ 14) If you tend to have trouble deciding what to eat, Aizle (the name is an old Scots word for 'spark' or 'ember') will do the job for you. There's no menu here, just a five-course dinner conjured from a monthly 'harvest' of the finest and freshest local produce (listed on a blackboard), and presented beautifully – art on a plate.

⭐**Locanda de Gusti** ITALIAN **££**

(Map p52; ☑ 0131-346 8800; www.locandade gusti.com; 102 Dalry Rd; mains £14-26; ⧖ 5.30-10pm Mon-Wed, 12.30-2pm & 5.30-10pm Thu-Sat; 🖶; ⧉ 2, 3, 4, 25, 33, 44) This bustling family bistro, loud with the buzz of conversation and the clink of glasses and cutlery, is no ordinary Italian but a little corner of Naples, complete with hearty Neapolitan home cooking by friendly head chef Rosario. The food ranges from light and tasty ravioli tossed with butter and sage to delicious platters of grilled seafood.

⭐**First Coast** SCOTTISH **££**

(Map p52; ☑ 0131-313 4404; www.first-coast.co.uk; 97-101 Dalry Rd; mains £13-20; ⧖ noon-2pm & 5-11pm Mon-Sat; 🕾☑🖶; ⧉ 2, 3, 4, 25, 33, 44) This popular neighbourhood bistro has a striking main dining area with sea-blue wood panelling and stripped stonework, and a short and simple menu offering hearty comfort food such as fish with creamy mash, brown shrimp and garlic butter, or pigeon breast with black pudding, pearl barley and beetroot. Lunchtime and early evening there's an excellent two-course meal for £13.50.

⭐**Loudon's Café & Bakery** CAFE **££**

(Map p52; www.loudons.co.uk; 94b Fountainbridge; mains £8-13; ⧖ 7.30am-5pm Mon-Fri, 8am-5pm Sat & Sun; 🕾☑🖶; ⧉ 1, 34, 300) Organic bread and cakes baked on the premises, ethically sourced coffee, daily and weekend newspapers scattered about, even some outdoor

tables – what's not to like? All-day brunch (8am to 4pm) served at weekends includes eggs Benedict, granola with yoghurt, and specials such as blueberry pancakes with fruit salad.

✘ **Leith**

Pitt MARKET **£**

(☑ 07736 281893; www.thepitt.co.uk; 125 Pitt St; entry £2; ⧖ noon-10pm Sat Mar-Dec; ⧉ 7, 11, 14) A weekly street-food market surrounded by industrial warehouses, The Pitt is a little bit of East London in north Edinburgh. The regularly changing food trucks sell anything from burgers stuffed with crab to halloumi bao buns to haggis to sweet-potato *pierogi* (dumplings). Choose a drink from the wine and gin bars, or the Barneys beer truck selling local craft ales.

The vibe is rustic and outdoorsy, with live bands, wooden pallet seating and fire barrels for warming your hands.

⭐**Fishers Bistro** SEAFOOD **££**

(☑ 0131-554 5666; www.fishersbistros.co.uk; 1 The Shore; mains £14-25; ⧖ noon-10.30pm Mon-Sat, 12.30-10.30pm Sun; 🕾☑🖶; ⧉ 16, 22, 36, 300) This cosy little restaurant, tucked beneath a 17th-century signal tower, is one of the city's best seafood places. The menu ranges widely in price, from cheaper dishes such as classic fish cakes with lemon-and-chive mayonnaise to more expensive delights such as Fife lobster and chips (£40).

⭐**Martin Wishart** FRENCH **£££**

(☑ 0131-553 3557; www.martin-wishart.co.uk; 54 The Shore; 3-course lunch £32, 4-course dinner £90; ⧖ noon-2pm & 7-10pm Tue-Fri, noon-1.30pm & 7-10pm Sat; ☑; ⧉ 16, 22, 36, 300) ✍ In 2001 this restaurant became the first in Edinburgh to win a Michelin star, and it's retained it ever since. The eponymous chef has worked with Albert Roux, Marco Pierre White and Nick Nairn, and brings a modern French approach to the best Scottish produce, from langoustines with white asparagus and confit onion to a six-course vegetarian tasting menu (£75).

⭐**Kitchin** SCOTTISH **£££**

(☑ 0131-555 1755; http://thekitchin.com; 78 Commercial Quay; 3-course lunch/dinner £33/75; ⧖ noon-2.30pm & 6-10pm Tue-Sat; ☑; ⧉ 16, 22, 36, 300) Fresh, seasonal, locally sourced Scottish produce is the philosophy that has won a Michelin star for this elegant but unpretentious restaurant. The menu moves with the seasons, of course, so expect fresh salads in summer and game in winter, and shellfish dishes such as baked scallops with white wine, vermouth and herb sauce when there's an 'r' in the month.

Chop House Leith STEAK £££

(☑ 0131-629 1919; www.chophousesteak.co.uk; 102 Constitution St; mains £17-29; ⊙ noon-3pm & 5-10.30pm Mon-Fri, 10am-10.30pm Sat & Sun; 🐾; 🖵 12, 16) A modern take on the old-fashioned steakhouse, this 'bar and butchery' combines slick designer decor (the ceramic brick tiles are a nod to traditional butcher shops) with a meaty menu of the best Scottish beef, dry-aged for at least 35 days and chargrilled to perfection. Sauces include bone-marrow gravy and Argentine *chimichurri*. Cool cocktails, too.

 Drinking & Nightlife

Edinburgh has always been a drinker's city. It has more than 700 pubs – more per square mile than any other UK city – and they are as varied and full of character as the people who drink in them, from Victorian palaces to stylish preclub bars, and from real-ale howffs (meeting places, often pubs) to cool cocktail lounges.

Old Town

★ **Cabaret Voltaire** CLUB

(Map p58; www.thecabaretvoltaire.com; 36-38 Blair St; ⊙ 5pm-3am Tue-Sat, 8pm-1am Sun; 🐾; 🖵 all South Bridge buses) An atmospheric warren of stone-lined vaults houses this self-consciously 'alternative' club, which eschews huge dance floors and egotistical DJ worship in favour of a 'creative crucible' hosting an eclectic mix of DJs, live acts, comedy, theatre, visual arts and the spoken word. Well worth a look.

★ **Bow Bar** PUB

(Map p58; www.thebowbar.co.uk; 80 West Bow; ⊙ noon-midnight Mon-Sat, to 11.30pm Sun; 🖵 2, 23, 27, 41, 42) One of the city's best traditional-style pubs (it's not as old as it looks), serving a range of excellent real ales, Scottish craft gins and a vast selection of malt whiskies, the Bow Bar often has standing-room only on Friday and Saturday evenings.

Bongo Club CLUB

(Map p58; www.thebongoclub.co.uk; 66 Cowgate; free-£7; ⊙ 11pm-3am Tue & Thu, 7pm-3am Fri-Sun;

🐾; 🖵 2) Owned by a local arts charity, the weird and wonderful Bongo Club boasts a long history of hosting everything from wild club nights and local bands to performance art and kids comedy shows.

Dragonfly COCKTAIL BAR

(Map p58; ☑ 0131-228 4543; www.dragonfly cocktailbar.com; 52 West Port; ⊙ 4pm-1am; 🐾; 🖵 2) A superstylish lounge bar with a Raffles of Singapore vibe – it's all crystal chandeliers, polished wood and oriental art – Dragonfly has won rave reviews for both its innovative cocktails and its designer decor. Grab a seat on the neat little mezzanine, from where you can look down on the bar as the Singapore Slings are being slung.

Jolly Judge PUB

(Map p58; www.jollyjudge.co.uk; 7a James Ct; ⊙ noon-11pm Mon-Thu, to midnight Fri & Sat, 12.30-11pm Sun; 🐾; 🖵 23, 27, 41, 42) A snug little howff tucked away down a close, the Judge exudes a cosy 17th-century atmosphere (low, timber-beamed painted ceilings) and has the added attraction of a cheering open fire in cold weather. No music or gaming machines, just the buzz of conversation.

Salt Horse Beer Shop & Bar BAR

(Map p58; ☑ 0131-558 8304; www.salthorse.beer; 57-61 Blackfriars St; ⊙ 4pm-midnight Mon-Fri, noon-1am Sat, 12.30pm-midnight Sun; 🖵 300) Tucked off the Royal Mile, this independent hybrid combines great beer, food, and a shop next door selling around 400 beers to drink in or take away. Work your way through 12 keg lines of local and imported beers and a small but perfectly formed menu of handmade burgers, Scotch eggs, and charcuterie and cheese platters.

Checkpoint BAR

(Map p58; ☑ 0131-225 9352; www.checkpoint edinburgh.com; 3 Bristo Pl; ⊙ 9am-1am; 🐾; 🖵 2, 47) A friendly cafe, bar and restaurant with a comprehensive menu including breakfasts, bar bites and substantial mains, Checkpoint is gaining a reputation as one of the coolest spots in Edinburgh. The utilitarian white-walled space is flooded with light from floor-to-ceiling windows and is vast enough to house, of all things, an old shipping container.

Liquid Room CLUB

(Map p58; www.liquidroom.com; 9c Victoria St; free-£20; ⊙ live music from 7pm, club nights

10.30pm-3am; 🚌 23, 27, 41, 42) Set in a subterranean vault deep beneath Victoria St, the Liquid Room is a superb club venue with a thundering sound system. There are regular club nights every Friday and Saturday, as well as DJs and live bands on other nights. Check the website for upcoming events.

New Town

Lucky Liquor Co   COCKTAIL BAR

(Map p66; ☎ 0131-226 3976; www.luckyliquorco. com; 39a Queen St; ⏱ 4pm-1am; 🚌 24, 29, 42) This tiny, black-and-white bar is all about the number 13: 13 bottles of base spirit are used to create a daily menu of 13 cocktails. The result is a playful list with some unusual flavours, such as tonka-bean liqueur, pea purée and lavender absinthe (though not all in the same glass!), served by a fun and friendly crew.

Bramble   COCKTAIL BAR

(Map p66; ☎ 0131-226 6343; www.bramblebar. co.uk; 16a Queen St; ⏱ 4pm-1am; 🚌 23, 27) One of those places that easily earn the sobriquet 'best-kept secret', Bramble is an unmarked cellar bar (just an inconspicuous brass nameplate beneath a dry-cleaner's shop) where a maze of stone and brick hideaways conceals what is arguably the city's best cocktail venue. No beer taps, no fuss, just expertly mixed drinks.

Joseph Pearce's   PUB

(Map p52; ☎ 0131-556 4140; www.bodabar.com/ joseph-pearces; 23 Elm Row; ⏱ 11am-midnight Sun-Thu, to 1am Fri & Sat; 🛜 🍴; 🚌 all Leith Walk buses) This traditional Victorian pub has been remodelled and given a new lease of life by the Swedish owners. It's a real hub of the local community, with good food (very family friendly before 5pm), a relaxed atmosphere, and events like Monday-night Scrabble games and August crayfish parties.

Right margin vertical text: EDINBURGH DRINKING & NIGHTLIFE

TOP FIVE TRADITIONAL PUBS

Bennet's Bar (Map p52; ☎ 0131-229 5143; www.bennetsbaredinburgh.co.uk; 8 Leven St; ⏱ 11am-1am; 🚌 all Tollcross buses) Situated beside the **King's Theatre** (Map p52; ☎ 0131-529 6000; www.capitaltheatres.com/kings; 2 Leven St; ⏱ box office 10am-6pm; 🚌 all Tollcross buses), Bennet's (established in 1839) has managed to hang on to almost all of its beautiful Victorian fittings, from the leaded stained-glass windows and the ornate mirrors to the wooden gantry and the brass water taps on the bar (for your whisky – there are over 100 malts from which to choose).

Café Royal Circle Bar (Map p66; ☎ 0131-556 1884; www.caferoyaledinburgh.co.uk; 17 W Register St; ⏱ 11am-11pm Mon-Wed, to midnight Thu, to 1am Fri & Sat, to 10pm Sun; 🛜; 🚌 Princes St) Perhaps *the* classic Edinburgh pub, the Café Royal's main claims to fame are its magnificent oval bar and its Doulton tile portraits of famous Victorian inventors. Sit at the bar or claim one of the cosy leather booths beneath the stained-glass windows, and choose from the seven real ales on tap.

Athletic Arms (Diggers; Map p52; ☎ 0131-337 3822; https://athleticarms.com; 1-3 Angle Park Tce; ⏱ 11am-1am; 🚌 1, 34, 300) Nicknamed for the cemetery across the street – gravediggers used to nip in and slake their thirst here – the Diggers dates from 1897. It's still staunchly traditional – the decor has barely changed in 100 years – and is a beacon for real-ale drinkers, serving locally brewed 80-shilling ale. Packed to the gills with football and rugby fans on match days.

Abbotsford (Map p66; ☎ 0131-225 5276; www.theabbotsford.com; 3 Rose St; ⏱ 11am-11pm Mon-Thu, to midnight Fri & Sat, 12.30-11pm Sun; 🛜; 🚌 all Princes St buses) One of the few pubs in Rose St that has retained its Edwardian splendour, the Abbotsford has long been a hang-out for writers, actors, journalists and media people, and has many loyal regulars. Dating from 1902, and named after Sir Walter Scott's country house, the pub's centrepiece is a splendid mahogany island bar. Good selection of real ales.

Sheep Heid Inn (www.thesheepheidedinburgh.co.uk; 43-45 The Causeway; ⏱ 11am-11pm Mon-Thu, to midnight Fri & Sat, noon-11pm Sun; 🍴; 🚌 42) Possibly the oldest inn in Edinburgh (with a licence dating back to 1360), the Sheep Heid feels more like an upmarket country pub than an Edinburgh bar. Set in the semirural shadow of Arthur's Seat (p63), it's famous for its 19th-century skittles alley and its lovely little beer garden.

Guildford Arms PUB
(Map p66; ✉ 0131-556 4312; www.guildfordarms. com; 1 W Register St; ⊙ 11am-11pm Mon-Thu, to 11.30pm Fri & Sat, 12.30-11pm Sun; 🖥; 🚇 St Andrew Sq) Located in a side alley off the east end of Princes St, the Guildford is a classic Victorian pub full of polished mahogany, brass and ornate cornices. The range of real ales is excellent – try to get a table in the unusual upstairs gallery, with a view over the sea of drinkers below.

Oxford Bar PUB
(Map p66; ✉ 0131-539 7119; www.oxfordbar.co.uk; 8 Young St; ⊙ noon-midnight Mon-Thu, 11am-1am Fri & Sat, 12.30-11pm Sun; 🖥; 🚇 all Princes St buses) The Oxford is that rarest of things: a real pub for real people, with no 'theme', no frills and no pretensions. 'The Ox' has been immortalised by Ian Rankin, author of the Inspector Rebus novels, whose fictional detective is a regular here. Occasional live folk music.

Cumberland Bar PUB
(Map p52; ✉ 0131-558 3134; www.cumberlandbar. co.uk; 1-3 Cumberland St; ⊙ noon-midnight Mon-Wed, to 1am Thu-Sat, 11am-11pm Sun; 🖥; 🚇 23, 27) Immortalised as the stereotypical New Town pub in Alexander McCall Smith's serialised novel *44 Scotland Street*, the Cumberland has an authentic, traditional wood-brass-and-mirrors look (despite being relatively new) and serves well-looked-after, cask-conditioned ales and a wide range of malt whiskies. There's also a pleasant little beer garden.

Leith

★ Roseleaf BAR
(✉ 0131-476 5268; www.roseleaf.co.uk; 23-24 Sandport Pl; ⊙ 10am-1am; 🖥 🚼; 🚇 16, 22, 36, 300) Cute, quaint, and decked out in flowered wallpaper, old furniture and rose-patterned china (cocktails are served in teapots), the Roseleaf could hardly be further from the average Leith bar. The real ales and bottled beers are complemented by a range of speciality teas, coffees and fruit drinks (including rose lemonade), and well-above-average pub grub (served from 10am to 10pm).

Lioness of Leith BAR
(✉ 0131-629 0580; www.thelionessofleith.co.uk; 21-25 Duke St; ⊙ noon-1am Mon-Thu, 11am-1am Fri-Sun; 🖥; 🚇 21, 25, 34, 49, 300) Duke St was always one of the rougher corners of Leith, but the emergence of pubs like the Lioness is a sure sign of gentrification. Distressed timber and battered leather benches are surrounded by vintage *objets trouvés*, a pin-

---

LGBTIQ+ EDINBURGH

Edinburgh has a small – but perfectly formed – gay and lesbian scene, centred on the area around Broughton St (known affectionately as the 'Pink Triangle') at the eastern end of New Town.

Scotsgay (www.scotsgay.co.uk) is the local magazine covering gay and lesbian issues, with listings of gay-friendly pubs and clubs.

Useful contacts:

Edinburgh LGBT Centre (✉ 0131-523 1100; www.lgbthealth.org.uk; 9 Howe St; 🚇 24, 29, 42)

Lothian LGBT Helpline (✉ 0300 123 2523; www.lgbthealth.org.uk/helpline; ⊙ noon-9pm Tue & Wed)

Pubs & Clubs

CC Blooms (Map p66; ✉ 0131-556 9331; http://ccblooms.co.uk; 23 Greenside Pl; ⊙ 11am-3am; 🖥; 🚇 all Leith Walk buses) The raddled old queen of Edinburgh's 1990s gay scene has been given a shot in the arm, with two floors of deafening dance and disco every night. It can get pretty crowded after 11pm and the drinks can be overpriced, but it's worth a visit – go early, or sample the wild Church of High Kicks cabaret show on Sunday nights.

Regent (Map p52; ✉ 0131-661 8198; 2 Montrose Tce; ⊙ noon-1am Mon-Sat, 12.30pm-1am Sun; 🚇 1, 4, 5, 15, 45, 300) This is a pleasant gay local with a relaxed atmosphere (no loud music), serving coffee and croissants as well as excellent real ales, including Deuchars IPA and Caledonian 80/-. Meeting place for the Lesbian and Gay Real Ale Drinkers club (first Monday of the month at 9pm).

ball machine and a pop-art print of Allen Ginsberg. Good beers and cocktails, and a tempting menu of gourmet burgers.

Teuchters Landing   PUB
(📲 0131-554 7427; www.aroomin.co.uk; 1 Dock Pl; ⊙ 10.30am-1am; 🕾; 🚌 16, 22, 36, 300) A cosy warren of timber-lined nooks and crannies housed in a single-storey red-brick building (once a waiting room for ferries across the Firth of Forth), this real-ale and malt-whisky bar also has tables on a floating terrace in the dock.

Port O'Leith   PUB
(📲 0131-554 3568; www.facebook.com/ThePort OLeithBar; 58 Constitution St; ⊙ 11am-1am Mon-Sat, noon-1am Sun; 🚌 12,16) This good old-fashioned local boozer has been sympathetically restored – it appeared in the 2013 film *Sunshine on Leith*. Its nautical history is evident in the form of flags and cap bands left behind by visiting sailors (Leith docks are just down the road). Pop in for a pint and you'll probably stay until closing time.

☆ Entertainment

Edinburgh has a number of fine theatres and concert halls, and there are independent art-house cinemas as well as mainstream movie theatres. Many pubs offer entertainment ranging from live Scottish folk music to pop, rock and jazz, as well as karaoke and quiz nights, while a range of stylish modern bars purvey house, dance and hip-hop to the pre-clubbing crowd.

Live Music
Edinburgh is a great place to hear traditional Scottish (and Irish) folk music, with a mix of regular spots and impromptu sessions. The Gig Guide (www.gigguide.co.uk) is a free email newsletter and listing website covering live music in Scotland.

★ Sandy Bell's   TRADITIONAL MUSIC
(Map p58; www.sandybellsedinburgh.co.uk; 25 Forrest Rd; ⊙ noon-1am Mon-Sat, 12.30pm-midnight Sun; 🚌 2, 23, 27, 41, 42, 45) This unassuming pub has been a stalwart of the traditional-music scene since the 1960s (the founder's wife sang with the Corries). There's music every weekday evening at 9pm, and from 2pm Saturday and 4pm Sunday, plus lots of impromptu sessions.

Caves   LIVE MUSIC
(Map p58; https://unusualvenuesedinburgh.com/venues/the-caves-venue-edinburgh; 8-12 Niddry St

ⓘ WHAT'S ON

The comprehensive source for what's-on info is *The List* (www.list.co.uk), an excellent listings website and magazine covering both Edinburgh and Glasgow. It's available from most newsagents, and is published every two months.

S; 🚌 300) A spectacular subterranean venue set in the ancient stone vaults beneath the South Bridge, the Caves stages a series of one-off club nights and live-music gigs, as well as *ceilidh* (traditional music) nights during the Edinburgh Festival. Check the What's On link on the website for upcoming events.

Jam House   LIVE MUSIC
(Map p66; 📲 0131-220 2321; www.thejamhouse. com; 5 Queen St; from £4; ⊙ 6pm-3am Fri & Sat; 🚇 St Andrew Sq) The brainchild of rhythm-and-blues pianist and TV personality Jools Holland, the Jam House is set in a former BBC TV studio and offers a combination of fine dining and live jazz and blues performances. Admission is for over-21s only, and there's a smart-casual dress code.

Henry's Cellar Bar   LIVE MUSIC
(Map p58; 📲 0131-629 2992; www.facebook.com/Henryscellarbar; 16 Morrison St; free-£10; ⊙ 9pm-3am Sun & Tue-Thu, 8pm-3am Mon, 7pm-3am Fri & Sat; 🚌 all Lothian Rd buses) One of Edinburgh's most eclectic live-music venues, Henry's has something going on most nights of the week, from rock and indie to 'Balkan-inspired folk' and from funk and hip-hop to hardcore, staging both local bands and acts from around the world.

Bannerman's   LIVE MUSIC
(Map p58; www.facebook.com/BannermansBar; 212 Cowgate; ⊙ noon-1am Mon-Sat, 12.30pm-1am Sun; 🕾; 🚌 45, 300) A long-established music venue – it seems like every Edinburgh student for the last four decades spent half their youth here – Bannerman's straggles through a warren of old vaults beneath South Bridge. It pulls in crowds of students, locals and backpackers with live rock, punk and indie bands five or six nights a week.

Jazz Bar   JAZZ, BLUES
(Map p58; www.thejazzbar.co.uk; 1a Chambers St; £3-7; ⊙ 5pm-3am Sun-Fri, 1.30pm-3am Sat; 🕾; 🚌 45, 300) This atmospheric cellar bar, with its polished parquet floors, bare stone walls,

candlelit tables and stylish steel-framed chairs, is owned and operated by jazz musicians. There's live music every night from 9pm to 3am, and on Saturday from 3pm. As well as jazz, expect bands playing blues, funk, soul and fusion.

Voodoo Rooms LIVE MUSIC
(Map p66; ☑ 0131-556 7060; www.thevoodoo rooms.com; 19a W Register St; free-£20; ☺ 4pm-1am Mon-Thu, noon-1am Fri-Sun; ☒ St Andrew Sq) Decadent decor of black leather, ornate plasterwork and gilt detailing creates a stylish setting for this complex of bars and performance spaces above the Café Royal (p91) that hosts everything from classic soul and Motown to blues nights, jam sessions and live local bands.

Cinemas
Film buffs will find plenty to keep them happy in Edinburgh's art-house cinemas, while popcorn munchers can choose from a range of multiplexes.

Filmhouse CINEMA
(Map p58; ☑ 0131-228 2688; www.filmhouse cinema.com; 88 Lothian Rd; ☎; ☒ all Lothian Rd buses) The Filmhouse is the main venue for the annual Edinburgh International Film Festival (p74) and screens a full program of art-house, classic, foreign and second-run films, with lots of themes, retrospectives and 70mm screenings. It has wheelchair access to all three screens.

Cameo CINEMA
(Map p52; ☑ 0871 902 5723; www.picturehouses. com/cinema/Cameo_Picturehouse; 38 Home St; ☎; ☒ all Tollcross buses) The three-screen, independently owned Cameo is a good old-fashioned cinema showing an imaginative mix of mainstream and art-house movies. There's a good program of late-night films and Sunday matinees, and the seats in screen 1 are big enough to get lost in.

Classical Music, Opera & Ballet
Edinburgh is home to the Scottish Chamber Orchestra (SCO; www.sco.org.uk), one of Europe's finest orchestras and well worth hearing. Its performances are usually held at **Queen's Hall** (Map p52; ☑ 0131-668 2019; www.thequeenshall.net; Clerk St; ☺ box office 10am-5.15pm Mon-Sat, or to 15min after show begins; ☒ all Newington buses) or Usher Hall.

Scottish Opera (www.scottishopera. org.uk) and the Royal Scottish National Orchestra (RSNO; www.rsno.org.uk) are based in Glasgow but regularly perform in Edinburgh, at the Edinburgh Festival Theatre and Usher Hall, respectively.

Edinburgh Festival Theatre THEATRE
(Map p58; ☑ 0131-529 6000; www.capital theatres.com/festival; 13-29 Nicolson St; ☺ box office 10am-7.30pm; ☒ all South Bridge buses) A beautifully restored art-deco theatre with a modern all-glass frontage, the Festival is the city's main venue for opera, dance and ballet, but also stages musicals, concerts, drama and children's shows.

Usher Hall CLASSICAL MUSIC
(Map p58; ☑ 0131-228 1155; www.usherhall. co.uk; Lothian Rd; ☺ box office 10am-5.30pm, to 8pm show nights; ☒ all Lothian Rd buses) The architecturally impressive Usher Hall hosts concerts by the Royal Scottish National Orchestra (RSNO) and performances of popular music.

St Giles Cathedral CLASSICAL MUSIC
(Map p58; www.stgilescathedral.org.uk; High St; ☒ 23, 27, 41, 42) The big kirk on the Royal Mile plays host to a regular and varied program of classical music, including popular lunchtime and evening concerts and organ recitals. The cathedral choir sings at the 10am and 11.30am Sunday services.

Theatre, Musicals & Comedy
★ Summerhall THEATRE
(Map p52; ☑ 0131-560 1580; www.summerhall. co.uk; 1 Summerhall; ☺ box office 10am-6pm; ☒ 41, 42, 67) Formerly Edinburgh University's veterinary school, the Summerhall complex is a major cultural centre and entertainment venue, with old halls and lecture theatres (including an original anatomy lecture theatre) now serving as venues for drama, dance, cinema and comedy performances. It's also one of the main venues for Edinburgh Festival (p75) events.

Royal Lyceum Theatre THEATRE
(Map p58; ☑ 0131-248 4848; www.lyceum.org.uk; 30b Grindlay St; ☺ box office 10am-5pm Mon-Sat, to 7pm show nights; ♿; ☒ all Lothian Rd buses) A grand Victorian theatre located beside the Usher Hall, the Lyceum stages drama, concerts, musicals and ballet.

Traverse Theatre THEATRE
(Map p58; ☑ 0131-228 1404; www.traverse.co.uk; 10 Cambridge St; ☺ box office 10am-6pm Mon-Sat, to 7pm show nights; ☎; ☒ all Lothian Rd buses) The Traverse is the main focus for

new Scottish writing; it stages an adventurous program of contemporary drama and dance. The box office is only open on Sunday (from 4pm) when there's a show on.

Stand Comedy Club　　　　　　COMEDY
(Map p66; ☑ 0131-558 7272; www.thestand.co.uk; 5 York Pl; tickets £3-18; ⊘ from 7.30pm Mon-Sat, from 12.30pm Sun; 🚇 St Andrew Sq) The Stand, founded in 1995, is Edinburgh's main independent comedy venue. It's an intimate cabaret bar with performances every night and a free Sunday lunchtime show.

Sport

Edinburgh has two rival football (soccer) teams playing in the Scottish Premier League – **Heart of Midlothian** (aka Hearts, nicknamed the Jam Tarts or Jambos), founded in 1874, and **Hibernian** (aka Hibs, Hibbies or Hi-bees), founded in 1875.

Hearts has its home ground at **Tynecastle Stadium** (www.heartsfc.co.uk; Gorgie Rd; 🚇 2, 3, 4, 25, 33, 44), southwest of the city centre in Gorgie. Hibernian's home ground is northeast of the city centre at **Easter Road Stadium** (www.hibernianfc.co.uk; 12 Albion Pl).

The domestic football season lasts from August to May and most matches are played at 3pm on Saturday or 7.30pm on Tuesday or Wednesday.

Each year, from January to March, Scotland's national rugby team takes part in the Six Nations Rugby Union Championship (www.sixnationsrugby.com). The most important fixture is the clash against England for the Calcutta Cup, which takes place in Edinburgh in even-numbered years (and at Twickenham in London in odd-numbered years). At club level, the season runs from September to May.

🏠 Shopping

Princes St is Edinburgh's principal shopping street, lined with all the big high-street stores, with many smaller shops along pedestrianised Rose St, and more expensive designer boutiques on George St and Thistle St.

For more off-beat shopping – including fashion, music, crafts, gifts and jewellery – head for the cobbled lanes of Cockburn, Victoria and St Mary's Sts, all near the Royal Mile in the Old Town; William St in the western part of the New Town; and the

Stockbridge district, immediately north of the New Town.

There are two big shopping centres in the New Town – **Waverley Mall** (Map p66; ☑ 0131-557 3759; www.waverleymall.com; Waverley Bridge; ⊘ 9am-7pm Mon-Sat, 10am-6pm Sun; 🚇 all Princes St buses), at the eastern end of Princes St, and the nearby **Edinburgh St James** (Map p66; www.edinburghstjames.com; 1 Leith St; 🚇 St Andrew Sq) at the top of Leith St, plus **Multrees Walk** (Map p66; www.multreeswalk.co.uk; St Andrew Sq; 🚇 St Andrew Sq), a designer shopping complex with a flagship Harvey Nichols store on the eastern side of St Andrew Sq.

The huge **Ocean Terminal** (☑ 0131-555 8888; www.oceanterminal.com; Ocean Dr; ⊘ 10am-8pm Mon-Fri, to 7pm Sat, 11am-6pm Sun; 📶; 🚇 11, 22, 34, 36, 200, 300) in Leith is the biggest shopping mall in the city.

🏠 Old Town

Armstrong's　　　　　　　　　　VINTAGE
(Map p58; ☑ 0131-220 5557; www.armstrongsvintage.co.uk; 83 Grassmarket; ⊘ 10am-5.30pm Mon-Thu, to 6pm Fri & Sat, noon-6pm Sun; 🚇 2) Armstrong's is an Edinburgh fashion institution (established in 1840, no less), a quality vintage-clothes emporium offering everything from elegant 1940s dresses to funky 1970s flares. Aside from the retro fashion, it's a great place to hunt for preloved kilts and Harris tweed, or to seek inspiration for that fancy-dress party.

Ragamuffin　　　　FASHION & ACCESSORIES
(Map p58; ☑ 0131-557 6007; www.facebook.com/pg/ragamuffinclothesandknitwear; 278 Canongate; ⊘ 10am-6pm Mon-Sat, noon-6pm Sun; 🚇 35) Quality Scottish knitwear and fabrics, including cashmere from Johnstons of Elgin, Fair Isle sweaters and Harris tweed.

> **DON'T MISS**
>
> ### EDINBURGH FARMERS MARKET
>
> This colourful weekly **event** (Map p58; ☑ 0131-652 5940; www.edinburghfarmersmarket.com; Castle Tce; ⊘ 9am-2pm Sat; 🚇 all Lothian Rd buses) attracts stallholders who sell everything from wild boar, venison and home-cured pedigree bacon to organic bread, free-range eggs, honey and handmade soap.

EDINBURGH BOOK SCULPTURES

In 2011 and 2012 an unknown artist left a series of intricate and beautiful paper sculptures in various Edinburgh libraries, museums and bookshops (more sculptures appeared in 2013 and 2014). Each was fashioned from an old book and alluded to literary themes; a message from the anonymous artist revealed they had been inspired by the poem 'Gifts', by Edinburgh poet Norman MacCaig. Two are on display at the **Scottish Poetry Library** (Map p52; ☑ 0131-557 2876; www.spl.org.uk; 5 Crichton's Cl; ◷ 10am-5pm Tue-Fri, to 4pm Sat; ▣ 6, 300) **FREE**, where you can pick up a self-guided walking-tour leaflet, *Gifted: The Edinburgh Book Sculptures* (also available on the library's website).

Geoffrey (Tailor) Inc FASHION & ACCESSORIES
(Map p58; ☑ 0131-557 0256; www.geoffreykilts. co.uk; 57-59 High St; ◷ 9.30am-6pm Mon-Sat, 10.30am-5.30pm Sun; ▣ 300) Geoffrey can fit you out in traditional Highland dress, or run up a kilt in your own clan tartan. The store's offshoot, 21st Century Kilts, offers modern fashion kilts in a variety of fabrics.

Bill Baber FASHION & ACCESSORIES
(Map p58; ☑ 0131-225 3249; www.billbaber.com; 66 Grassmarket; ◷ 9am-5.30pm Mon-Sat, 11am-4pm Sun; ▣ 2) This family-run designer-knitwear studio has been in the business for more than 30 years, producing stylish and colourful creations using linen, merino wool, silk and cotton.

Royal Mile Whiskies DRINKS
(Map p58; ☑ 0131-225 3383; www.royalmile whiskies.com; 379 High St; ◷ 10am-7pm Sun-Wed, to 8pm Thu-Sat; ▣ 23, 27, 41, 42) If it's a drap of the cratur ye're after, this place has a selection of single malts in miniature and full-size bottles. There's also a range of blended whiskies, Irish whiskey and bourbon, and you can buy online, too.

🏠 New Town

21st Century Kilts FASHION & ACCESSORIES
(Map p66; http://21stcenturykilts.com; 48 Thistle St; ◷ 10am-6pm Tue & Thu-Sat; ▣ 23, 27) With celebrity customers including Alan Cummings, Robbie Williams and Vin Diesel, 21st Century Kilts offers modern fashion kilts in a variety of fabrics, both off-the-peg and made to measure.

Jenners DEPARTMENT STORE
(Map p66; ☑ 0131-225 2442; www.houseof fraser.co.uk; 48 Princes St; ◷ 9.30am-6.30pm Mon-Wed, to 8pm Thu, to 7pm Fri, 9am-7pm Sat, 11am-6pm Sun; ▣ Princes St) Founded in 1838, and acquired by House of Fraser in 2005, Jenners is the *grande dame* of Scottish department stores. It stocks a wide range of quality goods, both classic and contemporary.

Harvey Nichols DEPARTMENT STORE
(Map p66; ☑ 0131-524 8388; www.harvey nichols.com; 30-34 St Andrew Sq; ◷ 10am-6pm Mon-Wed, to 8pm Thu, to 7pm Fri & Sat, 11am-6pm Sun; ▣ St Andrew Sq) The jewel in the crown of Edinburgh's shopping scene has four floors of designer labels and eye-popping price tags.

🏠 South Edinburgh

Meadows Pottery CERAMICS
(Map p52; ☑ 0131-662 4064; www.themeadows pottery.com; 11a Summerhall Pl; ◷ 10am-6pm Mon-Fri, to 5pm Sat; ▣ 2, 41, 42, 67) This little shop sells a range of colourful, high-fired oxidised stoneware, both domestic and decorative, all hand thrown on the premises. If you can't find what you want, you can commission custom-made pieces.

Backbeat MUSIC
(Map p52; ☑ 0131-668 2666; 31 E Crosscauseway; ◷ 10am-5.30pm Mon-Sat; ▣ all Newington buses) If you're hunting for secondhand vinyl from way back, this cramped little shop has a stunning and constantly changing collection of jazz, blues, rock and soul, plus lots of '60s and '70s stuff, though you'll have to take some time to hunt through the clutter.

Lighthouse BOOKS
(Map p58; ☑ 0131-662 9112; http://lighthouse bookshop.com; 43 W Nicolson St; ◷ 10am-6pm Mon-Sat, 11.30am-5pm Sun; ▣ 41, 42, 67) Lighthouse is a radical independent bookshop that supports both small publishers and local writers. It stocks a wide range of political, gay and feminist literature, as well as non-mainstream fiction and nonfiction.

🏠 Leith

Kinloch Anderson
FASHION & ACCESSORIES

(📞 0131-555 1390; www.kinlochanderson.com; 4 Dock St; ⏱ 9am-5.30pm Mon-Sat; 🚌 16, 22, 36, 300) One of the best tartan shops in Edinburgh, Kinloch Anderson was founded in 1868 and is still family run. It is a supplier of kilts and Highland dress to the royal family.

🏠 Stockbridge

⭐ Golden Hare Books
BOOKS

(Map p66; 📞 0131-629 1396; https://goldenhare books.com; 68 St Stephen St; ⏱ 10am-6pm; 🚌 24, 29, 42) Independent bookshops don't get lovelier than this. The Golden Hare boasts a top-notch selection of 'beautiful, unusual and interesting books', an enchanting children's nook, and a small but perfectly formed events program. A must if you love books, book design and beautiful shops.

Stockbridge Market
MARKET

(Map p66; www.stockbridgemarket.com; cnr Kerr & Saunders Sts; ⏱ 10am-5pm Sun; 🚌 24, 29, 36, 42) On Sunday the local community's focus is Stockbridge Market, set in a leafy square next to the bridge that gives the district its name. Wares range from fresh Scottish produce to handmade ceramics, jewellery, soaps and cosmetics. Grab an espresso from Steampunk Coffee, which operates out of a 1970s VW campervan.

Galerie Mirages
JEWELLERY

(Map p52; 📞 0131-315 2603; www.galeriemirages. com; 46a Raeburn Pl; ⏱ 10am-5.30pm Mon-Sat, 12-4.30pm Sun; 🚌 24, 29, 42) An Aladdin's cave packed with jewellery, textiles and handicrafts from all over the world, Mirages is best known for its silver, amber and gemstone jewellery in both culturally traditional and contemporary designs.

ℹ️ Information

EMERGENCY

Police Scotland (📞 non-emergency 101; www. scotland.police.uk; Gayfield Sq; ⏱ 24hr; 🚌 all Leith Walk buses) You can report a crime in person at this 24-hour police station, or by calling the non-emergency number (for crimes that have already taken place, eg a theft); use the emergency number (999 or 112) for crimes in progress or where there is a risk of injury or loss of life.

Police Scotland (📞 non-emergency 101; www. scotland.police.uk; 3-5 Torphichen Pl; ⏱ 9am-5pm Mon-Fri; 🚌 Haymarket)

INTERNET ACCESS

There are countless wi-fi hot spots all over Edinburgh. Internet cafes, such as **Coffee Home** (📞 0131-477 8336; www.coffeehome.co.uk; 28 Crighton Pl; per 20min 60p; ⏱ 10am-7pm Mon-Sat, noon-7pm Sun; 📶🐱; 🚌 all Leith Walk buses) in Leith, are spread around the city, and most cafes and bars offer free wi-fi for customers.

MEDIA

Newspapers *The Scotsman* (www.scotsman. com) is a quality daily covering Scottish, UK and international news, sport and current affairs; *Scotland on Sunday* is the weekend newspaper from the same publisher. The *Edinburgh Evening News* (www.edinburghnews. com) covers news and entertainment in the city and its environs.

Radio The BBC Radio Scotland (www.bbc. co.uk/radioscotland) program *Good Morning Scotland*, from 6am weekdays, covers Scottish current affairs.

MEDICAL SERVICES

For urgent medical advice you can call the **NHS 24 Helpline** (📞 111; www.nhs24.scot). Chemists (pharmacists) can advise you on minor ailments. At least one local chemist remains open round the clock – its location will be displayed in the windows of other chemists.

For urgent dental treatment, you can visit the walk-in **Chalmers Dental Centre** (📞 0131-536 4800; www.nhslothian.scot.nhs.uk; 3 Chalmers St; ⏱ 9am-4.45pm Mon-Thu, to 4.15pm Fri;

the Edinburgh Tourist Office (p98)

ℹ️ **CITY MAPS**

For coverage of the whole city in detail, the best maps are Collins' *Pocket Map Edinburgh* and Philip's *Edinburgh Street Atlas*. You can buy these at the Edinburgh Tourist Office (p98), bookshops and newsagents. Note that long streets may be known by different names along their length. For example, the southern end of Leith Walk is variously called Union Pl and Antigua St on one side, and Elm Row and Greenside Pl on the other.

The OS's 1:50,000 Landranger map *Edinburgh, Penicuik & North Berwick* (sheet No 66) covers the city and the surrounding region to the south and east at a scale of 1.25 inches to 1 mile; it's useful for walking in the Pentland Hills and exploring Edinburgh's fringes and East Lothian.

23, 27, 45, 47, 300). In the case of a dental emergency in the evenings or at weekends, call the **Lothian Dental Advice Line** (0131-536 4800; 5-10pm Mon-Fri, 9am-10pm Sat & Sun).

Boots (0131-225 6757; 48 Shandwick Pl; 7.30am-8pm Mon-Fri, 9am-6pm Sat, 10.30am-5pm Sun; West End) Chemist open longer hours than most.

Edinburgh Rape Crisis Centre (08088 01 03 02; www.rapecrisisscotland.org.uk)

Edinburgh Royal Infirmary (0131-536 1000; www.nhslothian.scot.nhs.uk/GoingToHospital/Locations/RIE; 51 Little France Cres, Old Dalkeith Rd; 24hr; 7, 8, 21, 24, 38) Edinburgh's main general hospital; has a 24-hour accident and emergency department.

Royal Hospital for Sick Children (0131-536 0000; www.nhslothian.scot.nhs.uk; 9 Sciennes Rd; 24hr; 41) Casualty department for children aged under 13; located in Marchmont. Scheduled to move to a new location near the Edinburgh Royal Infirmary by 2019.

Western General Hospital (0131-537 1000; www.nhslothian.scot.nhs.uk/GoingToHospital/Locations/WGH; Crewe Rd S; 8am-9pm; 19, 24, 29, 38 47) For non-life-threatening injuries and ailments, you can attend the Minor Injuries Clinic here without having to make an appointment.

POST

The UK postal system is generally reliable. You can find up-to-date rates at www.royalmail.com.

Frederick St Post Office (Map p66; 40 Frederick St; 9am-5.30pm Mon & Wed-Fri, 9.30am-5.30pm Tue, 9.30am-12.30pm Sat; 24, 29, 42)

St Mary's St Post Office (Map p58; 46 St Mary's St; 9am-5.30pm Mon-Fri, to 12.30pm Sat; 300)

Waverley Mall Post Office (Map p66; upper level, Waverley Mall; 9am-5.30pm Mon & Wed-Sat, 9.30am-5.30pm Tue; all Princes St buses)

TOURIST INFORMATION

Edinburgh Airport Tourist Office (0131-473 3690; www.visitscotland.com; East Terminal, Edinburgh Airport; 7.30am-7.30pm Mon-Fri, to 7pm Sat & Sun) VisitScotland Information Centre is in the airport's terminal extension.

Edinburgh Tourist Office (Edinburgh iCentre; Map p66; 0131-473 3868; www.visitscotland.com/info/services/edinburgh-icentre-p234441; Waverley Mall, 3 Princes St; 9am-7pm Mon-Sat, 10am-7pm Sun Jul & Aug, to 6pm Jun, to 5pm Sep-May; ; St Andrew Sq) Accommodation booking service, currency exchange, gift shop and bookshop, internet access, and counters selling tickets for

Edinburgh city tours and Scottish Citylink bus services.

USEFUL WEBSITES

Edinburgh Festival Guide (www.edinburghfestivalcity.com) Everything you need to know about Edinburgh's many festivals.

The List (www.list.co.uk) Local listings and reviews for restaurants, bars, clubs and theatres.

Lonely Planet (www.lonelyplanet.com/edinburgh) Destination information, hotel bookings, traveller forum and more.

VisitScotland Edinburgh (www.visitscotland.com/edinburgh) Official Scottish-tourist-board site.

Getting There & Away

AIR

Edinburgh Airport (EDI; 0844 448 8833; www.edinburghairport.com), 8 miles west of the city, has numerous flights to other parts of Scotland and the UK, Ireland and mainland Europe. There's a **VisitScotland Information Centre** in the airport's terminal extension.

Loganair (0344 800 2855; www.loganair.co.uk) operates daily flights to Wick, Orkney, Shetland and Stornoway.

BUS

Edinburgh Bus Station (Map p66; left-luggage lockers per 24hr £5-10; 4.30am-midnight Sun-Thu, to 12.30am Fri & Sat; St Andrew Sq) is at the northeastern corner of St Andrew Sq, with pedestrian entrances from the square and from Elder St. For timetable information, contact **Traveline** (0871 200 22 33; www.traveline-scotland.com).

Scottish Citylink (0871 266 3333; www.citylink.co.uk) buses connect Edinburgh with all of Scotland's cities and major towns. The following are sample one-way fares departing from Edinburgh.

DESTINATION	FARE (£)
Aberdeen	32.70
Dundee	17.50
Fort William	37
Glasgow	7.90
Inverness	32.20
Portree	58.30
Stirling	8.70

It's also worth checking with **Megabus** (0141-352 4444; www.megabus.com) for cheap intercity bus fares (from as little as £5) from Edinburgh to Aberdeen, Dundee, Glasgow, Inverness and Perth.

There are various buses to Edinburgh from London and the rest of the UK.

CAR & MOTORCYCLE

Arriving in or leaving Edinburgh by car during the morning and evening rush hours (7.30am to 9.30am and 4.30pm to 6.30pm Monday to Friday) is an experience you can live without. Try to time your journey to avoid these periods.

Major roads leading into and out of Edinburgh:
➡ M90 north to Perth
➡ M9 northwest to Stirling
➡ M8 west to Glasgow
➡ A7 south to Galashiels
➡ A68 south to Melrose and Jedburgh
➡ A1 southeast to Berwick-upon-Tweed

TRAIN

The main rail terminus in Edinburgh is **Waverley train station**, located in the heart of the city. Trains arriving from, and departing for, the west also stop at Haymarket station, which is more convenient for the West End.

You can buy tickets, make reservations and get travel information at the **Edinburgh Rail Travel Centre** (Waverley station; ⊙ 5am-midnight Mon-Sat, 7am-midnight Sun; 🚌 all Princes St buses). For fare and timetable information, phone the **National Rail Enquiry Service** (📱 03457 48 49 50; www.nationalrail. co.uk) or use the journey planner on the website.

If you're travelling as a pair, consider purchasing a **Two Together Railcard** (www.twotogether -railcard.co.uk; per year £30), which offers you up to 30% off your combined fares on train rides taken throughout Great Britain.

ScotRail (📱 0344 811 0141; www.scotrail.co.uk) operates regular train services to the following:
Aberdeen (£35.50, 2½ hours)
Dundee (£18.90, 1¼ hours)
Glasgow (£14.40, 50 minutes, every 15 minutes)
Inverness (£40, 3½ hours)

ⓘ Getting Around

TO/FROM THE AIRPORT
Bus

Lothian Buses' Airlink (https://lothianbuses. co.uk/airport) service 100 runs from Waverley Bridge, outside the train station, to the airport (one way/return £4.50/7.50, 30 minutes, every 10 minutes from 4am to midnight) via the West End and Haymarket. Skylink services 200 and 300 run from the airport to Ocean Terminal via north Edinburgh and west Edinburgh/the Royal Mile, respectively.

Taxi

An airport taxi to the city centre costs around £20 and takes about 20 to 30 minutes.

Tram

Edinburgh Trams (www.edinburghtrams.com) run from the airport to the city centre (one way/return £6/8.50, 33 minutes, every six to eight minutes from 6am to midnight).

BICYCLE

Thanks to the efforts of local cycling campaign group Spokes and a bike-friendly city council, Edinburgh is well equipped with bike lanes and dedicated cycle tracks. You can buy a map of the city's cycle routes from most bike shops.

Biketrax (p73) rents out mountain bikes, hybrid bikes, road bikes, Brompton folding bikes and electric bikes. You'll need a debit- or credit-card deposit and photographic ID.

BUS

Bus timetables, route maps and fare guides are posted at all main bus and tram stops, and you can pick up a copy of the free *Lothian Buses Route Map* from Lothian Buses Travelshops on **Waverley Bridge** (Map p58; 31 Waverley Bridge; ⊙ 9am-6pm Tue, Wed & Fri, to 7pm Mon & Thu, to 5.30pm Sat, 10am-5.30pm Sun; 🚌 6) and **Hanover St** (Map p66; 27 Hanover St; ⊙ 9am-6pm Mon-Fri, to 5.30pm Sat; 🚌 23, 27).

Adult fares within the city are £1.70; purchase from the bus driver. Children aged under five travel free and those aged five to 15 pay a flat fare of 80p.

On Lothian Buses you must pay the driver the exact fare, but First buses will give change. Lothian Bus drivers also sell a day ticket (£4) that gives unlimited travel on Lothian buses and trams for a day; a family day ticket (up to two adults and three children) costs £8.50.

Night-service buses, which run hourly between midnight and 5am, charge a flat fare of £3.50.

You can also buy a Ridacard (from Travelshops; not available from bus drivers) that gives unlimited travel for one week for £19.

The Lothian Buses lost-property office is in the Hanover St Travelshop.

CAR & MOTORCYCLE

Though useful for day trips beyond the city, a car in central Edinburgh is more of a liability than a convenience. There is restricted access on

---

ⓘ BUS INFO ON YOUR PHONE

Transport for Edinburgh has created free smartphone apps that provide route maps, timetables and live waiting times for city buses and trams. Search for Transport for Edinburgh on the App Store (iOS) or Google Play (Android). The companion m-tickets app allows you to buy bus and tram tickets on your phone.

Princes St, George St and Charlotte Sq, many streets are one way, and finding a parking place in the city centre is like striking gold. Queen's Dr around Holyrood Park is closed to motorised traffic on Sunday.

Car Rental

All the big international car-rental agencies have offices in Edinburgh, including **Avis** (☑ 0844 544 6059; www.avis.co.uk; 24 E London St; ☺ 8am-6pm Mon-Fri, to 3pm Sat, 10am-2pm Sun; ☒ 8, 13, 27) and **Europcar** (☑ 0871 384 3453; www.europcar.co.uk; Platform 2, Waverley station; ☺ 7am-5pm; ☒ all Princes St buses).

There are many smaller, local agencies that offer better rates. **Arnold Clark** (☑ 0141-237 4374; www.arnoldclarkrental.com) charges from £46/230 per day/week for a small car, including VAT and insurance.

Parking

There's no parking on main roads into the city from 7.30am to 6.30pm Monday to Saturday. Also, parking in the city centre can be a nightmare.

On-street parking is controlled by self-service ticket machines from 8.30am to 6.30pm Monday to Saturday, and costs from £2.20 to £4.20 per hour, with a 30-minute to four-hour maximum.

If you break the rules, you'll get a fine, often within minutes of your ticket expiring – Edinburgh's parking wardens are both numerous and notorious. The fine is £60, reduced to £30 if you pay up within 14 days. Cars parked illegally will be clamped or towed away. There are large, long-stay car parks at the Omni Centre, Blackfriars St, Castle Tce, Holyrood Rd and Fountain Park. Motorcycles can be parked free at designated areas in the city centre.

TAXI

Edinburgh's black taxis can be hailed in the street, ordered by phone (extra 80p charge) or picked up at one of the many central ranks. The minimum charge is £2.10 (£3.10 at night) for the first 450m, then 25p for every subsequent 184m – a typical 2-mile trip across the city centre will cost around £6 to £7. Tipping is up to you – because of the high fares, local people rarely tip on short journeys, but they occasionally round up to the nearest 50p on longer ones.

Central Taxis (☑ 0131-229 2468; www.taxis-edinburgh.co.uk)

City Cabs (☑ 0131-228 1211; www.citycabs.co.uk)

ComCab (☑ 0131-272 8001; www.comcab-edinburgh.co.uk)

TRAM

Edinburgh's tram system (www.edinburghtrams.com) consists of one line from Edinburgh Airport to York Pl, at the top of Leith Walk, via Haymarket, the West End and Princes St.

Tickets are integrated with the city's Lothian Buses, costing £1.70 for a single journey within the city boundary, or £6 to the airport. Trams run every eight to 10 minutes Monday to Saturday and every 12 to 15 minutes on Sunday, from 5.30am to 11pm.

DAY TRIPS ON THE BORDERS RAILWAY

The longest stretch of new railway line to be built in the UK for more than 100 years, the Borders Railway opened in 2015, linking Edinburgh with Tweedbank near Melrose. With trains running every 30 minutes, it's a great way to take day trips into the countryside south of the capital.

Top of the list of attractions is Abbotsford (p146), Sir Walter Scott's country house, which lies a pleasant 20-minute walk from the terminus at Tweedbank, most of it along the banks of the River Tweed. Other trips are described in the Borders Railway Guide (£9.90; https://bordersrailwayguide.co.uk), available from Edinburgh tourist offices.

AROUND EDINBURGH

Edinburgh is small enough that, when you need a break from the city, the beautiful countryside that surrounds it is right on your doorstep – and easily accessible by public transport, even by bike. The old counties around Edinburgh are called West Lothian, Midlothian and East Lothian, often referred to collectively as the Lothians. From royal births to bloody battles, they've played a rich part in Scottish history, and you'll see it writ large in some of the most impressive castles, churches and country houses in the land.

The region's landscapes make a fitting backdrop – a patchwork of rolling farmland, ancient forests and golden beaches (as well as industrialised pockets) bordered by the majestic Firth of Forth. Whether setting off to windswept islands under the iconic Forth bridges, following rivers through ancient woodland or wildlife spotting on the beautiful East Lothian coast, adventure awaits.

WORTH A TRIP

ROSSLYN CHAPEL

Many years may have passed since Dan Brown's novel *The Da Vinci Code* and the subsequent film came out, but floods of visitors still descend on Scotland's most beautiful and enigmatic church – **Rosslyn Chapel** (Collegiate Church of St Matthew; ☑ 0131-440 2159; www.rosslynchapel.com; Chapel Loan, Roslin; adult/child £9/free; ⊙ 9.30am-6pm Mon-Sat Jun-Aug, to 5pm Sep-May, noon-4.45pm Sun year-round; P; ☐ 37). Built in the mid-15th century for Sir William St Clair, third prince of Orkney, its ornately carved interior – at odds with the architectural fashion of its time – is a monument to the mason's art, rich in symbolic imagery. Hourly talks by qualified guides are included with admission.

As well as flowers, vines, angels and biblical figures, the carved stones include many examples of the pagan Green Man; other figures are associated with Freemasonry and the Knights Templar. Intriguingly, there are also carvings of plants from the Americas that predate Columbus' voyage of discovery. The symbolism of these images has led some researchers to conclude that Rosslyn is some kind of secret Templar repository, and it has been claimed that hidden vaults beneath the chapel could conceal anything from the Holy Grail or the head of John the Baptist to the body of Christ himself. The chapel is owned by the Scottish Episcopal Church and services are still held here on Sunday mornings.

The chapel is on the eastern edge of the village of Roslin, 7 miles south of Edinburgh's centre. Lothian Bus 37 to Penicuik Deanburn runs from Edinburgh's West End to Roslin (£1.70, one hour, every 15 minutes). Note that bus 37 to Bush does not go via Roslin – check the bus front and if in doubt ask the driver.

Queensferry

POP 9030

Queensferry, also known as South Queensferry, is at the narrowest part of the Firth of Forth, where ferries have crossed to Fife from the earliest times. The village takes its name from Queen Margaret (1046–93), who gave pilgrims free passage across the firth on their way to St Andrews. Ferries continued to operate until 1964, when the graceful **Forth Road Bridge** was opened; this was followed by a second road bridge, the **Queensferry Crossing** (2017).

Predating the first road bridge by 74 years, the magnificent **Forth Bridge** – only outsiders ever call it the Forth Rail Bridge – is one of the finest engineering achievements of the 19th century. Opened in 1890 as the world's first major steel structure, its three huge cantilevers span 1630m and took 53,000 tonnes of steel, 6.5 million rivets and the lives of 73 men to build.

Hopetoun House   HISTORIC BUILDING
(☑ 0131-331 2451; www.hopetoun.co.uk; house & grounds adult/child £10.50/5.50, grounds only £4.75/2.95; ⊙ 10.30am-5pm Easter-Sep, last entry 4pm; P) One of Scotland's finest stately homes, Hopetoun House has a superb location in lovely grounds beside the Firth of Forth. The family seat of the earls of Hopetoun, it has two parts: the older, built between 1699 and 1707 and dominated by a splendid stairwell with (modern) trompe l'oeil paintings, and the newer, designed between 1720 and 1750 by three members of the Adam family – William, and his sons, Robert and John. Guided tours run on weekdays at 2pm.

The highlights are the red and yellow Adam drawing rooms, lined in silk damask, and the view from the roof terrace. Britain's most elegant equine accommodation – where the earls once housed their pampered racehorses – is now the stylish **Stables Kitchen** (☑ 0131-331 3661; www.hopetoun.co.uk; Hopetoun House; mains £5-11, afternoon tea per person £22; ⊙ 11am-4.30pm Easter-Sep; ✈), a delightful spot for lunch or afternoon tea.

The 2428-hectare grounds, where red deer roam in summer, offer sweeping Firth of Forth views. Rangers lead walks on the last Sunday of the month at 3.30pm, as well as activities such as foraging, pond-dipping and bushcraft.

Hopetoun House is 2 miles west of Queensferry along the coast road. Driving

Rosslyn Chapel

DECIPHERING ROSSLYN

Rosslyn Chapel is a small building, but the density of decoration inside can be overwhelming. It's well worth buying the official guidebook by the Earl of Rosslyn first; find a bench in the gardens and have a skim through before going into the chapel – the background information will make your visit all the more interesting. The book also offers a useful self-guided tour of the chapel, and explains the legend of the Master Mason and the Apprentice.

Entrance is through the ❶ **north door**. Take a pew and sit for a while to allow your eyes to adjust to the dim interior; then look up at the ceiling vault, decorated with engraved roses, lilies and stars, (Can you spot the sun and the moon?). Walk left along the north aisle to reach the Lady Chapel, separated from the rest of the church by the ❷ **Mason's Pillar** and the ❸ **Apprentice Pillar**. Here you'll find carvings of ❹ **Lucifer**, the Fallen Angel, and the ❺ **Green Man**. Nearby are ❻ **carvings** that appear to resemble Indian corn (maize). Finally, go to the western end and look up at the wall – in the left corner is the head of the ❼ **Apprentice**; to the right is the (rather worn) head of the ❽ **Master Mason**.

EXPLORE SOME MORE

After visiting the chapel, head downhill to see the spectacularly sited ruins of Roslin Castle, then take a walk along leafy Roslin Glen.

Lucifer, the Fallen Angel
At head height, to the left of the second window from the left, is an upside-down angel bound with rope, a symbol often associated with Freemasonry. The arch above is decorated with the Dance of Death.

The Apprentice
High in the corner, beneath an empty statue niche, is the head of the murdered Apprentice, with a deep wound in his forehead above the right eye. Legend says the Apprentice was murdered in a jealous rage by the Master Mason. The worn head on the side wall to the left of the Apprentice is that of his mother.

North Door

The Master Mason ❽

Baptistry

ROSSLYN CHAPEL & THE DA VINCI CODE

Dan Brown was referencing Rosslyn Chapel's alleged links to the Knights Templar and the Freemasons – unusual symbols found among the carvings, and the fact that a descendant of its founder, William St Clair, was a Grand Master Mason – when he chose it as the setting for his novel's denouement. Rosslyn is indeed a coded work, written in stone, but its meaning depends on your point of view. See The Rosslyn Hoax? by Robert LD Cooper for an alternative interpretation of the chapel's symbolism.

PRACTICAL TIPS

Local guides give hourly talks throughout the day, which are included in the admission price. No photography is allowed inside the chapel.

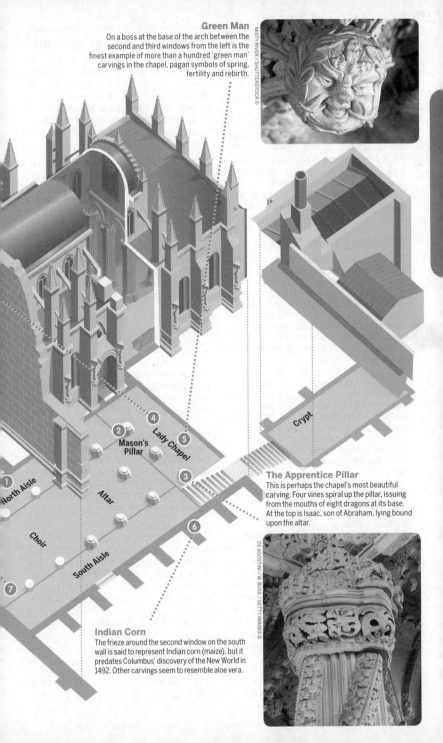

Green Man
On a boss at the base of the arch between the second and third windows from the left is the finest example of more than a hundred 'green man' carvings in the chapel, pagan symbols of spring, fertility and rebirth.

MISTY RIVER / SHUTTERSTOCK ©

Crypt

The Apprentice Pillar
This is perhaps the chapel's most beautiful carving. Four vines spiral up the pillar, issuing from the mouths of eight dragons at its base. At the top is Isaac, son of Abraham, lying bound upon the altar.

DE AGOSTINI / W. BUSS / GETTY IMAGES ©

Indian Corn
The frieze around the second window on the south wall is said to represent Indian corn (maize), but it predates Columbus' discovery of the New World in 1492. Other carvings seem to resemble aloe vera.

④
②
Mason's Pillar
⑤
Lady Chapel
③
①
North Aisle
Altar
⑥
Choir
South Aisle
⑦

from Edinburgh, turn off the A90 onto the A904 just before the Forth Bridge and follow the signs.

★ **Forth Boat Tours** BOATING
(🖱 0131-331 3030; www.forthtours.com; Hawes Pier; adult/child £15/8, with Inchcolm stopover £21/14; ⊙ Easter-Oct; 🐾) Forth Boat Tours runs daily 90-minute trips along the Firth of Forth, heading via its majestic bridges, storied islands and shoreline landmarks (including the epic Edinburgh skyline) to Inchcolm. Most voyages offer a 90-minute stopover (£6) on the island, a place of blond beaches, squawking seabirds and abandoned defences that's famed for its medieval abbey – it's well worth it.

ℹ Getting There & Away

Queensferry lies on the southern bank of the Firth of Forth, 8 miles west of Edinburgh city centre. Lothian Country (https://lothiancountry.co.uk) bus 43 runs from Edinburgh to the village centre (£2.70, 45 minutes, every 20 minutes). It's a 10-minute walk from the bus stop to the **Hawes Inn** (🖱 0131-331 1990; www.vintageinn.co.uk; 7 Newhalls Rd; mains £10-19; ⊙ noon-11pm Mon-Sat, to 10.30pm Sun; 🅿 🛜 🛗 🐾) and Hawes Pier.

Trains go from Edinburgh's Waverley and Haymarket stations to Dalmeny station (£4.70, 15 minutes, two to four hourly). From the station exit, the Hawes Inn is five minutes' walk along a footpath (across the road, behind the bus stop) that leads north beside the railway and then downhill under the Forth Bridge. The village centre is 15 minutes away – head left when the footpath forks, via the scenic woodland of Ferry Glen.

Inchcolm

Inchcolm Abbey ABBEY
(HES; www.historicenvironment.scot; adult/child £6/3.60; ⊙ 9.30am-5.30pm Apr-Sep, to 4pm Oct) Known as the 'Iona of the East', the island of Inchcolm (meaning 'St Columba's Island') lies east of the Forth bridges, less than a mile off the Fife coast. Only 800m long, it's home to the ruins of Inchcolm Abbey, one of Scotland's best-preserved medieval abbeys, founded by Augustinian priors in 1123.

Access is by **ferry** (www.maidoftheforth.co.uk; Hawes Pier, South Queensferry; adult/child £20/10.60) from Queensferry. The trip also gives you the chance to see the island's grey seals, as well as puffins and other seabirds.

North Berwick & Around

North Berwick is an attractive Victorian seaside resort with long sandy beaches and a small harbour. It's also a popular golfing destination, with three courses in and around the town and a dozen more within easy reach, including the world-famous Open Championship course at **Muirfield** (www.muirfield.org.uk).

Scottish Seabird Centre NATURE CENTRE
(🖱 01620-890202; www.seabird.org; The Harbour; adult/child £8.95/4.95; ⊙ 10am-6pm Apr-Aug, to 5pm Mon-Fri, to 5.30pm Sat & Sun Feb, Mar, Sep & Oct, to 4pm Mon-Fri, to 5pm Sat & Sun Nov-Jan; 🅿 🛗) 🏆 Top marks to the bright spark who came up with the idea for this centre, an ornithologist's paradise that uses remote-control video cameras sited on Bass Rock and other islands to relay live images of nesting gannets and other seabirds (including puffins if you're lucky). You can control the cameras yourself and zoom in on scenes of cosy gannet domesticity. For real-life close encounters of the bird kind, check out the Seabird Boat Trips offered by the centre.

Seabird Boat Trips BOATING
(🖱 01620-890202; www.seabird.org; The Harbour; adult £14-55, child £11-44; ⊙ Easter-autumn) The Scottish Seabird Centre runs catamaran and high-speed RIB boat trips exploring the Forth islands' riotous bird life – including the squawking, spiralling spectacle of the world's largest Northern gannet colony on Bass Rock, and a plethora of puffins on the Isle of May (the UK's top breeding site). Choose from short cruises or stopovers with several hours to get acquainted.

Tantallon Castle RUINS
(HS; 🖱 01620-892727; www.historicenvironment.scot; adult/child £6/3.60; ⊙ 9.30am-5.30pm Apr-Sep, 10am-4pm Oct-Mar; 🅿; 🚌 120) Perched on a cliff 3 miles east of North Berwick is the spectacular ruin of Tantallon Castle. Built around 1350, the red-sandstone fortress was the residence of the Douglas earls of Angus (the Red Douglases), defended on one side by a series of ditches and on the other by an almost sheer drop into the sea. Often attacked, it finally succumbed to an English bombardment in the 17th century – but its battlement views remain as mighty as ever.

Dirleton Castle CASTLE
(HS; ☑ 01620-850330; www.historicenvironment.
scot; Dirleton; adult/child £6/3.60; ⊙ 9.30am-
5.30pm Apr-Sep, 10am-4pm Oct-Mar; ℙ; ▣ 124,
X5) ✔ Two miles west of North Berwick
is this impressive medieval fortress with
massive round towers, a drawbridge and
a horrific pit dungeon, surrounded rather
incongruously by beautiful, manicured
gardens.

ℹ Getting There & Away

North Berwick is 24 miles east of Edinburgh.
East Coast operates two bus services between
Edinburgh and North Berwick: the 124 (£4.70,
1¼ hours, every 30 minutes) and the X5 (£4.70,
one hour, hourly Monday to Saturday).

There are frequent trains between North Berwick and Edinburgh (£6.70, 35 minutes, hourly).

Linlithgow

POP 13,460

This ancient royal burgh is one of Scotland's
oldest towns, though much of it 'only' dates
from the 15th to 17th centuries. Birthplace
of Mary, Queen of Scots, and other Stuart
monarchs, it's also traversed by the scenic
Union Canal on its journey from Falkirk to
Edinburgh.

The town centre radiates around the
ornately carved Cross Well, which dates
from the 19th century. Despite some ugly
modern buildings and occasional traffic
congestion, it retains a certain charm, and
the town makes an excellent day trip from
Edinburgh.

There's a self-service tourist office
(☑ 01506-282720; www.linlithgowburghhalls.com;
Linlithgow Burgh Halls, The Cross; ⊙ 9am-5pm
Mon-Sat, 11am-5pm Sun; 🛜) in the Burgh Halls,
near the Linlithgow Palace entrance.

Linlithgow Palace PALACE
(HS; ☑ 01506-842896; www.historicenvironment.
scot; Kirkgate; adult/child £6/3.60; ⊙ 9.30am-
5.30pm Apr-Sep, 10am-4pm Oct-Mar; ℙ) ✔ This
magnificent loch-side palace was begun by
James I in 1424, and became a favourite
royal residence – James V was born here in
1512, as was his daughter Mary (later Queen
of Scots) in 1542, and Bonnie Prince Charlie visited in 1745. The elaborately carved
King's Fountain, the centrepiece of the
palace courtyard, flowed with wine during
Charlie's stay; commissioned by James V in
1537, it's Britain's oldest fountain. Atop the
northwestern tower are sweeping views
from Queen Margaret's Bower.

Visit on a Sunday in July or August and
you'll be able to see the courtyard fountain
in action. Summer also sees the palace wind
the clock back to medieval times with its
two-day Spectacular Jousting tournament –
check dates online.

ℹ Getting There & Away

Linlithgow is 15 miles west of Edinburgh and
is served by frequent trains from the capital
(£5.40, 20 minutes, four every hour). The train
station is 250m east of the town centre.

You can also cycle from Edinburgh to Linlithgow along the Union Canal towpath (21 miles) –
allow two hours.

Glasgow

POP 596,500

Best Places to Eat

➡ Ubiquitous Chip (p126)
➡ Gamba (p125)
➡ Stravaigin (p125)
➡ Ox & Finch (p125)
➡ Saramago Café Bar (p124)
➡ Spanish Butcher (p125)

Best Places to Stay

➡ Dakota Deluxe (p122)
➡ Alamo Guest House (p123)
➡ Grasshoppers (p120)
➡ 15Glasgow (p124)
➡ Glasgow SYHA (p123)

Why Go?

Disarmingly blending sophistication and earthiness, Scotland's biggest city has evolved over the last couple of decades to become one of Britain's most intriguing metropolises.

The soberly handsome Victorian buildings, the legacy of wealth generated from manufacturing and trade, suggest a staid sort of place. Very wrong. They are packed with stylish bars, top-notch restaurants and one of Britain's best live-music scenes. The place's sheer vitality is gloriously infectious: the combination of edgy urbanity and the residents' legendary friendliness is captivating.

Glasgow also offers plenty by day. Its shopping – whether you're looking for Italian fashion or preloved denim – is famous and there are top-drawer museums and galleries. Charles Rennie Mackintosh's sublime designs dot the city, which – always proud of its working-class background – also innovatively displays its industrial heritage.

When to Go
Glasgow

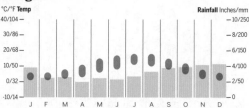

Feb The drizzle won't lift? Maroon yourself in one of Glasgow's fabulous pubs or clubs.

Jun The West End Festival and the Glasgow Jazz Festival make the city music heaven.

Aug Glasgow is superfriendly at any time, but when the sun is shining it's the happiest city in Britain.

History

The area where Glasgow now stands was bisected by the Romans in the 2nd century AD when they built the Antonine Wall to protect the fringes of their empire from the Caledonian wildlings beyond.

Glasgow grew around the religious site established in the 6th century by St Kentigern, better known as St Mungo (originally an affectionate nickname). It became an important bishop's seat, but the cathedral that was built here is one of the few remnants of the medieval city. It was swept away by the energies of a new age – the age of capitalism, the Industrial Revolution and the British Empire.

Glasgow's west-coast position led to it becoming an important port for trade with the Americas. In the 18th century much of the tobacco trade between Europe and the USA was routed through Glasgow, providing a great source of wealth. The tobacco barons were responsible for much construction around the city that remains today. Even after the tobacco trade declined in the 19th century, the city continued to prosper as a centre of textile manufacturing, shipbuilding and the coal and steel industries. Many of the city's major buildings and monuments were constructed during the Victorian period, when Glasgow was a byword for mercantile prosperity. The outward appearance, however, was tempered by the dire working conditions in the factories.

In the first half of the 20th century Glasgow was the centre of Britain's munitions industry, supplying arms and ships for the two world wars, in the second of which the city was carpet-bombed. Post–World War II, however, the port and heavy industries began to dwindle, and by the early 1970s the city looked doomed. Glasgow became synonymous with unemployment, economic depression and urban violence, centred around high-rise housing schemes such as the infamous Gorbals.

More recently, urban development and a booming cultural sector have injected style and confidence into the city; though the standard of living remains low for Britain and life continues to be tough for many, the ongoing regeneration process gives grounds for optimism. The successful hosting of the 2014 Commonwealth Games highlighted this regeneration to a wide global audience.

◉ Sights

Glasgow's major sights are fairly evenly dispersed across the city. These include standout museums and galleries, the cathedral and a range of architecturally notable buildings, in particular those designed by Charles Rennie Mackintosh. The city's parks and green spaces are also a significant highlight.

◉ City Centre

★**Glasgow School of Art**　HISTORIC BUILDING
(Map p110; ☑ 0141-353 4526; www.gsa.ac.uk; 167 Renfrew St) In 2018, Charles Rennie Mackintosh's greatest building was gearing up for reopening after a devastating 2014 fire when, unbelievably, another blaze destroyed the painstakingly reconstructed interiors and severely damaged the building. The school has committed to reconstructing it, but it will be a lengthy process. At time of research the visitor centre, shop and exhibitions in the neighbouring Reid building were closed to visitors; check the website to see if visits and tours have resumed.

★**City Chambers**　HISTORIC BUILDING
(Map p110; ☑ 0141-287 2000; www.glasgow.gov.uk; George Sq; ☺9am-5pm Mon-Fri) **FREE** The grand seat of local government was built in the 1880s at the high point of Glasgow's wealth. The interior is even more extravagant than the exterior, and the chambers have sometimes been used as a movie location to represent the Kremlin or the Vatican. You can have a look at the opulent ground floor during opening hours. To see more, free guided tours are held at 10.30am and 2.30pm Monday to Friday; it's worth popping in earlier that day to prebook.

★**Sharmanka Kinetic Theatre**　THEATRE
(Map p110; ☑ 0141-552 7080; www.sharmanka.com; 103 Trongate; adult/child short show £8/3, long show £10/8; ☺40-minute shows 5pm Wed & Thu, 1pm Fri, 3pm Sat & Sun, 60-minute shows 7pm Thu, 5pm Sun) This extraordinary mechanical theatre is located at the Trongate 103 arts centre. The amazing creativity of Russian sculptor and mechanic Eduard Bersudsky, now resident in Scotland, has created a series of large, wondrous figures sculpted from bits of scrap and elaborate carvings. Set to haunting music, each figure performs humorous and tragic stories of the human spirit. Great for kids and very moving for adults: inspirational one moment

See West End Map (p116)

Glasgow Highlights

1 Art (p114)
Exploring the city's fabulous wealth of paintings, sculpture and public art, beginning with the Kelvingrove Art Gallery & Museum.

2 Architecture (p114) Discovering the city's fine Victorian buildings and the Art Nouveau masterpieces of Charles Rennie Mackintosh.

3 Ubiquitous Chip (p126) Dining in the restaurant that set the scene for the West End's culinary excellence.

4 Live Music (p131) Seeing a band at King Tut's Wah Wah Hut or at any other venue in the city's legendary, diverse live-music scene.

5 Vintage Shops

N

0 — 2 km
0 — 1 mile

POSSILPARK

BARMULLOCH

Springburn

Barnhill

Hogganfield Loch

Hogganfield Park

Craighall Rd

Sighthill Park

RIDDRIE

Cumbernauld Rd

See Central Glasgow Map (p110)

Cowcaddens Rd

Castle St

Alexandra Pde

Alexandra Parade

Edinburgh Rd

Queen St

Cathedral St

7 Pot Still

George St

High St

Necropolis

DENNISTOUN

CARNTYNE

Carntyne Rd

9 Speakeasy

Duke St

Duke Street

Mr Ben

Argyle Street

Bellgrove

Carntyne

Clyde St

Saltmarket

Gallowgate

Shettleston Rd

Westmuir St

Gorbals St

London Rd

Glasgow Green

BRIDGETON

PARKHEAD

Celtic Park

6

Tollcross Rd

Cathcart Rd

HUTCHESONTOWN

Bridgeton

London Rd

Aikenhead Rd

Dalmarnock

DALMARNOCK

Dalmarnock Rd

Clyde Walkway 8

POLMADIE

Crosshill

Rutherglen

Cambuslang Rd

RUTHERGLEN

Main St

Hampden Park

BANKHEAD

Blantyre (4 mi)

(p135) Browsing the city's excellent selection of vintage shops – Mr Ben being among the favourites.

6 **Football** Catching a match at either of the local teams' massive cauldrons of football – Celtic Park (p134) or Ibrox Stadium (p134).

7 **Pub Culture** (p129) Diving into Glasgow's social life in traditional pubs such as the Pot Still.

8 **Clyde Walkway** (p119) Grabbing a bike for a leisurely exploration of Glasgow's industrial heritage and green surroundings on this great cycle route.

9 **Pink Triangle** (p128) Immersing yourself in Glasgow's friendly LGBT culture in one of the bars of the Pink Triangle such as Speakeasy.

Central Glasgow

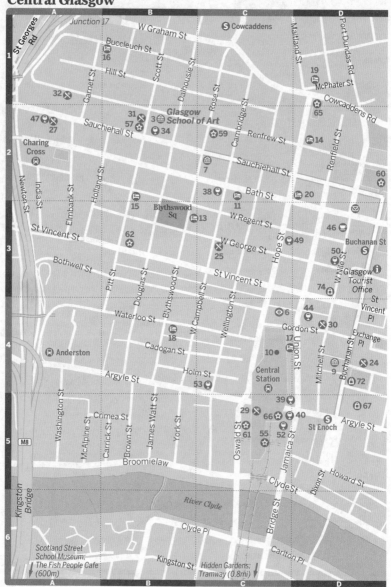

and macabre the next, but always colourful, thought provoking and clever.

The gallery opens just before performances on Wednesday to Sunday – the sculptures and their stories are fascinating even when not in motion.

Mackintosh at the Willow HISTORIC BUILDING
(Map p110; ☑ 0141-204 1903; www.mackintoshat thewillow.com; 217 Sauchiehall St; exhibition admission adult/child £5.50/3.50; ⊙ Opening: Tearoom 9am-5pm, exhibition 9am-5.30pm Mon-Sat, 10am-5pm Sun, last entry 1hr before)

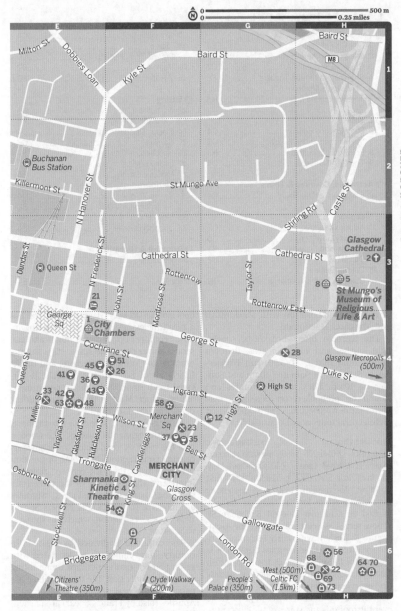

Opened in 2018, this reconstruction of the original Willow tearoom that Mackintosh designed and furnished in the early 20th century for restaurateur Kate Cranston offers authentic design splendour in its original location. You can admire the architect's distinctive touch in just about every element; he had free rein and even the teaspoons were given his attention. Alongside the tearoom is a visitor centre, with a two-level interactive exhibition about the historical context and Kate

Central Glasgow

◎ Top Sights

◎ Sights

⊕ Activities, Courses & Tours

⊜ Sleeping

⊗ Eating

⊚ Drinking & Nightlife

Cranston's collaboration with Mackintosh and Margaret Macdonald.

The tearoom offers breakfasts, snacks, light lunches and afternoon teas. Tearoom tours (adult/child £7.50/5.50) run Wednesday to Saturday at 9am and 10am and Sundays at 10am. They last 45 minutes and should be prebooked on bookings@mackintoshatthewillow.com. More specialised architectural tours are also available.

The Lighthouse HISTORIC BUILDING
(Map p110; ☎0141-276 5365; www.thelighthouse.co.uk; 11 Mitchell Lane; ◎10.30am-5pm Mon-Sat, from noon Sun) FREE Mackintosh's first building, designed in 1893, was a striking new headquarters for the *Glasgow Herald*. Tucked up a narrow lane off Buchanan St, it now serves as Scotland's Centre for Architecture & Design, with fairly technical temporary exhibitions (sometimes admission is payable for these), as well as the Mackintosh Interpretation Centre, a detailed (if slightly dry) overview of his life and work. On the top floor of the 'lighthouse', drink in great views over the rooftops and spires of the city centre.

◉ East End

★Glasgow Cathedral CATHEDRAL
(HES; Map p110; ☎0141-552 6891; www.historicenvironment.scot; Cathedral Sq; ◎9.30am-5.30pm Mon-Sat, 1-5pm Sun Apr-Sep, 10am-4pm Mon-Sat, from 1pm Sun Oct-Mar) Glasgow Cathedral has a rare timelessness. The dark, imposing interior conjures up medieval might and can send a shiver down the spine. It's a shining example of Gothic architecture, and unlike nearly all of Scotland's cathedrals, it survived the turmoil of the Reformation mobs almost intact. Most of the current building dates from the 15th century.

Entry is through a side door into the nave, hung with regimental colours. The wooden roof has been restored many times since its original construction, but some of the timber dates from the 14th century; note the impressive shields. Many of the cathedral's stunning, narrow stained-glass windows are modern; to your left is Francis Spear's 1958 work *The Creation*, which fills the west window.

The cathedral is divided by a late-15th-century stone choir screen, decorated with seven pairs of figures perhaps representing the seven deadly sins. The four stained-glass panels of the east window, depicting the Apostles (also by Francis Spear) are particularly evocative. At the northeastern corner is the entrance to the 15th-century upper chapter house, where the University of Glasgow was founded. It's now used as a sacristy.

The most interesting part of the cathedral, the lower church, is reached by a stairway. Its forest of pillars creates a powerful

113

GLASGOW SIGHTS

atmosphere around the tomb of St Mungo (who founded a monastic community here in the 6th century), the focus of a famous medieval pilgrimage that was believed to be as meritorious as a visit to Rome.

While here, don't miss a stroll in the necropolis.

★ **Glasgow Necropolis** CEMETERY
(⊙7am-4.30pm Apr-Oct, from 8am Nov-Mar) FREE Behind Glasgow Cathedral, this sizeable 19th-century necropolis stretches picturesquely up and over a green hill. The elaborate Victorian tombs of the city's wealthy industrialists, several of them designed by prominent architects of the day (including Alexander Thomson and Charles Rennie Mackintosh), make for an intriguing stroll and offer great views and a vague Gothic thrill. Walking tours run every couple of weeks; check www.glasgownecropolis.org.

★ **St Mungo's Museum of Religious Life & Art** MUSEUM
(Map p110; ☑0141-276 1625; www.glasgowmuseums.com; 2 Castle St; ⊙10am-5pm Tue-Thu & Sat, from 11am Fri & Sun) FREE Set in a reconstruction of the bishop's palace that once stood in the cathedral forecourt, this museum audaciously attempts to capture the world's major religions in an artistic nutshell. A startling achievement, it presents the similarities and differences of how various religions approach common themes such as birth, marriage and death. The attraction is twofold: firstly, impressive art that blurs the lines between religion and culture, and secondly, the opportunity to delve into different faiths, as deeply or shallowly as you wish.

Provand's Lordship HISTORIC BUILDING
(Map p110; ☑0141-276 1625; www.glasgowmuseums.com; 3 Castle St; ⊙10am-5pm Tue-Thu & Sat, from 11am Fri & Sun) FREE Near the cathedral is Provand's Lordship, the oldest house in Glasgow. This rare example of 15th-century domestic Scottish architecture was built in 1471 as a manse. The ceilings and doorways are low, and the rooms are furnished with period furniture and artefacts; upstairs a room recreates the living space of an early-16th-century chaplain. The building's biggest draw is its authentic feel, though it's a shame the original wooden floors have had to be covered for protection.

Provand's Lordship was once one of several dozen religious buildings in the immediate vicinity of the cathedral. It was built to house the master of the St Nicholas chapel and hospital, which once stood just to the south. Behind Provand's Lordship, the St Nicholas Garden recreates what a 15th-century hospital garden might have been like.

People's Palace MUSEUM
(☎0141-276 0788; www.glasgowmuseums.com; Glasgow Green; ◷10am-5pm Tue-Thu & Sat, from 11am Fri & Sun) FREE Set in the city's oldest park, Glasgow Green, is the solid orange stone People's Palace. It is an impressive museum of social history, telling the story of Glasgow from 1750 to the present through creative, inventive family-friendly displays. The palace was built in the late 19th century as a cultural centre for Glasgow's East End. The attached greenhouse, the **Winter Gardens** (open from 10am to 4.45pm daily), has tropical plants and is a nice spot for a coffee.

◉ West End

With its appealing studenty buzz, modish bars and cafes and bohemian swagger, the West End is for many the most engaging area of Glasgow – it's great for people-watching. Streets of elegant terraced houses and ample parkland cover large areas of the district, which is centred around the Victorian grandeur of the University of Glasgow and the Kelvingrove Art Gallery & Museum. Glasgow's key eat streets are also here.

★**Kelvingrove Art Gallery & Museum** GALLERY, MUSEUM
(Map p116; ☎0141-276 9599; www.glasgow museums.com; Argyle St; ◷10am-5pm Mon-Thu & Sat, from 11am Fri & Sun) FREE A magnificent sandstone building, this grand Victorian cathedral of culture is a fascinating and unusual museum, with a bewildering variety of exhibits. You'll find fine art alongside stuffed animals, and Micronesian shark-tooth swords alongside a Spitfire plane, but it's not mix 'n' match: rooms are carefully and thoughtfully themed, and the collection is of a manageable size. It has an excellent room of Scottish art, a room of fine French impressionist works, and quality Renaissance paintings from Italy and Flanders.

Salvador Dalí's superb *Christ of St John of the Cross* is also here. Best of all, nearly everything, including the paintings, has an easy-reading paragraph of interpretation. You can learn a lot about art here, and it's excellent for children, with plenty to do and displays aimed at a variety of ages. Free hour-long guided tours begin at 11am and 2.30pm. Be here at 1pm to hear the impressive organ being played. Bus 17, among many others, runs here from Renfield St.

★**Mackintosh House** HISTORIC BUILDING
(Map p116; ☎0141-330 4221; www.hunterian.gla. ac.uk; 82 Hillhead St; adult/child £6/3; ◷10am-5pm Tue-Sat, 11am-4pm Sun) Attached to the **Hunterian Art Gallery** (Map p116; ☎0141-330 4221; www.hunterian.gla.ac.uk; 82 Hillhead St; ◷10am-5pm Tue-Sat, 11am-4pm Sun) FREE, this is a reconstruction of the first home that Charles Rennie Mackintosh bought with his wife, noted designer/artist Margaret Macdonald. It's fair to say that interior decoration was one of their strong points; Mackintosh House is startling even today. The quiet elegance of the hall and dining room on the ground floor give way to a stun-

GLASGOW IN...

Two Days

On your first day, hit the East End for **Glasgow Cathedral** (p112), **St Mungo's Museum** (p113) and a wander through the hillside **necropolis** (p113). Later, take in one of the city's top museums: either the **Burrell Collection** (p117) or the **Kelvingrove**. As evening falls, head to trendy Merchant City for a stroll and dinner; try **Café Gandolfi** (p124). Check out **Artà** (p129) for a pre- or post-meal drink. The next day, visit whichever museum you missed yesterday, and then it's Mackintosh time. Check out **Mackintosh at the Willow** (p110): if you like his style, head to the West End for **Mackintosh House**. Hungry? Thirsty? Some of the city's best restaurants and bars are up this end of town, so you could make a night of it. Make sure to check out one of the numerous excellent **music venues** (p131) around the city.

Four Days

A four-day stay gives better scope to get to grips with Glasgow. Spend a day along the Clyde – the **Riverside Museum** and the **Glasgow Science Centre**. Plan your weekend around a night out at the Cathouse (p129) or the legendary **King Tut's Wah Wah Hut** (p131), and a day strolling the stylish city-centre clothing emporia or attending a football game. Don't miss trying at least one of the city's classic curry houses.

ning drawing room and bedroom upstairs. Visits are by guided tour in the morning and self guided in the afternoon.

The visual highlight is the white-as-white drawing room. There's something otherworldly about the very mannered style of the beaten silver panels, the long-backed chairs and the surface decorations echoing Celtic manuscript illuminations. You wouldn't have wanted to be the guest who spilled a glass of red on this carpet.

The house will perhaps become part of the new museum at Kelvin Hall, but likely not until at least 2023.

Hunterian Museum MUSEUM
(Map p116; ✐ 0141-330 4221; www.hunterian.gla. ac.uk; University Ave; ⊙ 10am-5pm Tue-Sat, 11am-4pm Sun) **FREE** Housed in the glorious sandstone university building, which is in itself reason enough to pay a visit, this quirky museum contains the collection of renowned one-time student William Hunter (1718–83). Hunter was primarily an anatomist and physician, but as one of those wonderfully well-rounded Enlightenment figures, he interested himself in everything the world had to offer.

Pickled organs in glass jars take their place alongside geological phenomena, potsherds gleaned from ancient brochs, dinosaur skeletons and a creepy case of deformed animals. The main halls of the exhibition, with their high vaulted roofs, are magnificent in themselves. Highlights include a display of artefacts from the Antonine Wall and the beautiful 1674 Chinese *Map of the Whole World* produced for the emperor by a Jesuit at the court.

This collection will perhaps become part of the new museum at Kelvin Hall but probably not until at least 2023.

Kelvin Hall MUSEUM
(Map p116; ✐ 0141-276 1450; www.glasgowlife. org.uk; 1445 Argyle St; ⊙ 6.30am-10pm Mon-Fri, 8am-5pm Sat, 8am-8pm Sun) **FREE** Opened in the 1920s as an exhibition centre, this enormous sandstone palace, renovated and reopened in 2016, is a mixed leisure-and-arts space. In addition to a gym and sports facilities, it hosts the audiovisual archive of the **National Library of Scotland** (Map p116; ✐ 0845 366 4600; www.nls.uk; Kelvin Hall, 1445 Argyle St; ⊙ 10am-5pm Tue & Thu-Sat, 1.30-8pm Wed) **FREE** and also stores items from the University of Glasgow's museum collection (available by appoint-

ment). The major exhibition halls are being developed and may end up holding the Hunterian collections as well as other city-related exhibits.

◉ The Clyde

Once a thriving shipbuilding area, the Clyde sank into dereliction during the postwar era but has been subject to extensive rejuvenation. There are noteworthy sights along the river, though the walk along its banks still isn't all that it could be.

★**Riverside Museum** MUSEUM
(✐ 0141-287 2720; www.glasgowmuseums.com; 100 Pointhouse Pl; ⊙ 10am-5pm Mon-Thu & Sat, from 11am Fri & Sun; ⊕) **FREE** This visually impressive modern museum at Glasgow Harbour owes its striking curved forms to late British-Iraqi architect Zaha Hadid. A transport museum forms the main part of the collection, featuring a fascinating series of cars made in Scotland, plus assorted railway locos, trams, bikes (including the world's first pedal-powered bicycle from 1847) and model Clyde-built ships. An atmospheric recreation of a Glasgow shopping street from the early 20th century puts the vintage vehicles into a social context. There's also a cafe.

It's west of the city centre. Get bus 100 from the north side of George Sq or walk (signposted) from the Kelvingrove Art Gallery & Museum – about half a mile.

The magnificent three-masted *Glenlee*, launched in 1896, is the **Tall Ship** (✐ 0141-357 3699; www.thetallship.com; Riverside Museum; ⊙ 10am-5pm Feb-Oct, to 4pm Nov-Jan; ⊕) **FREE**, which is berthed alongside the museum. On board are family-friendly displays about the ship's history, restoration and shipboard life during its heyday. Upkeep costs are high, so donate something or have a coffee below decks.

★**Glasgow Science Centre** MUSEUM
(Map p116; ✐ 0141-420 5000; www.glasgow sciencecentre.org; 50 Pacific Quay; adult/child £11.50/9.50, IMAX, Glasgow Tower or Planetarium extra £2.50-3.50; ⊙ 10am-5pm daily Apr-Oct, to 3pm Wed-Fri, to 5pm Sat & Sun Nov-Mar; ⊕) This brilliant science museum will keep the kids entertained for hours (that's middle-aged kids, too!). It brings science and technology alive through hundreds of interactive exhibits on four floors: a bounty of discovery for inquisitive minds. There's also an

West End

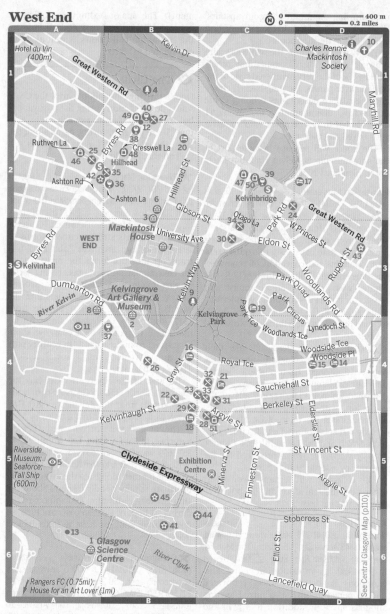

N 0 ___ 400 m
0 ___ 0.2 miles

IMAX theatre (see www.cineworld.com for current screenings), a rotating 127m-high **observation tower**, a **planetarium** and a **Science Theatre**, with live science demonstrations. To get here, take bus 89 or 90 from Union St.

Clydeside Distillery   DISTILLERY
(Map p116; ☎0141-212 1401; www.theclydeside. com; The Pumphouse, 100 Stobcross Rd; tour adult/child £15/5; ☺10am-4pm Sep-Jun, to 4.30pm Jul & Aug) It's great to see this old pumphouse by the Clyde being put to good

West End

GLASGOW SIGHTS

use as a new malt whisky distillery run by proper whisky folk. It's an impressive set-up, with the stills overlooking the river (don't worry, the water comes from Loch Katrine, not the Clyde). The tour (1¼ hours) is engaging, with some history of the Clyde. It includes a tasting of three malts (though you won't be able to taste whisky from here until at least 2020).

There's also a pleasant cafe and a well-stocked whisky shop.

◉ South Side

The Southside is an intriguingly multicultural part of Glasgow, with temples and mosques alongside sturdy episcopal churches. It's got an up-and-coming food scene and thriving cultural centres. Several excellent attractions are also dotted across the area.

Burrell Collection GALLERY
(☏ 0141-287 2550; www.glasgowlife.org.uk; Pollok Country Park; ◔ closed) FREE One of

Glasgow's top attractions, this outstanding museum 3 miles out of town houses everything from Chinese porcelain and medieval furniture to paintings by Cézanne. The tapestry collection is a particular highlight. It's closed for refurbishment, and is due to reopen in 2020. The new building will have double the exhibition space as well as a cafe. Meanwhile, some items are on display at the Kelvingrove Art Gallery & Museum (p114).

**Scotland Street
School Museum** NOTABLE BUILDING
(☏ 0141-287 0504; www.glasgowlife.org.uk; 225 Scotland St; ◔ 10am-5pm Tue-Thu & Sat, from 11am Fri & Sun) FREE Mackintosh's Scotland Street School seems a bit forlorn these days, on a windswept industrial street with no babble of young voices filling its corridors. Nevertheless, it's worth a visit for its stunning facade and the interesting museum of education that occupies the

interior. Reconstructions of classrooms from various points in the school's lifetime, combined with grumbling headmaster and cleaner, will have older visitors recalling their own schooldays. It's right opposite Shields Road subway station and there's also an OK cafe.

House for an Art Lover NOTABLE BUILDING
(☑ 0141-353 4770; www.houseforanartlover.co.uk; Bellahouston Park, Dumbreck Rd; adult/child £6/4.50; ⊘ check online, roughly 10am-4pm Mon-Fri, to noon Sat, to 2pm Sun) Although designed in 1901 as an entry in a competition run by a German magazine, this house in Bellahouston Park was not built until the 1990s. Mackintosh worked closely with his wife on the design and her influence is evident, especially in the rose motif. The overall effect of this brilliant architect's ideas is one of space and light. Buses 9, 10 and 38 all run here from downtown; check the website for opening hours, as it's regularly booked for events.

The house is the hub of an arts promotion program and there are regular workshops, exhibitions and events.

Scottish Football Museum MUSEUM
(The Hampden Experience; ☑ 0141-616 6139; www.scottishfootballmuseum.org.uk; Hampden Park; adult/child £8/3; ⊘ 10am-5pm Mon-Sat, from 11am Sun) At Hampden Park, the national stadium, this museum covers the history of the game in Scotland and the considerable influence of Scots on the world game. It's crammed full of impressive memorabilia, including a cap and match ticket from the very first international football game ever played, held in Glasgow in 1872. You can also take a tour of the stadium (adult/child £8/3.50; combined ticket with museum £13/5), home ground to both Scotland and lower-division outfit Queens Park.

THE GENIUS OF CHARLES RENNIE MACKINTOSH

Great cities have great artists, designers and architects contributing to their urban environment while expressing their soul and individuality. Charles Rennie Mackintosh was all of these and his quirky, linear and geometric designs have had an enormous influence on Glasgow. Many of the buildings Mackintosh designed are open to the public, and you'll see his tall, thin, art-nouveau typeface repeatedly reproduced.

Born in 1868, Mackintosh studied at the Glasgow School of Art. It was there that he met the influential artist and designer Margaret Macdonald, whom he married; they collaborated on many projects and were major influences on each other's work. Together with her sister Frances and Herbert MacNair, the artist who married her, they formed 'The Four', a pioneering group that developed the Glasgow Style. This contribution to art nouveau incorporated influences from the Arts and Crafts movement and Japanese design.

In 1896, aged only 27, Mackintosh won a competition for his design for the new building of the Glasgow School of Art (p107), where he had studied. This was his supreme architectural achievement. The first section was opened in 1899 and is considered to be the earliest example of art nouveau in Britain. The second section, opened a decade later, includes some of the earliest art deco. The building demonstrates his skill in combining function and style.

Another of Mackintosh's finest works is Hill House (p249), in Helensburgh. Other buildings around town include the **Daily Record Building** (Map p110; 20 Renfield Lane), Scotland Street School (p117), Mackintosh Queen's Cross church and House for an Art Lover. His reconstructed Willow Tearooms (p110) feature his design concept right down to the smallest level.

Although Mackintosh's genius was quickly recognised in the rest of Europe, he did not receive the same encouragement in Scotland. His architectural career here lasted only until 1914, when he moved to England to concentrate on furniture design. He died in 1928, and it is only since the last decades of the 20th century that Mackintosh's genius has been widely recognised. For more about the man and his work, contact the **Charles Rennie Mackintosh Society** (Map p116; ☑ 0141-946 6600; www.crmsociety.com; Mackintosh Queen's Cross, 870 Garscube Rd). Check its website and www.glasgowmackintosh.com for special events.

The museum is at Hampden Park, off Aikenhead Rd. Take a train to Mount Florida station or take bus 5, 31 or 75 from Stockwell St.

North Side

Mackintosh Queen's Cross
CHURCH

(Map p116; ☎0141-946 6600; www.mackintosh church.com; 870 Garscube Rd; adult/child £4/free; ⊙10am-5pm Mon-Fri Apr-Oct, to 4pm Mon, Wed & Fri Nov-Dec & Feb-Mar, closed Jan) Now headquarters of the Charles Rennie Mackintosh Society, this is the only one of Mackintosh's church designs to be built. It has an excellent stained-glass window and exquisite relief carvings, and the wonderful simplicity and grace of the barrel-shaped design is particularly inspiring. The luminous church hall is arguably even finer. It has a good gift shop and a detailed Mackintosh DVD playing. Garscube Rd is the northern extension of Rose St in the city centre.

Activities

There are numerous green spaces within the city. Pollok Country Park surrounds the Burrell Collection (p117) and has several woodland trails. Nearer the centre of the city, the **Kelvin Walkway** follows the River Kelvin through **Kelvingrove Park** (Map p116), the Botanic Gardens and on to Dawsholm Park.

The **Clyde Walkway** stretches from Glasgow upriver to the Falls of Clyde near New Lanark, about 40 miles away. The tourist office (p136) has information outlining different sections of this walk. The 10-mile section through Glasgow has interesting parts, though most of the old shipyards are no longer there. There are some beautiful sections further upstream.

The well-trodden, long-distance footpath **West Highland Way** begins in Milngavie, 8 miles north of Glasgow (you can walk to Milngavie from Glasgow along the River Kelvin), and runs for 95 spectacular miles to Fort William.

There are several long-distance pedestrian/cycle routes that begin in Glasgow and follow off-road routes for most of the way. Check www.sustrans.org.uk for more details.

The **Clyde–Loch Lomond route** traverses residential and industrial areas in a 20-mile ride from Bell's Bridge to Loch Lomond. This route continues to Inverness, part of the **Lochs and Glens National Cycle Route**.

The **Clyde to Forth cycle route** runs through Glasgow. One way takes you to Edinburgh via Bathgate, the other takes you via Paisley to Greenock and Gourock, the first section partly on roads. Another branch heads down to Irvine and Ardrossan, for the ferry to Arran. An extension via Ayr, Maybole and Glentrool leads to the Solway coast and Carlisle.

☞ Tours

Glasgow Central Tours
WALKING

(Map p110; www.glasgowcentraltours.co.uk; tour £13; ⊙check website for tour times) A passionate, entertaining guide takes you around, behind and under Glasgow Central station (p137). Hidden spaces, an abandoned Victorian platform and lots of intriguing information make this a fascinating experience even if railways don't get you excited. It lasts about an hour; check the website for dates. The minimum age is 12 years.

Rabbies
BUS

(www.rabbies.com) This popular outfit runs a range of minibus tours up to the Highlands, including popular long day trips that take in Glencoe and Loch Ness, or West Highland castles.

Glasgow Bike Tours
CYCLING

(Map p116; ☎0141-374 2342; www.glasgowbike tours.co.uk; 28 Vinicombe St; adult/child £30/15) A friendly guide runs a three-hour circuit around the city. It takes in several key sights around the periphery of the city centre and gets you an especially good look at the Clyde and the West End.

Seaforce
BOATING

(☎0141-221 1070; www.seaforce.co.uk; Riverside Museum) Departing from the Riverside Museum, Seaforce offers speedy all-weather powerboat jaunts along the Clyde. There's a variety of trips, including a 20-minute 'Clyde Ride' around central Glasgow (adult/child £10/5). They run year round but call ahead as they are weather dependent.

Waverley
BOATING

(Map p116; ☎0141-221 8152; www.waverley excursions.co.uk; ⊙mid-May–mid-Aug plus some Oct departures) The world's last ocean-going paddle steamer (built in 1947) cruises Scotland's west coast in summer, with many different routes; the website details days of departure. It serves several towns and the islands of Bute, Great Cumbrae, Arran and more. Its Glasgow departures are from the

Glasgow Science Centre, while it also has frequent departures from Largs and Ayr among other locations.

Festivals & Events

Celtic Connections MUSIC
(☎0141-353 8000; www.celticconnections.com; ⏲Jan) This two-week music festival focuses on roots music and folk from Scotland and around the world.

Glasgow Film Festival FILM
(www.glasgowfilm.org; ⏲Feb) Two-week film festival with screenings in various locations across the city.

Glasgow International Comedy Festival COMEDY
(☎0844 873 7353; www.glasgowcomedyfestival.com; ⏲Mar) Two weeks of quality comedy, both home-grown and imported, enlivens stages across the city in March.

West End Festival PERFORMING ARTS
(☎0141-341 0844; www.westendfestival.co.uk; ⏲Jun) This music and arts event is Glasgow's biggest festival. Runs for three weeks.

Glasgow Jazz Festival MUSIC
(www.jazzfest.co.uk; ⏲Jun) Excellent festival sees big-name international acts come to town, with stages set up in George Sq and Merchant City.

TRNSMT MUSIC
(www.trnsmtfest.com) Held over two consecutive weekends in late June and early July, this festival only started in 2017 but has been a huge success, drawing major indie rock acts to Glasgow Green.

Merchant City Festival STREET CARNIVAL
(www.merchantcityfestival.com; ⏲late Jul) Lively weeklong street festival in the Merchant City quarter, with lots of performances and stalls.

Sleeping

Glasgow has plenty of accommodation but can still fill up at weekends; booking ahead for weekends is essential, as well as in high season July and August.

Most providers set prices according to demand. Rates shoot up at weekends and reach stratospheric levels, even at mediocre places, if there's a big-name concert on a Saturday. By the same token, you can get excellent deals on quieter nights out of season.

City Centre

Glasgow Metro Youth Hostel HOSTEL £
(Map p110; ☎0141-354 0109; www.hostellingscotland.org.uk; 89 Buccleuch St; s £32-45; ⏲late Jun-Aug; 📶) Student accommodation belonging to the nearby Glasgow School of Art provides the venue for this summer hostel. All rooms are comfortable singles, many with an en suite, there are kitchen facilities, and it's a very good deal for solo travellers or groups. Rates vary by day and month.

★Z Hotel HOTEL ££
(Map p110; ☎0141-212 4550; www.thezhotels.com; 36 North Frederick St; r £90-165; ❄📶) Just off George Sq, the facade of a historic building conceals a stylish contemporary hotel. Chambers are modern but compact – the idea is that you sleep here and socialise in the bar area, especially during the afternoon wine-and-cheese session. Big flatscreens and pleasing showers add comfort to rooms that are often overpriced but can be great value if advance booked.

★Grasshoppers HOTEL ££
(Map p110; ☎0141-222 2666; www.grasshoppersglasgow.com; 87 Union St; r £90-138; ❄📶🐾) Discreetly hidden atop a timeworn railway administration building alongside Central station, this small, well-priced hotel is a modern, upbeat surprise. Rooms are compact (a few are larger) but well appointed, with unusual views over the station roof's glass sea. Numerous touches – friendly staff, interesting art, in-room cafetière, free cupcakes and ice cream, and weeknight suppers – make this one of the centre's homiest choices.

There's a very good deal available (£8 per day) at a car park a block away.

Citizen M HOTEL ££
(Map p110; ☎020-3519 1111; www.citizenm.com; 60 Renfrew St; r £90-180; @📶) This modern chain does away with some normal hotel accoutrements in favour of self-check-in terminals and minimalist, plasticky modern rooms with just two features: a big, comfortable king-sized bed and a decent shower with mood lighting. The idea is that guests make liberal use of the public areas, and why wouldn't you, with upbeat, supercomfortable designer furniture, a 24-hour cafe and iMacs?

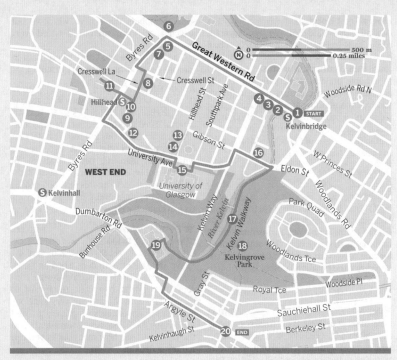

City Walk
West End

START KELVINBRIDGE SUBWAY STATION
END ARGYLE ST, FINNIESTON
LENGTH 3 MILES; 2 HOURS

Emerge from the subway and turn left across **1 Great Western Bridge (Kelvinbridge)**, emblazoned with the lion rampant of the Hillhead burgh on the south side and the city coat of arms on the north. Note the riverside bar **2 Inn Deep** (p130) to come back to.

Continue along Great Western Rd, stopping for a browse in **3 Glasgow Vintage Company** (p135) and **4 Caledonia Books** (p135). At the corner of Byres Rd, a former church is now **5 Oràn Mór** (p130); consider its lunchtime theatre session. Across the road stretch the **6 Botanic Gardens**.

Turn left down Byres Rd; investigate shops, like liquid deli **7 Demijohn** (382 Byres Rd; ☉10am-6pm Mon-Sat, 11.30am-5pm Sun). At Cresswell St, turn left and then right on Cresswell Lane to check out **8 De Courcy's Arcade** (☉10am-5.30pm Mon-Sat, noon-5pm Sun).

Continuing down this lane brings you to the bar-heavy **9 Ashton Lane**, where **10 Ubiquitous Chip** (p126) is still one of Scotland's best places to eat. Turn right opposite Jinty McGuinty's to reach Byres Rd again. Cross and examine the quirky shops down **11 Ruthven Lane**, accessed directly opposite.

Back on Byres Rd, head south, then turn left up University Ave. The ugly 1960s **12 Boyd Orr tower** is soon replaced by more typical sandstone terraces as you climb the hill. On the left is the **13 Hunterian Art Gallery** (p114) and **14 Mackintosh House** (p114); on the right, wander through the University of Glasgow's main building, home to the **15 Hunterian Museum** (p115).

At the bottom of University Ave, turn left, then right onto Gibson St, home to quality lunch stops like **16 Stravaigin** (p125). Cross the bridge and turn right into the park, bearing right down to the river and the **17 Kelvin Walkway**. Follow this for half a mile through lovely **18 Kelvingrove Park** (p119) to reach the **19 Kelvingrove Art Gallery & Museum** (p114). From here it's a short hop to the Finnieston eating strip on **20 Argyle St**.

Pipers' Tryst Hotel HOTEL **££**

(Map p110; ☑0141-353 5551; www.thepipingcentre.
co.uk; 30-34 McPhater St; s/d £90/120, without
breakfast £78/96; ☎) The name is no tartan
tourist trap; rather this intimate, cosy hotel
in a noble building is actually run by the
adjacent bagpiping centre, and profits go
towards maintaining it. Cheery staff, great
value and a prime city-centre location make
this a wise choice. You won't have far to migrate after a night of Celtic music and malts
in the snug bar-restaurant.

Babbity Bowster INN **££**

(Map p110; ☑0141-552 5055; www.babbity
bowster.com; 16-18 Blackfriars St; s/d £55/75;
P☎) Smack bang in the heart of vibrant
Merchant City, this lively, pleasant pub has
simple rooms with sleek furnishings and a
minimalist design (room 3 is a good one).
Staying here is an excellent Glaswegian experience – the building's design is attributed
to Robert Adam. The price is a steal given
that breakfast and parking are included.

Point A HOTEL **££**

(Map p110; ☑0141-352 2650; www.pointahotels.
com; 80 Bath St; r £80-149; ✳☎) Offering urban comfort without frills, Point A concentrates on doing the basics well, offering very
comfortable beds and reliable showers in
minimalist, functional modern rooms with
mood lighting, big flatscreens and climate
control. Prices vary hugely by demand;
some chambers don't have windows but
are cheaper. Rooms are only serviced every
third day.

The location is good, just where Bath St
morphs from down-at-heel to intriguing.

ABode Glasgow HOTEL **££**

(Map p110; ☑0141-221 6789; www.abodeglasgow.
co.uk; 129 Bath St; r £119-164; ✳@☎) A characterful listed building dating from the mid-
19th century holds this interesting hotel that
features plenty of original art, sweet rooms
with tartan blankets, period features all
over the public areas and helpful staff. Bathrooms are compact, but this is a good deal in
the heart of things and a far cry from your
typical chain hotel.

★**Dakota Deluxe** HOTEL **£££**

(Map p110; ☑0141-404 3680; www.dakotahotels.
co.uk; 179 West Regent St; r £150-200; ✳☎✷)
Suave and seductive in dark wood and grey
tones, Dakota carries a strong design concept from low-lit basement restaurant to
light-filled suites. Rooms are very spacious
and feature appealing sitting areas as well
as inviting beds. Service is excellent, and
the bar area – see how many Jacks you can
name – a delight.

Blythswood Square HOTEL **£££**

(Map p110; ☑0141-248 8888; www.blythswood
square.com; 11 Blythswood Sq; r £195-300;
P@☎✷✷) In a gorgeous Georgian terrace,

GLASGOW FOR CHILDREN

Glasgow is easy to visit with children due to its extensive public transport system and
friendly locals. The city boasts excellent family attractions and there are several apart-
ment-hotels around town. In general, restaurants are well geared for children, and lots of
places serve food throughout the day.

Family-oriented venues include the following:

➡ Glasgow Science Centre (p115)

➡ Sharmanka Kinetic Theatre (p107)

➡ Riverside Museum (p115)

➡ People's Palace (p114)

Need to Know

Childcare For suggestions for short-term child-care agencies, contact the council-run
Glasgow Family Information Service (☑0141-287 4702; www.gfis.org.uk).

Playgrounds Most parks in Glasgow have playgrounds for children.

Shopping centres Major shopping complexes are handy stops, with baby-changing
facilities and soft play areas.

Pubs In family-licensed pubs, accompanied children under 14 years old are admitted
between 11am and 8pm.

this elegant five-star offers inner-city luxury, with grey and cerise providing casual soft-toned style throughout. Rooms (recently refurbished) go from standard to penthouse with corresponding increases in comfort; it's hard to resist the traditional 'classic' rooms with windows onto the delightful square, but at weekends you'll have a quieter sleep in the new wing at the back.

It has an excellent bar and a superb restaurant, as well as a very handsome floor-boarded and colonnaded salon space on the 1st floor that functions as an evening spot for cocktails. Other facilities include valet parking and a seductive spa complex.

Indigo   HOTEL **£££**
(Map p110; ☑ 0141-226 7700; www.hinglasgow. co.uk; 75 Waterloo St; r £130-200; ☀ @ 🕾) Once the power station for early trams, this boutique-chain conversion of an elegant building has resulted in a satisfying, surprisingly quiet option in city centre. Rooms have mural-style artwork, great beds and a free minibar (the contents improve as you go up the room grades). Space is good, and bathrooms have rain shower heads. Prices vary; there are usually good online deals.

There is an upmarket grill restaurant attached.

🛏 West End

Glasgow SYHA   HOSTEL **£**
(Map p116; ☑ 0141-332 3004; www.hostelling scotland.org.uk; 8 Park Tce; dm/s/tw £29/52/69; @ 🕾) Perched on a hill overlooking Kelvingrove Park in a charming townhouse, this place is one of Scotland's best official hostels. Dorms are mostly four to six beds with padlock lockers, and all have their own en suite. The common rooms are spacious, plush and good for lounging about. There's no curfew, it has a good kitchen, and meals are available.

Heritage Hotel   HOTEL **£**
(Map p116; ☑ 0141-339 6955; www.theheritage hotel.net; 4 Alfred Tce, Great Western Rd; s/d £45/75; P 🕾) A stone's throw from all the action of the West End, this friendly hotel has an open, airy feel despite the rather dilapidated raised terrace it's located on. Generally, rooms on the 1st and 2nd floors are a bit more spacious and have a better outlook. The location, parking option and very fair prices mark it out.

★ Amadeus Guest House   B&B **££**
(Map p116; ☑ 0141-339 8257; www.amadeusguest house.co.uk; 411 North Woodside Rd; s £60-70, s without bathroom £42-45, d £80-100; 🕾) Just off the bustle of Great Western Rd, a minute's walk from the subway but on a quiet street by the riverside pathway, this B&B has compact bright rooms, all distinct, with a cheerful, breezy feel. There's a variety of types, including several singles. It offers excellent value and a genuine welcome. A good continental breakfast is included.

★ Alamo Guest House   B&B **££**
(Map p116; ☑ 0141-339 2395; www.alamoguest house.com; 46 Gray St; d £99-111, superior d £159-220, d without bathroom £69-79; @ 🕾) The Alamo may not sound like a peaceful spot, but that's exactly what this great place is. Opposite Kelvingrove Park, it feels miles from the city's hustle, but several of Glasgow's best museums and restaurants are right at hand. The decor blends antique furnishings and modern design, with excellent bathrooms, and the owners will make you very welcome.

Flower House   B&B **££**
(Map p116; ☑ 0141-204 2846; www.theflower house.net; 33 St Vincent Cres; s £50-70, d £70-120; 🕾) Cosy, old-style B&B is offered in this pretty Victorian terraced house fronted by a riot of creepers and flowers – you can't miss it. Just off the Finnieston strip, its comfortably dignified interior features antiques, curios, striped wallpaper and noble furniture. Bathrooms are exterior but private: they are extraordinary, particularly the 'penny wall'. Hospitality is good humoured and exceptional, with homemade treats for breakfast.

Sandyford Lodge   GUESTHOUSE **££**
(Map p116; ☑ 0141-332 9009; www.sandyford lodge.com; 21 Royal Cres; s £59-89, d £109-139; 🕾) This elegant Victorian building is handy for the West End's museums and the Finnieston restaurant strip. Rooms, which vary in size, offer decent value – except on busy weekends – with good facilities and comfort, while staff go out of their way to be helpful. Don't confuse with the nearby Sandyford Hotel, run by the same owners.

Acorn Hotel   HOTEL **££**
(Map p116; ☑ 0141-332 6556; www.acorn-hotel. com; 140 Elderslie St; s £60-80, d £80-110; @ 🕾) Enjoying a pretty location by a park, yet by a decent pub and just a block from Sauchiehall St, this smart little place has rooms that

are compact but boast stylish colours and comfortable beds. Staff are very welcoming. Room-only rates are available.

★15Glasgow
B&B £££

(Map p116; ☑0141-332 1263; www.15glasgow. com; 15 Woodside Pl; d/ste £130/160; P 🛜) Glasgow's 19th-century merchants certainly knew how to build a beautiful house, and this 1840s terrace is a sumptuous example. Huge rooms with lofty ceilings have exquisite period detail complemented by attractive modern greys, striking bathrooms and well-chosen quality furniture. Your welcoming host makes everything easy for you: the in-room breakfast, overlooking the park, is a real treat. They prefer no under-five-year-olds.

Hotel du Vin
HOTEL £££

(☑0141-378 0385; www.hotelduvin.com; 1 Devonshire Gardens; r £184-304; P @ 🛜 🛜) This is traditionally Glasgow's favoured hotel of the rich and famous, and the patriarch of sophistication and comfort. A study in elegance, it's sumptuously decorated and occupies three classical sandstone terrace houses. There's a bewildering array of room types, all different in style and size. The hospitality is old-school courteous, and there's an excellent restaurant on-site with a vast wine selection.

🍴 Eating

Glasgow is the best place to eat in Scotland, with a stupendous range of restaurants and cafes. The West End is a culinary centre, with Merchant City also boasting a high concentration of quality establishments. Pubs and bars (p127) are often good meal-time options too.

The excellent *Eating & Drinking Guide*, published by *The List* every second April, covers both Glasgow and Edinburgh.

🍴 City Centre

★Riverhill Coffee Bar
CAFE £

(Map p110; ☑0141-204 4762; www.riverhillcafe. com; 24 Gordon St; rolls £4-5; ⊙7am-5pm Mon-Fri, from 8am Sat, from 10am Sun; 🛜) 🧽 Chain cafes plaster Glasgow's centre, so it's a joy to come across this tiny place, which offers great coffee and hot chocolate as well as delicious filled rolls and tempting pastries. Ingredients are sustainably sourced and seriously tasty. It's extremely friendly; you'd come every day if you lived nearby.

★Saramago Café Bar
CAFE, VEGAN £

(Map p110; ☑0141-352 4920; www.cca-glasgow. com; 350 Sauchiehall St; mains £8-12; ⊙food noon-10pm Sun-Wed, to 11.30pm Thu-Sat; 🛜🛜) In the airy atrium of the Centre for Contemporary Arts, this place does a great line in eclectic vegan fusion food, with a range of top flavour combinations from around the globe. The upstairs bar (open from 4pm) has a great deck on steep Scott St and packs out inside with a friendly arty crowd enjoying the DJ sets and quality tap beers.

Chippy Doon the Lane
FISH & CHIPS £

(Map p110; ☑0141-225 6650; www.thechippy glasgow.com; McCormick Lane, 84 Buchanan St; meals £6-12; ⊙noon-9pm Sun-Thu, to 9.30pm Fri & Sat; 🛜) 🧽 Don't be put off by its location in a down-at-heel alleyway off the shopping precinct: this is a cut above your average chip shop. Sustainable seafood is served in a chic space: all old-time brick, metal archways and jazz. Otherwise, chow down on your takeaway at the wooden tables in the lane or out on Buchanan St itself.

Platform
STREET FOOD £

(Map p110; www.facebook.com/platformgla; 253 Argyle St; light meals £4-7; ⊙noon-10pm Fri & Sat, to 6pm Sun) This atmospheric series of brick-arched vaults under the railway lines at Central station comes into its own at weekends, when street-food vendors open up stalls and a bar doles out pints to those seeking an escape from the weather. It's family and dog friendly. During the week the cafe is still open.

★Singl-end
CAFE £££

(Map p110; ☑0141-353 1277; www.thesingl-end. co.uk; 265 Renfrew St; dishes £7-13; ⊙9am-5pm; 🛜🧽) There's something glorious about this long basement cafe with its cheery service and air of brunchy bonhomie. It coves a lot of bases, with good coffee, generous breakfasts and lunches, booze and baking. Dietary requirements are superbly catered for, with fine vegan choices and clear labelling. On a diet? Avert your eyes from the 'eat-me' cornucopia of meringues and pastries by the door.

Café Gandolfi
CAFE, BISTRO £££

(Map p110; ☑0141-552 6813; www.cafegandolfi. com; 64 Albion St; mains £10-18; ⊙8am-11pm Mon-Sat, from 9am Sun; 🛜) In Merchant City, this cafe was once part of the old cheese market. It's been pulling in the punters for years and attracts an interesting mix of die-hard Gandolfers, the upwardly mobile and tourists. It covers all the bases with excellent breakfasts and coffee, an enticing upstairs bar (p129), and top-notch bistro food, including Scottish and continental options, in an atmospheric medieval-like setting.

Loon Fung
CANTONESE ££

(Map p110; ☏0141-332 1240; www.loonfung glasgow.com; 417 Sauchiehall St; mains £11-15; ⊘noon-11pm; 🛜🅿) This elegant Cantonese oasis is one of Scotland's most authentic Chinese restaurants; indeed, it's quite a surprise after a traditional dining experience here to emerge to boisterous Sauchiehall St rather than Hong Kong. The dim-sum choices are toothsome, and the seafood – try the sea bass – really excellent.

★ Spanish Butcher
SPANISH £££

(Map p110; ☏0141-406 9880; www.spanish butcher.com; 80 Miller St; mains £16-22; ⊘noon-1am; 🛜) In a refined interior, moodily dark with industrial decor above retro wickerwork chairs, this is a fine venue for quality northern Spanish beef, with the best cuts designed for sharing. But there's plenty more to delight: whole baked fish, expertly deboned, are attractive and succulent, while the *secreto* and *presa* cuts redefine the pork genre.

There are some good Spanish wines by the glass and a range of tasty bar snacks if you just want a drink.

★ Gamba
SEAFOOD £££

(Map p110; ☏0141-572 0899; www.gamba.co.uk; 225a West George St; mains £21-30; ⊘noon-2.15pm & 5-9.30pm Mon-Sat, 5-9pm Sun; 🛜) This business-district basement is easily missed but is actually one of the city's premier seafood restaurants. Presentation is elegant, with carefully selected flavours allowing the fish, sustainably sourced from Scotland and beyond, to shine. Service is smart and solicitous. There's a good weekday lunch deal, costing £20/22 for two/three courses.

Hutchesons City Grill
STEAK £££

(Map p110; ☏0141-552 4050; www.hutchesons glasgow.com; 158 Ingram St; mains £14-30; ⊘food noon-10pm; 🅿) This upstairs dining room in a historic Merchant City building has real wow factor with superhigh ceilings, leadlights, ornamental fireplaces and 19th-century boardroom-style seating. Steaks are the order of the day with various delicious aged options available, but oysters, duck and other dishes are served too. A good portion

of the short menu is vegetarian. The bar downstairs is equally plush.

✖ West End

In many ways, the West End is the powerhouse of Glasgow's foodie scene, with the area around Byres Rd a hub of quality eating and Argyle St in Finnieston a heartland of fashionable new eating options. Great Western Rd and Gibson St also offer excellent choice.

78 Cafe Bar
CAFE, VEGETARIAN £

(Map p116; ☏0141-576 5018; www.the78cafebar. com; 10 Kelvinhaugh St; mains £5-9; ⊘food noon-9pm; 🛜🅿) More a comfortable lounge than your typical veggie restaurant, this cafe offers cosy couch seating and reassuringly solid wooden tables, as well as an inviting range of ales. The low-priced vegan food includes hearty stews and curries, and there's regular live music in a very welcoming atmosphere.

Bay Tree
CAFE £

(Map p116; ☏0141-334 5898; www.thebaytree westend.co.uk; 403 Great Western Rd; mains £7-16; ⊘11am-10pm Tue-Fri, from 10am Sat & Sun; 🛜🅿) There are many good cafes along this section of Great Western Road, but the Bay Tree is still a solid choice. It has lots of vegan and vegetarian options, smiling staff, filling mains (mostly Middle Eastern and Greek), generous salads and a good range of hot drinks. It's famous for its all-day breakfasts.

★ Stravaigin
SCOTTISH, FUSION ££

(Map p116; ☏0141-334 2665; www.stravaigin.co.uk; 28 Gibson St; bar dishes £6-12, restaurant mains £15-19; ⊘food 11am-11pm; 🛜) Stravaigin is a serious foodie's delight, with a menu constantly pushing the boundaries of originality and offering creative culinary excellence. With a range of eating spaces across three levels, it's pleasingly casual and easygoing. The entry level also has a buzzing bar with a separate menu. Scottish classics like haggis take their place alongside a range of Asian-influenced dishes. It's all delicious.

★ Ox & Finch
FUSION ££

(Map p116; ☏0141-339 8627; www.oxandfinch.com; 920 Sauchiehall St; small plates £4-10; ⊘noon-10pm; 🛜🅿) This fashionable place could almost sum up the thriving modern Glasgow eating scene, with a faux-pub name, sleek but comfortable contemporary decor, tapas-sized dishes and an open kitchen.

Grab a cosy booth and be prepared to have your tastebuds wowed with innovative, delicious creations aimed at sharing, drawing on French and Mediterreanean influences but focusing on quality Scottish produce.

★ Mother India INDIAN ££

(Map p116; ☑ 0141-221 1663; www.motherindia. co.uk; 28 Westminster Tce, Sauchiehall St; mains £11-16; ☺ 5.30-10.30pm Mon-Thu, noon-11pm Fri, 1-11pm Sat, 1-10pm Sun; ☎🍴👶) Glasgow curry buffs forever debate the merits of the city's numerous excellent South Asian restaurants; Mother India features in every discussion. It's been a stalwart for years, and the quality and innovation on show are superb. The three dining areas are all attractive and it makes an effort for kids, with a separate menu.

There are various other innovative, distinct sister restaurants around town.

Alchemilla MEDITERRANEAN ££

(Map p116; ☑ 0141-337 6060; www.thisis alchemilla.com; 1126 Argyle St; plates £5-14; ☺ food noon-10pm) The number of quality eating options opening on the Finnieston strip is phenomenal, and this is a fine example. The casual open-kitchen eatery offers small, medium and large plates with an eastern Mediterranean feel. Interesting ingredients and intriguing textures are key to delicious dishes ideal for sharing. There are lots of meat-free options and a list of hard-to-find natural wines.

Left Bank BISTRO ££

(Map p116; ☑ 0141-339 5969; www.theleftbank. co.uk; 33 Gibson St; mains £9-16; ☺ 9am-10pm Mon-Fri, from 10am Sat & Sun; ☎🍴👶) 🌱 Huge windows fronting the street reveal this outstanding eatery specialising in gastronomic delights and lazy afternoons. Lots of little spaces filled with couches and chunky tables make for intimacy. The wide-ranging menu is good for devising a shared meal of delightful creations using seasonal and local produce, with an eclectic variety of influences. Breakfasts and brunches are also highlights.

The Finnieston SEAFOOD ££

(Map p116; ☑ 0141-222 2884; www.thefinnieston bar.com; 1125 Argyle St; mains £13-23; ☺ food 11am-10pm Mon-Sat, to 9pm Sun; ☎) 🌱 A flagship of this increasingly vibrant strip, this gastropub recalls the area's sailing heritage with a cosily romantic below-decks atmosphere and artfully placed nautical motifs. It's been well thought through, with excellent G&Ts (slurp one in the little courtyard) and cocktails accompanying a short menu of high-quality upmarket pub fare focusing on sustainable Scottish seafood. Its brunches are also recommendable.

Six by Nico GASTRONOMY ££

(Map p116; ☑ 0141-334 5661; www.sixbynico.co.uk; 1132 Argyle St; tasting menu around £30, wine flight £25; ☺ noon-10pm Tue-Sun) Chefs are creative types and get easily bored whisking up the same menu day after day. Nico has fixed that by presenting a themed degustation that lasts for six weeks. Sometimes it will be focused on a specific national cuisine; other times it's a more whimsical subject, like Disney or childhood. Presentation and quality are impeccable.

Bothy SCOTTISH ££

(Map p116; ☑ 0845 166 6032; www.bothyglasgow. co.uk; 11 Ruthven Lane; mains £12-20; ☺ food noon-10pm Mon-Fri, from 10am Sat & Sun; ☎) This West End player, boasting a combo of modern design and comfy retro furnishings, blows apart the myth that Scottish food is stodgy and uninteresting. The Bothy dishes out traditional home-style fare with a modern twist. It's filling, but leave room for dessert. Smaller lunch plates are a good deal, and there's an attractive outdoor area.

★ Ubiquitous Chip SCOTTISH £££

(Map p116; ☑ 0141-334 5007; www.ubiquitouschip. co.uk; 12 Ashton Lane; 2-/3-course lunch £20/24, mains £20-30, brasserie mains £13-16; ☺ restaurant noon-2.30pm & 5-11pm Mon-Sat, 12.30-3pm & 5-10pm Sun; ☎) 🌱 The original champion of Scottish produce, Ubiquitous Chip is legendary for its still-unparalleled cuisine and lengthy wine list. Named to poke fun at Scotland's culinary reputation, it offers a French touch but resolutely Scottish ingredients, carefully selected and following sustainable principles. The elegant courtyard space offers some of Glasgow's best dining, while, above, the cheaper brasserie (longer hours) offers exceptional value for money.

Two bars, including the cute 'Wee Pub' down the side alley, offer plenty of drinking pleasure. There's always something going on at the Chip – check the website for upcoming events.

Butchershop Bar & Grill STEAK £££

(Map p116; ☑ 0141-339 2999; www.butchershop glasgow.com; 1055 Sauchiehall St; steaks £19-36; ☺ noon-10pm Sun-Thu, to 1am Fri & Sat; ☎) Offering several different cuts of traceably sourced, properly aged beef, this is one of the best spots in Glasgow for a tasty, served-as-you-want-it steak. It's a perfect lunch venue after the Kelvingrove Art Gallery & Museum. There are seats out the front if the weather happens to be fine. It also has a little seafood on the menu and decently mixed cocktails.

Cail Bruich SCOTTISH £££
(Map p116; ☑ 0141-334 6265; www.cailbruich. co.uk; 725 Great Western Rd; 2-/3-course lunch £22/28, set menus £45-55; ⊗ 6-9pm Mon & Tue, noon-2pm & 6-9pm Wed-Sat, 1-7pm Sun; 🖝) In an elegant if rather nondescript dining room, the kitchen here turns out some memorable modern Scottish fare. The forage ethos brings surprising, tangy, herbal flavours to plates that are always interesting but never pretentious. Everything from the amuse-bouche to the homemade bread is top-notch; the degustation menu (£55) with optional wine flight (£40) combines the best on offer.

Gannet SCOTTISH £££
(Map p116; ☑ 0141-204 2081; www.thegannetgla. com; 1155 Argyle St; mains £21-25; ⊗ 5-9.30pm Tue & Wed, noon-2pm & 5-9.30pm Thu-Sat, 1-7.30pm Sun; 🖝) 🍴 In vogue but not starchy, this jewel of the Finnieston strip offers a cosy wood-panelled ambience and gourmet food that excels on presentation and taste without venturing towards cutting-edge. The short, polished daily menu features quality produce sourced mostly from southern Scotland and the interesting wine list backs it up very well indeed. Solicitous, professional service is another plus point.

✖ East End

McCune Smith CAFE £
(Map p110; ☑ 0141-548 1114; www.mccunesmith. co.uk; 3 Duke St; light meals £4-8; ⊗ 8am-4pm; 🖝) This stellar cafe is named after a University of Glasgow graduate who was a noted abolitionist and the first African American to hold a medical degree. The hospitable owners take their coffee seriously and offer scrumptious breakfast and brunch fare, plus delicious sandwiches and soups in a luminous, high-ceilinged interior. They bake their own bread and half the menu or more is vegan.

A'Challtain SEAFOOD ££
(Map p110; ☑ 0141-237 9220; www.baadglasgow. com/achalltainn; Moncur St; mains £12-19; ⊗ food noon-9pm Tue-Sat, 11am-7pm Sun) Part of the Barras markets' revitalisation, A'Challtain is upstairs in the Art & Design Centre and is an enticing destination for quality seafood, with standout oysters and squat lobster, and superfresh fish specials. Balcony seating is great for lunch or when the market's on. There's a cocktail bar below too, and a bakery-cafe was shortly to open at the time of research.

The all-day Sunday brunch menu is aimed squarely at the hungover (apart from the raw oysters of course).

✖ Southside

Cafe Strange Brew CAFE £
(☑ 0141-440 7290; www.facebook.com/cafestrange brew; 1082 Pollokshaws Rd; dishes £5-11; ⊗ 9am-5pm Mon-Sat, to 4pm Sun) This has such cachet as the Southside's, if not the city's, best cafe, that you'll be waiting in line most days. It's worth the enforced contemplation though, with generous, vibrant, filling brunchy fare that draws on global influences as well as closer-to-home inspiration. Presentation is a high point; leave room for the sinfully sticky desserts.

The Fish People Cafe SEAFOOD ££
(☑ 0141-429 8787; www.thefishpeoplecafe.co.uk; 350 Scotland St; mains £15-23; ⊗ noon-9pm Tue-Thu, to 10pm Fri & Sat, to 4pm Sun) A subway-station forecourt is an unlikely spot to find a seafood restaurant of such quality, but pop out of Shields Rd and here it is. The adjacent fish shop supplies the raw materials for simple but perfectly prepared dishes that shine with quality. Service is also exceptionally welcoming. It's opposite Scotland Street School, but worth the trip from anywhere in town.

🍷 Drinking & Nightlife

Glaswegians are known to enjoy a beverage or two, and some of Britain's best nightlife is found in the din and sometimes roar of the city's pubs and bars. There are as many different styles of bar as there are punters to guzzle in them. Craft beer, single malt, Scottish gins; it's all here.

Glasgow's clubbing scene has been affected by recent closures, but it's still lively. Glaswegians usually hit clubs after the pubs have closed, so many clubs offer discounted admission and cheaper drinks if you go early. Entry costs £5 to £10 (up to £25 for big events), although bars often hand out free passes. There's a minimum age of 21 years to enter some of them. Clubs shut comparatively early, so ask around to find out where the after-parties are.

City Centre

★ DogHouse Merchant City
BAR

(Map p110; ☑ 0141-552 6363; www.brewdog.com; 99 Hutcheson St; ⊙ 11am-midnight Mon-Fri, from 10am Sat & Sun; ☎) Brewdog's zingy beers are matched by its upbeat attitude, so this Merchant City spot was always going to be a fun place. An open kitchen doles out slidery, burgery smoked-meat fare while 25 taps run quality craft beer from morning till night.

★ Sub Club
CLUB

(Map p110; ☑ 0141-248 4600; www.subclub.co.uk; 22 Jamaica St; ⊙ typically 11pm-3am Tue, Fri & Sat) Scotland's most famous house club is still going strong several decades on. Saturday

---

LGBTIQ+ GLASGOW

Glasgow has a vibrant LGBT scene, with the gay quarter found in and around the Merchant City (particularly Virginia, Wilson and Glassford Sts). The city's gay community has a reputation for being very friendly.

Most Glaswegians are very tolerant, but you may encounter disapproval away from central areas. Same-sex marriage was legalised in Scotland in 2014.

Many straight clubs and bars have gay and lesbian nights. To tap into the scene, check out *The List* (www.list.co.uk) and the free *Scots Gay* (www.scotsgay.co.uk) magazine and website.

Waterloo Bar (Map p110; ☑ 0141-248 7216; www.facebook.com/waterloobar1; 306 Argyle St; ⊙ noon-11pm Mon-Thu, to midnight Fri & Sat, 12.30-11pm Sun) This traditional pub is Scotland's oldest gay bar. It attracts punters of all ages. It's very friendly and, with a large group of regulars, a good place to meet people away from the scene.

Katie's Bar (Map p110; ☑ 0141-237 3030; www.katiesbar.co.uk; 17 John St; ⊙ noon-midnight; ☎) With an easily missed entrance between a Spanish and an Italian restaurant, this basement bar is a friendly LGBT pub with a pool table and regular gigs at weekends. It's a pleasant, low-key space to start off the night and especially popular with women.

Underground (Map p110; ☑ 0141-553 2456; www.facebook.com/undergroundglasgo; 6a John St; ⊙ noon-midnight; ☎) Downstairs on cosmopolitan John St, Underground sports a relaxed crowd and, crucially, a free jukebox. You'll be listening to indie rather than Abba here.

AXM (Map p110; ☑ 0141-552 5761; www.axmglasgow.com; 80 Glassford St; ⊙ 11pm-3am Wed & Sun, from 10pm Thu-Sat) This popular Manchester club's Glasgow branch is a cheery spot, not too scene-y, with all welcome. It makes for a fun place to finish off a night out.

Delmonica's (Map p110; ☑ 0141-552 4803; www.delmonicas.co.uk; 68 Virginia St; ⊙ noon-midnight Mon-Sat, from 12.30pm Sun) In the heart of the Pink Triangle, this is a popular bar with a good mix of ages and orientations. It packs out in the evenings when bingo, quizzes, drag shows and other fun keep things lively, and it's a pleasant spot for a quiet drink during the day. Come here before the adjacent Polo Lounge, as you might get a free pass.

Polo Lounge (Map p110; ☑ 0845 659 5905; www.pologlasgow.co.uk; 84 Wilson St; admission £3-7; ⊙ 9pm-3am) One of the city's principal gay clubs is an attractive spot, with opulent furnishings. The downstairs Polo Club and Club X areas pack out on weekends, when bouncers can be strict; just the main bars open on other nights. One of them, the **Riding Room** (Map p110; ☑ 0845 659 5904; www.theridingroom.co.uk; 58 Virginia St; ⊙ 9pm-3am Sun-Thu, from 7pm Fri & Sat), has cabaret shows.

Speakeasy (Map p110; ☑ 0845 166 6036; www.speakeasyglasgow.co.uk; 10 John St; ⊙ 5pm-3am Wed-Sat) Relaxed and friendly bar that starts out publike and gets louder with gay anthem DJs as the night progresses. Entry is free and it serves food until 9pm, so it's a good all-rounder. Upstairs from midnight on Saturdays is the Midnight Glory club night (£3).

at the Sub Club is one of Glasgow's legendary nights, offering serious clubbing with a sound system that aficionados usually rate as the city's best. The claustrophobic, last-one-in vibe is not for those faint of heart. Check the website for other nights.

Pot Still PUB
(Map p110; 0141-333 0980; www.thepotstill. co.uk; 154 Hope St; 11am-midnight;) The cheeriest and cosiest of places, the Pot Still has a time-warp feel with its creaky floor and old-style wrought-iron-legged tables. There's a superb whisky selection and knowledgeable staff – constantly up and down ladders to get at bottles – to back it up. Tasty pies (£4) are on hand for solid sustanance.

Shilling Brewing Co MICROBREWERY
(Map p110; 0141-353 1654; www.shillingbrewing company.co.uk; 92 West George St; noon-11pm Mon, to midnight Tue-Thu, to 1am Fri & Sat, 12.30-11pm Sun;) Drinking in former banks is a Glasgow thing and this central brewpub offers some of the best of it. The wooden, high-ceilinged space has huge windows out to the city centre and room to spare to try its beers; the almost grapefruity Unicorn IPA is a real palate cleanser. Another couple of dozen taps showcase guest craft brews from around Scotland.

ABC CLUB
(O₂ABC; Map p110; 0141-332 2232; www.o2abc glasgow.co.uk; 300 Sauchiehall St; 11pm-3am Thu-Sat;) Both nightclub and venue, this reference point on Sauchiehall has two large concert spaces with big-name gigs, plus several attractive bars. It's a good all-rounder, with three well-established club nights: Jellybaby on Thursday, Propaganda on Friday and Love Music on Saturday. Admission is around £5.

Laboratorio Espresso CAFE
(Map p110; 0141-353 1111; www.labespr.tumblr. com; 93 West Nile St; 7.30am-5.30pm Mon-Fri, from 9am Sat, from 11am Sun) A chic space, all concrete and glass, this cafe offers the best coffee we've tried in Glasgow. It's sourced properly, and served in delicious double-shot creations with authentically concentrated espresso; soy milk is available. There are a couple of tables outside even in the coldest weather. Pastries and biscotti are on hand, but it's all about the brew here.

Babbity Bowster PUB
(Map p110; 0141-552 5055; www.babbity bowster.com; 16-18 Blackfriars St; 11am-midnight Mon-Sat, from 12.30pm Sun;) In a quiet corner of Merchant City, this handsome spot is perfect for a tranquil daytime drink, particularly in the adjoining beer garden. Service is attentive, and the smell of sausages may tempt you to lunch; it also offers accommodation. This is one of the city centre's most charming pubs, in one of its noblest buildings. There's a regular folk-music scene here.

Bar Gandolfi COCKTAIL BAR
(Map p110; 0141-552 4462; www.cafegandolfi. com; 64 Albion St; noon-midnight;) Above the cafe of the same name, this little upstairs gem is far from the often-boisterous Merchant Sq pubs opposite. Pared-back unvarnished wooden stools and tables, offbeat art exhibitions and a large kitchen-bar area – there's far more space behind it than on the patrons' side – create a relaxing space for a quality cocktail or spirit. There's also tasty, well-sourced food available.

Artà BAR, CLUB
(Map p110; 0845 166 6018; www.arta.co.uk; 62 Albion St; 5pm-midnight Thu, to 3am Fri, 12.30pm-3am Sat;) Set in a former cheese market, this place is very OTT with its Mediterranean-villa decor; it really does have to be seen to be believed. Despite the luxury, it's got a relaxed, chilled vibe and makes a decent cocktail. It also does Spanish-influenced food but it's better visited as a bar and nightclub.

Horse Shoe PUB
(Map p110; 0141-248 6368; www.thehorseshoe barglasgow.co.uk; 17 Drury St; 10am-midnight Sun-Fri, from 9am Sat) This legendary city pub and popular meeting place dates from the late 19th century and is largely unchanged. It's a picturesque spot, with the longest continuous bar in the UK, but its main attraction is what's served over it – real ale and good cheer. Upstairs in the lounge is some of the best-value pub food (dishes £4 to £10) in town.

Cathouse CLUB
(Map p110; 0141-248 6606; www.cathouse. co.uk; 15 Union St; 10.30pm-3am Wed-Sun;) It's mostly rock, alternative and metal with a touch of Goth and post-punk at this

long-standing indie venue. There are two dance floors: upstairs is pretty intense with lots of metal and hard rock; downstairs is a little more tranquil. Admission ranges from free to £6.

Nice 'n' Sleazy
BAR, CLUB

(Map p110; ☑ 0141-333 0900; www.nicensleazy. com; 421 Sauchiehall St; ⊙ noon-3am Mon-Sat, from 1pm Sun; ☜) On the rowdy Sauchiehall strip, students from the nearby School of Art make the buzz here reliably friendly. If you're over 35, you'll feel like a professor not a punter, but retro decor, a big selection of tap and bottled beers, 3am closing and nightly alternative live music downstairs followed by a club at weekends make this a winner.

A couple of similar options on this strip mean that you can pick and choose. There's also popular, cheap Tex-Mex food here (dishes £6 to £9).

Butterfly & the Pig
PUB

(Map p110; ☑ 0141-221 7711; www.thebutterflyand thepig.com; 153 Bath St; ⊙ 11am-1am Mon-Thu, to 3am Fri & Sat, 12.30pm-midnight Sun; ☜) A breath of fresh air, this offbeat spot makes you feel comfortable as soon as you plunge into its basement depths. The decor is eclectic with a cosy retro feel. There's regular live jazz or similar and a sizeable menu – if you can decipher it – of pub grub, plus a rather wonderful tearoom upstairs, great for breakfast before the pub opens.

Corinthian Club
BAR

(Map p110; ☑ 0141-552 1101; www.thecorinthian club.co.uk; 191 Ingram St; ⊙ 11am-2am Sun-Thu, noon-3am Fri & Sat; ☜) A breathtaking domed ceiling and majestic chandeliers make this casino a special space. Originally a bank and later Glasgow's High Court, this regal building's main bar is a stunner. Cosy wrap-around seating and room to spare are complemented by a restaurant, a nightclub, a piano bar, a roof terrace and a champagne bar, as well as the casino area itself.

Classic Grand
CLUB

(Map p110; ☑ 0141-847 0820; www.classicgrand. com; 18 Jamaica St; ⊙ hours vary; ☜) Rock, industrial, electronic and powerpop grace the stage and the turntables at this unpretentious central venue. It doesn't take itself too seriously, drinks are cheap and the locals are welcoming. Hours vary according to events, but core opening is 11pm to 3am Thursday to Saturday.

☕ West End

★ Inn Deep
BAR

(Map p116; ☑ 0141-357 1075; www.inndeep.com; 445 Great Western Rd; ⊙ noon-midnight Mon-Sat, 12.30-11pm Sun) Descend the stairs to find yourself in a fabulous spot on the banks of the Kelvin. It's glorious on a fine day (and Glaswegians set that bar pretty low) to grab a craft beer and spill out onto the riverside path in a happy throng. The vaulted interior spaces under the bridge are also characterful.

Brewdog Glasgow
PUB

(Map p116; ☑ 0141-334 7175; www.brewdog.com; 1397 Argyle St; ⊙ noon-midnight; ☜) Perfect for a pint after the Kelvingrove Art Gallery & Museum, this great spot offers the delicious range of artisanal beers from the brewery of the same name. Punk IPA is refreshingly hoppy, with other favourites, new releases and guest beers also to explore. Tasting flights mean you can try several, while burgers and dogs are on hand to soak it up.

Òran Mór
BAR, CLUB

(Map p116; ☑ 0141-357 6200; www.oran-mor. co.uk; cnr Byres & Great Western Rds; ⊙ 9am-2am Mon-Wed, to 3am Thu-Sat, 10am-3am Sun; ☜) Now some may be uncomfortable with the thought of drinking in a church. But we say: the Lord giveth. This bar, restaurant, club and theatre venue is a likeable and versatile spot with an attractive interior and a fine whisky selection to replace the holy water. The lunchtime **A Play, a Pie and a Pint** (www.playpiepint.com; £10-14 incl pie & pint; ⊙ 1pm Mon-Sat) is an excellent feature.

Brel
BAR

(Map p116; ☑ 0141-342 4966; www.brelbar.com; 39 Ashton Lane; ⊙ noon-midnight Sun-Thu, to 1am Fri & Sat; ☜) Perhaps the best bar on Ashton Lane, Brel can seem tightly packed, but there's a conservatory for eating out the back so you can pretend you're sitting outside when it's raining, and when the sun does peek through, there's an appealing tiered beer garden. Its got a huge range of Belgian beers, and also does mussels and langoustines among other tasty fare.

Hillhead Bookclub
BAR

(Map p116; ☑ 0141-576 1700; www.hillheadbook club.co.uk; 17 Vinicombe St; ⊙ 11am-midnight Mon-Fri, from 10am Sat & Sun; ☜) Atmosphere in spades is the call sign of this easygoing West End bar. An ornate wooden ceiling overlooks two levels of well-mixed cocktails, seriously cheap drinks, comfort food and numerous intriguing decorative touches. There's even a ping-pong table in a cage.

☆ Entertainment

Glasgow is Scotland's entertainment city, from classical music, fine theatres and ballet to an amazing range of live music venues. To tap into the scene, check out *The List* (www.list.co.uk), an invaluable free events guide.

For theatre tickets, book directly with the venue. For concerts, a useful booking centre is **Tickets Scotland** (Map p110; ☑ 0141-204 5151; www.tickets-scotland.com; 237 Argyle St; ⊙ 9am-6pm Mon-Wed & Fri-Sat, to 7pm Thu, 11.30am-5.30pm Sun).

Live Music

Glasgow is the king of Scotland's live music scene. Year after year, touring musicians and travellers alike name Glasgow one of their favourite cities in the world to enjoy live music. Much of Glasgow's character is encapsulated in the soul and humour of its inhabitants, and the main reason for the city's musical success lies within its audience and the musical community it has bred and nurtured for years.

There are so many venues it's impossible to keep track of them all. For the latest listings, pick up a copy of the *Gig Guide* or check its website (www.gigguide.co.uk). It's available free in most pubs and venues.

★ King Tut's Wah Wah Hut   LIVE MUSIC
(Map p110; ☑ 0141-221 5279; www.kingtuts.co.uk; 272a St Vincent St; ⊙ noon-midnight) One of the city's premier live-music pub venues, hosting bands every night of the week. A staple of the local scene, and a real Glasgow highlight.

Hug & Pint   LIVE MUSIC
(Map p116; ☑ 0141-331 1901; www.thehugandpint.com; 171 Great Western Rd; ⊙ noon-midnight; ⊛) With bands almost daily in the downstairs space, this comfortable local is a great destination. It would be anyway for its excellent atmosphere, highly original Asian-influenced vegan food and colourful interior.

Hydro   LIVE PERFORMANCE
(Map p116; ☑ 0844 395 4000; www.thessehydro.com; Finnieston Quay; ⊛) A spectacular modern building to keep the adjacent 'Armadillo' company, the Hydro amphitheatre is a phenomenally popular venue for big-name concerts and shows.

13th Note Café   LIVE MUSIC
(Map p110; ☑ 0141-553 1638; www.13thnote.co.uk; 50-60 King St; ⊙ noon-11pm or midnight; ⊛) Cosy basement venue with small independent bands as well as weekend DJs and regular comedy and theatre performances. At street level the pleasant cafe does decent vegetarian and vegan food (£7 to £10, until 9pm).

Barrowland Ballroom   CONCERT VENUE
(The Barrowlands; Map p110; www.glasgow-barrowland.com; 244 Gallowgate) A down-at-heel but exceptional old dancehall above the Barras market catering for some of the larger acts that visit the city. It's one of Scotland's most atmospheric venues with its sprung floor and authentic character.

Clyde Auditorium   LIVE PERFORMANCE
(Map p116; ☑ 0844 395 4000; www.sec.co.uk; Finnieston Quay) Also known as the Armadillo because of its bizarre shape, the Clyde adjoins the SEC Centre auditorium, and caters for big national and international acts.

SEC Centre   LIVE PERFORMANCE
(Map p116; ☑ 0844 395 4000; www.sec.co.uk; Finnieston Quay) The headquarters of the complex that includes the Clyde Auditorium and Hydro is an exhibition space and sometime concert venue.

Audio   CONCERT VENUE
(Map p110; www.facebook.com/audioglasgow; 14 Midland St) In the bowels of Central station, this is an atmospheric venue for regular concerts by touring acts, particularly of the rock and metal varieties.

Ivory Blacks   LIVE MUSIC
(Map p110; ☑ 07538 463752; www.reverbnation.com/venue/ivoryblacks; 56 Oswald St) Inside Central station, this sweaty, atmospheric space is an unpretentious venue for gigs, which are regular and mostly of the rock and metal variety.

Cinemas

★ Glasgow Film Theatre   CINEMA
(Map p110; ☑ 0141-332 6535; www.glasgowfilm.org; 12 Rose St; adult/child £10.50/5.50) This much-loved three-screener off Sauchiehall St shows art-house cinema and classics.

Grosvenor Cinema   CINEMA
(Map p116; ☑ 0845 166 6002; www.grosvenorwestend.co.uk; Ashton Lane) This sweet cinema puts you in the heart of West End eating and nightlife for post-show debriefings.

ANDRYSPB21/SHUTTERSTOCK ©

1. Glasgow Cathedral (p112)
This is a fine example of Gothic architecture, with some roof timbers dating from the 14th century.

2. West End (p114)
This studenty, bohemian neighbourhood is for many the most engaging area of Glasgow. It's centred on the Victorian grandeur of the University of Glasgow (pictured) and Kelvingrove Art Gallery & Museum (p114).

3. Mackintosh at the Willow (p110)
This elaborate recreation of the famous Sauchiehall St tearoom was launched in 2018 to celebrate Charles Rennie Mackintosh's 150th anniversary.

4. Sharmanka Kinetic Theatre (p107)
This extraordinary mechanical theatre features a series of large, wondrous figures – sculpted from bits of scrap and elaborate carvings – that perform humorous and tragic stories of the human spirit.

ROBIN MITCHELL ©

Theatres & Concert Halls

Citizens' Theatre
THEATRE

(☑ 0141-429 0022; www.citz.co.uk; 119 Gorbals St) South of the Clyde, this is one of the top theatres in Scotland. It's well worth trying to catch a performance here. A major redevelopment was about to begin at last visit and the theatre will be closed until 2020.

Tramway
PERFORMING ARTS

(☑ 0845 330 3501; www.tramway.org; 25 Albert Dr; ⊙ 9.30am-8pm Mon-Sat, 10am-6pm Sun; ☎) Occupying a former tram depot, this buzzy cultural centre has performance and exhibition spaces as well as a popular cafe. It's a real Southside community hub, with an unusual garden (☑ 0141-433 2722; www.the hiddengardens.org.uk; ⊙ 10am-8pm Tue-Sat, noon-6pm Sun Apr-Sep, 10am-4pm Tue-Sat, noon-4pm Sun Oct-Mar) FREE out the back. It attracts cutting-edge theatrical groups, is the home of Scottish Ballet and hosts a varied range of artistic exhibitions. It's very close to Pollokshields East train station.

Theatre Royal
CONCERT VENUE

(Map p110; ☑ 0844 871 7647; www.glasgowtheatre royal.org.uk; 282 Hope St) Proudly sporting an eye-catching modern facelift, Glasgow's oldest theatre is the home of Scottish Opera.

City Halls
CONCERT VENUE

(Map p110; ☑ 0141-353 8000; www.glasgow concerthalls.com; Candleriggs) In the heart of Merchant City, there are regular performances in this beautiful rectangular auditorium by the Scottish Chamber Orchestra and the Scottish Symphony Orchestra.

Glasgow Royal Concert Hall
CONCERT VENUE

(Map p110; ☑ 0141-353 8000; www.glasgow concerthalls.com; 2 Sauchiehall St; ☎) A feast of classical music is showcased at this concert hall, the modern home of the Royal Scottish National Orchestra. There are also regular pop, folk and jazz performances, typically by big-name solo artists.

Centre for Contemporary Arts
ARTS CENTRE

(Map p110; ☑ 0141-352 4900; www.cca-glasgow. com; 350 Sauchiehall St; ⊙ 10am-midnight Mon-Thu, noon-1am Fri & Sat, to midnight Sun, galleries until 6pm Tue-Sun) This is a chic venue making terrific use of space and light. It showcases the visual and performing arts, including movies, talks and galleries. There's a good cafe-bar here too.

Sport

Two football clubs – Rangers and Celtic – totally dominate the sporting scene in Scotland, having vastly more resources than other clubs and a long history (and rivalry). This runs along traditionally partisan lines, with Rangers representing Protestant supporters, and Celtic, Catholic. It's worth going to a game; both play in magnificent arenas with great atmosphere. Games between the two (normally four a year) are fiercely contested, but tickets aren't sold to the general public; you'll need to know a season-ticket holder. In recent years, Rangers have had to work their way back up the divisions after a financial meltdown, returning to the top flight in 2016.

Celtic FC
FOOTBALL

(☑ 0871 226 1888; www.celticfc.net; Celtic Park, Parkhead) Playing in green and white hoops, Celtic are one of Glasgow's big two football clubs and traditionally represent the Catholic side of the divide. There are daily stadium tours (adult/child £12.50/7.50). Catch bus 61 or 62 from outside St Enoch centre.

Rangers FC
FOOTBALL

(☑ 0871 702 1972; www.rangers.co.uk; Ibrox Stadium, 150 Edmiston Dr) One of Glasgow's big two football clubs, Rangers play in blue and traditionally represent the Protestant, pro-Union side of the divide. They recently returned to the top division after a financial meltdown. Tours of the stadium and trophy room run Friday to Sunday (£15/5 per adult/child). Take the subway to Ibrox station.

🛍 Shopping

Boasting the UK's largest retail phalanx outside London, Glasgow is a shopaholic's paradise. The 'Style Mile' around Buchanan and Argyle Sts and Merchant City (particularly upmarket Ingram St) is a fashion hub, while the West End has quirkier, more bohemian shopping options: it's great for vintage clothing. The weekend Barras market in the East End is very worthwhile.

The Barras
MARKET

(Map p110; ☑ 0141-552 4601; www.glasgow-barrow land.com; btwn Gallowgate & London Rd; ⊙ 10am-5pm Sat & Sun) Glasgow's legendary weekend flea market, the Barras on Gallowgate, is a fascinating mixture of on-trend openings and working-class Glasgow. Genuine old stalls flogging time-faded glasses, posters

DON'T MISS

VINTAGE & RETRO SHOPPING

Snag a bargain and bring out the hipster in you with Glasgow's fabulous range of retro rag stores.

Mr Ben (Map p110; ☑ 0141-553 1936; www.mrbenretroclothing.com; 101 King St; ⊘12.30-6pm Mon & Tue, from 10.30am Wed-Sat, 12.30-5.30pm Sun) This cute place is one of Glasgow's best destinations for vintage clothing, with a great selection of brands like Fred Perry, as well as more glam choices and even outdoor gear.

Randall's Antique & Vintage Centre (Map p110; ☑ 07752 658045; www.facebook.com/randallsantiqueandvintagecentre; Stevenson St West; ⊘9am-5pm Sat & Sun) This is a real treasure trove of the once loved, the tacky, the tawdry, the magnificent and the curious from the not-so-recent past. It's an excellent set-up with several sellers and a top spot to browse. Don't take the kids; they'll make you feel ancient with their incredulity at items that you remember using not so very long ago.

Glasgow Vintage & Flea Market (Map p110; www.theglasgowmarkets.com; 17 Bain St; ⊘10am-4pm 4th Sun of month) Normally taking place on one Sunday per month, this market packs out St Luke's (Map p110; ☑ 0141-552 8378; www.stlukesglasgow.com; 17 Bain St; ⊘noon-midnight; ☎) with quality vintage and secondhand stalls. Check the website for upcoming dates.

Glasgow Vintage Company (Map p116; ☑ 0141-338 6633; www.facebook.com/theglasgow vintagecompany; 453 Great Western Rd; ⊘11am-6pm Mon-Sat, to 5pm Sun) With a little more breathing room than some of Glasgow's vintage shops, this one offers relaxed browsing.

Caledonia Books (Map p116; ☑ 0141-334 9663; www.caledoniabooks.co.uk; 483 Great Western Rd; ⊘10.30am-6pm Mon-Sat) This characterful spot is just what a secondhand bookshop should be, with a smell of dust and venerability and a wide range of intriguing volumes on the slightly chaotic shelves.

Antiques & Interiors (Map p116; www.antiques-atlas.com; Ruthven Lane; ⊘11am-5.30pm Mon-Sat, noon-5pm Sun) Up the back of the quirky Ruthven Lane complex, this arcade has several shops specialising in antiques, design and retro items.

and DVDs that you'd struggle to give away are juxtaposed with vintage classics, very earthy traders' pubs and a street scene where fake designer gear is marked down and dodgy characters peddle smuggled cigarettes.

It's an intriguing stroll, as much for the assortment of local characters as for what's on offer. People come here just to wander, and parts of it have a real feel of a nearly vanished Britain of whelk stalls and rag-and-bone merchants. Watch your wallet.

Barras Art & Design　　ARTS & CRAFTS (BAaD; Map p110; ☑ 0141-237 9220; www.baad glasgow.com; Moncur St; ⊘noon-midnight Tue-Sat, 11am-10pm Sun) This workshop zone for artists and designers in the heart of the Barras has helped pep up the area and bring a new wave of folk in. It's a lovely covered courtyard with a bar, cafe and restaurant, as well as pop-up and other shops. There are events on most weekends, including a monthly farmers market.

Adjacent to the main building, converted shipping containers hold more workshops and creative spaces.

Princes Square　　SHOPPING CENTRE (Map p110; ☑ 0141-221 0324; www.princessquare. co.uk; 48 Buchanan St; ⊘10am-7pm Mon-Fri, 9am-6pm Sat, 11am-5pm Sun) Set in a magnificent 1841 renovated square with elaborate ironwork and an exuberant metal leaf-and-peacock facade, this place has lots of beauty and fashion outlets, including Vivienne Westwood. There's a good selection of restaurants and cafes, as well as a bar with a roof terrace.

Argyll Arcade　　JEWELLERY (Map p110; ☑ 0141-248 5257; www.argyll-arcade. com; Buchanan St; ⊘10am-5.30pm Mon-Sat, noon-5pm Sun) This splendid historic arcade doglegs between Buchanan and Argyle Sts and has done since before Victoria reigned. It's quite a sight with its end-to-end jewellery and watch shops. Top-hatted doorpeople greet nervously excited couples shopping for diamond rings.

Hidden Lane
ARTS & CRAFTS

(Map p116; www.thehiddenlaneglasgow.com; 1103 Argyle St) Well concealed down a passageway off the Finnieston strip, these back alleys house a colourful mix of arty shops and studios well worth investigating. There's a tearoom, jewellery store, yoga centre and plenty more.

Slanj Kilts
CLOTHING

(Map p110; ☑ 0141-248 5632; www.slanjkilts.com; 80 St Vincent St; ☺ 9.30am-5.30pm Mon-Wed, Fri & Sat, to 6.30pm Thu, 11am-4pm Sun) This upbeat shop is a top spot to hire or buy kilts both traditional and modern, as well as other tartan wear and a range of T-shirts and other accessories. Always worth a look.

ℹ Information

INTERNET ACCESS

There's a free wi-fi zone across the city centre. You can get a local SIM card for about a pound and data packages are cheap.

Gallery of Modern Art (☑ 0141-229 1996; www.glasgowlife.org.uk; Royal Exchange Sq; ☺ 10am-5pm Mon-Thu, to 8pm Thu, 11am-5pm Fri & Sun; 🛜) Basement library; free internet access. Bookings recommended.

Hillhead Library (☑ 0141-276 1617; www. glasgowlife.org.uk; 348 Byres Rd; ☺ 10am-8pm Mon-Thu, to 5pm Fri & Sat, noon-5pm Sun; 🛜) Free internet terminals.

iCafe (☑ 0141-353 6469; www.icafe.uk.com; 250 Woodlands Rd; per hr £2.50; ☺ 8.30am-9.30pm; 🛜) Sip a coffee and munch on a pastry while you check your emails on superfast internet connections. It's actually a very good cafe in its own right. There are other branches, including one on **Sauchiehall St** (☑ 0141-353 1553; www.icafe.uk.com; 315 Sauchiehall St; ☺ 7am-10pm Mon-Fri, from 8am Sat & Sun; 🛜).

Mitchell Library (☑ 0141-287 2999; www. glasgowlife.org.uk; North St; ☺ 9am-8pm Mon-Thu, to 5pm Fri & Sat) Free internet access; bookings recommended.

Yeeha Internet Cafe (www.yeeha-internet-cafe.co.uk; 2nd fl, 48 West George St; per hr £2.50; ☺ 9.30am-6pm Mon-Fri, from 10am Sat) Upstairs location in the heart of the city.

MEDICAL SERVICES

Glasgow Dental Hospital (☑ 0141-211 9600; www.nhsggc.org.uk; 378 Sauchiehall St)

Glasgow Royal Infirmary (☑ 0141-211 4000; www.nhsggc.org.uk; 84 Castle St) Medical emergencies and outpatient facilities.

Queen Elizabeth University Hospital (☑ 0141-201 1100; www.nhsggc.org.uk; 1345 Govan Rd) Modern; south of the river.

POST

Many shops across the city centre offer postal service, including some supermarkets that are open Sundays. Service is reliable.

Post Office (Map p110; ☑ 0345 611 2970; www.postoffice.co.uk; 136 West Nile St; ☺ 9am-5.30pm Mon-Sat) The most central full-service post office.

TOURIST INFORMATION

Glasgow Tourist Office (Map p110; www. visitscotland.com; 158 Buchanan St; ☺ 9am-5pm Mon-Sat, 10am-4pm Sun Nov-Apr, 9am-6pm Mon-Sat, 10am-4pm Sun May, Jun, Sep & Oct, 9am-7pm Mon-Sat, 10am-5pm Sun Jul & Aug; 🛜) The city's tourist office is in the centre of town. It opens at 9.30am on Thursday mornings.

USEFUL WEBSITES

Glasgow Food Geek (www.glasgowfoodgeek. co.uk) Likeably unpretentious food blog with restaurant reviews and the odd recipe.

Herald Scotland (www.heraldscotland.com) Online edition of Glasgow's broadsheet, printed since 1783.

The List (www.list.co.uk) Comprehensive entertainment listings and restaurant reviews.

Lonely Planet (www.lonelyplanet.com/ scotland/glasgow) Destination information, hotel bookings, traveller forum and more.

People Make Glasgow (www.peoplemake glasgow.com) Good city-run website with events and more.

SPT (www.spt.co.uk) Glasgow public transport information.

ℹ Getting There & Away

AIR

Ten miles west of the city in Paisley, **Glasgow International Airport** (GLA; ☑ 0344 481 5555; www.glasgowairport.com; 🛜) handles international and domestic flights. Facilities include car hire, ATMs and a supermarket where you can buy SIM cards.

Thirty miles southwest of Glasgow near Ayr, **Glasgow Prestwick Airport** (PIK; ☑ 0871 223 0700; www.glasgowprestwick.com) is used by Ryanair and some other budget airlines, with connections mostly to southern Europe.

BUS

All long-distance buses arrive at and depart from **Buchanan bus station** (Map p110; ☑ 0141-333 3708; www.spt.co.uk; Killermont St; 🛜), which has pricey lockers, ATMs and wi-fi.

GLASGOW INFORMATION

Megabus (☏ 0141-352 4444; www.megabus. com) Your first port of call if you're looking for the cheapest fare. Megabus offers very cheap demand-dependent prices on many major bus routes, including to Edinburgh and London.

National Express (☏ 0871 781 8181; www. nationalexpress.com) Runs daily to several English cities.

Scottish Citylink (☏ 0871 266 3333; www. citylink.co.uk) Has buses to Edinburgh (£7.90, 1¼ hours, every 15 minutes) and most major towns in Scotland.

There are also buses from Buchanan bus station direct to/from Edinburgh Airport (£12, one hour, half-hourly).

TRAIN

As a general rule, **Glasgow Central station** (www.scotrail.co.uk; Gordon St) serves southern Scotland, England and Wales, and **Queen Street station** (www.scotrail.co.uk; George St) serves the north and east (including Edinburgh). Buses run between the two stations every 10 minutes. There are direct trains more than hourly to London Euston station; they're much quicker (4½ hours) and more comfortable than the bus. The fare is £65/142/183 for advance/off-peak/ any-time singles.

ScotRail (p468) runs Scottish trains. Destinations include the following:

Aberdeen (£41.80, 2½ to 3½ hours, hourly)
Dundee (£23.20, 1½ hours, hourly)
Edinburgh (£14.40, 50 minutes, every 15 minutes)
Fort William (£30.80, 3¾ hours, four daily)
Inverness (£92.50; 3½ to four hours; five direct daily, three on Sunday)
Oban (£25.30, three hours, three to six daily)

ⓘ Getting Around

TO/FROM THE AIRPORT
Glasgow International Airport

Bus 500 runs every 10 or 15 minutes (half-hourly or hourly late at night) from Glasgow International Airport to Buchanan bus station via Central and Queen Street train stations (single/ return £8/12, 25 minutes). This is a 24-hour service. You can include a day ticket on the bus network for £12 total or a four-day ticket for £18.

Another bus, the 77, covers the same route via the West End twice hourly, taking longer.

A taxi costs around £25.

Glasgow Prestwick Airport

There's a dedicated train station at the airport, with four trains an hour (two on Sundays) to Glasgow (£8.30, 40 to 55 minutes). You get a 50% discount from the airport by showing your boarding pass.

At night, bus X99 replaces the train.

A taxi to the centre of Glasgow costs £55 to £65.

BICYCLE

The **Nextbike** (www.nextbike.co.uk; per 30min £1) citybike scheme is easy; download the app for the most convenient use.

There are several places to hire a bike; the tourist office has a full list.

Gear Bikes (☏ 0141-339 1179; www.gearbikes. com; 19 Gibson St; half-day/day/week £15/20/80; ⊙10am-6pm Mon-Sat, noon-5pm Sun)

Bike for Good (☏ 0141-248 5409; www. bikeforgood.org.uk; 65 Haugh Rd; half-day/ day/week £15/20/70; ⊙ 9am-5pm Mon-Sat, to 8pm Wed)

BUS

City bus services, mostly run by **First Glasgow** (☏ 0141-420 7600; www.firstglasgow.com), are frequent. You can buy tickets when you board buses, but on most you must have the exact change. Short journeys in town cost £1.60 or £2.30; a day ticket (£4.50) is good value and is valid until 1am, when a night network starts. A weekly ticket is £17. Check route maps online at www.spt.co.uk.

CAR & MOTORCYCLE

The most difficult thing about driving in Glasgow is the sometimes-confusing one-way system. For short-term parking (up to two hours), you've got a decent chance of finding something on the street, paying at the meters, which cost up to £4 per hour. Otherwise, multistorey car parks are probably your best bet and are not so expensive. Ask your hotel in advance if it offers parking discounts.

There are numerous car-rental companies; both big names and discount operators have airport offices.

Arnold Clark (☏ 0141-423 9559; www.arnold clarkrental.com; 43 Allison St; ⊙8am-5.30pm Mon-Fri, to 4pm Sat, 11am-4pm Sun)

Avis (☏ 0344 544 6064; www.avis.co.uk; 70 Lancefield St; ⊙8am-6pm Mon-Fri, to 3pm Sat, 10am-2pm Sun)

Enterprise (☏ 0141-221 2124; www.enterprise. co.uk; 40 Oswald St; ⊙7am-9pm Mon-Fri, 8am-4pm Sat, 10am-3pm Sun)

Europcar (☏ 0371 384 3471; www.europcar. co.uk; 76 Lancefield Quay; ⊙8am-6pm Mon-Fri, to 4pm Sat)

Hertz (☏ 0141-229 6120; www.hertz.co.uk; Jury's Inn, 80 Jamaica St; ⊙8am-6pm Mon-Fri, to 1pm Sat, 10am-2pm Sun)

TAXI

There's no shortage of taxis, and if you want to know anything about Glasgow, striking up a conversation with a cabbie is a good place to start. Fares are very reasonable – you can get across the city centre for around £6, and there's no surcharge for calling a taxi. You can pay by credit card with **Glasgow Taxis** (🖉 0141-429 7070; www.glasgowtaxis.co.uk) if you order by phone; most of its taxis are wheelchair accessible. Download its app to make booking easy.

TRAIN

There's an extensive suburban network of trains in and around Glasgow; tickets should be purchased before travel if the station is staffed, or from the conductor if it isn't.

There's also an underground line, the subway, that serves 15 stations in the city centre, and west and south of the city (single £1.70). The train network connects with the subway at Buchanan Street underground station, next to Queen Street overground station (p137), and St Enoch underground station, near Glasgow Central station (p137). The All Day Ticket (£4.10) gives unlimited travel on the subway for a day, while the Roundabout ticket gives a day's unlimited train and subway travel for £7. The subway runs roughly from 6.30am to 11.30pm Monday to Saturday but annoyingly runs only from 10am to 6pm on Sunday.

AROUND GLASGOW

Good transport connections mean it's easy to plan day trips out of Glasgow. Around the city are varied attractions – the noble abbey at Paisley, home of the eponymous patterned fabric; the estuary mouth twin towns of Greenock and Gourock, and Blantyre, home to an evocative castle and birthplace of David Livingstone.

Paisley

POP 76,600

Once a proud weaving town, but these days effectively a southwestern suburb of Glasgow, Paisley gave its name to the distinctive teardrop-patterned fabric. Though flanked by green countryside, it's not an engaging place, but has an ace up its sleeve in the shape of the magnificent abbey, which is well worth the short trip from Glasgow to see. The museum is also recommendable.

Trains run from Glasgow Central station to Paisley (£3.60, 10 minutes, eight hourly).

★ **Paisley Abbey**   ABBEY
(🖉 0141-889 7654; www.paisleyabbey.org.uk; Abbey Close; ⊙ 10am-3.30pm Mon-Sat) **FREE**
Paisley Abbey is well worth the short trip

from Glasgow. This majestic Gothic building was founded in 1163 by Walter Fitzalan, first high steward of Scotland and ancestor of the Stuart dynasty. Apart from the magnificent perspective down the nave, points of interest include royal tombs, some excellent 19th- and 20th-century stained glass, including three windows by Edward Burne-Jones, and the 10th-century Celtic Barochan Cross.

A monastery for Cluny monks, it was damaged by fire during the Wars of Independence in 1306 but rebuilt soon after. Most of the nave is 14th or 15th century. The building was mostly a ruin from the 16th century until the 19th-century restoration, completed in 1928. A window commemorates the fact that William Wallace was educated by monks from this monastery.

Paisley Museum   MUSEUM
(🖉 0300 300 1210; www.renfrewshireleisure.com; High St; ⊙ 11am-4pm Tue-Sat, 2-5pm Sun) **FREE**
At the western end of High St, worthwhile Paisley Museum is housed in an elegant Victorian Grecian edifice and has a decent collection of 19th-century Scottish art as well as a bit of everything else, from dinosaur footprints to a stuffed terrier, and plenty of information on the town's textile history and the famous Paisley pattern's origins in ancient Mesopotamia.

Greenock & Gourock

POP 53,700

Fused together these days, the towns of Gourock and Greenock were always warming sights to a Glasgow mariner's heart as their ships rounded the point from the Firth of Clyde into the river proper and thence to home. Gourock's firthside views are spectacular, and Greenock's historical sandstone buildings – despite the scrappy shopping complexes in its centre – invite a stop. Before the Clyde was dredged, larger ships couldn't progress further than Greenock, which consequently raked in considerable customs dues. In summer and on fine days, these become little resort towns for Glasgow families looking for a day out.

Greenock was the birthplace of James Watt, the inventor whose work on the steam engine was one of the key developments of the Industrial Revolution. A statue of him marks his birthplace; behind this looms the spectacular Italian-style Victoria Tower on the municipal buildings, constructed in 1886.

McLean Museum & Art Gallery   MUSEUM, GALLERY

(☑ 01475-715624; www.inverclyde.gov.uk; 15 Kelly St, Greenock; ⊙10am-5pm Mon-Sat) FREE In the historic centre of Greenock, this was closed for refurbishment at the time of research and due to reopen in 2019. There's quite an extensive collection, with displays charting the history of steam power and Clyde shipping. The art gallery has some fine pieces, and several canvases give you an idea of just how busy Greenock's harbour once was. There's also a pictorial history of Greenock through the ages, displays from China, Japan and Egypt, and a natural history section.

❶ Getting There & Away

Greenock is 27 miles west of Glasgow, and Gourock is 3 miles further west. The Glasgow–Greenock–Gourock leg of the Clyde to Forth pedestrian and cycle route follows an old train track for 10 miles.

There are trains from Glasgow Central station (£7.30, 35 to 50 minutes, two to three hourly) and hourly buses stopping in both towns.

Gourock's train station is next to the ferry terminal. Gourock is an important ferry hub:

Argyll Ferries (☑ 0800 066 5000; www. argyllferries.co.uk) A passenger service to Dunoon (£4.65, 25 minutes, half-hourly Monday to Saturday, hourly Sunday) on Argyll's Cowal Peninsula.

Caledonian MacBrayne (CalMac; ☑ 0800 066 5000; www.calmac.co.uk) From Wemyss Bay (pronounced 'weemz'), 8 miles south of Gourock, ferries run to Rothesay on Bute (per passenger/car £3.15/11.30, 35 minutes, hourly or better). Trains from Glasgow (£7.60, 50 minutes, more than hourly) connect with ferries.

Kilcreggan Ferry (☑ 01475-721281; www.spt. co.uk) A passenger-only ferry service to Kilcreggan (adult/child £2.60/1.30, 15 minutes, 12 to 13 daily Monday to Saturday); buy tickets on board.

Western Ferries (☑ 01369-704452; www. western-ferries.co.uk) Has a car service (adult/ child/car £4.60/2.30/17.60, 20 minutes, two to three hourly) to Dunoon from McInroy's Point, 2 miles south from Gourock train station on the Irvine road; Scottish Citylink buses run here.

Blantyre

POP 17,000

Though technically part of Lanarkshire, Blantyre, birthplace of David Livingstone, is an outlying suburb of Glasgow these days. It was founded as a cotton mill in the late 18th century. Livingstone, a zealous and pious doctor, missionary and explorer, was raised in a one-room tenement and worked in the mill by day from the age of 10, going to the local school at night. Amazingly for a time in which most mill workers were barely able to write their names, he managed to get himself into university to study medicine.

Trains run from Glasgow Central station to Blantyre (20 minutes, three hourly).

David Livingstone Centre   MUSEUM

(www.david-livingstone-trust.org; 165 Station Rd, Blantyre; ⛟) This museum tells the story of David Livingstone's life from his early days in Blantyre to the 30 years he spent in Africa, where he named the Victoria Falls on one of his numerous journeys. A major redevelopment was in place at our last visit; it's scheduled to reopen in 2019. The grassy park the museum is set in makes a perfect picnic spot. Head straight down the hill from the station to reach the museum.

Bothwell Castle   CASTLE

(HES; ☑ 01698-816894; www.historicenvironment. scot; Castle Ave, Uddingston; adult/child £5/3; ⊙9.30am-5.30pm Apr-Sep, 10am-4pm Sat-Wed Oct-Mar) It's a 30-minute walk from Blantyre along the river to Bothwell Castle, regarded as the finest 13th-century castle in Scotland. The stark, roofless, red-sandstone ruins are substantial and, largely due to their beautiful green setting, romantic.

Southern Scotland

Best Places to Eat

➡ Cobbles (p152)
➡ Auld Alliance (p171)
➡ Coltman's (p144)
➡ Night Safe Bistro (p148)
➡ La Vigna (p157)

Best Places to Stay

➡ Corsewall Lighthouse Hotel (p175)
➡ Knockinaam Lodge (p176)
➡ Old Bank House (p145)
➡ Old Priory (p151)
➡ Edenbank House (p151)

Why Go?

Though wise folk are well aware of its charms, for many people southern Scotland is just something to drive through on the way to northern Scotland. Big mistake. But it does mean you'll find breathing room here in summer, and peaceful corners.

Proximity to England brought raiding and strife; grim borderland fortifications saw skirmishes aplenty. There was loot to be had in the Borders, where large prosperous abbeys ruled over agricultural communities. Regularly ransacked before their destruction in the Reformation, the ruins of these churches, linked by cycling and walking paths, are among Scotland's most atmospheric historic sites.

The rolling west enjoys extensive forest cover between bustling market towns. The hills cascade down to sandy stretches of coastline blessed with Scotland's sunniest weather. It's the land of Robert Burns, whose verse reflected his earthy attitudes and active social life.

When to Go
Ayr

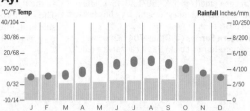

May Take a fortnight to cross the whole region, hiking the gorgeous Southern Upland Way.

Jun The perfect time to visit the region's numerous stately homes, with spectacular blooming gardens.

Oct Hit Galloway's forests to see red deer battling it out in the rutting season.

BORDERS REGION

The Borders has had a rough history: centuries of war and plunder have left a battle-scarred landscape, encapsulated by the magnificent ruins of the Border abbeys. Their wealth was an irresistible magnet during cross-frontier wars, and they were destroyed and rebuilt numerous times. Today these massive stone shells are the region's finest attraction. And don't miss Hermitage Castle: nothing encapsulates the region's turbulent history like this spooky stronghold.

But the Borders is also genteel. Welcoming villages with ancient traditions pepper the countryside and grandiose mansions await exploration. It's fine walking and cycling country too, the hills lush with shades of green. Offshore you'll find some of Europe's best cold-water diving.

Peebles

POP 8600

With a picturesque main street set on a ridge between the River Tweed and the Eddleston Water, Peebles is one of the most handsome of the Border towns. Though it lacks a major sight, the agreeable atmosphere and good walking options in the rolling, wooded hills thereabouts will entice you to linger for a couple of days.

◉ Sights & Activities

The riverside walk along the River Tweed has plenty of grassed areas ideal for a picnic, and there's a children's playground (near the main road bridge).

Nearby in Glentress forest is the busiest of the 7stanes mountain-biking hubs, as well as osprey viewing and marked walking trails. There are also swing and zip-line forest routes, not to mention camping huts (see www.glentressforestlodges.co.uk). In town, you can hire bikes to explore the region from Bspoke Cycles (p144).

There are further mountain-biking trails at Innerleithen, 7 miles east of Peebles.

★ **7stanes Glentress**   MOUNTAIN BIKING
(www.7stanesmountainbiking.com) FREE Two miles east of Peebles off the A72, in Glentress forest, this is the busiest of the 7stanes mountain-biking hubs, and also offers osprey viewing and marked walking trails. The **shop** (☑ 01721-724522; www.tweedvalleybikehire.com;

Glentress Forest; hardtail per day £25; ⊘ 9am-5pm or 6pm) here hires rigs and will put you on the right trail for your ability. You can arrange courses with **Dirt School** (☑ 07545 339938; www.dirtschool.co.uk). These are some of Britain's best biking routes.

You can also hire bikes from Bspoke (p144) in Peebles itself. There's on-site cabin accommodation at Glentress too.

Go Ape   ADVENTURE SPORTS
(www.goape.co.uk; Glentress Forest; adult/child £33/25; ⊘ Feb-Nov) This forest-top adventure course features rope bridges, swings and a glorious long zip line over trees and a reservoir. Opening times and days vary widely through the season, so check the website and book ahead online.

🛏 Sleeping

Rosetta Holiday Park   CAMPSITE £
(☑ 01721-720770; www.rosettaholidaypark.com; Rosetta Rd; tent site for 1/2 people £12/20; ⊘ mid-Mar–Oct; P 🞀 🖘 🐾) This campsite, about 800m north of the town centre, has an appealing green setting with lots of trees and grass. There are plenty of amusements for the kids, such as a bowling green and a games room. It also has static caravans of various grades for weeklong stays.

Lindores Guest House   B&B ££
(☑ 01721-729040; www.lindoresgh.co.uk; 60 Old Town; s £50-60, d £70-80; 🖘) Run by an interesting, kind couple, this rather striking house offers commodious, flowery rooms. Both en-suite and shared bathrooms are available and showers are great. Breakfast features really delicious home-baked bread among other goodies. There's secure parking for bikes and motorbikes.

Cringletie House   HOTEL £££
(☑ 01721-725750; www.cringletie.com; Edinburgh Rd/A703; r £175-210; P 🞀 🐾) Luxury without snobbery is this hotel's hallmark, and more power to it. To call this a house is being coy: it's an elegant baronial mansion, 2 miles north of Peebles, set in lush, wooded grounds. Rooms are plush and feature genteel elegance and linen so soft you could wrap a newborn in it. There's an excellent restaurant on site.

A delightful cottage here sleeps six people and has a deck and a hot tub. Dogs are also exceptionally well catered for at Cringletie.

Southern Scotland Highlights

1 Border Abbeys (p146) Exploring the noble, evocative ruins – Dryburie is our favourite – and the area's other excellent historic sights.

2 Culzean Castle (p162) Admiring the 18th-century architectural genius of a castle perched on wild sea cliffs.

3 Hermitage Castle (p149) Pondering the tough old life on the England–Scotland frontier at this desolate castle.

4 Kirkcudbright (p170) Exploring this charming, dignified town, marvelling at the creative flair of its inhabitants.

EDINBURGH

EAST LOTHIAN

Cockburnspath

A1

St Abbs ⑨

Coldingham ⑨

Eyemouth

MIDLOTHIAN

A701

A702

Lammermuir Hills

Duns

Moorfoot Hills

Lauder

M8

Lanark

New Lanark ⑦

SOUTH LANARKSHIRE

Biggar

Peebles

A72

Tweed

Galashiels

Melrose

Abbotsford

Dryburgh Abbey

Selkirk

Smailholm

Coldstream

Kelso

A698

Kirk Yetholm

Border Abbeys ①

Town Yetholm

M74

Clyde

Abington

A74(M)

A708

B709

SCOTTISH BORDERS

Teviot

Jedburgh

A68

Hawick

Sanquhar

A76

Moffat

Eskdalemuir

White Esk

Teviot

Hermitage Castle ③

Northumberland National Park

Border Forest Park

Thornhill

Southern Upland Way ⑧

Esk

Newcastleton

Nith

A74(M)

Langholm

Cairn Water

Lockerbie

NORTHUMBERLAND

Dumfries

Gretna Green

Gretna

Caerlaverock Castle

New Abbey

Carlisle

ENGLAND

Solway Firth

CUMBRIA

Kirkoswald

Lake District National Park

N

0   40 km
0   20 miles

Eating

Cocoa Black　　　　　　　　CAFE £
(☎ 01721-723764; www.cocoablack.com; 1 Cuddy Bridge; sweets £2-5; ⏰ 9.30am-5pm Mon-Fri, 9am-5pm Sat, 10.30am-5pm Sun; 🕸️🍴) Chocaholics should make a beeline for this friendly cafe, where exquisite cakes and other patisserie offerings will satisfy any cacao-focused cravings. It also runs a school where you can learn to make them yourself.

★ Coltman's　　　　　BISTRO, DELI ££
(☎ 01721-720405; www.coltmans.co.uk; 71 High St; mains £13-16; ⏰ 10am-5pm Sun-Wed, to 10pm Thu-Sat; 🕸️) 🍴 This main street deli has numerous temptations, such as excellent cheeses and Italian smallgoods, as well as perhaps Scotland's tastiest sausage roll. Behind the shop, the good-looking dining area serves up confident bistro fare and light snacks with a variety of culinary influences, using top-notch local ingredients. Upstairs is a cosy bar.

Osso　　　　　　　　　　BISTRO ££
(☎ 01721-724477; www.ossorestaurant.com; Innerleithen Rd; light meals £8-14, dinner mains £17-24; ⏰ 10am-4.30pm & 6-9pm Tue-Sat, 10am-4.30pm Sun & Mon) A good stop for home baking, coffee, light meals or sandwiches at any time of day, this bistro comes into its own at dinner time. A short, regularly changed menu of delicious dishes offers a quality dining experience. Everything is prepared with patience; slow-cooked meats are a highlight.

ℹ️ Information

Peebles Tourist Office (☎ 01721-728095; www.visitscottishborders.com; 23 High St; ⏰ 9am-5pm Mon-Sat, 11am-4pm Sun Apr-Jun, Sep & Oct, 9am-5.30pm Mon-Sat, 10am-4pm Sun Jul & Aug, 9am-5pm Mon-Fri, 9.30am-4pm Sat, 11am-4pm Sun Nov & Dec, 9am-5pm Mon-Fri, 9.30am-4pm Sat Jan-Mar) Helpful office in the centre of town, although its future was in doubt at the time of research.

ℹ️ Getting There & Around

The bus stop is beside the post office on Eastgate. Bus X62 runs half-hourly (hourly on Sundays) to Edinburgh (£5.60, 1¼ hours). In the other direction it heads for Melrose (£6.20, 1¼ hours).

Bspoke Cycles (☎ 01721-723423; www.bspokepeebles.co.uk; Old Tweeddale Garage, Innerleithen Rd; bikes per day from £25; ⏰ 9am-5.30pm Mon-Sat) Rents hybrid bikes (£25 per day), road bikes (£35), hardtail mountain bikes (£35) and e-bikes (£60).

Melrose

POP 2500

Tiny, charming Melrose is a polished village running on the well-greased wheels of tourism. Sitting at the feet of the three heather-covered Eildon Hills, Melrose has a classic market square and one of the great abbey ruins. Just outside town is Abbotsford (p146), the home of Sir Walter Scott, which makes another superb visit.

◎ Sights & Activities

There are many attractive walks in the **Eildon Hills**, accessible via a footpath off Dingleton Rd (the B6359) south of Melrose, or via the trail along the River Tweed.

The St Cuthbert's Way (p150) long-distance walking path starts in Melrose, while the coast-to-coast Southern Upland Way (p150) passes through town. You can do a day's walk along St Cuthbert's Way as far as Harestanes (16 miles), on the A68 near Jedburgh, and return to Melrose on the hourly Jedburgh–Galashiels bus. The Tweed Cycle Route (p150) also passes through Melrose.

★ Melrose Abbey　　　　　　　RUINS
(HES; ☎ 01896-822562; www.historicenvironment.scot; adult/child £6/3.60; ⏰ 9.30am-5.30pm Apr-Sep, 10am-4pm Oct-Mar) Perhaps the most interesting of the Border abbeys, red-sandstone Melrose was repeatedly destroyed by the English in the 14th century. The remaining broken shell is pure Gothic and the ruins are famous for their decorative stonework – look out for the pig gargoyle playing the bagpipes. Though Melrose had a monastery way back in the 7th century, this abbey was founded by David I in 1136 for Cistercian monks, and later rebuilt by Robert the Bruce, whose heart is buried here.

The ruins date from the 14th and 15th centuries, and were repaired by Sir Walter Scott in the 19th century. The adjoining museum has many fine examples of 12th- to 15th-century stonework and pottery found in the area. Note the impressive remains of the 'great drain' outside – a medieval sewerage system.

🎊 Festivals & Events

Melrose Rugby Sevens　　　　　SPORTS
(www.melrose7s.com; ⏰ mid-Apr) Rugby followers fill the town to see this famous one-day sevens competition.

TRAQUAIR HOUSE

One of Scotland's great country houses, **Traquair House** (☑ 01896-830323; www.traquair.co.uk; Innerleithen; adult/child/family £9/4.50/25; ☉ 11am-5pm Easter-Sep, to 4pm Oct, to 3pm Sat & Sun Nov) has a powerful, ethereal beauty, and exploring it is like time travel. Odd, sloping floors and a musty odour bestow a genuine feel, and parts of the building are believed to have been constructed long before the first official record of its existence in 1107. The massive tower house was gradually expanded but has remained virtually unchanged since the 17th century. Traquair is about 6 miles southeast of Peebles.

Since the 15th century, the house has belonged to various branches of the Stuart family, and the family's unwavering Catholicism and loyalty to the Stuart cause led to famous visitors like Mary, Queen of Scots and Bonnie Prince Charlie, but also to numerous problems after the deposal of James II of England in 1688. The family's estate, wealth and influence were gradually whittled away, as life as a Jacobite became a furtive, clandestine affair.

One of Traquair's most interesting places is the concealed room where priests secretly lived and performed Mass – up until 1829 when the Catholic Emancipation Act was finally passed. Other beautiful, time-worn rooms hold fascinating relics, including the cradle used by Mary for her son, James VI of Scotland (who also became James I of England), and fascinating letters from the Jacobite Earls of Traquair and their families, including one particularly moving one written from death row in the Tower of London.

The main gates to the house were locked by one earl in the 18th century until the day a Stuart king reclaimed the throne in London, so meanwhile you'll have to enter by a side gate.

In addition to the house, there's a garden **maze**, a small **brewery** producing the tasty Bear Ale, and a series of **craft workshops**. You can also stay here in one of three opulent B&B rooms (single/double £130/190).

Bus X62 runs from Edinburgh via Peebles to Innerleithen and on to Galashiels and Melrose.

Borders Book Festival　　LITERATURE
(www.bordersbookfestival.org; Harmony House, St Mary's Rd; ☉ mid-Jun) This book festival is run in Melrose over four days at Harmony House, a 19th-century mansion in a pretty garden.

🛏 Sleeping & Eating

★ Old Bank House　　B&B ££

(☑ 01896-823712; www.oldbankhousemelrose.co.uk; 27 Buccleuch St; s/d £55/70; 🛜🍽) Right in the centre, this is a superb B&B in a charming old building. The owner's artistic touch is evident throughout, from walls covered with paintings, some his own, to a house full of curios and tasteful art-nouveau features, and a sumptuous breakfast room. Rooms are spacious with comfortable furniture and modern bathrooms; they're complemented by a generous can-do attitude.

This place goes the extra mile, and that makes it a great Borders base.

Dunfermline House　　B&B ££

(☑ 01896-822411; www.dunfermlinehouse.co.uk; Buccleuch St; d £65; 🛜) Very close to Melrose Abbey, this place offers a genuinely warm welcome and comfortable, flowery rooms in classic B&B style. It's very walker- and cyclist-friendly and breakfast is well above average, with plenty of fruit on hand.

★ Townhouse　　BOUTIQUE HOTEL £££

(☑ 01896-822645; www.thetownhousemelrose.co.uk; Market Sq; s/d/superior d £100/138/159; 🅿🛜) The classy Townhouse exudes warmth and professionalism, and has some of the best rooms in town, tastefully furnished with attention to detail. The superior rooms are enormous in size with lavish furnishings and excellent en suites. Standard rooms are a fair bit smaller but they're refurbished and very comfortable. It's well worth the price.

There is an excellent restaurant (p146) located on-site.

Burts Hotel　　HOTEL £££

(☑ 01896-822285; www.burtshotel.co.uk; Market Sq; s/d/superior d £78/145/155; 🅿🛜🍽) Set in an early-18th-century house, Burts is a famously reliable central hotel that retains

THE RIDING OF THE MARCHES

The Riding of the Marches, also known as the Common Riding, takes place in early summer in the major Borders towns. Like many Scottish festivals, it has ancient origins, dating back to the Middle Ages when riders would be sent to the town boundary to check on the common lands. The colourful event normally involves extravagant convoys of horse riders following the town standard as it is paraded along a well-worn route. Festivities vary between towns but usually involve lots of singing, sport, pageants and concerts, and plenty of whisky. If you want to zero in on the largest of the Ridings, head to Jedburgh for the Jethart Callant's Festival (p149).

much of its period charm. Rooms vary – the renovated ones with modern plaid fabrics are very smart, and the superiors are extra spacious. There are plenty of singles too. The air of friendly formality makes it a favourite with older visitors. Appealing food is also on hand.

Townhouse SCOTTISH ££

(☑ 01896-822645; www.thetownhousemelrose.co.uk; Market Sq; mains £14-18; ⊙noon-2pm & 6-9pm; ☎) The brasserie and restaurant here turn out just about the best gourmet cuisine in town and offer decent value. There's some rich, elaborate, beautifully presented fare, with plenty of venison and other game choices, but for a lighter feed you can always opt for the range of creative lunchtime sandwiches.

It is found within the boutique hotel (p145) of the same name.

ⓘ Getting There & Away

The Borders Railway runs from Edinburgh to Tweedbank (£10.70, one hour, half-hourly), which is 1.5 miles from Melrose. Buses run half-hourly from here into Melrose.

Regular X62 buses run to/from Edinburgh (£7.50, 2½ hours, half-hourly Monday to Saturday) via Peebles. On Sundays this service runs hourly but only from nearby Galashiels, connected to Melrose by regular buses.

For other Borders destinations, you'll most likely need to change in Galashiels.

Around Melrose

★**Abbotsford** HISTORIC BUILDING

(☑ 01896-752043; www.scottsabbotsford.com; visitor centre free, house adult/child £11/5; ⊙10am-5pm Apr-Oct, to 4pm Nov-Mar, house closed Dec-Feb) Just outside Melrose, this is where to discover the life and works of Sir Walter Scott, to whom we arguably owe both the modern novel and our mind's-eye view of Scotland. This whimsical, fabulous house where he lived – and which ruined him when his publishers went bust – really brings this 19th-century writer to life. The grounds on the banks of the Tweed are lovely, and Scott drew much inspiration from rambles in the surrounding countryside.

A modern visitor centre displays memorabilia and gives an intriguing overview of the man; the smart audio-guide system – with one designed for kids – will then show you round the house. In the house are some gloriously over-the-top features, with elaborate carvings, enough swords and dirks to equip a small army, a Chinese drawing room and a lovely study and library.

A wing of the house offers luxurious self-catering accommodation designed for large groups.

Abbotsford is 2 miles west of Melrose; buses between Galashiels and Melrose will drop you at the nearby Tweedbank roundabout. It's an easy walk from Tweedbank station, reachable in under an hour from Edinburgh. You can also walk from Melrose along the southern bank of the Tweed. There's a cafe-restaurant atop the visitor centre.

★**Dryburgh Abbey** RUINS

(HES; ☑ 01835-822381; www.historicenvironment.scot; adult/child £6/3.60; ⊙9.30am-5.30pm Apr-Sep, 10am-4pm Oct-Mar) This is the most beautiful and complete of the Border abbeys, partly because the neighbouring town of Dryburgh no longer exists (another victim of the wars) and partly because of its lovely site by the Tweed in a sheltered birdsong-filled valley. Dating from about 1150, the abbey belonged to the Premonstratensians, a religious order founded in France, and evokes 12th-century monastic life more successfully than its nearby counterparts. The pink-hued stone ruins are the burial place of Sir Walter Scott.

The abbey is 5 miles southeast of Melrose on the B6404, which passes the famous Scott's View outlook. Hike there along the southern bank of the River Tweed, or take a bus to the nearby village of Newtown St Boswells.

Selkirk

POP 5600

While the noisy throb of machinery once filled the valleys below Selkirk, a prosperous mill town in the early 19th century, today it sits placid and pretty – apart from busy traffic through the centre – atop its steep ridge. Naughty millworkers who fell foul of the law would have come face to face in court with Sir Walter Scott, sheriff here for three decades.

Sights

Halliwell's House Museum MUSEUM
(☑ 01750-726456; www.scotborders.gov.uk; Halliwell's Close; ⊙ 11am-4pm Mon-Sat, noon-3pm Sun Apr-Oct) FREE Halliwell's House Museum is the oldest building (1712) in Selkirk. The museum charts local history with an engrossing exhibition, and the **Robson Gallery** has changing exhibitions. There's some local information available here too.

Sir Walter Scott's Courtroom MUSEUM
(☑ 01750-726456; www.scotborders.gov.uk; Market Sq; ⊙ 10am-4pm Mon-Fri, 11am-3pm Sat late Mar-Sep, plus 11am-3pm Sun May-Aug, noon-3pm Mon-Sat Oct) FREE Drop into Sir Walter Scott's Courtroom, where there's an exhibition on the man's life and writings, plus a fascinating account of the courageous explorer Mungo Park (born near Selkirk) and his search for the River Niger.

Sleeping & Eating

County Hotel INN £
(☑ 01750-721233; www.countyhotelselkirk.co.uk; 1 High St; s/d/executive d incl breakfast £50/60/77; P🞀🞀) Located in the centre of town, this is a former coaching inn. It has the odd Norwegian touch and comfortable, modernised rooms that vary in size. Executive rooms are superspacious and handsome. It has a stylish restaurant and lounge with original art. Room-only rates are also available for £7.50 less per person.

Philipburn House Hotel HOTEL ££
(☑ 01750-720747; www.bw-philipburnhousehotel.co.uk; Linglie Rd/A708; r incl breakfast £110-190; P🞀🞀) On the edge of town, this former dower house has a jazzy 21st-century look that hasn't ruined its historic features, as well as appealing renovated rooms and a snug bar and restaurant. The luxury rooms are particularly good – some have a jacuzzi, while another is a split-level affair with a double balcony. Room-only rates are available, and tariffs range widely.

Self-catering facilities are on offer in the separate lodges, where pets are also welcome.

SIR WALTER SCOTT

Sir Walter Scott (1771–1832) is one of Scotland's greatest literary figures. Born in Edinburgh, he spent time on his grandparents' farm at Sandyknowe in the Borders as a child. It was here, rambling around the countryside, that he developed a passion for historical ballads and Scottish heroes. After studying in Edinburgh he bought Abbotsford, a country house in the Borders.

The Lay of the Last Minstrel (1805) was an early critical success. Further works earning him an international reputation included *The Lady of the Lake* (1810), set around Loch Katrine and the Trossachs. He later turned his hand to novels and was instrumental in their development. His first novel, *Waverley* (1814), which dealt with the 1745 Jacobite rebellion, set the classical pattern of the historical novel. Other works included *Guy Mannering* (1815) and *Rob Roy* (1817). He became something of an international superstar, and heavily influenced writers and artists such as Austen, Dickens and Turner. His writings virtually single-handedly revived interest in Scottish history and legend, and much of our Scottish clichés of today – misty glens, fierce warriors, tartan – are largely down to him. His organisation of the visit of George IV to Edinburgh reintegrated Highland dress into society.

Later in life Scott wrote obsessively to stave off bankruptcy. Tourist offices stock a *Sir Walter Scott Trail* booklet, which details many places associated with him in the Borders.

Fleece　　　　　　　　　　　　　　BISTRO **££**

(☑01750-725501; www.thefleecebarandkitchen. co.uk; 1 Ettrick Tce; mains £10-16; ⊙noon-2pm & 5-9pm Tue-Sat, noon-6pm Sun) Selkirk's best place to eat is in the heart of things. It has a bar as well as a well-thought-out range of classic Scottish and other British ingredients. Presentation is strong and it manages to cover both pub-style meals and more innovative combinations.

ⓘ Getting There & Away

Bus X95 runs at least hourly between Carlisle and Edinburgh (£7.40, two hours) via Hawick, Selkirk and Galashiels. It's usually faster to hop off a bus at Galashiels and catch the train into Edinburgh.

Hawick

POP 13,900

Straddling the River Teviot, Hawick (pronounced 'hoik') is one of the largest towns in the Borders and has long been a major production centre for knitwear. There are several large outlets to buy jumpers and other woollens around town. Hawick is also famous for rugby; the local club has produced dozens of Scotland internationals.

⊙ Sights

Heart of Hawick　　　　　　　VISITOR CENTRE

(www.heartofhawick.co.uk; Kirkstile) Three buildings form the 'heart' of Hawick. A former mill holds a cafe and cinema. Opposite, historic **Drumlanrig's Tower**, once a major seat of the Douglas clan, now houses the **Borders Textile Towerhouse** (☑01450-377615; www.heartofhawick.co.uk; 1 Tower Knowe; ⊙10am-4.30pm Mon-Sat, noon-3pm Sun Apr-Oct, 10am-4pm Mon & Wed-Sat Nov-Mar) FREE. This tells the story of the town's knitwear-producing history. Behind the mill, the **Heritage Hub** (☑01450-360699; www.heartofhawick.co.uk; Kirkstile; ⊙9.30am-4.45pm Mon-Fri) FREE is a state-of-the-art facility open to anyone wishing to trace their Scottish heritage or explore other local archives.

Hawick Museum & Art Gallery　　　　　　MUSEUM, GALLERY

(☑01450-364747; www.scotborders.gov.uk; Wilton Lodge Park; ⊙10am-noon & 1-5pm Mon-Fri, 2-5pm Sat & Sun Apr-Sep, noon-3pm Mon-Fri, 1-3pm Sun Oct-Mar) FREE This museum has an interesting collection of mostly 19th-century manufacturing and domestic memorabilia as well as details on a tragic pair of local motorcycling legends. There are usually a couple of temporary exhibitions on as well.

🛏 Sleeping & Eating

Bank Guest House　　　　　　　　　B&B **££**

(☑01450-363760; www.thebankno12highst.com; 12 High St; s £55-65, d £85-100; 🅿 🐝) This posh boutique B&B in the centre of Hawick brings out the best in this solid 19th-century building with modish wallpapers and designer furniture and fabrics. Modern comforts as well as numerous thoughtful extras make this a great place to stay.

Teviotside Guest House　　　　　　B&B **££**

(☑01450-363393; www.teviotsideguesthouse.co.uk; 1 Teviotside Tce; s £35, d £70-90; 🐝 🐾) Alan runs a relaxed and cheerful ship at this six-room B&B near the river. Room 1 is especially lovely with a wraparound outlook and upmarket bathroom. Breakfast is an easygoing buffet affair. There's some noise at weekends from a nearby nightclub.

Damascus Drum　　　　　　　　　　CAFE **£**

(☑07707-856123; www.damascusdrum.co.uk; 2 Silver St; light meals £5-10; ⊙10am-5pm Mon-Sat; 🐝 🐾) The Middle East meets the Borders in this enticing cafe behind the tourist office. Patterned rugs and a secondhand bookshop make for a relaxing environment to enjoy breakfasts, bagels, burgers and tasty Turkish-style meze options.

★ **Night Safe Bistro**　　　　　　　　BISTRO **££**

(☑01450-377045; www.hawicknightsafebistro. co.uk; 12 High St; dinner mains £15-19; ⊙10am-4pm & 5.30-9pm Tue-Thu, 10am-9pm Fri & Sat; 😊) Lively and attractive, this High St coffee stop and restaurant occupies the ground level of a handsome bank building. Morning coffees and light lunches give way to sturdier dinner mains based around well-sourced duck, fish and meat. Service is very welcoming. You'd better book ahead.

Le 2016　　　　　　　　　　　　　FRENCH **££**

(☑01450-370094; www.le2016.net; Sandbed; mains £12-15; ⊙noon-2.30pm & 6-9pm Tue-Fri, 6-9.30pm Sat) Interior design isn't a strong point at this restaurant, which has taken over a too-large space, but the food certainly is. A young French couple produces a short but interesting menu of seasonal Gallic cuisine, with stylish but unfussy presentation and delicious flavours.

HERMITAGE CASTLE

The 'guardhouse of the bloodiest valley in Britain', **Hermitage Castle** (HES; ☑ 01387-376222; www.historicenvironment.scot; B6357; adult/child £5/3; ☉ 9.30am-5.30pm Apr-Sep) embodies the brutal history of the Scottish Borders. Desolate but proud with its massive squared stone walls, it looks more like a lair for orc raiding parties than a home for Scottish nobility, and is one of the bleakest and most stirring of Scottish ruins. The castle is about 12 miles south of Hawick on the B6357.

Strategically crucial, the castle was the scene of many a dark deed and dirty deal with the English invaders, all of which rebounded heavily on the perfidious Scottish lord in question. Here, in 1338, Sir William Douglas imprisoned his enemy Sir Alexander Ramsay and deliberately starved him to death. Ramsay survived for 17 days by eating grain that trickled into his pit (which can still be seen) from the granary above. In 1566 Mary, Queen of Scots famously visited the wounded tenant of the castle, Lord Bothwell, here. Fortified, he recovered to (probably) murder her husband, marry her himself, then abandon her months later and flee into exile.

ℹ️ Getting There & Away

Hourly bus X95 connects Hawick with Galashiels, Selkirk and Edinburgh (£7.80, two hours). Buses leave from Mart St at the northern end of the town centre.

Jedburgh

POP 4000

Attractive Jedburgh, where many old buildings and wynds (narrow alleys) have been intelligently restored, invites exploration by foot. It's centred on the noble skeleton of its ruined abbey.

◎ Sights & Activities

The tourist office has handy booklets for walks around the town, including sections of the Southern Upland Way (p150) or Borders Abbeys Way (p150). Jedburgh is also a popular stop for walkers on St Cuthbert's Way (p150), which passes nearby.

★ Jedburgh Abbey   RUINS

(HES; ☑ 01835-863925; www.historicenvironment. scot; Abbey Rd; adult/child £6/3.60; ☉ 9.30am-5.30pm Apr-Sep, 10am-4pm Oct-Mar; 👶) Dominating the town skyline, this was the first of the great Border abbeys to be passed into state care, and it shows – audio and visual presentations telling the abbey's story are scattered throughout the carefully preserved ruins (good for the kids). The red-sandstone ruins are roofless but relatively intact, and the ingenuity of the master mason can be seen in some of the rich (if somewhat faded) stone carvings in the nave.

The abbey was founded in 1138 by David I as a priory for Augustinian canons.

Mary, Queen of Scots'
Visitor Centre   HISTORIC BUILDING

(Queen St; ☉ 9.30am-4.30pm Mon-Sat, 10.30am-4pm Sun early Mar–late Nov) **FREE** Mary stayed at this beautiful 16th-century tower house in 1566 after her famous ride to visit the injured Earl of Bothwell, her future husband, at Hermitage Castle. The interesting exhibition evokes the sad saga of Mary's life and death. Various objects associated with her – including a lock of her hair – are on display.

Jedburgh Castle Jail   MUSEUM

(☑ 01835-864750; www.scotborders.gov.uk; Castlegate; ☉ 10am-4.30pm Mon-Sat, 1-4pm Sun Easter-Oct) **FREE** Jedburgh Castle was a victim of Scotland's wars for independence but this smart 1820s prison was built on the site as part of a jail reform program. You can check out the original cells and some prisoners' stories and browse the town museum here.

✦ Festivals & Events

Jethart Callant's Festival   CULTURAL

(www.jethartcallantsfestival.com; ☉ late Jun–mid-Jul) This two-week cavalcade recalls the perilous time when people rode out on horseback checking for English incursions. It's perhaps the most notable of the Common Riding festivals of the Borders. There are various rides and processions over the fortnight, involving hundreds of costumed horse riders. Other events continue for another week afterwards.

🛏 Sleeping & Eating

Maplebank
B&B £

(📞 01835-862051; maplebank3@btinternet.com; 3 Smiths Wynd; s/d £30/50; P 🛜 🐾) It's pleasing to come across places where it feels like you're staying in someone's home. Here, that someone is like your favourite aunt: friendly, chaotic and generous. There's lots of clutter and it's very informal. Rooms are comfortable and large, sharing a good bathroom. Breakfast (including fruit, yoghurts and homemade jams) is brilliant – much better than at most posher places.

Willow Court
B&B ££

(📞 01835-863702; www.willowcourtjedburgh.co.uk; The Friars; s/d £75/86; P 🛜) It seems inadequate to call this impressive option a B&B; it's more like a boutique hotel. Impeccable rooms with elegant wallpaper, showroom bathrooms and great beds are complemented by a courteous, professional welcome. The conservatory lounge is great for admiring the views over garden and town.

For sale at the time of research, so things may change.

Glenbank House Hotel
HOTEL ££

(📞 01835-862258; www.jedburgh-hotel.com; Castlegate; d £65-99; P 🛜) This lovely old building has modernised, comfortable rooms – some of which are rather compact – shiny contemporary bathrooms, and nice views over the town and hills. It's a likeable place, with very welcoming people running it. There's no restaurant service but you're in the centre of town.

Capon Tree
SCOTTISH ££

(📞 01835-869596; www.thecapontree.com; 61 High St; mains £14-20; ⏰ food 6-9pm Mon-Fri, noon-2.30pm & 5.30-9pm Sat, noon-2.30pm & 5.30-8pm Sun; 🛜) Attractively combining smart and casual, this welcoming bistro and bar does modern Scottish cuisine. Plates are beautifully, though not fussily, presented and ingredients are of high quality. The overall package is appealing, the service good and the ambience romantic. There are handsome rooms available too.

WALKING & CYCLING IN SOUTHERN SCOTLAND

Walking

The region's most famous walk is the challenging 212-mile **Southern Upland Way** (📞 01387-273987; www.southernuplandway.gov.uk), which runs coast to coast from Portpatrick to Cockburnspath. If you want a sample, one of the best bits is the three- to four-day section from Dalry to Beattock.

Another long-distance walk is 62-mile **St Cuthbert's Way** (http://stcuthbertsway.info), inspired by the travels of St Cuthbert, a 7th-century saint who lived at the first Melrose monastery. It crosses some superb scenery between Melrose and Lindisfarne (in England).

From Glasgow to Galloway via Ayrshire, the 143-mile Whithorn Way (p173) follows in the footsteps of ancient pilgrims.

The **Borders Abbeys Way** (www.bordersabbeysway.com) links all the great Border abbeys in a 65-mile circuit. For shorter walks and especially circular loops in the hills, the towns of Melrose, Jedburgh and Kelso all make ideal bases. On the Borders coast, the Berwickshire Coastal Path (p154) takes in splendid scenery.

For baggage transfer on these walks, contact **Walking Support** (📞 01896-822079; www.walkingsupport.co.uk). In early September, look out for the **Scottish Borders Walking Festival** (www.borderswalking.com; ⏰ early Sep), with a week of walks for all abilities and an instant social scene.

Cycling

With the exception of the main A-roads, traffic is sparse, which, along with the beauty of the countryside, makes this ideal cycling country.

The **Tweed Cycle Route** is 95 waymarked miles along the beautiful Tweed Valley, following minor roads from Biggar to Peebles (22 miles), Melrose (25 miles), Coldstream (28 miles) and Berwick-upon-Tweed (20 miles). The **4 Abbeys Cycle Route** is a 55-mile circuit of the Border abbeys. Local tourist offices have route maps; these and other routes are also detailed at www.cyclescottishborders.com. Further west, the Whithorn Way (p173) is also a cycling route.

ℹ Information

Jedburgh Tourist Office (☎ 01835-863170; www.visitscotland.com; Murray's Green; ⊙ 9am-5pm Mon-Sat, 10am-4pm Sun Apr-Jun, Sep & Oct, 9am-5.30pm Mon-Sat, 10am-5pm Sun Jul & Aug, 10am-4pm Mon-Sat Nov-Mar; ☎) Head tourist office for the Borders region. Very helpful.

ℹ Getting There & Away

Jedburgh has good bus connections to Hawick, Melrose and Kelso (all around 25 minutes, roughly hourly, two-hourly on Sunday). Buses also run to Edinburgh (£7.80, two hours, six daily, three on Sunday).

Kelso

POP 5600

Kelso, a prosperous market town with a broad, cobbled square flanked by Georgian buildings, has a cheery feel and historic appeal. During the day it's a busy little place, but after 8pm you'll have the streets to yourself. The town has a lovely site at the junction of the Tweed and Teviot, and is one of the most enjoyable places in the Borders.

◉ Sights & Activities

The Kelso–Jedburgh section (12 miles) of the Borders Abbeys Way is a fairly easy walk, largely following the River Teviot. The tourist office has a free leaflet with map and route description.

For a shorter ramble, leave the Square by Roxburgh St and take the signposted alley to **Cobby Riverside Walk**, a pleasant stroll along the river to Floors Castle (rejoin Roxburgh St to gain admission to the castle).

Floors Castle HISTORIC BUILDING
(☎ 01573-223333; www.floorscastle.com; adult/child castle & grounds £11.50/6; ⊙ 10.30am-5pm May-Sep, Sat & Sun Oct) Grandiose Floors Castle is Scotland's largest inhabited mansion, home to the Duke of Roxburghe, and overlooks the Tweed about a mile west of Kelso. Built by William Adam in the 1720s, the original Georgian simplicity was 'improved' in the 1840s with the addition of somewhat OTT battlements and turrets. Inside, view the vivid colours of 17th-century Brussels tapestries in the drawing room and intricate oak carvings in the ornate ballroom. The walled garden is a highlight of the extensive grounds.

Kelso Abbey RUINS
(HES; www.historicenvironment.scot; Bridge St; ⊙ 9.30am-5.30pm Apr-Sep, 10am-4pm Sat-Wed Oct-Mar) FREE Once one of the richest abbeys in southern Scotland, Kelso Abbey was built by the Tironensians, an order founded in Picardy and brought to the Borders around 1113 by David I. English raids in the 16th century reduced it to ruins, though what little remains today is some of the finest surviving Romanesque architecture in Scotland.

🛏 Sleeping

⭐ **Edenbank House** B&B ££
(☎ 01573-226734; www.edenbank.co.uk; Stichill Rd; s/d £50/90; 🅿 ☎) A half-mile down the Stichill road, this grand Victorian house sits in spacious grounds where only bleating lambs in the fields and birds in the garden break the silence. It's a fabulous place, with huge opulent rooms, lovely views over the fields and incredibly warm hospitality. Breakfast features homemade produce, and a laissez-faire attitude makes for an utterly relaxing stay.

Don't just show up: call ahead.

⭐ **Old Priory** B&B ££
(☎ 01573-223030; www.theoldpriorykelso.com; 33 Woodmarket; s/d £80/90; 🅿 ☎) Fantastic rooms here are allied with numerous personal details – the operators turn down the beds at night and make you feel very welcome. Doubles are top-notch and the family room really excellent. The huge windows flood the rooms with natural light. The wonderful library room (£120) is huge and luxurious, with a super bathroom. Top-class B&B.

Inglestone House B&B ££
(☎ 01573-225800; www.inglestonehouse.co.uk; Abbey Row; s/d/f £60/90/150; ☎) The Northumbrian owners here are welcoming and very cordial but also leave you space for yourself, giving this spot behind the main street an appealing blend of hotel and guesthouse. Rooms are a good size with firm mattresses and – unusually for the Borders – the wi-fi is fast.

Central Guest House GUESTHOUSE ££
(☎ 07410-515514; www.thecentralguesthousekelso. co.uk; 51 The Square; s/d/apt £45/65/95; ☎) A reasonable cheaper option in sometimes pricey Kelso and just on the central square. The owners live off site, so call ahead first. The rooms are fine: spacious, with firm

beds, carpets and good bathrooms. Rates are room-only, but you get a fridge, toaster and microwave, so you can create your own breakfast.

✖ Eating & Drinking

★ Cobbles
BISTRO ££

(☑ 01573-223548; www.thecobbleskelso.co.uk; 7 Bowmont St; mains £10-17; ☺ food noon-2.30pm & 5.45-9pm Mon-Fri, noon-9pm Sat, noon-8.30pm Sun; ☎) This inn off the main square is so popular you will need to book a table at weekends. It's cheery, very welcoming and warm, and serves excellent upmarket pub food in generous portions. Pick and mix from bar menu, steaks and gourmet options. Leave room for cheese and/or dessert. The bar's own microbrewed ales are excellent. A cracking place.

★ Contented Vine
SCOTTISH, ITALIAN ££

(☑ 01573-224777; www.contentedvine.co.uk; 60 Horsemarket; mains £10-20; ☺ 6-10pm Mon-Thu, 5-10pm Fri-Sun; ☎) Upmarket pasta dishes take their place alongside quality dishes of Scottish produce with a Mediterranean inflection at this popular, welcoming central restaurant that has a real throwback vibe and a curious setting in a former cinema. Early evening dining deals are generous. The wine list could be a lot more inspiring.

★ Rutherfords
PUB

(☑ 07803-208460; www.rutherfordsmicropub. co.uk; 38 The Square; ☺ noon-10pm Sun-Thu, to 11pm Fri & Sat, reduced hours Nov-Mar) This enchanting small bar prioritises conversation and has no TV or music. It's a charming place with gin on tap poured through a microscope, carefully selected craft beers and spirits, and a warm, convivial atmosphere. Unusual and excellent.

ⓘ Getting There & Away

There are six daily direct bus services to Edinburgh (£7.70, two hours, two on Sunday) and regular routes to other Borders towns and Berwick-upon-Tweed.

Around Kelso

The area around Kelso has two starkly contrasting historic buildings to visit, and the twin walkers' villages of Town Yetholm and Kirk Yetholm.

Mellerstain House
HISTORIC BUILDING

(☑ 01573-410225; www.mellerstain.com; Gordon; adult/child £10/5; ☺ noon-5pm Fri-Mon Easter & May-Sep) Finished in 1778, this is considered to be Scotland's finest Robert Adam–designed mansion. It is huge and famous for its classic elegance, ornate interiors and plaster ceilings; the library in particular is outstanding. The upstairs bedrooms are less attractive, but have a peek at the bizarre puppet-and-doll collection in the gallery.

It's about 6 miles northwest of Kelso, near Gordon. There are concerts held here through the summer months.

Smailholm Tower
TOWER

(HES; ☑ 01573-460365; www.historicenvironment. scot; Sandyknowe Farm, Smailholm; adult/child £5/3; ☺ 9.30am-5.30pm Apr-Sep) Perched on a rocky knoll above a small lake, this narrow stone tower provides one of the most evocative sights in the Borders and keeps its bloody history alive. Although displays inside are sparse, the panoramic view from the top is worth the climb. The tower is 6 miles west of Kelso, a mile south of Smailholm village on the B6397.

The nearby privately owned farm, **Sandyknowe**, was owned by Sir Walter Scott's grandfather. As Scott himself recognised, his imagination was fired by the ballads and stories he heard as a child at Sandyknowe, and by the ruined tower a stone's throw away.

Eyemouth

POP 3500

Eyemouth is a busy fishing port and popular domestic holiday destination. The harbour itself is very atmospheric – you may even spot seals frolicking in the water, as well as tourists frolicking around the boats, snapping pics of old fishing nets accompanied by the cry of seagulls.

The community here suffered its greatest catastrophe in October 1881, when a terrible storm destroyed the coastal fishing fleet, killing 189 fishermen, 129 of whom were locals. Peter Aitchison's *Black Friday* is a good book about the disaster.

◉ Sights & Activities

Gunsgreen House
MUSEUM

(☑ 01890-752062; www.gunsgreenhouse.org; Gunsgreen Quay; adult/child £6.80/4.50; ☺ 11am-5pm Apr-Oct; ◉) Standing proud and four-

PAXTON HOUSE

Six miles west of Berwick-upon-Tweed, **Paxton House** (☏ 01289-386291; www.paxton house.co.uk; B6461; adult/child £10/4; ☉ 10am-5pm Easter-Oct, grounds 10am-sunset; 🚼) is located beside the River Tweed and surrounded by parkland and gardens. It was built in 1758 by Patrick Home for his intended wife, the daughter of Prussia's Frederick the Great. Unfortunately, she stood him up, but it was her loss; designed by the Adam family – brothers John, James and Robert – it's acknowledged as one of the finest 18th-century Palladian houses in Britain. Four tours run daily; see the website for limited winter visiting.

It contains a large collection of Chippendale and Regency furniture, and its picture gallery houses paintings from the national galleries of Scotland. The nursery is a feature designed to provide insight into a child's 18th-century life. In the grounds are walking trails, a restored waterwheel and a riverside museum on salmon fishing. There's plenty to keep the kids entertained here, including boat trips on the Tweed.

Bus 32 runs past here every couple of hours from Berwick.

square across the harbour, this elegant 18th-century John Adam mansion was built on the profits of smuggling: Eyemouth was an important landing point for illegal cargoes from northern Europe and the Baltic. The house has been beautifully restored to reflect this and other aspects of its varied past. The hands-on exhibition makes a special effort to keep the kids entertained. Both the house and the adjacent tower-like dovecote can be hired out as self-catering accommodation.

Eyemouth Museum   MUSEUM
(☏ 01890-751701; www.eyemouthmuseum.co.uk; Manse Rd; adult/child £3.50/free; ☉ 11am-4pm Mon-Sat Apr-Oct) Set in a church, the town museum has intriguing local history displays, particularly relating to the town's fishing heritage. Its centrepiece is the tapestry commemorating the 1881 fishing disaster.

Eyemouth RIB Trips   BOATING
(☏ 07941-441995; www.eyemouthribtrips.co.uk; Harbour Rd; ☉ Apr-Oct; 🚼) Provides a range of fun boat trips, some focused on coastal scenery and wildlife spotting (adult/child £20/15), others on giving you a thrill and a soaking from the spray (adult/child £20/15, minimum age 10). It also offers shuttle services to St Abbs (£5 each way; you can walk back).

🛏 Sleeping & Eating

Bantry   B&B ££
(Mackays; ☏ 01890-751900; www.mackaysof eyemouth.co.uk; 20 High St; s/d/f £50/75/80; P 🛜) Above a restaurant on the main drag, this B&B has acceptable modern rooms (some with shared bathroom) with muted tones. It is positioned right on the waterfront; try to get room No 3 for sea views. There's a fabulous deck, with loungers and a summer hot tub, overlooking the lapping waves. No-breakfast rates available too.

Oblò   BISTRO ££
(☏ 01890-752527; www.oblobar.com; Manse Rd; mains £11-17; ☉ food 10am-8.30pm Sun-Tue, to 9pm Wed-Sat; 🛜🚼) For a meal any time, find your way upstairs to this modern Mediterranean-fusion bar-bistro with comfy seating and a modish interior. It's just down from the museum, and it's got a great deck to lap up the sunshine. Service is attentive and the food is delicious. Try the local seafood.

ℹ Getting There & Away

Eyemouth is 5 miles north of the Scotland–England border. Buses go to Berwick-upon-Tweed (£3, 15 minutes, frequent), which has a train station, and to Edinburgh (£11, 1¾ hours, six to eight daily Monday to Saturday, three Sunday).

Coldingham & St Abbs

This picturesque area is fantastic for those who love the great outdoors. Some of the UK's best diving is here, as well as great cycling, walking, angling and birdwatching. From the village of Coldingham, with its twisting streets, take the B6438 downhill to the small fishing village of St Abbs, a gorgeous, peaceful little community with a picture-perfect harbour nestled below the cliffs.

◉ Sights & Activities

St Abbs & Eyemouth Voluntary Marine Reserve
NATURE RESERVE

(☑ 01890-771443; www.marine-reserve.co.uk) The clear, clean waters around St Abbs form part of St Abbs & Eyemouth Voluntary Marine Reserve, one of the best cold-water diving sites in Europe. The reserve is home to a variety of marine life, including grey seals and porpoises. Visibility is about 7m to 8m but has been recorded at up to 24m. Beds of brown kelp form a hypnotically undulating forest on the seabed.

St Abbs Visitor Centre
MUSEUM

(☑ 01890-771672; www.stabbsvisitorcentre.co.uk; Coldingham Rd, St Abbs; ⊙ 10am-5pm Easter–mid-Oct) FREE This modern exhibition in St Abbs has interesting interactive displays on the often stormy history of this harbour village. Spoken reminiscences from locals like a fisherman and lighthouse keeper are the highlight.

St Abb's Head National Nature Reserve
BIRDWATCHING

(www.nts.org.uk) This 78-hectare reserve is an ornithologist's wonderland, with large colonies of guillemots, kittiwakes, herring gulls, fulmars, razorbills and some puffins. The clifftop walks here are spectacular. You get to the reserve by following the 2-mile circular trail from the car park on the road just west of St Abbs, where there's a good **nature exhibition** (www.nts.org.uk; Old Smiddy, St Abbs; ⊙ 10am-5pm Apr-Oct) FREE in the Old Smiddy complex.

Coldingham Bay
BEACH

In Coldingham, a signposted turn-off to the east leads just under a mile down to away-from-it-all Coldingham Bay, which has a sandy beach and a clifftop walking trail to Eyemouth (3 miles). At **St Vedas Surf Shop** (☑ 01890-771679; www.stvedas.co.uk; Coldingham Bay; surfboard hire per hour £6, kayaks per hour/half-/full day £14/32/49; ⊙ 9am-dusk) you can hire surfboards, sea kayaks and snorkelling gear; there's a hotel here that serves cheap food. Surfing lessons (£35) are also available.

Berwickshire Coastal Path
WALKING

(www.scotborders.gov.uk) Thirty miles of spectacular coastal walking link Berwick-upon-Tweed in the south with Cockburnspath in the north, where you can continue on the Southern Upland Way (p150). A pretty 3½-mile section links St Abbs and Eyemouth.

Scuba Diving

The sea around St Abbs forms part of the St Abbs & Eyemouth Voluntary Marine Reserve. Three dive boats operate out of St Abbs. You can charter them whole, or phone to book a spot on a boat; these spots cost around £45 per person for two dives.

Dive St Abbs (Paul Crowe; ☑ 07710 961050, 01890-771945; http://divestabbs.com; Rock House, St Abbs; 2 dives £45)

St Abbs Diving (Paul O'Callaghan; ☑ 07780 980179, 01890-771525; www.stabbsdiving.com; The Harbour, St Abbs; 2 dives £45)

St Abbs Charters (Barry White; ☑ 01890-771384; www.stabbscharters.com; The Harbour, St Abbs; 2 dives £45)

The St Abbs Visitor Centre can provide some diving advice. A guide to local dive sites costs £7.50.

🛏 Sleeping & Eating

Rock House
HOSTEL, B&B £

(☑ 01890-771945; www.divestabbs.com; Harbour, St Abbs; dm £23, d £60, cottage £70; 🛜) Right by St Abbs' harbour, this is run by a friendly dive skipper and family; you can almost roll out of bed onto the boat. The bunkhouse (usually booked up by groups at the weekend) sleeps a total of 10. There's also a pretty B&B room and a cute cottage with a little deck overlooking the heart of the village.

Priory View
B&B ££

(☑ 01890-771525; www.prioryview.com; Eyemouth Rd, Coldingham; d £70-75, f £110; P 🛜 🐾) Once a police station, this solid house offers five comfortable B&B rooms decked out in wood. There's a pleasant garden with a games room and a genuine welcome from the owners, who also have a dive boat in St Abbs.

Ebbcarrs Cafe
CAFE £

(☑ 01890-771302; Harbour, St Abbs; light meals £4-7; ⊙ 10am-5pm Apr-Oct, 10am-4pm Tue-Sun Nov-Mar) A stone cottage by the harbour in St Abbs, sweet Ebbcarrs does tasty rolls with local crab, cullen skink and other sweet and savoury bites. Grab one of the picnic tables outside or head upstairs for indoor seating.

Ebba's Bistro
CAFE £

(☑ 01890-771413; www.ebbacentre.weebly.com; Ebba Centre, Briery Law, St Abbs; light meals £4-11; ⊙ 10am-4pm; 🛜) This very welcoming cafe in what was once the village school, now a community centre, offers tasty home-baked

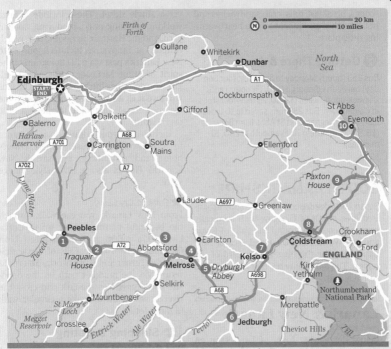

Driving Tour
Historic Sights

START EDINBURGH
END EDINBURGH
LENGTH 155 MILES; ONE TO THREE DAYS

This drive takes in several of the principal sites of the Borders region. You could do it in a long day, but to give yourself time to explore the historic buildings, take two or three. All the towns mentioned have good overnighting options.

Starting in Edinburgh, head south on the A701 to ① **Peebles** (p141); Rosslyn Chapel is an easy detour along the way. Stroll around Peebles, a typically pretty Borders town, then head east along the A72, deviating at Innerleithen to historic ② **Traquair House** (p145), offering 10 centuries of history and great insights into the Jacobite cause and rebellions. Continue eastwards on the A72, pausing at excellent ③ **Abbotsford** (p146), Sir Walter Scott's one-time home. The attractive bijou village of ④ **Melrose** (p144), with its fabulous abbey, is a must-see and a good meal or overnight stop. Head east again, then south down the A68 to ⑤ **Dryburgh Abbey** (p146), perhaps the most evocative of the great Borders ruins.

Continue to attractive ⑥ **Jedburgh** (p149), dominated by the skeleton of the third of the abbeys. The turbulent history of these once-powerful communities tells of the constant strife in these frontier lands.

Take the A698 northeast to ⑦ **Kelso** (p151), a historic market town and the location of grandiose Floors Castle, the last and least intact of the abbey ruins. Several other historic buildings are close by, so this makes an appealing stop for a night or two to explore them: the classical elegance of Mellerstain House and the contrastingly grim Smailholm Tower are particularly worthwhile.

Beyond Kelso, the A698 takes you to ⑧ **Coldstream**, which gives its name to the famous regiment once based here. Here the road crosses the Tweed into England and leads eventually to the coast near Berwick-upon-Tweed. Head north and take the left turn to the magnificent 18th-century ⑨ **Paxton House** (p153), just back over the border in Scotland. Continue north to ⑩ **Eyemouth** (p152), with its fascinating maritime history. Here, Gunsgreen House is an elegant 18th-century mansion with an intriguing smuggling past. From here, take the A1 back to Edinburgh.

scones, breakfast rolls, crab sandwiches and hot brunches and lunches. It's a heartwarming little place.

❶ Getting There & Away

Bus 253 (hourly Monday to Saturday, four Sunday) between Edinburgh (£10, 1¾ hours) and Berwick-upon-Tweed (£3.80, 25 minutes) stops in Coldingham. Bus 235 runs seven to 10 times daily to Coldingham and St Abbs from Berwick (£3.80, 25 minutes) via Eyemouth (£2.10, 10 minutes).

SOUTH LANARKSHIRE

South Lanarkshire combines a highly urbanised area south of Glasgow with scenically gorgeous country around the Falls of Clyde and the World Heritage–listed area of New Lanark, by far the biggest drawcard of the region. The handsome town of Biggar is also worth a visit.

Lanark & New Lanark

POP 8900

Below the market town of Lanark, in an attractive gorge by the River Clyde, is the World Heritage Site of New Lanark – an intriguing collection of restored mill buildings and warehouses.

Once Britain's largest cotton-spinning complex, it's better known for the pioneering social experiments of Robert Owen, who managed the mill from 1800. New Lanark is really a memorial to this enlightened capitalist. He provided his workers with housing, a cooperative store, the world's first nursery school, adult-education classes, a sick-pay fund for workers and a social centre he called the New Institute for the Formation of Character. Devote half a day to exploring this site as there's plenty to see and do, including appealing walks along the riverside. What must once have been a thriving, noisy, industrial village is now a peaceful oasis with only the swishing of trees and the rushing of the River Clyde to be heard.

⊙ Sights & Activities

★New Lanark Visitor Centre   MUSEUM
(☑01555-661345; www.newlanark.org; adult/child/family £12.50/9/38; ⊙10am-5pm Apr-Oct, to 4pm Nov-Mar; ⊕) The main attractions of this World Heritage mill town are accessed via a single ticket. These include a huge working spinning mule, producing woollen yarn, and the Historic Schoolhouse, which contains an innovative, high-tech journey to New Lanark's past via a 3D hologram of the spirit of Annie McLeod, a 10-year-old mill girl who describes life here in 1820. The kids will love it as it's very realistic, although the 'do good for all mankind' theme is a little overbearing.

Included in your admission is entrance to a millworker's house, Robert Owen's home and exhibitions on 'saving New Lanark'. There's also a 1920s-style village store.

★Falls of Clyde   WALKING
From New Lanark, you can walk through the beautiful nature reserve up to Corra Linn (0.75 miles) and Bonnington Linn (1½ miles), two of the Falls of Clyde that inspired Turner and Wordsworth. You could return via the muddier path on the opposite bank, pass New Lanark and cross the river downstream to make a circular walk (5 miles total).

🛏 Sleeping & Eating

Wee Row Hostel   HOSTEL £
(☑01555-666710; www.newlanarkhostel.co.uk; Rosedale St, New Lanark; tw/q/studio £55/79/89; ⊙Mar-Oct; ⓟ@🛜) This hostel has a great location in an old mill building in the heart of the New Lanark complex. It has comfortable en-suite rooms with both beds and bunks and a really good downstairs common area. Prices come down substantially outside high season. Closed between 11am and 3pm. You can use the nearby hotel spa for a small charge.

New Lanark Mill Hotel   HOTEL £££
(☑01555-667200; www.newlanarkhotel.co.uk; New Lanark; r £109-179; ⓟ@🛜🏊🏋) Cleverly converted from an 18th-century mill, this hotel is full of character and is a stone's throw from the major attractions. It has smart rooms (the deluxe ones are quite a bit more spacious), with contemporary art and views (and sounds) of the churning Clyde below. There's also self-catering accommodation in charming cottages, and a pool, spa and fitness area.

There are good facilities for people with disabilities. The hotel also serves good meals (mains £11 to £17). Rooms are quite a bit cheaper midweek.

★ **La Vigna** ITALIAN £££
(☑ 01555-664320; www.lavigna.co.uk; 40 Wellgate,
Lanark; mains £17-25; ☺ noon-2.30pm & 5-10pm
Mon-Sat, noon-3pm & 5-9.30pm Sun; ☎) This
long-established local favourite is a great
spot, seemingly plucked from some bygone
age with its quietly efficient service and
classy, welcoming ambience. The food is distinctly Italian, albeit using Scottish venison,
beef and fish, and there are also vegetarian
options. Lunch and early dining specials are
great value.

ℹ **Getting There & Away**

Lanark is 25 miles southeast of Glasgow.
Express bus 240X runs hourly Monday to Saturday (£6.50, one hour); trains from Glasgow
Central also run (£7.30, 55 minutes, every 30
minutes, hourly on Sundays).

It's a pleasant walk to New Lanark, but there's
also a half-hourly bus service from the train
station (daily). If you need a taxi, call **Clydewide**
(☑ 01555-666333; www.clydewidetaxis.co.uk).

Biggar

POP 2300

Biggar is a pleasant town in a rural setting
overlooked by Tinto Hill. The town has a
worthwhile museum and a famous puppet
theatre. It's also known for the nationalist,
leftist poet Hugh MacDiarmid, who lived
near here for nearly 30 years until his death
in 1978.

**Biggar & Upper
Clydesdale Museum** MUSEUM
(☑ 01899-221050; www.biggarmuseumtrust.
co.uk; 156 High St; adult/child £5/2; ☺ 10am-5pm
Tue-Sat, 1-5pm Sun Mar-Oct, to 4pm Nov–mid-Dec,
10am-4pm Sat, 1-4pm Sun mid-Dec–Feb) This
museum is an enthusiastic community
project that is well worth a visit. The pièce
de résistance is Gladstone Court, a reconstructed street with historic Victorian-era
nook-and-cranny shops that you can pop
into to steal a glimpse of the past. A working telephone exchange is an impressive
highlight. Other displays cover the archaeology, geography and history of the area, with
features both on the Covenanters and the
Polish soldiers billeted in Biggar in WWII.

Biggar Puppet Theatre THEATRE
(☑ 01899-220631; www.purvespuppets.com;
Broughton Rd; adult/child £10/8; ☺ Easter-Sep)
A well-loved local institution that runs mat-
inée shows every couple of days through-

out the summer using miniature Victorian
puppets and bizarre glow-in-the-dark modern ones over 1m high. Different shows are
suitable for varying age groups, so enquire
before you take the kids along. Check the
website for performance times.

Tinto Hill WALKING
The 712m hill dominates the town from a
distance. It is a straightforward ascent by
the northern ridge from the car park, just off
the A73 by Thankerton Crossroads. Look out
for the Stone Age fort on your way up. Allow
two hours for the return trip (4½ miles).

ℹ **Getting There & Away**

Biggar is 33 miles southeast of Glasgow. There
are hourly buses (four on Sunday) to/from
Edinburgh (£5.20, 1¼ hours); some services
continue to Dumfries (£6.70, 1½ hours). For
Glasgow, change at Lanark (30 minutes). Other
buses run to Peebles.

AYRSHIRE

Ayrshire is synonymous with golf and
Robert Burns – and there's plenty on offer
here to satisfy both of these pursuits. Troon
and Turnberry have world-famous courses,
and there's enough Burns memorabilia in
the region to satisfy even his most fanatical
admirers.

The best way to appreciate the Ayrshire
coastline is on foot: the **Ayrshire Coastal
Path** (www.ayrshirecoastalpath.org; ☀) offers
100 miles of spectacular waterside walking.

Largs

POP 11,300

On a sunny day, there are few places in
southern Scotland more beautiful than
Largs, where green grass meets the sparkling water of the Firth of Clyde. It's a
resort-style waterfront town that harks
back to seaside days in times of gentler
pleasures, and the minigolf, amusements,
old-fashioned eateries and bouncy castle

ℹ **ARDROSSAN**

Ardrossan, an otherwise unremarkable
coastal town, is the main ferry port
for Arran. There are also seasonal services to Campbeltown on the Kintyre
peninsula.

OFF THE BEATEN TRACK

IRVINE

Boat lovers should check out the **Scottish Maritime Museum** (☑ 01294-278283; www.scottishmaritimemuseum.org; Harbour Rd; adult/child £7.50/free; ⊙ 10am-5pm; ⬛) by the train station in Irvine, which long ago was west Scotland's busiest port. In the massive Linthouse Engine Shop – an old hangar with a cast-iron framework – is an absorbing collection of boats and machinery. Displays cover ropeworking, the age of steam and the Clyde's shipbuilding industry. Every boat here has a story – some tragic. Free guided tours take you down to the dock where you can clamber over various ships, and visitors can also see a shipyard worker's restored flat.

Further along the appealing harbour road, be sure to drop into the **Ship Inn** (☑ 01294-279722; www.theshipinnirvine.co.uk; 120 Harbour St; mains £9-13; ⊙ food noon-2.30pm & 5-9pm Mon-Fri, 10am-9pm Sat & Sun; ☎). It's the oldest pub in Irvine, serves tasty bar meals and has bucket-loads of character.

Irvine is 26 miles from Glasgow. There are frequent buses from Ayr (30 to 40 minutes) and Largs (one hour). Trains run to/from Glasgow Central station; the other way they go to Ayr.

mean you should get into the spirit, buy an ice cream and stroll around this slice of retro Scotland.

◉ Sights & Activities

In summer, the Waverley (p119), the last ocean-going paddle steamer ever built, runs spectacular coastal voyages. There are several departures a week from Largs; book online.

Víkingar! MUSEUM
(☑ 01475-689777; www.kaleisure.com; Greenock Rd; adult/child £4.50/3.50; ⊙ 11.30am-2.30pm Sat & Sun Feb & Nov, 11.30am-1.30pm Mar, 10.30am-2.30pm Apr-Jun, Sep & Oct, 10.30am-3.30pm Jul & Aug; ⬛) The town's main attraction is a multimedia exhibition describing Viking influence in Scotland until its demise at the Battle of Largs in 1263. It's got a slightly downbeat municipal feel these days, but tours with staff in Viking outfits run every hour; ring ahead to check, though. It also has a swimming pool, soft play area and leisure centre. It's on the waterfront road; you can't miss it, as it's the only place with a longship outside.

✶ Festivals & Events

Largs Viking Festival CULTURAL
(www.largsvikingfestival.org; ⊙ 1st week Sep) This festival celebrates the Battle of Largs and the end of Viking political domination in Scotland. The highlights are the authentic Viking village peopled by costumed locals and the re-enactment of the battle, complete with longship aflame.

🛏 Sleeping & Eating

Glendarroch B&B ££
(☑ 01475-676305; www.glendarrochlargs.com; 24 Irvine Rd; d £70; ℗☎) This B&B on the main road through town has warm and friendly owners who keep their prices fair and their four lovely rooms very shipshape. All are en suite and the kingsized double is particularly desirable.

St Leonards Guest House B&B ££
(☑ 01475-673318; www.stleonardsguesthouse.com; 9 Irvine Rd; d £65-80; ℗☎) On the main road through town, but excellently soundproofed, this spot offers a cordial welcome and spotless, well-decorated rooms, two of which share a top-notch modern bathroom. Breakfast is a pleasure.

Lounge BISTRO ££
(☑ 01475-689968; www.loungeatlargs.com; 33 Main St; mains £11-16; ⊙ food noon-3.30pm & 5-9.30pm Mon-Fri, noon-4pm & 5-9.30pm Sat & Sun; ☎) Tucked away above the Royal Bank of Scotland on the main road, this stunningly attractive bar and bistro comes as quite a surprise. Eating is done in an elegant tearoom space, with hardwood floor, ceramic fireplace and leather seats. Service is willing, and there's a nice range of classic Scottish pub fare alongside tasty seafood and a few fusion dishes.

There's also a roof terrace with gas heaters, a fine spot for a drink.

Nardini's BISTRO ££
(☑ 01475-675000; www.nardinis.co.uk; 2 Greenock Rd; mains £8-16; ⊙ 9am-9pm or 10pm Apr-Oct, to 8pm Nov-Mar; ☎⬛) Nothing typifies the

old-time feel of Largs more than this giant art-deco gelateria. The ice creams are decadently delicious, with rich flavours that'll have parents licking more than their fair share from their kids' cones. It also has a cafe with outdoor seating, and a franchise restaurant that does decent pizza and pasta, and some more elaborate mains and tapas.

❶ Getting There & Away

Largs is 32 miles west of Glasgow by road. There are trains from Glasgow Central (£8.40, one hour, hourly). Buses run the route more slowly via Greenock and Gourock. Buses also run once or twice hourly to Ayr (£7.20, 1¾ hours) via Ardrossan and Irvine. You can also reach these by rail, some with a change at Kilwinning.

Troon

POP 14,640

Troon, a major sailing centre on the coast 7 miles north of Ayr, has excellent sandy beaches and six golf courses, including one of the world's finest. Nearby Dundonald Castle is also well worth a visit.

Dundonald Castle CASTLE
(HES; ☑ 01563-851489; www.dundonaldcastle.org. uk; Winehouse Yett, Dundonald; adult/child £5/3; ☺ 9.30am-5.30pm Apr-Oct, 10am-4pm Nov-Mar) Dundonald Castle commands impressive views and, in its main hall, has one of the finest barrel-vaulted ceilings preserved in Scotland. It was the first home of the Stuart kings, built by Robert II in 1371, and reckoned to be the third most important castle in Scotland in its time, after Edinburgh and Stirling. The visitor centre has good information on prior settlements, and scale models of the castle and its predecessors. Buses running between Troon and Kilmarnock stop in Dundonald.

There are ongoing archaeological investigations here that, it is hoped, will reveal remains of an earlier castle.

Winter opening hours are changeable; call ahead.

★ Royal Troon GOLF
(☑ 01292-311555; www.royaltroon.co.uk; Craigend Rd; ☺ mid-Apr–early Oct) The demanding championship Old Course here hosted the 2016 Open Championship and is one of golf's classic links challenges. The standard green fee is £250 but there are sometimes offers on the website. The second course, Portland, can be played for £85.

★ MacCallum's SEAFOOD ££
(☑ 01292-319339; www.maccallumsoftroon.co.uk; Harbour Rd; seafood mains £14-20, fried fish £4-7; ☺ restaurant noon-2.30pm & 6.30-9.30pm Wed-Sat plus Tue in summer, noon-2.30pm Sun, chip shop noon-8pm Sun & Tue-Thu, noon-9pm Fri & Sat) Right at the end of the harbour road, where yachts have given way to fishing boats, this set-up has two parts, both worthwhile. The Oyster Bar offers excellent fresh seafood in a smart, uncluttered setting. Next door, the Wee Hurrie does fish and chips, with excellent fish choices like sea bass. Order the fritto misto to try different varieties.

❶ Getting There & Away

There are half-hourly trains to Ayr (£3.40, 10 minutes) and Glasgow (£8.10, 40 minutes). The ferry service to Northern Ireland is no longer running.

Ayr

POP 46,710

Ayr's long sandy beach has made it a popular family seaside resort since Victorian times, but the town has struggled in recent years. Parts of the centre have a neglected air, though there are many fine Georgian and Victorian buildings, and it makes a convenient base for exploring this section of coast. The huge drawcard is Alloway, 3 miles south, with its Robert Burns heritage. Most things to see in Ayr are also Robert Burns related.

◉ Sights

St John's Tower TOWER
(Eglinton Tce) This is the only remnant of the church that hosted a parliament in 1315, the year after the celebrated victory at the

---

A DAY AT THE RACES

Ayr Racecourse (☑ 01292-264179; www.ayr-racecourse.co.uk; Whitletts Rd), Scotland's premier racecourse, is a fun day out, with both flat and jump racing days and good facilities. The biggest event is the Scottish Grand National in April. Check the website for a list of race days. As well as racing, other events, including a popular car boot sale, are regularly held here.

Established in 1576 and in its current location since 1907, the racecourse is an easy 15-minute walk from Ayr town centre.

Ayr

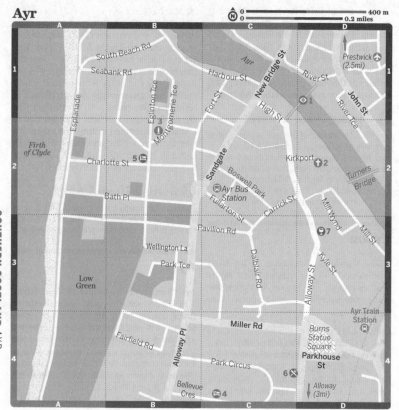

SOUTHERN SCOTLAND AYR

battle of Bannockburn. John Knox' son-in-law was the minister here, and Mary, Queen of Scots, stayed overnight in 1563. You can only admire it from the street, but it's very photogenic.

Auld Brig   BRIDGE

(Old Bridge) Several of Burns' poems are set here in Ayr; in *Twa Brigs,* Ayr's old and new bridges argue with one another. The Auld Brig was built in 1491 and spans the river just north of the church.

Auld Kirk   CHURCH

(Old Church; www.auldkirk.org; Blackfriars Walk; ⊙1-2pm Tue Mar-Jun & Sep-Nov, 10.30am-12.30pm Sat Jul & Aug) FREE Robert Burns was baptised in the Auld Kirk. The atmospheric cemetery here overlooks the river and is good for a stroll, offering an escape from the bustle of High St.

🎉 Festivals & Events

Burns an' a' That   CULTURAL

(www.burnsfestival.com) This festival encompasses several events that take place throughout the year. There's a bit of everything, from wine tasting and horse racing to concerts, some of it Burns related. Burnsfest is the major live-music event, held on a Saturday in May.

Sleeping

Heads of Ayr Caravan Park CAMPSITE £
(☎ 01292-442269; www.headsofayr-caravanpark. co.uk; Dunure Rd; sites £21-25; ☻ Mar-Oct; P ☎ ☎) This caravan park is in a lovely, quiet location close to the beach. There are various caravans and chalets available to rent by the week or for a few days. From Ayr take the A719 south for about 5 miles.

26 The Crescent B&B ££
(☎ 01292-287329; www.26crescent.co.uk; 26 Bellevue Cres; d £84-99; ☎) When the blossoms are out, this is Ayr's prettiest street, and it boasts an excellent place to stay. The rooms are impeccable – an upgrade to the spacious four-poster room is a sound investment. Bathrooms are excellent. Though there's more space on the 1st floor, we like the top-floor chambers with sloping roof. The welcome is genuinely friendly.

Arrandale Hotel GUESTHOUSE ££
(☎ 01292-289959; www.arrandalehotel.co.uk; 2 Cassillis St; s £38, d £70-85; ☎) In a quiet and pleasant part of town, the mixture of new and old here doesn't always work, but it's a relaxed, friendly place offering comfort at a reasonable price. Sparklingly clean bathrooms are a highlight, and the large lounge is an appealing space. Room-only rates are the norm, with breakfast £7 per person. There's a cafe here too.

Eating & Drinking

XXII BISTRO ££
(No 22 Bar & Grill; ☎ 01292-280820; www.22ayr. com; 22 Beresford Tce; mains £11-17; ☻ food 9am-9.30pm; ☎) Buzzy and attractive, XXII serves a wide-ranging fusion menu as well as cocktails, breakfasts and more. Mediterranean and, particularly, Italian influences take pride of place, backed up by things like tempura and steaks. It can be hit-and-miss but outranks the local competition (not a tough task). There's a wide choice of wines by the glass.

Tam O'Shanter PUB
(☎ 01292-611684; 230 High St; ☻ 11am-11pm Mon-Sat, 12.30-11pm Sun; ☎) In Robert Burns' poem 'Tam o' Shanter', Tam spends a boozy evening in this pub, which now bears his name. Opened in the mid-18th century, it's

an atmospheric old place with a good vibe as well as mediocre pub grub (served noon to 9pm).

Getting There & Away

BUS
Ayr is 33 miles from Glasgow and is Ayrshire's major transport hub. There are frequent express services to Glasgow (£6.70, one hour) via Prestwick Airport, as well as services to Stranraer (£8.40, two hours, four to eight per day) and several Ayrshire towns. The **bus station** (Sandgate) sits at the corner of Fullarton St and Sandgate.

TRAIN
There are at least two trains an hour that run between Ayr and Glasgow Central station (£8.70, 50 minutes), and some trains continue south from Ayr to Stranraer (£11.50, 1¼ hours).

Alloway
POP 6100

The pretty, lush village of Alloway (3 miles south of Ayr) should be on the itinerary of every Robert Burns fan – he was born here on 25 January 1759. Even if you haven't been seduced by Burnsmania, it's still well worth a visit, as the Burns-related exhibitions give a good impression of life in Ayrshire in the late 18th century.

Alloway Auld Kirk RUINS
(Monument Rd; ☻ 24hr) FREE Near the Robert Burns Birthplace Museum (p162) are the ruins of the kirk, the setting for part of Burns' verse tale 'Tam o' Shanter'. Burns' father, William, is buried in the kirkyard; read the poem on the back of the gravestone.

Burns Monument & Memorial Gardens GARDENS
(☻ 24hr) FREE Within these gardens near the Robert Burns Birthplace Museum (p162) is a striking neo-Grecian monument to the poet, completed in 1823. It affords a view of the nearby 13th-century Brig o' Doon, another Burns landmark.

Getting There & Away

Buses heading south to Girvan and Stranraer run roughly hourly from Ayr to Alloway (£2.20, 10 minutes). Some X77 services run direct here from Glasgow via Prestwick airport and Ayr. Otherwise you can easily walk or cycle here from Ayr.

ROBERT BURNS' BIRTHPLACE

The impressive **Robert Burns Birthplace Museum** (NTS; ☑ 01292-443700; www.burns museum.org.uk; Murdoch's Lone; adult/child £10.50/7.50; ⊙10am-5pm) has collected a solid range of Burns memorabilia, including manuscripts and possessions of the poet, like the pistols he packed for his work as a taxman. There's good biographical information, and a series of displays that bring to life poems via background snippets, translations and recitations. Appropriately, the museum doesn't take itself too seriously: there's plenty of humour that the poet surely would have approved of, and entertaining audio and visual performances will keep the kids amused.

The admission ticket also covers the atmospheric **Burns Birthplace Cottage** (open 11am to 5pm), connected via a walkway to the Birthplace Museum. Born in the little box-bed in this cramped thatched dwelling, the poet spent the first seven years of his life here. It's an attractive display that gives you a context for reading plenty of his verse. Much-needed translation of some of the more obscure Scots farming terms he loved to use decorate the walls.

Culzean Castle

★ **Culzean Castle & Country Park** PALACE (NTS; ☑01655-884455; www.nts.org.uk; Culzean; castle adult/child/family £16.50/12.25/41; ⊙castle 10.30am-5pm Apr-Oct, last entry 4pm, park 9.30am-sunset year-round; 🖝) The Scottish National Trust's flagship property, magnificent Culzean (kull-*ane*) is one of the most impressive of Scotland's stately homes. On approach the castle floats into view like a mirage. Designed by Robert Adam, encouraged to exercise his romantic genius, this 18th-century mansion is perched dramatically on a clifftop.

There's a great play area for kids, which recreates the castle on a smaller scale, as well as a recreation of a Victorian vinery, an orangery, a deer park and an aviary.

Robert Adam was the most influential architect of his time, renowned for his meticulous attention to detail and the elegant classical embellishments with which he decorated his ceilings and fireplaces.

The beautiful oval staircase here is regarded as one of his finest achievements. On the 1st floor, the opulence of the circular saloon contrasts violently with the views of the wild sea below. Lord Cassillis' bedroom is said to be haunted by a lady in green, mourning for a lost baby. Even the bathrooms are palatial: the dressing room beside the state bedroom is equipped with a Victorian state-of-the-art shower.

If you really want to experience the magic of this place, it's possible to stay in the **castle** (☑ 01655-884455; www.culzean-eisenhower.com; s/d from £255/275, Eisenhower ste s/d £375/400;

⊙Apr-Oct; 🅿🛜) from April to October. There's also a **campsite** (☑ 01655-760627; www. campingandcaravanningclub.co.uk; sites per adult/ child members from £11.20/5.60, non-members £16/8; ⊙Apr-Oct; 🅿🛜🐾) at the entrance to the park, offering grassy pitches with great views.

Wildlife in the area includes otters.

Stagecoach buses running between Ayr and Girvan stop outside the gates, from where it's a 1-mile walk to the castle itself.

Crossraguel Abbey

Between the towns of Maybole and Kirkoswald, by the A77, **Crossraguel Abbey** (HES; ☑ 01655-883113; www.historicenvironment. scot; A77, near Maybole; adult/child £5/3; ⊙9.30am-5.30pm Apr-Sep) is a substantial ruin dating back to the 13th century that's good fun to explore. The renovated 16th-century gatehouse is the best part – you'll find decorative stonework and superb views from the top. Inside, if you have the place to yourself, you'll hear only the whistling wind – an apt reflection of the abbey's long-deceased monastic tradition. Don't miss the echo in the chilly sacristy.

Turnberry

Turnberry basically consists of one of Scotland's great golf links and a massive, superluxurious resort and self-catering complex opposite it. The whole thing was bought by Donald Trump in 2015 and has had a recent facelift.

Turnberry's **Ailsa** (☑01655-334060; www. turnberry.co.uk; Maidens Rd) is one of Scotland's most prestigious links courses, with spectacular views of Ailsa Craig offshore. You don't need a handicap certificate to play, just plenty of pounds – the summer weekend green fee is £375. In summer though, take advantage of the after-3pm 'sunset' rate and you can go round for less than half that.

Ailsa Craig

The curiously shaped island of Ailsa Craig can be seen from much of southern Ayrshire. While its unusual blue-tinted granite – famous for making the best curling stones – has been used by geologists to trace the movements of the great Ice Age ice sheet, birdwatchers know Ailsa Craig as the world's second-largest gannet colony – around 10,000 pairs breed annually on the island's sheer cliffs.

To see the island close up, take a cruise from Girvan on the **MV Glorious** (07773 794358, 01465-713219; www.ailsacraig.org.uk; 7 Harbour St; May–mid-Oct). It's possible to land if the sea is reasonably calm; a four-hour trip costs £25/15 per adult/child.

Trains going to Girvan run approximately hourly (less frequently on Sundays) from Ayr (£5.70, 25 minutes).

DUMFRIES & GALLOWAY

Some of southern Scotland's finest attractions lie in the gentle hills and lush valleys of Dumfries and Galloway. It's an ideal destination for families, as there's plenty on offer for the kids. Galloway Forest – with its sublime views, mountain-biking and walking trails, red deer, kites and other wildlife – is a highlight, as are the dream-like ruins of Caerlaverock Castle. Adding to the appeal of this enticing region is a string of southern Scotland's most idyllic towns, which are charming when the sun shines. And shine it does. This is the mildest region in Scotland and is warmed by the Gulf Stream, a phenomenon that has allowed the development of some famous gardens.

Dumfries

POP 32,900

Lovely, red-hued sandstone bridges crisscross the wide, grassy-banked River Nith, which runs through the centre of pleasant Dumfries. Historically the town held a strategic position in the path of vengeful English armies; consequently, although it has existed since Roman times, the oldest standing building dates from the 17th century. Plenty of famous names have passed through: Robert Burns lived here and worked as a tax collector, Peter Pan creator JM Barrie was schooled here and DJ Calvin Harris hails from the town.

◉ Sights

★**Burns House** MUSEUM
(01387-255297; www.dumgal.gov.uk; Burns St; 10am-5pm Mon-Sat, 2-5pm Sun Apr-Sep, 10am-1pm & 2-5pm Tue-Sat Oct-Mar) FREE This is a place of pilgrimage for Burns enthusiasts. It's here that the poet spent the last years of his life, and there are various possessions of his in glass cases, as well as manuscripts and, entertainingly, letters: make sure you have a read.

Dumfries Museum & Camera Obscura MUSEUM
(01387-253374; www.dumgal.gov.uk; Rotchell Rd; museum free, camera obscura adult/child £3.40/1.70; 10am-5pm Mon-Sat, 2-5pm Sun Apr-Sep, 10am-1pm & 2-5pm Tue-Sat Oct-Mar) FREE

> **WORTH A TRIP**
>
> ### DUMFRIES HOUSE
>
> A Palladian mansion designed in the 1750s by the Adam brothers, **Dumfries House** (01290-425959; www.dumfries-house.org.uk; Cumnock; house tour adult/child £9/4; tours 10.45am-3.30pm Sun-Fri, 10.45am & noon Sat Easter-Oct, 12.15pm & 1.45pm Sat & Sun Nov-Feb, closed mid-Dec–early Jan) is an architectural jewel: such is its preservation that Prince Charles personally intervened to ensure its protection. It contains an extraordinarily well-preserved collection of Chippendale furniture and numerous objets d'art. Visits are by guided tour; book ahead. There's a discount for Historic Environment Scotland members. The daily Grand Tour (adult/child £13/4) also takes you to the bedrooms upstairs and the grounds. There's a cafe here.
>
> The house is located 13 miles east of Ayr, near Cumnock. Bus it from Ayr or Dumfries to Cumnock and walk or cab it the 2 miles to the house; you can also get a train from Glasgow to Auchinleck.

Dumfries

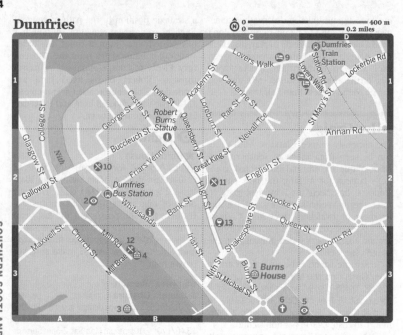

Dumfries

⊙ Top Sights
1 Burns House C3

⊙ Sights
2 Devorgilla Bridge A2
3 Dumfries Museum & Camera
   Obscura B3
4 Robert Burns Centre B3
5 Robert Burns Mausoleum D3
6 St Michael's Kirk C3

🛏 Sleeping
7 Ferintosh Guest House D1
8 Huntingdon D1
9 Torbay Lodge C1

🍴 Eating
10 Cavens Arms A2
11 Kings C2
12 Willows B3

🍸 Drinking & Nightlife
13 Globe Inn C2

This museum covers local history and pre-history with a wide range of displays from fossils to farm implements. In the tower is a camera obscura, built in 1836, giving an intriguing view, even in this digital age, of the surrounding area.

Devorgilla Bridge   BRIDGE
The red sandstone bridges arching over the River Nith are the most attractive feature of the town. Devorgilla Bridge (1431) is one of the oldest bridges in Scotland. Built into its southwestern end is the city's oldest extant house.

Robert Burns Centre   MUSEUM
(✆01387-264808; www.dumgal.gov.uk; Mill Rd; audiovisual presentation £2.30; ⊙10am-5pm Mon-Sat, 2-5pm Sun Apr-Sep, 10am-1pm & 2-5pm Tue-Sat Oct-Mar) **FREE** A worthwhile Burns exhibition in an old mill on the banks of the River Nith; it tells the story of the poet and Dumfries in the 1790s. The optional audiovisual presentations give more background on Dumfries, and explain the exhibition's contents. The centre functions as a cinema in the evenings.

Ellisland Farm   MUSEUM
(✆01387-740426; www.ellislandfarm.co.uk; Holywood Rd, Auldgirth; adult/child £5/free; ⊙10am-1pm & 2-5pm Mon-Sat, 2-5pm Sun Apr-Sep, 10am-1pm & 2-5pm Tue-Sat Oct, Nov & early Jan-Mar) Six miles northwest of Dumfries, you can visit the farm that Robert Burns leased in 1788 by the River Nith. He had the house built for his family and lived here until 1791. The farmhouse still preserves plenty of atmosphere

of the time. There's an exhibition and short film. Ellisland is signposted off the A76 to Kilmarnock; bus 246 will get you there too.

Robert Burns Mausoleum TOMB

(St Michael's Kirk, Brooms Rd) FREE Burns' mausoleum is in the graveyard at St Michael's Kirk (www.stmichaelschurchdumfries.org; Brooms Rd; ☉10.30am-3.30pm Mon-Fri Apr-Sep). It's in the far corner (ie eastern corner) from the entrance. There's a grisly account of his reburial on the information panel.

🛏 Sleeping

★ Ferintosh Guest House B&B ££

(☏01387-252262; www.ferintosh.net; 30 Lovers Walk; s £35-42, d £66-74; ☏ ☏) A typically lovely Dumfries sandstone Victorian villa opposite the train station, Ferintosh is a good-humoured place with excellent rooms and a warm welcome. These people have the right attitude towards hospitality, with comfortable plush beds, a free dram on arrival, and plenty of good chat on distilleries. The owner's original artwork complements the decor.

Cyclists are welcomed with a shed and bike-washing facilities. It was for sale at the time of research so things may change.

Huntingdon B&B ££

(☏01387-249071; www.thehuntingdonbandb.co.uk; 32 Lovers Walk; r £90; ℗ ☏) This smart modernisation of a sturdy sandstone former day hospital offers high-standard B&B in four attractive, very commodious rooms with good modern bathrooms right by the train station. There's a pleasant front lawn and a gracious host. Room-only rates are available.

Torbay Lodge B&B ££

(☏01387-253922; www.torbaylodge.co.uk; 31 Lovers Walk; s £45-55, d/f £79/100; ℗ ☏) This high-quality guesthouse has beautifully presented bedrooms with big windows, elegant bedsteads and generously sized en suites (and a single without); the good vibe is topped off by an excellent breakfast. It's handy for the train station and there's a laundry service.

🍴 Eating & Drinking

Cavens Arms PUB FOOD £

(☏01387-252896; www.facebook.com/cavens. arms.9; 20 Buccleuch St; mains £8-12; ☉food 11.30am-8.30pm Tue-Sat, noon-8.30pm Sun; ☏) Engaging staff, 10 real ales on tap and a warm, contented buzz make this a legendary Dumfries pub. Generous portions of typical pub nosh backed by a long list of more adventurous daily specials make it one of the town's most enjoyable places to eat too. Gets packed on weekends (but staff will still try to find you a table).

If you were going to move to Dumfries, you'd make sure you were within a block or two of this place. There's no food on Monday, but the pub's still open. Under-14s aren't allowed to eat here.

Kings CAFE £

(☏01387-254444; www.kings-online.co.uk; 12 Queensberry St; snacks £2-6; ☉8am-5.30pm Mon-Sat, noon-4pm Sun; ☏) This buzzy cafe in the centre of town doubles as a bookshop. It does tasty fair-trade coffee, has big windows for observing Dumfries life passing by and serves toothsome sweet things, breakfasts and filled rolls.

Willows BRITISH ££

(☏01387-216688; www.facebook.com/thewillows restaurantdumfries; Mill Rd; dinner mains £14-20; ☉food 5-9pm Mon, 11am-3pm & 5-9pm Tue-Sat; ☏) In the Robert Burns Centre, this new restaurant has an enviable riverside location. A short menu of quality lamb, fish and the like is on offer in the evenings, while lunch features tapas and home baking. It's also a nice spot for a coffee or a drink.

Globe Inn PUB

(☏01387-252335; www.globeinndumfries.co.uk; 56 High St; ☉10am-11pm Mon-Wed, to midnight Thu, to 1am Fri & Sat, 11.30am-midnight Sun) A traditional, rickety old nook-and-cranny pub down a narrow wynd off the main pedestrian drag, this was reputedly Burns' favourite watering hole, and scene of one of his numerous seductions. It's not an upmarket place, but can have good atmosphere created more by its welcoming locals and staff than the numerous pictures of the 'ploughman poet' himself.

---

❶ DUMFRIES & GALLOWAY BUS PASS

Buses are the main mode of local transport with Stagecoach (☏01387-253496; www.stagecoachbus.com) the primary operator. Its Megarider ticket costs £23.50 and gives you unlimited travel on Stagecoach buses within Dumfries and Galloway for a week – not a bad deal.

ℹ️ Information

Dumfries Tourist Office (☎ 01387-253862;
www.visitscotland.com; 64 Whitesands;
🕑 9.30am-4.30pm Mon-Sat Nov-Mar,
9.30am-5pm or 5.30pm Mon-Sat, 11am-4pm
Sun Apr-Oct) By the river. Offers plenty of
information on the region including a leaflet
on the local Robert Burns trail. You can get a
parking disc here to use in the riverside car
park opposite.

ℹ️ Getting There & Away

BUS

Buses (Whitesands) run via towns along the
A75 to Stranraer (£7.80, 2¼ hours, seven daily
Monday to Saturday, three on Sunday) as well
as to Castle Douglas and Kirkcudbright. Buses
101 and 102 run to/from Edinburgh (£10, 2¾
to three hours, four to seven daily), via Moffat
and Biggar.

TRAIN

There are trains between Carlisle and Dumfries
(£11.40, 40 minutes, every hour or two), and
direct trains between Dumfries and Glasgow
(£17.10, 1¾ hours, nine daily Monday to Saturday). Services are reduced on Sundays.

Ruthwell Cross

Seven miles east of Caerlaverock Castle, in
tiny Ruthwell, a church holds one of Europe's most important early Christian monuments. The 6m-high 7th-century **Ruthwell**

THE SCOTTISH BARD

I see her in the dewy flowers,
I see her sweet and fair:
I hear her in the tunefu' birds,
I hear her charm the air:
There's not a bonnie flower that springs
By fountain, shaw, or green;
There's not a bonnie bird that sings,
But minds me o' my Jean.

Robert Burns, 'Of a' the Airts', 1788

Best remembered for penning the words of 'Auld Lang Syne', Robert Burns (1759–96) is
Scotland's most famous poet and a popular hero; his birthday (25 January) is celebrated
as Burns Night by Scots around the world.

Burns was born in Alloway to a poor family, who scraped a living gardening and farming. At school he soon showed an aptitude for literature and a fondness for the folk song.
He later began writing his own songs and satires. When the problems of his arduous
farming life were compounded by the threat of prosecution from the father of Jean Armour, with whom he'd had an affair, he decided to emigrate to Jamaica. He gave up his
share of the family farm and published his poems to raise money for the journey.

The poems were so well reviewed in Edinburgh that Burns decided to remain in Scotland and devote himself to writing. He went to Edinburgh in 1787 to publish a 2nd edition,
but the financial rewards were not enough to live on and he had to take a job as an ex-
cise man in Dumfriesshire. Though he worked well, he wasn't a taxman by nature, and
described his job as 'the execrable office of whip-person to the blood-hounds of justice'.
He contributed many songs to collections, and a 3rd edition of his poems was published
in 1793. A prodigious writer, Burns composed more than 28,000 lines of verse over 22
years. He died (probably of heart disease) in Dumfries in 1796, aged 37, having fathered
more than a dozen children to several different women. Generous-spirited Jean bore nine
of them and took in another, remarking 'Oor Robbie should hae had twa wives'.

Many of the local landmarks mentioned in the verse tale 'Tam o' Shanter' can still be
visited. Farmer Tam, riding home after a hard night's drinking in a pub in Ayr, sees witches dancing in Alloway churchyard. He calls out to the one pretty witch, but is pursued by
them, and has to reach the other side of the River Doon to be safe. He just manages to
cross the Brig o' Doon, but his mare loses her tail to the witches.

The Burns connection in southern Scotland is milked for all it's worth and tourist offices have a *Burns Heritage Trail* leaflet leading you to every place that can claim some link
with the bard. Burns fans should have a look at www.robertburns.org.

Cross (HES; www.historicenvironment.scot; B724; ☉ daylight hours) **FREE** is carved top to bottom in New Testament scenes and is inscribed with a poem called 'The Dream of the Rood'; written in a Saxon runic alphabet, it's considered one of the earliest examples of English-language literature. Bus 79 running between Dumfries and Annan stops in Ruthwell.

Caerlaverock

The ruins of **Caerlaverock Castle** (HES; ☎ 01387-770244; www.historicenvironment.scot; Glencaple; adult/child £6/3.60; ☉ 9.30am-5.30pm Apr-Sep, 10am-4pm Oct-Mar), by Glencaple on a beautiful stretch of the Solway coast, are among the loveliest in Britain. Surrounded by a moat, lawns and stands of trees, the unusual pink-stoned triangular castle looks impregnable. In fact, it fell several times, most famously when it was attacked in 1300 by Edward I: the siege became the subject of an epic poem, 'The Siege of Caerlaverock'.

The current castle dates from the late 13th century but, once defensive purposes were no longer a design necessity, it was refitted as a luxurious Scottish Renaissance mansion house in 1634. Ironically, the rampaging Covenanter militia sacked it a few years later. With nooks and crannies to explore, passageways and remnants of fireplaces, this castle is great for the whole family.

Nearby the **Caerlaverock Wetland Centre** (☎ 01387-770200; www.wwt.org.uk/caerlaverock; Eastpark Farm; adult/child £7.90/4.54, free for WWT members; ☉ 10am-5pm; ◉) protects 546 hectares of salt marsh and mud flats, the habitat for numerous birds, including barnacle geese. There are various activities, including badger-watching, dawn goose flights and child-focused events. It also has a good nature-watching bookshop and a coffee shop that serves organic food. Accommodation in private rooms with a shared kitchen (double £60 to £84) is available too.

New Abbey

The small, picturesque whitewashed village of New Abbey lies 7 miles south of Dumfries and has several worthwhile things to see and do in and around it. The centre is dominated by the ruins of Sweetheart Abbey, while a working watermill is nearby. Outside town are a popular farm park and mountain biking trails.

Mabie Farm Park FARM
(☎ 01387-259666; www.mabiefarmpark.co.uk; Burnside Farm, Mabie; adult/child/family £8/7.50/30; ☉ 10am-5pm Apr-Oct, plus Sat & Sun Mar; ◉) If your kids are complaining about historic sights and Robert Burns, pack up the clan and get down to this spot, between Dumfries and New Abbey off the A710. It's a brilliantly run complex with plenty of animals and activities, including petting-and-feeding sessions, donkey rides, go-karting, slides, a soft play area, picnic spots...the list goes on. Put a full day aside.

New Abbey Corn Mill NOTABLE BUILDING
(☎ 01387-850260; www.historicenvironment.scot; adult/child £5/3; ☉ 9.30am-5.30pm Apr-Sep, 10am-4pm Sat-Wed Oct-Mar) This 18th-century watermill in the centre of the village is very well preserved. A video sets it in context, and cordial guides will show you the workings. On summer days it is often running.

Sweetheart Abbey RUINS
(HES; ☎ 01387-850397; www.historicenvironment. scot; adult/child £5/3; ☉ 9.30am-5.30pm Apr-Sep, 10am-4pm Sat-Wed Oct-Mar) The shattered red-sandstone remnants of this 13th-century Cistercian abbey stand in stark contrast to the manicured lawns surrounding them. The abbey, the last of Scotland's major monasteries to be established, was founded by Devorgilla of Galloway in 1273 in honour of her dead husband John Balliol. On his death, she had his heart embalmed and carried it with her until she died 22 years later. She and the heart were buried by the altar: hence the name.

The couple founded Balliol College, Oxford.

7stanes Mabie MOUNTAIN BIKING
(www.7stanesmountainbiking.com; A710) **FREE** Mabie Forest Park is one of southern Scotland's 7stanes mountain-biking hubs, set among forested hills a couple of miles north of New Abbey. There are nearly 40 miles of trails for all levels; the closest bike hire is in Dumfries. It's very close to the Mabie Farm Park, which is handy if you've got kids of different ages.

Annandale & Eskdale

These valleys, in Dumfries and Galloway's east, form part of two major routes that cut across Scotland's south. Away from the highways, the roads are quiet and there are some interesting places to visit, especially if you're looking to break up a road trip.

WORTH A TRIP

MUSEUM OF LEAD MINING

'Lead mining': even the phrase has a sort of dulling effect on the brain, and you'd think it'd be a tough ask to make the subject interesting. But the **Museum of Lead Mining** (☑01659-74387; www.leadminingmuseum.co.uk; Wanlockhead; adult/child £12.50/7.90, mine or cottages only £5.50/4.50; ⊙11am-4.30pm Apr-Sep; ⓓ), signposted 10 miles off the motorway northwest of Moffat, manages to pull it off. The place is fascinating, and family friendly, offering a tour of a real mine, recreated miners' cottages, a remarkable 18th-century library, and a display on lead mining and other minerals.

It's apparently Scotland's highest village, set amid a striking landscape of treeless hills and burbling streams. In summer the museum also runs gold-panning activities. The palpable enthusiasm and personableness of the staff bring the social history of the place alive. It's really rather special, and is one of our favourite museums in Scotland.

Buses running between Ayr and Dumfries stop in Sanquhar, from where there's a bus to Wanlockhead five times daily Monday to Saturday. Wanlockhead is also a stop on the Southern Upland Way (p150) walking route.

Gretna & Gretna Green

POP 3100

Firmly on the coach-tour circuit for its romantic associations, Gretna Green is on the outskirts of the town of Gretna, just across the river from Cumbria in England. Historically famous as a destination at which eloping couples get married, it's still one of Britain's most popular wedding venues.

Famous Blacksmith's Shop   MUSEUM
(☑01461-338441; www.gretnagreen.com; Gretna Green; exhibition adult/child £3.75/free; ⊙9am-5pm Oct-Mar, to 5.30pm Apr & May, to 6pm Jun-Sep) At the centre of the village of Gretna Green, the touristy Famous Blacksmith's Shop complex has a number of mediocre shops and eateries, a maze, and a quite entertaining multilingual exhibition on Gretna Green's history, with tales of intrigues, elopements, scoundrels and angry parents arriving minutes too late. There's a recreation of a blacksmith's forge, a collection of handsome carriages and a few marriage rooms: you may well run into a modern-day wedding as you walk through.

Smith's at Gretna Green   HOTEL ££
(☑01461-337007; www.smithsgretnagreen.com; s/d from £98/108; ᴘ ⓦ) A large contemporary hotel close to the Gretna Green complex. Though the blocky exterior won't delight everybody, the interior is much more stylish; rooms are decorated in a chic, restrained style with king-sized beds. Various grades are available; the rates here represent typical online booking offers. The **restaurant** (☑01461-337007; www.smiths gretnagreen.com; restaurant mains £22-31, bar mains £12-18; ⊙10am-10pm; ⓦ ⓓ) is the best around. There's a little noise from the adjacent motorway.

Castle Douglas & Around

POP 4100

Castle Douglas attracts a lot of day trippers but hasn't been 'spruced up' for tourism. It's an open, attractive, well-cared-for town, with some remarkably beautiful areas close to the centre, such as the small Carlingwark Loch. The town was laid out in the 18th century by Sir William Douglas, who had made a fortune in the Americas.

Northwest of the town, long Loch Ken is a good destination for water sports and, along its eastern shore, spotting red kites.

⊙ Sights & Activities

Loch Ken   LAKE
Stretching for 9 miles northwest of Castle Douglas between the A713 and A762, Loch Ken is a popular outdoor recreational area. The range of water sports includes windsurfing, sailing, canoeing, power-boating and kayaking. There are also walking trails and rich bird life. The Royal Society for the Protection of Birds (RSPB) has a nature reserve on the western bank, north of Glenlochar. The eastern shore is great for watching red kites.

Threave Castle   CASTLE
(HES; ☑07711 223101; www.historicenvironment. scot; adult/child incl ferry £5/3; ⊙10am-5pm Apr-Sep, to 4pm Oct) Two miles west of Castle Douglas, this impressive tower sits on a small river island. Built in the late 14th

century, it became a principal stronghold of the Black Douglases, including the excellently named Archibald the Grim. It's now basically a shell, having been badly damaged by the Covenanters in the 1640s, but it's a romantic ruin nonetheless. It's a 15-minute walk from the car park to the ferry landing, where you ring a bell to be taken across.

Also from the car park, where there's a small nature exhibition, a 1.5-mile circular **nature path** gives you the chance to spot deer and ospreys, as well as waterbirds from hides. At dusk it's good for batwatching.

★ **Galloway**
Activity Centre　　　WATER SPORTS, OUTDOORS
(☑ 01556-502011; www.lochken.co.uk; Parton; ⊙ 10am-5pm, plus evening session Jun-Aug; ▣) On the eastern bank of Loch Ken north of Parton, this excellent set-up runs a very wide range of activities on water and land, and also provides equipment and a variety of **accommodation** (dm £18-19.50, cabin for 2/6 people £40/85, yurt £90; ▣ 🛜 🛉) 🐾. Activities run in sessions of 1½ hours; one session costs £21.50 each for two, and the price reduces substantially for further sessions. Best to book in advance.

Activities include but are not limited to windsurfing, foiling, sailing, kayaking, paddle boarding, archery and mountain biking. There's also a cafe here.

Ken-Dee Marshes
Nature Reserve　　　BIRDWATCHING
(☑ 01556-670464; www.rspb.org.uk) FREE This birdwatching reserve is on the western bank of Loch Ken, 3½ miles north of Glenlochar. It's a scenic spot where the River Dee meets

the loch, and a nature trail and hides allow you to view a range of species, including pied flycatchers, redstarts and wintering geese.

🛏 Sleeping & Eating

Lochside Caravan
& Camping Site　　　CAMPSITE £
(☑ 01556-504682; www.dumgal.gov.uk/caravan andcamping; Lochside Park; tent sites £12.50, plus car £4; ⊙ Apr-Oct; ▣ 🛉) Very central campsite attractively situated beside Carlingwark Loch; there's plenty of grass and fine trees provide shade.

★ **Douglas House**　　　B&B ££
(☑ 01556-503262; www.douglas-house.com; 63 Queen St; s £41, d £78-87; 🛜 🛉) This beautiful 200-year-old stone house has big beautiful bathrooms that complement the light, stylish chambers. The two upstairs doubles are lovely and the downstairs double is huge with a super-king-sized bed – it could sleep four! There are numerous little extras and prices are very fair for this high standard. Breakfast is recommended, with locally sourced produce.

★ **Designs**　　　CAFE £
(☑ 01556-504552; www.designsgallery.com; 179 King St; lunches £6.50; ⊙ 9.30am-5pm; 🛜) This excellent cafe under a gallery and shop is the best spot in town for a coffee, with cosy wood fittings offset by a garden space out the back. There's a nice line in ciabatta and bruschetta options complemented by chalkboard lunch specials. The carrot cake also comes warmly recommended.

SOUTHERN SCOTLAND CASTLE DOUGLAS & AROUND

TYING THE KNOT IN GRETNA GREEN

The *Marriage Act* that passed in England in 1754 suddenly required couples that did not have their parents' consent to be 21 years of age before they could marry. But cunning teenage sweethearts soon realised that the law didn't apply in Scotland, where a simple declaration in front of a pair of witnesses would suffice. As the first village in Scotland, Gretna Green's border location made it the most popular venue for eloping couples to get hitched.

Locals competed for the incoming trade, and marriages were performed by just about anyone who could round up a couple of witnesses from the nearest pub. One legendary Gretna vow-taker was the local blacksmith, who became known as the 'Anvil Priest'. In 1856 eloping was made more difficult when a law was passed obliging couples to have spent at least three weeks in Scotland prior to tying the knot, but Gretna Green remained popular. And it still is: some 5000 couples annually take or reaffirm their marriage vows in the village. If you want to get married over the famous anvil in the Old Blacksmith's Shop at Gretna Green, check out www.gretnagreen.com or www.gretnaweddings.co.uk.

Mr Pook's Kitchen
BRITISH **££**

(☑ 01556-504000; www.mrpooks.co.uk; 38 King St; mains £16-21; ⊙ 5-9pm Tue-Fri, noon-9pm Sat, 11am-4pm Sun) This converted bank on the main street had just opened when we last passed by. It was still finding its feet but we liked the way it was shaping up: solid British produce served with a bit of style and flair, with slow-roasting a speciality. There's also a bottle shop here.

ⓘ Getting There & Away

Buses run roughly hourly from Castle Douglas to Dumfries (from £3.40, 30 to 50 minutes); there are also services to Kirkcudbright (20 minutes), Stranraer, New Galloway and Ayr.

Kirkcudbright

POP 3400

Kirkcudbright (kirk-*coo*-bree), with its dignified streets of 17th- and 18th-century merchants' houses and appealing harbour, is the ideal base from which to explore the south coast. Look out for the nook-and-cranny closes and wynds in the elbow of beautifully restored High St. With its architecture and setting, it's easy to see why Kirkcudbright has been an artists colony since the late 19th century.

⊙ Sights

Broughton House
GALLERY

(NTS; ☑ 01557-330437; www.nts.org.uk; 12 High St; adult/child £7.50/6.50; ⊙ 10am-5pm Apr-Oct) The 18th-century Broughton House displays paintings by EA Hornel, one of the Glasgow Boys (he lived and worked here). The library, with its wood panelling and stone carvings, is probably the most impressive room. Behind the house is a lovely Japanese-style garden (also open 11am to 4pm Monday to Friday in February and March).

Kirkcudbright Galleries
GALLERY

(☑ 01557-331276; www.kirkcudbrightgalleries.org. uk; St Mary St; ⊙ 10am-5pm Mon-Sat, noon-5pm Sun) **FREE** This new conversion of the town hall into a shiny new gallery opened just after we last passed by. There's a permanent exhibition on this town's artistic heritage and a collection of art and design by notable former residents. Two other galleries host high-quality temporary exhibitions. There's also a cafe and shop. Disabled facilities are excellent.

Tolbooth Art Centre
GALLERY

(☑ 01557-331556; www.dumgal.gov.uk; High St; ⊙ 10am-4pm Mon-Sat, 1-4pm Sun mid-Apr-Sep, 11am-4pm Mon-Sat Oct–mid-Apr) **FREE** As well as catering for today's local artists and holding a cinema, this centre has an exhibition on the history of the town's artistic development. The place is as interesting for the building itself as for the artistic works on display: it's one of the oldest and best-preserved tolbooths (a building that served as both town hall and courthouse in Scottish towns) in the country. There are interpretative signboards to explain its past.

MacLellan's Castle
CASTLE

(HES; ☑ 01557-331856; www.historicenvironment. scot; Castle St; adult/child £5/3; ⊙ 9.30am-1pm & 2-5.30pm Apr-Sep) Near the harbour, this is a large, atmospheric ruin built in 1577 by Thomas MacLellan, then provost of Kirkcudbright, as his town residence. Inside, look for the 'lairds' lug', a 16th-century hidey-hole designed for the laird to eavesdrop on his guests.

🎊 Festivals & Events

Thursdays in high summer are Scottish theme nights, with music, dancing and more in the centre of town.

Art & Crafts Trail
ART

(www.artandcraftstrail.com; ⊙ late Jul or early Aug) Each year the town revels in a four-day community artistic extravaganza with a theme that changes annually. There's something quirky – sculpture, music, handcraft workshops – going on all over the place in numerous venues: people's homes, improvised outdoor spaces, the castle. Infectious fun is guaranteed.

Kirkcudbright Jazz Festival
MUSIC

(☑ 01557-330467; www.kirkcudbrightjazzfestival. co.uk; ⊙ Jun) Four days of swing, trad and dixie across several venues.

🛌 Sleeping

Silvercraigs Caravan & Camping Site
CAMPSITE **£**

(☑ 01557-332050; www.silvercraigscaravanpark. co.uk; Silvercraigs Rd; tent sites £10-16; P 🐾) There are brilliant views from this year-round campsite; you feel like you're sleeping on top of the town. It's great for stargazing on clear nights, and there are good facilities, including a laundry. Both powered and unpowered sites are available. Call ahead in the low season.

★ **Selkirk Arms Hotel**   HOTEL **££**
(☑ 01557-330402; www.selkirkarmshotel.co.uk;
High St; s/d £90/120, compact d £99; **P @ 🛜 🌂**)
What a haven of hospitality this is. Rooms
look great with a stylish purply finish and
slate-floored bathrooms. Wood furnishings
and views over the back garden give some of
them an extra rustic appeal. There's a good
restaurant as well as a cute gin and prosecco
bar. Staff are happy to be there, and you will
be too.

Anchorlee   B&B **££**
(☑ 01557-330197; www.anchorlee.co.uk; 95 St Mary
St; s/d £68/80; ☺ Easter-Dec; **P 🛜 🌂**) This elegant residence on the main road offers great
hospitality from its cordial hosts. Four lovely
rooms offer plenty of space; number four is
an appealing split-level affair overlooking
the garden. Breakfast is excellent.

Garret   BOUTIQUE HOTEL **££**
(☑ 01557-330797; www.thegarrethotel.co.uk; 116
High St; s/d £75/95, superior d £105; 🛜) This
hotel wasn't quite open when we last passed
by but should be well worth a look. It's a
noble Georgian town house with eight spacious, light rooms. There's also a cafe-bar
with garden seating. The location on this
lovely street is excellent.

Kirkcudbright Bay Hotel   PUB **££**
(☑ 01557-339544; www.kirkcudbrightbayhotel.com;
25 St Cuthbert St; s/d £65/80; 🛜) This well-
run central pub is a very pleasant place to
lay your head, with comfortable modernised
en-suite rooms – the large room 1 is especially appealing – and an attractive downstairs bar and restaurant. Room-only rates
are offered too but breakfast is generous and
includes haggis. Some cheaper rooms without bathroom (£40) are also available.

✗ Eating

★ **Auld Alliance**   SCOTTISH, FRENCH **££**
(☑ 01557-330888; www.auldalliancekirkcudbright.
co.uk; 29 St Cuthbert St; mains £14-23; ☺ 6-9pm
Thu-Sat, plus Wed Jul-Sep; 🛜) Overlooking
the heart of town, this restaurant's cuisine is
true to its name, which refers to the historic
bond between Scotland and France. Local
produce is given a Gallic and Mediterranean
twist, with dishes like Galloway lamb tagine
or local haddock encrusted with oatmeal
and black olive tapenade.

Selkirk Arms Hotel   BISTRO **££**
(☑ 01557-330402; www.selkirkarmshotel.co.uk;
High St; mains £11-17; ☺ noon-2pm & 6-9pm;

P 🛜 🛗) Cheery servers and a wide-ranging
menu of well-presented dishes give you
plenty of options here; you can sit in the
more formal restaurant area (dinner only)
or the casual bar zone. Local scallops are a
highlight, and some fairly elaborate mains
can round out the meal, but you can also
chow down on upmarket fish and chips. All
positive. Located in the hotel.

ℹ Information

Check out www.kirkcudbright.town for heaps of
information on the town.
Kirkcudbright Tourist Office (☑ 01557-
330494; www.visitscotland.com; Harbour Sq;
☺ 11am-3pm Mon-Sat, 11am-5pm Sun Apr–mid-
Jun, 9.30am-6pm Mon-Sat, 10am-5pm Sun
mid-Jun–Aug, 10am-5pm Mon-Sat, 11am-3pm
Sun Sep & Oct, 11am-4pm Mon-Sat Nov-Mar)
Handy office with useful brochures detailing
walks and road tours in the surrounding district. Its future was in doubt at the time of
research.

ℹ Getting There & Away

Kirkcudbright is 28 miles southwest of Dumfries.
Buses run to Dumfries (£4.50, 1¼ hours) via or
changing in Castle Douglas (£2.50, 15 minutes).
Change at Ringford or Gatehouse of Fleet for
Stranraer.

Galloway Forest Park

South and northwest of the small town of
New Galloway is 300-sq-mile Galloway Forest Park, with numerous lochs and great
whale-backed mountains covered in heather
and pine. The highest point is **Merrick**
(843m). The park is criss-crossed by off-road
bike routes (p172) and some superb signposted walking trails, from gentle strolls to
long-distance paths, including the Southern
Upland Way (p150).

Walkers and cyclists should head for
Glentrool in the park's west, accessed by
the forest road east from Bargrennan off the
A714, north of Newton Stewart. Located just
over a mile from Bargrennan is the Glentrool Visitor Centre (p172). The road then
winds and climbs up to Loch Trool, where
there are magnificent views.

The park is very family focused; look out
for the booklet of annual events in tourist offices. It's also great for **stargazing**;
it has been named a Dark Sky Park by the
International Dark-Sky Association (www.
darksky.org).

🏃 Activities

7stanes Kirroughtree
MOUNTAIN BIKING

(www.7stanesmountainbiking.com; Visitor Centre, Kirroughtree) FREE Three miles east of Newton Stewart, this centre offers plenty of singletrack at four different skill levels. You can also hire bikes here (www.thebreakpad.com).

Stargazing Scotland
OUTDOORS

(📞07340 518498; www.stargazingscotland.com) This couple will take you out under the dark skies of Galloway Forest Park for a stargazing session. They run a few public sessions through the year (adult/child £15/8) so check their online calendar, but you're more likely to have to book a private tour (for one/two £75/89).

Galloway Red Deer Range
WILDLIFE WATCHING

(https://scotland.forestry.gov.uk; A712) FREE At the Galloway Red Deer Range you can observe Britain's largest land-based beast from a hide and viewing area. During rutting season in autumn, it's a bit like watching a bullfight as snorting, charging stags compete for the harem. From April to September there are guided ranger-led visits (adult/child £8/5) to see these impressive beasts.

Red Kite Feeding Station
BIRDWATCHING

(📞01644-450202; www.bellymackhillfarm.co.uk; Bellymack Hill Farm, Laurieston; adult/child £5/free; ⊙noon-4pm) Just off the B795, this farm has daily feedings of red kites at 2pm. There's a visitor centre (with cafe) here, from which you can observe these beautiful raptors, which congregate from about 1pm. There are often RSPB volunteers present who can inform you about the birds' lifestyles.

Raiders' Road
SCENIC DRIVE

(http://scotland.forestry.gov.uk; per vehicle £2; ⊙vehicles Apr-Oct; 🚻) About a mile west of Clatteringshaws Visitor Centre, Raiders' Rd is a 10-mile drive through the forest with various picnic spots, child-friendly activities and short walks marked along the way. Drive slowly as there's plenty of wildlife about. One of the nicest spots is a cascade where you might spot otters. Walkers and cyclists can access the road year-round.

ℹ Information

Clatteringshaws Visitor Centre (📞01644-420285; https://scotland.forestry.gov.uk; A712; ⊙10am-4pm) On the shore of Clatteringshaws Loch, 6 miles west of New Galloway, this is basically a cafe but has the odd display panel. From the visitor centre you can walk to a replica of a Romano-British **homestead** (0.5 miles), and to **Bruce's Stone** (1 mile), where Robert the Bruce is said to have rested after defeating the English at the Battle of Rapploch Moss in 1307. Pick up a copy of the *Galloway Kite Trail* leaflet here, which details a circular route through impressive scenery that offers a good chance to spot the majestic reintroduced red kite.

Glentrool Visitor Centre (📞01671-840302; https://scotland.forestry.gov.uk; ⊙10.30am-4.30pm) Located just over a mile from Bargrennan, this place stocks information on activities, including mountain biking, in the area. This is one of the **7stanes mountain-biking hubs**. There is a coffee shop with snacks.

Kirroughtree Visitor Centre (📞01671-402165; https://scotland.forestry.gov.uk; off A75, Palnure; ⊙10am-5pm) This park tourist office 3 miles southeast of Newton Stewart has a cafe and a nature-watching hide. This is also one of the **7stanes mountain-biking hubs**, and there's a good bike shop here that does hires and repairs.

MOUNTAIN-BIKING HEAVEN

A brilliant way to experience southern Scotland's forests is by pedal power. The **7stanes** (stones) are seven mountain-biking centres around southern Scotland, featuring trails through some of the finest forest scenery you'll find in the country.

Glentrool (www.7stanesmountainbiking.com; Visitor Centre, Glentrool) FREE is one of these centres; the **Blue Route** here is 5.6 miles in length and is a lovely ride climbing up to Green Torr Ridge overlooking Loch Trool. If you've more serious intentions, the **Big Country Route** is 36 miles of challenging ascents and descents that afford magnificent views of the Galloway Forest. It takes a full day and is not for wimps.

Another of the trailheads is at Kirroughtree Visitor Centre, 3 miles southeast of Newton Stewart. This centre offers plenty of singletrack at four different skill levels. You can also hire bikes here (www.thebreakpad.com). For more information on routes see www.7stanesmountainbiking.com.

ⓘ Getting There & Away

The scenic 19-mile A712 (Queen's Way) between New Galloway and Newton Stewart slices through the southern section of the park. It's the only road through the park, but no buses run along it. The nearest public-transport point for the western part of this road is Newton Stewart, for the east New Galloway. There's **bike hire** (☑ 01671-401529; www.kirkcowancycles.co.uk; Victoria Lane; half-/full day £13/20; ◷ 9am-5pm Mon-Sat) available in Newton Stewart.

The Machars

South of Newton Stewart, the Galloway Hills give way to the softly rolling pastures of the triangular peninsula known as the Machars. The south has many early Christian sites and the 25-mile Pilgrims Way walk.

Bus 415 runs every hour or so (only twice on Sundays) between Newton Stewart and Isle of Whithorn (£3.20, one hour) via Wigtown (15 minutes) and Whithorn. There are some intermediate services also.

Wigtown

POP 900

Little Wigtown, officially Scotland's National Book Town, has more than a dozen bookshops offering an astonishingly wide selection of volumes, giving book enthusiasts the opportunity to get lost here for days. A major book festival is also held here.

Wigtown Book Festival   LITERATURE
(www.wigtownbookfestival.com; ◷ late Sep) This major 10-day book festival is held in Wigtown. As well as events with writers, there's a poetry competition and programs for children and young adults.

Hillcrest House   B&B ££
(☑ 01988-402018; www.hillcrest-wigtown.co.uk; Station Rd; s/d £55/85; P🅿🛜🐕) A noble stone building in a quiet part of town, this offers a genuine welcome and a lovely interior featuring high ceilings and huge windows. Spend extra for one of the superior rooms, which have stupendous views overlooking rolling green hills and the sea. This is all complemented by a ripper breakfast involving fresh local produce. Dinners also often available.

ReadingLasses   CAFE £
(☑ 01988-403266; www.facebook.com/reading lasses; 17 South Main St; light meals £4-8; ◷ 10am-4pm Thu-Tue; 🛜🍽) 🍽 This bookshop is set around a brilliantly welcoming cafe serving decent coffee to prolong your reading time, as well as really delicious baking and other sweet treats. Soups, sandwiches and other light meals add a savoury side.

The Bookshop   BOOKS
(☑ 01988-402499; www.the-bookshop.com; 17 North Main St; ◷ 9am-5pm Mon-Sat) This claims to be Scotland's largest secondhand bookshop, and has a great collection of Scottish and regional titles. The owner's *Diary of a Bookseller* tells it like it is.

ⓘ Getting There & Away

Bus 415 runs every hour or so (thrice on Sundays) between Newton Stewart and Wigtown (£2.20, 15 minutes). Buses continue to Whithorn and Isle of Whithorn.

Whithorn

POP 800

Whithorn has a broad, attractive High St that is virtually closed at both ends (it was designed to enclose a medieval market). There are few facilities in town, but it's worth visiting because of its fascinating history.

In 397, while the Romans were still in Britain, St Ninian established the first Christian mission beyond Hadrian's Wall in Whithorn (pre-dating St Columba on Iona by 166 years). After his death, **Whithorn Priory**, the earliest recorded church in Scotland, was built to house his remains, and Whithorn became the focus of an important medieval pilgrimage.

★**Whithorn Timescape**   MUSEUM
(The Whithorn Trust; ☑ 01988-500508; www.whithorn.com; 45 George St; adult/child £6/3.60; ◷ 10.30am-5pm Apr-Oct) Ruined **Whithorn Priory** is part of this excellent complex, which introduces you to the history of the place with a very informative audiovisual and exhibition. A highlight is the brilliant replica Iron Age longhouse (three charismatic tours daily) based on nearby excavations. There's also a museum with some fascinating early Christian stone sculptures, including the **Latinus Stone** (c 450), reputedly Scotland's oldest Christian artefact.

Whithorn Way   WALKING
(www.whithornway.org) This recently signposted route covers 143 miles of ancient pilgrimage trail from Glasgow's cathedral to Whithorn via Paisley and the Ayrshire coast.

Isle of Whithorn

POP 300

The Isle of Whithorn, once an island but now linked to the mainland by a causeway, is a curious place with an attractive natural harbour and colourful houses.

St Ninian's Chapel

RUINS

(www.historicenvironment.scot; ⊙24hr) **FREE** The roofless 13th-century St Ninian's Chapel, probably built for pilgrims who landed nearby on their way to the shrine at Whithorn, sits evocatively on the windswept rocky headland. Modern-day pilgrims are invited to add a stone to the Witness Cairn nearby.

St Ninian's Cave

CAVE

(Physgill; ⊙24hr) **FREE** Around Burrow Head, to the southwest but accessed off the A747 before you enter the Isle of Whithorn, is St Ninian's Cave, where the saint apparently went to pray. You can walk here along the coast from Isle of Whithorn.

Steam Packet Inn

PUB ££

(☑01988-500334; www.thesteampacketinn.biz; Harbour Row; r per person £30-45; ⊙food noon-2pm & 6.30-9pm; 🛜🐾) The quayside Steam Packet Inn is a popular pub with real ales, scrumptious bar meals (mains £7 to £11) and comfy-enough lodgings with no single supplement. Try to get a room at the front of the building as they have lovely views over the little harbour (No 2 is a good one).

Stranraer

POP 10,400

The friendly but somewhat ramshackle port of Stranraer has seen its tourist mainstay, the ferry traffic to Northern Ireland, move up the road to Cairnryan. The town's still wondering what to do with itself, but there are good places to stay and lots to explore in the surrounding area.

⊙ Sights

Castle Kennedy Gardens GARDENS, CASTLE

(☑01776-702024; www.castlekennedygardens.com; Sheuchan; adult/child £5.50/2; ⊙10am-5pm Apr-Oct, Sat & Sun Feb & Mar) Three miles east of Stranraer, these magnificent gardens are among Scotland's most renowned. They cover 30 hectares and are set on an isthmus between two lochs and two castles. The landscaping was undertaken in 1730 by the Earl of Stair, who used unoccupied soldiers to do the work. Buses heading east from Stranraer stop at the gate on the main road; it's a pleasant 20-minute stroll from here to the gardens' entrance.

Some open-air cinema events are staged here during summer.

Stranraer Museum

MUSEUM

(☑01776-705088; www.dumgal.gov.uk; 55 George St; ⊙10am-5pm Mon-Fri, 10am-1pm & 1.30-4.30pm Sat) **FREE** This museum houses exhibits on local history and you can learn about Stranraer's polar explorers. The highlight is the carved stone pipe from Madagascar. Temporary exhibitions by local artists are also on display.

🛏 Sleeping & Eating

Ivy House

B&B £

(☑01776-704176; www.ivyhouse-ferrylink.co.uk; 3 Ivy Pl; s/d £35/55, s without bathroom £30; 🛜) This is a great guesthouse that does Scottish hospitality proud, with excellent facilities, tidy en-suite rooms and a smashing breakfast. Nothing is too much trouble for the genial host, who always has a smile for her guests. Prices are excellent. The room at the back overlooking the churchyard is particularly light and quiet.

★Thornbank House

B&B ££

(☑01776-706168; www.thornbankhouse.co.uk; Thornbank Rd; r £80; 🅿🛜🐾🐾) An exceptional place offering extremely comfortable and well-furnished modern rooms (one with a jacuzzi), Thornbank also offers excellent breakfasts and friendly, casual hospitality. It's already well out of the ordinary before you even consider the large indoor swimming pool and absolutely sensational vista over the bay to Ailsa Craig. One room has an outdoor deck to enjoy the view.

Cairnryan B&B

B&B ££

(☑07759-498130; www.cairnryan-bb.co.uk; Cairnryan Rd; s/d £65/78; 🅿🛜) Overlooking the water in the centre of little Cairnryan, this is a modern bungalow with two comfortable en-suite rooms. The double has a lovely outlook over the bay, but it's the genuinely welcoming hosts – old hands at excellent B&B, and providing pick-up/drop-off at the nearby ferry – who make this a special experience. Breakfast features the odd home-grown treat.

Henrys Bay House

SCOTTISH ££

(☑01776-707388; www.henrysbayhouse.co.uk; Cairnryan Rd; mains £11-20; ⊙noon-2pm & 5-9pm Tue-Sat) Just east of the centre, this is Stranraer's best place to eat, with hearty portions of well-sourced meat and seafood and a welcoming vibe. There's a pleasingly old-fashioned feel to some of the dishes, while others have a more contemporary style. If the weather's fine, the deck is a great spot to be, overlooking the bay.

ℹ Getting There & Away

Stranraer is 6 miles south of the ferry port of Cairnryan, which is on the eastern side of Loch Ryan. A bus service coinciding with Stena Line ferries runs between Stranraer and Cairnryan. Buses running frequently between Stranraer and Ayr also stop in Cairnryan. For a taxi, call **McLean's Taxis** (☑ 01776-703343; www. mcleanstaxis.com; 21 North Strand St; ⊙ 24hr) , which should cost about £8.

BOAT

P&O (☑ 01304-448888; www.poferries.com) Runs six to eight fast ferries a day from Cairnryan to Larne (Northern Ireland). The crossing takes two hours.

Stena Line (☑ 08447 70 70 70; www.stenaline. co.uk) Runs five to six daily fast ferries from Cairnryan to Belfast (2¼ hours).

Prices for crossings vary but in the high season are around £35/105 per person/car.

BUS

Scottish Citylink (www.citylink.co.uk) buses run to Glasgow (£18.50, 2½ hours, four daily) and Edinburgh (£21.50, four hours, two daily).

There are also several daily local buses to Kirkcudbright and the towns along the A75, such as Newton Stewart (£4.30, 40 minutes, at least hourly) and Dumfries (£7.80, 2¼ hours, seven daily Monday to Saturday, three on Sunday).

TRAIN

Scotrail (www.scotrail.co.uk) runs to/from Glasgow (£13.60, 2¾ hours). There are four direct services Monday to Saturday and none on Sunday; more frequent daily connections (also a little quicker) change in Ayr.

The Rhinns of Galloway

The Rhinns (or Rhins) of Galloway is a hammerhead-shaped peninsula west of Stranraer that runs 25 miles from north to south. Its coastal scenery includes rugged cliffs, tiny harbours and sandy beaches. Dairy cattle graze on the greenest grass you've ever seen, and the warm waters of the Gulf Stream give the peninsula the mildest climate in Scotland.

CORSEWALL LIGHTHOUSE HOTEL

It's just you and the cruel sea out here at this fabulously romantic 200-year-old **lighthouse** (☑ 01776-853220; www. lighthousehotel.co.uk; Kirkcolm; d £140-250; P 🖵). On a sunny day, the water shimmers with light, and you can see Ireland, Kintyre, Arran and Ailsa Craig. But when wind and rain beat in, it's just great to be cosily holed up in the bar-restaurant or snuggling under the covers in your room.

It's right at the northwest tip of the peninsula, 13 miles northwest of Stranraer down a potholed road. Rooms in the lighthouse building itself are attractive if necessarily compact; chalets are also available. Dinner, bed and breakfast rates are available for an extra £20 per person.

Pretty Portpatrick, set around a harbour, is a big drawcard. Further south, sleepy **Port Logan** has an excellent sandy beach and a famous botanical garden. From **Drummore**, a fishing village on the east coast, it's another 5 miles to the spectacular **Mull of Galloway**, Scotland's most southerly point.

★ Mull of Galloway   NATURE RESERVE

(www.mull-of-galloway.co.uk) Scotland's southernmost point is a spectacular spot, with windswept green grass and views of Scotland, England, the Isle of Man and Northern Ireland. The lighthouse here was built by Robert Stevenson, grandfather of the writer, in 1826. The Mull of Galloway RSPB nature reserve, home to thousands of seabirds, is also important for its wildflowers. At the entrance to the reserve is a spectacular **clifftop cafe** (☑ 01776-840558; www.galliecraig.co.uk; light meals £3-8; ⊙ 11am-4pm Sat-Wed Feb & Mar, 10am-5pm daily Apr-Oct, 11am-4pm Sat & Sun Nov). The former homes of the lightkeepers are available as accommodation; check out www.lighthouseholiday cottages.co.uk.

Logan Botanic Garden   GARDENS

(☑ 01776-860231; www.rbge.org.uk/logan; Port Logan; adult/child £6.50/free; ⊙ 10am-5pm Mar-Oct, to 4pm early Nov) The mild climate in this southwestern part of Scotland is demonstrated at Logan Botanic Garden, a mile north of Port Logan, where an array of subtropical flora includes tree ferns and cabbage palms. The garden is an outpost of the Royal Botanic Garden in Edinburgh. There's a good cafe here.

Mull of Galloway Lighthouse   LIGHTHOUSE
(www.mull-of-galloway.co.uk; Mull of Galloway; adult/child £3/1, with exhibition £5/1.50; ☉10am-4pm Sat & Sun Apr-Oct, daily Jul & Aug) You can climb the lighthouse at the Mull of Galloway for views over four different political entities: Northern Ireland, Scotland, England and the Isle of Man. Check the website to coincide with a blast on the newly restored foghorn (outside of seabird nesting season).

Portpatrick

POP 500

Portpatrick is a charming harbour village on the rugged west coast of the Rhinns of Galloway peninsula. It is a good base from which to explore the area, and it's the starting or finishing point for the Southern Upland Way (p150). You can follow part of the Way to Stranraer (9 miles). It's a clifftop walk, with sections of farmland and heather moor.

Mount Stewart Hotel   BOUTIQUE HOTEL ££
(☑01776-810291; www.themountstewarthotel.co.uk; South Crescent; d without/with view £106/126; P🤶) If you thought the views harbourside were good, stroll up the hill to this hotel and they're even better. You can see Northern Ireland on a good day, or Belfast's lights at night. The rooms have been recently fitted out and

look very smart, with lots of blacks and greys. It's notably friendly with a restaurant and good bar.

⭐**Knockinaam Lodge**   HOTEL £££
(☑01776-810471;   www.knockinaamlodge.com; dinner & B&B s £215, d £360-460; P🤶) For a real dose of luxury, head 3 miles southeast to this former hunting lodge in a dramatic, secluded location with grassy lawns rolling down to a sandy cove. It's where Churchill plotted the endgame of WWII – you can stay in his suite – and it's a very romantic place to get away from it all.

Excellent   French-influenced   cuisine (lunch/dinner for nonguests £40/70) is backed up by a great range of wines and single malts, and breakfast features homemade jams.

Campbell's   SEAFOOD ££
(☑01776-810314; www.campbellsrestaurant.co.uk; 1 South Crescent; mains £13-23; ☉noon-2.30pm & 6-9pm Tue-Sat, noon-2.30pm & 6.30-9pm Sun; 🤶) Fresh local seafood is the stock-in-trade of this unpretentious local favourite. With Melba toast, prawn cocktails and curious cutlery, it's got a retro vibe, and the old-fashioned portion sizes are impressive too. Choose one of the sharing platters and enjoy the flavour burst of locally caught fish or shellfish with harbour views. For sale at time of research.

ℹ Getting There & Away

Bus 367 runs to Stranraer (£2, 20 minutes, hourly Monday to Saturday, three Sunday).

Central Scotland

Best Places to Eat

→ Cellar Restaurant (p198)
→ Peat Inn (p196)
→ 63 Tay Street (p203)
→ Loch Leven's Larder (p207)
→ Adamson (p194)
→ Barley Bree (p208)

Best Places to Stay

→ Old Fishergate House (p193)
→ Spindrift (p197)
→ Merlindale (p208)
→ Pitcullen Guest House (p203)
→ Victoria Square Guesthouse (p180)
→ Murray Library Hostel (p197)

Why Go?

The country's historic roots are deeply embedded in central Scotland. Key battles around Stirling shaped the nation's fortunes; significant castles from the region's history pepper the landscape; and Perth, the former capital, is where kings were crowned on the Stone of Destiny.

Arriving from Glasgow and Edinburgh, visitors begin to get a sense of the country further north as the Lowland scenery ramps up towards Highland splendour. It is here that the majesty of Scotland's landscape begins to unfold among woodlands and waterfalls, craggy hills and rushing rivers, with the silhouettes of soaring, sentinel-like peaks on the northern horizon.

Whether in the softly wooded country of lowland Perthshire or the green Fife coastline dotted with fishing villages, opportunities to enjoy the outdoors abound: walking, cycling and angling are all easy possibilities. The region also has some of the country's best pubs and restaurants, which greet weary visitors at day's end.

When to Go
Stirling

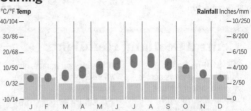

May A magical time to explore before summer crowds arrive, and to enjoy the Perth Arts Festival.

Jul & Aug Seafood feasts in Fife, and fresh raspberries in Blairgowrie.

Oct & Nov Autumn colours enliven walks in the Perthshire woods around Crieff, Comrie and Blairgowrie.

STIRLING REGION

Covering Scotland's wasp-like waist, this region has always been a crucial strategic point connecting the Lowlands to the Highlands. Scotland's two most important independence battles were fought here, within sight of Stirling's hilltop castle. William Wallace's victory over the English at Stirling Bridge in 1297, followed by Robert the Bruce's triumph at Bannockburn in 1314, established Scottish nationhood, and the region remains a focus of much national pride.

Stirling

POP 36,150

With an impregnable position atop a mighty wooded crag (the plug of an extinct volcano), Stirling's beautifully preserved Old Town is a treasure trove of historic buildings and cobbled streets winding up to the ramparts of its impressive castle, which offer views for miles around. Clearly visible is the brooding Wallace Monument, a strange Victorian Gothic creation honouring the legendary freedom fighter of *Braveheart* fame. Nearby is Bannockburn, scene of Robert the Bruce's pivotal triumph over the English in 1314.

The castle makes a fascinating visit, but make sure you also spend time exploring the Old Town and the picturesque Back Walk footpath that encircles it. Below the Old Town, retail-oriented modern Stirling doesn't offer the same appeal; stick to the high ground as much as possible and you'll love the place.

Sights

★ Stirling Castle

CASTLE

(HES; www.stirlingcastle.gov.uk; Castle Wynd; adult/child £15/9; ⊙ 9.30am-6pm Apr-Sep, to 5pm Oct-Mar, last entry 45min before closing; P) Hold Stirling and you control Scotland. This maxim

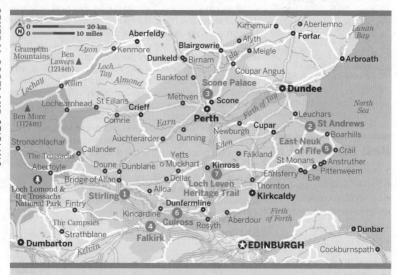

Central Scotland Highlights

1 Stirling Castle
Admiring the views across ancient independence battlefields from this magnificent castle.

2 St Andrews (p190)
Pacing through the historic birthplace of golf to play the famous Old Course.

3 Scone Palace (p200)
Strutting with the peacocks

at this elegant palace, near where Scottish kings were once crowned.

4 Falkirk Wheel (p186)
Taking a canal-boat trip through an engineering marvel.

5 East Neuk of Fife (p196) Feasting on local seafood in picturesque fishing villages.

6 Culross (p187)
Exploring the set of TV series *Outlander* in this perfectly preserved medieval village.

7 Loch Leven Heritage Trail (p206) Hiking or biking around lovely Loch Leven on a scenic all-abilities trail.

has ensured that a fortress of some kind has existed here since prehistoric times. You cannot help drawing parallels with Edinburgh Castle, but many find Stirling's fortress more atmospheric – the location, architecture, historical significance and commanding views combine to make it a grand and memorable sight. It's best to visit in the afternoon; many tourists come on day trips, so you may have the castle almost to yourself by about 4pm.

The current castle dates from the late 14th to the 16th century, when it was a residence of the Stuart monarchs. The undisputed highlight of a visit is the fabulous **Royal Palace**, which underwent a major restoration in 2011. The idea was that it should look brand new, just as when it was constructed by French masons under the orders of James V in the mid-16th century with the aim of impressing his new (also French) bride and other crowned heads of Europe.

The suite of six rooms – three for the king, three for the queen – is a sumptuous riot of colour. Particularly notable are the **Stirling Heads** – reproductions of painted oak roundels in the ceiling of the king's audience chamber (originals are in the Stirling Heads Gallery). The **Stirling tapestries** are modern reproductions, painstakingly woven by expert hands over many years, and based on 16th-century originals in New York's Metropolitan Museum. They depict the hunting of a unicorn – an event ripe with Christian metaphor – and are breathtakingly beautiful. An exhibition at the far end of the Nether Bailey (at the castle's northern end) describes their creation, often with a weaver on hand to demonstrate the techniques used.

The **Stirling Heads Gallery**, above the royal chambers, displays some of the original carved oak roundels that decorated the king's audience chamber – a real rogue's gallery of royals, courtiers, and biblical and classical figures. In the vaults beneath the palace is a child-friendly **exhibition** on various aspects of castle life.

The other buildings surrounding the main castle courtyard are the vast **Great Hall**, built by James IV; the **Royal Chapel**, remodelled in the early 17th century by James VI and with the colourful original mural painting intact; and the King's Old Building. The latter is now home to the **Argyll & Sutherland Highlanders Regimental Museum** (www.argylls.co.uk; Stirling Castle; with Stirling Castle admission free; ⊘9.30am-5pm Apr-Sep, 10am-4.15pm Oct-Mar).

Other displays include the **Great Kitchens**, bringing to life the bustle and scale of the enterprise of cooking for the king, and, near the entrance, the **Castle Exhibition**, which gives good background information on the Stuart kings and updates on current archaeological investigations. There are magnificent vistas from the ramparts towards the Highlands and the Ochil Hills.

Admission includes an audioguide, and free guided tours leave regularly from near the entrance. Your ticket also includes admission to nearby Argyll's Lodging.

★**Old Town Jail**   HISTORIC BUILDING
(http://oldtownjail.co.uk; St John St; adult/child £6.50/4.50; ⊘10.15am-5.15pm Jul–mid-Sep) This impressive Victorian prison building lay derelict from the 1960s until 2015, when it was reopened as a visitor attraction. Costumed guides lead tours around the former prison cells and up to the top of the observation tower, recounting gruesome tales of prisoners, punishments and executions along with fascinating facts about Stirling's history. Tours depart every 30 minutes.

Argyll's Lodging   HISTORIC BUILDING
(www.stirlingcastle.gov.uk; Castle Wynd; with Stirling Castle admission free; ⊘12.45-4pm) This elegant building is Scotland's most impressive 17th-century town house, built for a wealthy local merchant and later acquired by the Earl of Argyll when he thought that Charles II might use Stirling Castle as a royal residence. It has been tastefully restored and gives an insight into the lavish lifestyle of 17th-century aristocrats. You can join a 20-minute guided tour (included in the Stirling Castle admission fee) or wander through the house at your leisure.

National Wallace Monument   MONUMENT
(🖉01786-472140; www.nationalwallacemonument. com;AbbeyCraig;adult/child£9.99/6.25;⊘9.30am-5pm Apr-Jun, Sep & Oct, to 6pm Jul & Aug, 10am-4pm Nov-Feb, 10am-5pm Mar; P🖩) Perched high on a crag above the floodplain of the River Forth, this Victorian monument is so Gothic it deserves circling bats and croaking ravens. In the shape of a medieval tower, it commemorates William Wallace, the hero of the bid for Scottish independence depicted in the film *Braveheart*. The view from the top over the flat, green gorgeousness of the Forth Valley, including the site of Wallace's 1297 victory over the English at Stirling Bridge, almost justifies the steep entry fee.

CENTRAL SCOTLAND STIRLING

The climb up the narrow staircase inside leads through a series of galleries, including the Hall of Heroes, a marble pantheon of lugubrious Scottish luminaries. Admire Wallace's 66 inches of broadsword and see the man himself recreated in a 3D audiovisual display.

Buses run from Stirling bus station to the visitor centre (£2.60, 10 minutes, every 30 minutes). From the visitor centre, walk or shuttle-bus up the hill to the monument itself.

Bannockburn Heritage Centre MUSEUM
(NTS; http://battleofbannockburn.com; Glasgow Rd; adult/child £11.50/8.50; ☉10am-5.30pm Mar-Oct, to 5pm Nov-Feb; P⛟) Robert the Bruce's defeat of the English army on 24 June 1314 at Bannockburn established Scotland as a separate nation. The Bannockburn Heritage Centre uses interactive technology to bring the battle to life. The highlight is a digital projection of the battlefield onto a 3D landscape that shows the movements of infantry and cavalry (entry is by prebooked time slots). Bannockburn is 2 miles south of Stirling; buses run from Stirling bus station (£2.20, 10 minutes, three per hour).

Outside the centre, the 'battlefield' itself is no more than an expanse of neatly trimmed grass, crowned with a circular monument inscribed with a poem by Kathleen Jamie, and a Victorian statue of the victor astride his horse. There has been much debate over exactly where the Battle of Bannockburn took place, but it was definitely somewhere near here on the southern edge of Stirling's urban sprawl. Exploiting the marshy ground around the Bannock Burn, Bruce won a great tactical victory against a much larger and better-equipped force.

Stirling Old Bridge BRIDGE
(HES; ☉24hr) FREE Dating from the 15th century, this graceful arched stone bridge is one of the oldest in Scotland, now reserved for pedestrians and cyclists only. An earlier wooden bridge, which once lay a short distance upstream, was the site of the Battle of Stirling Bridge (1297), at which William Wallace defeated England's Edward I and laid the ground for Scottish independence.

🛏 Sleeping

Willy Wallace Backpackers Hostel HOSTEL £
(☑01786-446773; www.willywallacehostel.com; 77 Murray Pl; dm/tw from £16/48; @☎) This highly convenient, central hostel is friendly,

roomy and sociable – there's a piano and guitar in the common room. The colourful, spacious dormitories are clean and light, and it has free tea and coffee, a good kitchen and a laissez-faire atmosphere. Other amenities include bicycle hire and laundry service.

Stirling SYHA HOSTEL £
(☑01786-473442; www.syha.org.uk; St John St; dm/tw £17.50/44; P@☎) This hostel has an unbeatable location and great facilities. Though its facade is that of a former church, the interior is modern and efficient. The dorms are compact but comfortable, with lockers and en-suite bathrooms; other highlights include pool table, bike shed and, at busy times, cheap meals on offer. Lack of atmosphere is a possible downside.

Munro Guesthouse B&B £
(☑01786-472685; www.munroguesthouse.co.uk; 14 Princes St; s/d from £60/75; ☎) Cosy and cheery, Munro Guesthouse is right in the centre of town but located on a quiet side street. Things are done with a smile here, and the smallish rooms are most inviting, particularly the cute attic ones. The breakfast is also better than the norm, with fruit salad on hand. There's easy (pay) parking opposite.

★Victoria Square Guesthouse B&B ££
(☑01786-473920; www.victoriasquareguesthouse. com; 12 Victoria Sq; s/d from £84/120; P☎) Though close to the centre of town, Victoria Sq is a quiet oasis of elegant Victorian buildings surrounding a verdant park. This luxury guesthouse's huge rooms, bay windows and period features make it a winner – there's a great four-poster room (from £145) for romantic getaways, and some bedrooms have views to the castle towering above. No children.

Neidpath B&B B&B ££
(☑01786-469017; www.accommodationinstirling. co.uk; 24 Linden Ave; s/d/f £55/70/95; P☎) Offering excellent value and a genuine welcome, this fine choice is easily accessed by car. The spacious and appealing 'Campbell' room is the best of three excellent modernised bedrooms with fridges and good bathrooms. The owners also run various self-catering apartments around town; details are available via the website. Two-night minimum stay in July and August.

Stirling

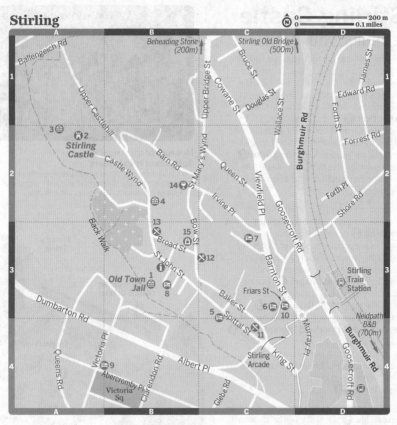

Stirling

◎ Top Sights
1 Old Town Jail	B3
2 Stirling Castle	A2

◎ Sights
3 Argyll & Sutherland Highlanders Regimental Museum	A2
4 Argyll's Lodging	B2

⬤ Sleeping
5 Colessio Hotel	C3
6 Friars Wynd	C3
7 Munro Guesthouse	C3
8 Stirling SYHA	B3
9 Victoria Square Guesthouse	B4
10 Willy Wallace Backpackers Hostel	C3

⊗ Eating
11 Breá	C4
12 Darnley Coffee House	C3
13 Hermann's	B3

◉ Drinking & Nightlife
Brewdog	(see 11)
14 Settle Inn	B2

ⓐ Shopping
15 Stirling Bagpipes	B3

★ **Friars Wynd**   HOTEL £££
(☑ 01786-473390; www.friarswynd.co.uk; 17 Friars St; r from £119; ☎) Set in a lovingly restored 19th-century town house just a short walk from the train station, Friars Wynd offers eight bedrooms of varying size, many with period features such as Victorian cast-iron fire surrounds or exposed patches of original red-brick walls. The 1st-floor rooms are directly above the bar and restaurant, so they can be a little noisy at weekends.

Stirling Castle

PLANNING YOUR ATTACK

Stirling's a sizeable fortress, but not so huge that you'll have to decide what to leave out – there's time to see it all. Unless you've got a working knowledge of Scottish monarchs, head to the **Castle Exhibition ❶** first: it'll help you sort one James from another. That done, take on the sights at leisure. First, stop and look around you from the **ramparts ❷**; the views high over this flat valley, a key strategic point in Scotland's history, are magnificent.

Track back towards the citadel's heart, stopping for a quick tour through the **Great Kitchens ❸**; looking at all that fake food might make you seriously hungry, though. Then enter the main courtyard. Around you are the principal castle buildings, including the **Royal Chapel ❹**. During summer there are events (such as Renaissance dancing) in the **Great Hall ❺** – get details at the entrance. The **Museum of the Argyll & Sutherland Highlanders ❻** is a treasure trove if you're interested in regimental history, but missable if you're not. Leave the best for last – crowds thin in the afternoon – and enter the sumptuous **Royal Palace ❼**.

Take time to admire the beautiful **Stirling Tapestries ❽**, skillfully woven by hand on-site between 2001-2014.

THE WAY UP & DOWN

If you have time, take the atmospheric Back Walk, a peaceful, shady stroll around the Old Town's fortifications and up to the castle's imposing crag-top position. Afterwards, wander down through the Old Town to admire its facades.

TOP TIPS

» **Admission** Entrance is free for Historic Scotland members. If you'll be visiting several Historic Scotland sites a membership will save you plenty.

» **Vital Statistics** First constructed: before 1110; number of sieges: at least nine; last besieger: Bonnie Prince Charlie (unsuccessful); money spent refurbishing the Royal Palace: £12 million.

BRIAN JANNSEN / GETTOSTOCK ©

Museum of the Argyll & Sutherland Highlanders
The history of one of Scotland's legendary regiments – now subsumed into the Royal Regiment of Scotland – is on display here, featuring memorabilia, weapons and uniforms.

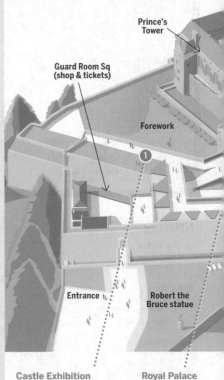

Prince's Tower

Guard Room Sq (shop & tickets)

Forework

❶

Entrance

Robert the Bruce statue

Castle Exhibition
A great overview of the Stewart dynasty here will get your facts straight, and also offers the latest archaeological titbits from the ongoing excavations under the citadel. Analysis of skeletons has revealed surprising amounts of biographical data.

Royal Palace
The impressive highlight of a visit to the castle is this recreation of the royal lodgings originally built by James V. The finely worked ceiling, ornate furniture and sumptuous unicorn tapestries dazzle.

Great Hall & Royal Chapel

Creations of James IV and VI, respectively, these elegant spaces around the central courtyard have been faithfully restored. The vast Great Hall, with its imposing beamed roof, was the largest medieval hall in Scotland.

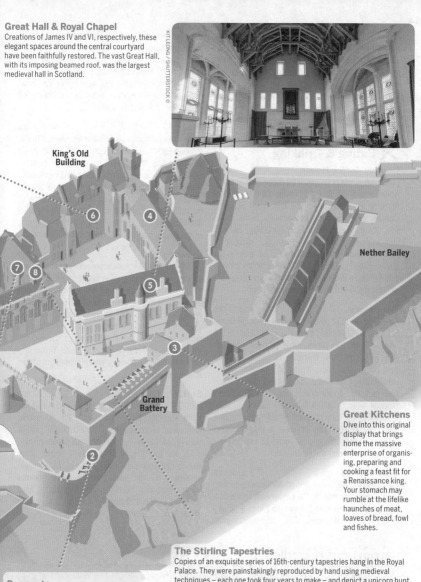

King's Old Building

(6) (4)

(7) (8)

(5)

(3)

Nether Bailey

Grand Battery

(2)

Great Kitchens

Dive into this original display that brings home the massive enterprise of organising, preparing and cooking a feast fit for a Renaissance king. Your stomach may rumble at the lifelike haunches of meat, loaves of bread, fowl and fishes.

The Stirling Tapestries

Copies of an exquisite series of 16th-century tapestries hang in the Royal Palace. They were painstakingly reproduced by hand using medieval techniques – each one took four years to make – and depict a unicorn hunt rich with Christian symbolism.

Ramparts

Perched on the wall you can appreciate the utter dominance of the castle's position atop this lofty volcanic crag. From its vantage points, you can see the site of Robert the Bruce's victory at Bannockburn and the monument to William Wallace.

Colessio Hotel
BOUTIQUE HOTEL **£££**

(☑ 01786-448880; www.hotelcolessio.com; 33 Spittal St; r from £119; ☜) This luxury hotel and spa occupies a landmark neoclassical building (a former hospital) in the heart of the Old Town. The tasteful conversion includes sumptuous rooms and suites with a touch of designer decadence, and a sophisticated cocktail bar and restaurant.

Eating & Drinking

Darnley Coffee House
CAFÉ **£**

(☑ 01786-474468; www.facebook.com/Darnley CoffeeHouse; 18 Bow St; mains £4-6; ☺ 10am-4pm; ☜☑) Just down the hill from Stirling Castle, this is a good pit stop for home baking, soup, vegan food and speciality coffees (no espresso machine, though) during a walk around the Old Town. The cafe is in the vaulted cellars of a 16th-century house where Darnley, the lover and later husband of Mary, Queen of Scots, once stayed.

Hermann's
AUSTRIAN, SCOTTISH **££**

(☑ 01786-450632; www.hermanns.co.uk; 58 Broad St; mains £12-20, 2/3-course lunch £12.50/15.50; ☺ noon-3pm & 6-10pm; ☑☝) This elegant Scottish-Austrian restaurant is a reliable and popular choice, with conservative decor oddly offset by magazine-spread skiing photos, but the food doesn't miss a beat and ranges from Scottish favourites such as Cullen skink to Austrian schnitzel and *spätzle* noodles. Vegetarian options are good, and quality Austrian wines provide an out-of-the-ordinary accompaniment.

Birds & Bees
PUB FOOD **££**

(☑ 01786-473663; www.thebirdsandthebees-stirling. com; Easter Cornton Rd, Causewayhead; mains £11-22; ☺ food served noon-2.30pm & 5-10pm; P ☜☝) A bit of a local secret, this – a country pub in a converted barn, hidden away on a back road on the city's northern fringes. There's faux-rustic decor and a crowd-pleasing pub-grub menu that runs from nachos and tempura king prawns to steaks, burgers, ribs and fish and chips. Outdoor seating and plenty of space for kids to run around.

Breá
SCOTTISH **££**

(www.brea-stirling.co.uk; 5 Baker St; mains £15-22; ☺ noon-9pm Sun-Thu, to 10pm Fri & Sat; ☜☑☝) ☝ Bringing a bohemian touch to central Stirling, this busy bistro has pared-back contemporary decor and a short menu showcasing carefully sourced Scottish produce, including beef, venison, seafood, haggis and Brewdog beers, as well as gourmet burgers, pizza and a handful of vegetarian dishes.

Brewdog
BAR

(☑ 01786-440043; www.brewdog.com/bars/uk/ stirling; 7 Baker St; ☺ noon-midnight Sun-Thu, to 1am Fri & Sat; ☜) The burgeoning Brewdog empire has come to Stirling, with a cool bar done out in designer-distressed timber offering no fewer than 16 taps dispensing craft beers from all over the world, including several from its own famously crowdfunded brewery near Fraserburgh in Aberdeenshire.

Settle Inn
PUB

(☑ 01786-474609; 91 St Mary's Wynd; ☺ 11am-11pm Mon-Sat, 12.30-11pm Sun; ☜) A warm welcome is guaranteed at Stirling's oldest pub (1733), a spot redolent with atmosphere, with its log fire, vaulted back room, low-slung ceilings and Friday-night folk-music sessions. Guest ales, atmospheric nooks where you can settle in for the night, and a blend of local characters make it a classic of its kind.

STIRLING'S OLD TOWN

Sloping steeply down from Stirling Castle, the Old Town has a remarkably different feel to modern Stirling, its cobblestone streets packed with 15th- to 17th-century architectural gems, and surrounded by Scotland's best-surviving town wall. Its growth began when Stirling became a royal burgh (about 1124), and reached a peak in the 15th and 16th centuries when rich merchants built their houses here.

Stirling's **town wall** was built around 1547 when Henry VIII of England began the 'Rough Wooing' – attacking Scottish towns in order to force Mary, Queen of Scots, to marry his son so the two kingdoms could be united. The wall can be explored on the **Back Walk**, which follows the line of the wall from Dumbarton Rd to the castle. You pass the town cemeteries (check out the **Star Pyramid**, an outsized affirmation of Reformation values dating from 1863), then continue around the back of the castle to Mote Hill and the **Beheading Stone**.

WILLIAM WALLACE – SCOTTISH PATRIOT

William Wallace is one of Scotland's best-known historical figures, a patriot whose exploits set the scene for Scotland's wars of independence. Born in 1270, he was catapulted to fame and into a place in history as a highly successful guerrilla commander who harassed the English invaders for many years.

In the wake of his victory over the English at Stirling Bridge in 1297, Wallace was knighted by Robert the Bruce and proclaimed Guardian of Scotland. However, it was only a short time before English military superiority and the fickle loyalties of the Scots nobility turned against the defender of Scottish independence.

Disaster struck in July 1298 when Edward I's forces defeated the Scots at the Battle of Falkirk. Wallace went into hiding and travelled throughout Europe to drum up support for the Scottish cause. But many Scottish nobles were prepared to side with Edward, and Wallace was betrayed after his return to Scotland in 1305; he was found guilty of treason at Westminster and hanged, beheaded and disembowelled at Smithfield, London.

🛍 Shopping

Stirling Bagpipes　　　　　　　　　MUSIC
(📞 01786-448886; www.stirlingbagpipes.com; 8 Broad St; ⊙ 10am-6pm Mon, Tue & Thu-Sat) Bagpipes are handmade and repaired in this combined shop and workshop, which also houses a collection of antique bagpipes and piping paraphernalia. The place is a focus for local pipers, and sells books and CDs of bagpipe music.

ℹ Information

Stirling Community Hospital (📞 01786-434000; www.nhsforthvalley.com; Livilands Rd) is south of the town centre. The nearest emergency department is at Forth Valley Royal Hospital in Larbert, 9 miles southeast of Stirling.

Information can be found and accommodation booked at **Stirling Tourist Office** (📞 01786-475019; www.destinationstirling.com; Old Town Jail, St John St; ⊙ 10am-5pm).

ℹ Getting There & Away

BUS

The **bus station** is on Goosecroft Rd. **Citylink** (📞 0871 266 3333; www.citylink.co.uk) offers a number of services to/from Stirling, including:

Dundee £15.20, 1¾ hours, hourly
Edinburgh £8.70, 1¼ hours, hourly
Glasgow £8.20, 45 minutes, hourly
Perth £9.70, 50 minutes, at least hourly

Some buses continue to Aberdeen, Inverness and Fort William; more frequently a change will be required.

TRAIN

ScotRail (www.scotrail.co.uk) has services to/from a number of destinations, including:

Aberdeen £34.40, 2¼ hours, hourly weekdays, every two hours Sunday
Dundee £15, one hour, hourly weekdays, every two hours Sunday
Edinburgh £9.10, one hour, twice hourly Monday to Saturday, hourly Sunday
Glasgow £8.30, 40 minutes, twice hourly Monday to Saturday, hourly Sunday
Perth £8.30, 35 minutes, hourly weekdays, every two hours Sunday

Dunblane

POP 8800

Dunblane, 5 miles northwest of Stirling, is a pretty town with a notable cathedral. It's difficult not to remember the horrific massacre that took place in the primary school in 1996, but happier headlines have come the town's way with the success of Dunblane-born tennis star Andy Murray – a gold-painted letterbox at the north end of the High St commemorates his 2012 Olympic gold medal.

Dunblane Cathedral　　　　　　　CHURCH
(HES; www.dunblanecathedral.org.uk; Cathedral Sq; ⊙ 9.30am-5.30pm Mon-Sat, 2-5.30pm Sun Apr-Sep, 10am-4pm Mon-Sat, 2-4pm Sun Oct-Mar) FREE Dunblane Cathedral is a superbly elegant example of Gothic architecture – the lower parts of the bell tower date from the 11th century and the rest mainly from the 13th century, though it was all restored in late-Victorian times. There are fine 15th-century carved-wood misericord stalls in the chancel, and a 9th-century carved Celtic cross stands in the north aisle; a modern standing stone commemorates the town's slain children.

Leighton Library
LIBRARY

(www.leightonlibrary.org.uk; 61 High St; ⊘ 11am-1pm Mon-Sat May-Sep) FREE The musty old Leighton Library, dating from 1684, is the oldest purpose-built library in Scotland. In the company of a guide, visitors get to handle and read books from the original collection of Robert Leighton, the late-17th-century bishop of Dunblane. The oldest volume dates from 1504.

Cromlix House
HISTORIC HOTEL £££

(☎ 01786-822125; www.cromlix.com; Kinbuck; d/ ste from £290/475; P ⊚) Wimbledon tennis champion Andy Murray (born in nearby Dunblane) has invested some of his winnings in this luxurious country-house hotel, signposted 4 miles north of Dunblane. Guests can enjoy walking and fishing in the extensive grounds; elegant, understated bedrooms; a restaurant overseen by legendary French chef Albert Roux; and – of course – a tennis court laid out in Wimbledon colours.

Riverside
PUB FOOD ££

(☎ 01786-823318; www.theriversidedunblane. co.uk; Stirling Rd; mains £10-22; ⊘ food 10am-2.30pm & 5-9pm Mon-Fri, 10am-9pm Sat & Sun; ⊚ ⊘ ⊛) ⊘ The name describes the location of this pub-cafe-restaurant that champions local produce and serves everything from free-range eggs Benedict for breakfast and pulled-pork sandwiches for lunch to seafood risotto for dinner or just a glass of local beer on the terrace overlooking the Allan Water.

ℹ Getting There & Away

There are frequent trains from Stirling to Dunblane (£3.60, 12 minutes, every 30 minutes). Bus services are slower and less convenient.

Doune

POP 1630

Doune is best known for its castle, which was famously used as a film set for *Monty Python and the Holy Grail* (1975), and more recently for the TV series *Outlander*. But it's a picturesque village in its own right, with a cluster of craft shops and some lovely walks along the River Teith.

Doune Castle
CASTLE

(HES; www.historicenvironment.scot; adult/child £6/3.60; ⊘ 9.30am-5.30pm Apr-Sep, 10am-4pm Oct-Mar; P) Magnificent Doune Castle is

---

WORTH A TRIP

FALKIRK WHEEL & THE KELPIES

Scotland's canals were once vital avenues for goods transport, but the railway age left them to fall into dereliction. A millennium project restored two of Scotland's major canals, the Union and the Forth & Clyde, which were once linked by an arduous series of 11 locks covering the difference in level of 115ft. The construction of the unique Falkirk Wheel changed all that. Its rotating arms literally scoop boats up and lift them to the higher waterway.

Falkirk is a large town about 10 miles southeast of Stirling. Regular buses and trains link the two, and also connect Falkirk with Glasgow and Edinburgh.

Completed in 2002, the **Falkirk Wheel** (www.thefalkirkwheel.co.uk; Lime Rd, Falkirk; visitor centre free, boat trips adult/child £13.50/7.50; ⊘ 10am-5.30pm Mar-Oct, 11am-4pm Wed-Sun Nov-Feb; P) is a modern engineering marvel, a rotating boat lift that raises vessels the 115ft from the Forth & Clyde Canal to the Union Canal. Boat trips depart from the lower basin (eight daily March to October, three daily in winter) and travel into the wheel, which delivers you to the Union Canal high above. Boats then go through Roughcastle Tunnel before the return descent on the wheel. Anyone with an interest in engineering should not miss this boat ride – it's great for kids, too.

There's also a water play park, a cafe and a visitor centre that explains the workings of the mighty wheel – it only takes the power of about eight toasters for a full rotation!

A pair of stunning equine statues gracing the eastern entrance to the Forth & Clyde Canal, **the Kelpies** (☎ 01324-590600; www.thehelix.co.uk; The Helix, Falkirk; tours adult/child £7.50/free; ⊘ visitor centre 9.30am-5pm, tours 11.30am, 1.20pm & 3.30pm; P) are named after mythical Scottish water-horses. The two 30m-tall horse heads are fashioned out of stainless steel, and are a tribute to the working horses that once hauled barges along the canal. You can view them for free (indeed, they are clearly visible from the M9 motorway between Edinburgh and Stirling), but the 45-minute guided tour takes you inside the sculptures.

one of the best-preserved medieval fortresses in Scotland, having remained largely unchanged since it was built for the duke of Albany in the 14th century. It has been used as a set for the movie *Monty Python and the Holy Grail* (1975) – the audioguide is narrated by Python member Terry Jones – and the TV series *Outlander* and *Game of Thrones*. Highlights include the cathedral-like Great Hall, and a kitchen fireplace big enough to roast a whole ox.

The castle was a favourite royal hunting lodge, but it was also of great strategic importance because it controlled the route between the Lowlands and Highlands. Mary, Queen of Scots, once stayed here, as did Bonnie Prince Charlie. There are great views from the castle walls, and the lofty gatehouse is very impressive, rising nearly 30m.

Buttercup Cafe   CAFE £
(☑ 01786-842511; www.buttercupcafe.co.uk; 7 Main St; mains £4-10; ◷ 9am-4pm Mon-Fri, 9am-5pm Sat, 10am-4pm Sun; 🛜🚼) Right in the middle of the village, this cute cafe serves good breakfasts (including eggs Benedict, pancakes, omelettes and gluten-free options; until 11.30am) and hot lunches. It is licensed, so you can enjoy a glass of Prosecco with your smoked-salmon sandwiches.

❶ Getting There & Away

Doune is 8 miles northwest of Stirling. Buses run from Stirling to Doune every hour or two (£4.60, 25 minutes) Monday to Saturday, less frequently on Sunday.

FIFE

The Kingdom of Fife (www.visitfife.com) as it calls itself – it was home to Scottish monarchs for 500 years – is a tongue of land protruding between the Firths of Forth and Tay that has managed to maintain an individual Lowland identity quite separate from the rest of the country. Though southern Fife is part of Edinburgh's commuter-belt territory, eastern Fife's rolling green farmland and quaint fishing villages are prime turf for exploration, and the fresh sea air feels like it's doing you a power of good. Fife's biggest attraction, St Andrews, has Scotland's most venerable university and a wealth of historic buildings. It's also, of course, the headquarters of golf and draws professionals and keen slashers alike to take on the Old Course – the classic links experience.

CASTLE CAMPBELL

One of central Scotland's most dramatically situated castles, **Castle Campbell** (HES; www.historicenvironment.scot; adult/child £6/3.60; ◷ 9.30am-5.30pm Apr-Sep,10am-4pm Oct, 10am-4pm Sat-Wed Nov-Mar; 🅿) is located on a spur between two deep, wooded ravines known as the Burn of Sorrow and the Burn of Care. A former stronghold of the dukes of Argyll, it was originally known as 'Castle Gloom'. There are interesting rooms in the 15th-century tower house, but the main attraction is the spectacular view from the top. The castle lies a mile north of charming Dollar village, about 11 miles west of Kinross.

There's a superb circular walk (30 minutes) from the lower car park, up the track to the castle and then back down via a walkway through the ravine.

❶ Getting Around

The main bus operator here is Stagecoach East Scotland (www.stagecoachbus.com). The Fife Dayrider ticket (£9.10) gives one day's unlimited travel around Fife on Stagecoach buses.

Fife Council produces a useful transport map, *Getting Around Fife*, available from tourist offices. Good public-transport information can be found at www.fifedirect.org.uk.

If you are driving from the Forth bridges to St Andrews, a slower but much more scenic route than the M90/A91 is along the signposted Fife Coastal Tourist Route.

Culross

POP 400

Instantly familiar to fans of the TV series *Outlander,* in which it appears as the fictional village of Cranesmuir, Culross (*koo-ross*) is Scotland's best-preserved example of a 17th-century town. Limewashed white and yellow-ochre houses with red-tiled roofs stand amid a maze of cobbled streets, and the winding Back Causeway to the abbey is lined with whimsical cottages. The National Trust for Scotland (NTS) owns no fewer than 20 of the town's buildings.

As the birthplace of St Mungo, Glasgow's patron saint, Culross was an important religious centre from the 6th century. The burgh developed under local laird Sir George Bruce by extracting coal through ingenious tunnels

LINDORES ABBEY DISTILLERY

Of the many new distilleries popping up all over Scotland, **Lindores Abbey Distillery** (☑ 01337-842547; http://lindoresabbeydistillery.com; Abbey Rd, Newburgh; tours per person £12.50; ⊙10am-4pm Apr-Sep, 11am-4pm Oct-Mar; P) – opened in 2017 – has a unique historical claim. It's a stunning modern building (made using local stone and timber) that stands beside the ruins of Lindores Abbey, the site of the earliest written reference to Scotch whisky, which dates from 1494.

extending under the seabed. When mining was ended by flooding of the tunnels, the town switched to making linen and shoes.

Culross Palace   HISTORIC SITE
(NTS; www.nts.org.uk; Low Causewayside; adult/child £10.50/7.50; ⊙11am-5pm Jul & Aug, to 4pm Apr-Jun, Sep & Oct) More large house than palace, the 17th-century residence of local laird Sir George Bruce features an interior largely unchanged since his time. The decorative wood panelling and painted timber ceilings are of national importance, particularly the allegorical scenes in the Painted Chamber, which survive from the early 1600s. Don't miss the recreation of a 17th-century garden at the back, with gorgeous views from the top terrace.

The Town House (with ticket and information desk downstairs) and the Study, both dating from the early 17th century, can be visited on a 45-minute guided tour of the town (£2 per person, available between 1pm and 3pm).

Culross Abbey   RUINS
(HES; www.historicenvironment.scot; Back Causeway; ⊙dawn-dusk) FREE Ruined Culross Abbey, founded by the Cistercians in 1217, sits atop a hill in a lovely peaceful spot with vistas of the firth. The choir was converted into the parish church in the 16th century; it's worth a peek inside for the stained glass and the Gothic Argyll tomb.

❶ Getting There & Away

Culross is 16 miles east of Stirling, and 12 miles west of the Forth bridges. Buses run from Dunfermline (£3.20, 30 minutes, hourly) to Culross. Buses from Stirling (£9, 1½ hours, three daily) require a change at Falkirk.

Dunfermline

POP 49,700

Dunfermline is a large and unlovely town, but it's rich in history, boasting the evocative Dunfermline Abbey, its neighbouring palace and the attractive grounds of Pittencrieff Park, the latter gifted to the city by local boy made good Andrew Carnegie (1835–1919), of US-steel-industry fame.

Dunfermline Abbey & Palace   RUINS
(HES; www.historicenvironment.scot; St Catherine's Wynd; adult/child £5/3; ⊙9.30am-5.30pm Apr-Sep, 10am-4pm Sat-Wed Oct-Mar) Dunfermline Abbey was founded by David I in the 12th century as a Benedictine monastery. The abbey and its neighbouring palace were already favoured by religious royals: Malcolm III married the exiled Saxon princess Margaret here in the 11th century, and both chose to be interred here. More royal burials followed, none more notable than that of Robert the Bruce, whose remains were interred here in 1329.

What remains of the abbey are the ruins of the impressive three-tiered refectory building, and the atmosphere-laden nave of the old church, endowed with geometrically patterned columns and fine Romanesque and Gothic windows. It adjoins the 19th-century **abbey church** (https://dunfermlineabbey.com; St Catherine's Wynd; ⊙10am-4.30pm Mon-Sat, 2-4.30pm Sun Apr-Oct) FREE where Robert the Bruce lies entombed beneath the ornate pulpit.

Next to the refectory (and included in your abbey admission) is **Dunfermline Palace**. Once the abbey guesthouse, it was converted for James VI, whose son, the ill-fated Charles I, was born here in 1600. Below stretches the leafy, strollable **Pittencrieff Park**.

Andrew Carnegie Birthplace Museum   MUSEUM
(www.carnegiebirthplace.com; Moodie St; ⊙10am-5pm Jul & Aug, 10am-5pm Mon-Sat, 1-4pm Sun Mar-Jun, Sep & Oct, shorter hours Nov) FREE The cottage where the great American industrialist and philanthropist Andrew Carnegie was born in 1835 is now a museum. Carnegie emigrated to the United States in 1848 and by the late 19th century had become the richest man in the world, but he gave away 90% of his wealth to build libraries, universities and schools all around the world. Dunfermline benefited by his purchase of Pittencrieff Park, beside the palace.

Dunfermline Carnegie Library & Galleries　　　MUSEUM
(www.onfife.com/venues/dunfermline-carnegie-library-galleries; 1-7 Abbot St; ⊙10am-7pm Mon & Thu, to 5pm Tue & Fri, to 2pm Wed, to 4pm Sat, noon-4pm Sun) FREE Opened in 2017, this award-winning building houses a museum that charts the history of Dunfermline, with a massive Meldrum weaving loom as its centrepiece. There are also galleries that host art exhibitions, and a decent cafe.

❶ Getting There & Away

There are frequent buses between Dunfermline and Edinburgh (£6.50, 50 minutes), Stirling (£5.50, 1¼ hours) and St Andrews (£11.50, 1½ hours), plus trains to/from Edinburgh (£5.60, 35 minutes, half-hourly).

Aberdour

☑ 01383 / POP 1630
Aberdour is a popular seaside town with an impressive castle and a lovely family beach, known as the Silver Sands.

Aberdour Castle　　　CASTLE
(HES; www.historicenvironment.scot; adult/child £6/3.60; ⊙9.30am-5.30pm Apr-Sep, 10am-4pm Sat-Wed Oct-Mar; P) Long a residence of the Douglases of Morton, this impressive structure exhibits several architectural phases, from tumbled 12th-century masonry with oyster shells poking from the mortar to a 17th-century painted timber ceiling. Most charming of all is the elaborate 16th-century *doocot* (dovecote) at the far end of the gardens. Be sure to pop into the beautiful Romanesque **church of St Fillan's**, next door to the castle.

❶ Getting There & Away

There are hourly trains to Edinburgh (£6.30, 35 minutes) and Dundee (£14.80, 1¼ hours) from Aberdour, as well as buses to nearby Dunfermline (£4.50, 45 minutes, twice hourly).

Falkland

POP 1100
Below the soft ridges of the Lomond Hills in the centre of Fife lies the charming village of Falkland, a cluster of whitewashed cottages with red pantile roofs and crowstep gables. A handful of tearooms and antique shops dot the narrow street, and rising majestically over the village square is Falkland Palace, a 16th-century country residence of the Stuart monarchs.

Falkland Palace　　　PALACE
(NTS; www.nts.org.uk; High St; adult/child £13/9; ⊙11am-5pm Mon-Sat, noon-5pm Sun Mar-Oct) Falkland Palace, a 16th-century country residence of the Stuart monarchs, is prettier and in many ways more impressive and interesting than the Palace of Holyroodhouse (p61) in Edinburgh. Mary, Queen of Scots, is said to have spent the happiest days of her life here 'playing the country girl' in the surrounding woods and parks, and James V, James VI and Charles II all stayed here on various occasions. Don't miss the world's oldest surviving **real tennis court**, dating from 1539.

OUTLANDER TOURS

The worldwide popularity of *Outlander*, a historical fantasy TV series set in 18th-century Scotland, has seen a huge surge in visitors to the places where it was filmed. Numerous operators will take you on guided location tours that last anything from a day to a week or more. The main locations are listed by VisitScotland (www.visitscotland.com/see-do/attractions/tv-film/outlander).

Top Five Outlander Locations

➡ Doune Castle (p186) stars as Castle Leoch, the main location in season one.

➡ Culross (p187) doubles as the village of Cranesmuir.

➡ Glasgow Cathedral (p112) features as L'Hôpital des Anges in Paris in season two.

➡ **Blackness Castle** (HS; ☑ 01506-834807; www.historicenvironment.scot; Blackness; adult/child £6/3.60; ⊙9.50am-5.30pm Apr-Sep, 10am-4pm Sat-Wed Oct-Mar; P; ☐ F49) ✎ was used as the Fort William headquarters of Black Jack Randall.

➡ Highland Folk Museum (p315) – the replicas of turf-roofed Highland cottages here were used for several period scenes.

FIFE COASTAL PATH

The **Fife Coastal Path** (www.fifecoastal path.co.uk) runs for 117 miles, following the entire Fife coastline from Kincardine to Newburgh. It's well waymarked, picturesque and not too rigorous, though winds can buffet. It's easily accessed for shorter sections or day walks, and long stretches of it can also be tackled on a mountain bike.

The palace was built between 1501 and 1541 to replace a castle dating from the 12th century; French and Scottish craftspeople were employed to create a masterpiece of Scottish Gothic architecture. The **keeper's bedroom** houses an extraordinary royal four-poster bed made for James VI in 1618, richly carved with figures of Faith, Hope, Justice and Prudence.

The **Chapel Royal**, an extravaganza of carved wood and painted ceilings, has been restored to its original glory (and still serves as a Roman Catholic place of worship), while the neighbouring hall is hung with prodigious 17th-century Flemish hunting **tapestries**. In the grounds, the **real tennis court** that was built in 1539 for James V is the oldest still in use anywhere in the world (the one at London's Hampton Court Palace was originally built in 1528 but was renovated for Charles II in the 17th century).

❶ Getting There & Away

Falkland village is 11 miles north of Kirkcaldy. Stagecoach (www.stagecoachbus.com) bus 64 links St Andrews to Falkland direct (£6.50, 1¾ hours, hourly Monday to Saturday, five on Sunday). If travelling from Edinburgh (£14, two hours, hourly Monday to Saturday, five on Sunday), change buses at Glenrothes.

St Andrews

POP 16,900

For a small town, St Andrews has made a big name for itself: firstly as a religious centre and place of pilgrimage, then as Scotland's oldest (and Britain's third-oldest) university town. But it is its status as the home of golf that has propelled it to even greater fame, and today's pilgrims mostly arrive with a set of clubs in hand. Nevertheless, it's a lovely place to visit even if you've no interest in the game, with impressive medieval ruins, stately university buildings, idyllic white sands and excellent guesthouses and restaurants.

The Old Course, the world's most famous golf links, has a striking seaside location at the western end of town – it's a thrilling experience to stroll the hallowed turf. Nearby is magnificent West Sands beach, made famous by the film *Chariots of Fire*.

History

St Andrews is said to have been founded by St Regulus (also known as St Rule), who arrived from Greece in the 4th century, bringing with him the bones of St Andrew, Scotland's patron saint. The town soon grew into a major pilgrimage centre and later developed into the ecclesiastical capital of Scotland. The university, the oldest in Scotland, was founded in 1410.

Golf has been played at St Andrews for more than 600 years; the game's governing body, the Royal & Ancient Golf Club, was founded here in 1754 and the imposing Royal & Ancient Clubhouse was built 100 years later.

◉ Sights

St Andrews Cathedral   RUINS
(HES; www.historicenvironment.scot; The Pends; adult/child £5/3, incl castle £9/5.40; ⊙9.30am-5.30pm Apr-Sep, 10am-4pm Oct-Mar) All that's left of one of Britain's most magnificent medieval buildings are ruined fragments of wall and arch, and a single towering gable, but you can still appreciate the scale and majesty of the edifice from these scant remains. There's also a **museum** with a collection of superb 17th- and 18th-century grave slabs, 9th- and 10th-century Celtic crosses, and the late-8th-century **St Andrews Sarcophagus**, Europe's finest example of early medieval stone carving.

Founded in 1160 and consecrated in 1318, the cathedral stood as the focus of this important pilgrimage centre until 1559, when it was pillaged during the Reformation. The bones of St Andrew himself lie beneath the altar; until the cathedral was built, they had been enshrined in the nearby **Church of St Regulus** (or Rule). All that remains of this church is **St Rule's Tower**, worth the claustrophobic climb for the view across St Andrews. The admission fee only applies for the museum and tower; you can wander freely around the atmospheric ruins.

St Andrews Castle CASTLE
(HES; www.historicenvironment.scot; The Scores;
adult/child £6/3.60, incl cathedral £9/5.40;
⊙9.30am-5.30pm Apr-Sep, 10am-4pm Oct-Mar)
The castle is mainly in ruins, but the site
itself is evocative and has dramatic coastline
views. It was founded around 1200 as a fortified home for the bishop of St Andrews. After
the execution of Protestant reformers in 1545,
other reformers retaliated by murdering Cardinal Beaton and taking over the castle. They
spent almost a year holed up, during which
time they and their attackers dug a complex
of **siege tunnels**; you can walk (or stoop)
along their damp, mossy lengths.

The visitor centre gives a good audiovisual introduction and has a small collection
of Pictish stones.

British Golf Museum MUSEUM
(www.britishgolfmuseum.co.uk; Bruce Embankment;
adult/child £8.50/free; ⊙9.30am-5pm Mon-Sat,
10am-5pm Sun Apr-Oct, 10am-4pm daily Nov-Mar)
This museum provides a comprehensive
overview of the history and development of
the game and the role of St Andrews in it. The
huge collection ranges from the world's oldest set of clubs (late 17th century, used with
feather-stuffed golf balls) to modern equipment, trophies and clothing, and there's a
large collection of memorabilia from Open
winners both male and female, including
Tiger Woods' sweat-stained Nike cap.

🏃 Activities
Apart from the obvious activity – golf – the
tourist office has a list of local **walks** and
also sells OS maps. **Fergus Cook** (⊉07921
577137; www.guidedtoursofstandrews.co.uk; per
person £10-30) offers guided walking tours of
the town.

All the main East Neuk attractions are
within reasonable **cycling** distance.

The section of the Fife Coastal Path located between St Andrews and the East
Neuk is fun, either on foot or by mountain
bike. Parts of the track are tricky and can
be covered by the tide, so check tide times
before you go. The tourist office has a detailed map.

EatWalk St Andrews FOOD
(⊉07740 869359; www.eatwalkstandrews.co.uk;
per person from £63; ⊙1pm daily) Three-hour
guided food tours of the town, taking in five
places where you stop to sample locally produced food and drink.

🎉 Festivals & Events
Open Championship SPORTS
(www.theopen.com; ⊙Jul) One of international
golf's four major championships. The tournament venue changes from year to year,
and comes to St Andrews every five years
(next in 2021) – check the website for future
venues.

DON'T MISS

PLAYING THE OLD COURSE

The **St Andrews Old Course** (⊉Reservations Department 01334-466718; www.standrews.
com; Golf PI) is the oldest and most famous golf course in the world. Golf has been played
here since the 15th century – by 1457 it was apparently so popular that James II had to
ban it because it was interfering with his troops' archery practice. Although it lies beside
the Royal & Ancient Golf Club, the Old Course is a public course.

To play the Old Course, you'll need to book in advance via the website, or by contact-
ing the Reservations Department. Reservations open on the last Wednesday in August
the year before you wish to play. No bookings are taken for weekends or the month of
September (check the latest guidelines on the website).

Unless you've booked months in advance, getting a tee-off time is literally a lottery;
enter the ballot at the **caddie office** (⊉01334-466666; West Sands Rd) (or by phone)
before 2pm two days before you wish to play (there's no Sunday play). Be warned that
applications by ballot are normally heavily oversubscribed, and green fees are £180 in
summer.

A caddie for your round costs £50 plus tip. If you play on a windy day, expect
those scores to balloon: Nick Faldo famously stated, 'When it blows here, even the
seagulls walk'.

There are **guided walks** (www.standrews.com/walk; per person £10; ⊙11am & 2pm daily
Apr-Sep) of the Old Course, and you are free to walk over the course on Sunday, or follow
the footpaths around the edge at any time.

St Andrews

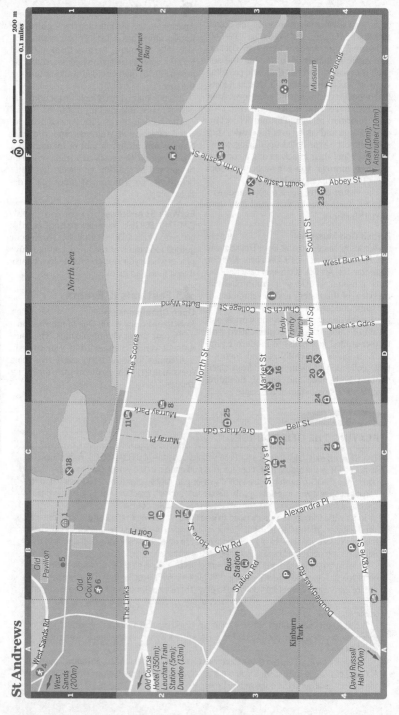

N

0   200 m
0   0.1 miles

West Sands Rd

West Sands (200m)

Old Course Hotel (350m); Leuchars Train Station (5mi); Dundee (33mi)

Old Pavilion

Old Course

The Links

Golf Pl

Hope St

City Rd

Bus Station

Station Rd

Kinburn Park

Doubledykes Rd

Argyle St

David Russell Hall (700m)

Alexandra Pl

Bell St

St Mary's Pl

Greyfriars Gdn

Murray Pl

Murray Park

The Scores

North Sea

St Andrews Bay

North St

Market St

South St

North Castle St

South Castle St

Abbey St

West Burn La

Butts Wynd

College St

Church St

Church Sq

Queen's Gdns

Holy Trinity Church

Museum

The Pends

Crail (10mi); Anstruther (10mi)

St Andrews

St Andrews Highland Games CULTURAL
(www.standrewshighlandgames.co.uk; adult/child £7/4; ☉ Jul) Held on the North Haugh on the last Sunday in July.

🛏 Sleeping

St Andrews' accommodation is expensive and often heavily booked, especially in summer, at weekends, and during golfing events and university graduations, so reserve well ahead. Almost every house on supercentral Murray Park and Murray Pl is a guesthouse.

During summer (June to August), three student residences become visitor accommodation – **Agnes Blackadder Hall** (☎ 01334-463000; https://ace.st-andrews.ac.uk; North Haugh; s/d £65/85; ☉ Jun-Aug; 🅿 @ ☎) 🍴, **David Russell Hall** (☎ 01334-463000; https://ace.st-andrews.ac.uk; Buchanan Gardens; s/d £65/85; ☉ Jun-Aug; 🅿 @ ☎) 🍴 and **McIntosh Hall** (☎ 01334-467035; https://ace.st-andrews.ac.uk; Abbotsford Cres; s/tw £49/69; ☉ Jun-Aug; 🅿 @ ☎) 🍴. Prices are good value for the standard of accommodation on offer.

St Andrews Tourist Hostel HOSTEL £
(☎ 01334-479911; www.hostelsstandrews.com; St Marys Pl; dm £14.50-18.50; @ ☎) Laid back and central, this hostel is the only backpacker accommodation in town. Occupying a stately old building, it has high corniced ceilings, especially in the huge lounge. There's a laissez-faire approach that can verge on chaotic at times, but the staff and location can't be beaten. Reception closed between 2pm and 5pm.

★ **Fairways of St Andrews** B&B ££
(☎ 01334-479513; www.fairwaysofstandrews.co.uk; 8a Golf Pl; d £105-140; ☎) Just a few paces from golf's most famous 18th green, this is more like a boutique hotel than a B&B, despite its small size. There are just three superstylish rooms; the best, on the top floor, is huge and has its own balcony with views over the Old Course (p191).

★ **Old Fishergate House** B&B ££
(☎ 01334-470874; www.oldfishergatehouse.co.uk; North Castle St; r £115-125; ☎) This historic 17th-century town house, furnished with period pieces, is in the oldest part of town, close to the cathedral. The two twin rooms are very spacious and even have their own sitting room. On a scale of one to 10 for quaintness, we'd rate it a 9½. The cracking breakfast menu features pancakes with maple syrup, and smoked-haddock omelette.

Five Pilmour Place B&B ££
(☎ 01334-478665; www.5pilmourplace.com; 5 Pilmour Pl; s/d from £80/120; ☎) Just around the corner from the Old Course (p191), this luxurious and intimate spot offers stylish, compact rooms with plenty of designer touches. The king-size beds are especially comfortable, and the lounge area is an Edwardian-style retreat of leather armchairs, polished wood and swagged curtains.

Cameron House B&B ££
(☎ 01334-472306; www.cameronhouse-sta.co.uk; 11 Murray Park; s/d from £60/100; ☎)

Beautifully decorated rooms and warm, cheerful hosts make this a real home away from home. The two single rooms share a bathroom. Prices drop £10 per person outside peak season.

★ 34 Argyle St
B&B £££

(📞 07712 863139; www.34argylestreet.com; 34 Argyle St; r from £150; 📶) Set in a fine old stone-built house just west of the town centre, the Argyle has four luxurious, hotel-quality bedrooms with huge modern bathrooms of dark tile, chrome and glass (two of the four have free-standing bath tubs). Little touches like drinks offered on arrival, fresh flowers and sweets add to the atmosphere of hospitality.

Old Course Hotel
HOTEL £££

(📞 01334-474371; www.oldcoursehotel.co.uk; Old Station Rd; r from £399; 🅿️📶🏊) A byword for golfing luxury, this hotel is right alongside the famous 17th green (Road Hole) on the Old Course (p191) and has huge rooms, excellent service and a raft of facilities, including a spa complex. Fork out the extra £50 or so for a view over the Old Course. You can usually find good deals online.

Hazelbank Hotel
HOTEL £££

(📞 01334-472466; www.hazelbank.com; 28 The Scores; d £149-219; 📶) Offering a genuine welcome, the family-run Hazelbank is the most likeable of the pleasingly old-fashioned hotels along The Scores. The more expensive front rooms have marvellous views along the beach and out to sea; prices drop significantly outside the summer season. There's good karma if you are playing golf – Bobby Locke won the Open (p191) in 1957 while a guest here.

✕ Eating

Tailend
FISH & CHIPS £

(www.thetailend.co.uk; 130 Market St; takeaway £5-9; ⏱ 11.30am-10pm) 🍴 Delicious fresh fish sourced from Arbroath, just up the coast, puts this place a class above most chippies. It fries to order and the food's worth the wait. The array of exquisite smoked delicacies at the counter will have you planning a picnic or fighting for a table in the licensed cafe out the back.

Balgove Larder
CAFE £

(📞 01334-898145; www.balgove.com; Strathtyrum; mains £6-9; ⏱ 9am-5pm; 🅿️📶🍴) A bright and spacious agricultural shed in a rural setting a mile west of St Andrews houses this farm shop and cafe, serving good coffee, hearty breakfasts, and lunch dishes that use local produce such as roast-beetroot salad (grown on the farm itself), and smoked-haddock chowder (with fish from St Monans).

Northpoint Cafe
CAFE £

(📞 01334-473997; www.facebook.com/northpointcafe; 24 North St; mains £4-8; ⏱ 8.30am-5pm Mon-Fri, 9am-5pm Sat, 10am-4pm Sun; 📶) The cafe where Prince William famously met his future wife, Kate Middleton, while they were both students at St Andrews serves good coffee and a broad range of breakfast fare, from porridge topped with banana to toasted bagels, pancake stacks and classic fry-ups. It's a bit too busy for its own good these days, so get in early for lunch.

★ Adamson
BRASSERIE ££

(📞 01334-479191; http://theadamson.com; 127 South St; mains £13-27; ⏱ noon-3pm & 5pm-midnight Mon-Fri, 11am-midnight Sat & Sun; 📶🍴) Housed in the former post-office building, this loud and bustling brasserie panders to a youngish clientele of local families, well-heeled students and tourists with a crowd-pleasing menu of steaks and seafood. Service can be overeager or occasionally chaotic, but it all adds to the hectic buzz.

Mitchell's Deli
DELI, SCOTTISH ££

(📞 01334-441396; www.mitchellsdeli.co.uk; 110-112 Market St; mains £8-20; ⏱ 8am-10pm Sun-Thu, to 11pm Fri & Sat; 📶🍴) 🍴 Railway-sleeper floors, cut-down-workbench tables and seats upholstered with old tweed jackets lend a utilitarian air to this excellent deli-cafe-restaurant where local produce is king. Breakfast (served till noon, 2pm on Sunday) includes free-range eggs Benedict, and avocado on sourdough toast, while the evening menu runs to fish and chips, mac and cheese, and burgers.

★ Vine Leaf
SCOTTISH £££

(📞 01334-477497; www.vineleafstandrews.co.uk; 131 South St; 2/3-course dinner £28/33; ⏱ 6-11pm Tue-Sat; 🍴) 🍴 Classy, comfortable and well established, the friendly Vine Leaf offers a changing menu of sumptuous Scottish seafood, game and vegetarian dishes. There's a wide selection within the set-price menu, all well presented, and an interesting, mostly old-world wine list. Reservations recommended.

Seafood Ristorante
SEAFOOD £££

(☎01334-479475; www.theseafoodrestaurant.com; The Scores; mains £25-36; ⊙noon-9.30pm Mon-Sat, 12.30-9.30pm Sun) ✒ This stylish restaurant occupies a glass-walled room, built out over the sea, with polished wooden floors, crisp white linen, an open kitchen and panoramic views of St Andrews Bay. It offers top-notch seafood and an excellent wine list; an all-day menu offers smaller dishes between lunch and dinner service. There's a three-course lunch (£25) on weekdays only.

⬤ Drinking & Entertainment

St Andrews Brewing Co
MICROBREWERY

(www.standrewsbrewingcompany.com; 177 South St; ⊙11am-midnight; 📶🍴🐕) Good beer, good food and good company are the order of the day in this friendly, modern brewpub, with 18 beers and ciders on tap (including several of its own brews), more than 170 varieties in bottles, and around 30 craft gins.

Eden Mill Distillery
DISTILLERY

(☎01334-834038; www.edenmill.com; Main St, Guardbridge; tours per person £10; ⊙10am-6pm) This brewery-distillery produces beer and whisky but is best known for its range of craft gins made using locally grown botanicals. One-hour tours of the gin distillery depart from 11am to 4pm, beginning with a G&T and ending with a tasting session (there are whisky and beer tours, too). Eden Mill is 4 miles northwest of St Andrews, towards Leuchars.

Vic
BAR

(www.vicstandrews.co.uk; 1 St Mary's Pl; ⊙10am-2am; 📶) Warehouse chic meets medieval conviviality in this strikingly restored student favourite. Walls plastered with black-and-white pop culture give way to a handsome, high-ceilinged bar with sociable long tables down the middle and an eclectic assortment of seating. Other spaces include a more romantic bar, a dance floor and a deck for smokers. There are regular events, including weekend club nights.

Byre Theatre
THEATRE

(☎01334-475000; www.byretheatre.com; Abbey St; 📶) This theatre company started life in a converted cow byre in the 1930s, but it now occupies flashy modern premises making clever use of light and space.

⬤ Shopping

Topping & Co
BOOKS

(☎01334-585111; www.toppingbooks.co.uk; 7 Greyfriars Garden; ⊙9am-8.30pm) As befits a university town, this is a classic old-school bookshop crammed floor to ceiling with a huge range of titles, with free tea and coffee, armchairs and sofas tucked into hidden corners, and a packed calendar of readings, signings and other literary events.

IJ Mellis
CHEESE

(☎01334-471410; www.mellischeese.net; 149 South St; ⊙9am-5.30pm Mon-Sat, 11am-5pm Sun) IJ Mellis has a wealth of mouth-watering Scottish, British, Irish and continental cheeses you can smell from halfway down the street.

❶ Information

The helpful staff at **St Andrews Tourist Office** (☎01334-472021; www.visitscotland.com; 70 Market St; ⊙9.15am-6pm Mon-Sat, 10am-5pm Sun Jul & Aug, shorter hours rest of year) have good knowledge of the city and Fife.

❶ Getting There & Away

BUS

All buses leave from the **bus station** (Station Rd). Services include:

Anstruther £4.50, 25 minutes, hourly

Crail £4.50, 25 minutes, hourly

Dundee £8, 40 minutes, at least half-hourly

Edinburgh £12.50, two hours, hourly

Glasgow £12.50, 2½ hours, hourly

Stirling £9, two hours, every two hours Monday to Saturday

TRAIN

There is no train station in St Andrews itself, but you can take a train from Edinburgh (grab a seat on the right-hand side of the carriage for great sea views) to Leuchars (£14.70, one hour, half-hourly), 5 miles to the northwest. From here, buses leave regularly for St Andrews (£3.20, 10 minutes, every 10 minutes), or a taxi costs around £13.

❶ Getting Around

To order a cab, call **Golf City Taxis** (☎01334-477788; www.golfcitytaxis.co.uk).

Spokes (☎01334-477835; www.spokescycles.com; 37 South St; per day/week £20/95; ⊙8.45am-5.30pm Mon-Sat) hires out mountain bikes.

THE PEAT INN

This superb Michelin-starred **restaurant** (☑ 01334-840206; www.thepeatinn.co.uk; 3-course lunch/dinner £25/55; ☉ 12.30-2pm & 6.30-9pm Tue-Sat; P), backed by a commodious suite of **bedrooms** (s/d £230/250; P☎), makes an ideal gourmet break. The chef makes a great effort to source premium-quality Scottish produce and presents it in innovative ways that never feel pretentious or overmodern. The inn is 6 miles from St Andrews; head southwest on the A915, then turn right onto the B940.

The split-level bedrooms look over the garden and fields beyond. Various all-inclusive offers are available.

East Neuk

This charming stretch of coast runs south from St Andrews to the headland at Fife Ness, then as far west as Earlsferry. Neuk is an old Scots word for 'corner', and it's certainly an appealing nook of the country to investigate, with picturesque fishing villages whose distinctive red pantiled roofs and crowstep gables are a legacy of centuries-old trading links with the Low Countries.

The Fife Coastal Path's most scenic stretches are in this area (p190). It's easily visited from St Andrews, or even as a day trip from Edinburgh, but also offers many pleasant places to stay.

❶ Getting There & Away

The East Neuk is best explored with your own car, though finding a place to park in the villages on summer weekends can be difficult.

Stagecoach (www.stagecoachbus.com) bus 95 runs hourly from St Andrews to Leven along the coast via Crail, stopping at all the East Neuk villages on the way.

Crail

POP 1640

Pretty and peaceful, little Crail has a much-photographed stone-built harbour surrounded by quaint cottages with red-tiled roofs. The village's history is outlined in the **Crail Museum** (www.crailmuseum.org.uk; 62 Marketgate; ☉ 11am-4pm Mon-Sat, 1.30-4pm Sun Jun-Oct, Sat & Sun only Apr & May) FREE, but the main attraction is just wandering the winding streets and hanging out by the harbour. There are views across to the Isle of May.

Cambo Walled Garden GARDENS
(www.camboestate.com; Cambo Estate; adult/child £5.50/free; ☉ 10am-5pm; P🚼🐕) Cambo Estate, 2.5 miles north of Crail, is the country seat of the Erskine family. Its walled garden, with an ornamental stream running through the middle, is famously beautiful in spring and summer, but also in January and February, when its spectacular displays of snowdrops are in flower. There's a visitor centre and cafe, and woodland walks that lead to the Fife Coastal Path, plus the kids can feed potatoes to the estate's pigs.

Kingsbarns Distillery DISTILLERY
(☑ 01333-451300; www.kingsbarnsdistillery.com; East Newhall Farm, Kingsbarns; guided tour £10; ☉ 10am-6pm Apr-Sep, to 5pm Mar & Oct, shorter hours Nov-Feb; P) This distillery opened in 2015 and uses Fife-grown barley to create a distinctive Lowland whisky – it takes a minimum of three years' maturation to create a single malt, so the first bottles went on sale in 2018. Meanwhile, one-hour tours explain the process and offer tasting sessions, while the on-site cafe serves excellent tea and scones.

Selcraig House B&B ££
(☑ 01333-450697; www.selcraighouse.co.uk; 47 Nethergate; s/d £40/80; ☎🐕) Eighteenth-century Selcraig House is a characterful, well-run place with a variety of rooms and a friendly resident cat. Curiously shaped top-floor chambers will appeal to those who appreciate the quirky, while the fantastic four-poster-bed rooms will charm those with a taste for luxury and beautiful furnishings.

Crail Harbour Gallery & Tearoom CAFE £
(www.crailharbourgallery.co.uk; Shoregate; mains £6-12; ☉ 10.15am-4.30pm) Set in an original 17th-century pantiled cottage, with a low ceiling and quirkily uneven stone floor, this cosy cafe goes beyond the usual coffee and cake by serving locally caught dressed crab, and hot-smoked salmon salad.

Lobster Store SEAFOOD ££
(☑ 01333-450476; 34 Shoregate; mains £4-15; ☉ noon-4pm Tue-Sun Jun-Sep, Sat & Sun only Oct-Apr) This quaint little shack overlooking Crail harbour serves dressed crab and freshly boiled lobster that has been caught locally. You can have a whole lobster (split)

or lobster rolls. This is no-fuss takeaway – there's a single table out the front, but you can find a place to sit and eat your catch anywhere around the harbour.

ⓘ Getting There & Away

Crail is 10 miles southeast of St Andrews. Stagecoach (www.stagecoachbus.com) bus 95 linking Leven, Anstruther, Crail and St Andrews passes through Crail hourly every day (£4.50, 35 minutes to St Andrews).

Anstruther

POP 3450

Once among Scotland's busiest fishing ports, cheery Anstruther (pronounced *en-ster* by locals) has ridden the tribulations of the declining fishing industry better than some, and now offers a pleasant mixture of bobbing boats, historic streets, and visitors ambling around the harbour grazing on fish and chips or contemplating a boat trip to the Isle of May.

⊙ Sights & Activities

Scottish Fisheries Museum   MUSEUM
(www.scotfishmuseum.org; East Shore; adult/child £9/free; ⊙10am-5.30pm Mon-Sat, 11am-5pm Sun Apr-Sep, 10am-4.30pm Mon-Sat, noon-4.30pm Sun Oct-Mar) This excellent museum covers the history of the Scottish fishing industry in fascinating detail, including plenty of hands-on exhibits for kids. Displays include the **Zulu Gallery**, which houses the huge, partly restored hull of a traditional 19th-century Zulu-class fishing boat, redolent with the scents of tar and timber. Afloat in the harbour outside the museum is the **Reaper**, a fully restored Fifie-class fishing boat built in 1902.

Isle of May   NATURE RESERVE
(www.nature.scot) The mile-long Isle of May, 6 miles southeast of Anstruther, is a spectacular nature reserve. Between April and July the island's cliffs are packed with breeding kittiwakes, razorbills, guillemots, shags and more than 80,000 puffins. Inland are the remains of the 12th-century St Adrian's Chapel, dedicated to a monk who was murdered on the island by the Danes in 875. Several boats operating out of Anstruther harbour offer trips to the island.

May Princess   BOATING
(☑07957 585200; www.isleofmayferry.com; adult/child £26/13; ⊙Apr-Sep) A five-hour boat trip to the Isle of May, including two to three

hours ashore, sails three to seven times weekly from April to September, daily from July to September. You can make reservations and buy tickets at the harbour kiosk at least an hour before departure. Departure times vary depending on the tide – call, or check the website.

Osprey   BOATING
(☑07473 631671; www.isleofmayboattrips.co.uk; adult/child non-landing trip £25/18, with time ashore £30/22; ⊙Apr-Sep) The 12-seater high-speed rigid-hull inflatable *Osprey* offers one-hour non-landing circuits of the Isle of May as well as 4½-hour trips with time ashore.

🛏 Sleeping & Eating

★**Murray Library Hostel**   HOSTEL £
(☑01333-311123; http://murraylibraryhostel.com; 7 Shore St; dm/d from £20/52; 🛜) Set in a handsome, red-sandstone waterfront building that once housed the local library, this hostel is beautifully furnished and equipped. There are four- to six-bed dorms, many with sea views, plus private twins and doubles, a gorgeous modern kitchen and a comfortable lounge.

★**Spindrift**   B&B ££
(☑01333-310573; www.thespindrift.co.uk; Pittenweem Rd; d/f £100/150; 🅿🛜🐾) Arriving from the west, there's no need to go further than Anstruther's first house on the left, a redoubt of Scottish cheer and warm hospitality. The rooms are elegant and extremely comfortable – some have views across to Edinburgh, and one is a wood-panelled recreation of a ship's cabin, courtesy of the sea captain who once owned the house.

There are DVD players and teddies for company, an honesty bar with characterful ales and malts, and fine company from your hosts. Breakfast includes porridge once voted the best in the kingdom. Dinner (£26 per person) is also available but must be booked in advance.

Lahloo   B&B ££
(☑01333-312202; www.lahloobandb.co.uk; 15 East Green; s/d £60/90; 🛜🐾) The unusual name comes from the clipper ship whose captain once lived in this lovely Georgian house, but there's nothing spartan or sailor-like about the accommodation here – there are spotless, supercomfy rooms decorated in soothing shades of cream and taupe, waterfall showers in the en-suite bathrooms, and tea and scones on arrival.

Anstruther Fish Bar FISH & CHIPS £
(✆01333-310518; www.anstrutherfishbar.co.uk; 42-44 Shore St; mains £5-9; ⏰11.30am-9.30pm Sun-Thu, to 10pm Fri & Sat; 🖆) An award-winning chippie famous for its deep-fried haddock and chips, this place also offers classy takes on traditional takeaway dishes, including dressed crab and battered prawns (both locally caught).

★**Cellar Restaurant** SCOTTISH £££
(✆01333-310378; www.thecellaranstruther.co.uk; 24 East Green; 5-course lunch/7-course dinner £35/60; ⏰6.30-9pm Wed, 12.30-1.45pm & 6.30-9pm Thu-Sun, no lunch Thu Oct-Mar) 🍴 Tucked away in an alley behind the Scottish Fisheries Museum (p197), the elegant and upmarket Cellar has been famous for its superb food and fine wines since 1982; the recipient of a Michelin star in 2015, it is at the top of its game, offering a creative menu built around Scottish seafood, lamb, pork and beef. Advance booking essential.

🛈 Getting There & Away

Stagecoach (www.stagecoachbus.com) bus X60 runs hourly from Edinburgh to Anstruther (£12.50, 2¼ hours) and on to St Andrews (£4.50, 25 minutes). Bus 95 links Anstruther to all the other East Neuk villages, including Crail (£2.40, 15 minutes, hourly).

Around Anstruther

Scotland's Secret Bunker MUSEUM
(www.secretbunker.co.uk; Troywood; adult/child £12.50/8.50; ⏰10am-6pm Mar-Oct, last entry 5pm; 🅿) This fascinating – and chilling – monument to Cold War paranoia was built in the 1950s to serve as one of Britain's regional command centres in the event of a nuclear war. Hidden 30m underground and encased in nearly 5m of reinforced concrete, it houses two levels of austere operations rooms, communication centres, broadcasting studios, weapons stores and dormitories, filled with period artefacts and museum displays. The bunker is 3 miles north of Anstruther, off the B9131 to St Andrews.

You can book a **Go-Flexi** (✆01382-540624; www.go-flexi.org) 'taxibus' from Anstruther (£2.30) or take a standard taxi (around £20) from St Andrews.

Kellie Castle CASTLE
(NTS; www.nts.org.uk; adult/child £10.50/7.50; ⏰castle 11am-5pm daily Jun-Aug, Sat-Thu Apr, May, Sep & Oct; 🅿) An authentic example of Lowland Scottish domestic architecture, Kellie Castle has creaky floors, crooked little doorways, superb decorative plasterwork and some marvellous works of art. The original part of the building dates from 1360; it was enlarged to its present dimensions around 1606. It's set amid beautiful gardens (open year-round from 9.30am to 6pm or dusk), 3 miles northwest of Pittenweem on the B9171.

Pittenweem
POP 1490

Pittenweem is the main fishing port on the East Neuk coast, and there are lively morning fish sales at its harbour. The village is a great place to wander, with boats bobbing along the harbour front, and art galleries, cafes and craft shops on the High St a block above, the two linked by steep, narrow alleys.

The village name means 'place of the cave', referring to St Fillan's Cave.

St Fillan's Cave CAVE
(Cove Wynd; adult/child £1/free; ⏰10am-6pm) St Fillan's Cave was used as a chapel by a 7th-century missionary who reputedly possessed miraculous powers – apparently, when he wrote his sermons in the dark cave, his arm would throw light on his work by emitting a luminous glow. The cave is protected by a locked gate, but a key and an information leaflet are available from the nearby Cocoa Tree Cafe.

Cocoa Tree Cafe CAFE £
(www.pittenweemchocolate.co.uk; 9 High St; mains £5-9; ⏰10am-6pm; 🛜🖆🍴) This artisan chocolatier also houses a cafe that serves deliciously decadent hot chocolate, as well as freshly prepared focaccia sandwiches and salads.

St Monans
POP 450

This ancient fishing village is named after a cave-dwelling saint who was probably killed by pirates. Apart from a historic **windmill** overlooking the sea, its main sight is the picturesque **parish church**, built in 1362 on the orders of a grateful David II, who was rescued by villagers from a shipwreck in the Firth of Forth. It was burned by the English in 1544 but restored. The church commands sweeping views of the firth, and the past echoes inside its cold, whitewashed walls.

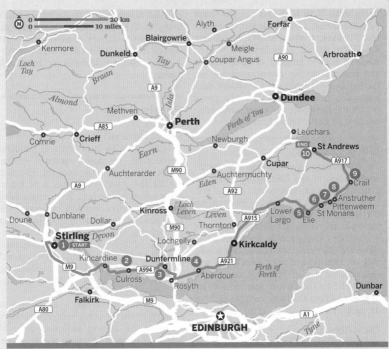

Driving Tour
The Fife Coast

START STIRLING
END ST ANDREWS
LENGTH 76 MILES; ONE DAY

This tour links two of the most popular tourist towns in Central Scotland via the scenic delights of the Fife coast.

Head south from **① Stirling** (p178) on the M9 and at Junction 7 turn east towards Kincardine Bridge. As you approach the bridge, follow signs for Kincardine and Kirkcaldy; then once across the Firth of Forth, follow the Fife Coastal Tourist Rte signposts to the historic village of **② Culross** (p187). Spend an hour or so exploring the medieval buildings of Culross before continuing via the A994 to **③ Dunfermline** (p188), for a look at its fine abbey and palace ruins.

From Dunfermline take the M90 towards the Forth Road Bridge, but leave at Junction 1 (signposted A921 Dalgety Bay) and continue to the attractive seaside village of **④ Aberdour** (p189) for lunch at the Aberdour Hotel or the Room with a View restaurant. Stay on the A921 as far as Kirkcaldy, then take the

faster A915 (signposted St Andrews) as far as Upper Largo, where you'll follow the A917 towards Elie; from here on, you will be following the brown Fife Coastal Tourist Rte signs.

⑤ Elie (p200), with its sandy beaches and coastal footpaths, is a great place to stretch your legs and take in some bracing sea air before driving just a couple of miles further on to explore the neighbouring fishing villages of **⑥ St Monans** and **⑦ Pittenweem**. Just 1 mile beyond Pittenweem, **⑧ Anstruther** (p197) deserves a slightly longer stop for a visit to the Scottish Fisheries Museum, a stroll by the harbour and an ice cream. If time allows, you may want to detour inland a couple of miles to visit Kellie Castle or Scotland's Secret Bunker.

The final stop before St Andrews is the pretty fishing village of **⑨ Crail** (p196), where the late-afternoon or early-evening light will provide ideal conditions for capturing one of Scotland's most photographed harbours. A brisk hike along the coastal path towards Fife Ness, keeping an eye out for seals and seabirds, will round off the day before you drive the last 10 miles into **⑩ St Andrews** (p190).

Craig Millar @ 16 West End SEAFOOD £££
(☑ 01333-730327; www.16westend.com; 16 West End; 3-course lunch/dinner £28/45; ⊘ 12.30-2pm & 6.30-9pm Wed-Sat, 12.30-2pm Sun) ✐ The range of seafood on offer changes daily at this comfortable but classy restaurant on the harbour – it could include oysters, scallops, cod, turbot or monkfish (the menu details the provenance of these sustainable catches, so just swim with the tide.

Elie & Earlsferry

These two attractive villages mark the southwestern end of the East Neuk. There are great sandy beaches, two golf courses and good walks along the coast – seek out the **Chain Walk**, an adventurous scramble along the rocky shoreline at Kincraig Point, west of Earlsferry, using chains and steel rungs cemented into the rock (allow two hours, and ask local advice about tides before setting off). On a more relaxing note, there's nothing better than a lazy summer Sunday in Elie, watching the local team play cricket on the beach.

Elie Watersports WATER SPORTS
(☑ 01333-330962; www.eliewatersports.com; Elie Harbour, Elie; ⊘ May-Sep, ring ahead other times) Elie Watersports hires out windsurfers (£30 per two hours), sailing dinghies (£25 per hour), canoes (£14 per hour) and mountain bikes (£15 per day), and offers instruction (at extra cost).

Ship Inn PUB FOOD ££
(☑ 01333-330246; www.shipinn.scot; The Toft, Elie; mains £11-22; ⊘ food served noon-3pm & 5-9pm; ⊞ 🐾) The Ship Inn, down by Elie harbour, is a pleasant and popular place for a pint at the outside tables overlooking the wide sweep of the bay, but there's also a restaurant area with an above-average menu based on local seafood, beef and lamb.

LOWLAND PERTHSHIRE & KINROSS

For sheer scenic variety, Perthshire is the pick of Scotland's counties and a place where everyone will find a special, personal spot. The county straddles the Highland border, with Highland Perthshire (p320) stretching north from Dunkeld, while Lowland Perthshire ranges from the sedate streets of Perth itself, a fair city with a fabulous attraction

in lavish Scone Palace, to the rural market towns of Crieff and Blairgowrie. Kinross, once one of Scotland's smallest counties, is famous for lovely Loch Leven, with a historic island castle, scenic walks and good trout fishing.

Perth

POP 46,970

Elegantly arranged along the Tay, Perth is a pleasant city with large tracts of parkland surrounding an easily navigated centre. The Scottish Parliament once sat here and, but for the murder of James I at Blackfriars monastery in 1437, Perth might have been the capital of Scotland. Instead it built its fortune on the weaving, dyeing, fishing and brewing industries, and gave the country some of its most famous brand names, including Pullars (dry cleaning), Dewars and Bells (both whisky). To learn more about the city's history, pick up the *Walks Around Historic Perth* booklet at the museum.

On the outskirts lies Scone Palace, a country house of staggering luxury built alongside the ancient crowning place of Scotland's kings. The palace is a must-see, and the town itself – known as the Fair City – is endowed with fine galleries and good restaurants, and is within easy striking distance of Edinburgh and Glasgow.

◉ Sights

★ **Scone Palace** PALACE
(☑ 01738-552300; www.scone-palace.co.uk; Scone Estate; adult/child £12/8.50, grounds only £7.50/5.50; ⊘ 9.30am-6pm May-Sep, 10am-5pm Apr & Oct, last entry 1hr before closing; 🅿) 'So thanks to all at once and to each one, whom we invite to see us crowned at Scone.' This line from *Macbeth* indicates the importance of Scone (pronounced 'skoon') as the coronation place of Scottish monarchs. The original palace of 1580, laying claim to this historic site, was rebuilt in the early 19th century as a Georgian mansion of extreme elegance and luxury. The self-guided tour takes you through a succession of sumptuous rooms filled with fine French furniture and noble portraits.

Scone has belonged for centuries to the Murray family, earls of Mansfield, and many of the objects have a fascinating history attached to them (friendly guides are on hand to explain). Each room has comprehensive multilingual information; there are also panels relating histories of some of the Scottish kings crowned at Scone over the centuries. Outside, peacocks – each named after a monarch – shriek and strut around the magnificent grounds, which incorporate woods, a butterfly garden and a maze.

Ancient kings were crowned on **Moot Hill**, now topped by a chapel next to the palace. It's said that the hill was created by bootfuls of earth, brought by nobles attending the coronations as an acknowledgement of the king's rights over their lands, although it's more likely the site of an ancient motte-and-bailey castle. Here in 838 Kenneth MacAlpin became the first king of a united Scotland and brought to Scone the **Stone of Destiny**, on which Scottish kings were ceremonially invested. In 1296 Edward I of England carted this talisman off to Westminster Abbey, where it remained for 700 years before being returned to Scotland in 1997 (it now sits in Edinburgh Castle, but there are plans afoot to return it to Perth).

Scone Palace is 2 miles north of Perth; from the town centre, cross the bridge, turn left, and bear left along the footway beside the A93 until you reach the gates of the estate. From here, it's another half-mile to the palace (about 45 minutes' walk). Various buses from town stop here; the tourist office (p206) can advise.

Perth Museum & Art Gallery   MUSEUM
(www.culturepk.org.uk/museums-and-galleries/perth-museum-and-art-gallery; cnr George & Charlotte Sts; ⊙10am-5pm Tue-Sat year-round, plus 10am-5pm Sun Apr-Oct) **FREE** This elegant neoclassical building, based on the Pantheon in Rome, houses one of the oldest purpose-built museums in Britain. There's a varied range of exhibits covering the city's history and natural environment, from portraits of dour lairds to carved Pictish stones and a plaster cast of Britain's record rod-caught salmon (29kg, hooked on the River Tay in 1922) along with an account of its capture by the angler, Georgina Ballantine.

Fergusson Gallery   GALLERY
(www.culturepk.org.uk/museums-and-galleries/the-fergusson-gallery; cnr Marshall Pl & Tay St; ⊙10am-5pm Tue-Sat year-round, plus noon-4.30pm Sun Apr-Oct) **FREE** Beautifully set in a circular cast-iron building that was once a waterworks, this gallery exhibits an extensive collection of paintings by the Scottish Colourist JD Fergusson in a most impressive display. Fergusson spent time in Paris, and

the influence of artists such as Matisse on his work is evident; his voluptuous female portraits against a tropical-looking Riviera background are memorable, as is the story of his lifelong relationship with noted Scottish dancer Margaret Morris.

Black Watch Museum   MUSEUM
(☑01738-638152; www.theblackwatch.co.uk; Hay St; adult/child £8/3.50; ⊙9.30am-4.30pm Apr-Oct, 10am-4pm Nov-Mar; **P**) Housed in Balhousie Castle on the edge of North Inch park, this museum honours what was once Scotland's foremost army regiment (it was subsumed into the new Royal Regiment of Scotland in 2006). Formed in 1725 to control rebellious Highlanders following the Jacobite uprising of 1715, the Black Watch fought in numerous famous campaigns, recreated here with paintings, memorabilia and anecdotes.

There's justifiable pride in the regiment's role in the gruelling trench warfare of WWI, where it suffered nearly 30,000 casualties, but no little sense of historical perspective on less glorious colonial engagements, such as those against the 'Fuzzy Wuzzies' of Sudan.

St John's Kirk   CHURCH
(www.st-johns-kirk.co.uk; St John's St; ⊙10am-4pm Mon-Sat May-Sep) **FREE** Imposing St John's Kirk was founded in 1126 and is still the centrepiece of the town. In 1559 John Knox preached a powerful sermon here that helped begin the Reformation, inciting a frenzied destruction of Scone abbey and other religious sites; the church itself, restored in the 19th century, is a rare example of a surviving medieval Scottish kirk.

Perth used to be known as St John's Town after this church, and the local football team is still called St Johnstone.

Perth

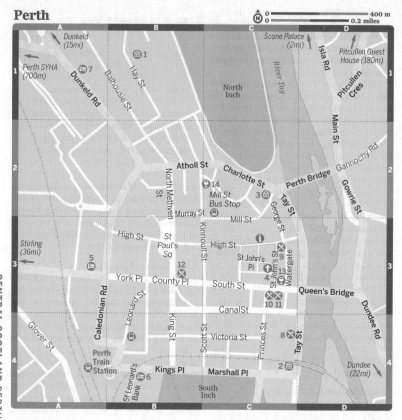

Perth

◎ Sights

🛏 Sleeping

🍴 Eating

🍸 Drinking & Nightlife

🛏 Sleeping

Heidl Guest House   B&B £

(☏ 01738-635031; http://heidlguesthouse.co.uk;
43 York Pl; s/d/f from £60/70/105; ℗ 🛜) It may
lack a little character from outside, but the
Heidl is an excellent guesthouse, and the
enthusiastic owners have renovated it well,
leaving the seven bedrooms very spruce
indeed. Most rooms are en suite; the two
that aren't have separate but private bathrooms. Writer John Buchan (of *The Thirty-
Nine Steps* fame) was born in the house
opposite.

Perth SYHA   HOSTEL £

(☏ 01738-877800; www.syha.org.uk; Crieff Rd; s/
tw/q £20/49/69; ☉ late Jun–late Aug) A 20-minute
stroll from the centre, this summer-only
hostel is set in a student residence at Perth

College. The rooms are all en-suite twins and four-bed apartments, with good shared kitchens and common rooms. Turn into the Brahan entrance on Crieff Rd; the hostel is by the large car park. Numerous buses stop outside.

★ Pitcullen Guest House — B&B ££
(☑ 01738-626506; www.pitcullen.co.uk; 17 Pitcullen Cres; d/f £70/130; P ⊛) This excellent B&B has a much more contemporary look than other guesthouses on this strip. Great-looking fabrics and modern styling give the rooms an upbeat feel, and lots of thought has gone into making your stay more comfortable, with things like fridges with free drinks in the rooms, plenty of plugs to make recharging easy and handy maps on the walls.

Parklands — HOTEL ££
(☑ 01738-622451; www.theparklandshotel.com; 2 St Leonard's Bank; s/d £98/119; P ⊛) This relaxing hotel occupies a luxurious villa set amid lush hillside gardens overlooking the parklands of the South Inch. While the rooms preserve the character of this beautiful building, formerly the residence of the town's mayors, they also offer modern conveniences and plenty of style. There's a great terrace and garden area in which to lap up the Perthshire sun.

Rosebank — B&B ££
(☑ 01738-301707; www.rosebankguesthouseperth. co.uk; 53 Dunkeld Rd; s/d from £70/87; P ⊛) One of several B&Bs on the northern approach to the city centre, the Rosebank impresses with its warm welcome and brightly decorated rooms. Hearty breakfasts are served in an elegant dining room with original Victorian cornices and fireplace.

✗ Eating & Drinking

★ Tabla — INDIAN ££
(☑ 01738-444630; http://tablarestaurant.co.uk; 173 South St; mains £10-15; ⊗ noon-2pm & 5-10pm Mon-Sat, 5-10pm Sun) Tabla is one of the best Indian restaurants in the whole of central Scotland, its bustling, modern dining room catering to a loyal clientele of locals tucking into authentic dishes such as *andhra wada* (lentil patties with chilli, coriander and cumin) and railway *boti* (curried lamb on the bone with curry leaves and star anise, as served on Indian trains).

Duo — ITALIAN ££
(☑ 01738-628152; 2 Princes St; mains £9-13; ⊗ 10am-9pm Tue-Sun; ⊛) A wood-fired pizza oven is the pride of the kitchen at this cosy, informal restaurant. A few French dishes muscle onto the menu alongside the pizza and pasta (try French onion soup, or scallops with black pudding and apple compote), and the gourmet platter of charcuterie and cheese is a delight.

Breizh — BISTRO, FRENCH ££
(☑ 01738-444427; www.breizhrestaurant.com; 28 High St; mains £10-20; ⊗ 9am-9.30pm Mon-Thu, to 10pm Fri & Sat, 11am-9.30pm Sun; ⊛) This funkily French bistro – the name is Breton for Brittany – is a treat. Dishes are served with real panache, and the salads, featuring all sorts of delicious ingredients, are a feast of colour, texture and subtle flavours. The blackboard specials offer great value and an authentic taste of northwestern France, including traditional *galettes* (Breton buckwheat pancakes with savoury fillings).

★ 63 Tay Street — SCOTTISH £££
(☑ 01738-441451; www.63taystreet.com; 63 Tay St; mains lunch £14, dinner £19-24; ⊗ 6.30-9pm Tue & Wed, noon-2pm & 6.30-9pm Thu-Sat; ⊛) ⊘ Classy and warmly welcoming, this understated restaurant is Perth's best, featuring a lightly decorated dining area, excellent service and quality food. In a culinary Auld Alliance, French influence is applied to the best of Scottish produce to create memorable game, seafood, beef and vegetarian dishes.

Greyfriars Bar — PUB
(☑ 01738-633036; www.perth-bars.co.uk; 15 South St; ⊗ 2.30-11pm Mon-Wed, noon-12.30am Thu-Sat, noon-11pm Sun) The smallest and friendliest pub in Perth offers great entertainment every week (open-mic Thursdays from 9pm, live-music Saturdays from 9pm), fine ales from several nearby breweries, and local gins and whiskies.

King James — PUB
(www.kingjamesbar.com; 73 Kinnoull St; ⊗ 11am-11pm Mon-Wed, to midnight Thu, to 12.30am Fri & Sat, noon-11.30pm Sun) The basement of this pub contains a crime scene – the medieval stonework here is all that survives of Blackfriars monastery, where James I of Scotland was murdered in 1437. A glass panel in the floor of the bar allows drinkers to look down on this piece of Perth history, though most regulars will be watching sport on the large-screen TVs.

1. Doune Castle (p186) 2. Dunstaffnage Castle (p292)
3. Glamis Castle (p219) 4. Caerlaverock Castle (p167)

Scottish Castles

Scotland is home to more than 1000 castles, ranging from meagre 12th-century ruins to magnificent Victorian mansions. They all began with one purpose: to serve as fortified homes for the landowning aristocracy. But as society became more settled and peaceful, defensive features gave way to ostentatious displays of wealth and status.

Curtain Wall Castles

Norman castles of the 12th century were mainly of the 'motte-and-bailey' type, consisting of earthwork mounds and timber palisades. The first wave of stonebuilt castles emerged in the 13th century, characterised by massive curtain walls up to 3m thick and 30m tall to withstand sieges, well seen at Dunstaffnage Castle and Caerlaverock Castle.

Tower Houses

The appearance of the tower house in the 14th century marks the beginning of the development of the castle as a residence. Clan feuds, cattle raiders and wars between Scotland and England meant that local lords built fortified stone towers in which to live, from diminutive Smailholm Tower in the Borders to impressive Doune Castle near Stirling.

Artillery Castles

The arrival of gunpowder and cannon in the 15th century transformed castle design, with features such as gun loops, round towers, bulwarks and bastions making an appearance. Forbidding Hermitage Castle is a prime example of a castle adapted for artillery defence.

Status Symbols

The Scottish Baronial style of castle architecture, characterised by a profusion of pointy turrets, crenellations and stepped gables, had its origins in 16th- and 17th-century castles such as Craigievar and Castle Fraser, and reached its apotheosis in the royal residences of Glamis and Balmoral.

GLENEAGLES

Deep in rural Perthshire near the town of Auchterarder lies **Gleneagles Hotel** (☎ 01764-662231; www.gleneagles.com; r from £530; P @ 🛜 🐆), one of Scotland's most famous resorts. Not your typical bed-and-breakfast, this is a no-holds-barred luxury retreat with three championship **golf courses** (☎ 01764-662231; www.gleneagles.com/golf; green fees from £145), Michelin-starred Andrew Fairlie – often referred to as Scotland's best restaurant (open for dinner Tuesday to Saturday) – and a variety of extravagantly elegant rooms and suites.

Despite the imposing building and kilted staff snapping to attention, it's welcoming to non-VIPs, and family friendly to boot, with lots of activities available. There's Gleneagles train station if you wish to arrive sustainably; if not, limousine transfers are available. Check the website for deals.

Phoenix Falconry (☎ 01764-682823; www.scottishfalconry.co.uk; Easterton Farm; per person £30-180), just along the road from Gleneagles Hotel near Auchterarder, offers experiences that range from one-hour bird-handling sessions to all-day adventures, flying harris hawks and other raptors over the owner's estate.

ⓘ Information

Perth Tourist Office (☎ 01738-450600; www.perthshire.co.uk; 45 High St; ⏱ 9.30am-4.30pm Mon-Sat, 11am-4pm Sun, longer hours Jul & Aug)

ⓘ Getting There & Away

BUS

Citylink (www.citylink.co.uk) and **Stagecoach** (www.stagecoachbus.com) intercity buses operate from the **bus station** (Leonard St), with services to/from the following:

Dundee £7.70, 40 minutes, hourly
Edinburgh £11.30, 1¾ hours, hourly
Glasgow £13, 1¾ hours, hourly
Inverness £23.20, three hours, five daily
Stirling £9.70, 55 minutes, hourly

Further buses run from the Broxden Park & Ride on Glasgow Rd; this is connected regularly with the bus station by shuttle bus. These include **Megabus** (www.megabus.com) discount services to Aberdeen, Edinburgh, Glasgow, Dundee and Inverness.

Stagecoach buses serving local Perthshire destinations depart from **Mill St**. An East Scotland Dayrider ticket gives you one day of unlimited bus travel in Perthshire, Fife, Dundee and Angus for £14.90.

TRAIN

Trains run between Perth and various destinations, including:

Dundee £8.30, 25 minutes, hourly
Edinburgh £17.10, 1½ hours, at least hourly Monday to Saturday, every two hours Sunday
Glasgow £17.10, 1½ hours, at least hourly Monday to Saturday, every two hours Sunday
Pitlochry £14.40, 30 minutes, 10 daily
Stirling £8.30, 30 minutes, one or two per hour

Kinross & Loch Leven

The town of Kinross sits on the banks of pretty Loch Leven, a haven for walkers, cyclists and anglers. Just east of the town sits the gorgeously restored **Kinross House** (http://kinrosshouse.com), the finest Palladian mansion in Scotland, built by Sir William Bruce in 1693. Sadly, it's not open to the public (it can be rented for a princely sum), but you can get a glimpse of it from the loch-side trail.

Lochleven Castle   CASTLE
(HES; www.historicenvironment.scot; Kinross Pier; adult/child incl boat ride £7.50/4.50; ⏱ 10am-5.15pm Apr-Sep, to 4.15pm Oct, last sailing 1hr before closing; P) Evocative Lochleven Castle served as an island fortress and prison from the late 14th century; its most famous captive was Mary, Queen of Scots, who was incarcerated here in 1567. Her famous charms bewitched Willie Douglas, who managed to get hold of the cell keys to release her, then rowed her across to the shore. The castle is now roofless but basically intact and makes for an atmospheric destination; visitors cross to the island by boat (included in admission fee).

Loch Leven Heritage Trail   WALKING, CYCLING
(www.lochlevenheritagetrail.co.uk) One of the best all-abilities hiking and biking routes in Scotland, this scenic 14-mile circuit of Loch Leven links Kinross Pier, the RSPB Loch Leven nature reserve, and Loch Leven's Larder. Allow two hours to cycle the trail or five hours to walk it; you can hire bikes and mobility scooters at Kinross Pier.

The circuit offers great views of the Lomond Hills, and there's a sandy beach northeast of Kinross.

Loch Leven Fisheries FISHING
(☑ 01577-863467; www.fishlochleven.co.uk; Kinross Pier; boat hire per day £21-52) World famous among anglers for more than 100 years for its hard-fighting, pink-fleshed brown trout, Loch Leven has been stocked in recent years with rainbow trout as well. Fishing is by fly only, from boats that can be hired at Kinross Pier (one to three anglers per boat).

★ Loch Leven's Larder SCOTTISH £
(☑ 01592-841000; http://lochlevenslarder.com; Channel Farm; mains £6-11; ⊙ 9.30am-5.30pm; P 🛜 🐕 🍽) 🧀 Three miles east of Kinross, off the A911, this family-run farm shop and restaurant overlooking Loch Leven is the ideal place to enjoy fresh local food, much of it from the family's own farm, whether it's a breakfast of soft-boiled free-range eggs with hot buttered toast, a platter of Scottish cheeses, or a lunch of Arbroath smoked-haddock quiche with potato salad.

There's a terrace with a panorama over the loch, a children's playground, and a footpath that connects to the Loch Leven Heritage Trail, making it an ideal break on a walking or cycling circuit of the loch.

Upper Strathearn

The Highland villages of Comrie and St Fillans in upper Strathearn are surrounded by forests and bare, craggy hilltops where deer and mountain hares live in abundance.

Comrie is a cute little village that has played its part in the history of science – on its western edge stands **Earthquake House** (www.strathearn.com/pl/earthquake.htm), the world's first seismic observatory. There are many excellent local walks, a favourite being to the spectacular gorge and waterfall known as the **Deil's Cauldron**, 1 mile north of the village.

St Fillans enjoys a scenic location at the eastern end of **Loch Earn**, which reflects the silhouettes of surrounding peaks. The loch has good **fishing** for brown trout and pike – you can buy permits (£11 for one day) from the village shop in St Fillans.

Four Seasons Hotel HOTEL ££
(☑ 01764-685333; www.thefourseasonshotel. co.uk; St Fillans; d from £99; ⊙ closed Jan–mid-Feb; P 🛜 🍽) The historic Four Seasons (the Beatles stayed here while on tour in 1964) has been given a classy modern makeover. Two beautifully appointed lounges and an atmospheric wee bar enjoy great views over the loch. The superior rooms – worth the upgrade – have the best vistas, and there are six chalets nestled in the slopes behind the hotel.

There are many activities to choose from, including waterskiing, quad biking and pony trekking, and a noted fine-dining restaurant.

★ Hansen's Kitchen DELI, CAFE £
(☑ 01764-670253; www.facebook.com/hansens kitchen; Drummond St, Comrie; mains £4-6; ⊙ 8am-5pm Mon-Sat, 10am-4pm Sun; 🍽) 🧀 The foodie epicentre of Upper Strathearn, Hansen's is a hugely popular delicatessen and cafe (there's barely a dozen seats crammed into the interior) serving superb coffee, cheese and charcuterie platters, and lunch dishes such as home-baked panini stuffed with salami, mozzarella and pesto. If you can't get a table, grab some takeaway and head for the riverside benches beneath the church.

ⓘ Getting There & Away

Comrie is 24 miles west of Perth, and St Fillans is about 5 miles further west. Buses run from Perth via Crieff to Comrie (£3.80, one hour, hourly Monday to Saturday, every two hours Sunday) and St Fillans (£3.80, 1½ hours, five daily Monday to Saturday).

Crieff

POP 7370

Elegant Crieff is an old resort-style town, known for golf, fishing and its whisky distillery, and it's as popular with tourists today as it was in Victorian times. It sits in a valley amid some glorious Perthshire countryside and, with excellent eating and accommodation options, it's a fine base for exploring this part of the country.

🛏 Sleeping

Comrie Croft HOSTEL, CAMPSITE £
(☑ 01764-670140; www.comriecroft.com; Braincroft; campsites per person £10, dm £18, s/d £32/60; P @ 🛜 🍽) 🧀 A rustic, hospitable place, Comrie Croft has a bit of everything: camping; a pleasant, airy hostel; and Nordic katas (£99 per night), with wood stoves, that sleep up to six. Activities include mountain biking (purpose-built trails; bike hire available),

fishing, walking, and lots of games for the kids. It's 4 miles west of Crieff on the A85.

★**Merlindale** B&B ££

(☏ 01764-655205; www.merlindale.co.uk; Perth Rd; s/d £70/95; ☼ Mar-Nov; P 🛜) Georgian architecture meets generous hospitality at this excellent guesthouse at the eastern end of town. The four fabulous rooms all have individual character, and two have sumptuous bathrooms with free-standing tubs. There's a comfy lounge-library, the owner is a Cordon Bleu–trained chef, and thoughtful touches abound.

Yann's at Glenearn House B&B ££

(☏ 01764-650111; www.yannsatglenearnhouse. com; Perth Rd; r £100; P 🛜 🐾) This luxury B&B is a most welcoming establishment, offering four large, bright rooms with plenty of understated style, an atmospheric lounge stuffed with armchairs, and French crêpes on the breakfast menu. The owner is a French chef, and there's an excellent **restaurant** (☏ 01764-650111; www.yannsatglenearnhouse.com; Perth Rd; mains £14-22; ☼ 6-9pm Wed-Sun; P 🛜 🐾) on the premises.

Crieff Hydro HOTEL ££

(☏ 01764-655555; www.crieffhydro.com; Ferntower Rd; r from £108; P @ 🛜 🐾 🐾) This enormous spa hotel is nearly 150 years old, but apart from its monumental exterior it looks very different from its mannered Victorian past. It's attractively functional and really does have everything for a family holiday, from cinema and gym to restaurants, activities and pools. It's exceptionally child friendly, with free daily childcare.

Room rates vary substantially, so check the website. There are also self-catering cottages dotted around the extensive grounds offering a quieter stay in a cosier, more couple-focused environment (and you can still access all the leisure facilities at the hotel).

✖ Eating

Delivino CAFE, DELI ££

(www.delivino.co.uk; 6 King St; mains £8-12, sharing platters £17; ☼ 9am-6pm Mon-Thu, to 9pm Fri & Sat, noon-4pm Sun) Just down from the square on the main street, elegant Delivino offers something for everyone, from Crieff locals to travellers looking for a light bite. An extensive selection of antipasti allows you to graze on several flavours at a time, while delicious bruschetta and pizza, accompanied by a glass of Italian red, make this a great lunch option.

Lounge BISTRO ££

(☏ 01764-654407; www.loungeincrieff.co.uk; 1 West High St; mains £9-17; ☼ 10am-8pm Tue-Thu, to 10pm Fri & Sat; 🛜) Enter the romantic interior of this informal lounge bar and bistro for anything from a cup of tea to good wines by the glass to an interesting array of gourmet sandwiches, tapas and other delights – notably *galettes au sarrasin* (delicious French buckwheat pancakes with savoury fillings). Run by Delphine, sister of Yann, owner of Crieff's top restaurant.

Pura Maison SCOTTISH ££

(☏ 01764-650762; www.puramaison.co.uk; 26 James Sq; mains £11-14; ☼ 10am-8pm Wed & Thu, to 9pm Fri & Sat, noon-8pm Sun) Simply styled in shades of coffee and cream, this plain and unpretentious place takes the best of Scottish produce and serves it with a French flourish in dishes such as venison Scotch egg with beetroot and Dijon-mustard purée, or grilled salmon with tarragon hollandaise.

★**Barley Bree** SCOTTISH £££

(☏ 01764-681451; www.barleybree.com; 6 Willoughby St, Muthill; mains lunch £11-15, dinner £20-25; ☼ noon-2pm & 6.45-9pm Wed-Sat, noon-3pm & 6-9pm Sun; P 🛜) 🍴 Set in the pretty village of Muthill (pronounced *mooth*-il), 3 miles south of Crieff, the Barley Bree is a delightfully rustic restaurant with rooms. Wooden floorboards, stone fireplace, stacked logs and deer antlers set the scene for dishes of fine Scottish seafood, beef and game; half a dozen luxurious bedrooms (doubles from £115) tempt you to stay the night.

🛍 Shopping

Crieff Food Company FOOD & DRINKS

(☏ 01764-655817; www.thecriefffoodco.co.uk; cnr High St & James Sq; ☼ 9am-5pm Mon-Sat, 10am-4pm Sun; 🛜) This food hall and delicatessen is a showcase for local producers, and it's a great place to stock up on Scottish delicacies such as Heather Hills honey, Strathearn cheeses, Perthshire oatcakes and smoked venison from Rannoch Smokery. There's a good **cafe** here, too.

Gordon & Durward FOOD

(www.scottishsweets.co.uk; 14 West High St) On the go since 1925, this old-fashioned sweet shop is lined with jars of traditional Scottish sweets (candies) such as boilings, macaroons, Edinburgh rock, sugar mice and tablet (a crumbly, buttery fudge).

THE LIBRARY OF INNERPEFFRAY

Scotland's oldest lending **library** (📞 01764-652819; www.innerpeffraylibrary.co.uk; Inner-peffray; adult/child £7.50/free; ⊙ 10am-12.45pm & 2-4.45pm Wed-Sat, 2-4pm Sun Mar-Oct, by appointment Nov-Feb; 🅿) – founded in 1680 – houses a huge collection of rare, interesting and ancient books, some of them 500 years old. If you have any interest in books you could easily spend half a day here in the company of voluntary guides, who will point out interesting volumes or find books on subjects that interest you. The library is signposted along a farm road about 5 miles southeast of Crieff, off the B8062.

Next to the library is **Innerpeffray Chapel**, built in 1507 as a private Catholic chapel for the Drummond family (who also founded the library). It contains some fragments of painted plaster, and the remarkable **Faichney monument** (1707), an ornately carved gravestone that reveals the mason's pride in his family.

❶ Getting There & Away

Buses link Crieff with Perth (£3, 40 minutes, hourly Monday to Saturday, less frequently on Sunday) and Stirling (£3.40, one hour, four to 10 daily).

Blairgowrie & Around

POP 8950

Blairgowrie is a compact market town on the banks of the River Ericht, famed for its salmon fishing. Formerly a flax-spinning centre, the town today is the hub of Scotland's soft-fruits industry – the fields for miles around are ripe with raspberries and strawberries, for sale in season from kiosks on the edge of town.

About 5 miles east of Blairgowrie, **Alyth** is a charming historic village clustered along the banks of the Alyth Burn, which is crossed by a 15th-century stone bridge and a couple of modern footbridges. Ask at Blairgowrie's tourist office for the *Walk Auld Alyth* leaflet.

Off the A94 and 8 miles east of Blairgowrie, **Meigle** is well worth the trip for those with a fascination for Pictish sculptured stones, which can be viewed at the **Meigle Museum** (HES; 📞 01828-640612; www.historic environment.scot; Dundee Rd, Meigle; adult/child £5/3; ⊙ 9.30am-5.30pm Apr-Sep, 10am-4pm Oct).

Cateran Trail　　　　　　　　　WALKING
(www.caterantrail.org) Blairgowrie is the start and finish point for the Cateran Trail, a circular 64-mile waymarked path that leads through the mountains around Glenshee on the southern fringes of the Cairngorms National Park. The first mile or so along the River Ericht, as far as the waterfall at **Cargill's Leap** and the former flax mill at Keathbank, makes an excellent short walk.

Gilmore House　　　　　　　　B&B ££
(📞 01250-872791; www.gilmorehouse.co.uk; Perth Rd; d £75-84; 🅿🛜) 🌿 Blairgowrie's prosperous past has left a legacy of spacious Victorian villas. Many, like Gilmore House, have been turned into B&Bs, but few as successfully as this welcoming haven. There are three gorgeously fitted-out en-suite bedrooms, two guest lounges and a hearty breakfast built around seasonal local produce.

Dalmore Inn　　　　　　　　　SCOTTISH ££
(📞 01250-871088; www.dalmoreinn.com; Perth Rd; mains £10-28; ⊙ 10am-9pm; 🅿🚼) 🌿 One of Blairgowrie's most popular eateries, the Dalmore finds inventive ways to present the best of local produce, with dishes such as Arbroath smokie (hot-smoked haddock) and smoked-trout risotto, and braised leg of rabbit with madeira jus. The inn is on the southern edge of town, on the A93 towards Perth.

❶ Information

Blairgowrie Tourist Office (📞 01250-872960; www.perthshire.co.uk; 26 Wellmeadow; ⊙ 10am-5pm Mon-Sat, 10.30am-3.30pm Sun Apr-Aug, 10am-4pm Mon-Sat Sep-Mar)

❶ Getting There & Away

Buses run to Blairgowrie from Perth (£3.50, 50 minutes, half-hourly) and from Dundee (£3.70, one hour, hourly), and there are hourly buses between Blairgowrie and Alyth (£1.90, 17 minutes), and Blairgowrie and Meigle (£2.50, 30 minutes).

Northeast Scotland

Why Go?

Many visitors pass by this corner of the country in their headlong rush to the tourist honeypots of Loch Ness and Skye. But they're missing out on a part of Scotland that's just as beautiful and diverse as the more obvious attractions of the west.

Within its bounds you'll find two of Scotland's four largest cities: Dundee, the city of jute, jam and journalism, home to Captain Scott's Antarctic research ship, the *Discovery*, and the stunning V&A Dundee museum of design; and Aberdeen, the granite city, an economic powerhouse fuelled by the riches of North Sea oil.

Angus is a region of rich farmland and scenic glens dotted with the mysterious stones left behind by the ancient Picts, while Aberdeenshire and Moray are home to the greatest concentration of Scottish Baronial castles in the country, and dozens of whisky distilleries along the River Spey.

Best Places to Eat

➡ Drouthy Cobbler (p237)

➡ Castlehill (p216)

➡ 88 Degrees (p224)

➡ Tolbooth Restaurant (p235)

➡ Café 52 (p230)

➡ Tayberry (p219)

Best Places to Stay

➡ Dutch Mill Hotel (p229)

➡ 24 Shorehead (p234)

➡ Malmaison (p215)

➡ Jays (p229)

➡ Sail Loft Bunkhouse (p240)

When to Go
Aberdeen

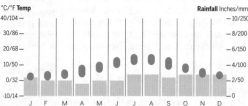

Jun & Jul Classic boats large and small fill Portsoy harbour for the Scottish Traditional Boat Festival.

Sep Revellers gather for a whisky and music festival in Dufftown.

Dec Spectacular fireball ceremony in Stonehaven on Hogmanay (New Year's Eve).

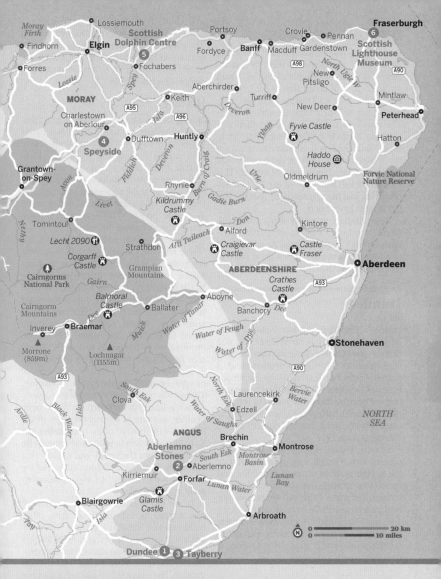

Northeast Scotland Highlights

1 **V&A Dundee** (p212) Discovering the best of Scottish and international design at this architecturally stunning museum in the heart of Dundee's redeveloped waterfront.

2 **Aberlemno Stones** (p221) Meditating on the meaning of these mysterious Pictish stones, carved with strange symbols and scenes of battle.

3 **Tayberry** (p219) Tucking into the cream of Scottish cuisine at this restaurant in Broughty Ferry.

4 **Speyside** (p238) Being initiated into the mysteries of malt whisky on a tour of a Speyside distillery.

5 **Scottish Dolphin Centre** (p236) Learning about the Moray Firth's bottlenose dolphins at Spey Bay.

6 **Scottish Lighthouse Museum** (p235) Exploring the heritage of Scotland's maritime tradition and visiting the country's oldest lighthouse, set atop a 16th-century castle.

DUNDEE & ANGUS

Angus is a fertile farming region stretching north from Dundee – Scotland's fourth-largest city – to the Highland border. It's an attractive area of broad straths (valleys) and low, green hills contrasting with the rich, red-brown soil of freshly ploughed fields. The romantic Angus Glens finger their way into the foothills of the Grampian Mountains, while the scenic coastline ranges from the red-sandstone cliffs of Arbroath to the long, sandy beaches around Montrose. This was the Pictish heartland of the 7th and 8th centuries, and many interesting Pictish symbol stones survive here.

Apart from the crowds visiting newly confident Dundee and the coach parties shuffling through Glamis Castle, Angus is a bit of a tourism backwater and a good place to escape the crowds.

Dundee

POP 147,300

London's Trafalgar Sq has Nelson, Edinburgh's Princes St has Sir Walter Scott and Belfast has Queen Victoria outside City Hall. Dundee's City Sq, on the other hand, is graced – rather endearingly – by the bronze figure of Desperate Dan. Familiar to generations of British schoolchildren, Dan is one of the best-loved cartoon characters from the comic *Dandy,* published by Dundee firm DC Thomson since 1937.

Dundee enjoys perhaps the finest location of any Scottish city, spreading along the northern shore of the Firth of Tay, and boasts tourist attractions of national importance in Discovery Point and Verdant Works. Add attractive seaside town Broughty Ferry and the Dundonians themselves – among the friendliest, most welcoming and entertaining people you'll meet – and Dundee is definitely worth a stopover.

The waterfront around Discovery Point has undergone a massive redevelopment, centred on the construction of the architecturally outstanding V&A Dundee museum of design, opened in 2018.

History

During the 19th century Dundee grew from its trading-port origins to become a major player in the shipbuilding, whaling, textile and railway engineering industries. Dundonian firms owned and operated most of the jute mills in India (jute is a natural fibre used to make ropes and sacking), and the city's textile industry employed as many as 43,000 people – little wonder Dundee earned the nickname 'Juteopolis'.

Dundee is often called the city of the 'Three Js' – jute, jam and journalism. According to legend, it was a Dundee woman, Janet Keillor, who invented marmalade in the late 18th century; her son founded the city's famous Keillor jam factory. Jute is no longer produced, and when the Keillor factory was taken over in 1988, production was transferred to England. Journalism still thrives, however, led by the family firm of DC Thomson. Best known for children's comics such as the *Beano* and the *Dandy,* and regional newspapers including the *Press and Journal,* Thomson is now the city's largest employer.

In the late 19th and early 20th centuries Dundee was one of the richest cities in the country – there were more millionaires per head of population here than anywhere else in Britain – but the textile and engineering industries declined in the second half of the 20th century, leading to high unemployment and urban decay.

In the 1960s and '70s Dundee's cityscape was scarred by ugly blocks of flats, office buildings and shopping centres linked by unsightly concrete walkways; most visitors passed it by. Since the mid-1990s, however, Dundee has reinvented itself as a tourist destination, and a centre for banking, insurance and high-tech industries, while its waterfront has undergone a major redevelopment. It also has more university students – one in seven of the population – than any other town in Europe, except Heidelberg.

◉ Sights & Activities

★**V&A Dundee**   MUSEUM

(☏01382-305665; www.vandadundee.org; Riverside Esplanade; ⊙10am-5pm) **FREE** The centrepiece of Dundee's revitalised waterfront is this stunning building designed by Japanese architect Kengo Kuma. Opening in September 2018, it houses an outpost of London's Victoria & Albert Museum of art and design with exhibitions showcasing the work of Scottish designers past and present, from famous names such as Charles Rennie Mackintosh to modern creatives such as fashion designer Holly Fulton, alongside the best of art and design from around the world.

★ **Discovery Point**   MUSEUM
(www.rrsdiscovery.com; Discovery Quay; adult/child £11.25/6.25; ☉10am-6pm Mon-Sat, 11am-6pm Sun Apr-Oct, to 5pm Nov-Mar; P 🚼) The three masts of Captain Robert Falcon Scott's famous polar expedition vessel the RRS *Discovery* provide a historic counterpoint to the modern architecture of the V&A Design Museum. Exhibitions and audiovisual displays in the neighbouring visitor centre provide a fascinating history of both the ship and Antarctic exploration, but *Discovery* is the star attraction. You can visit the bridge, the galley and the mahogany-panelled officers' wardroom, and poke your nose into the cabins used by Scott and his crew.

The ship was built in Dundee in 1900, with a wooden hull at least half a metre thick to survive the pack ice, and sailed for the Antarctic in 1901 where it spent two winters trapped in the ice. From 1931 it was laid up in London where its condition steadily deteriorated, until it was rescued by the efforts of Peter Scott (Robert's son) and the Maritime Trust, and restored to its 1925 condition. In 1986 the ship was given a berth in its home port of Dundee, where it became a symbol of the city's regeneration.

A joint ticket that gives entry to both Discovery Point and the Verdant Works costs £18.25/10.25/46 per adult/child/family.

★ **Verdant Works**   MUSEUM
(www.verdantworks.com; West Henderson's Wynd; adult/child £11.25/6.25; ☉10am-6pm Mon-Sat, 11am-6pm Sun Apr-Oct, shorter hours Nov-Mar; 🚼) One of the finest industrial museums in Europe, the Verdant Works explores the history of Dundee's jute industry. Housed in a restored jute mill, complete with original machinery in working condition, the museum's exhibits follow the raw material from its origins in India through to the manufacture of a wide range of finished products, from sacking to sailcloth to wagon covers for the pioneers of the American West. The museum is 250m west of the city centre.

McManus Galleries   MUSEUM
(www.mcmanus.co.uk; Albert Sq; ☉10am-5pm Mon-Sat, 12.30-4.30pm Sun) FREE Housed in a solid Victorian Gothic building designed by Gilbert Scott in 1867, the McManus Galleries are a city museum on a human scale – you can see everything there is to see in a single visit, without feeling rushed or overwhelmed. The exhibits cover the history of the city from the Iron Age to the present day, including relics of the Tay Bridge Disaster and the Dundee whaling industry.

Computer geeks will enjoy the Sinclair ZX81 and Spectrum (pioneering personal computers with a whole 16Kb of memory!) which were made in Dundee in the early 1980s.

HM Frigate Unicorn   MUSEUM
(www.frigateunicorn.org; Victoria Dock; adult/child £6.50/2.50; ☉10am-5pm Apr-Oct, noon-4pm Thu-Sun Nov-Mar) Dundee's second floating tourist attraction – unlike the polished and much-restored RRS *Discovery* – retains the authentic atmosphere of a salty old sailing ship. Built in 1824, the 46-gun *Unicorn* is the oldest British-built ship still afloat – she was mothballed soon after launching and never saw action. Wandering around below deck gives you an excellent impression of what it must have been like for the crew forced to live in such cramped conditions.

By the mid-19th century sailing ships were outclassed by steam and the *Unicorn* served as a gunpowder store, then later as a training vessel. When it was proposed to break up the ship for scrap in the 1960s, a preservation society was formed. The ship is berthed in Victoria Dock, just northeast of the Tay Road Bridge. The entry price includes a self-guided tour (also available in French and German).

Dundee Contemporary Arts   ARTS CENTRE
(www.dca.org.uk; Nethergate; ☉10am-6pm Fri-Wed, to 8pm Thu) FREE Pioneering the development of the city's Cultural Quarter from its opening in 1999, Dundee Contemporary Arts is a centre for modern art, design and cinema. The galleries here exhibit work by contemporary UK and international artists, and there are printmakers' studios where you can watch artists at work, or even take part in craft demonstrations and workshops. There's also the Jute Café-Bar (p217).

City Square   SQUARE
The heart of Dundee is City Sq, flanked to the south by the 1930s facade of **Caird Hall**, which was gifted to the city by a textile

Dundee

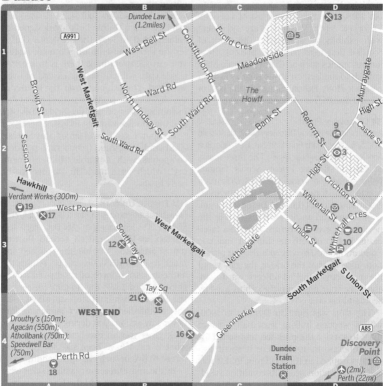

magnate and is now home to the City Chambers. A more recent addition to the square, unveiled in 2001, is a bronze statue of **Desperate Dan**, the lantern-jawed hero of children's comic the *Dandy* (he's clutching a copy in his right hand).

Dundee Law   PARK
It's worth making the climb up Dundee Law (174m) for great views of the city, the two Tay bridges and across to Fife. The **Tay Rail Bridge** – at just over 2 miles long, it was the world's longest when it was built – was completed in 1887. The 1.5-mile **Tay Road Bridge** was opened in 1966. Dundee Law is a steep 1.5-mile walk northwest of the city centre, or you can drive to the summit.

The railway bridge replaced an earlier structure whose stumps can be seen alongside. The original bridge collapsed during a storm in 1879 less than two years after it was built, in the infamous **Tay Bridge Disaster**, taking a train and 75 lives along with it.

Foxlake   WATER SPORTS
(☎ 01382-214484; www.foxlakedundee.co.uk; West Victoria Dock; 15min session per adult/child £25/18; ⊙ 9am-9pm Jul-Aug, 10am-dusk Sat & Sun Apr-Jun & Sep) The former dock in front of the Apex Hotel (p216) is home to this cable-towed wakeboarding park. You can also try your hand at stand-up paddleboarding (SUP, per session £15).

🛏 Sleeping

Most city-centre hotels are business-oriented and cheaper on weekends. B&Bs are concentrated along Broughty Ferry Rd and Arbroath Rd east of the city centre, and Perth Rd to the west. If you don't fancy a night in the city, consider nearby seaside town, Broughty Ferry.

Dundee accommodation is usually booked solid during the Open golf tournament at Carnoustie or St Andrews – check www.theopen.com for dates (it's in St Andrews in 2021).

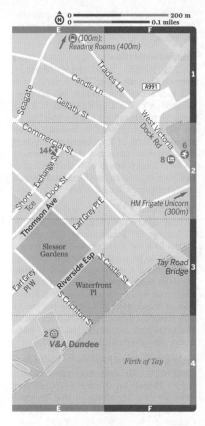

Dundee Backpackers HOSTEL **£**
(☏ 01382-224646; www.hoppo.com/dundee; 71 High St; dm £18, s/tw from £25/45; @ 🛜) This hostel is set in a beautifully converted historic building, with a clean, modern kitchen, a pool room and an ideal location right in the city centre. It can get a bit noisy at night, but that's because it's close to pubs and nightlife.

Athollbank B&B **£**
(☏ 01382-801118; www.athollbank.com; 19 Thomson St; s/d £30/48; 🛜🐾) A great-value B&B set on a quiet side street in the city's West End, Athollbank has smart, good-sized bedrooms (none are en suite, though) and is close to local pubs and restaurants.

Aabalree B&B **£**
(☏ 01382-223867; www.aabalree.com; 20 Union St; s/d £35/50; 🛜) This is a pretty basic B&B – there are no en suites, and no lift to the three floors – but the owners are welcoming (don't be put off by the dark entrance). It couldn't be more central, close to both the train and bus stations, but that makes it popular, so book ahead.

★Malmaison BOUTIQUE HOTEL **££**
(☏ 01382-339715; www.malmaison.com/locations/dundee; 44 Whitehall Cres; r from £85; 🛜) Housed in a Victorian hotel building, this place has been refurbished in typical Malmaison style with period features such as intricate wrought-iron balustrades complemented by delightfully over-the-top modern decor. The rooms on the south side overlook the redeveloped waterfront and the V&A museum. Room rates are excellent value; check website for special offers.

Urban Quarters APARTMENT **££**
(☏ 07876 450961; www.urbanquarters.co.uk; 26 South Tay St; 2-bedroom apt from £140; 🛜) This complex contains four two-bedroom apartments, all stylishly decorated with clean, modern lines and kitted out with

modern kitchens (including Nespresso coffee machines) and smart TVs with access to Netflix. There's a two-night minimum stay.

Shaftesbury Lodge
HOTEL ££

(☑ 01382-669216; www.shaftesburylodge.co.uk; 1 Hyndford St; s/d from £60/80; 🐾) The family-run, 12-room Shaftesbury is set in a Victorian mansion that was built for a jute baron and has many authentic period features, including a fine marble fireplace in the dining room. It's 1.5 miles west of the city centre, just off Perth Rd.

Errolbank Guest House
B&B ££

(☑ 01382-462118; www.errolbank-guesthouse.com; 9 Dalgleish Rd; s/d from £64/74; 🅿🐾) A mile east of the city centre, just north of the road to Broughty Ferry, Errolbank is a lovely Victorian family home with smallish, but nicely decorated, en-suite rooms set on a quiet street.

Apex City Quay Hotel
HOTEL £££

(☑ 01382-202404; www.apexhotels.co.uk/dundee-hotel; 1 West Victoria Dock Rd; r from £130; 🅿🐾🏊) Though it looks plain and boxy from the outside, the Apex sports the sort of stylish, spacious, sofa-equipped rooms that make you want to lounge around all evening munching chocolate in front of the TV. If you can drag yourself away from your room, there are spa treatments, saunas and Japanese hot tubs to enjoy.

The hotel is just east of the city centre, overlooking the city's redeveloping waterfront and close to HMS *Unicorn*.

✕ Eating

★ Bach
CAFE £

(https://the-bach.com; 31 Meadowside; mains £5-11; ⊙ 9am-5pm; 🐾🍴) Easily the best breakfast spot in town (served till 11.45am weekdays, all-day brunch at weekends), this place sports a mix of Scottish, New Zealand, Asian and Mexican influences with delightful dishes such as Hebridean eggs (with Stornoway black pudding), homemade Kiwi burgers, nachos and banh mi (Vietnamese baguette sandwiches).

Parlour Cafe
CAFE £

(☑ 01382-203588; 58 West Port; mains £6-9; ⊙ 8am-6pm Mon-Sat, 10am-3pm Sun; 🐾🍴) 🌱 Tiny but terrific, this friendly neighbourhood cafe is bursting with good things to eat including filled tortillas, savoury tarts, bean burgers, bagels and homemade soup, all freshly prepared using seasonal produce.

Great coffee and cakes too, but be prepared to wait for a table or squeeze in among the locals.

Bridgeview Station
SCOTTISH £

(☑ 01382-660066; www.bridgeviewstation.com; Riverside Dr; lunch mains £7-11, 3-course dinner £23; ⊙ 8am-6pm Sun-Tue, to 10pm Wed-Sat; 🅿🍴) Bridgeview enjoys a lovely setting in a red-brick Victorian railway station building on the western fringes of Dundee, with a view across the Firth of Tay. Covering everything from breakfast to dinner, the menu majors on fresh local produce with the lunch platters (fish, vegetarian, or cheese and ploughman's) offering unbeatable value.

★ Castlehill
MODERN SCOTTISH ££

(☑ 01382-220008; www.castlehillrestaurant.co.uk; 22 Exchange St; 3-course dinner £38; ⊙ noon-2.30pm Fri & Sat, 5.30-10pm Wed-Sat) Thought by many to be worthy of earning Dundee's first Michelin star, the Castlehill is passionate about Scottish produce (the chef is a keen forager for wild herbs and fungi) and invests a lot of imagination into turning out beautifully presented dishes made with Angus lamb, Perthshire pork and Shetland scallops – art on a plate. Five-course tasting menu is £55.

Innis & Gunn Beer Kitchen
PUB FOOD ££

(☑ 01382-202070; www.innisandgunn.com/bars/dundee; 10 South Tay St; mains £9-16; ⊙ kitchen noon-9pm; 🐾) The decor in this brewpub is designed to appeal to fans of craft beer, all bare bricks, dark browns, stainless-steel pipes and brewing equipment, but the menu edges towards the gourmet end of pub grub where steaks, burgers and hot dogs sit alongside devilled mushrooms, seared scallops and pan-fried fillet of hake.

Agacán
TURKISH ££

(☑ 01382-644227; www.agacan.co.uk; 113 Perth Rd; mains £11-19; ⊙ 5-9.30pm Tue-Sun; 🍴) With a charismatic owner, quirky decor and wonderfully aromatic Turkish specialities (İskender kebab is a favourite), it's no wonder that you have to book ahead at this colourful little restaurant, a 20-minute walk up Perth Rd from the centre. If you can't get a table, you can settle for takeaway.

Avery & Co
CAFE ££

(☑ 01382-201533; www.averyandco.co.uk; 34 South Tay St; mains £7-15; ⊙ 9am-9pm Mon-Fri, 10am-10pm Sat, 10am-4pm Sun; 🐾🍴) Fresh, natural and local (with the occasional dash of Mexican) is the mantra at this utilitarian cafe, which serves everything from breakfast burritos to lunch platters of roast vegetable and hummus wholemeal wraps, to dinner dishes such as roast Scottish lamb on a bed of spiced quinoa, purple sprouting broccoli and salsa verde. There's a good vegan menu too.

Jute Café Bar BISTRO **££**
(✆01382-909246; www.jutecafebar.co.uk; 152 Nethergate; mains £8-18; ⊙10am-9.30pm; 🖻🖶) The industrial-chic cafe-bar in the Dundee Contemporary Arts centre (p213) serves excellent deli sandwiches and burgers, as well as more adventurous Mediterranean-Asian fusion cuisine. Tables spill out into the sunny courtyard in summer.

🍷 Drinking & Nightlife

D'Arcy Thompson BAR
(http://thedarcythompson.co.uk; 21-23 Old Hawk-hill; ⊙11.30am-11pm Sun-Thu, to midnight Fri & Sat; 🖻🖶) Bentwood chairs, old laboratory stools and a handful of discreetly displayed Victorian zoological specimens pay tribute to the eponymous Dundee professor of natural history (1860–1948) who once worked at the university across the road. Craft beers, coffee and cocktails are on the menu, as well as an above-average choice of pub grub.

Speedwell Bar PUB
(www.facebook.com/thespeedwellbar; 165-167 Perth Rd; ⊙11am-midnight Mon-Sat, 12.30pm-midnight Sun; 🖻) Known to generations of Dundonians as 'Mennie's' (Mrs Mennie was a former bar-keeper), this university district pub, 1.5 miles west of the city centre, is the city's best pre-served Edwardian bar, complete with acres of polished mahogany, real ale on tap and a choice of 150 malt whiskies.

Braes BAR
(✆01382-226344; www.braesdundee.co.uk; 14-18 Perth Rd; ⊙11am-midnight Sun-Thu, to 1am Fri & Sat; 🖻) Students from the nearby university crowd the tables at this modern bar with its cute, Scandinavian-style decor (lots of col-ourfully painted wood panelling) and views across the rooftops to the Tay Bridge. A good range of craft beers and coffee are com-plemented by a decent choice of pub grub (mains £7 to £14, good vegetarian options).

Drouthy's PUB
(✆01382-202187; www.drouthysdundee.co.uk; 142 Perth Rd; ⊙10am-midnight; 🖻) A perfectly un-pretentious local pub, serving a wide range of Scottish and international craft beers and an all-day menu of tempting pub grub (mains

WORTH A TRIP

NEWPORT RESTAURANT

The setting is fabulous, with vast win-dows overlooking the Firth of Tay, and quirky 'recycled' decor that includes the clever use of an old piano to store cutlery and wine glasses. Graze on an assort-ment of 'small plates' showcasing the best of local produce, or opt for the six-course tasting menu (per person £55). It has vegetarian and pescatarian options.

The **restaurant** (✆01382-541449; http://thenewportrestaurant.co.uk; 1 High St, Newport-on-Tay; small plates £6-14; ⊙noon-2.30pm Thu-Sat, noon-3pm Sun, 6-9.30pm Wed-Sat; P✆) is across the water from Dundee, a short drive (or just a 30-minute walk) away over the Tay Road Bridge.

£8 to £10), including irresistible gourmet burgers. Live music in the basement club.

Empire State Coffee COFFEE
(www.empirestatecoffee.com; 28 Whitehall Cres; ⊙7.30am-6pm Mon-Sat, 9am-5pm Sun; 🖻) Get your morning caffeine hit at this small arti-san roastery – if the street-level cafe looks full up, head to the back and down the stairs where you'll find a nifty basement lounge decorated to look like a railway carriage. Good hot chocolate too.

⭐ Entertainment

Reading Rooms LIVE MUSIC
(www.readingroomsdundee.com; 57 Blackscroft; free–£10) Dundee's hippest venue is an arty, bohemian hang-out in a rundown former library that hosts some of Scotland's best indie club nights. Live gigs have ranged from island singer-songwriter Colin MacIntyre (aka Mull Historical Society) to Glasgow guitar band Franz Ferdinand and Ayrshire rockers Biffy Clyro.

Dundee Rep Theatre THEATRE
(✆01382-223530; www.dundeerep.co.uk; Tay Sq; ⊙box office 9.30am-6pm Mon-Sat) Dundee's main venue for the performing arts, the Rep is home to Scotland's only full-time repertory company and to the Scottish Dance Theatre.

ⓘ Information

Ninewells Hospital (✆01382-660111; www.nhstayside.scot.nhs.uk) At Menzieshill, west of the city centre.

Post Office (30 Whitehall St; ⊙ 8.30am-6pm Mon-Fri, 9am-5.30pm Sat)

Dundee Tourist Office (☑ 01382-527527; www.angusanddundee.co.uk; 16 City Sq; ⊙ 9.30am-5pm Mon-Sat)

❶ Getting There & Away

AIR

Two and a half miles west of the city centre, **Dundee Airport** (www.hial.co.uk/dundee-airport) has daily scheduled services to London Stansted airport, Jersey and Amsterdam. A taxi from the city centre to the airport takes 10 minutes and costs around £5.

BUS

The bus station is northeast of the city centre. Some Aberdeen buses travel via Arbroath, others via Forfar.

Aberdeen £18.30, 1½ hours, hourly

Edinburgh £17.50, 1½ hours, hourly, some change at Perth

Glasgow £17.50, 1¾ hours, hourly

London from £21, 11 to 12 hours, National Express, daily

Perth £8.20, 35 minutes, hourly

Oban £38.20, 5½ hours, three daily, change at Glasgow

TRAIN

Trains from Dundee to Aberdeen travel via Arbroath and Stonehaven.

Aberdeen £20.90, 1¼ hours, twice hourly

Edinburgh £18.90, 1¼ hours, at least hourly

Glasgow £23.20, 1½ hours, hourly

Perth £8.30, 20 minutes, hourly

❶ Getting Around

The city centre is compact and easy to get around on foot. For information on local public transport, check **Dundee Travel Info** (www.dundeetravelinfo.com).

BUS

City bus fares cost £1.70 to £2.20 depending on distance; buy your ticket from the driver (exact fare only – no change given).

CAR

Rental agencies include the following.

Arnold Clark (☑ 01382-225382; www.arnoldclarkrental.com; East Dock St; ⊙ 8am-6pm Mon-Sat, 9am-4pm Sun)

Europcar (☑ 01382-373939; www.europcar.co.uk; 45-53 Gellatly St; ⊙ 8am-6pm Mon-Fri, to 1pm Sat)

TAXI

Tele Taxis (☑ 01382-825825; www.tele-taxis.co.uk)

Broughty Ferry

Dundee's attractive seaside suburb, known locally as 'the Ferry', lies 4 miles east of the city centre. It has a castle, a long, sandy beach and a number of good places to eat and drink. It's also handy for the golf courses at nearby **Carnoustie** (☑ 01241-802270; www.carnoustiegolflinks.co.uk; 20 Links Pde, Carnoustie, Angus).

◉ Sights

Broughty Castle Museum   MUSEUM
(www.leisureandculturedundee.com; Castle Green; ⊙ 10am-4pm Mon-Sat, 12.30-4pm Sun, closed Mon Oct-Mar; ℗) **FREE** A 16th-century tower that looms imposingly over Broughty Ferry harbour, guarding the entrance to the Firth of Tay, houses a fascinating exhibit on Dundee's whaling industry, and the view from the top offers the chance of spotting seals and dolphins offshore.

🛏 Sleeping & Eating

Broughty Ferry is a more attractive place to stay than central Dundee, and has a good choice of B&Bs and hotels. There are campsites too, a few miles further east at Monifeith.

Ashley House   B&B ££
(☑ 01382-776109; www.ashleyhousebroughtyferry.com; 15 Monifieth Rd; s/d from £55/77; ℗ 🤶 🐾) This spacious and comfortable guesthouse has long been one of Broughty Ferry's best. Its five cheerfully decorated bedrooms come equipped with hotel-grade beds and DVD players; one has a particularly grand bathroom.

Hotel Broughty Ferry   HOTEL ££
(☑ 01382-480027; www.hotelbroughtyferry.com; 16 W Queen St; s/d from £79/88; ℗ 🤶 🐾) It may not look like much from the outside, but this is the Ferry's swankiest place to stay, with 16 beautifully decorated bedrooms, a sauna, solarium and a small heated pool. It's only a five-minute stroll from the waterfront.

Fisherman's Tavern   B&B ££
(☑ 01382-775941; www.fishermanstavern-broughtyferry.co.uk; 10-16 Fort St; r from £73; 🤶) A delightful 17th-century terraced cottage just a few paces from the seafront, the Fisherman's was converted into a pub in 1827. It now has 12 stylishly modern rooms, most with en suite, and an atmospheric pub.

★ Tayberry MODERN SCOTTISH ££
(☑ 01382-698280; www.tayberryrestaurant.
com; cnr Brook St & Esplanade; 3-courses £30;
☺ noon-2pm & 6-9pm Tue-Sat) ✎ Neutral decor
enriched with splashes of berry purple create
an understated atmosphere in which accomplished chef Adam Newth presents gorgeous
and colourful confections using fresh and
foraged local produce – dishes such as monkfish cheeks with salad of capers, pecans and
pomegranate seeds, or pork belly with confit
beetroot and toffee apple syrup, delight the
eye as much as the palate.

Afternoon tea (from £19 per person) is
served in the delightful upstairs dining room,
with views across the dunes to the Firth of Tay.

Ship Inn PUB FOOD ££
(☑ 01382-779176; www.theshipinn-broughtyferry.
co.uk; 121 Fisher St; mains £9-19; ☺ food served
noon-3pm & 5-9.30pm) The Ship Inn is a snug,
wood-panelled, 19th-century pub on the
waterfront, which serves top-notch dishes
ranging from gourmet haddock and chips to
venison steaks; you can eat in the upstairs
restaurant, or down in the bar (bar meals £8
to £13). It's always busy, so get there early to
grab a seat.

❶ Getting There & Away

Dundee city bus 5 and Stagecoach bus 73 run
from Dundee High St to Broughty Ferry (£2.20,
20 minutes) several times an hour from Monday
to Saturday, and hourly on Sunday.

There are five trains daily from Dundee (£1.60,
five to 10 minutes).

Glamis Castle

Looking every inch the Scottish Baronial
castle, with its roofline sprouting a forest
of pointed turrets and battlements, **Glamis Castle** (www.glamis-castle.co.uk; adult/
child £12.50/9; ☺ 10am-5.30pm Apr-Oct, last entry
4.30pm; ℗ ♿) claims to be the legendary
setting for Shakespeare's *Macbeth*. A royal
residence since 1372, it is the family home of
the earls of Strathmore and Kinghorne – the
Queen Mother (born Elizabeth Bowes-Lyon,
1900–2002) spent her childhood at Glamis
(pronounced 'glams') and Princess Margaret
(the Queen's sister, 1930–2002) was born here.

The five-storey, L-shaped castle was given
to the Lyon family in 1372, but was significantly altered in the 17th century. Inside,
the most impressive room is the **drawing room**, with its vaulted plasterwork ceiling.

There's a display of armour and weaponry in
the haunted crypt and frescoes in the chapel
(also haunted). **Duncan's Hall** is named for
the murdered King Duncan from *Macbeth*
(though the scene actually takes place in
Macbeth's castle in Inverness). As with Cawdor Castle, the claimed Shakespeare connection is fictitious – the real Macbeth had
nothing to do with either castle, and died
long before either was built.

You can also look around the **royal apartments**, including the Queen Mother's bedroom. Hour-long guided tours (included in
admission) depart every 15 minutes; the last
tour is at 4.30pm.

Glamis Castle is 12 miles north of Dundee. There are two to four buses a day from
Dundee (£6.85, 1½ hour) to Glamis; change
at Forfar.

Arbroath

POP 23,900
Arbroath is an old-fashioned seaside resort
and fishing harbour, home of the famous
Arbroath smokie (a form of smoked
haddock). The humble smokie achieved
European Union 'Protected Geographical
Indication' status in 2004 – the term
'Arbroath smokie' can only be used legally to
describe haddock smoked in the traditional
manner within an 8km radius of Arbroath.

◉ Sights

Arbroath Abbey HISTORIC BUILDING
(HES; www.historicenvironment.scot; Abbey St;
adult/child £6/3.60; ☺ 9.30am-5.30pm Apr-
Sep, 10am-4pm Oct-Mar) The picturesque,

LOCAL KNOWLEDGE

THE ANGUS FOOD SCENE

Angus takes in the broad valley of Strathmore, which stretches northeast from Blairgowrie to Stonehaven. The region contains some of the most fertile farmland in Scotland, and has long been famous for producing Aberdeen Angus beef, soft fruits, barley, potatoes and other vegetables which, along with the harvest of the sea (landed at Arbroath), has encouraged the rise of a thriving artisan food and drink scene.

The List (https://food.list.co.uk/guides/angus-larder) publishes a booklet called *The Angus Larder*, listing local producers, markets and eating places.

red-sandstone ruins of Arbroath Abbey, founded in 1178 by King William the Lion, dominate the town of Arbroath. It is thought that Bernard of Linton, the abbot here in the early 14th century, wrote the famous Declaration of Arbroath in 1320, asserting Scotland's right to independence; an exhibition in the beautifully preserved Abbot's House includes a replica of the declaration. You can climb part way up one of the towers for a grand view over the ruins.

St Vigeans Museum   MUSEUM
(HES; ☑ 01241-878756; www.historicenvironment.scot; St Vigeans Lane; adult/child £5/3; ⊙ by appointment) About a mile north of Arbroath town centre, this cottage museum houses a superb collection of Pictish and medieval sculptured stones. The museum's masterpiece is the **Drosten Stone**, beautifully carved with animal figures and hunting scenes on one side, and an interlaced Celtic cross on the other (look for the devil perched in the top left corner). Check the website for open days; otherwise phone ahead or ask at Arbroath Abbey to arrange a visit.

🏃 Activities

The coast northeast of Arbroath consists of dramatic red-sandstone cliffs riven by inlets, caves and natural arches. An excellent **clifftop walk** follows the coast for 3 miles to the quaint fishing village of **Auchmithie**, which claims to have invented the Arbroath smokie; you can try it at the village's But'n'Ben Restaurant.

If you fancy catching your own fish, the **Mari Dawn** (☑ 01241-873957, 07836 770609; ianswankie@yahoo.co.uk), **MV Ardent** (☑ 07543 005908; www.arbroathangling.co.uk) and **Girl Katherine II** (☑ 07752 470621; www.sea-angling.net) offer three-hour sea-angling trips (usually from 2pm to 5pm) out of Arbroath harbour for around £15 to £20 per person, including tackle and bait.

🛏 Sleeping

Harbour Nights Guest House   B&B ££
(☑ 01241-434343; www.harbournights-scotland.com; 4 The Shore; s/d from £55/75; 🖥) With a superb location overlooking the harbour, four stylishly decorated bedrooms and a gourmet breakfast menu, Harbour Nights is our favourite place to stay in Arbroath. Rooms 2 and 3, with harbour views, are a bit more expensive (from £80), but well worth asking for when booking.

Townhouse Hotel   HOTEL ££
(☑ 01241-431577; www.townhousehotelarbroath.co.uk; 99 High St; r from £79; 🖥) The Townhouse, set in a restored Georgian-style building on Arbroath's main street, offers stylishly decorated if somewhat smallish rooms but with a superb location just a few minutes walk from Arbroath Abbey.

🍴 Eating & Drinking

Smithie's Deli   CAFE £
(www.facebook.com/smithiesdeli1; 16 Keptie St; mains £4-7; ⊙ 9.30am-4.30pm Mon-Fri, to 4pm Sat; 🖥🌱) 🍃 Housed in a former butcher's shop, with hand-painted tiles and meat hooks on the ceiling, Smithie's is a great little neighbourhood deli and cafe serving fair-trade coffee, pancakes, wraps and an Italian charcuterie and cheese platter. Sadly, no espresso or breakfast menu.

But'n'Ben Restaurant   SCOTTISH ££
(☑ 01241-877223; www.thebutnben.com; 1 Auchmithie; mains £8-26; ⊙ noon-2pm Wed-Mon, 6-9pm Wed-Sat, 4-5.30pm Sun; 🅿🚼) 🍃 Above the harbour in Auchmithie, this cosy cottage restaurant with open fireplace, rustic furniture and sea-themed art serves the best of local seafood – the Arbroath smokie pancakes are recommended – plus great homemade cakes and desserts, and high teas on Sunday (£16). Best to book.

Old Brewhouse   SCOTTISH ££
(☑ 01241-879945; www.oldbrewhousearbroath.co.uk; 1 High St; mains £10-20; ⊙ noon-8.30pm

Mon-Fri, to 9pm Sat, 12.30-8.30pm Sun; 🛜) Located on the seafront east of the harbour, the Old Brewhouse has the scent of the North Sea in its nostrils, and also on its menu – choose from a Cullen skink, crab salad, haddock and chips, or Arbroath smokie done half a dozen ways (speciality of the house is a ramekin of Arbroath smokie and bacon topped with cheese).

Also offers B&B at £90 for a double room.

Gordon's Restaurant
SCOTTISH £££

(📞 01241-830364; www.gordonsrestaurant.co.uk; Main St, Inverkeillor; 3-course lunch £35, 4-course dinner £65; ⏰12.30-1.30pm Sun, 7-8.30pm Tue-Sun, closed Sun dinner Oct-Apr) 🚗 Six miles north of Arbroath, in the tiny and unpromising-looking village of Inverkeillor, lies this hidden gem – an intimate and rustic eatery serving gourmet-quality Scottish cuisine. There are five comfortable **bedrooms** (single/double from £85/110) for those who don't want to drive after dinner.

Old Bean Coffee House & Cocktail Bar
CAFE

(www.facebook.com/oldbeancoffeehouse1; 1b Millgate; ⏰9am-5pm Tue-Fri, 10am-4.30pm Sat, 11am-4.30pm Sun, also 6.30pm-midnight Fri & Sat; 🛜) This laid-back little cafe serves the best coffee in town (using locally roasted Sacred Grounds coffee beans), along with a menu of bagels, waffles, salads and panini. On Friday and Saturday evenings it morphs into a cocktail bar, with occasional DJ nights.

ℹ Getting There & Away

Bus 140 runs from Arbroath to Auchmithie (£1.60, 15 minutes, six daily Monday to Friday, three daily on Saturday and Sunday).

Trains from Dundee to Arbroath (£5.90, 20 minutes, two per hour) continue to Aberdeen (£20.50, 55 minutes) via Montrose and Stonehaven.

Kirriemuir

POP 6100

Known as the Wee Red Town because of its close-packed, red-sandstone houses, Kirriemuir is famed as the birthplace of JM Barrie (1860–1937), writer and creator of the much-loved *Peter Pan*. A bronze statue of the 'boy who wouldn't grow up' graces the intersection of Bank and High Sts.

Tourist information is available in the Gateway to the Glens Museum.

◉ Sights

JM Barrie's Birthplace
MUSEUM

(NTS; www.nts.org.uk; 9 Brechin Rd; adult/child £6.50/5.50; ⏰11am-4pm Thu-Mon Jul & Aug, Sat & Sun only Apr-Jun & Sep) This is Kirriemuir's big attraction, a place of pilgrimage for *Peter Pan* fans from all over the world. The two-storey house where Barrie was born has been furnished in period style, and preserves Barrie's writing desk and the wash house at the back that served as his first 'theatre'.

Camera Obscura
HISTORIC BUILDING

(www.kirriemuircameraobscura.com; by donation; ⏰11am-4pm Sat-Mon Apr-Sep) This 1930s cricket pavilion on the hilltop northeast of the town centre was gifted to the town by famous son JM Barrie, and is now managed by local volunteers. The camera obscura incorporated into the pointed turret uses a lens to project live images of the surrounding countryside on to a viewing table, and is one of only four in Scotland.

Gateway to the Glens Museum
MUSEUM

(kirriemuirmuseum@angusalive.scot; 32 High St; ⏰10am-5pm Tue-Sat) **FREE** The old Town House opposite the Peter Pan statue dates from 1604 and houses the Gateway to the Glens Museum, a useful introduction to local history, geology and wildlife for those planning to explore the Angus Glens. It also contains a shrine to local boy made good, Bon Scott (1946–80), former lead singer of rock band AC/DC.

ABERLEMNO PICTISH STONES

The mysterious **Aberlemno Stones** (⏰Apr-Sep) are among Scotland's finest Pictish carved stones. By the roadside there are three 7th- to 9th-century slabs with various symbols, including the z-rod and double disc; in the churchyard at the bottom of the hill there's a magnificent 8th-century stone displaying a Celtic cross, interlace decoration, entwined beasts and, on the reverse, scenes of the Battle of Nechtansmere (where the Picts vanquished the Northumbrians in 685). The site is 5 miles northeast of Forfar, on the B9134.

The stones are covered up from October to March, otherwise there's free access at all times.

NORTHEAST SCOTLAND KIRRIEMUIR

222

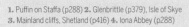
1. Puffin on Staffa (p288) 2. Glenbrittle (p379), Isle of Skye
3. Mainland cliffs, Shetland (p416) 4. Iona Abbey (p288)

MICHAEL FOLLAN · MGFOTOUK.COM/GETTY IMAGES ©

JUTAPORN CHONGCHAROENSIRI/SHUTTERSTOCK ©

Scotland's Islands

Scotland's sweeping array of islands – 790 at last count, around a hundred of which are inhabited – defines the country's complex coastline. Ruins, from prehistoric religious centres to staunch castles, overlook landscapes where sheep crop lush grass, the scant remaining fisherfolk take on powerful seas, and urban professionals looking for a quieter life battle with unreliable wi-fi.

Geography & History

Though in the modern world these islands might seem remote outposts, Scotland's complex geography has meant that, from Celts through to Vikings and the Lords of the Isles, transport, trade and power are intimately tied to the sea. Today's lonely island stronghold was yesteryear's hub of connections spreading right across western and northern Britain and beyond.

Sights & Activities

For the visitor, there's bewildering scope. The once-Norse islands of Orkney and Shetland are Britain's northernmost parts, while the Hebrides guard the west coast like a storm shield against the mighty Atlantic. The choice is yours: for scenic splendour with hills to climb and memorable walks you might choose spectacular Skye, diverse Mull, accessible Arran or lonely Jura. Neolithic villages, standing stones, evocative prehistoric monuments? Head to far-flung Orkney, Shetland or the Outer Hebrides. Abbeys, castles or stately homes? Magical Iona, Bute, Coll, Barra or Westray. Beaches? Pick Harris or Tiree. Birdlife? Unst, the Uists, Fair Isle, Noss, North Ronaldsay or Staffa. Whisky? It's got to be Islay. A convivial pub, local seafood and a warm welcome? Take your pick of any, then find yourself a snug cottage with a scent of the salty breeze and call it home for a day or three.

Bon Scott Statue   MONUMENT
(Bellies Brae) Bon Scott (1946–80), the former lead singer of rock band AC/DC, grew up in Kirriemuir. His local origins are celebrated in the annual Bonfest rock festival (www.bonfest.com) held in the village, and by this life-size statue, installed in 2016.

Eating

★ **88 Degrees**   CAFE, DELI **£**
(☑01575-570888; www.facebook.com/88kirriemuir; 17 High St; mains £4-8; ☺9.30am-4pm Wed-Sat, 10am-4pm Sun; ☑) 🅿 This tiny deli serves the best cafe cuisine in the county – superb coffee (the cafe is named for the ideal temperature of an espresso), delicious cakes and tray bakes, and handmade chocolates. Breakfast (served till 11.30am) includes buttermilk waffles with banana and maple syrup.

🔒 Shopping

Star Rock Shop   FOOD & DRINKS
(☑01575-572579; 25 Roods; ☺10am-4pm Tue-Sat) For generations of local school kids, the big treat when visiting Kirriemuir was a trip to the Star Rock Shop. Established in 1833, it specialises in traditional Scottish 'sweeties', arranged in colourful jars along the walls –

including humbugs, cola cubes, pear drops and the original Star Rock candy, still made to an 1833 recipe.

ℹ Getting There & Away

Stagecoach bus 20 runs from Dundee to Kirriemuir (£4.50, one hour, hourly Monday to Saturday, every two hours Sunday) via Forfar (25 minutes, change here for Glamis).

Edzell

POP 900

The picturesque village of Edzell, with its broad main street and grandiose **monumental arch**, dates from the early 19th century when Lord Panmure decided that the original medieval village, a mile to the west, spoiled the view from Edzell Castle. The old village was razed and the villagers moved to this pretty, planned settlement.

Two miles north of Edzell, the B966 to Fettercairn crosses the River North Esk at Gannochy Bridge. From the lay-by just over the bridge, a wooden door in the stone wall gives access to a delightful footpath that leads along the wooded river gorge for 1.5 miles to a picturesque spot known as the **Rocks of Solitude**.

PICTISH SYMBOL STONES

The mysterious carved stones that dot the landscape of eastern Scotland are the legacy of the warrior tribes who inhabited these lands 2000 years ago. The Romans occupied the southern half of Britain from AD 43 to 410, but the region to the north of the firths of Forth and Clyde – known as Caledonia – was abandoned as being too dangerous, and sealed off behind the ramparts of the Antonine Wall and Hadrian's Wall.

Caledonia was the homeland of the Picts, a collection of tribes named by the Romans for their habit of painting or tattooing their bodies. In the 9th century they were culturally absorbed by the Scots, leaving behind only a few archaeological remains, a scattering of Pictish place names beginning with 'Pit', and hundreds of mysterious carved stones decorated with intricate symbols, mainly in northeast Scotland. The capital of the ancient Southern Pictish kingdom is said to have been at Forteviot in Strathearn; Pictish symbol stones are found throughout this area and all the way up the eastern coast of Scotland into Sutherland and Caithness.

It is thought that the stones were set up to record Pictish lineages and alliances, but no one is sure exactly how the system worked. They are decorated with unusual symbols, including z-rods (a lightning bolt?), circles (the sun?), double discs (a hand mirror?) and fantastical creatures, as well as figures of warriors on horseback, hunting scenes and (on the later stones) Christian symbols.

Local museums provide a free leaflet, *Angus Pictish Trail,* which will guide you to the main sites (there are similar leaflets for Aberdeenshire and Moray). The finest assemblage of stones in their natural outdoor setting is at Aberlemno (p221), and there are excellent indoor collections at St Vigeans Museum (p220) and the Meigle Museum (p209).

The Pictish Trail by Anthony Jackson lists 11 driving tours, while *The Symbol Stones of Scotland* by the same author provides more detail on the history and meaning of the Pictish stones.

Edzell Castle
CASTLE

(HES; www.historicenvironment.scot; adult/child £6/3.60; ⊙9.30am-5.30pm Apr-Sep; ℗) The Lindsay earls of Crawford, Lord Panmure's predecessors as owners of Edzell Castle, built the L-plan tower house in the 16th century. Sir David Lindsay, a cultured and well-travelled man, laid out this castle's beautiful **pleasance** in 1604 as a place of contemplation and learning. Unique in all of Scotland, this Renaissance walled garden is lined with niches for nesting birds, and sculptured plaques illustrating the cardinal virtues, the arts and the planetary deities.

Glenesk Hotel
SLEEPING ££

(☑ 01356-647333; www.gleneskhotel.com; High St; s/d from £85/120; ℗ 🛜) The Glenesk is a grand old country-house hotel with a solidly traditional atmosphere. The bedrooms range from no-surprises standard to four-poster luxury, while the bar reflects the twin passions of the owner – commercial aviation (aircraft portraits on the walls) and malt whisky (one of Scotland's largest collections, with more than 1000 varieties).

ⓘ Getting There & Away

Stagecoach buses 21 and 21A from Dundee (via Forfar and Brechin) stop at Edzell (£7.80, 1½ hours, seven daily Monday to Friday, five on Saturday).

ABERDEENSHIRE

Since medieval times Aberdeenshire and its northwestern neighbour Moray have been the richest and most fertile regions of the Highlands. Aberdeenshire is famed for its Aberdeen Angus beef cattle, its many fine castles and the prosperous 'granite city' of Aberdeen.

North of Aberdeen, the Grampian Mountains fall away to rolling agricultural plains pocked with small, craggy volcanic hills. This fertile lowland corner of northeastern Scotland is known as Buchan; the old Scots dialect, the Doric, is in everyday use here (if you think the Glaswegian accent is difficult to understand, just try listening in on a conversation in Fraserburgh).

The Buchan coast alternates between rugged cliffs and long, long stretches of sand, dotted with picturesque little fishing villages such as Pennan, where parts of the film *Local Hero* were shot.

Aberdeen

POP 195,000

Aberdeen is northeast Scotland's powerhouse, fuelled by the North Sea petroleum industry. Oil money made the city as expensive as London, with prices charged to match the depth of oil-wealthy pockets, though regular downturns in the industry see prices fall. Fortunately, most cultural attractions, such as the Maritime Museum and Aberdeen Art Gallery, are free.

Known throughout Scotland as the granite city, much of the town was built using silvery-grey granite hewn from the now-abandoned Rubislaw Quarry, at one time the biggest artificial hole in the ground in Europe. On a sunny day the granite lends an attractive glitter to the city, but when low, grey rain clouds scud in off the North Sea it can be hard to tell where the buildings stop and the sky begins.

Royal Deeside is easily accessible to the west, Dunnottar Castle to the south, sandy beaches to the north and whisky country northwest.

⊙ Sights & Activities

⊙ City Centre

Union St is the city's main thoroughfare, lined with solid, Victorian granite buildings. The oldest area is Castlegate, at the eastern end, where the castle once stood. When it was captured from the English for Robert the Bruce, the password used by the townspeople was 'Bon Accord' (good fellowship), which is now the city's motto.

In the centre of Castle St stands the 17th-century **Mercat Cross** (Castle St), bearing a sculpted frieze of portraits of Stuart monarchs. The Baronial heap towering over the eastern end of Castle St is the **Salvation Army Citadel** (www.salvationarmy.org.uk/aberdeen-citadel; Castle St), which was modelled on Balmoral Castle.

On the northern side of Union St, 200m west of Castlegate, is 17th-century **Provost Skene's House** (☑ 01224-641086; www.aagm.co.uk; Guestrow) FREE, one of the city's oldest buildings (closed to the public until completion of the surrounding Marischal Sq redevelopment). Another 100m to the west is **St Nicholas Church**, the so-called 'Mither Kirk' (Mother Church) of Aberdeen. The granite spire dates from the 19th century, but there has been a church on this site since

Aberdeen

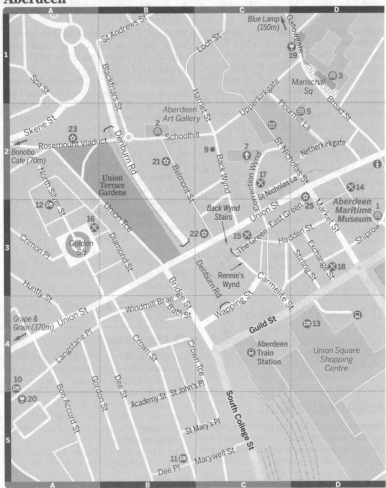

the 12th century; the early-15th-century **St Mary's Chapel** survives in the eastern part of the church.

⭐**Aberdeen Maritime Museum** MUSEUM
(☎ 01224-337700; www.aagm.co.uk; Shiprow; ⊙ 10am-5pm Mon-Sat, noon-3pm Sun) **FREE**
Overlooking the nautical bustle of Aberdeen harbour is the Maritime Museum, centred on a three-storey replica of a North Sea oil-production platform, which explains all you ever wanted to know about the petroleum industry. Other galleries, some situated in **Provost Ross's House**, the oldest building

in the city and part of the museum, cover the shipbuilding, whaling and fishing industries.

Sleek and speedy **Aberdeen clippers** were a 19th-century shipyard speciality, used by British merchants to import tea, wool and exotic goods (opium, for instance) to Britain, and, on the return journey, transport emigrants to Australia.

⭐**Gordon Highlanders Museum** MUSEUM
(www.gordonhighlanders.com; St Lukes, Viewfield Rd; adult/child £8/4.50; ⊙ 10am-4.30pm Tue-Sat Feb-Nov; **P ♿**) This excellent museum records the history of one of the British Army's most

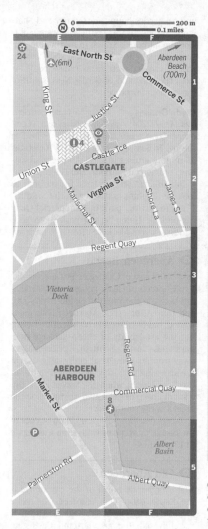

Aberdeen

famous fighting units, described by Winston Churchill as 'the finest regiment in the world'. Originally raised in the northeast of Scotland by the 4th Duke of Gordon in 1794, the regiment was amalgamated with the Seaforths and Camerons to form the Highlanders regiment in 1994. The museum is about a mile west of the western end of Union St – take bus 11 or X17 from Union St.

Aberdeen Art Gallery GALLERY
(☏ 01224-523700; www.aagm.co.uk; Schoolhill; ⊙ 10am-5pm Tue-Sat, 2-5pm Sun) **FREE** Behind the grand facade of Aberdeen Art Gallery

(closed for a major redevelopment until early 2019) is a cool, marble-lined space exhibiting the work of contemporary Scottish and English painters, such as Gwen Hardie, Stephen Conroy, Trevor Sutton and Tim Ollivier. There are also several landscapes by Joan Eardley, who lived in a cottage on the cliffs near Stonehaven in the 1950s and '60s and painted tempestuous oils of the North Sea and poignant portraits of slum children.

Among the Pre-Raphaelite works upstairs, look out for the paintings by Aberdeen artist William Dyce (1806–64), ranging from religious works to rural scenes.

Marischal College HISTORIC BUILDING
(Broad St) Marischal College, founded in 1593 by the 5th Earl Marischal, merged with King's College (founded 1495) in 1860 to

---

POTARCH & THE DINNIE STONES

Named after Donald Dinnie (1837–1916), a famous Aberdeenshire athlete and strongman, the **Dinnie Stones** (www.thedinniestones.com; Potarch) are a pair of granite boulders weighing 733lb (335.5kg) in total. Dinnie famously carried them (one in each hand) across Potarch Bridge in 1860, a feat of strength that went unrepeated until the 1970s. The current record for lifting and holding the stones sits at 34 seconds, set in May 2018. The stones sit outside Potarch Lodge, 10 miles west of Crathes Castle.

A pleasantly rustic spot set beside a venerable stone bridge over the Dee, **Potarch Cafe & Restaurant** (☑ 01339-884468; www.ballogie-estate.co.uk; Potarch Lodge; mains £10-20; ☺ 10am-5pm Sun-Thu, to 11pm Fri & Sat; P ় ়) serves Scottish pub grub such as Cullen skink, haddock and chips and a couple of vegetarian dishes. There are pleasant riverside and forest walks nearby, and the famous Dinnie Stones outside.

---

create the modern University of Aberdeen. The college's huge and impressive facade overlooking Broad St, in perpendicular Gothic style – unusual in having such elaborate masonry hewn from notoriously hard-to-work granite – dates from 1906 and is the world's second-largest granite structure (after El Escorial near Madrid).

A renovation project saw the facade returned to its original silvery-grey glory, and the building now houses Aberdeen City Council's headquarters. Outside, Marischal Sq is undergoing redevelopment as a pedestrian plaza, creating controversy over plans for modern architecture juxtaposed with the college's neo-Gothic facade.

Nick Nairn Cook School   COOKING
(☑ 01877-389900; www.nicknairncookschool.com; 15 Back Wynd; 1-day course per person £149) One-day courses in modern Scottish cooking at the school owned by Scotland's top TV chef, Nick Nairn, author of *Wild Harvest* and *Island Harvest*.

◉ Aberdeen Harbour

Aberdeen has a busy, working harbour crowded with survey vessels and supply ships servicing the offshore oil installations, and car ferries bound for Orkney and Shetland. Despite all this traffic, the waters outside the harbour are rich in marine life – in summer dolphins, porpoises and basking sharks can be seen from cruise boats or from the headland of Girdle Ness, south of the harbour entrance.

Clyde Cruises   WILDLIFE WATCHING
(☑ 01475-722204; www.clydecruises.com; Commercial Quay; adult/child from £16/8; ☺ Tue-Sun Jul-Aug, Fri-Sun Apr-Jun & Sep-Oct) Operates 45-minute cruises around Aberdeen's bustling commercial harbour, and 1½-hour trips (adult/child £25/12) outside the harbour to look for dolphins and other marine wildlife. If you're driving, park in Commercial Quay car park or Union Sq car park (both paid parking) across Market St from the harbour.

◉ Aberdeen Beach

Just 800m east of Castlegate is a spectacular 2-mile sweep of clean, golden sand stretching between the mouths of the Rivers Dee and Don. At one time Aberdeen Beach was a good, old-fashioned British seaside resort, but the availability of cheap package holidays has lured Scottish holidaymakers away from its somewhat chilly delights. On a warm summer's day, though, it's still an excellent beach; when the waves are right, a small group of dedicated **surfers** ride the breaks at the south end.

Bus 15 (eastbound) from Union St goes to the beach, or you can walk from Castlegate in 10 minutes.

◉ Old Aberdeen

Just over a mile north of the city centre is the district called Old Aberdeen. The name is misleading – although Old Aberdeen is certainly old, the area around Castlegate in the city centre is older still. This part of the city was originally called Aulton, from the Gaelic for 'village by the stream', and this was Anglicised in the 17th century to Old Town.

Bus 20 from Littlejohn St (just north of Marischal College) runs to Old Aberdeen every 15 to 20 minutes.

St Machar's Cathedral   CATHEDRAL
(www.stmachar.com; The Chanonry; ☺ 9.30am-4.30pm) FREE The 15th-century St Machar's, with its massive twin towers, is a rare example of a fortified cathedral. According to legend, St Machar was ordered to establish

a church where the river takes the shape of a bishop's crook, which it does just here. The cathedral is best known for its impressive **heraldic ceiling**, dating from 1520, which has 48 shields of kings, nobles, archbishops and bishops. Sunday services are held at 11am and 6pm.

Festivals & Events

True North
MUSIC

(www.aberdeenperformingarts.com/truenorth; ⊙ Sep) Held over the last weekend in September, this four-day festival celebrates the balladeer tradition of northeast Scotland with a program devoted to singer-songwriters from Scotland and all around the world.

Sound Festival
MUSIC

(http://sound-scotland.co.uk; ⊙ Oct-Nov) Festival dedicated to new music – classical, electroacoustic, improvised, experimental and jazz – performed at a range of venues large and small across Aberdeen and northeast Scotland, held over 10 days in late October/early November.

Sleeping

There are clusters of B&Bs on Bon Accord St and Springbank Tce (both 400m southwest of the train station) and along Great Western Rd (the A93, a 25-minute walk southwest of the city centre). With so many oil-industry workers staying the night before flying offshore, single rooms are at a premium, and rates tend to be significantly lower at weekends.

Aberdeen SYHA
HOSTEL £

(SYHA; ☑ 01224-646988; www.syha.org.uk; 8 Queen's Rd; dm/tw from £15.50/36; @ 🕿) This unexceptional but good-value hostel, set in a granite Victorian villa, is a mile west of the train station. Walk west along Union St and take the right fork along Albyn Pl until you reach a roundabout; Queen's Rd continues on the western side of the roundabout.

⭐ Globe Inn
B&B ££

(☑ 01224-624258; www.the-globe-inn.co.uk; 13-15 North Silver St; s/d £72/78; 🕿) This popular pub has seven appealing, comfortable guest bedrooms upstairs, done out in dark wood with burgundy bedspreads. There's live music in the pub on weekends so it's not a place for early-to-bed types, but the price versus location factor can't be beaten. No dining room, so breakfast is continental, served on a tray in your room. Cheaper at weekends.

⭐ Dutch Mill Hotel
HOTEL ££

(☑ 01224-322555; www.dutchmill.co.uk; 7 Queen's Rd; s £60-85, d £70-95; 🅿 🕿) The grand, granite-hewn, Victorian-era mansions that line Queens Rd house financial offices, private schools, medical practices and the occasional hotel – this one has nine bedrooms with beautifully understated modern decor, a popular bar and a conservatory restaurant. Rates are cheaper at weekends.

⭐ Jays
B&B ££

(☑ 01224-638295; www.jaysguesthouse.co.uk; 422 King St; s/d from £70/100; ⊙ Mon-Thu; 🅿 🕿) Located halfway between the city centre (a 15-minute walk) and Old Aberdeen (a 10-minute walk), this elegantly decorated Edwardian villa is a cosy nest of hospitality, with welcoming owners who seemingly can't do enough to help their guests enjoy their stay. Popular, so book well in advance (note – open Monday to Thursday nights only).

Bauhaus Hotel
BOUTIQUE HOTEL ££

(☑ 01224-212122; www.thebauhaus.co.uk; 52-60 Langstane Pl; d/ste from £75/120; 🕿) Decor of exposed brick and leather wall panels, slate-lined bathrooms, and Corbusier armchairs in the more expensive suites add a designer's touch to this centrally located, good-value hotel. Rates vary hugely, so check the website for special offers.

Butler's Guest House
B&B ££

(☑ 01224-212411; www.butlersguesthouse.com; 122 Crown St; s/d from £55/70; 🕿) Butler's is a cosy place with a big breakfast menu that includes fresh fruit salad, kippers and kedgeree as alternatives to the traditional fry-up (rates include a continental breakfast – cooked breakfast costs extra). There are cheaper rooms with shared bathrooms.

Jurys Inn
HOTEL £££

(☑ 01224-381200; www.jurysinns.com; Union Sq, Guild St; r from £127; 🕿) Conveniently located between the train and bus stations, this business-oriented hotel has stylish, spacious rooms with plenty of space for unpacking suitcases.

Eating

Bonobo Cafe
VEGAN £

(www.bonobotribe.co.uk; 73-75 Skene St; mains £4-7; ⊙ 8am-4pm Tue-Fri, 9am-5pm Sat, 10am-4pm Sun; 🍴) 🌿 Aberdeen has lagged behind a bit in the vegetarian-restaurant stakes, so it was good to see this 100% vegan cafe open in 2017. The menu runs from breakfast (served till noon, and all day on Sunday) of avocado on toast or smoked carrot and cream-cheese bagel, to lunch dishes such as smoky pinto bean and sweetcorn wraps.

★ **Café 52**　　　　　　　BISTRO ££
(☎ 01224-590094; www.cafe52.co.uk; 52 The Green; mains lunch £5, dinner £13; ⊘ noon-midnight Mon-Sat, to 4pm Sun; ☎🍴) This little haven of laid-back industrial chic – a high, narrow space lined with bare stonework, rough plaster and exposed ventilation ducts – serves some of the finest and best-value cuisine in the northeast (beetroot falafel with crispy capers and red-pepper aioli), and at incredible prices considering the quality on offer.

★ **Silver Darling**　　　　SEAFOOD ££
(☎ 01224-576229; www.thesilverdarling.co.uk; Pocra Quay, North Pier; mains £15-21; ⊘ noon-2pm & 5.30-9.30pm Mon-Fri, noon-9.30pm Sat, noon-8pm Sun; 🖫) 🍴 The Silver Darling (an old Scottish nickname for herring) is the place for a special meal, housed in a former Customs office at the entrance to Aberdeen harbour with picture windows overlooking the sea. Here you can enjoy fresh Scottish seafood while you watch the porpoises playing in the harbour mouth. Bookings are recommended.

Granite Park　　　　MODERN SCOTTISH ££
(☎ 01224-478004; www.granitepark.co.uk; 8 Golden Sq; 2-/3-course lunch £23/28, dinner mains £18-33; ⊘ noon-2.30pm & 5-9.30pm Tue-Sat) 🍴 This smart and sophisticated restaurant and cocktail bar, tucked away on a quiet square, takes Scottish favourites such as sea trout, scallops and Aberdeen Angus beef and gives them a sprinkling of French or Mediterranean flair. Best to book.

Angus & Ale　　　　MODERN SCOTTISH ££
(☎ 01224-643324; www.angusale.com; 28 Adelphi Lane, Union St; mains £10-30; ⊘ noon-10.30pm; 🖫) 🍴 Aberdeen Angus beef and craft beers are the speciality of this little gem in an alley off Union St, a small but sophisticated space decorated with weathered stone and muted natural colours. Charcoal grilling is a strength, with 28-day aged steaks, burgers and barbecue pork ribs on the menu alongside blackened cod fillet and whole roast poussin.

Sand Dollar Café　　　　CAFE ££
(☎ 01224-572288; www.sanddollarcafe.com; 2 Beach Esplanade; mains day £7-13, evening £16-29; ⊘ 7.30am-6pm Sun-Thu, 7.30am-4pm &

6-9pm Fri & Sat; 🖫) A cut above your usual seaside cafe – on sunny days you can sit at the wooden tables on the prom and share a bottle of chilled white wine, or choose from a menu that includes pancakes with maple syrup, homemade burgers and chocolate brownies with Orkney ice cream.

An evening bistro menu offers steak and seafood dishes; best to book for this. The cafe is on the esplanade, 800m northeast of the city centre.

Musa Art Cafe　　　　MODERN SCOTTISH ££
(☎ 01224-571771; www.musaaberdeen.com; 33 Exchange St; mains £12-25; ⊘ 11am-11pm Mon-Sat, noon-4pm Sun; ☎🍴) 🍴 The bright paintings on the walls match the vibrant furnishings and smart gastronomic creations at this great cafe-restaurant, set in a former church. In addition to a menu that focuses on quality local produce cooked in a quirky way – think haggis spring rolls with tomato and chilli jam – there are Brewdog beers from Fraserburgh, and interesting music, sometimes live.

★ **Moonfish Café**　　　　MODERN SCOTTISH £££
(☎ 01224-644166; www.moonfishcafe.co.uk; 9 Correction Wynd; 2-/3-course dinner £30/36; ⊘ noon-2pm & 6-9.30pm Tue-Sat) 🍴 The menu of this funky little eatery hidden on a backstreet concentrates on good-quality Scottish produce but draws its influences from cuisines all around the world, from simple scallops with chorizo, pine kernels and fennel, to rump of lamb with Jerusalem artichoke, mint and hazelnuts. Two-course lunch £16.50.

🍷 **Drinking & Nightlife**

Aberdeen is a great city for a pub crawl – it's more a question of knowing when to stop than where to start. There are lots of preclub bars in and around Belmont St and Langstane Pl, with more traditional pubs scattered throughout the city centre.

★ **Orchid**　　　　COCKTAIL BAR
(www.orchidaberdeen.com; 51 Langstane Pl; ⊘ 6pm-2am Sun-Thu, 5pm-3am Fri, 6pm-3am Sat) The winner of Scotland's Best Cocktail Bar 2017 is a relaxed and welcoming spot, quietly confident in its wide-ranging knowledge and expertise. Offers regular gin- and whisky-tasting sessions as well as mixology classes – the house cocktail is the Pink Orchid (vanilla vodka, black raspberry liqueur, cranberry, lime, sugar and egg white, shaken with ice and strained into a chilled glass).

Globe Inn PUB
(www.the-globe-inn.co.uk; 13-15 North Silver St; ⊙11am-midnight, to 1am Fri & Sat) This lovely Edwardian-style pub with wood panelling, marble-topped tables and walls decorated with old musical instruments is a great place for a quiet afternoon drink. It serves good coffee, as well as real ales and malt whiskies, and has live folk music Tuesdays, and rock bands Friday and Saturday. It also has probably the poshest pub toilets in the country.

BrewDog BAR
(www.brewdog.com/bars/aberdeen; 17 Gallowgate; ⊙noon-midnight Mon-Thu, to 1am Fri & Sat, 12.30pm-midnight Sun; 🖳🖶) The original flagship bar of northeast Scotland's most innovative craft brewery brings a bit of industrial chic to Aberdeen's pub scene along with a vast range of guest beers from around the world.

Grape & Grain WINE BAR
(www.grapeandgrain.wine; 31 Thistle St; ⊙4-11pm Mon-Thu, noon-11pm Fri & Sat, noon-8pm Sun) Decadent decor of deep blue-green panelling, designer copper light fittings and mirrored walls tempts you to linger in this classy wine bar – there are even wireless phone chargers built into the tabletops. The cellar is stocked with a wide but carefully curated selection of wines, plus craft beers and gins. It also serves tempting platters of Scottish cheeses.

Blue Lamp PUB
(www.jazzatthebluelamp.com; 121 Gallowgate; ⊙11am-midnight Mon-Thu, to 1am Fri & Sat, 12.30-11pm Sun) A long-standing feature of the Aberdeen pub scene, the Blue Lamp is a favourite student hang-out – a cosy drinking den with good beer and *craic* (lively conversation) and regular sessions of live jazz and stand-up comedy. The pub is 150m north of the city centre, along Broad St.

☆ Entertainment

Belmont Filmhouse CINEMA
(www.belmontfilmhouse.com; 49 Belmont St; 🖳) The Belmont is a great little art-house cinema, with a lively program of cult classics, director's seasons, foreign films and mainstream movies.

His Majesty's Theatre BALLET, OPERA
(www.aberdeenperformingarts.com; Rosemount Viaduct) The main theatre in Aberdeen hosts everything from ballet and opera to pantomimes and musicals.

Lemon Tree Theatre PERFORMING ARTS
(www.aberdeenperformingarts.com; 5 West North St) Hosts an interesting program of dance, music and drama, and often has live rock, jazz and folk bands playing. There are also children's shows, ranging from comedy to drama to puppetry.

Tunnels LIVE MUSIC
(www.facebook.com/tunnelsaberdeen; Carnegie's Brae) This cavernous, subterranean club – the entrance is in a road tunnel beneath Union St – is a great live-music venue, with a packed program of up-and-coming Scottish bands. It also hosts regular DJ nights – check its Facebook page for the latest events.

Cafe Drummond LIVE MUSIC
(www.facebook.com/drummondsab10; 1 Belmont St) A long-established stalwart of Aberdeen's alternative music scene, Drummond is a crowded, grungy student hang-out offering live gigs from up-and-coming local talent, and regular club nights extending into the wee hours of the night.

ℹ Information

Books & Beans (www.booksandbeans.co.uk; 22 Belmont St; per 15min £1; ⊙7.45am-4.30pm Mon-Sat, 9.45am-4pm Sun; 🖳) Internet access; also fair-trade coffee and secondhand books.

Aberdeen Royal Infirmary (☑0345 456 6000; www.nhsgrampian.org; Foresterhill) Medical services. About a mile northwest of the western end of Union St.

Main Post Office (St Nicholas Shopping Centre, Upperkirkgate; ⊙9am-5.30pm Mon-Sat, noon-4pm Sun)

Aberdeen Tourist Office (☑01224-269180; www.aberdeen-grampian.com; 23 Union St; ⊙9am-6.30pm Mon-Sat, 10am-4pm Sun Jul & Aug, 9.30am-5pm Mon-Sat Sep-Jun; 🖳) Handy for general information; has internet access (£1 per 20 minutes).

ℹ Getting There & Away

AIR

Aberdeen Airport (ABZ; ☑0844 481 6666; www.aberdeenairport.com) is at Dyce, 6 miles northwest of the city centre. There are regular flights to numerous Scottish and UK destinations, including Orkney and Shetland, and international flights to the Netherlands, Norway, Denmark, Germany and France.

Stagecoach Jet bus 727 runs regularly from Aberdeen bus station to the airport (single £3.40, 35 minutes). A taxi from the airport to the city centre takes 25 minutes and costs around £15.

BOAT

Car ferries from Aberdeen to Orkney and Shetland are run by **Northlink Ferries** (www.north linkferries.co.uk). The ferry terminal is a short walk east of the train and bus stations.

BUS

The **bus station** (Guild St) is next to Jurys Inn, close to the train station.

Braemar £12.10, 2¼ hours, every two hours; via Ballater and Balmoral

Dundee £18.30, 1½ hours, hourly

Edinburgh £32.70, three hours, three daily direct, more frequent changing at Perth

Glasgow £32.70, three hours, at least hourly

Inverness £13.45, four hours, hourly; via Huntly, Keith, Fochabers, Elgin and Nairn

London from £36, 13½ hours, twice daily; National Express

Perth £25.70, two hours, hourly

TRAIN

The **train station** is south of the city centre, next to the massive Union Sq shopping mall.

Dundee £20.90, 1¼ hours, twice an hour

Edinburgh £35.50, 2½ hours, hourly

Glasgow £35.50, 2¾ hours, hourly

Inverness £29.70, 2¼ hours, eight daily

London King's Cross £175, seven to 11 hours, hourly; some direct, most change at Edinburgh

ⓘ Getting Around

BUS

The main city bus operator is **First Aberdeen** (www.firstgroup.com/aberdeen). Local fares cost from £1.50 to £2.70; pay the driver as you board the bus. A FirstDay ticket (£4) allows unlimited travel from the time of purchase until midnight on all First Aberdeen buses. Information, route maps and tickets are available from the **First Travel Centre** (47 Union St; ⊙ 9am-5.30pm Mon-Fri, to 4.30pm Sat).

The most useful services for visitors are buses 15 and 19 from Union St to Great Western Rd (for B&Bs); bus 11 from Union St to Aberdeen SYHA and the airport; and bus 20 from Marischal College to Old Aberdeen.

CAR

Car-rental companies include the following.

Arnold Clark (✆ 01224-622714; www.arnold clarkrental.com; Canal Rd; ⊙ 8am-7pm Mon-Fri, 8am-4.30pm Sat, 9am-4.30pm Sun)

Enterprise Car Hire (✆ 01224-642642; www.enterprise.co.uk; 80 Skene Sq; ⊙ 7am-7pm Mon-Fri, 8am-4pm Sat, 10am-3pm Sun)

The Aberdeen Western Peripheral Route (AWPR), a new road that allows motorists heading north to bypass the city centre, is scheduled to open by 2019.

TAXI

The main city-centre taxi ranks are at the train station and on Back Wynd, off Union St. To order a taxi, phone **ComCab** (✆ 01224-353535; www.comcab-aberdeen.co.uk) or **Rainbow City Taxis** (✆ 01224-878787; www.rainbowcitytaxis.com).

Around Aberdeen

The atmospheric, 16th-century **Crathes Castle** (NTS; ✆ 01330-844525; www.nts.org.uk; adult/child £13/9.50; ⊙ 10.30am-5pm daily Apr-Oct, 11am-4pm Sat & Sun Nov-Mar; 🅿🚻) is famous for its Jacobean painted ceilings, magnificently carved canopied beds, and the 'Horn of Leys', reputedly presented to the Burnett family by Robert the Bruce in the 14th century. The beautiful formal gardens include 300-year-old yew hedges and colourful herbaceous borders. The castle is signposted off the A93; Stagecoach buses 201 and 202 from Aberdeen stop at the castle entrance (£5.30, 45 minutes, every 30 minutes).

Designed in Georgian style by William Adam in 1732, **Haddo House** (NTS; ✆ 0844-493 2179; www.nts.org.uk; adult/child £11/9.50; ⊙ tours noon-2pm Mon-Fri, 11.30am-3.30pm Sat & Sun Apr-Oct; 🅿) is best described as a classic English stately home transplanted to Scotland. Home to the Gordon family, it has sumptuous Victorian interiors with wood-panelled walls, Persian-rug-scattered floors and a wealth of period antiques. The beautiful grounds and terraced gardens are open all year (9am to dusk). The house is accessed by guided tour only, best booked in advance. Haddo is 19 miles north of Aberdeen, near Ellon.

Buses run hourly Monday to Saturday from Aberdeen to Tarves/Methlick (£6.15, one hour), stopping at the end of the Haddo House driveway; it's a 1-mile walk from bus stop to house.

Though a magnificent example of Scottish Baronial architecture, **Fyvie Castle** (NTS; www.nts.org.uk; Fyvie; adult/child £13/9.50; ⊙ 11am-5pm daily Jun-Aug, Sat-Wed Apr, May, Sep & Oct; 🅿) is probably more famous for its ghosts, including a phantom trumpeter and the mysterious Green Lady, and its art collection, which displays portraits by Thomas Gainsborough and Sir Henry Raeburn. The grounds are open all year (9am to dusk).

The castle is 25 miles north of Aberdeen on the A947 towards Turriff. A bus runs hourly from Aberdeen to Banff and Elgin via Fyvie village (£8.35, 1½ hours), a mile from the castle.

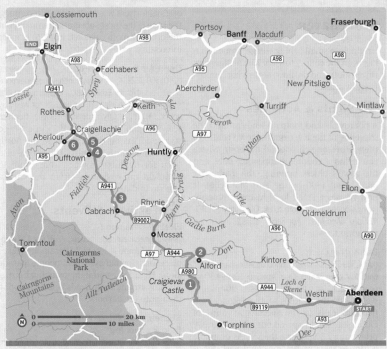

Driving Tour
Aberdeen to Elgin

START ABERDEEN
END ELGIN
LENGTH 80 MILES; ONE DAY

Head out of Aberdeen on the A944 and, just before Westhill, bear left on to the B9119 towards Tarland. As you leave behind the fringes of the city you enter the sheep pastures, woods and barley fields of rural Aberdeenshire, with the foothills of the Cairngorm Mountains rising ahead.

Follow signs for Tarland for 18 miles, then turn right on the A980 towards Alford. A few miles along this road you'll see ❶ **Craigievar Castle** (p236) across the fields to your left; stop for an hour's visit (time your departure to arrive for opening at 10.30am). Continue 4 miles north to the village of ❷ **Alford** (p235) where you can explore the Grampian Transport Museum and have lunch at the Alford Bistro.

From Alford take the A944 and A97 west and north for 10 miles then turn left on to the B9002 (signposted Craig and Cabrach). This minor road climbs across heather-clad hills to reach the A941; turn left towards Cabrach and Dufftown. This is remote country, but a few miles beyond the tiny hamlet of Cabrach you'll find the ❸ **Grouse Inn** (p239), a pub and tearoom famed for its whisky collection – there are 235 bottles behind the bar, all different.

Continue on the A941 as it climbs through a narrow pass in the hills and descends into the glen of the River Fiddich – the name tells you that you are now entering whisky country. Eight miles after the Grouse Inn you reach ❹ **Dufftown** (p237), the whisky capital of Speyside. Visit the town's whisky museum or, better yet, take a tour of ❺ **Glenfiddich Distillery** (p238).

From Dufftown, head north on the A941 for 4 miles to Craigellachie, and detour west for a mile and a half on the A95 to ❻ **Aberlour** (p238) to round off your trip with a stroll along the banks of the River Spey, and perhaps a meal at the Mash Tun before driving the last 15 miles north to Elgin.

Stonehaven

POP 11,430

Originally a small fishing village, Stonehaven has been the county town of Kincardineshire since 1600 and is now a thriving family-friendly seaside resort.

Sights & Activities

A boardwalk and footpath leads around the shoreline of the bay from the town centre to the picturesque cliff-bound **harbour**, where you'll find a couple of appealing pubs and the town's oldest building, the **Tolbooth**, built about 1600 by the Earl Marischal. It now houses a small local history **museum** (www.stonehaventolbooth.co.uk; Old Quay; ⊙ 1.30-4.30pm Wed-Mon Apr-Sep) FREE and a restaurant.

Dunnottar Castle   CASTLE
(☑ 01569-762173; www.dunnottarcastle.co.uk; adult/child £7/3; ⊙ 9am-5.30pm Apr-Sep, 10am-4.30pm or dusk Oct-Mar; P) A pleasant, 20-minute walk along the clifftops south of Stonehaven harbour leads to the spectacular ruins of Dunnottar Castle, spread out across a grassy promontory 50m above the sea. As dramatic a film set as any director could wish for, it provided the backdrop for Franco Zeffirelli's *Hamlet* (1990), starring Mel Gibson. The

---

SAND DUNES & SAND TRAPS

Coastal sand dunes extend north from Aberdeen for more than 14 miles, one of the largest areas of dunes in the UK, and the least affected by human activity. **Forvie National Nature Reserve** (www.nnr.scot; P) has wildlife hides and waymarked trails through the dunes to an abandoned medieval village where only the ruins of the church survive. The dunes form an important nesting and feeding area for birds – don't wander off the trails during the nesting season (April to August).

Donald Trump sparked a major controversy when he opened Trump International Golf Links in 2012, amid a 'protected' area of sand dunes just 4 miles south of Forvie. The development has split the community between those who welcome the potential economic benefits, and those worried about the environmental damage.

---

original fortress was built in the 9th century; the keep is the most substantial remnant, but the drawing room (restored in 1926) is more interesting.

Open-Air Swimming Pool   SWIMMING
(☑ 01569-762134; www.stonehavenopenairpool.co.uk; adult/child £5.40/3.30; ⊙ 10am-6pm Sat & Sun late May–early Sep, see website for weekday hours; ⊞) This Olympic-size (50m), heated, seawater pool was built in 1934 in art-deco style, and sits on the seafront to the north of Stonehaven town centre. The pool is also open for 'midnight swims' from 10pm to midnight on Wednesday from the end of June to mid-August.

Festivals & Events

Fireball Ceremony   CULTURAL
(www.stonehavenfireballs.co.uk; ⊙ 31 Dec) Stonehaven's famous Fireball Ceremony takes place on Hogmanay, when people parade along High St at midnight swinging blazing fireballs around their heads before throwing them into the harbour.

**Stonehaven Midsummer
Beer Happening**   BEER
(www.midsummerbeerhappening.co.uk; ⊙ late Jun) Home to the Six Degrees North craft brewery and several excellent real ale pubs, Stonehaven makes a great setting for this convivial three-day celebration of artisan beers.

Stonehaven Folk Festival   MUSIC
(www.stonehavenfolkfestival.co.uk; ⊙ mid-Jul) The town fills with musicians for this lively four-day folk festival.

Sleeping & Eating

★ **24 Shorehead**   B&B ££
(☑ 01569-767750; www.twentyfourshorehead.co.uk; 24 Shorehead; s/d £80/90; ☎) Location makes all the difference, and the location of this former cooperage offering peaceful and very stylish B&B accommodation can't be beaten – it's the last house at the end of the road, overlooking the harbour with lovely sea views. Using the binoculars provided, you can even spot seals from your bedroom. No credit cards.

Bayview B&B   B&B ££
(☑ 07791 224227; www.bayviewbandb.co.uk; Beachgate Lane; d £85-125; ☎) The bedrooms at this luxurious B&B are characterised by bright modern decor and original artwork, but the big selling point is that most have

floor-to-ceiling windows and a balcony with views over the bay.

Beachgate House
B&B **££**

(☏01569-763155; www.beachgate.co.uk; Beachgate Lane; s/d £75/95; **P**) This luxurious modern bungalow is right on the seafront, just a few paces from the tourist office; two of its five rooms have sea views, as does the lounge/dining room.

★ Creel Inn
SEAFOOD **££**

(☏01569-750254; www.thecreelinn.co.uk; Catterline; mains £13-27, 2-course lunch £16; ⊙noon-2pm & 6-9pm Mon-Fri, noon-9.30pm Sat, noon-8.30pm Sun; **P**🖶) 🖉 Set in the tiny fishing village of Catterline, 5 miles south of Stonehaven, the Creel is a rustic pub with thick stone walls, low ceilings and open fireplaces, famous for its menu of locally caught fish and shellfish – the lobster and crab come from the bay below the village.

Marine Hotel
SEAFOOD **££**

(☏01569-762155; www.marinehotelstonehaven.co.uk; 9-10 The Shore; mains £14-25; ⊙food served noon-2.30pm & 6-9pm Mon-Sat, noon-9pm Sun; 🖶) Polished wood, brass taps, bare stone and muted colours give this popular harbourside pub, run by Stonehaven's own Six Degrees North craft brewery, a trad-meets-boutique look; there are half a dozen real ales on tap, and a menu that includes fresh seafood specials served both in the bar and in the upstairs restaurant.

★ Tolbooth Restaurant
SEAFOOD **£££**

(☏01569-762287; www.tolbooth-restaurant.co.uk; Old Pier; mains £18-33; ⊙noon-3pm & 6-9.30pm Wed-Sat & noon-3pm Sun year-round, lunch & dinner Tue-Sun May-Sep) 🖉 Set in the 17th-century Tolbooth building overlooking the harbour, and decorated with local art and crisp white linen, this is one of the best seafood restaurants in the region. Daily specials include dishes such as scallops with crispy bacon and pea puree. From Wednesday to Saturday you can get a two-/three-course lunch for £20/24. Reservations recommended.

❶ Getting There & Away

Stonehaven is 15 miles south of Aberdeen and is served by frequent buses travelling between Aberdeen (£5.30, 45 minutes, hourly) and Dundee (£9, 1¾ hours).

Hourly trains to Dundee (£16, 55 minutes) and Aberdeen (£5.40, 20 minutes) are faster and offer a more scenic journey.

WORTH A TRIP

SCOTTISH LIGHTHOUSE MUSEUM

The fascinating **Scottish Lighthouse Museum** (☏01346-511022; www.lighthousemuseum.org.uk; Kinnaird Head; adult/child £8.80/4.40; ⊙10am-5pm daily Apr-Oct, to 4.30pm Tue-Sun Nov-Mar; **P**🖶) provides an insight into the network of lights that have safeguarded the Scottish coast for over 100 years, and the men and women who built and maintained them (plus a sobering fact – that *all* the world's lighthouses are to be decommissioned by 1 January 2080). A guided tour takes you to the top of the old Kinnaird Head lighthouse, built on top of a converted 16th-century castle.

The engineering is so precise that the 4.5-ton light assembly can be rotated by pushing with a single finger. The anemometer here measured the strongest wind speed ever recorded in the UK, with a gust of 123 knots (142mph) on 13 February 1989.

Strathdon

Strathdon – the valley of the River Don – is home to several of Aberdeenshire's finest castles, and stretches westward from Kintore, 13 miles northwest of Aberdeen, taking in the villages of Kemnay, Monymusk, Alford (*ah*-ford) and the tiny hamlet of Strathdon. The A944 parallels the lower valley; west of Alford, the A944, A97 and A939 follow the river's upper reaches.

The A939, known as the **Cockbridge–Tomintoul road** – a magnificent roller coaster of a route much loved by motorcyclists – runs from Strathdon across the Lecht pass (637m), where there's a small skiing area with lots of short easy and intermediate runs.

Grampian Transport Museum
MUSEUM

(☏01975-562292; www.gtm.org.uk; Alford; adult/child £10/1.50; ⊙10am-5pm Apr-Sep, to 4pm Oct; **P**🖶) This museum houses a fascinating collection of vintage vehicles, including a Triumph Bonneville in excellent nick, a couple of Model T Fords (including one used by Drambuie), a Ferrari F40 and an Aston Martin V8 Mk II. More unusual exhibits include a 19th-century horse-drawn sleigh from Russia, a 1942

SCOTTISH DOLPHIN CENTRE

Based in a historic icehouse that used to store ice for preserving local salmon catches, the **Scottish Dolphin Centre** (☎01343-820339; https://dolphincentre. whales.org; Tugnet Ice House, Spey Bay; ⊙10.30am-5pm Apr-Oct; P) is one of the best land-based dolphin-spotting places in the country. The indoor attractions include feeds from nearby wildlife cameras, a 'dry dive' audiovisual experience that takes you beneath the waves of the Moray Firth, and a pleasant cafe. Outdoors, you can watch for dolphins, seals and other marine creatures at the mouth of the River Spey, or join a guided wildlife walk.

The centre is in the tiny village of Spey Bay, 4 miles north of Fochabers, at the mouth of the River Spey.

Mack snowplough and a steam-powered tricycle built in 1895 by a local postman.

Since 2017 the museum's centrepiece has been TV presenter Guy Martin's collection of cars and bikes, including the pedal cycle on which he set the British cycle speed record of 112mph (drafting behind a racing truck) in 2014.

Castle Fraser CASTLE
(NTS; www.nts.org.uk; adult/child £11/9.50; ⊙10am-4pm daily Jul & Aug, Wed-Sun Apr-Jun, Sep & Oct; P) The impressive 16th- to 17th-century Castle Fraser, 16 miles west of Aberdeen, is the ancestral home of the Fraser family. The largely Victorian interior includes the **great hall** (with a hidden opening where the laird could eavesdrop on his guests), the library, bedrooms and an ancient kitchen, plus a secret room for storing valuables. Fraser family relics on display include needlework hangings and a 19th-century artificial leg. The 'Woodland Secrets' area in the castle grounds is designed as a kids' adventure playground.

Craigievar Castle CASTLE
(NTS; www.nts.org.uk; adult/child £12.50/9; ⊙10.30am-5pm daily Jul-Sep, Fri-Tue Apr-Jun; P) A superb example of the original Scottish Baronial style, Craigievar has managed to survive pretty much unchanged since its completion in the 17th century. The lower half is a plain tower house, the upper half

sprouts corbelled turrets, cupolas and battlements – an extravagant statement of its builder's wealth and status. It's 6 miles south of Alford and last admission is at 4pm.

Alford Bistro CAFE £
(☎01975-563154; thealfordbistro@btconnect.com; 40 Main St; mains £5-11; ⊙9am-5pm Mon & Tue, 9am-8pm Wed-Sat, 10am-8pm Sun; ⊕) ⊘ This great-value family bistro is always crowded, and it's easy to see why – bright, modern decor in muted shades of pale green and grey, friendly service and a menu of lovingly prepared, classic comfort food – yellow pea soup, macaroni cheese, beef stew with skirlie (oatmeal and onion fried in butter), homemade sausage rolls – wear trousers with an elastic waistband.

ⓘ Getting There & Away

Stagecoach bus X20 runs from Aberdeen to Alford (£9.95, 1¼ hours, six daily Monday to Friday, three on Saturday).

MORAY

The old county of Moray (*murr*-ay), centred on the county town of Elgin, lies at the heart of an ancient Celtic earldom and is famed for its mild climate and rich farmland – the barley fields of the 19th century once provided the raw material for the Speyside whisky distilleries, one of the region's main attractions for present-day visitors.

Elgin

POP 23,130

Elgin has been the provincial capital of Moray for over eight centuries and was an important town in medieval times. Dominated by a hilltop monument to the 5th Duke of Gordon, Elgin's main attractions are its impressive ruined cathedral, where the tombs of the duke's ancestors lie, and its fine museum.

◉ Sights

★**Elgin Museum** MUSEUM
(www.elginmuseum.org.uk; 1 High St; donations accepted; ⊙10am-5pm Mon-Fri, 11am-4pm Sat Apr-Oct) FREE Scotland's oldest independent museum is an old-fashioned cabinet of curiosities, a captivating collection artfully displayed in a beautiful, purpose-built Victorian building. Exhibits range from Ecuadorian shrunken heads to Peruvian mummies, and

include mysterious Pictish carved stones and internationally important fish and reptile fossils discovered in local rocks.

Elgin Cathedral
CATHEDRAL

(HES; www.historicenvironment.scot; King St; adult/child £7.50/4.50; ⊙9.30am-5.30pm Apr-Sep, 10am-4pm Oct-Mar) Many people think that the ruins of Elgin Cathedral, known as the 'lantern of the north', are the most beautiful and evocative in Scotland; its octagonal chapter house is the finest in the country. Consecrated in 1224, the cathedral was burned down in 1390 by the infamous Wolf of Badenoch, the illegitimate son of Robert II, following his excommunication by the Bishop of Moray. Guided tours are available on weekdays.

🛏️ Sleeping & Eating

Moraydale
B&B ££

(⌨01343-546381; www.moraydaleguesthouse.com; 276 High St; s/d/f from £70/85/95; 🅿🛜🐾) The Moraydale is a spacious Victorian mansion filled with period features – check out the stained glass and the cast-iron and tile fireplaces. The bedrooms are all en suite and equipped with modern bathrooms – the three large family rooms are particularly good value.

Southbank Guest House
B&B ££

(⌨01343-547132; www.southbankguesthouse.co.uk; 36 Academy St; s/d/tr from £70/90/145; 🅿🛜) The family-run, 15-room Southbank is set in a large Georgian town house in a quiet street south of Elgin's centre, just five minutes' walk from the cathedral and other sights. There may be a three-night minimum stay in high season.

Johnstons Coffee Shop
CAFE £

(www.johnstonsofelgin.com; Newmill; mains £6-10; ⊙10am-5pm Mon-Sat, to 4.30pm Sun; 🅿🛜🛝) The coffee shop at Johnstons woollen mill is one of the best places to eat in town, serving breakfast till 11.45am, hot lunches from noon to 3pm (crepes with a range of fillings, including smoked salmon with cream cheese and dill) and cream teas.

Batchen Street Coffee
CAFE £

(www.facebook.com/batchenstreetcoffee; 33 Batchen St; mains £4-7; ⊙8.30am-4pm Mon-Fri, 9.30am-4.30pm Sat; 🛜) 🍴 A great little coffee shop that serves superb espresso (it also offers Chemex brews), good-value breakfasts (scrambled eggs on toast), light lunches (soup, quiche) and great home baking.

⭐ Drouthy Cobbler
CAFE, BAR ££

(⌨01343-596000; http://thedrouthycobbler.uk; 48a High St; mains £10-18; ⊙food served 5-9.30pm daily, noon-4.30pm Sat & Sun; 🛜🛝🐾) This cafe-bar has a bistro-style menu that changes regularly but includes quality versions of popular dishes such as Cullen skink, mussels, bangers and mash, fish and chips and homemade burgers. It's tucked away up a side alley. It also hosts live music and comedy gigs in the evenings.

🛍️ Shopping

Gordon & MacPhail
FOOD & DRINKS

(⌨01343-545110; www.gordonandmacphail.com; 58-60 South St; ⊙8.30am-5pm Mon-Sat, alcohol on sale from 10am) Gordon & MacPhail is the world's largest specialist malt-whisky dealer. More than a century old and offering around 1000 different varieties, its Elgin shop is a place of pilgrimage for whisky connoisseurs, and it also houses a mouthwatering delicatessen.

Johnstons of Elgin
FASHION & ACCESSORIES

(⌨01343-554009; www.johnstonscashmere.com; Newmill; ⊙9am-5.30pm Mon-Sat, 10am-5pm Sun) Founded in 1797, Johnstons is famous for its cashmere woollen clothing, and is the only UK woollen mill that still sees the manufacturing process through from raw fibre to finished garment. There's a retail outlet and coffee shop, and free guided tours of the works.

ℹ️ Getting There & Away

The **bus station** (Alexandra Rd) is a block north of High St, and the train station is 900m south of the town centre.

BUS

Aberdeen £13.45, 2½ hours, hourly

Banff & Macduff £11.30, 1¾ hours, hourly

Dufftown £5.95, 50 minutes, hourly Monday to Saturday

Inverness £11.30, 1½ hours, hourly

TRAIN

Aberdeen £19.90, 1¾ hours, five daily

Inverness £13.10, 40 minutes, five daily

Dufftown & Aberlour

Rome may be built on seven hills, but Dufftown's built on seven stills, say the locals. Founded in 1817 by James Duff, 4th Earl of Fife, Dufftown is 17 miles south of Elgin and lies at the heart of the Speyside whisky-distilling region. With seven working distilleries nearby, Dufftown has been dubbed Scotland's malt-whisky capital and is host to the biannual Spirit of Speyside whisky festival. Ask at the whisky museum about the **Malt Whisky Trail** (www.maltwhiskytrail.com), a self-guided tour around the local distilleries.

Aberlour (www.aboutaberlour.co.uk) – or Charlestown of Aberlour, to give it its full name – is even prettier than Dufftown, straggling along the banks of the River Spey. It is famous as the home of Walkers Shortbread, and has the Aberlour Distillery right on the main street. Attractions include salmon fishing on the Spey, nearby Knockando Woolmill and some lovely walks along the Speyside Way.

◎ Sights & Activities

Knockando Woolmill MUSEUM
(☑ 01340-810345; www.kwc.co.uk; Knockando; ⊙ 10am-4pm Tue-Sun Apr-Oct; 🅿 👫) 🖋 FREE
Hidden in a fold of the hills 5 miles west of Aberlour, Knockando is a rare survival of an 18th-century woollen mill that has been lovingly restored to full working order. The ancient looms clank away Tuesday to Friday, turning out plaid and tweed textiles that can be purchased in the neighbouring shop. Guided tours cost £5; book in advance.

Whisky Museum MUSEUM
(☑ 01340-821097; www.whisky.dufftown.co.uk; 12 Conval St; ⊙ 10am-4pm Apr-Oct) FREE As well as housing a selection of distillery memorabilia (try saying that after a few drams), the Whisky Museum holds 'nosing and tasting evenings' in the Commercial Hotel, where you can learn what to look for in a fine single malt (£15 per person, 8pm Wednesday July and August).

You can test your new-found skills at the nearby Whisky Shop, which stocks hundreds of single malts.

Keith & Dufftown Railway HERITAGE RAILWAY
(☑ 01340-821181; www.keith-dufftown-railway.co.uk; Dufftown Station; adult/child return £11/5; 🅿 👫) A line running for 11 miles from Dufftown to Keith sees trains hauled by 1950s diesel motor units running on weekends from

---

BLAZE YOUR OWN WHISKY TRAIL

Visiting a distillery can be memorable, but only hardcore malthounds will want to go to more than one or two. Here are the top five whisky sights in the area.

Aberlour (☑ 01340-881249; www.aberlour.com; tours from £15; ⊙ 9.30am-5pm daily Apr-Oct, 10am-4pm Mon-Fri Nov-Mar; 🅿) Has an excellent, detailed tour with a proper tasting session. It's on the main street in Aberlour.

Glenfarclas (☑ 01807-500257; https://glenfarclas.com; tours £7.50; ⊙ 10am-5pm Mon-Fri Apr-Sep, to 4pm Sat Jul-Sep, Mon-Fri Oct-Mar; 🅿) Small, friendly and independent, Glenfarclas is 5 miles south of Aberlour on the Grantown road; the last tour leaves 90 minutes before closing. The in-depth Connoisseur's Tour (Fridays only, July to September) is £40.

Glenfiddich (☑ 01340-820373; www.glenfiddich.co.uk; admission free, tours from £10; ⊙ 9.30am-4.30pm; 🅿) It's big and busy, but handiest for Dufftown and foreign languages are available. The standard tour (£10) starts with an overblown video, but it's fun and informative. The in-depth half-day Pioneer's Tour (£95) must be prebooked.

Macallan (☑ 01340-872280; www.themacallan.com; Easter Elchies, Craigellachie; tours £15; ⊙ 9.30am-5pm Mon-Fri; 🅿) Macallan opened a new distillery and visitor centre in 2018. The 1¾-hour tours (maximum group of 10) should be prebooked. Lovely location 1 mile west of Craigellachie.

Speyside Cooperage (☑ 01340-871108; www.speysidecooperage.co.uk; tours £4; ⊙ 9am-5pm Mon-Fri, closed Christmas–early Jan) Here you can see the fascinating art of barrel-making in action. It's a mile from Craigellachie on the Dufftown road.

The biannual **Spirit of Speyside** (www.spiritofspeyside.com; ⊙ May & Sep) whisky festival in Dufftown has a number of great events. It takes place in early May and late September; both accommodation and events should be booked well ahead.

Easter to September, plus Fridays from June onward. There are also two 1930s 'Brighton Belle' Pullman coaches, and a cafe housed in two 1950s British Railways coaches.

Sleeping & Eating

Davaar B&B
B&B **££**

(☏ 01340-820464; www.davaardufftown.co.uk; 17 Church St; d/f £65/80; ☎) Davaar is a sturdy Victorian villa with three smallish but comfy rooms. The breakfast menu is superb, offering the option of Portsoy kippers as well as the traditional fry-up (which uses eggs from the owners own chickens).

Mash Tun
B&B **££**

(☏ 01340-881771; www.mashtun-aberlour.com; 8 Broomfield Sq; s/d from £85/120; ☎) Housed in a curious stone building made for a sea captain in the outline of a ship, this luxurious B&B has a famous whisky bar – a place of pilgrimage for whisky enthusiasts – which has a collection of old and rare single malts. There's also an excellent restaurant (mains £12 to £23, lunch and dinner daily) that serves posh pub grub.

Craigellachie Hotel
HOTEL **£££**

(☏ 01340-881204; www.craigellachiehotel.co.uk; Craigellachie; r from £150; P ☎) The Craigellachie has a wonderfully old-fashioned, hunting-lodge atmosphere, from the wood-panelled lobby to the opulent drawing room where you can sink into a sofa in front of the log fire. But the big attraction for whisky connoisseurs is the **Quaich Bar**, a cosy nook filled with handcrafted furniture and lined with around 900 varieties of single malt whisky.

The hotel is a mile northeast of Aberlour, overlooking the River Spey.

Grouse Inn
PUB

(☏ 01466-702200; Lower Cabrach; ⊗ 10am-11pm Easter-Oct) A pub famed for its whisky collection, the Grouse has an astounding 235 different malt whiskies on the optic behind the bar, and more than 700 to choose from. There's also a tearoom (open 10am to 6pm Saturday to Thursday, 1pm to 6pm Friday). The inn is 8 miles south of Dufftown on the A941 road.

🛍 Shopping

Spey Larder
FOOD & DRINKS

(☏ 01340-871243; www.speylarder.com; 96-98 High St; ⊗ 9.30am-5pm Mon-Sat) This deli is the

WORTH A TRIP

PENNAN

Pennan is a picturesque harbour village tucked beneath red-sandstone cliffs, 12 miles west of Fraserburgh. It featured in the 1983 film *Local Hero*, and fans of the film still come to make a call from the red telephone box that played a prominent part in the plot (the box in the film was just a prop, and it was only later that film buffs and locals successfully campaigned for a real one to be installed).

The interior of the village hotel, the Pennan Inn, also appeared in the film, though one of the houses further along the seafront to the east doubled for the exterior of the fictional hotel. The beach scenes were filmed on the other side of the country, at Camusdarach Beach (p341) in Arisaig.

place to shop for picnic goodies to eat on the banks of the River Spey – a great selection of Scottish artisan cheeses, smoked salmon, venison charcuterie, delicious home-baked bread and local craft beers.

Whisky Shop
FOOD & DRINKS

(☏ 01340-821097; www.whiskyshopdufftown.co.uk; 1 Fife St; ⊗ 10am-6pm Mon-Sat year-round, plus Sun Easter-Oct) A fantastic shop that stocks hundreds of single malts and runs tasting sessions and other events.

ⓘ Getting There & Away

Buses link Elgin to Dufftown (£6.25, 50 minutes) hourly Monday to Saturday, continuing to Huntly and Aberdeen.

On summer weekends, you can take a train from Inverness or Aberdeen to Keith (£16.30, one hour, five daily), and then ride the Keith and Dufftown Railway to Dufftown.

There are hourly buses to Aberlour from Elgin (£5.95, 40 minutes), and from Dufftown (£2.95, 15 minutes).

Banff & Macduff

POP 9100

The handsome Georgian town of Banff and the busy fishing port of Macduff lie on either side of Banff Bay, separated only by the mouth of the River Deveron. **Banff Links** – 800m of clean golden sand

NORTHEAST 250 DRIVING ROUTE

Encouraged by the success of the North Coast 500, local tourism bodies have come up with the **Northeast 250** (www.northeast250.com), a circular driving route that takes in the Aberdeenshire and Moray coastline, Speyside, Royal Deeside and the southern Cairngorms. Highlights include grand coastal scenery, picturesque fishing villages, baronial castles and heather-clad mountains.

stretching to the west – Duff House and Macduff's impressive aquarium pull in the holiday crowds.

★ Duff House
GALLERY

(📞 01261-818181; www.nationalgalleries.org/visit/duff-house; adult/child £7.50/4.50; ⏱ 11am-5pm Apr-Oct, to 4pm Thu-Sun Nov-Mar; 🅿) One of Scotland's underappreciated treasures, Duff House is home to an art gallery with a superb collection of Scottish and European art, including important works by Raeburn and Gainsborough. The house is an impressive baroque mansion on the southern edge of Banff, built between 1735 and 1740 as the seat of the Earls of Fife. It was designed by William Adam and bears similarities to that other Adam masterpiece, Hopetoun House (p101) near Edinburgh.

Macduff Marine Aquarium
AQUARIUM

(www.macduff-aquarium.org.uk; 11 High Shore, Macduff; adult/child £7.25/4.25; ⏱ 10am-5pm Mon-Fri, 11am-5pm Sat & Sun Apr-Oct, 11am-4pm Sat-Wed Nov-Mar; 🅿🚻) The centrepiece of Macduff's aquarium is a 400,000L open-air tank, complete with kelp-coated reef and wave machine. Marine oddities on view include the brightly coloured cuckoo wrasse, the warty-skinned lumpsucker and the vicious-looking wolf fish. There's also a live CCTV feed from the seabird nesting colonies at the RSPB's Troup Head nature reserve.

ℹ Getting There & Away

Bus 35 runs from Banff to Elgin (£11.30, 1¾ hours, every two hours) and Aberdeen (£13.45, two hours), while bus 272 runs to Fraserburgh (£8.90, 55 minutes, three daily) on weekdays only.

Portsoy

POP 1750

The pretty fishing village of Portsoy has an atmospheric **17th-century harbour** and a maze of narrow streets lined with picturesque cottages. An ornamental stone known as Portsoy marble – actually a beautifully patterned green-and-pale-pink serpentine – was quarried near Portsoy in the 17th and 18th centuries, and was reputedly used in the decoration of some rooms in the Palace of Versailles.

Portsoy Salmon Bothy
MUSEUM

(https://salmonbothy.org; Links Rd; ⏱ 2-4pm Fri-Mon Apr-Sep) **FREE** Built in 1834 as a workshop, icehouse and storage space for nets and equipment, the bothy now houses a museum that records the history of salmon fishing in the local area.

Scottish Traditional Boat Festival
CULTURAL

(www.stbfportsoy.com; ⏱ Jun or Jul) Each year on the last weekend in June or first weekend in July, Portsoy harbour is home to this lively gathering of historic wooden sailing boats accompanied by sailing races, live folk music, crafts demonstrations, street theatre and a food festival.

★ Sail Loft Bunkhouse
HOSTEL £

(📞 01261-842222; http://portsoysailloft.org; Back Green; dm/tw £23/48; 🅿🛜) Housed in a row of restored 18th-century cottages and a former sail-making loft, this bunkhouse offers luxurious accommodation in four- and six-bed dorms and a choice of private doubles and twins. There's a large modern kitchen, comfortable lounge with wood-burning stove, outdoor deck and barbecue, and even a wood-fired hot tub (£7.50 per person per hour). Check-in at the neighbouring caravan park.

Portsoy Pottery
ARTS & CRAFTS

(Shorehead; ⏱ 10am-5pm Mon-Sat Apr-Oct) Beside the harbour (entrance around the back of the big stone building), the Portsoy Pottery sells handmade stoneware objects made from the local marble and a range of crafts and gifts.

ℹ Getting There & Away

Portsoy is 8 miles west of Banff; the hourly bus between Banff (£5.30, 25 minutes) and Elgin (£11.05, 1½ hours) stops here.

Southern Highlands & Islands

Best Places to Eat

➡ Ninth Wave (p287)

➡ Café Fish (p285)

➡ Callander Meadows (p252)

➡ Starfish (p259)

➡ Ee-Usk (p278)

Best Places to Stay

➡ Monachyle Mhor (p252)

➡ Calgary Farmhouse (p286)

➡ Iona Hostel (p288)

➡ Highland Cottage (p284)

➡ Knap Guest House (p259)

➡ Glenartney (p271)

Why Go?

The impossibly complex coastline of Scotland's southwest harbours some of its most inspiring corners. Here, sea travel is key – dozens of ferries allow you to island-hop from the scenic splendour of Arran to majestic Mull or Tiree's lonely sands, via the whisky distilleries of Islay, the wild mountains of Jura, the scenic delights of diminutive Colonsay and Oban's sustainable seafood scene.

On fresh water too, passenger ferries, vintage steamboats, canoes and kayaks ply Loch Lomond and the Trossachs National Park, a memorable concentration of scenery that's very accessible but possessed of a wild beauty.

Wildlife experiences are a highlight here, from the rasping spout of a minke whale to the 'krek-krek' of a corncrake. Spot otters tumbling in the kelp, watch sea eagles snatch fish from a lonely loch and thrill to the sight of dolphins riding the bow-wave of your boat.

When to Go
Oban

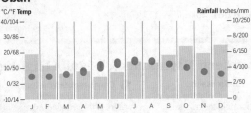

May Fèis Ìle (Islay Festival) celebrates traditional Scottish music and whisky.

Jun Roadsides and gardens become a blaze of colour with deep-pink rhododendron blooms.

Aug The best month of the year for whale watching off the west coast.

Southern Highlands & Islands Highlights

1 The Trossachs
(p248) Exploring the lovely lochscapes and accessible walking and cycling routes.

2 Islay (p262) Visiting the smoky heavyweights of the whisky world on their peaty turf.

3 Arran (p270) Blowing away the cobwebs on this scenic, activity-packed island.

4 Corryvreckan Whirlpool
(p268) Visiting the white waters of this maelstrom at the north end of lonely Jura.

5 Iona (p287) Journeying through wildlife-rich Mull to reach this holy emerald isle.

6 West Highland Way
(p243) Hiking along the eastern shore of Loch Lomond.

7 Seafood Restaurants
(p278) Tucking into a platter of fresh local langoustines at Ee-Usk or another one of Oban's eating establishments.

8 Machrihanish (p262) Teeing off on the great-value old and new golf courses down the Kintyre peninsula.

LOCH LOMOND & THE TROSSACHS

The 'bonnie banks' and 'bonnie braes' of Loch Lomond have long been Glasgow's rural retreat – a scenic region of hills, lochs and healthy fresh air within easy reach of Scotland's largest city. Today the loch's popularity shows no sign of decreasing. The scenic Trossachs have likewise long been popular for their wild Highland beauty, set so close to the southern population centres. With the region covered by a large national park, it makes a fine destination for outdoor activity, with some excellent walking and cycling on offer and lots of high-quality accommodation and eating choices.

Loch Lomond

Loch Lomond is mainland Britain's largest lake and, after Loch Ness, the most famous of Scotland's lochs. Its proximity to Glasgow (20 miles away) means that the tourist honey pots of Balloch and Luss get pretty crowded in summer. The eastern shore, which is followed by the West Highland Way long-distance footpath, is quieter and offers a better chance to appreciate the loch away from the busy main road.

Loch Lomond straddles the Highland border. The southern part is broad and island-studded, fringed by woods and Lowland meadows. However, north of Luss the loch narrows, occupying a deep trench gouged out by glaciers during the Ice Age, with 900m mountains crowding either side.

Activities

Walking

The **West Highland Way** (www.west-highland-way.org) runs along the loch's eastern shore, while the **Rob Roy Way** (www.robroyway.com) heads from Drymen to Pitlochry via the Trossachs. The **Three Lochs Way** (www.threelochsway.co.uk) loops west from Balloch through Helensburgh and Arrochar before returning to Loch Lomond at Inveruglas. The **Great Trossachs Path** (www.lochlomond-trossachs.org) links the loch with the Trossachs. There are numerous shorter walks around: get further information from tourist offices.

Rowardennan is the starting point for ascents of Ben Lomond (p248), a popular and relatively straightforward (if strenuous) climb.

Other Activities

The mostly traffic-free **Clyde and Loch Lomond Cycle Way** links Glasgow to Balloch (20 miles), where it joins the **West Loch Lomond Cycle Path**, which continues along the loch shore to Tarbet (10 miles). The park website (www.lochlomond-trossachs.org) details some other local routes.

Loch Lomond Leisure   WATER SPORTS
(☑ 0333 577 0715; www.lochlomond-scotland.com; Luss) From Luss pier, Loch Lomond Leisure runs speedboat tours of the loch (short trip £10/5 per adult/child) as well as water-skiing or wakeboarding (both £40/105 for one/three sets) and other splashy activities. Kayaks (£20/65 per hour/day) and various boats are also available for hire.

Balmaha Boatyard   BOATING
(☑ 01360-870214; www.balmahaboatyard.co.uk; Balmaha; ⊙ 9am-5pm Apr-Oct, to 4pm Nov-Mar) The operator runs an on-demand ferry to the island of Inchcailloch, just offshore (£5 return). It also rents out rowing boats (£40 per day) and motorboats (£60 per day).

Tours

Sweeney's Cruises   BOATING
(☑ 01389-752376; www.sweeneyscruiseco.com; Balloch Rd, Balloch) Offers a range of trips including a one-hour return cruise to Inchmurrin (adult/child £10.50/7, five times daily April to October, twice daily November to March) and a two-hour cruise around the islands (£19/10.50, twice daily May to September plus weekends April and October). The quay is directly opposite Balloch train station. It also runs summer trips from a dock at Loch Lomond Shores (p245). Piped commentary is by Neil Oliver.

Cruise Loch Lomond   BOATING
(☑ 01301-702356; www.cruiselochlomond.co.uk; Tarbet; ⊙ 8.30am-5.30pm Easter-Oct) With departures from Tarbet and Luss, this operator runs short cruises and two-hour trips to Arklet Falls and Rob Roy's Cave (adult/child £15/8). There are several options. You can also be dropped off at Rowardennan to climb Ben Lomond (£15/9), getting picked up in the afternoon, or after a 7-mile hike along the West Highland Way (£15/9). From its Tarbet office, it also rents out bikes (half-/full day £13/17).

Loch Lomond Seaplanes   SCENIC FLIGHTS
(☑ 01436-675030; www.lochlomondseaplanes.com; flights from £119) Loch Lomond Seaplanes

Loch Lomond & the Trossachs NP

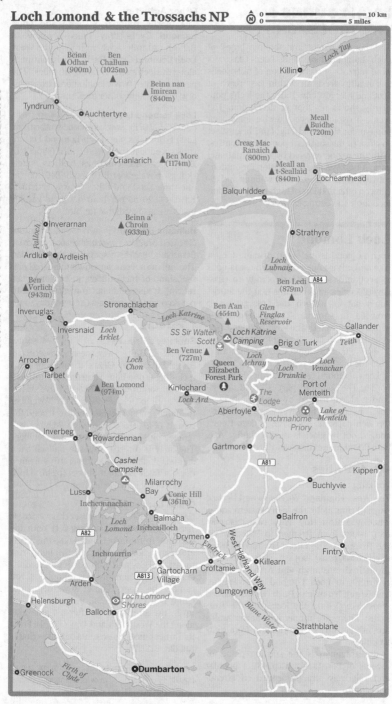

N

| 0 | | 10 km |
| 0 | | 5 miles |

Beinn Odhar (900m)
Ben Challum (1025m)
Killin
Loch Tay
Tyndrum
Auchtertyre
Beinn nan Imirean (840m)
Meall Buidhe (720m)
Creag Mac Ranaich (800m)
Crianlarich
Ben More (1174m)
Meall an t-Seallaid (840m)
Locheamhead
Balquhidder
Beinn a' Chroin (933m)
Inverarnan
Falloch
Strathyre
Ardlui
Ardleish
Loch Lubnaig
Ben Vorlich (943m)
Ben Ledi (879m)
A84
Inveruglas
Stronachlachar
Loch Katrine
Ben A'an (454m)
Glen Finglas Reservoir
Callander
Inversnaid
Loch Arklet
SS Sir Walter Scott
Loch Katrine Camping
Brig o' Turk
Teith
Arrochar
Loch Chon
Ben Venue (727m)
Loch Achray
Loch Drunkie
Loch Venachar
Tarbet
Queen Elizabeth Forest Park
Port of Menteith
Ben Lomond (974m)
Kinlochard
Loch Ard
The Lodge
Aberfoyle
Inchmahome Priory
Lake of Menteith
Inverbeg
Rowardennan
Gartmore
A81
Kippen
Cashel Campsite
Milarrochy Bay
Conic Hill (361m)
Buchlyvie
Luss
Inchconnachan
Balmaha
Balfron
Loch Lomond
Inchcailloch
A82
Drymen
Fintry
Inchmurrin
Gartocharn Village
Croftamie
Killearn
West Highland Way
Endrick
A813
Arden
Dumgoyne
Helensburgh
Loch Lomond Shores
Balloch
Blane Water
Strathblane
Greenock
Firth of Clyde
Dumbarton

offers a variety of scenic flights over the loch and western Scotland, leaving from the Cameron House Hotel just north of Balloch.

ℹ Information

Balloch Tourist Office (☎ 01389-753533; www.visitscotland.com; Balloch Rd; ⊙ 9.30am-6pm Jul & Aug, to 5.30pm Jun & Sep, 10am-5pm Oct-May) Opposite Balloch's train station.

Balmaha National Park Centre (☎ 01389-722100; www.lochlomond-trossachs.org; Balmaha; ⊙ 9.30am-4pm Apr-Oct, 9.30am-4pm Sat & Sun Nov-Mar) Has maps showing local walking routes.

ℹ Getting There & Away

BUS

First Glasgow (www.firstglasgow.com) Bus 1/1A runs from Argyle St in central Glasgow to Balloch (£5.30, 1½ hours, at least two per hour).

Scottish Citylink (☎ 0871 266 3333; www.citylink.co.uk) Coaches from Glasgow stop at Luss (£9.40, 55 minutes, 9 to 18 daily), Tarbet (£9.40, 65 minutes, 9 to 18 daily) and Ardlui (£16.90, 1½ hours, four to nine daily).

TRAIN

Glasgow–Balloch (£5.60, 45 minutes, every 30 minutes)

Glasgow–Arrochar & Tarbet (£12.40, 1¼ hours, four to seven daily)

Glasgow–Ardlui (£16.30, 1½ hours, four to seven daily, continuing to Oban or Fort William)

ℹ Getting Around

Bus 309 runs from Balloch to Drymen and Balmaha (£2.60, 20 minutes, nine to 10 daily), while bus 305 heads to Luss (£2.80, 20 minutes, nine to 10 daily). Bus 207 connects Balloch with Loch Lomond Shores and Alexandria. An **SPT Daytripper ticket** gives a family group unlimited travel for a day on most bus and train services in the Glasgow, Loch Lomond and Helensburgh area. Buy the ticket (£12.30 for one adult and two children, £21.80 for two adults and up to four children) from any train station or Glasgow bus station.

Tarbet and Ardlui are accessible by train and by Citylink buses between Glasgow and north-western destinations.

Local buses run from Helensburgh to Arrochar via Luss and Tarbet four times daily Monday to Friday.

Western Shore

Balloch, straddling the River Leven at Loch Lomond's southern end, is the loch's main population centre and transport hub. A

ℹ LOCH LOMOND WATER BUS

From mid-March to October a network of boats criss-crosses Loch Lomond, allowing you to explore the loch's hiking and biking trails using public transport. The Loch Lomond Water Bus timetable is available from tourist offices and on-line (www.lochlomond-trossachs.org).

Victorian resort once thronged by day trippers transferring between the train station and the steamer quay, it is now a 'gateway centre' for Loch Lomond and the Trossachs National Park. Visitors still arrive in abundance. On its edge, the overblown Loch Lomond Shores complex provides family-friendly attractions, boat trips, eating establishments and lots of retail.

Leaving Balloch behind, the road along the western shore offers great views of Loch Lomond. There's also busy traffic along what is a major route to north and west Scotland.

Some would say that the western shore of the loch serves a purpose: to take one for the team, accept the tour coaches and leave other parts of the lake comparatively traffic-free.

Head first for the picture-postcard village of **Luss**. Stroll among the pretty cottages, built by the local laird in the 19th century for his estate workers, and admire the lochside vistas. You won't be alone: to live in one of these cute cottages must occasionally feel like being a celeb with paparazzi camped outside the door.

Beyond Luss, **Tarbet** sits at the junction where you choose between Argyll and Kintyre or Oban and the Highlands. Following the shore brings you to **Ardlui** and thence Crianlarich.

⊙ Sights & Activities

Loch Lomond Shores   AREA
(www.lochlomondshores.com; ⊙ 9.30am-6pm) Loch Lomond Shores, a major tourism development situated a half-mile north of Balloch, sports various visitor attractions, outdoor activities and boat trips. The heart of the development is a large shopping mall.

Loch Lomond Sea Life   AQUARIUM
(☎ 01389-721500; www.visitsealife.com; Loch Lomond Shores; £13.95, per person for 2 or more £12.30; ⊙ 10am-5pm Mar-Oct, to 4pm Nov-Feb) The centrepiece of Loch Lomond Shores is this aquarium, which has displays on the

wildlife of Loch Lomond, an otter enclosure (housing short-clawed Asian otters, not Scottish ones), and a host of sea-life exhibits ranging from sharks to stingrays to sea turtles. It's a lot cheaper if you book online.

Maid of the Loch SHIP
(www.maidoftheloch.com; ⊙11am-5pm school holidays & weekends Easter-Oct) FREE The vintage paddle steamer *Maid of the Loch,* built in 1953, is moored at Loch Lomond Shores while awaiting full restoration – you can nip aboard for a look around. With any luck, it might be operational for the 2019 summer.

🍴 Sleeping & Eating

Glenview B&B ££
(☑01389-528878; www.glenview-luss.co.uk; Luss; d £100-140; P🖙) In the centre of things on the road through Luss village, this white house offers a genuine welcome and three highly appealing suites. All are showroom-spotless: one comes with a full kitchen and dining area, the others with spacious lounge areas, with one also having a modish four-poster bed. Breakfast is continental, with a cooked option available in their cafe around the corner.

Loch Lomond Arms INN £££
(☑01436-860420; www.lochlomondarmshotel. com; Main Rd, Luss; r £190-250; P🖙) Though you're paying quite a bit for the location, there's something very likeable about the modernised but still traditional rooms here, with their artful design, intriguing fabrics and creature comforts. There's a suite and self-catering options in nearby buildings. The bar and restaurant areas are attractive without pulling up any culinary trees.

Drover's Inn PUB FOOD ££
(☑01301-704234; www.thedroversinn.co.uk; Inverarnan; bar meals £9-14; ⊙11.30am-10pm Mon-Sat, to 9.30pm or 10pm Sun; P🖙) Don't miss this low-ceilinged howff (drinking den), just north of Ardlui, with its smoke-blackened stone, kilted bartenders, and walls festooned with moth-eaten stags' heads and stuffed birds. The convivial bar, where Rob Roy allegedly dropped by for pints, serves hearty hill-walking fuel and hosts live folk music on weekends.

Rooms could do with an upgrade but there are some newer ones in a separate building, the Stagger Inn.

Luss Seafood Bar SEAFOOD ££
(☑01436-860524; www.luss-seafoodbar.com; Church Rd, Luss; dishes £8-20; ⊙9am-6pm Feb-Oct; 🖙) Curiously the eating establishments in Luss are tucked safely away from the lake; this place is no exception, set behind a shop on the main street. But it's a light, cheerful spot serving tasty fresh oysters, potted fish and smoked salmon. Prices are on the high side, but the produce is good. In winter it becomes a coffee shop.

Eastern Shore

Away from the busy western road, the loch's eastern shore is a quieter spot populated mostly by walkers and campers. Nevertheless, the narrow road gets busy. It runs from **Drymen** through attractive **Balmaha**, where you can hire boats.

There are several lochside picnic areas; **Milarrochy Bay** (1.5 miles north of Balmaha), has a nice gravel beach and superb views across the loch to the Luss hills.

The road ends at **Rowardennan**, where there's a hotel, hostels and boat hire, but the hiking trail West Highland Way (p243) continues north along the shore of the loch. It's 7 miles to **Inversnaid**, reachable by road from the Trossachs, and 15 miles to **Inverarnan** at the loch's northern end. Rowardennan is also the launchpad for climbing Ben Lomond.

🍴 Sleeping & Eating

Book your accommodation ahead in the walking season, as it packs out. There are hostel, hotel and camping options as well as B&Bs along this stretch.

From March to September, wild camping is restricted on the eastern shore of Loch Lomond between Drymen and Ptarmigan Lodge (just north of the Rowardennan SYHA). There are campsites at Milarrochy, Cashel and Sallochy, and a hostel at Inversnaid.

Rowardennan SYHA HOSTEL £
(☑01360-870259; www.syha.org.uk; Rowardennan; dm/tw/q £23.50/60/112; ⊙mid-Mar–mid-Oct; P🖙) Where the road ends on the eastern side of Loch Lomond, this is a postcard-quality retreat in an elegant ex-hunting lodge with lawns stretching right down to the water's edge. Whether you're walking the West Highland Way, climbing Ben Lomond or just putting your feet up, it's a great choice, with a huge lounge that has windows overlooking the loch.

Meals are available, including packed lunches for walkers, and there's a pub a short walk away. The wi-fi is a patchy satellite link.

Inversnaid Bunkhouse HOSTEL £
(☎01877-386249; www.inversnaid.com; Inversnaid; dm £20-23, d without bathroom £48-59, tent site per person £10; ⊙Mar-Oct; P 📶 🐾) This former church is now a remote, welcoming hostel in a peaceful streamside location. It's popular with walkers and offers simple accommodation in crowded dorms, very pleasant doubles and grassy campsites (pre-pitched tents available). It's 15 miles from Aberfoyle by road, or by ferry from Loch Lomond's western side, or via an 8-mile walk north from Rowardennan on the West Highland Way.

A hot tub is great for aching muscles and the cafe serves simple meals (noon to 4pm and 6pm to 8pm), packed lunches and decent beers; you can also self-cater evening meals. It's a 15-minute uphill trudge from the lakeshore and trail, but they offer free transfers. A modern self-catering cabin is also available.

Cashel Campsite CAMPSITE £
(☎01360-870234; www.campingintheforest.co.uk; Rowardennan; site for 1/2 £18/25.45; ⊙Mar-late Oct; P 🐾) The most attractive campsite in this eastern shore area is 3 miles north of Balmaha, on the loch shore.

Oak Tree Inn INN ££
(☎01360-870357; www.theoaktreeinn.co.uk; Balmaha; s/d £80/100; P 📶) An attractive traditional inn built in slate and timber, this place offers bright, modern bedrooms for pampered hikers, plus super-spacious superior chambers, self-catering cottages and glamping pods with their own deck. The rustic restaurant brings locals, tourists and walkers together and dishes up hearty meals that cover lots of bases (mains £10 to £13; noon to 9pm). There's plenty of outdoor seating.

But it doesn't end there; the Oak Tree is an impressive set-up that brews its own beers, makes its own ice cream (and sells it in an adjacent cafe), and smokes its own fish. In fact, Balmaha basically is the Oak Tree these days.

Crianlarich & Tyndrum

POP 400

Surrounded by spectacular hillscapes at the northern edge of Loch Lomond and the Trossachs National Park, these villages are popular pit stops on the main A82 road for walkers on the West Highland Way and Munro-baggers. Crianlarich has a train station and more community atmosphere. Tyndrum (*tyne*-drum), 5 miles up the road, has two stations, a bus interchange, a petrol station and late-opening motorists' cafes, and is popular for the ascent of Munros **Cruach Ardrain** (1046m), **Ben More** (1174m) and magnificent **Ben Lui** (1130m).

Sleeping & Eating

Strathfillan Wigwams CAMPSITE, CABIN £
(☎01838-400251; www.wigwamholidays.com; A82, Strathfillan; sites per adult/child £8/3, wigwam d small/large/en suite £40/50/75, lodge d £70-80; P @ 📶 🐾) A working farm off the A82 between Crianlarich and Tyndrum, this place has heated 'wigwams': wooden A-frame cabins, with fridges and foam mattresses, that can sleep four at a pinch. More upmarket are the self-contained lodges with their own bathrooms and kitchen facilities. It also has camping and a shop. There's a two-night minimum on summer weekends. Wi-fi costs a small extra amount.

Crianlarich SYHA HOSTEL £
(☎01838-300260; www.syha.org.uk; Station Rd, Crianlarich; dm/tr/q £21/71/94; P @ 📶) Well run and comfortable, with a spacious kitchen, dining area and lounge, this hostel is a real haven for walkers or anyone passing through. Dorms vary in size – there are some great en suite family rooms that should be booked in advance – but all are clean and roomy.

Ewich Guest House B&B ££
(☎01838-300536; www.ewich.co.uk; A82, Strathfillan; s £45, d £70-80; P 📶 🐾) This lovely Swiss-run stone farmhouse is just below the main road between Crianlarich and Tyndrum, but has a fabulous outlook over a valley, with uplifting views and a large garden. It's very handy for walking and cycling routes and boasts enticing rooms with cheerful fabrics and floorboards. Breakfast has home-laid eggs and there's a personable pooch.

Walker-friendly features like packed lunches, laundry and a drying room are also available.

Real Food Café CAFE £
(☎01838-400235; www.therealfoodcafe.com; A82, Tyndrum; mains £7-10; ⊙7.30am-8pm Nov-Mar, to 9pm Apr-Oct; 📶 👪) 🌿 Hungry hillwalkers throng the tables in this justifiably popular cafe. The menu looks familiar – fish and chips, soups, salads and burgers – but the owners make an effort to source sustainably and locally, and the quality shines through.

ℹ️ Getting There & Away

BUS

Scottish Citylink (www.citylink.co.uk) runs several buses daily to Glasgow (£18.70, 1¾ hours), Fort William (£15.70, 1¼ hours) and Skye (£41.20, four to five hours) from both Crianlarich and Tyndrum. One bus a day goes to Oban in summer (£12.70, 1¼ hours).

TRAIN

Trains run to Tyndrum and Crianlarich from Fort William (£19.90, 1¾ hours, four daily Monday to Saturday, two on Sunday), Oban (£11.70, 1¼ hours, four or six daily) and Glasgow (£21.10, two hours, three to seven daily).

Arrochar

The village of Arrochar has a wonderful location, looking across the head of Loch Long to the jagged peaks of the **Cobbler** (Ben Arthur). The mountain takes its name from the shape of its north peak (the one on the right, seen from Arrochar), which looks like a cobbler hunched over his bench. The village makes a picturesque overnight stop.

Cobbler   HIKING

(Ben Arthur) To climb the Cobbler, an impressively handsome mountain of 884m, start from the roadside car park at Succoth near the head of Loch Long. A steep uphill hike through woods is followed by an easier section heading into the valley below the triple peaks. Then it's steeply uphill again to the saddle between the north and central peaks.

The central peak is higher, but awkward to get to – scramble through the hole and along the ledge to reach the airy summit. The north peak to the right is an easy walk. Allow five to six hours for the 5-mile round trip.

Village Inn   INN ££

(☎ 01301-702279; www.villageinnarrochar.co.uk; Shore Rd; d £120-125; 🅿️🛜🐕) The black-and-white 19th-century Village Inn is a gloriously convivial pub boasting a beer garden with a great view of the Cobbler. There are 14 en suite bedrooms, lovely renovated chambers, some with loch views and most with decent bathrooms. Meals (11am to 9pm) are bar standards supplemented by more ambitious blackboard specials – they're somewhat overpriced (mains £10 to £17) but tasty enough.

The Trossachs

The Trossachs region has long been a favourite weekend getaway, offering outstanding natural beauty and excellent walking and cycling routes within easy reach of the country's southern population centres. With thickly forested hills, romantic lochs, national-park status and an interesting selection of places to stay and eat, its popularity is sure to continue.

The Trossachs first gained cachet in the early 19th century, when curious visitors came from across Britain, drawn by the romantic language of Walter Scott's poem 'Lady of the Lake', inspired by Loch Katrine and Rob Roy, about the derring-do of the region's most famous son.

In summer, the Trossachs can be overburdened with coach tours, but many of these are for day trippers – peaceful, long evenings gazing at the reflections in the nearest loch are still possible. If you can, it's worth timing your visit to avoid weekends.

Aberfoyle & Around

POP 700

Little Aberfoyle has lots to do close at hand and has great accommodation options nearby. It's also a stop on the Rob Roy Way

---

> ### CLIMBING BEN LOMOND
>
> Standing guard over the eastern shore of Loch Lomond is **Ben Lomond** (www.nts.org.uk; 974m), Scotland's most southerly Munro. It's a popular climb: most follow the Tourist Route up and down from Rowardennan car park. It's a straightforward route on a well-used and maintained path; allow five hours for the 7-mile round trip.
>
> The Ptarmigan Route is less crowded and has better views, following a narrow but clearly defined path up the western flank, directly overlooking the loch, to a curving ridge leading to the summit. You can then descend via the Tourist Route, making this option a satisfying circuit.
>
> To find the start of the Ptarmigan path, head north from Rowardennan car park 600m, past the SYHA hostel; cross the bridge after Ben Lomond Cottage and immediately turn right along a path through the trees. The route is then easy to follow.

(p243). However, it's crawling with visitors on most weekends and dominated by a huge car park, and is easily overwhelmed by day trippers. Callander or other Trossachs towns appeal more as a base.

Sights & Activities

Inchmahome Priory RUINS
(☎01877-385294; www.historicenvironment.scot; Lake of Menteith; incl ferry adult/child £7.50/4.50; ⊙10am-5pm Apr-Sep, to 4pm Oct, last ferry to island 45min before closing) From the **Lake of Menteith** (called 'lake' not 'loch' due to a mistranslation from Gaelic), 3 miles east of Aberfoyle, a ferry takes visitors to these substantial ruins. Mary, Queen of Scots was kept safe here as a child during Henry VIII's 'Rough Wooing'. Henry attacked Stirling, trying to force Mary to marry his son in order to unite the kingdoms.

★**Loch Katrine Circuit** CYCLING
An excellent 20-mile circular cycle route from Aberfoyle starts on the **Lochs & Glens Cycle Way** on the forest trail. Following the southern shore of Loch Achray, you reach the pier on Loch Katrine. The 10.30am boat (or afternoon sailings in summer) takes you to the western shore, from where you can follow the beautiful B829 via Loch Ard back to Aberfoyle.

Instead of getting the boat, you could bike it along the loch's northern shore, adding an extra 14 miles to the trip. An alternative to the forest trail from Aberfoyle is taking the A821 over Duke's Pass.

The Lodge OUTDOORS
(David Marshall Lodge; ☎0300 067 6615; www.forestry.gov.uk; A821; car park £1-3; ⊙10am-4pm Oct-Dec & Mar-Apr, to 3pm Jan & Feb, to 5pm May-Jun & Sep, to 6pm Jul & Aug) Half a mile north of Aberfoyle, this nature centre has info about the many walks and cycle routes in and around the **Queen Elizabeth Forest Park**. There are live wildlife cameras offering a peek at osprey and barn-owl nests among others. The centre is worth visiting solely for the views.

Picturesque but busy waymarked trails start from here, ranging from a light 20-minute stroll to a nearby waterfall – with great interactive play options for kids – to a hilly 4-mile circuit. The centre has a popular cafe. Also here, **Go Ape!** (☎0333 920 4859; www.goape.co.uk; adult/child £33/25; ⊙Sat & Sun Nov & Feb-Easter, Wed-Mon Easter-Oct) will bring out the monkey in you on its exhilarating adventure course of long ziplines, swings and rope bridges through the forest. Look out, too, for the spooky mirror sculptures by local artist Rob Mulholland.

> WORTH A TRIP
>
> ### HILL HOUSE
>
> Built in 1902 for Glasgow publisher Walter Blackie, **Hill House** (☎01436-673900; www.nts.org.uk; Upper Colquhoun St, Helensburgh; adult/child £10.50/7.50; ⊙11.30am-5pm Mar-Oct) is perhaps architect Charles Rennie Mackintosh's finest creation – its timeless elegance still feels chic today. The interiors are stunning, with rose motifs and fabulous furniture. Water soaking through the rendered cement exterior means that you'll find the house enclosed in a giant covering structure. You can stay on the top floor here – check the Holidays section of the NTS website. It's near Upper Helensburgh station, though not all trains stop there.
>
> The house also has a beautiful garden. Mackintosh was very protective of his creation: he once chided Mrs Blackie for putting the wrong-coloured flowers in a vase in the hall.
>
> If you're arriving at Helensburgh Central station, it's about a 1-mile uphill walk to Hill House. Buses 302 and 306 can get you close.

Sleeping & Eating

Bield B&B ££
(☎01877-382351; www.thebield.net; Trossachs Rd, Aberfoyle; s/d £50/65; P ᯤ) With a kind, genuine welcome, the Bield is exactly the sort of place you want after a long day's walking or cycling. This striking sandstone house has large, comfortable rooms, a sociable breakfast table and views from its hillside location just above Aberfoyle's centre. Prices are very reasonable.

★**Lake of Menteith Hotel** HOTEL £££
(☎01877-385258; www.lake-hotel.com; Port of Menteith; r £150-255; P ᯤ 🐾) Soothingly situated on a lake (yes, it's the only non-loch in Scotland) 3 miles east of Aberfoyle, this genteel retreat makes a great romantic getaway. Though all rooms are excellent, with a contemporary feel, it's worth an upgrade to the enormous 'lake heritage' ones with a view of the water: it really is a sensational outlook.

Even if you're not staying, head down to the waterside bar-restaurant (mains £10 to £17;

open noon to 2.30pm and 5.30pm to 9pm, closed Monday and Tuesday from November to February). Check the website for packages.

★ Aberfoyle Delicatessen & Trossachs Butcher
DELI £

(☑ 01877-382242; www.aberfoyledelibutcher.co.uk; 3 Dukes Ct, Aberfoyle; pies £2.20; ☺ 8.30am-1.30pm & 2-5pm) This main-street shop is a cut above most of Aberfoyle's culinary offerings. There's good produce for self-caterers and excellent sandwiches, but the pies are a step beyond even those. Steak and black pudding? Venison? It's all delicious, and ingredients are specified for those with dietary needs.

ℹ Information

Aberfoyle Tourist Office (☑ 01877-381221; www.visitscotland.com; Main St; ☺ 10am-5pm Apr-Oct, to 4pm Nov-Mar; ☎) A large office with a good selection of walking information.

ℹ Getting There & Away

First (www.firstgroup.com) has six daily buses (Monday to Saturday) from Stirling (£5.20, 55 minutes).

DRT operates in the Aberfoyle area.

Lochs Katrine & Achray

This rugged area, 7 miles north of Aberfoyle and 10 miles west of Callander, is the heart of the Trossachs. **Loch Katrine Cruises** (☑ 01877-376315; www.lochkatrine.com; 1hr cruise adult £12-14, child £6.50-7.50) run from Trossachs Pier at the eastern tip of beautiful Loch Katrine. One of these is the fabulous centenarian steamship *Sir Walter Scott;* check the website for departures, as it's worth taking a trip on this veteran if possible. There are various one-hour afternoon sailings, and at 10.30am (plus additional summer departures) there's a trip to Stronachlachar at the other end of the loch. From Stronachlachar (accessible by car via a 12-mile road from Aberfoyle), you can reach Loch Lomond's

---

ℹ TROSSACHS TRANSPORT

DRT (Demand Responsive Transport; ☑ 01786-404040; www.stirling.gov.uk) covers the Trossachs area. It sounds complex, but basically it means for the price of a bus you get a taxi to where you want to go. There are various zones. Taxis should preferably be booked 24 hours in advance by phone.

---

eastern shore at isolated Inversnaid. A tarmac path links Trossachs Pier with Stronachlachar, so you can take the boat out and walk/cycle back (14 miles). At Trossachs Pier, **Katrinewheelz** (☑ 01877-376366; www.katrinewheelz.co.uk; bike hire per half-/full day from £15/20; ☺ 9am-5pm Apr-Oct, 11am-3pm Sat & Sun Nov-Dec & Feb-Mar) hires out good bikes. The cafe is mediocre so bring a picnic or eat at the other end of the loch.

Loch Achray Walks
HIKING

The path to the rocky cone called **Ben A'an** (454m) begins at a car park just east of the Loch Katrine turn-off. It's easy to follow and the return trip is just under 4 miles. A tougher walk is up rugged **Ben Venue** (727m). Start walking from the signed car park just south of the Loch Katrine turn-off (7.5 miles return).

Loch Katrine Camping
CABIN £

(☑ 01877-376317; www.lochkatrinecamping.com; Loch Katrine; pods £40-80; P ☎ 😊) Just beyond the ferry pier on Loch Katrine, this is a pleasing new place to stay, offering tent and motorhome pitches as well as cute camping pods with a little deck. They sleep two or four and come in two categories, one with underfloor heating and en suite bathroom. Book them well ahead. It's cheaper if you bring your own linen.

There's a two-night minimum stay for the en suite ones, one of which is adapted for wheelchair use.

Callander

POP 3100

Callander, the principal Trossachs town, has been pulling in tourists for over 150 years, and has a laid-back ambience along its main thoroughfare that quickly lulls visitors into lazy pottering. There's an excellent array of accommodation options here, and some intriguing places to eat. Good walking and cycling routes are close at hand.

◉ Sights & Activities

★ Hamilton Toy Collection
MUSEUM

(☑ 01877-330004; www.thehamiltontoycollection.co.uk; 111 Main St; adult/child £3/1; ☺ 10.30am-5pm Mon-Sat, noon-5pm Sun Apr-Oct; ☻) The Hamilton Toy Collection is a powerhouse of 20th-century juvenile memorabilia, chock-full of dolls houses, puppets and toy soldiers. It's an amazing collection and a guaranteed nostalgia trip. Phone ahead in winter as it opens some weekends.

Bracklinn Falls & Callander Crags   WALKING
Impressive Bracklinn Falls are reached by track and footpath from Bracklinn Rd (30 minutes each way from the car park). Also off Bracklinn Rd, a woodland trail leads up to Callander Crags, with great views over the surroundings; a return trip from the car park is about 4 miles.

Wheels Cycling Centre   CYCLING
(☎01877-331100; www.scottish-cycling.com; bike per hour/day/week from £8/20/90; ⊙10am-6pm Mar-Oct) The Trossachs is a lovely area to cycle around. On a cycle route, excellent Wheels Cycling Centre has a wide range of hire bikes. To get here from the centre of Callander, take Bridge St off Main St, turn right onto Invertrossachs Rd and continue for a mile.

🛏 Sleeping

★Callander Hostel   HOSTEL £
(☎01877-331465; www.callanderhostel.co.uk; 6 Bridgend; dm/d £19.50/60; P@🛜) ⏎ This hostel in a mock-Tudor building has been a major labour of love by a local youth project and is now a top-class facility. Well-furnished dorms offer bunks with individual lights and USB charge ports, while en suite doubles have super views. Staff are lovely, and it has a spacious common area and share kitchen as well as a cafe and garden.

Abbotsford Lodge   HOTEL ££
(☎01877-330066; www.abbotsfordlodge.com; Stirling Rd; d £75-85; ⊙mid-Feb-early Nov; P🛜) Offering excellent value for stylish contemporary rooms in a handsome Victorian house, this main-road choice has energetic owners who provide first-class hospitality and have a real eye for design. There are fabulous, spacious superiors (from £125) as well as cheaper top-floor rooms – with shared bathroom – that have lovably offbeat underroof shapes. It caters to cyclists and walkers with bike storage and packed lunches.

Room-only rates are available, but breakfast is top-notch. There are some appealing options for families, though no under-6s are allowed.

Arden House   B&B ££
(☎01877-339405; www.ardenhouse.org.uk; Bracklinn Rd; d £100-125; ⊙Mar-Oct; P🛜) This elegant home has a fabulous hillside location with verdant garden and lovely vistas; close to Callander's centre but far from the crowds. The rooms are impeccable, with lots of natural light and include large upstairs doubles with great views. Welcoming owners, noble architectural features – super bay windows – and a self-catering studio make this a top option.

There's a two-night minimum stay in summer.

Callander Meadows   B&B ££
(☎01877-330181; www.callandermeadows.co.uk; 24 Main St; s £60, d £75-95; P🛜🐾) Upstairs at this recommended restaurant (p252) are some very appealing chambers, elegantly kitted out with solid furniture and good modern shower rooms. One, which can serve as a family room, has a four-poster bed. The owners are very welcoming and you are right in the heart of Callander. Breakfast is excellent.

★Roman Camp Hotel   HOTEL £££
(☎01877-330003; www.romancamphotel.co.uk; off Main St; s/d/superior £135/160/260; P🛜🐾) Callander's best hotel is centrally located but feels rural, set by the river in beautiful grounds. Endearing features include a lounge with blazing fire and a library with a tiny secret chapel. It's an old-fashioned warren of a place with four grades of rooms; standards are certainly luxurious, but superiors are even more appealing, with period furniture, excellent bathrooms, armchairs and fireplace.

The upmarket restaurant is open to the public. Reassuringly, the name refers not to toga parties but to a ruin in the adjacent fields.

🍴 Eating

Mhor Bread   CAFE, BAKERY £
(☎01877-339518; www.mhorbread.net; 8 Main St; light meals £2-6; ⊙7am-5pm Mon-Sat, 8am-5pm Sun; 🛜) ⏎ Great bread (sourdough, seeded, local) for picnics is baked at this high-street spot, which is also a good stop for decent coffee, pies and filled rolls. The steak and haggis pie is a treat.

★Venachar Lochside   SCOTTISH ££
(☎01877-330011; www.venachar-lochside.com; Loch Venachar; mains £13-18; ⊙noon-4pm Jan-Nov, plus 5.30-8.30pm Fri & Sat Jun-Sep; 🛜♿) On lovely Loch Venachar, 4.5 miles west of Callander, this cafe-restaurant has a stunning waterside setting and does a nice line in carefully sourced produce (including delicious local trout) prepared in innovative ways. It opens from 10am for coffees, teas and baked goods. You can also hire boats and tackle to go fishing for trout on the loch. Check its Facebook page for dinner openings.

★ **Callander Meadows** SCOTTISH ££
(☑01877-330181; www.callandermeadows.co.uk; 24 Main St; dinner mains £13-19; ☺10am-2.30pm & 6-8.30pm Thu-Sun year-round, plus Mon May-Sep; ☎) Informal and cosy, this well-loved restaurant in the centre of Callander occupies the front rooms of a Main St house. It's truly excellent; there's a contemporary flair for presentation and unusual flavour combinations, but a solidly British base underpins the cuisine. There's a great beer/coffee garden out the back, where you can also eat. Lighter lunches such as sandwiches are also available.

Poppy Seed SCOTTISH ££
(☑01877-330329;www.poppyseedrestaurant.co.uk; Leny Rd; mains £12-18; ☺noon-9pm Thu-Tue; ☎) A revamp has seen this restaurant of a small main-road hotel invigorated by young owners. Start with an aperitif from the fine spirit selection of the handsome bar, then move through to dine on a short menu of quality ingredients prepared with imagination and deftly presented. In winter it's closed lunchtimes except on Sundays.

Mhor Fish SEAFOOD ££
(☑01877-330213; www.mhorfish.net; 75 Main St; mains £9-18; ☺noon-9pm Tue-Sun, closed Tue also Nov–mid-Feb; ☎) ✿ This simply decorated spot, with formica tables and a hodgepodge of chairs, sources brilliant sustainable seafood. Browse the fresh catch then eat it pan-seared in the dining area accompanied by a decent wine selection, or fried and wrapped in paper with chips to take away. It's all great, and calamari and oysters are wonderfully toothsome starters.

❶ Getting There & Away

First (www.firstgroup.com) operates buses from Stirling (£5.80, 45 minutes, hourly Monday to Saturday, every two hours Sunday).

Kingshouse (☑01877-384768; www.kingshousetravel.com) has buses between Callander and Killin (£5.30, 40 minutes, five to six Monday to Saturday).

For Aberfoyle, use DRT (p250) or get off a Stirling-bound bus at Blair Drummond safari park, cross the road and pick up an Aberfoyle-bound bus.

Balquhidder & Around

North of Callander, you'll skirt past the shores of gorgeous **Loch Lubnaig**. Not as famous as some of its cousins, it's still well worth a stop for its sublime views of forested

hills. In the small village of Balquhidder (ball-whidder), 9 miles north of Callander off the A84, there's a churchyard with – perhaps – Rob Roy's grave. In the church itself is the 8th-century St Angus' stone, probably a marker to the original tomb of St Angus.

🛏 Sleeping

Mhor 84 INN ££
(☑01877-384646; www.mhor84.net; A84, Kingshouse; r without breakfast £90; ℗☎☎) ✿ At the A84 junction, this 18th-century inn has been given a modern-retro revamp and is an upbeat place with bags of facilities, simple, good-value rooms and a delicious menu of hearty, nourishing meals following the Mhor philosophy of local and sustainable. A great pit stop for drivers, walkers and cyclists. Some rooms are in a rear cottage; there's also a self-catering one.

There are three menus served: breakfast from 8am to noon, a daytime one from noon to 5pm and dinner to 9pm.

★ **Monachyle Mhor** HOTEL £££
(☑01877-384622; www.monachylemhor.net; d £195-285, wagon £125; ☺Feb-Dec; ℗☎☎) ✿ A luxury hideaway with a fantastically peaceful location overlooking two lochs, Monachyle Mhor is a great fusion of country Scotland and contemporary attitudes to design and food. Rooms are superb and feature quirkily original decor, particularly the fabulous 'feature rooms'. Otherwise, go glamping in a retro wagon or kip in a romantic...ferry waiting room. The restaurant is excellent.

It's an enchanting combination of top-class hospitality with a relaxed rural atmosphere: dogs and kids happily romp on the lawns, and no one looks askance if you come in flushed and muddy after a day's fishing or walking.

❶ Getting There & Away

Local buses between Callander and Killin stop at the main-road turn-off to Balquhidder, as do daily buses with **Scottish Citylink** (www.citylink.co.uk) between Edinburgh and Oban/Fort William.

Balquhidder is part of the DRT scheme (p250), which you can use to get to Monachyle Mhor from the main road.

Killin

POP 800

A fine base for the Trossachs or Perthshire, this lovely village sits at the western end of Loch Tay and has a spread-out, relaxed feel, particularly around the scenic **Falls of**

Dochart, which tumble through the centre. On a sunny day people sprawl over the rocks by the bridge, with pint or picnic in hand. Killin offers fine walking around the town, and there are mighty mountains and glens close by.

Activities

Five miles northeast of Killin, **Ben Lawers** (1214m) rises above Loch Tay. Walking routes abound; one rewarding **circular walk** heads up into the Acharn forest south of town, emerging above the treeline to great views of Loch Tay and Ben Lawers. **Killin Outdoor Centre** (☎01567-820652; www.killinoutdoor.co.uk; Main St; bike per 24hr £25, kayak/canoe per 2hr £25; ⏲8.45am-5.30pm) provides walking advice.

Glen Lochay runs westwards from Killin into the hills of Mamlorn. You can take a **mountain bike** up the glen; the scenery is impressive and the hills aren't too difficult. It's possible, on a nice summer day, to climb over the top of **Ben Challum** (1025m) and descend to Crianlarich, but it's hard work. A potholed road, not maintained and no longer suitable for cars, also connects Glen Lochay with Glen Lyon.

Killin is on the **Lochs & Glens Cycle Way** from Glasgow to Inverness. Hire bikes from helpful Killin Outdoor Centre (which also has canoes and kayaks and, in winter, crampons and snowshoes).

Loch Tay Fish 'n' Trips FISHING
(☎07967 567347; www.lochtayfishntrips.co.uk) Loch Tay is famous for its fishing – salmon, trout and pike are all caught here. Fish 'n' Trips can kit you out for a day's fishing with a boat, tackle and guide for £120 for two people, or rent you a boat for £60 a day.

Sleeping & Eating

High Creagan CAMPSITE £
(☎01567-820449; www.facebook.com/highcreagancaravanpark; Aberfeldy Rd; per person tent/caravan sites £7/9; ⏲Apr-Oct; P) High Creagan is a long-established favourite with a good-humoured boss and a well-kept, sheltered campsite with plenty of grass set high on the slopes overlooking sparkling Loch Tay, 3 miles east of Killin. Under-15s aren't allowed in the tent area (for insurance reasons), as there's a stream running through it.

★**Courie Inn** INN ££
(☎01567-831000; www.thecourieinn.com; Main St; d £99-140; P 📶) An excellent all-round choice, Courie Inn has quality, comfortable rooms decorated with restrained modern elegance; they come in a variety of sizes, including a sumptuous suite with views. It artfully blends the traditional and contemporary. Downstairs, the restaurant does smart bistro food (mains £11 to £15; daily 5pm to 8.30pm, plus noon to 3pm Friday to Sunday), and there's a bar.

Old Bank B&B ££
(☎01567-829317; www.theoldbankkillin.co.uk; Manse Rd; s/d £55/80; P 📶) This four-square building with a pretty garden stands proud above the main street in Killin. It's a genuinely welcoming place, with a host who does everything in her power to make you feel welcome. Breakfast is abundant and the rooms are super-comfortable, with contemporary colours, hill views and thoughtful extras.

Getting There & Away

Kingshouse (www.kingshousetravel.com) runs five to six buses Monday to Saturday to Callander (£5.30, 40 minutes), where you can change for Stirling.

ROB ROY

Nicknamed Red (*'ruadh'* in Gaelic, anglicised to 'roy') for his ginger locks, Robert MacGregor (1671–1734) was the wild leader of the wildest of Scotland's clans, outlawed by powerful neighbours, hence their sobriquet, Children of the Mist. Incognito, Rob became a prosperous livestock trader, before a dodgy deal led to a warrant for his arrest.

A legendary swordsman, the fugitive from justice then became notorious for daring raids into the Lowlands to carry off cattle and sheep. Forever hiding from potential captors, he was twice imprisoned, but escaped dramatically on both occasions. He finally turned himself in and received his liberty and a pardon from the king. He lies buried – perhaps – in the churchyard at Balquhidder; his uncompromising later epitaph reads 'MacGregor despite them'. His life has been glorified over the years due to Walter Scott's novel and the 1995 film. Many Scots see his life as a symbol of the struggle of the common folk against the inequitable ownership of vast tracts of the country by landed aristocrats.

SOUTH ARGYLL

The impossibly tortuous coastline of the mainland and islands of South Argyll would confuse the most adept geographer. Sea lochs slice the rugged land into peninsulas that offer some of Scotland's most spectacular coastal scenery. The archipelago of islands includes the whisky Shangri La of Islay, the brooding hills of lonely Jura and the retro charms of Bute.

Cowal

The remote and picturesque Cowal Peninsula is cut off from the rest of the country by the lengthy fjords of Loch Long and Loch Fyne. It comprises rugged hills and narrow lochs, with only a few small villages and the old-fashioned, down-at-heel holiday resort of Dunoon. It makes for great, off-the-beaten-track exploration at a very accessible range from busier Glasgow and Loch Lomond.

The attractive Cowal Way (www.cowalway. co.uk) is a 57-mile walking path crossing the region.

From Arrochar, the A83 to Inveraray loops around the head of Loch Long and climbs into spectacular Glen Croe. The pass at the head of the glen is called the Rest and Be Thankful. As you descend Glen Kinglas on the far side, the A815 forks to the left just before Cairndow; this is the main overland route into Cowal.

There are ferries to Cowal from Gourock and Tarbert. Buses run from Glasgow to Dunoon via the ferry. Other buses run by West Coast Motors (☑01586-559135; www. westcoastmotors.co.uk) head overland into and around the peninsula.

Dunoon & Around

Like Rothesay on Bute, Dunoon is a Victorian seaside resort that owes its existence to the steamers that once carried thousands of Glaswegians on pleasure trips 'doon the watter' in the 19th and 20th centuries. Fortunes declined when cheap foreign holidays stole the market and Dunoon is still a bit down in the dumps. Bypass its ugly town centre and take in the magnificent perspectives along the long waterfront.

The town's main attraction is still, as it was in the 1950s, strolling along the promenade, licking an ice-cream cone and watching the yachts at play in the Firth of Clyde.

Benmore Botanic Garden   GARDENS
(☑01369-706261; www.rbge.org.uk; A815; adult/child £6.50/free; ⊙10am-6pm Apr-Sep, to 5pm Mar & Oct) This garden, 7 miles north of Dunoon, contains Scotland's finest collection of flowering trees and shrubs, including impressive displays of rhododendrons and azaleas, and is entered along a spectacular avenue of giant redwoods. A highlight is the Victorian fernery, nestled in an unlikely fold in the crags. The cafe here (which also opens through some of the winter) appeals for lunch or coffee. Buses run between here and Dunoon.

Cowal Highland Gathering   CULTURAL, SPORTS
(www.cowalgathering.com; Hillfoot St, Dunoon; ⊙late Aug) One of the closest Highland Games to the southern cities, this Dunoon extravaganza is held in late August. The spectacular finale features more than 1000 bagpipers saluting the chieftain.

❶ Getting There & Away

BOAT

Dunoon is served by two competing ferry services from Gourock (near Greenock). Argyll Ferries is better if you are travelling on foot and want to arrive in the town centre.

Argyll Ferries (www.argyllferries.co.uk; adult/child £4.65/2.35, 25 minutes, half-hourly Monday to Saturday, hourly Sunday)

Western Ferries (www.western-ferries.co.uk; adult/child/car £4.60/2.30/17.60, 20 minutes, two to three hourly) Arrives at a pier just over a mile from the centre of Dunoon. Departs from McInroy's Point, 2 miles south of Gourock train station on the Irvine road; Scottish Citylink buses run to here.

BUS

McGill's Buses (☑08000 51 56 51; www. mcgillsbuses.co.uk) run from Glasgow to Dunoon (£9.80, two hours, five to seven daily) via the ferry. It's quicker between Gourock and Glasgow to jump on the train.

Buses around the Cowal Peninsula, to Inveraray (£3.90) and to Rothesay on Bute (£3.50), are operated by West Coast Motors.

Tighnabruaich

POP 200

Sleepy little seaside Tighnabruaich (tinna-broo-ah) is one of the most attractive villages on the Firth of Clyde and by far the most appealing place at which to overnight on the Cowal Peninsula.

★ **Botanica** BISTRO ££

(📞 01700-811186; www.botanicafood.co.uk; Main St; dinner mains £14-23; ⏱ 8.30am-4pm Wed, Thu & Sun, to 11pm Fri & Sat, extended summer hours; 🛜 🅿) In the centre of Tighnabruaich village, this place offers a touch of eclecticism focused on solid British ingredients, with simple classics like asparagus with Bearnaise sauce making a lovely lunchtime treat, and a changing dinner menu featuring locally landed fish. Understandably, it tends to pack out for dinner, so it's best to book. It also has four rooms available.

Bute

POP 6500

The scenic island of Bute lies pinched between the thumb and forefinger of the Cowal Peninsula, separated from the mainland by a narrow, picturesque strait. The Highland Boundary Fault cuts through the middle of the island so that, geologically speaking, the northern half is in the Highlands and the southern half is in the central Lowlands. The main town, Rothesay, is a Victorian resort with a long waterfront and noteworthy castle; south of here is the grand pile of Mount Stuart, one of Scotland's finest stately homes. The west side of the island features dreamy outlooks across to the hills of Arran.

❶ Information

Isle of Bute Discovery Centre (📞 01700-507043; www.visitscotland.com; Victoria St; ⏱ 9.30am-5.30pm Jul & Aug, to 5pm Apr-Jun & Sep, 10am-5pm Oct, 10am-4pm Mon-Sat & 11am-3pm Sun Nov-Mar; 🛜) There's a free audiovisual display here that provides an upbeat introduction to the island. It's in Rothesay's restored Winter Gardens building – once an entertainment venue and still serving as a cinema.

❶ Getting There & Away

Buses run by West Coast Motors cross to Bute from the Cowal Peninsula.

CalMac (📞 0800 066 5000; www.calmac. co.uk) has ferries between Wemyss Bay and Rothesay (adult/car £3.15/11.30, 35 minutes, roughly hourly). Another crosses the short stretch of water between Rhubodach in the north of the island and Colintraive (adult/car £1.15/5.95, five minutes, half-hourly) in Cowal.

Rothesay

POP 4500

From the mid-19th century until the 1960s, Rothesay was one of Scotland's most popular holiday resorts, bustling with day trippers disembarking from numerous steamers crowded around the pier. Its hotels were filled with elderly holidaymakers and convalescents taking advantage of the famously mild climate.

Cheap foreign holidays saw Rothesay's fortunes decline, but a nostalgia-fuelled resurgence of interest has seen many Victorian buildings restored. The grassy, flowery waterfront and row of noble villas make it a lovely place to be once again.

◉ Sights

Rothesay Castle CASTLE

(📞 01700-502691; www.historicenvironment.scot; King St; adult/child £5/3; ⏱ 9.30am-5.30pm Apr-Sep, 10am-4pm Sat-Wed Oct-Mar) The splendid, ruined 13th-century Rothesay Castle, with seagulls and jackdaws nesting in the walls, was once a favourite residence of the Stuart kings. It is unique in Scotland in having a circular plan, with four stocky round towers. The landscaped moat, with manicured turf, flower gardens and lazily cruising ducks, makes a picturesque setting.

Victorian Toilets HISTORIC BUILDING

(Rothesay Pier; adult/child 40p/free; ⏱ 9am-3.45pm Mon-Thu, to 4.45pm Fri-Sun Oct-Apr, 8am-5.45pm Mon-Thu, to 7.30pm Fri-Sun May-Sep) Dating from 1899, these toilets are a monument to lavatorial luxury – a disinfectant-scented temple of green and black marbled stoneware, glistening white enamel, glass-sided cisterns and gleaming copper pipes. The attendant will escort you into the bathrooms of the opposite sex for a look around when unoccupied. You can shower here, too.

🛏 Sleeping

Bute Backpackers Hotel HOSTEL £

(📞 01700-501876; www.butebackpackers.co.uk; 36 Argyle St; s/tw/d £25/45/50, s without bathroom £20; 🅿 🛜 🐾) An appealing budget option on Rothesay's main thoroughfare, this large, well-equipped place has private rooms of various sizes at bargain prices. Some are en suite, but the shared bathrooms are modern and spotless, with power showers. The kitchen is huge, and there's a barbecue as well.

★ Boat House
B&B ££

(☑01700-502696; www.theboathouse-bute.co.uk; 15 Battery Pl; d £80-90; 🛜🏵) Boat House brings a touch of class to Rothesay's guesthouse scene, with quality fabrics and furnishings and an eye for design that makes it feel like a boutique hotel, without the expensive prices. Rooms are very swish, with a kitchenette and breakfast provided. Other features include a garden, sea views, a central location and a ground-floor room kitted out for wheelchair users. There's a two-night minimum stay on weekends.

Glendale Guest House
B&B ££

(☑01700-502329; www.glendale-guest-house. com; 20 Battery Pl; s £47, d £66-90, f £125; 🅿🛜) This grand Victorian waterfront villa, complete with turret, offers very generous rooms with plush furniture and good family options. Front-facing bedrooms offer superb sea views from large windows, as do the lavishly elegant lounge and the breakfast room, where you'll find homemade smoked haddock fishcakes on the menu among other interesting options. Genial hosts make for a pleasurable stay.

St Ebba
B&B ££

(☑01700-500059; www.rothesayaccommodation. co.uk; 37 Mountstuart Rd; s/d £45/70; 🅿🛜) Turn left from the ferry in Rothesay and follow the shoreline to reach this typically noble Victorian lodge, divided into two B&Bs. This place, entered down the right, takes full advantage of the lovely views with its spacious rooms with big windows. Sea-view rooms cost an extra £10. Courteous hosts.

✗ Eating

★ Musicker
CAFE £

(☑01700-502287; www.musicker.co.uk; 11 High St; mains £3-7; ⊙10am-5pm Mon-Sat; 🛜🎵) This cool little cafe serves Bute's best coffee, alongside a range of home baking, soups and sandwiches with imaginative fillings. It also sells CDs, books and guitars, and sports an old-fashioned jukebox.

Harry Haw's
BISTRO ££

(☑01700-505857; www.harryhawsbute.co.uk; 23 High St; mains £9-15; ⊙noon-9pm; 🛜🎵) There are great scenes at this welcoming modern bistro with an attractive interior and views over Rothesay Castle. Its moderate prices and pleasing range of deli-style fare plus burgers, local roast meat and tasty pastas make it a standout. The staff are very friendly and so cheerful you'll wonder if there's something in the water.

Around Rothesay

★ Mount Stuart
HISTORIC BUILDING

(☑01700-503877; www.mountstuart.com; adult/child £13/7.50; ⊙11am-4pm Apr, May & Oct, to 5pm Jun-Sep, see website for winter hours, grounds 10am-6pm Mar-Oct) The family seat of the Stuart Earls of Bute is one of Britain's more magnificent 19th-century stately homes, the first to have a telephone, underfloor heating and a heated pool. Its eclectic interior, with an imposing central hall and chapel in Italian marble, is heavily influenced by the third Marquess' interests in Greek mythology and astrology. The drawing room has paintings by Titian and Tintoretto among other masters. Mount Stuart is 5 miles south of Rothesay; bus 490 runs here hourly.

Buy tickets at the visitor centre (or book online), from where it's a 15-minute stroll (a courtesy bus is also available) through lovely grounds to the house. Entry is either by guided tour or free visit, depending on the time. Private tours (£20 or £40) offer glimpses of the pool and more bedrooms.

There's a cafe serving famously opulent afternoon teas (book ahead).

Discounted ferry-plus-entrance tickets are available from **CalMac** (www.calmac.co.uk).

Inveraray

POP 600

There's no fifty shades of grey around here: this historic planned village is all black and white – even logos of high-street chain shops conform. Spectacularly set on the shores of Loch Fyne, Inveraray was built by the Duke of Argyll in Georgian style when he revamped his nearby castle in the 18th century.

⊙ Sights

Inveraray Castle
CASTLE

(☑01499-302203;www.inveraray-castle.com;adult/child/family £11/8/32; ⊙10am-5.45pm Apr-Oct) This visually stunning castle on the north side of town has been the seat of the Dukes of Argyll – chiefs of Clan Campbell – since the 15th century. The 18th-century building, with its fairy-tale turrets and fake battlements, houses an impressive armoury hall, its walls patterned with more than 1000 pole arms, dirks, muskets and Lochaber axes. Entry is slightly cheaper if you book online.

Inveraray Jail MUSEUM

(☎01499-302381; www.inverarayjail.co.uk; Church Sq; adult/child £11.50/7; ☻9.30am-6pm Apr-Oct, 10am-5pm Nov-Mar; ☷) At this entertaining interactive tourist attraction you can sit in on a trial, try out a cell and discover the harsh tortures that were meted out to unfortunate prisoners. The attention to detail – including a life-sized model of an inmate squatting on a 19th-century toilet – is excellent, and actors enliven things during busy periods. Last admission is an hour before closing.

🛏 Sleeping & Eating

⭐ George Hotel INN ££

(☎01499-302111; www.thegeorgehotel.co.uk; Main St E; d £90-135; P☎☷☀) The George boasts a magnificent choice of opulent, individual rooms decorated with sumptuous period furniture. Some feature four-poster beds, Victorian roll-top baths and/or private jacuzzis (superior rooms and suites cost £145 to £180 per double; the library suite is quite a sight). Some rooms are in an annexe opposite and there are also self-catering options.

The cosy wood-panelled bar, with rough stone walls, flagstone floor and peat fires, is a delightful place for all-day bar meals, and has a beer garden.

Samphire SEAFOOD ££

(☎01499-302321; www.samphireseafood.com; 6a Arkland; dinner mains £11-21; ☻noon-2.30pm & 5.30-9pm Wed-Fri, noon-2.30pm & 5-11pm Sat, noon-2.30pm & 5-9pm Sun; ☎) 🌱 There's lots to like about this compact restaurant that makes an effort to source sustainable local seafood. There's a fairly light touch from the kitchen, which tends to let the natural flavours shine through, with very pleasing results.

❶ Getting There & Away

Scottish Citylink (www.citylink.co.uk) has buses running from Glasgow to Inveraray (£13, 1¾ hours, up to nine daily). Some continue to Campbeltown (£14.20, 2¼ hours); others to Oban (£10.80, 1¼ hours). There are also buses to Dunoon (£3.90, 1¼ hours, three daily Monday to Saturday)

Crinan Canal

Completed in 1801, picturesque Crinan Canal runs for 9 miles from Ardrishaig to Crinan allowing seagoing vessels – mostly yachts, these days – to take a short cut from the Firth of Clyde and Loch Fyne to the west coast of

> ## FYNE FOOD & DRINK
>
> Eight miles north of Inveraray, at the head of Loch Fyne, it pays to stop by two great local establishments:
>
> **Loch Fyne Oyster Bar** (☎01499-600482; www.lochfyne.com; Clachan, Cairndow; mains £13-26; ☻9am-5pm; ☎) The success of this cooperative is such that it now lends its name to dozens of restaurants throughout the UK. But the original is still the best, with large, salty, creamy oysters straight out of the lake, and fabulous salmon dishes. The atmosphere and decor is simple, friendly and unpretentious; it also has a shop and deli where you can eat casually.
>
> **Fyne Ales** (☎01499-600120; www. fyneales.com; Achadunan, Cairndow; tours £5; ☻10am-6pm) The friendly folk here do a great range of craft beers in this attractive modern brewery off the A83 9 miles northeast of Inveraray. There's a lovely bar-cafe (with outdoor seating) where you can taste them all: the light, citrussy Jarl is a standout. Call ahead to book tours, which run for about 45 minutes. A range of walks tackle the pretty glen from a car park nearby.

Scotland, avoiding the long passage around the Mull of Kintyre. You can easily walk or cycle the **canal towpath** in an afternoon.

⭐ Venture West BOATING

(☎07789 071188; www.venture-west.co.uk; Crinan Harbour; 2½-hour trip adult/child £35/25; ☻Mar-Oct) Venture West has really enjoyable boat trips run from Crinan (other pick-up points are available) out to Jura, the Garvellach islands and the Corryvreckan Whirlpool. Highlights include sea eagles and (tide-dependent) landings on remote islands. Note that trips run from the old harbour, a little further west than the harbour at the end of the canal. Longer trips head to Iona and Staffa.

⭐ Crinan Hotel HOTEL £££

(☎01546-830261; www.crinanhotel.com; Crinan; s £155, d £230-290; ☻Mar-Dec; P☎☷☀) Romantic Crinan Hotel boasts one of the west coast's most spectacular views. All the bright, light rooms enjoy wonderful perspectives, and the somewhat faded old-world atmosphere is beguiling, with paintings throughout and a top-floor gallery. You're paying for the ambience and view here: don't expect five-star luxury. It's run with welcoming good humour and offers various eating options.

The restaurant Westward (set dinner £45; ⊘7-8.30pm; 🔊) does posh set dinners, the cosy Crinan Seafood Bar (mains £13-19; ⊘noon-2.30pm & 6-8.30pm; 🔊) does great fresh food, including excellent local mussels with white wine and garlic, and the nearby Crinan Coffee Shop (snacks £3-7; ⊘9am-6pm Apr-Oct; 🔊) has great home baking. Upstairs, Lock 16 opens for seafood dinners with spectacular views on summer weekends.

❶ Getting There & Away

West Coast Motors (www.westcoastmotors. co.uk) has the 425/426 service from Lochgilphead that runs along the canal to Crinan once or twice Monday to Friday. This allows you to walk the canal one way and get the bus back the other.

Kilmartin Glen

This magical glen is the focus of one of the biggest concentrations of prehistoric sites in Scotland. Burial cairns, standing stones, stone circles, hill forts and cup-and-ring-marked rocks litter the countryside. Within

<table>
<tr><td>

RETURN OF THE BEAVER

Beavers had been extinct in Britain since the 16th century. But in 2009 they returned to Scotland, when a population of Norwegian beavers was released into the hill lochs of Knapdale, Argyll. After a broadly successful trial, the beavers are now here to stay; the first successful reintroduction of a previously extinct mammal to Britain.

If the beavers are still present, you can try to get a glimpse of them on the Beaver Detective Trail. This circular walk starts from the Barnluasgan forestry car park on the B8025 road to Tayvallich, about 1.5 miles south of the Crinan Canal. There's an information hut here. The trail is 3 miles, but you might glimpse them at pretty Dubh Loch just half a mile down the track.

Near here, the Heart of Argyll Wildlife Organisation (📞01546-810218; www.heartofargyllwildlife.org; Barnluasgan; ⊘10am-5pm Apr-Oct) has a visitor centre and runs guided wildlife walks, including beaver-oriented ones.
</td></tr>
</table>

a 6-mile radius of Kilmartin village there are 25 sites with standing stones and more than 100 rock carvings.

In the 6th century, Irish settlers arrived in this part of Argyll and founded the kingdom of Dál Riata (Dalriada), which eventually united with the Picts in 843 to create the first Scottish kingdom. Their capital was the hill fort of Dunadd, on the plain to the south of Kilmartin.

Kilmartin House Museum   MUSEUM
(📞01546-510278; www.kilmartin.org; adult/child £6.50/2.50; ⊘10am-5.30pm Mar-Oct, 11am-4pm Nov-late Dec) This museum, in Kilmartin village, is a fascinating interpretive centre that provides a context for the ancient monuments you can go on to explore, alongside displays of artefacts recovered from various sites. Funding has nearly been achieved for a major redevelopment of the museum, so check the website for the latest details before visiting. It also has a cafe (mains £5-9; 🔊🌿) 🍴 and a good shop with handicrafts and books on Scotland.

Dunadd Fort   ARCHAEOLOGICAL SITE
(⊘24hr) FREE This hill fort, 3.5 miles south of Kilmartin village, was the seat of power of the first kings of Dál Riata, and may have been where the Stone of Destiny was originally located. Faint rock carvings of a boar and two footprints with an ogham inscription may have been used in inauguration ceremonies. The prominent little hill rises straight out of the boggy plain of Moine Mhor Nature Reserve.

A slippery path leads to the summit, where you can gaze out on much the same view that the kings of Dál Riata enjoyed 1300 years ago.

❶ Getting There & Away

Bus 423 between Oban and Ardrishaig (three to five Monday to Friday, two on Saturday) stops at Kilmartin (from Oban £5.60, one hour).

You can walk or cycle along the Crinan Canal from Ardrishaig, then turn north at Bellanoch on the minor B8025 road to reach Kilmartin (12 miles one way). It's a lovely journey.

Kintyre

The 40-mile long Kintyre peninsula is almost an island, with only a narrow isthmus at Tarbert connecting it to Knapdale. During the Norse occupation of the Western Isles, the Scottish king decreed that the Vikings could claim as their own any island they circumnavigated in a longship. So in 1098 the wily Magnus Barefoot stood at the helm while his men dragged their boat across this neck of land, validating his claim to Kintyre.

The coastline is spectacular on both sides, with stirring views of Arran, Islay, Jura and Northern Ireland. On a sunny day the water shimmers beyond the stony shore. Hiking the Kintyre Way is a great means of experiencing the peninsula, which has a couple of cracking golf courses at Machrihanish near Campbeltown.

Tarbert

POP 1100

The attractive fishing village and yachting centre of Tarbert is the gateway to Kintyre, and is most scenic, with buildings strung around its excellent natural harbour. A crossroads for nearby ferry routes, it's a handy stepping stone to Arran or Islay, but is well worth a stopover on any itinerary.

The picturesque harbour is overlooked by the crumbling, ivy-covered ruins of **Tarbert Castle** (⊙24hr) **FREE**, rebuilt by Robert the Bruce in the 14th century. You can hike up via a signposted footpath beside **Loch Fyne Gallery** (☑01880-820390; www.lochfynegallery. com; Harbour St; ⊙10am-5pm Mon-Sat, 10.30am-5pm Sun), which showcases the work of local artists.

🎎 Festivals & Events

Tarbert Seafood Festival　　　FOOD & DRINK
(www.tarbertfestivals.co.uk; ⊙1st weekend Jul) Food stalls, cooking demonstrations, music and family entertainment.

Tarbert Music Festival　　　　　　　MUSIC
(www.tarbertfestivals.co.uk; ⊙3rd weekend Sep) A festival of live folk, blues, jazz, rock, beer, *ceilidhs* (evenings of traditional Scottish entertainment), more beer...

🛏 Sleeping & Eating

Starfish Rooms　　　　　　　　　　B&B £
(☑01880-820304; www.starfishtarbert.com; Castle St; s/d without breakfast £35/70; 🛜) Above the restaurant of the same name, but run separately, this corridor of compact, floorboarded en suite rooms is a good deal, particularly for single travellers. Rooms 6 and 7 are doubles with attractive exposed stone walls. Breakfast isn't included, but there are cafes very close at hand.

OFF THE BEATEN TRACK

WALK KINTYRE

Tarbert is the starting point for the 103-mile **Kintyre Way** (www.kintyreway.com), a walking route that meanders the length of the peninsula to Southend at the southern tip and around to Machrihanish. It's very scenic, with wonderful coastal views nearly the whole way.

★**Knap Guest House**　　　　　　　　B&B ££
(☑01880-820015; www.knapguesthouse.co.uk; Campbeltown Rd; d £90-99; 🛜) This cosy upstairs spot at the bend in the main road offers faultless hospitality, luxurious furnishings and an attractive blend of Scottish and Far Eastern decor, with wooden elephants especially prominent. The welcome is warm, and there are great harbour views from the breakfast room, where the open kitchen allows you to admire the host at work. Prices drop in low season.

Rooms are plush, with the owner's years in hospitality paying dividends for guests. One is a suite (£135 to £180), which has an excellent, spacious lounge area with vistas.

Moorings　　　　　　　　　　　　　B&B ££
(☑01880-820756; www.themooringsbb.co.uk; Pier Rd; s £50-60, d £80; 🅿🛜) Follow the harbour just past Tarbert's centre to this spot, which is beautifully maintained and decorated by one man and his dogs. It has great views over the water and an eclectic menagerie of ceramic and wooden animals and offbeat artwork; you can't miss it from the street.

★**Starfish**　　　　　　　　　　　SEAFOOD ££
(☑01880-820733; www.starfishtarbert.com; Castle St; mains £12-23; ⊙6-9pm Sun-Thu, noon-2pm & 6-9pm Fri & Sat mid-Mar–Oct; 🛜) ✏ This attractive, very welcoming restaurant does simple, stylish seafood of brilliant quality. A great variety of specials – anything from classic French fish dishes to Thai curries – are prepared with whatever's fresh off the Tarbert boats that day. There are options for vegetarians and meat-eaters too, and decent cocktails. Closed Sunday and Monday early and late in the season.

ⓘ Getting There & Away

BOAT

CalMac (www.calmac.co.uk) operates a car ferry from Tarbert to Portavadie on the Cowal

SOUTHERN HIGHLANDS & ISLANDS KINTYRE

Peninsula (adult/car £2.70/8.40, 25 minutes, six to 12 daily). From late October to March there are also ferries to Lochranza on Arran (adult/car £2.90/9.70, 1¼ hours, one daily) that must be booked in advance.

Ferries to Islay and Colonsay depart from Kennacraig ferry terminal, 5 miles southwest.

BUS

Tarbert is served by four to five daily coaches with **Scottish Citylink** (www.citylink.co.uk), between Campbeltown (£8.40, one hour) and Glasgow (£17.70, 3¼ hours).

Gigha

POP 200

Gigha (*ghee*-ah; www.gigha.org.uk) is a low-lying island, 6 miles long by about 1 mile wide, famous for its sandy beaches, pristine turquoise water and mild climate – subtropical plants thrive in **Achamore Gardens** (✆ 01583-505275; www.gigha.org.uk; Achamore House; suggested donation adult/child £6/3; ⊙ dawn-dusk). Other highlights include the ruined **church** at Kilchattan, the **bible garden** at the manse, and Gigha's picturesque northern end.

The island was famously purchased by its residents in 2002, though they have had some financial problems since. Local **Gigha cheeses** include goats cheese and oak-smoked cheddar.

Gigha Hotel INN ££
(✆ 01583-505254; www.gighahotel.com; Ardminish; s £65, d £92-98; [P][♚][♟][♨]) The island's quirky hotel, just south of the central junction, has a variety of cosy rooms, some

with views. It also serves breakfasts, bar meals and restaurant dishes (mains £10 to £16).

★ **The Boathouse** SEAFOOD ££
(✆ 01583-505123; www.boathouseongigha.com; Ardminish; mains £10-20; ⊙ 11.30am-9pm mid-Mar-Oct; ♚) This picturesque stone cottage is right by the water near the ferry slip. It's *the* place to go for fresh seafood: local lobster, delicious oysters and sustainable, organic Gigha-farmed halibut are the highlights. Sit at the deck outside and admire the idyllic view. You can also camp here (£4/2 per adult/child), but space is limited so call in advance.

❶ Getting There & Away

CalMac (www.calmac.co.uk) runs from Tayinloan in Kintyre (adult/car £2.60/7.60, 20 minutes, roughly hourly). Stopping at the terminal are four to five daily buses with **Scottish Citylink** (www.citylink.co.uk), in each direction between Glasgow/Tarbert and Campbeltown

Campbeltown & Around

POP 4800

Blue-collar Campbeltown is set around a beautiful harbour. It still suffers from the decline of its fishing and whisky industries and the closure of the nearby air-force base, but is rebounding on the back of golf tourism, increased distillery action and a ferry link to Ayrshire. The spruced-up seafront backed by green hills lends the town a distinctly optimistic air.

OFF THE BEATEN TRACK

SKIPNESS

Tiny Skipness, 13 miles south of Tarbert, is pleasant and quiet with great views of Arran. Beyond the village rise the substantial remains of 13th-century **Skipness Castle** (www.historicenvironment.scot; ⊙ castle & chapel 24hr, tower 9.30am-5.30pm Apr-Sep, 10am-4pm Oct) FREE, a former possession of the Lords of the Isles.

Attached to Skipness House, near the castle, **Skipness Seafood Cabin** (✆ 01880-760207; www.skipnessseafoodcabin.co.uk; dishes £3-18; ⊙ 11am-7pm Sun-Fri late May-Sep) has a great summer scene on a fine day, serving no-frills but delicious local fish and shellfish dishes at outdoor picnic tables that have grand views over the grassy coast across to Arran. It's famous for its crab rolls, which are on the small side: add on a pot of mussels or plate of gravadlax.

The hot smoked salmon from **Skipness Smokehouse** (✆ 01880-760378; www.creelers.co.uk; ⊙ noon-5pm Sun-Fri Mar-Dec) behind Skipness Castle was one of the highlights of a long-standing seafood restaurant on Arran. That's closed, but you can get hold of it at their new smokehouse here, along with other treats. There's usually somebody around even outside the official opening hours.

Sights & Activities

Springbank   DISTILLERY
(☑01586-551710; www.springbankwhisky.com; 85 Longrow; tours from £7; ⊙tours 10am, 11.30am, 1.30pm & 3pm Mon-Fri, 10am & 11.30am Sat) There were once no fewer than 32 distilleries around Campbeltown, but most closed in the 1920s. Today this is one of only three still in operation. It is also one of the few around that distills, matures and bottles all its whisky on the one site, making for an interesting tour. It produces a quality malt, one of Scotland's finest. Various premium tours take you deeper into the process.

Davaar Cave   CAVE
(⊙24hr) FREE A very unusual sight awaits in this cave on the southern side of Davaar island, at the mouth of Campbeltown Loch. On the wall of the cave is an eerie painting of the Crucifixion by local artist Archibald MacKinnon, dating from 1887. You can walk to the island at low tide: check tide times with the tourist office.

Sleeping & Eating

★**Campbeltown Backpackers**   HOSTEL £
(☑01586-551188; www.campbeltownbackpackers. co.uk; Big Kiln St; dm £20; P🐾) 🐾 This beautiful hostel occupies a central former school building: it's great, with a modern kitchen, state-of-the-art wooden bunks and access for people with disabilities. Profits go to maintain the Heritage Centre (opposite) that runs it. Rates are £2 cheaper if you book ahead.

Argyll Hotel   INN ££
(☑01583-421212; www.argylehotelkintyre.co.uk; A83, Bellochantuy; s £45, d £80-90; P🐾🍽) Right on a fine stretch of beach with a magnificent outlook to Islay and Jura, this traditional inn 10 miles north of Campbeltown on the main road is run with cheery panache. Rooms are cosy and breakfast is a highlight, with creative egg dishes and a wealth of homemade jams, as you gaze over the water. The restaurant does some inventive fusion fare.

The water reaches the heady heights (for Scotland) of 11°C in summer if you fancy a dip. Don't confuse this place with the Argyll Arms Hotel in Campbeltown itself.

Royal Hotel   HOTEL £££
(☑01586-810000; www.machrihanishdunes.com; Main St; r £185-215; P🐾) Historically Campbeltown's best address, this reddish sandstone hotel opposite the harbour is looking swish again. It caters mostly to yachties and

> **WORTH A TRIP**

MULL OF KINTYRE

A narrow winding road, 15 miles long, leads south from Campbeltown to the **Mull of Kintyre**, passing good sandy beaches near Southend. This remote headland was immortalised in the famous song by Paul McCartney and Wings; the former Beatle owns a farmhouse in the area. From the road's end, a 30-minute steep downhill walk leads to a clifftop lighthouse, with Northern Ireland, only 12 miles away, visible across the channel. Don't leave the road when the frequent mists roll in; it's easy to become disoriented.

golfers. Although rack rates feel overpriced, there are often online specials and rooms are very spacious and attractive. There are some excellent midweek specials that include golf at Machrihanish Dunes and a couple of extras.

Food is served noon to 9pm Sunday to Thursday, and to 10pm Friday and Saturday.

Drinking & Nightlife

Ardshiel Hotel   BAR
(☑01586-552133; www.ardshiel.co.uk; Kilkerran Rd; ⊙noon-11pm Mon-Sat, from 12.30pm Sun; 🛜) This friendly hotel has one of Scotland's best whisky bars, the perfect place to learn more about the Campbeltown distilling tradition and to taste the local malts. With over 700 whiskies to choose from, it's not a place for the indecisive.

Getting There & Away

AIR

Loganair (www.loganair.co.uk) flies between Glasgow and Campbeltown's mighty runway at Machrihanish.

BOAT

Kintyre Express (☑01586-555895; www. kintyreexpress.com; ⊙Apr-Sep) operates a small, high-speed passenger ferry from Campbeltown to Ballycastle in Northern Ireland (£50/90 one way/return, 1½ hours, daily May to August, Friday to Sunday April and September). You must book in advance. From Ballycastle it heads on to Islay (£60/95 one way/return from Ballycastle) and back before the return trip to Campbeltown. It also runs charters.

CalMac (www.calmac.co.uk) runs thrice weekly May to September between Ardrossan in Ayrshire and Campbeltown (adult/car £7.90/41.70, 2¾ hours); the Saturday return service stops at Brodick on Arran.

BUS

Scottish Citylink (www.citylink.co.uk) runs from Campbeltown to Glasgow (£21.60, 4¼ hours, four to five daily) via Tarbert, Inveraray and Loch Lomond. Change at Inveraray for Oban.

Islay
POP 3200

The home of some of the world's greatest and peatiest whiskies, whose names reverberate on the tongue like a pantheon of Celtic deities, Islay (*eye*-lah) is a wonderfully friendly place whose welcoming inhabitants offset its lack of scenic splendour compared to Mull or Skye. The distilleries are well geared-up for visits, but even if you're not a fan of single malt, the birdlife, fine seafood, turquoise bays and basking seals are ample reasons to visit. Locals are among Britain's most genial: a wave or cheerio to passersby is mandatory, and you'll soon find yourself unwinding to relaxing island pace. The only drawback is that the waves of well-heeled whisky tourists have induced many sleeping options to raise prices to eye-watering levels.

Tours

Islay Sea Safaris   BOATING
(☑01496-840510; www.islayseasafari.co.uk; Port Ellen) Customised tours (£25 to £30 per person per hour) by sea from Port Ellen to spot some or all of Islay and Jura's distilleries in a single day, as well as birdwatching trips, coastal exploration, and trips to Jura's remote west coast and the Corryvreckan Whirlpool.

✱ Festivals & Events

Fèis Ìle   MUSIC, FOOD & DRINK
(Islay Festival; www.islayfestival.com; ☉ late May) A weeklong celebration of traditional Scottish music and whisky. Events include *ceilidhs* (evenings of traditional Scottish entertainment), pipe-band performances, distillery tours, barbecues and whisky tastings. The island packs out; book accommodation well in advance.

Islay Jazz Festival   MUSIC
(www.islayjazzfestival.co.uk; ☉ 2nd weekend Sep) This three-day festival features a varied line-up of international talent playing at various venues across the island.

ℹ Information

Bowmore Tourist Office (☑ 01496-305165; www.islayinfo.com; The Square; ☉10am-5pm Mon-Sat, noon-3pm Sun Mar-Jun, 9.30am-5.30pm Mon-Sat, noon-3pm Sun Jul & Aug, 10am-5pm Mon-Sat Sep-Oct, 10am-3pm Mon-Fri Nov-Feb) One of the nation's best tourist offices. The staff will bend over backwards to find you accommodation if things look full up.

ℹ Getting There & Away

There are two ferry terminals: Port Askaig on the east coast, and Port Ellen in the south. Islay airport lies midway between Port Ellen and Bowmore.

AIR

Loganair (www.loganair.co.uk) flies up to three times daily from Glasgow to Islay, while **Hebridean Air Services** (☑ 0845 805 7465; www.hebrideanair.co.uk; Oban Airport, North Connel) operates twice daily on Tuesday and Thursday from Oban to Colonsay and Islay.

BOAT

CalMac (www.calmac.co.uk) runs ferries from Kennacraig to Port Ellen or Port Askaig (adult/

GOLF AT MACHRIHANISH

Machrihanish, 5 miles northwest of Campbeltown, is home to a couple of classic golf courses:

Machrihanish Golf Club (☑01586-810277; www.machgolf.com; Machrihanish; green fee £75) Machrihanish Golf Club is a classic links course, designed by Old Tom Morris. It's remarkably good value compared to courses of a similar standard elsewhere in Scotland. The famous first hole requires a very decent drive across the bay, or you'll literally end up on the beach. Nearby is an upmarket hotel and restaurant, as well as self-catering villas.

Machrihanish Dunes (☑01586-810000; www.machrihanishdunes.com; Machrihanish; green fee £75) Much newer than its venerable neighbour Machrihanish Golf Club, the Dunes is an impressive seaside experience and commendably light on snobbery: the clubhouse is a convivial little hut, kids play free and there are always website offers. Good packages including accommodation are available.

car £6.70/33.45, two hours, three to five daily). On Wednesday and Saturday in summer you can travel to Colonsay (adult/car £4.15/17.30, 1¼ hours, day trip possible) and Oban (adult/car £9.60/51.45, four hours).

Book car space on ferries several days in advance.

❶ Getting Around

BICYCLE

There are various places to hire bikes, including **Islay Cycles** (📞07760 196592; www.islaycycles. co.uk; 2 Corrsgeir Pl, Port Ellen; bikes per day/ week from £20/70) and **Port Charlotte Bicycle Hire** (📞01496-850488; Main St, Port Charlotte; 1/3 days £15/35; ⏰9am-6pm).

BUS

A bus links Ardbeg, Port Ellen, Bowmore, Port Charlotte, Portnahaven and Port Askaig (Monday to Saturday only). You can get unlimited travel for 24 hours for £10, but fares are low anyway. Pick up a copy of the *Islay & Jura Public Transport Guide* from the Bowmore Tourist Office or on the ferry on the way over.

CAR

Islay Car Hire (📞01496-810544; www.islay carhire.com; Islay Airport) offers car hire from £35 a day and can meet ferries.

TAXI

There are various taxi services on Islay; **Carol's Cabs** (📞07775 782155, 01496-302155; www. carols-cabs.co.uk) is one that can take bikes.

Port Ellen & Around

Port Ellen is Islay's principal entry point. The coast stretching northeast is one of the loveliest parts of the island, where within 3 miles you'll find three of whisky's biggest names: Laphroaig, Lagavulin and Ardbeg.

The kelp-fringed skerries (small rocky islands or reefs) of the **Ardmore Islands**, near Kildalton, are a wildlife haven and home to Europe's second-largest colony of common seals.

◉ Sights

The three southern distilleries of Laphroaig, Lagavulin and Ardbeg are arrayed in an easy succession east of town. The Port Ellen distillery itself, dismantled apart from its malting works in 1983, is due to reopen by 2021.

Ardbeg   DISTILLERY
(📞01496-302244; www.ardbeg.com; tours from £6; ⏰9.30am-5pm Mon-Fri year-round, plus Sat & Sun Apr-Oct) Ardbeg's iconic peaty whiskies

GONE FISHIN'
A lifetime's experience of exploring his native rivers, lochs and coastline means there isn't much that professional guide Duncan Pepper of **Fishinguide Scotland** (📞07714-598848; www.fishinguide.co.uk; daily per person from £150; 🚣) doesn't know about Scottish fishing. Though based in Argyll, he leads fishing trips all over Scotland for salmon, trout, pike, pollack and more. Packages include travel, instruction, permits, tackle and a lavish picnic lunch.

start with their magnificent 10-year-old. The basic tour is good, and it also offers longer tours involving walks, stories and extended tastings. It's 3 miles northeast of Port Ellen; there's a good cafe (p264) for lunch here, too.

Lagavulin   DISTILLERY
(📞01496-302749; www.lagavulindistillery.com; tours from £6; ⏰9am-6pm Mon-Fri, to 5pm Sat & Sun May-Sep, 9am-5pm daily Apr & Oct, 10am-4pm Mon-Sat Nov-Mar) Peaty and powerful, this is one of the triumvirate of southern distilleries near Port Ellen. The Core Range tour (£15) is a good option, cutting out much of the distillery mechanics that you might have already experienced elsewhere and replacing it with an extended tasting.

Laphroaig   DISTILLERY
(📞01496-302418; www.laphroaig.com; tours from £10; ⏰9.45am-5pm daily Mar-Oct, to 4.30pm daily Nov & Dec, to 4.30pm Mon-Fri Jan & Feb) Laphroaig produces famously peaty whiskies just outside Port Ellen. Of the various premium tastings that it offers, the 'Water to Whisky' tour (£100) is recommended – you see the water source, dig peat, have a picnic and try plenty of drams.

Kildalton Cross   MONUMENT
(Kildalton; ⏰24hr) FREE A pleasant drive or ride leads past the distilleries to ruined **Kildalton Chapel**, 8 miles from Port Ellen. In the kirkyard is the exceptional late 8th-century Kildalton Cross. There are carvings of biblical scenes on one side and animals on the other.

🛏 Sleeping & Eating

Kintra Farm   CAMPSITE, B&B £
(📞01496-302051; www.kintrafarm.co.uk; tent site £6-8, plus adult/child £4/2; ⏰May-Sep; 🅿🐾) At the southern end of Laggan Bay, 3.5 miles northwest of Port Ellen, Kintra is a basic but

Islay, Jura & Colonsay

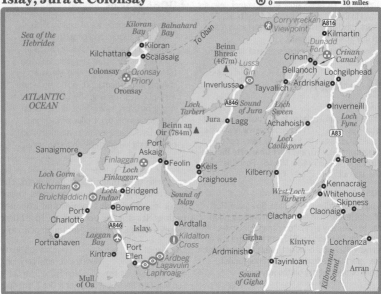

beautiful campsite on buttercup-sprinkled turf amid the dunes, with sunset views across the beach. There's also B&B and self-catering cottages at this working farm.

Askernish B&B B&B ££
(☏01496-302536; www.askernishbandb.co.uk; 49 Frederick Cres, Port Ellen; s £50, d £90-100; ☏) Very handy for the Port Ellen ferry slip, this dark-stone Victorian house was once the local medical practice; indeed, one of the rooms is in the former surgery, while another is the waiting room. Rooms are generous, with old-style flowery decor but modern bathroom fittings. The owner takes real interest in her guests and is a delight.

Old Kiln Café CAFE £
(☏01496-302244; www.ardbeg.com; Ardbeg; mains £8-13; ☉10am-3.45pm Mon-Fri year-round, plus Sat & Sun Apr-Oct; ☏) Housed in the former malting kiln at Ardbeg distillery, this cafe serves homemade soups, tasty light meals, heartier daily specials and a range of desserts, including traditional clootie dumpling (a rich steamed pudding filled with currants and raisins).

SeaSalt BISTRO, PIZZA ££
(☏01496-300300; www.seasalt-bistro.co.uk; 57 Frederick Cres, Port Ellen; mains £10-16; ☉noon-2.30pm & 5-8.45pm) This buzzy modern place

represents an unusual combination in Port Ellen: a takeaway doing kebabs, pizzas and bacon rolls, but also a bistro. High-backed dining chairs are comfortable for devouring local seafood off a menu of daily specials. The prawn and crayfish cocktail is a great place to start. It also opens from 10am to noon for coffee and breakfasty fare.

Bowmore

POP 700

Islay's attractive Georgian capital was built in 1768 to replace the village of Kilarrow, which just had to go – it was spoiling the view from the laird's house. Its centrepieces are the **Bowmore Distillery** (☏01496-810441; www.bowmore. com; School St; tours from £10; ☉9.30am-5pm Mon-Sat, noon-4pm Sun Mar-Oct, 10am-5pm Mon-Sat Nov-Feb) and distinctive **Round Church** at the top of Main St, built in circular form to ensure that the devil had no corners to hide in. He was last seen in one of the island's distilleries.

⌂ Sleeping

★**Lambeth House** B&B ££
(☏01496-810597; lambethguesthouse@tiscali.co.uk; Jamieson St; s/d £70/98; ☏) Cheerily welcoming, and with smart modern rooms with top-notch en suite bathrooms, this is a sound option in

the centre of town. The host is a long-time expert in making guests feel at home, and her breakfasts are reliably good. Rooms vary substantially in size but their prices are the same, so ask for a larger one when booking.

Dha Urlar B&B ££

(📞07967505991;www.dha-urlar-bed-and-breakfast. co.uk; Cruach; r £125-150; 🅿🤶) Just a mile out of Bowmore, this place sits in an elevated position granting spectacular perspectives across moorland to Jura, the Mull of Kintyre and the coast of Ireland. Rooms have lots of space, comfortable beds and modern bathrooms. Breakfast is served from an open kitchen while your hosts helpfully supply you with lots of local information.

Island Bear B&B ££

(📞 01496-301462; www.islandbear.co.uk; Shore St; s/d £75/100; 🤶) As central as you can be in Bowmore, this house is compact and built very vertically, though some ground-floor accommodation is on the way. Rooms are cosy and inviting, with modern decor and stylish en suite bathrooms. There are views from two of the rooms, a kindly welcome and tasty breakfasts.

Bowmore House B&B £££

(📞 01496-810324; www.thebowmorehouse.co.uk; Shore St; s/d from £85/135; 🅿🤶) This stately former bank building has plenty of character and super water views. It's a top-level B&B, with coffee machines in the rooms, an honesty minibar with bottles of wine and local ales, and plush king-sized beds. Rooms are spacious, high-ceilinged and light. Further rooms are in adjacent cottages, also available on a self-catering basis.

✖ Eating

Peatzeria ITALIAN ££

(📞01496-810810; www.peatzeria.com; 22 Shore St; mains £11-18; ⊙noon-10pm, closed Mon in winter; 🤶) This is one of those names that just had to be...nice work, punsters! An impressively realised church conversion has created a warmly welcoming Italian restaurant that specialises in toothsome stone-baked pizzas but also does a great line in antipasti, lasagne and other pasta dishes. The weatherproof conservatory seating area has special views over the bay.

Harbour Inn BRITISH ££

(📞01496-810330; www.bowmore.com; The Square; mains £15-20; ⊙ noon-2.30pm & 6-9.30pm; 🤶) Owned by the Bowmore Distillery, this restaurant at the **Harbour Inn** (s/d from £115/145) is

the classiest in town. The conservatory-style dining area offers wonderful sunset views over the water. Islay oysters are a delicious and obvious choice; the rest of the menu could benefit from a little more seasonal and local focus, but is competently prepared and presented.

It's also open in the morning for pretty good breakfasts and all afternoon for sandwiches and light meals.

Port Charlotte & Around

Eleven miles from Bowmore, on the opposite shore of Loch Indaal, is attractive Port Charlotte, a former distillery town that appeals as a base. Museums in town and distilleries close by mean there's plenty to do.

Six miles southwest of Port Charlotte the road ends at **Portnahaven**, a picturesque fishing village. For seal-spotting, you can't do better; there are frequently dozens of the portly beasts basking in the small harbour.

◉ Sights

★**Bruichladdich** DISTILLERY

(📞01496-850190; www.bruichladdich.com; Bruichladdich; tours from £5; ⊙9am-6pm Mon-Fri, to 5pm Sat, 10am-4pm Sun Apr-Sep, reduced hours Oct-Mar) A couple of miles from Port Charlotte, Bruichladdich (brook-*lad*-dy) is an infectiously fun distillery to visit and produces a mind-boggling range of bottlings; there's always some new experiment cooking. The standard expression is lightly peated, but they turn out some phenolic monsters under the Port Charlotte and Octomore labels. They also make a gin here, the Botanist, infused with local herbs. A generous attitude to tastings makes for an uplifting visit.

Kilchoman DISTILLERY

(📞 01496-850011; www.kilchomandistillery.com; Rockfield Farm, Kilchoman; tours from £7; ⊙ 9.45am-5pm Apr-Oct, closed Sat & Sun Nov-Mar) 🍸 Likeable Kilchoman, set on a farm, is one of Scotland's smallest distilleries. It grows and malts some of its own barley here and does its own bottling by hand. It has a wide variety of attractively packaged expressions: the 100% Islay whiskies are the ones produced from the home-grown barley. The tour is informative and the tasting generous. There's also a good cafe.

Museum of Islay Life MUSEUM

(📞01496-850358; www.islaymuseum.org; Port Charlotte; adult/child £4/1; ⊙10.30am-4.30pm Mon-Fri

DON'T MISS

ISLAY'S DISTILLERIES

Islay has nine working distilleries, with a tenth, the back-from-the-dead Port Ellen, on the way. All welcome visitors and run tours, which you should definitely book ahead by phone, as they have maximum numbers and can fill up days in advance. More expensive, specialised tours let you taste more malts and take you further behind the scenes. Pick up the invaluable pamphlet listing tour times from the Bowmore Tourist Office (p262). Five of the nine distilleries can be reached by the island's buses; a bit of walking, hitching or cabbing will easily get you to the others.

Apr-Oct) Islay's long history is lovingly recorded in this museum, housed in the former Free Church. Prize exhibits include an illicit still, 19th-century crofters' furniture, and a set of leather boots once worn by the horse that pulled the lawnmower at Islay House (so it wouldn't leave hoof prints on the lawn!).

🛌 Sleeping & Eating

Islay SYHA HOSTEL £
(📞01496-850385; www.syha.org.uk; Main St, Port Charlotte; dm/tw/q £20/48/90; ⊙Apr-Oct; @🛜) This clean and modern brick hostel has spotless dorms with washbasins and a large kitchen and living room. It's housed in a former distillery building with views over the loch. The bus stops nearby. Breakfast and heatable dinners are available. Have a crack at Islay Monopoly, one of the board games on hand.

Distillery House B&B £££
(📞01496-850495; mamak@sky.com; Main St, Port Charlotte; s £38, d £80, tw without bathroom £76; P🛜) For genuine islander hospitality at a fair price, head to this homely B&B, on the right as you enter Port Charlotte from the north. Set in part of the former Lochindaal distillery, it's run by a kindly local couple who make their own delicious marmalade and oatcakes. Rooms are well kept and most comfortable. The cute single has sea views. Minimum two-night stay.

Port Charlotte Hotel HOTEL £££
(📞01496-850360; www.portcharlottehotel.co.uk; Main St, Port Charlotte; s/d/f £175/240/290; P🛜🐾) This lovely old Victorian hotel has individually decorated bedrooms – modern but classic in style – with crisp white sheets, good toiletries and sea views. It's a friendly place with a plush lounge, cosy bar and quality restaurant.

Yan's Kitchen BISTRO ££
(📞01496-850230; www.yanskitchen.co.uk; Main St, Port Charlotte; tapas £4-7, mains £13-22; ⊙food noon-3pm & 5.30-9pm Tue-Sun Apr-Oct; 🐾) On the left as you enter Port Charlotte from the north, this cabin-like restaurant offers confident bistro cuisine, using ingredients like duck breast and local scallops to create satisfying, well-presented plates, whether Spanish tapas or evening seafood specials. The appealing wooden-floored interior takes full advantage of the coastal views. It's also open from 10.30am to noon for coffee and scones.

Port Askaig & Around

Port Askaig is set in a picturesque nook halfway along the Sound of Islay. It's little more than a hotel, shop (with ATM), petrol pump and ferry pier. There are three distilleries within reach and ferry connections to the mainland and Jura, just across the strait.

Three miles southwest, lush meadows swathed in buttercups and daisies slope down to reed-fringed **Loch Finlaggan**. This bucolic setting was once the most important settlement in the Hebrides, the central seat of power of the Lords of the Isles from the 12th to the 16th centuries.

★ Finlaggan RUINS
(📞01496-840644; www.finlaggan.org; adult/child £4/2; ⊙ruins 24hr, museum 10.30am-4.15pm Mon-Sat Apr-Oct) Three miles from Port Askaig, tumbledown ruins of houses and a chapel on an islet in a shallow loch mark what remains of the stronghold of the Lords of the Isles. A wooden walkway leads over the reeds and water lilies to the island, where information boards describe the remains. Start your exploration at the visitor centre, which has some good explanations of the site's history and archaeology and a video featuring Tony Robinson. The island itself is open at all times.

The setting is beautiful and the history fascinating. The MacDonald clan, descendants of the legendary warrior Somerled, administered their island territories from here from the 12th to the 15th centuries and entertained visiting chieftains in their great hall. A smaller island, Eilean na Comhairle, was reserved for solemn councils. Though this unassuming inland loch seems a strange place from which to wield serious political power, it had likely been an important place since prehistoric times. A crannog, fort and early Christian chapel were all located here, and the presence of ritual stones possibly aligned to the brooding Paps of Jura means the MacDonalds may have appropriated a place that already had strong ritual significance.

Buses between Bowmore and Port Askaig stop at the road junction, from where it's a 15-minute walk to the loch.

Ballygrant Inn
PUB

(☏ 01496-840277; www.ballygrant-inn.co.uk; Ballygrant; ⏱ 11am-1am Mon-Sat, 12.30pm-midnight Sun; 🛜) If you're serious about whisky, you'll want to stop by this attractive bar to try one of its 700-plus malts. Though customer service can vary, the owners have a deep knowledge of local whisky and can guide your selection. There are also quality ales on tap and good food here, with outdoor tables to admire the view.

Jura
POP 200

Jura lies long, dark and low off the coast like a vast Viking longship, its billowing sail the distinctive triple peaks of the Paps of Jura. A magnificently wild and lonely island, it's the perfect place to get away from it all –

as George Orwell did in 1948. Orwell wrote his masterpiece *Nineteen Eighty-Four* while living at the remote farmhouse of Barnhill in the north of the island.

Jura takes its name from the Old Norse *dyr-a* (deer island) – an apt appellation, as the island supports a population of around 6000 red deer, outnumbering their human cohabitants by about 30 to one.

There's a shop but no ATM on Jura; you can get cash back with debit cards at the Jura Hotel.

◎ Sights

Isle of Jura Distillery
DISTILLERY

(☏ 01496-820385; www.jurawhisky.com; Craighouse; tours from £6; ⏱ 10am-4.30pm Apr-Oct, to 4pm Mon-Fri Nov-Mar) There aren't a whole lot of indoor attractions on the island of Jura apart from visiting the Isle of Jura Distillery. The standard tour runs twice a day, while specialist tours (£15 to £25) take you deeper into the production process and should be booked in advance.

Lussa Gin
DISTILLERY

(☏ 01496-820323; www.lussagin.com; Ardlussa) At the northern end of Jura island, three local women have set up this distillery in the former stables of the Ardlussa estate. It produces gin that's flavoured with local botanicals. Phone ahead to book a tour (£6), which includes a taste of the refreshing lemony spirit.

THE SCOTTISH MAELSTROM

The Gulf of Corryvreckan – the channel (0.6 miles wide) between the northern end of Jura and the island of Scarba – is home to one of the most notorious tidal whirlpools in the world.

On Scotland's west coast, the rising tide – the flood tide – flows northwards. As it moves up the Sound of Jura, to the east of the island, it is forced into a narrowing bottleneck jammed with islands and builds up to a greater height than the open sea to the west of Jura. As a result, millions of tonnes of sea water pour westwards through the Gulf of Corryvreckan at speeds of up to 8 knots – an average sailing yacht is going fast at 6 knots.

The **Corryvreckan Whirlpool** forms where this mass of moving water hits an underwater pinnacle, which rises from the 200m-deep sea bed to within just 28m of the surface, and swirls over and around it. The turbulent waters create a magnificent spectacle, with white-capped breakers, standing waves, bulging boils and overfalls, and countless miniature maelstroms whirling around the main vortex.

Corryvreckan is at its most violent when a flooding spring tide, flowing west through the gulf, meets a westerly gale blowing in from the Atlantic. In these conditions, standing waves up to 5m high can form and dangerously rough seas extend more than 3 miles west of Corryvreckan, a phenomenon known as the Great Race.

You can see the whirlpool by making the long hike to the northern end of Jura (p268), or by taking a boat trip from Islay, Ardfern or the Isle of Seil.

For tide times, see www.whirlpool-scotland.co.uk.

🏃 Activities

There are few proper footpaths, and off-path exploration often involves rough going through giant bracken, knee-deep bogs and thigh-high tussocks. Hill access may be restricted during the deer-stalking season (July to February); the Jura Hotel can provide details. Look out for adders – the island is infested with them, but they're shy snakes and will move away as you approach.

Corryvreckan Viewpoint   HIKING
A good Jura walk is to a viewpoint for the Corryvreckan Whirlpool. From the northern end of the public road (a 16-mile return trip from here) hike past Barnhill to Kinuachdrachd Farm (6 miles). Just before the farm a footpath forks left and climbs before traversing rough and boggy ground, a natural grandstand for viewing the turbulent waters of the **Gulf of Corryvreckan**.

If you've timed it right (check tide times at the Jura Hotel) you will see the whirlpool as a writhing mass of white water.

Jura Island Tours   BUS
(📞 01496-820314;   www.juraislandtours.co.uk; short/long tours from Craighouse £15/25, from Feolin £25/35) Alex runs informative tours of the island in a modern minibus. Minimum numbers apply, but call regardless as he can put groups together.

🛏 Sleeping & Eating

Places to stay are very limited, so book ahead. As well as the Jura Hotel, there's a handful of B&Bs and several self-catering cottages let by the week (see www.juradevelopment.co.uk). One of these is remote Barnhill, where Orwell stayed.

You can camp (£5 per person) in the field below the Jura Hotel; there's a toilet and shower block that walkers, yachties and cyclists can also use. From July to February check on the deer-stalking situation before wild camping.

The Jura Hotel, a cafe and shop are basically the only places to get a bite to eat on the island. Some B&B providers offer evening meals.

Jura Hotel   HOTEL ££
(📞 01496-820243; www.jurahotel.co.uk; Craighouse; s £65, d £100-130; P🐾) The heart of Jura's community is this hotel, which is warmly welcoming and efficiently run. Rooms vary in size and shape, but all are renovated and inviting. The premier rooms, which all have sea views, are just lovely, with understated elegance and polished modern bathrooms. Eat in the restaurant or the convivial pub.

Barnhill   COTTAGE ££
(📞 01786 850274; www.escapetojura.com; per week from £1200; P🐾) The cottage where George Orwell stayed is in a gloriously remote location in Jura's north. It sleeps eight and is 7 miles from the main road on a rough 4WD track, and 25 miles from the pub. It's pretty basic but has a generator.

Ardlussa Estate   B&B £££
(📞 01496-820323; www.ardlussaestate.com; Ardlussa; d £150; P🐾) This grand shooting lodge in Jura's north offers B&B accommodation in two plush rooms with beautiful vistas. Lavish four-course dinners made with estate produce cost £50 per head. There's also a substantial self-catering wing sleeping up to 10 people.

Antlers   CAFE £
(📞 01496-820496;   www.facebook.com/antlers.jura; Craighouse; light meals £4-9; ⊙10am-4pm Easter-Oct) 🍴 This community-owned cafe has a craft shop and displays on Jura heritage. It does tasty home baking, venison burgers, sandwiches and more. Sit out on the deck to enjoy the view. It does takeaway dinners on Fridays and sometimes opens for sit-ins. Not licensed – £3 corkage.

ℹ Getting There & Away

A **car ferry** (📞 01496-840681; www.argyll-bute.gov.uk) shuttles between Port Askaig on Islay and Feolin on Jura (adult/car/bicycle £1.85/9.60/free, five minutes, hourly Monday to Saturday, every two hours Sunday). There is no direct car-ferry connection to the mainland.

From April to September, **Jura Passenger Ferry** (📞 07768 450000; www.jurapassengerferry.com; one way £20; ⊙Apr-Sep) runs from Tayvallich on the mainland to Craighouse on Jura (one hour, one or two daily except Wednesday). Booking is recommended (you can do this online).

ℹ Getting Around

The island's only **bus service** (📞 01436-810200; www.garelochheadcoaches.co.uk) runs between the ferry slip at Feolin and Craighouse (20 minutes, six to seven Monday to Saturday), timed to coincide with ferry arrivals and departures. Some of the runs continue north as far as Inverlussa.

Hire bikes from **Jura Bike Hire** (📞 07768 450000; Craighouse; bike hire per day £15) in Craighouse.

Colonsay

POP 100

Legend has it that when St Columba set out from Ireland in 563, his first landfall was Colonsay. But on climbing a hill he found he could still see the distant coast of his homeland, and pushed on north to Iona, leaving behind only his name (Colonsay means 'Columba's Isle').

Colonsay is a little jewel-box of varied delights, none exceptional but each exquisite – an ancient priory, a woodland garden, a golden beach – set amid a Highland landscape in miniature: rugged, rocky hills, cliffs and sandy strands, machair and birch woods, even a trout loch.

Sights & Activities

There are several good sandy beaches, but **Kiloran Bay** in the northwest, a scimitar-shaped strand of dark golden sand, is outstanding.

★ Oronsay Priory RUINS
(⊙24hr) FREE If the tide is right, don't miss walking across the half-mile of cockleshell-strewn sand linking Colonsay to smaller Oronsay. Here you can explore the 14th-century ruins of one of Scotland's best-preserved medieval priories. There are two beautiful 15th-century stone crosses in the kirkyard, but the highlight is the collection of superb carved grave slabs in the Prior's House. The island is accessible on foot for about 1½ hours either side of low tide; there are tide tables at the ferry terminal and hotel.

Colonsay House Gardens GARDENS
(⊘01951-200316; www.colonsayholidays.co.uk; Kiloran; ⊙gardens dawn-dusk, walled garden noon-5pm Wed & Fri, 2-5pm Sat Easter-Sep, 2-4.30pm Wed Oct) FREE Situated at Colonsay House, 1.5 miles north of Scalasaig, these gardens are tucked in an unexpected fold of the landscape and are famous for their outstanding collection of hybrid rhododendrons and unusual trees. The formal walled garden around the mansion has a terrace cafe.

Colonsay Brewery BREWERY
(⊘01951-200190; www.colonsaybrewery.co.uk; Scalasaig; ⊙call for hours) The Colonsay Brewery gives you the chance to have a look at how it produces its hand-crafted ales – the Colonsay IPA is a grand pint.

Kevin Byrne WALKING
(⊘01951-200320; byrne@colonsay.org.uk) Kevin Byrne offers customised guided tours on foot (£15) or in your own car (£40). There are also special tours focusing on Colonsay island's fern life.

Sleeping & Eating

Accommodation is limited and should be booked before coming to the island. Wild camping is allowed. See www.colonsay.org.uk for self-catering listings.

As well as the Colonsay Hotel, there are a couple of cafes on the island for food.

Backpackers Lodge HOSTEL £
(⊘01951-200312; www.colonsayholidays.co.uk; Kiloran; dm/tw £22/56; P⊛) Set in a former gamekeeper's house, this lodge is a 30-minute walk from the ferry on Colonsay (you can arrange to be picked up). Smart refurbished twin rooms are a great deal and are set in the house, with bunk rooms in a smaller stone building alongside. There's a kitchen in another building.

★ Colonsay Hotel HOTEL ££
(⊘01951-200316; www.colonsayholidays.co.uk; Scalasaig; s/d from £85/115; ⊙mid-Mar–Oct; P⊛⊛) ✔ This wonderfully laid-back hotel is set in an atmospheric old inn dating from 1750, a short walk uphill from the ferry pier in Scalasaig. It's a plush 18th-century place with well-appointed rooms, some with lovely views and four-poster beds. The bar and restaurant are the island's main social centres.

Information

General information is available at www.colonsay.org.uk and at the ferry waiting room (the ferry pier is at Scalasaig, the main village, which has a shop but no ATM).

Colonsay Bookshop (⊘01951-200320; www.houseoflochar.com; Scalasaig; ⊙3-5.30pm Mon-Sat Apr-Oct, or by appointment) This tiny bookshop near the ferry pier in Scalasaig has an excellent range of books on Hebridean history and culture.

Getting There & Around

AIR

Hebridean Air Services (www.hebrideanair.co.uk) operates flights from Oban's airport (at North Connel) to Colonsay and Islay twice daily on Tuesday and Thursday.

BICYCLE

You can hire bikes from **Archie McConnell** (☑ 01951-200355; www.colonsaycottage.co.uk; Colnatarun Cottage, Kilchattan; per day £8-10) – book in advance and he'll deliver them to anywhere on the island.

BOAT

CalMac (www.calmac.co.uk) runs ferries from Oban to Colonsay (passenger/car £7.40/37.60, 2¼ hours, seven weekly in summer, three in winter). From April to October, on Wednesday and Saturday, the ferry from Kennacraig to Islay continues to Colonsay (adult/car £4.15/17.30, 1¼ hours) and on to Oban. A day trip from Islay allows you six to seven hours on the island.

BUS

Colonsay Minibus Tour (☑ 01951-200141; adult/child £10/5), a service aimed at day trippers, makes two circuits of the island on Wednesdays, to meet the arriving and departing ferries – you can be dropped off/picked up at any point on the circuit.

ARRAN

POP 4600

Enchanting Arran is a jewel in Scotland's scenic crown. The island is a visual feast, and boasts culinary delights, its own brewery and distillery, and stacks of accommodation options. The variations in Scotland's dramatic landscape can all be experienced on this one island, best explored by pulling on the hiking boots or jumping on a bicycle. Arran offers some challenging walks in the mountainous north, while the island's circular coastal road is very popular with cyclists.

ⓘ Information

The **tourist office** (☑ 01770-303774; www.visitscotland.com; ⓧ 9am-5pm Mon-Sat Mar-Oct, plus 10am-5pm Sun Apr-Sep, 10am-4pm Mon-Sat Nov-Feb) is in Brodick. The ferry from Ardrossan also has some tourist information. Useful websites include www.visitarran.com.

ⓘ Getting There & Away

CalMac runs ferries between Ardrossan and Brodick (adult/car £3.90/15.55, 55 minutes, four to nine daily). From April to late October services also run between Claonaig on the Kintyre peninsula and Lochranza (adult/car £2.90/9.70, 30 minutes, seven to nine daily). In winter this service runs to Tarbert (1¼ hours) once daily and must be reserved.

ⓘ Getting Around

BICYCLE

Several places hire out bicycles, including these in Brodick:

Arran Adventure Company (☑ 01770-303349; www.arranadventure.com; Auchrannie Rd) Has good mountain bikes.

Arran Bike Hire (☑ 07825-160668; www.arranbikehire.com; Shorehouse, Shore Rd; per half-day/full day/week £11/15/65; ⓧ 10am-4pm Apr-Oct) On the waterfront in Brodick. Hires out trail bikes and hybrids and can offer advice on mountain-biking routes.

BUS

Four to seven buses daily go from Brodick pier to Lochranza (£3.15, 45 minutes), and many head the other way to Lamlash (£2) and Whiting Bay (£2.75, 30 minutes), then on to Kildonan and Blackwaterfoot. Pick up a timetable from the tourist office.

An Arran Dayrider costs £6.30 from the driver, giving a day's travel. Download a bus timetable from www.spt.co.uk.

CAR

Island of Arran Car Hire (☑ 01770-302839; www.arran-motors.com; car part-day/24hr from £35/38; ⓧ 8am-5.30pm Mon-Sat, 10am-5pm Sun) is at the service station by Brodick ferry pier.

Arran

N
0 — 5 km
0 — 2.5 miles

To Claonaig/Tarbet
Cock of Arran
Lochranza
Sound of Bute
Catacol
Isle of Arran Distillery
Mid Thundergay
A841
Sannox
Coire Fhionn Lochan
Caisteal Abhail (859m)
Cir Mhòr (798m)
Corrie
Beinn Tarsuinn (826m)
Goatfell (874m)
Merkland Point
Beinn Nuis (792m)
Isle of Arran Brewery
Brodick Castle
To Ardrossan
Auchagallon
The String Rd
Brodick
King's Cave
Machrie Moor Stone Circle
Lamlash
Holy Island
Blackwaterfoot
The Ross Rd
Whiting Bay
Kilmory/Lagg
Kilbrannan Sound
Torrylinn Cairn
Kildonan

Brodick & Around

POP 800

Most visitors arrive in Brodick, the beating heart of the island of Arran, and congregate along the coastal road to admire the town's long curving bay. On a clear day it's a spectacular vista, with Goatfell looming over the forested shore.

◉ Sights & Activities

Brodick Castle   CASTLE
(NTS; ☑01770-302202; www.nts.org.uk; castle & park adult/child £14/10, park only £7.50/6.50; ☉castle 11am-4pm May-Aug, 11am-3pm Apr & Sep, park 9.30am-sunset year-round) This elegant castle 2 miles north of Brodick evolved from 13th-century origins into a stately home and hunting lodge for the Dukes of Hamilton. You enter via the hunting gallery, wallpapered with deer heads. The rest of the interior is characterised by fabulous 19th-century wooden furniture and an array of horses 'n' hounds paintings. Helpful guides and laminated sheets – the kids' ones are more entertaining – add info. At last visit it was closed for renovations, due to reopen in spring 2019.

The extensive grounds, now a country park with various trails among the rhododendrons, justify the steep entry fee.

Isle of Arran Brewery   BREWERY
(☑01770-302353; www.arranbrewery.com; tours £5; ☉10am-5pm Mon-Sat, 12.30-5pm Sun Apr-Sep, 10am-3.30pm Mon & Wed-Sat Oct-Mar) This brewery, 1.5 miles from Brodick off the Lochranza road, produces the excellent Arran beers, which include the addictive Arran Dark. Tours run daily: call for times as they vary by season. They last about 45 minutes and include a tasting of all the beers.

Isle of Arran Heritage Museum   MUSEUM
(☑01770-302636; www.arranmuseum.co.uk; Rosaburn; adult/child £4/2; ☉10.30am-4.30pm Apr-Oct) This museum has a varied collection of historical and ethnographic items, from prehistoric stone tools to farming implements. There's quite a bit to see across several heritage buildings, with good background on the island and its people. Gardens and a cafe round out the experience. It's on the way to the castle from Brodick.

★Goatfell   HIKING
The walk up and down Goatfell (874m), the island's highest point, is 8 miles return (up

to eight hours), with trailheads at Brodick and Brodick Castle among others. In fine weather there are superb views to Ben Lomond and Northern Ireland. It can, however, be very cold and windy up here; take appropriate maps (available at the tourist office), waterproofing and a compass.

⚑ Festivals & Events

Arran Mountain Festival   SPORTS
(☑01770-303347; www.arranmountainfestival. co.uk; ☉mid-May) This four-day event offers a wide range of walking and climbing activities led by experienced mountain guides, with events for all abilities. Most cost between £15 and £25 and can be booked online.

Arran Folk Festival   MUSIC
(www.arranevents.com; ☉Jun) A three-day festival with concerts and great atmosphere in Brodick. Free daytime sessions are usually in the Douglas hotel, with evening concerts (tickets around £20) in Brodick Hall.

⏁ Sleeping

Brodick Bunkhouse   HOSTEL £
(☑01770-302968; www.brodickbunkhouse.co.uk; Alma Rd; dm £25; P🤍) A short stroll from the ferry, behind the Douglas hotel, this handy hostel has attractive, comfortable triple-decker bunks with individual plugs and USB ports. It's generally unstaffed, with keycode entry. It has a simple kitchen and access for people with disabilities. No under-18s are admitted.

★Glenartney   B&B ££
(☑01770-302220; www.glenartney-arran.co.uk; Mayish Rd; d £75-100; ☉Easter-Oct; P🤍🐾) 🌿 Uplifting bay views and genuine, helpful hosts make this a cracking option. Airy, stylish rooms make the most of the natural light at the top of the town. Comfortable lounges, help-yourself home baking and pod coffee plus a sustainable ethos make for a very pleasurable stay. Top facilities for cyclists, plus drying rooms and trail advice for hikers are added bonuses.

Broomage   B&B ££
(☑01770-302115; www.facebook.com/the.broomage; r £80; P🤍) Run by a young family, this luminous modern spot has two rooms with huge beds (they can become twins) and shiny modern bathrooms (one exterior to the room). There's a large lounge, amiable hospitality and breakfast featuring local produce. Downstairs is a self-catering apartment. It's fairly

discreetly signposted; turn down the road by the Royal Bank of Scotland.

Belvedere Guest House B&B ££

(📞01770-302397; www.belvedere-guesthouse. co.uk; Alma Rd; s £50, d £90-100; 🅿🛜) Overlooking town, bay and surrounding mountains, this place has very well-presented rooms with comfortable mattresses. Make sure you pay extra to grab room 1 or 2, each of which is spacious and has fabulous vistas over the water. Breakfast has plenty of choice; there's also a self-catering cottage. It's a likeable Brodick base with a laid-back and helpful host.

Douglas HOTEL £££

(📞01770-302968; www.thedouglashotel.co.uk; Shore Rd; r £160-200, ste £230; 🅿🛜🍽) Opposite the ferry, the Douglas is a smart, stylish haven of island hospitality. Views are magnificent and luxurious rooms with smart contemporary fabrics make the most of them. There are numerous thoughtful touches such as binoculars to admire the vistas, and bathrooms are great. The downstairs **bar and bistro** (bistro mains £13-20, bar meals £10-15; ⏰bistro 6-9.30pm, bar noon-9.30pm; 🛜🍽) are also recommended. Prices drop midweek and in winter.

Eating

Wineport CAFE £

(📞01770-302101; www.wineport.co.uk; Cladach Centre; light meals £4-11; ⏰11am-5pm Apr-Oct, Sat & Sun only Feb & Mar) Located 1.5 miles from Brodick, next to the Isle of Arran Brewery, whose ales are offered on tap, this summer-only cafe-bar has great outdoor tables for sunny days and does a nice line in pleasing pub-style fare, such as wings, wedges, pork burgers, local mussels and sharing platters. It opens for dinner some nights, but hours vary widely each year.

⭐ **Brodick Bar & Brasserie** BRASSERIE ££

(📞01770-302169; www.brodickbar.co.uk; Alma Rd; mains £13-22; ⏰noon-2.30pm & 5.30-9pm Mon-Sat; 🛜) This is one of Arran's most enjoyable eating experiences. The regularly changing blackboard menu brings modern French flair to a Brodick pub, with great presentation, efficient service and delicious flavour combinations. You'll have a hard time choosing, as it's all brilliant. It's very buzzy on weekend evenings. It was for sale at the time of research so things may change.

Fiddlers' Music Bar CAFE, BISTRO ££

(📞01770-302579; www.fiddlersmusicbar.com; Shore Rd; mains £10-15; ⏰food 11am-9pm; 🛜🍽) A likeable little place with a really cheerful vibe, Fiddlers' is run by local musicians and does an all-round job as pub, venue, cafe and bistro. It hosts live folk music every evening and there's a range of tasty food with some decent vegetarian choices. Check out the appropriate toilet seats.

Shopping

Arran Art Trail ARTS & CRAFTS

(www.arranopenstudios.com) Arran is home to quite a few creatives making a wide variety of art and handicrafts. This trail maps out a couple of dozen studios that you can visit around the island; grab the brochure from the tourist office or see the website.

Corrie to Lochranza

The coast road heads north from Brodick to small, pretty Corrie, where there's a Goatfell trailhead. After **Sannox**, with a sandy beach and great mountain views, the road cuts inland. Heading to the very north, on the island's main road, visitors weave through lush glens flanked by Arran's towering mountain splendour. This is perhaps the most beautiful section of the whole Arran coastal circuit.

Lochranza

POP 200

The village of Lochranza has a stunning location in a small bay on Arran island's north coast. It's characterised by the ruined 13th-century **Lochranza Castle** (www.historicenvironment.scot; ⏰24hr) FREE, a ruin standing proud on a little promontory. The nearby **Isle of Arran Distillery** (📞01770-830264; www.arranwhisky.com; tours adult/child £8/free; ⏰10am-5pm Mar-Oct, 10.30am-4pm Nov-Feb) produces a light, aromatic single malt. The Lochranza area bristles with red deer, who wander insouciantly into the village to crop the grass.

⭐ **Lochranza SYHA** HOSTEL £

(📞01770-830631; www.syha.org.uk; dm/d/q £24.50/64/108; ⏰mid-Mar–Oct, plus Sat & Sun year-round; 🅿@🛜🍽) 🌱 An excellent hostel in a charming spot with lovely views. Rooms sport chunky wooden furniture, keycards and lockers. Rainwater toilets, energy-saving heating solutions and a wheelchair-accessible room show thoughtful design, while plush lounging areas, a kitchen you could run a restaurant out of, a laundry, a drying room, red deer in the garden and welcoming management combine for a top option.

★ Butt Lodge
B&B **££**

(☎01770-830333; www.buttlodge.co.uk; s from £72, d £85-95, ste £110-125; ☺Mar–mid-Oct; [P][☎]) Down a short potholed road, this Victorian hunting lodge has been adapted by keen young owners to offer contemporary comfort with relaxed style and genuine hospitality. Rooms give perspectives over hills, garden and the rustic village golf course, with its red deer greenkeepers. The Castle suite is a fabulous space with views three ways and a mezzanine seating area.

Treats include tea and cake in the afternoons, and a spacious lounge to stretch out in. Look out for yoga and other retreats in low season.

West Coast

Blackwaterfoot is the largest village on the west coast of Arran, with a shop and hotel. It's pleasant enough, though not the most scenic of the island's settlements. You can walk to **King's Cave** (☺24hr) **FREE** from here (6 miles), and this walk can easily be extended to the **Machrie Moor Stone Circle** (☺24hr) **FREE**, the highlight of the area.

★ Cafe Thyme
CAFE **£**

(☎01770-840608; www.oldbyre.co.uk; Old Byre Visitor Centre, Machrie; dishes £8-12; ☺10am-5pm, reduced winter hours; [☎][🖉]) At the Old Byre Visitor Centre, this is a very pleasant spot, with chunky wooden tables, outdoor seating and sweeping views from its elevated position. It has home baking, a wide tea selection and decent coffee. Less predictably, the food menu features great Turkish pizza, meze boards and smartly priced daily specials. Lunches are served from noon to 3pm.

South Coast

The landscape in the south of Arran is gentler than in the north; the road drops into little wooded valleys, and it's particularly lovely around **Kilmory** and **Lagg**, from where a 10-minute walk will take you to **Torrylinn Cairn**, a chambered tomb over 4000 years old. **Kildonan** has pleasant sandy beaches, a gorgeous water outlook, a hotel, a campsite and an ivy-clad ruined castle.

In genteel **Whiting Bay**, strung out along the water, you'll find small sandy beaches and easy one-hour walks through the forest to the **Giant's Graves** and **Glenashdale**

Falls – keep an eye out for golden eagles and other birds of prey.

Lagg Distillery
DISTILLERY

(☎01786-431900; www.laggwhisky.com; Lagg) Still under construction when we last passed by, this new malt-whisky distillery will open to visitors in 2019. Run by the same folk who operate the distillery in Lochranza, it will focus on a peatier style. There's also an orchard being planted, so look out for cider and apple brandy further down the track.

★ Sealshore Campsite
CAMPSITE **£**

(☎01770-820320; www.campingarran.com; Kildonan; 1-/2-person tents £9/16, pods for 2 people £35; ☺Mar-Oct; [P][☎][🐾]) Living up to its name, this excellent small campsite is right by the sea (and the Kildonan Hotel) and has one of Arran's finest views from its grassy camping area. There are good facilities, including BBQs, power showers and a day room; the breeze keeps the midges away. Cosy camping pods or a fabulously refurbished Roma caravan offer non-tent choices.

Lamlash
POP 1000

Lamlash, just 3 miles south of Brodick, is in a dazzling setting strung along the beachfront. The bay was used as a safe anchorage by the navy during WWI and WWII.

Holy Island
ISLAND

Just off Lamlash, this island is owned by the Samye Ling Tibetan Centre and used as a retreat, but day visits are allowed. A tide-dependent **ferry** (☎01770-700463, 07970 771960; tomin10@btinternet.com; return adult/child £12/6; ☺daily Apr-Oct; by arrangement Tue & Fri Nov-Mar) zips across from Lamlash. No dogs, bikes, alcohol or fires are allowed on Holy Island. A good walk to the top of the hill (314m), takes two or three hours return. You can stay at the **Holy Island Centre for World Peace & Health** (☎01770-601100; www.holyisle.org; dm/s/d £32/55/80; ☺Apr-Oct). Prices include full (vegetarian) board.

★ Glenisle Hotel
HOTEL **£££**

(☎01770-600559; www.glenislehotel.com; Shore Rd; s/d/superior d £102/157/207; [☎]) This stylish hotel offers great service and high comfort levels. Rooms are decorated with contemporary fabrics; 'cosy' rooms under the sloping roof are a little cheaper. All feel fresh and include binoculars for scouring the seashore; upgrade to a 'superior' for the best

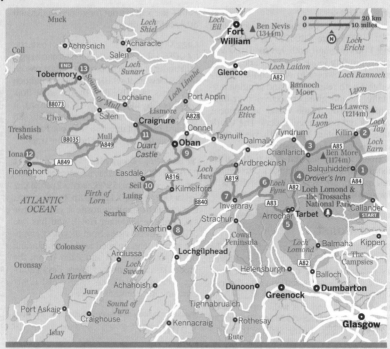

Driving Tour
The Trossachs to Mull

START CALLANDER
END TOBERMORY
LENGTH 240 MILES; TWO TO FOUR DAYS

Having explored the southern part of the Trossachs, head north out of Callander on the A84, following pretty Loch Lubnaig before optional detours of a few miles to see Rob Roy's grave at **1 Balquhidder** (p252) and the Falls of Dochart at pretty **2 Killin** (p252).

Continue on the A85 to **3 Crianlarich** (p247), surrounded by Highland majesty, then turn left on the A82 to follow the western shore of Loch Lomond. Stop for a look and/or pint at the quirky **4 Drover's Inn** (p246), then deviate right at Tarbet onto the A83 – shortly thereafter, **5 Arrochar** (p248) makes for a scenic lunch stop.

Head through scenic Glen Croe, over the pass and into Glen Kinglas, then follow the shore of Loch Fyne – stops at the **6 Fynes Ales brewery** (p257) and/or oyster bar obligatory! – to picturesque **7 Inveraray**

(p256). Go right through the arch here on the A819, then left onto the B840, a lonely road following stiletto-like Loch Awe. You'll eventually reach **8 Kilmartin** (p258), with its great museum and evocative prehistoric sights.

Follow the A816 north to **9 Oban**, where good accommodation options, a handsome harbour and delicious seafood await. You may want to deviate to see the island of **10 Seil** (p280) en route: from here, great boat trips can take you out to the Corryvreckan Whirlpool. Catch a ferry from Oban to Mull and follow the A849 southwest via **11 Duart Castle** (p283) to the island's tip at Fionnphort, where you cross to the emerald jewel of **12 Iona** (p287) and can take a boat trip to the spectacular rock formations of Staffa.

Retrace your steps, then follow Mull's winding west coast on the B8035 and B8073 via spectacular coastline and the beach at Calgary to arrive at the colourful shorefront houses of the main town, **13 Tobermory** (p283).

water views. Downstairs is excellent **food** (mains £12-18; ⊙ noon-8.45pm; 🐾 ✍) and lovely outdoor seating by the garden.

OBAN, MULL, IONA & TIREE

The Victorian harbour town of Oban is a pretty place in its own right, with an excellent seafood scene, and is also a major gateway to the Hebrides. The big island drawcard is Mull, whose majestic scenery, birdlife and pretty capital Tobermory are complemented by the enchanting holy island of Iona just offshore. But the attributes of other islands really merit exploration: the strange rock formations of uninhabited Staffa, the walking on Kerrera, the intriguing slate-quarrying communities of Seil, the peace of Coll and the glorious windswept beaches of Tiree.

Oban

POP 8600

Oban, the main gateway to many of the Hebridean islands, is a waterfront town on a delightful bay, with sweeping views to Kerrera and Mull. It's peaceful in winter, but in summer the town centre is jammed with traffic and crowded with holidaymakers and travellers headed for the archipelago. But the setting is still lovely, and Oban's brilliant seafood restaurants are marvellous places to be as the sun sets over the bay. There's a real magic to the location.

⊙ Sights

Oban Distillery   DISTILLERY
(✍ 01631-572004; www.malts.com; Stafford St; tours £10; ⊙ noon or 12.30-4.30pm Dec-Feb, 9.30am-5pm Mar-Jun & Oct-Nov, 9.30am-7.30pm Mon-Fri & 9.30am-5pm Sat & Sun Jul-Sep) This handsome distillery has been in operation since 1794. The standard guided tour leaves regularly (worth booking) and includes a dram, a take-home glass and a taste straight from the cask. Specialist tours (£40) run once on Mondays to Fridays in summer. Even without a tour, it's still worth looking at the small exhibition in the foyer.

Dunollie Castle   CASTLE
(✍ 01631-570550; www.dunollie.org; Dunollie Rd; adult/child £6/3; ⊙ 10am-5pm Mon-Sat, noon-5pm Sun Apr-Oct) A pleasant 1-mile stroll north

along the coast road leads to Dunollie Castle, built by the MacDougalls of Lorn in the 13th century and unsuccessfully besieged for a year during the 1715 Jacobite rebellion. It's ruined, but ongoing conservation work is offering increasing access. The nearby 1745 House – seat of Clan MacDougall – is an intriguing museum of local and clan history, and there are pleasant wooded grounds and a cafe. Free tours run twice daily.

McCaig's Tower   HISTORIC BUILDING
(cnr Laurel & Duncraggan Rds; ⊙ 24hr) Crowning the hill above town is this Colosseum-like Victorian folly, commissioned in 1890 by local worthy John Stuart McCaig, with the philanthropic intention of providing work for unemployed stonemasons. To reach it on foot, make the steep climb up Jacob's Ladder (a flight of stairs) from Argyll St; the bay views are worth the effort.

Pulpit Hill   VIEWPOINT
An excellent viewpoint to the south of Oban Bay; the footpath to the summit starts by Maridon B&B on Dunuaran Rd.

🏃 Activities

Hire a bike – try **Oban Cycles** (✍ 01631-566033; www.obancyclescotland.com; 87 George St; per day/week £25/125; ⊙ 10am-5pm Tue-Sat Feb-Dec) – for the local bike rides listed in a leaflet at the tourist office, including a 16-mile route to Seil.

Various operators offer boat trips (adult/child £10/5) to spot seals and other marine wildlife, departing from North Pier.

Oban has lots of outdoor shops and is a good place to get kitted out for the Highland and island outdoors.

Sea Kayak Oban   KAYAKING
(National Kayak School; ✍ 01631-565310; www.seakayakoban.com; Argyll St; ⊙ 10am-5pm Mon-Fri, 9am-5pm Sat, 10am-4pm Sun, winter hours greatly reduced) Sea Kayak Oban has a well-stocked shop, great route advice and sea-kayaking courses, including an all-inclusive two-day intro for beginners (£170 per person). It also has full equipment rental for experienced paddlers – trolley your kayak from the shop to the ferry (kayaks carried free) to visit the islands. Three-hour excursions (adult/child £50/35) leave regularly in season.

Puffin Adventures   DIVING
(✍ 01631-566088; www.puffin.org.uk; Port Gallanach) If you fancy exploring the underwater world, Puffin Adventures offers a two-hour

Oban

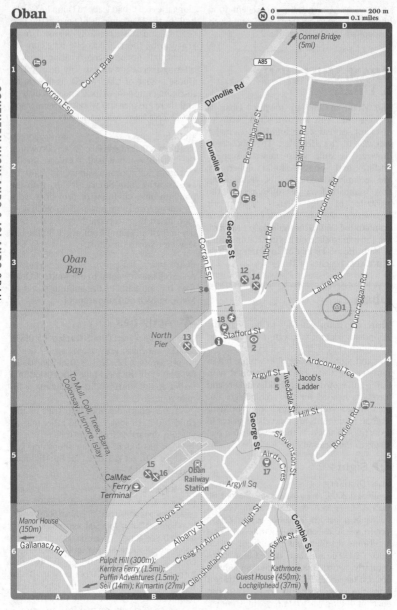

package (£90) for complete beginners, often with same-day availability, as well as four-day diving courses. A serious professional set-up, it has training services and excursions for more experienced divers as well. It's located south of Oban near the Kerrera ferry.

Tours

★ **Basking Shark Scotland** BOATING
(📞 07975 723140; www.baskingsharkscotland.
co.uk; ⊙ Apr-Oct) Runs boat trips focused on finding and observing basking sharks – the world's second-largest fish – and other

Oban

notable marine species. The one-day options leave from Coll, synchronised with the ferry from Oban, and cost £140, or £195 with swimming/snorkelling. Multiday trips are available, as are low-season research trips. It also offers excursions allowing you to swim or kayak with seals.

Coastal Connection BOATING
(☏01631-565833; www.coastal-connection.co.uk) Runs wildlife-spotting trips (adult/child £30/20), fast day trips to Tobermory (£40/25) and custom excursions to many west coast islands in a speedy, comfortable boat.

Festivals & Events

Highlands & Islands Music & Dance Festival MUSIC
(www.obanfestival.org; ⊙early May) An exuberant celebration of traditional Scottish music and dance, when Oban packs out.

West Highland Yachting Week SAILING
(www.whyw.co.uk; ⊙late Jul or early Aug) Oban becomes the focus of one of Scotland's biggest yachting events, when hundreds of yachts cram into the harbour and the town's bars are jammed with thirsty sailors.

Oban Games CULTURAL, SPORTS
(Argyllshire Gathering; www.obangames.com; adult/child £10/5; ⊙late Aug) A key event in the Highland games calendar, the Oban Games include a prestigious pipe-band competition.

Sleeping

Despite having lots of B&B accommodation, Oban can still fill up quickly in July and August, so try to book ahead. Avoid the substandard, tourist-trap B&Bs south of the roundabout on Dunollie Rd. If you can't find a bed in Oban, consider Connel, 4 miles north.

★**Backpackers Plus** HOSTEL £
(☏01631-567189; www.backpackersplus.com; Breadalbane St; dm/s/tw/d incl bathroom & breakfast £20/29/54/60; @⌂) This is a friendly place in an old church with a good vibe and a large and attractive communal lounge with lots of sofas and armchairs. A buffet breakfast is included, plus there's free tea and coffee, a laundry service and powerful showers. Private rooms are available in adjacent buildings: they are a very good deal.

Brand-new en suite doubles are in the old church hall, while a former guesthouse has sweet shared-bathroom options with a good common kitchen.

Oban Backpackers HOSTEL £
(☏01631-562107; www.obanbackpackers.com; Breadalbane St; dm £18.50-20.50; @⌂) Simple, colourful, relaxed and casual, this hostel has plenty of atmosphere. Dorms are basic, with high ceilings and plenty of space; prices vary according to size. Top bunks are wall-mounted. There's a sociable downstairs lounge with big windows and zebra-patterned couches, plus a sizeable kitchen. Breakfast is available for £3 and a safe is on hand (no lockers).

Oban SYHA HOSTEL £
(☏01631-562025; www.syha.org.uk; Corran Esplanade; dm/tw £24/58, plus £3 per person for non-members; P@⌂) Set in a grand Victorian villa on the Esplanade, 0.75 miles north of Oban's train station, this hostel is modernised to a high standard, with comfy wooden bunks, lockers, good showers and a lounge with great views across Oban Bay. All dorms are en suite; the neighbouring lodge has three- and four-bedded rooms. Breakfast is available. Dorm rates drop substantially in low season.

★ **Elderslie Guest House** B&B ££

(☎01631-570651; www.obanbandb.com; Soroba Rd; s £50-56, d £75-88; ☻Apr–mid-Oct; P🛜) A B&B can be a difficult balancing act: making things modern without losing cosiness, being friendly and approachable without sacrificing privacy. At this spot a mile south of Oban the balance is absolutely right, with a variety of commodious rooms with big showers, large towels and lovely outlooks over greenery. Breakfast is great, there's outdoor lounging space and the hosts are excellent.

Old Manse Guest House B&B ££

(☎01631-564886; www.obanguesthouse.co.uk; Dalriach Rd; s/d £80/98; ☻Mar-Oct; P🛜) Set on the hillside above town, this Oban B&B commands magnificent views over to Kerrera and Mull. It's run with genuine enthusiasm, and the owners are constantly adding thoughtful new features to the bright, cheerful rooms, such as binoculars, DVDs, poetry, corkscrews and tartan hot-water bottles. There are breakfast menus, with special diets catered for.

It was for sale at the time of research so things may change.

Fàilte B&B ££

(☎01631-570219; www.failtebedandbreakfastoban. co.uk; Rockfield Rd; s £50, d £80-90; ☻Feb-Nov; P🛜) Solicitous host Thomas knows a thing or two about guest comfort and the thoughtful extras here (powerpoints, disposable razors, real milk in the mini-fridge) make for a very comfortable stay. Rooms are pleasingly contemporary with a white-and-blond Scandinavian feel and modern showers. The family's quality artworks decorate the building and breakfast features fresh fruit and homemade breads and jams.

Kathmore Guest House B&B ££

(☎01631-562104; www.kathmore.co.uk; Soroba Rd; s £50, d £65-75; P🛜) A 10-minute stroll from Oban's centre, this warmly welcoming place mixes traditional Highland hospitality and hearty breakfasts with a wee touch of boutique flair in its stylish bedspreads and colourful artwork. It's actually two adjacent houses combined. There's a comfortable lounge and outdoor garden deck where you can enjoy a glass of wine on long summer evenings.

Sandvilla Guesthouse B&B ££

(☎01631-564483; www.holidayoban.co.uk; Breadalbane St; d £75-90; P🛜) Upbeat, bright and modern, this well kept B&B is our favourite of several options on this street. Enthusiastic owners guarantee a personal welcome and service with a smile. No young children are allowed.

Manor House HOTEL £££

(☎01631-562087; www.manorhouseoban.com; Gallanach Rd; r £195-270; P🛜🍽) Built in 1780 for the Duke of Argyll, the old-fashioned Manor House is Oban's finest hotel. It has small but elegant Georgian-style rooms – the majority with lovely sea views – with antiques and period-style wallpaper, plus a classy restaurant serving Scottish/French cuisine (table d'hôte dinner £49). Rates include access to a local gym and golf course. No under-12s.

✕ Eating

Oban Seafood Hut SEAFOOD £

(☎07881418565; www.facebook.com/obanseafood. hut.9; Railway Pier; mains £3-13; ☻10am-6pm mid-Mar–Oct) If you want to savour superb Scottish seafood without the expense of an upmarket restaurant, head for Oban's famous seafood stall – it's the green shack on the quayside near the ferry terminal. Here you can buy fresh and cooked seafood to take away, such as excellent prawn sandwiches, dressed crab and fresh oysters, for a pittance.

Little Potting Shed Cafe CAFE, VEGETARIAN £

(☎01631-358150; www.facebook.com/thelittle pottingshedcafeoban; 5 John St; light meals £4-9; ☻9am-5pm daily, to 9pm Fri & Sat Jul & Aug; 🛜🍽) Up a side alley off Oban's main street, this sweet spot has wooden tables and an excellent choice of vegetarian and vegan savoury and sweet bites. The vegan breakfast is also tasty, the coffee is good and strong, there's a wide selection of teas, and the non-dairy ice-cream is perfect for a summer's day. It's dog-friendly.

★ **Ee-Usk** SEAFOOD ££

(☎01631-565666; www.eeusk.com; North Pier; mains £14-24; ☻noon-3pm & 5.45-9.30pm Apr-Oct, noon-2.30pm & 5.45-9pm Nov-Mar; 🛜) 🖋 Bright and modern Ee-Usk (how you pronounce *iasg*, Gaelic for fish) occupies a prime pier location. Floor-to-ceiling windows allow diners on two levels to enjoy sweeping views while sampling local sustainable seafood ranging from fragrant fish cakes to langoustines and succulent fresh fish. A bevy of serving staff make it swift and efficient, and they'll try to give you the best view available. Both the food and location are first-class.

Waterfront Fishouse Restaurant SEAFOOD ££

(☑01631-563110; www.waterfrontfishouse.co.uk; 1 Railway Pier; mains £13-20; ⊙noon-2pm & 5.30-9pm, extended hours Jun-Aug; 🖥🚲) Waterfront is housed on the top floor of a converted seamen's mission, and the stylish, unfussy decor, bathed by the summer evening sun, does little to distract from the seafood freshly landed at the quay just a few metres away. The menu ranges from classic haddock and chips to fresh oysters, scallops and langoustines. It's best to book for dinner.

Coast SCOTTISH ££

(☑01631-569900; www.coastoban.co.uk; 104 George St; mains £17-20; ⊙noon-2pm & 5.30-9pm Tue-Sat Feb-late Dec; 🖥) With a stylishly casual contemporary interior, this place in a former bank offers well-integrated plates with a focus on local game and seafood. Dishes are presented with flair but don't stray into pretension; the flavours are trusty and quality combinations that work very well.

Drinking & Nightlife

Oban Inn PUB

(☑01631-567441; www.facebook.com/theobaninn; 1 Stafford St; ⊙11am-1am; 🖥) It's a pleasure to see this four-square 18th-century pub open again after some years closed, with its solid walls, flagstone floor and roof beams in the cosy front bar. It has Fyne Ales on tap, making it a prime spot for a waterfront pint, with a good mix of locals, visitors and yachties.

Aulay's Bar PUB

(☑01631-562596; www.aulaysbar.com; 8 Airds Cres; ⊙11.30am-11pm; 🖥) An authentic Scottish pub, Aulay's is cosy and low-ceilinged, its walls covered with old photographs of Oban ferries and other ships. It pulls in a mixed crowd of locals and visitors with its warm atmosphere and wide range of malt whiskies. There are two sides: the left door leads to a quieter lounge bar.

ⓘ Information

Large areas of central Oban have free wi-fi. **Oban Library** (☑01631-571444; www.argyll-bute.co.uk; 77 Albany St; ⊙10am-1pm & 2-7pm Mon & Wed, to 6pm Thu, to 5pm Fri, to 1pm Sat; 🖥) has computer terminals and wi-fi.

Lorn & Islands District General Hospital (☑01631-567500; www.obanhospital.com; Glengallan Rd) At the southern end of town, clearly signposted off the main road.

Oban Tourist Office (☑01631-563122; www.oban.org.uk; 3 North Pier; ⊙10am-5pm Mon-Sat, 11am-3pm Sun Nov-Mar, 9am-5.30pm

---

ARGYLL SEA KAYAK TRAIL

This 96-mile **route** (www.paddleargyll.org.uk) promoted by the local government runs from Oban to Helensburgh via sea lochs and the Crinan canal. It's a spectacular paddle; the only annoyance is not being able to traverse the canal's locks: bookable trolleys are provided for easy portage. Paddlers are encouraged to register online.

Mon-Sat, 10am-5pm Sun Apr-Oct) Helpful; on the waterfront.

ⓘ Getting There & Away

AIR

Hebridean Air Services (www.hebrideanair.co.uk) Flies from North Connel airfield to the islands of Coll, Tiree, Colonsay and Islay.

BOAT

Oban is a major gateway to the Hebrides. The **CalMac Ferry Terminal** (☑01631-562244; www.calmac.co.uk; Railway Pier) is in the centre, close to the train station, with ferries running from here to Mull, Islay, Colonsay, Coll, Tiree, Barra and Lismore.

BUS

Scottish Citylink (www.citylink.co.uk) has two to five buses connecting Glasgow (£20.50, three hours) with Oban. Most of these travel via Tarbet and Inveraray; in summer, one goes via Crianlarich. Two buses Monday to Saturday head north to Fort William (£9.40, 1½ hours).

TRAIN

ScotRail trains run to Oban from Glasgow (£25.30, three hours, three to six daily). Change at Crianlarich for Fort William.

ⓘ Getting Around

Hazelbank Motors (☑01631-566476; www.obancarhire.co.uk; Lynn Rd; car hire per day/week from £40/225; ⊙8.30am-5pm Mon-Sat) Hires out cars. You might get a van cheaper than a hatchback.

Lorn Taxis (☑01631-564744)

Around Oban

Kerrera

POP 50

Some of the area's best **walking** is on Kerrera, which faces Oban across the bay. There's a 6-mile circuit (allow three hours),

OFF THE BEATEN TRACK

LUING

A ferry hop from Seil's southern end takes you to the neighbouring island of Luing, a quiet backwater that has no real sights but is appealing for wildlife walks and easy-going bike rides.

which follows tracks or paths and offers the chance to spot wildlife such as Soay sheep, wild goats, otters, golden eagles, peregrine falcons, seals and porpoises. At the island's southern end, there's a ruined castle.

Kerrera Bunkhouse HOSTEL £
(☑01631-566367; www.kerrerabunkhouse.co.uk; Lower Gylen; dm £16, tent £45; ☺Easter-Sep; 🐾) This charming seven-bed bunkhouse in a converted 18th-century stable is near Gylen Castle, a 2-mile walk south from the ferry on Kerrera (keep left at the fork just past the telephone box). Booking ahead is recommended. There's also a spacious platform-pitched tent with a double bed and stove. You can get snacks and light meals at the neighbouring Kerrera Tea Garden (light meals £2-9; ☺10.30am-4.30pm) 🍴.

ⓘ Getting There & Away

CalMac run a daily passenger ferry to Kerrera from Gallanach, 2 miles southwest of the Oban town centre (adult single/return £3.10/4.65, 5 minutes, half-hourly in summer, eight to nine daily in winter).

Seil

POP 600

The small island of Seil, 10 miles southwest of Oban, is best known for its connection to the mainland – the graceful Bridge over the Atlantic, designed by Thomas Telford and opened in 1793.

On the west coast is the pretty conservation village of Ellenabeich, with white-washed cottages and rainwater barrels backed by a wee harbour and rocky cliffs. It was built to house local slate workers, but the industry collapsed in 1881 when the sea broke into the main quarry – the flooded pit can still be seen. The Scottish Slate Islands Heritage Trust (☑01852-300449; www.slateislands.org.uk; ☺10.30am-4.30pm) displays fascinating old photographs illustrating life in the village in the 19th and early 20th centuries.

Just offshore is small Easdale Island, which has more old slate-workers' cottages and the interesting Easdale Island Folk Museum (☑01852-300370; www.easdalemuseum.org; suggested donation £3; ☺11am-4pm Apr–mid-Oct). The island once housed 450 people, but the population fell to just seven old-timers by 1950. It now has a healthier 50-odd after a program welcoming incomers.

Confusingly Ellenabeich is also referred to as Easdale, so 'Easdale Harbour', for example, is on the Seil side.

🏃 Activities

★ Sealife Adventures BOATING
(☑01631-571010; www.sealife-adventures.com; B844; 3/4/5hr trip £52/69/80) Sealife Adventures, based on the eastern side of Seil island near the bridge, has a large, comfortable boat offering wildlife cruises with knowledgable guides and trips to the Corryvreckan Whirlpool.

★ Seafari Adventures BOATING
(☑01852-300003; www.seafari.co.uk; Ellenabeich; ☺Apr-Oct) Runs a series of exciting boat trips in high-speed rigid inflatables to Corryvreckan Whirlpool (adult/child £42/32; call about dates for 'Whirlpool Specials', when the tide is strongest). There are also three-hour summer whale-watching trips (£53/40), day-long cruises to Iona and Staffa (£90/68) and private charters available to other islands. There's a minimum of six passengers required for low-season departures.

Sea Kayak Scotland KAYAKING
(☑01852-300770; www.seakayakscotland.com; courses for 1/2/4 people per person £125/90/70) Year-round hire, instruction and guided sea-kayaking trips run by an experienced operator.

🎉 Festivals & Events

World Stone-Skimming Championships SPORTS
(www.stoneskimming.com; ☺Sep) Anyone who fancies their hand at ducks and drakes should try to attend a flooded slate quarry in Easdale on a Sunday in late September. There's no use boasting about the number of skips: once it's hit the water a minimum of three times it's all about the distance reached.

🛏 Sleeping & Eating

An Lionadh
RENTAL HOUSE ££

(✏ 01688-400388; www.anlionadh.co.uk; Easdale; per week £1000; 🛜🐾) Occupying a comparatively lofty position on the tranquil island of Easdale, this is a standout self-catering option with views both ways: over the village and out to the west, where a grassy lawn lets you contemplate the vistas at great leisure. There are four bedrooms, a lounge and a very attractive kitchen/dining area.

★ Puffer
CAFE ££

(✏ 01852-300022; www.pufferbar.com; Easdale; mains £8-15; ⏰ food 11am-4pm & 6-8pm Mon-Sat, 11am-4pm Sun Easter-Oct, call for winter opening; 🛜✏) 🍴 Easdale Island is fed and watered by the Puffer, named after the boats that once served the community. It combines pub, tearoom and restaurant. There are front and back decks, both very pleasant, and all-day sandwiches, burgers, and deli platters (appropriately served on a slate). Evening meals step it up a notch, with quality dishes based on regional produce.

ℹ Getting There & Around

West Coast Motors (✏ 01586-555885; www.westcoastmotors.co.uk) Bus 418 runs four to five times a day, except Sunday, from Oban to Ellenabeich (£3, 45 minutes), and on to North Cuan (£3, 53 minutes) at Seil's southern tip for the ferry to Luing.

Easdale Ferry (✏ 01631-562125; www.argyll-bute.gov.uk) Has a daily passenger-only ferry service from Ellenabeich to Easdale Island (£2.10 return, bicycles free, five minutes, shuttle service at busy times, otherwise every 30 minutes).

Luing Ferry (www.argyll-bute.gov.uk; North Cuan; return per person/car £2.10/8.50) Departs every 30 minutes from Seil's southern tip for the three-minute trip to Luing.

Mull

POP 2800

From the rugged ridges of Ben More and the black basalt crags of Burg to the blinding white sand, rose-pink granite and emerald waters that fringe the Ross, Mull can lay claim to some of the finest and most varied scenery in the Inner Hebrides. Noble birds of prey soar over mountain and coast, while the western waters provide good whale watching. Add a lovely waterfront 'capital', an impressive castle, the sacred island of Iona and easy access from Oban, and you can see why it's sometimes impossible to find a spare bed on the island.

🛱 Tours

Mull's varied landscapes and habitats offer the chance to spot some of Scotland's rarest and most dramatic wildlife, including sea eagles, golden eagles, otters, dolphins and whales. Numerous operators offer walking or road trips to see them; email mull@visitscotland.com for a full list.

Nature Scotland
WILDLIFE

(✏ 07743 956380; www.naturescotland.com) Young, enthusiastic guides offer a range of excellent wildlife tours, including afternoon trips that can link to ferries (adult/child £30/25, four hours), evening otter-spotting trips (£40/35, three to four hours), all-day walking trips (£60/50, seven hours) and winter stargazing excursions (£40/30, two to three hours).

Mull Eagle Watch
BIRDWATCHING

(✏ 01680-812556; www.mulleaglewatch.com; adult/child £8/4; ⏰ Apr-Sep) Britain's largest bird of prey, the white-tailed eagle, or sea eagle, has been successfully reintroduced to Mull, and the island is crowded with birdwatchers raptly observing the raptor. Two-hour tours to observe this bird are held in the mornings and afternoons, and must be booked in advance.

Turus Mara
BOATING

(✏ 01688-400242; www.turusmara.com; ⏰ Apr-mid-Oct) Offers trips from Ulva Ferry in central Mull to Staffa and the Treshnish Isles (adult/child £65/32.50, six hours), with an hour ashore on Staffa and two hours on Lunga, where you can see seals, puffins, kittiwakes, razorbills and many other species of seabird. There are also trips to Staffa alone (£32.50/18, 3¾ hours) and birdwatching-focused trips (£75/37.50, eight hours).

Transfer is also available from the Craignure ferry terminal, allowing you to visit as a day trip from Oban.

Staffa Tours
BOATING

(✏ 07831 885985; www.staffatours.com; ⏰ Apr-mid-Oct) Runs boat trips from Fionnphort and Iona to Staffa (adult/child £35/17.50, three hours), or Staffa plus the Treshnish Isles (also available from Tobermory and Ardnamurchan; £65/32.50, six hours). Before and after the seabird season, the trip is shorter (£50/30, five hours), not landing on Lunga. There are also connection-plus-tour options leaving from Oban.

Mull, Coll & Tiree

Mull Magic   WALKING

(☑ 01688-301213; www.mullmagic.com) Offers guided walking tours in the Mull country-side to spot eagles, otters, butterflies and other wildlife. Customised tours are also available; check the website for the different itineraries.

Isle of Mull Wildlife Expeditions   WILDLIFE

(☑ 01688-500121; www.torrbuan.com; adult/child £44.50/39.50) Six-hour Land Rover tours of the island with the chance of spotting red deer, golden eagles, peregrine falcons, white-tailed sea eagles, hen harriers, otters and perhaps dolphins and porpoises. The cost includes pick-up from your accommodation or the ferry, a picnic lunch and binoculars. It's possible as a day trip from Oban.

🎆 Festivals & Events

Mull Music Festival   MUSIC

(www.facebook.com/mullmusicfestival; ⊘ last weekend Apr) Four days of foot-stomping traditional Scottish and Irish folk music at Tobermory's pubs.

Mendelssohn on Mull   MUSIC

(www.mendelssohnonmull.com; ⊘ early Jul) A weeklong festival of chamber music, with performances around Mull island.

❶ Information

There's a bank with an ATM in Tobermory; otherwise you can get cash back with a purchase from Co-op food stores.

Craignure Tourist Office (☑ 01680-812377; www.visitscotland.com; Craignure; ⊘ 9am-5pm Mon, 8.30am-5pm Tue-Sat, 10am-5pm Sun Sep-Jun, 9am-6.15pm Mon, 8.30am-6.15pm Tue-Sat, 10am-4.15pm Sun Jul & Aug) Opposite the ferry slip.

Explore Mull (☑ 01688-302875; www.isle-of-mull.net; Ledaig; ⊘ 9am-5pm Easter-Jun & Sep–mid-Oct, to 7pm Jul & Aug; 🐟) In Tobermory car park. Has local information, can book all manner of island tours and hires out bikes.

Mull & Iona Community Hospital (☑ 01680-300392; www.nhshighland.scot.nhs.uk; Craignure) Has an A&E department.

❶ Getting There & Away

CalMac (www.calmac.co.uk) has three car ferries that link Mull with the mainland:

Oban to Craignure (adult/car £3.60/13.40, 40 minutes, every two hours) The busiest route – bookings are advised if you have a car.

Lochaline to Fishnish (adult/car £2.40/7.15, 15 minutes, at least hourly, except four daily on winter Sundays) On the east coast of Mull.

Tobermory to Kilchoan (adult/car £2.75/8.65, 35 minutes, seven daily Monday to Saturday, five Sunday April to October, three Monday to Saturday November to March) Links to the Ardnamurchan peninsula.

ℹ️ Getting Around

BICYCLE

You can hire bikes for around £20 per day from various places around the island, including Explore Mull in Tobermory.

BUS

West Coast Motors (☑01680-812313; www. westcoastmotors.co.uk) connects ferry ports and main villages. Its Discovery Day Pass (adult/child £15/7.50) is available from April to October and grants a day's unlimited bus travel.

The routes useful for visitors are bus 95/495 from Craignure to Tobermory, bus 96/496 from Craignure to Fionnphort, and bus 494 from Tobermory to Dervaig and Calgary.

CAR

Almost all of Mull's road network consists of single-track roads. There are petrol stations at Craignure, Fionnphort, Salen and Tobermory.

Mull Car Hire (☑07425 127900; www.mullcar hire.co.uk; car hire per day/week £50/280) Rents out small cars. Will bring cars to the ferry terminal.

Mull Taxi (☑07760 426351; www.mulltaxi. co.uk) Based in Tobermory.

Craignure & Around

POP 200

Located 3 miles south of Craignure, where the principal ferries from the mainland arrive, is Duart Castle, the ancestral seat of the Maclean clan, enjoying a spectacular position on a rocky outcrop overlooking the Sound of Mull. Otherwise there's not much to see at Craignure.

Duart Castle　　　　　　　　　　CASTLE
(☑01680-812309; www.duartcastle.com; adult/ child £7/3.50; ⊙10.30am-5pm daily May–mid-Oct, 11am-4pm Sun-Thu Apr) Originally built in the 13th century, it was abandoned for 160 years before a 1912 restoration. As well as dungeons, courtyard and battlements with memorable views, there's lots of clan history – none worse than the story of Lachlan Cattanach, who took his wife on an outing to an island in the strait, then left her there to drown when the tide came in.

A bus to the castle meets some of the incoming ferries at Craignure (£11 return including castle entrance), but it's a pretty walk to get here, too.

★ **Craignure Bunkhouse**　　　　HOSTEL £
(☑01680-812043; www.craignure-bunkhouse.co.uk; Craignure; dm/q £24/90; P🐾) An excellent hostel near the ferry slip, this purpose-built accommodation features top en suite dorms fetchingly decked out in wood. Bunks have lots of headroom and individual USB chargers, lamps and powerpoints. There are also double bunks for families. The ecologically minded design means sustainable sleeping, and the hostel has a great kitchen, sociable common area and enthusiastic staff.

Tobermory

POP 1000

Mull's main town is a very picturesque little fishing and yachting port with brightly painted houses arranged around a sheltered harbour. It's a great base, with good places to eat, inviting pubs and an array of quality accommodation both along the harbourfront and on the hill behind.

◎ Sights & Activities

The children's TV program *Balamory* was set here, and while the series stopped filming in 2004, regular repeats mean that the town still swarms in summer with toddlers (and nostalgic teenagers) towing parents around the locations (you can get a *Balamory* info sheet from tourist offices).

Whale-watching boat trips run out of Tobermory harbour. A range of tours can be booked at Explore Mull in the waterfront car park.

Hebridean Whale & Dolphin Trust　MUSEUM
(☑01688-302620; www.whaledolphintrust.co.uk; 28 Main St; ⊙10.30am-4.30pm Mar-Nov) 🐾 FREE
This place has displays, videos and interactive exhibits on whale and dolphin biology and ecology, and is a great place for kids to learn about sea mammals. It also provides information about volunteering and reporting sightings of whales and dolphins. Opening times are rather variable.

Mull Aquarium　　　　　　　AQUARIUM
(☑01688-302876; www.mullaquarium.co.uk; Ledaig; adult/child £5/4; ⊙9.30am-5pm Easter-Oct; 👶) 🐾 By the harbour car park, this aquarium has good information on the local marine environment, and little touch pools with crabs, starfish and the like for kids. All the creatures are returned to the sea after they've done a four-week shift here.

Mull Museum   MUSEUM

(☑ 01688-301100; www.mullmuseum.org.uk; Main St; ⊙ 10am-4pm Mon-Sat Easter-Oct) **FREE** Mull Museum, which records the history of the island, is a good place to go on a rainy day. There are interesting exhibits on crofting, and on the *Tobermory Galleon,* a ship from the Spanish Armada that sank in Tobermory Bay in 1588 and has been the object of treasure seekers ever since. Donations are appreciated in this volunteer-run set-up.

Tobermory Distillery   DISTILLERY

(☑ 01688-302647; www.tobermorymalt.com; Ledaig; tours £8; ⊙ 10am-5pm) This bijou distillery was established in 1798. It doesn't always open on winter weekends; phone ahead to check or book. There are two whisky lines here: the standard Tobermory and the lightly peated Ledaig. The standard tour lets you taste one of them; for £10, you can try them both.

Sea Life Surveys   WILDLIFE

(☑ 01688-302916; www.sealifesurveys.com; Ledaig) Whale-watching trips head from Tobermory harbour to the waters north and west of Mull. An all-day whale-watch allows up to seven hours at sea (£80), and has a 95% success rate for sightings. The four-hour Whalewatch cruise (adult/child £60/30) is better for families. Shorter seal-spotting excursions are also available (£25/12.50, two hours).

🛏 Sleeping

Tobermory has dozens of B&Bs, but the place can still be booked solid any time from May through to August, especially at weekends. Most options close in winter.

Tobermory SYHA   HOSTEL £

(☑ 01688-302481; www.syha.org.uk; Main St; dm/tw/q £20/60/112; ⊙ Mar-Oct; @ 🛜) This hostel has a great location in a Victorian house right on the waterfront. It's got an excellent kitchen and spotless if somewhat austere dorms, as well as good triples and quads for families. It books out fast in summer.

★ Sonas House   B&B ££

(☑ 01688-302304; www.sonashouse.co.uk; Fairways, Erray Rd; s/d £90/130, apt for 2 excl/incl breakfast £100/130; P 🛜 ⛱) Here's a treat: a B&B with a heated, indoor 10m swimming pool! Sonas is a large, modern house (follow signs to the golf course) offering luxury in a beautiful setting with superb Tobermory Bay views. Both rooms are beautifully done out with blond wood and other colours; 'Blue Poppy' has its own balcony. There's

also a self-contained studio apartment. Hospitality is faultless.

Harbour Guesthouse   B&B ££

(☑ 01688-302209; www.harbourguesthouse -tobermory.com; 59 Main St; s £65-70, d £90-110; ⊙ Easter–mid-Oct; 🛜) On the harbourfront, this is a cute Tobermory base that offers rooms varying in size and shape that have been refurbished and are most comfortable. Great harbour views and cordial hosts.

Cuidhe Leathain   B&B ££

(☑ 01688-302504; www.cuidhe-leathain.co.uk; Breadalbane St; r £100; ⊙ Apr-Oct; 🛜) A handsome 19th-century house in Tobermory's 'upper town', Cuidhe Leathain (coo-lane), which means Maclean's Corner, exudes a cosily cluttered Victorian atmosphere. The rooms are beautifully plush, with plunger coffee and decent teas. Breakfasts will set you up for the rest of the day, and the owners are a fount of knowledge about Mull and its wildlife. Minimum two-night stay.

★ Highland Cottage   BOUTIQUE HOTEL £££

(☑ 01688-302030; www.highlandcottage.co.uk; Breadalbane St; d £160-175; ⊙ Apr–mid-Oct; P 🛜 ⛱) Antique furniture, four-poster beds, embroidered bedspreads, fresh flowers and candlelight lend this small hotel (only six rooms) an appealingly old-fashioned cottage atmosphere, but with all mod cons, including cable TV, full-size baths and room service. There's also an excellent restaurant here (dinner £42.50), and the personable owners are experts in guest comfort.

🍴 Eating

Pier Café   CAFE £

(☑ 07786 197377; www.facebook.com/thepiercafe tobermory; The Pier; light meals £7-10; ⊙ 9.30am-5pm Mon-Thu, to 7pm Fri & Sat, 10.30am-5pm Sun mid-Mar–Oct; 🛜 ♿) A cosy wee corner with local art on the walls, tucked beneath Café Fish at the north end of Tobermory village, the Pier serves great coffee and breakfast rolls, top baguettes that may feature local squat lobster or other seafood, plus tasty lunches such as haddock and chips, pasta and sandwiches.

Fish & Chip Van   FISH & CHIPS £

(☑ 01688-301109; www.tobermoryfishandchipvan. co.uk; Main St; fish & chips £6-10; ⊙ 12.30-9pm Mon-Sat Apr-May, 12.30-9pm daily Jun-Sep, 12.30-7pm Mon-Thu, to 8pm Fri & Sat Oct-Mar) If it's takeaway you're after, you can tuck into some of Scotland's best gourmet fish and chips down on the Tobermory waterfront. And where else will you find a chip van selling freshly cooked scallops?

★ **Café Fish**   SEAFOOD **££**
(☑ 01688-301253; www.thecafefish.com; The Pier; mains £15-26; ☉noon-3pm & 5.30-11pm mid-Mar–Oct; 🐸) ✈ Seafood doesn't come much fresher than the stuff served at this warm and welcoming little restaurant overlooking Tobermory harbour. Crustaceans go straight from boat to kitchen to join rich seafood stew, fat scallops, fish pie and catch-of-the-day on the daily-changing menu, where confident use of Asian ingredients adds an extra dimension. Book ahead.

Hebridean Lodge   SCOTTISH **££**
(☑ 01688-301207; www.hebrideanlodge.co.uk; Salen Rd, Baliscate; mains £17-21; ☉ 6.30-8.30pm Mon-Fri Easter-Dec) Above a gallery and shop, this mezzanine restaurant offers delicious local produce at chunky wooden tables. There's a warm welcome and fine, fresh seafood and lamb, with daily specials complementing the short menu of generous-spirited Scottish cuisine. Book ahead.

🍷 **Drinking & Entertainment**

★ **Mishnish Hotel**   PUB
(☑01688-302500; www.mishnish.co.uk; Main St; ☉11am-1am; 🐸) 'The Mish', near the pier on the harbourfront, is a favourite hang-out for visiting yachties and a great place for a pint, with a very convivial atmosphere. Wood-panelled and flag-draped, this is a good old traditional pub where you can listen to live folk music, toast your toes by the open fire or challenge locals to a game of pool.

★ **Comar**   PERFORMING ARTS
(☑01688-302211; www.comar.co.uk) Mull's lively arts scene includes a famous theatre group, regular art exhibitions and concerts. This arts organisation puts on exhibitions, plays and concerts in Tobermory's **An Tobar Arts Centre** (☑01688-302211; www.comar. co.uk; Argyll Tce; ☉10am-5pm Mon-Sat May-Sep, 11am-4pm Tue-Sat Oct-Apr) FREE and elsewhere. Check its website for upcoming events.

North Mull

The road from Tobermory west to Calgary cuts inland, leaving most of Mull's north coast wild and inaccessible. It continues through the settlement of Dervaig to the glorious beach at Calgary. From here onwards

you are treated to spectacular coastal views; it's worth doing the route in reverse from Gruline for the best vistas.

◎ **Sights**

Calgary Beach   BEACH
Mull's best (and busiest) silver-sand beach, flanked by cliffs and with views out to Coll and Tiree, is about 12 miles west of Tobermory. And yes – this is the place from which Canada's more famous Calgary takes its name.

Glengorm Castle   GALLERY, PARK
(☑01688-302321; www.glengormcastle.co.uk; Glengorm; ☉buildings 10am-5pm Easter-Oct) FREE A long, single-track road leads north for 4 miles from Tobermory to majestic Glengorm Castle, with views across the sea to Ardnamurchan, Rum and the Outer Hebrides. The castle outbuildings house a **nature centre, farm shop** and the excellent **Glengorm Coffee Shop** (light meals £3-9; 🐸✈) ✈. The castle, which also has upmarket B&B acccommodation (p286), is not open to the public, but you're free to explore the beautiful grounds, where several good walks are signposted. Guided nature walks also run from here; check the website for times.

WHALE WATCHING ON MULL

The North Atlantic Drift – a swirling tendril of the Gulf Stream – carries warm water into the cold, nutrient-rich seas off the Scottish coast, resulting in huge plankton blooms. Small fish feed on the plankton, and bigger fish feed on the smaller fish; this huge seafood smorgasbord attracts large numbers of marine mammals, from harbour porpoises and dolphins to minke whales and even – though sightings are rare – humpback and sperm whales.

There are dozens of operators around the coast offering **whale-watching** boat trips lasting from a couple of hours to all day; some have sighting success rates of 95% in summer.

While seals, porpoises and dolphins can be seen year-round, minke whales are migratory. The best time to see them is from June to August, with August being the peak month for sightings. The website of the **Hebridean Whale & Dolphin Trust** (www.whale dolphintrust.co.uk) has lots of information on the species you are likely to see, and how to identify them.

Calgary Art in Nature
GALLERY

(📞01688-400256; www.calgary.co.uk; Calgary; entry by donation; ⏰10am-5pm Mar-Nov) Run with enthusiasm and vision, this place just back from Calgary beach is an excellent art space, and also has great self-catering accommodation. On-site silversmiths and wood sculptors ply their trade in their workshops, while a luminous gallery exhibits high-quality work from local artists. Other pieces dot the woodland ramble on the hill behind. There's also the good **Calgary Farmhouse Tearoom** (light meals £5-9; ⏰10am-5pm Easter-Oct, to 2pm Mon-Fri Nov-Mar; 📶) here.

🍴 Sleeping & Eating

Dervaig Hostel
HOSTEL £

(📞01688-400313; dervaigbunkrooms@gmail.com; Dervaig; dm/q £18/60; ⏰Apr-Oct; P📶) Comfortable bunkhouse accommodation in Dervaig's village hall, with self-catering kitchen and sitting room. The dorms have good en suite bathrooms and comfortable bunks.

★ Calgary Farmhouse
COTTAGE ££

(📞01688-400256; www.calgary.co.uk; Calgary; per week summer apt & cottages £500-2000, per 3 days studios & cabin £200-270; P📶🐾) This brilliant complex near Calgary beach offers a number of fantastic apartments, cottages and houses, beautifully designed and fitted out with timber furniture and wood-burning stoves. The Hayloft is spectacular, with noble oak and local art, while the wood-clad longhall-like Beach House has luxury and dreamy views. Romantic Kittiwake, a beautiful wooden camping cabin among trees, has bay views and a boat ceiling.

There are options sleeping from two to 10. The larger ones go by the week in summer, but smaller ones are available for shorter stays. There's a good on-site cafe that sells some foodstuffs too. Bikes are available for hire.

Bellachroy
INN ££

(📞01688-400314; www.thebellachroy.co.uk; Dervaig; s/d £85/125; ⏰Easter-Oct; P📶🐾) The Bellachroy is an atmospheric 17th-century droving inn with seven comfortable bedrooms with stripy carpets; they vary in size. The bar is a focus for local social life and serves decent food (noon to 2.30pm and 6pm to 8.30pm). Management are very helpful.

Glengorm Castle
B&B £££

(📞01688-302321; www.glengormcastle.co.uk; r £135-290; P📶🐾) Bristling with turrets as a real castle should, this accommodation enjoys an unforgettable location, with huge windows framing green fields sloping down to the water. The attractive interior has 20th-century art instead of stags' heads. Bedrooms are all different, with lots of space and character. It's got lively, genuinely friendly owners, and kids will have a ball running around the grounds.

Rooms are £30 more expensive if you only stay one night. There are also various self-catering cottages available (£495 to £890 per week).

Am Birlinn
SCOTTISH ££

(📞01688-400619; www.ambirlinn.com; Penmore, Dervaig; mains £14-24; ⏰noon-2.30pm & 5-9pm Wed-Sun mid-Mar–Oct; 📶) Occupying a spacious and modern wooden building between Dervaig and Calgary, this is an interesting dining option. Locally caught crustaceans and molluscs are the way to go here, though there are burgers, venison and other meat dishes available. Free pick-up and drop-off from Tobermory or other nearby spots is offered. There's also a bar.

South Mull

The road from Craignure to Fionnphort climbs through wild and desolate scenery before reaching the southwestern part of the island, which consists of a long peninsula called the **Ross of Mull**. The Ross has a spectacular south coast lined with black basalt cliffs that give way further west to white-sand beaches and pink granite crags. The cliffs are highest at Malcolm's Point, near the superb **Carsaig Arches**.

The village of **Bunessan** is home to a cottage museum; a minor road leads south from here to the beautiful white-sand bay of **Uisken**, with views of the Paps of Jura.

At the western end of the Ross, 35 miles from Craignure, is **Fionnphort** (*finn*-a-fort) and the Iona ferry. The coast here is a beautiful blend of pink granite rocks, white sandy beaches and vivid turquoise sea.

👁 Sights

Ardalanish Weavers
WORKSHOP

(📞01681-700265; www.ardalanish.com; ⏰10am-5pm Apr-Oct, to 4pm Mon-Fri Nov-Mar) Fleeces from the Hebridean sheep on this farm are woven into fine woollen products using venerable looms, which you can see at work in the old cowshed. Hot drinks and snacks are available at the shop, which sells weaving and farm produce. You can also feed the Highland cattle here. It's on a remote rural backroad 2 miles south of Bunessan.

Ross of Mull Historical Centre MUSEUM
(Tigh na Rois; ☑ 01681-700659; www.romhc.org.uk; Bunessan; entry by donation; ☉ 10am-4pm Mon-Fri Apr-Oct, other times by arrangement) The little village of Bunessan is home to the Ross of Mull Historical Centre, a cottage museum by a ruined mill that houses displays on local history, geology, archaeology, genealogy and wildlife.

🛏 Sleeping & Eating

Ross of Mull Bunkhouse HOSTEL £
(☑ 07759 615200; www.rossofmullbunkhouse. co.uk; Fionnphort; dm/s/tw £24/48/70; P🛜) Run by enthusiastic young owners, this excellent year-round bunkhouse about a mile from the Iona ferry offers a rural atmosphere, top-notch modern bathrooms and spacious, comfortable four-berth rooms with sturdy metal bunks, USB ports and bedside lights. There's an attractive common room with fireplace, guitars and loch views, plus a brilliant kitchen and a drying room.

Fidden Farm CAMPSITE £
(☑ 01681-700427; Fidden, Fionnphort; sites per adult/child £10/5; ☉ Easter-Aug; P🐾) A basic but popular and beautifully situated campsite, with views over pink granite reefs to Iona and Erraid. It's just over a mile south of Fionnphort. It can be very blowy when the wind gets up. Opening months vary a little from year to year.

★ Seaview B&B ££
(☑ 01681-700235; www.iona-bed-breakfast-mull. com; Fionnphort; s £65, d £90-105; ☉ mid-Mar–Oct; P🛜🐾) ⌀ Just up from the ferry, Seaview has beautifully decorated bedrooms and a breakfast conservatory with grand views across to Iona. The rooms are compact and charming, with gleaming modern bathrooms. The owners are incredibly helpful and also offer tasty three-course dinners (not in summer), often based around local seafood, while breakfasts include locally sourced produce.

Achaban House B&B ££
(☑ 01681-700205; www.achabanhouse.co.uk; Fionnphort; s/d £46/75; P🛜) This super refurbished rural house has very pleasing contemporary rooms with modern fabrics and a light, uncluttered feel. Some rooms look over the loch below. It's casual and friendly;

the ideal base for visiting Iona with the ferry less than a mile away. Guests have use of an excellent kitchen and a lounge with wood-burning stove. Continental breakfasts feature homemade bread.

★ Ninth Wave SCOTTISH £££
(☑ 01681-700757; www.ninthwaverestaurant.co.uk; Bruach Mhor, Fionnphort; 3-/4-/5-course dinner £48/56/68; ☉ sittings 7pm Wed-Sun May-Oct) ⌀ This excellent croft restaurant is owned and operated by a lobster fisherman and his Canadian wife. The daily menu makes use of locally landed shellfish and crustaceans, vegetables and salad grown in the garden, and quality local meats with a nose-to-tail ethos. It's all served in a stylishly converted bothy. Advance bookings (a couple of weeks at least) are essential. No under-12s.

It's worth going all-in and taking on the superb cheeseboard if you've got room. Don't miss the handmade chocolates infused with locally foraged flavours.

Iona

POP 200

Like an emerald teardrop off Mull's western shore, enchanting, idyllic Iona, holy island and burial ground of kings, is a magical place that lives up to its lofty reputation. From the moment you embark on the ferry towards its sandy shores and green fields, you'll notice something different about it. To appreciate its charms, spend the night: there are some excellent places to do it. Iona has declared itself a fair-trade island and actively promotes ecotourism.

History

St Columba sailed from Ireland and landed on Iona in 563, establishing a monastic community with the aim of Christianising Scotland. It was here that the *Book of Kells* – the prize attraction of Dublin's Trinity College – is believed to have been transcribed. It was taken to Ireland for safekeeping from 9th-century Viking raids.

The community was re-founded as a Benedictine monastery in the early 13th century and prospered until its destruction during the Reformation. The ruins were given to the Church of Scotland in 1899, and by 1910 a group of enthusiasts called the Iona Community Council had reconstructed the abbey. It's still a flourishing spiritual community offering regular courses and retreats.

STAFFA

Felix Mendelssohn, who visited the uninhabited island of Staffa, off Mull, in 1829, was inspired to compose his 'Hebrides Overture' after hearing waves echoing in the impressive and cathedral-like **Fingal's Cave**. The cave walls and surrounding cliffs are composed of vertical, hexagonal basalt columns that look like pillars (Staffa is Norse for 'Pillar Island'). You can land on the island and walk into the cave via a causeway. Nearby **Boat Cave** can be seen from the causeway, but you can't reach it on foot. Staffa also has a sizeable puffin colony, north of the landing place.

Northwest of Staffa lies a chain of uninhabited islands called the Treshnish Isles. The two main islands are the curiously shaped **Dutchman's Cap** and **Lunga**. You can land on Lunga, walk to the top of the hill, and visit the shag, puffin and guillemot colonies on the west coast at Harp Rock.

Unless you have your own boat, the only way to reach Staffa and the Treshnish Isles is on an organised boat trip from Fionnphort, Iona, Tobermory, Ardnamurchan, Seil or the Ulva ferry slip. Operators include Turus Mara (p281), Staffa Tours (p281), Staffa Trips and Seafari Adventures (p280).

◉ Sights

Past the abbey, look for a footpath on the left signposted **Dun I** (dun-ee). An easy 15-minute walk leads to Iona's highest point, with fantastic 360-degree views.

★ **Iona Abbey** HISTORIC BUILDING
(☑ 01681-700512; www.historicenvironment.scot; adult/child £7.50/4.50; ☺ 9.30am-5.30pm Apr-Sep, 10am-4pm Oct-Mar) Iona's ancient but heavily reconstructed abbey is the spiritual heart of the island. The spectacular **nave**, dominated by Romanesque and early Gothic vaults and columns, is a powerful space; a door on the left leads to the beautiful **cloister**, where medieval grave slabs sit alongside modern religious sculptures. Out the back, the **museum** displays fabulous carved high crosses and other inscribed stones, along with lots of background information. A replica of the intricately carved St John's Cross stands outside the abbey.

Next to the abbey is an ancient **graveyard** where there's an evocative Romanesque chapel, as well as a mound that marks the burial place of 48 of Scotland's early kings, including Macbeth. Former Labour party leader John Smith is also buried in this cemetery. The ruined **nunnery** nearby was established at the same time as the Benedictine abbey. The museum is closed Sundays in winter.

Iona Heritage Centre MUSEUM
(☑ 01681-700576; www.ionaheritage.co.uk; entry by donation; ☺ 10am-5.15pm Mon-Sat Easter-Oct) This place covers the history of Iona, crofting and lighthouses; there's also a craft shop and a cafe serving delicious home baking.

☞ Tours

Alternative Boat Hire BOATING
(☑ 01681-700537; www.boattripsiona.com; ☺ Mon-Thu Apr–mid-Oct) Offers cruises in a traditional wooden sailing boat for fishing, birdwatching, picnicking or just admiring the scenery. Three-hour afternoon trips cost £30/10 per adult/child; on Wednesday there's a full-day cruise (£50/20; 10am to 5pm). Bookings are essential.

Staffa Trips BOATING
(☑ 01681-700358; www.staffatrips.co.uk; ☺ Apr–mid-Oct) Runs three-hour boat trips to Staffa (adult/child £35/17.50) on the MV *Iolaire*, departing Iona pier at 9.45am and 1.45pm, and from Fionnphort at 10am and 2pm, with one hour ashore on Staffa.

🛏 Sleeping & Eating

There are B&B options, camping, a hostel and a pair of hotels on the island. It's imperative to book accommodation well ahead in spring and summer. Very little is open in winter apart from the hostel.

There are a couple of hotel restaurants, and the abbey has a cafe, as does the heritage centre. There's also a supermarket and a mediocre fast-food place by the ferry.

★ **Iona Hostel** HOSTEL £
(☑ 01681-700781; www.ionahostel.co.uk; dm adult/child £21/17.50, tw £42, bothy s/d £40/60; [P] [⛽] 🛜) 🌿 This working ecological croft and environmentally sensitive hostel is one of Scotland's most rewarding and tranquil places to stay. Lovable black Hebridean sheep surround the building, which features pretty, practical

and comfy dorms and an excellent kitchen-lounge. There's a fabulous beach nearby, and a hill to climb for views. It's just over a mile from the ferry on Iona, past the abbey.

There's also a cute wheeled bothy nearby, perfect for a bit of solitude.

★ Argyll Hotel
HOTEL **££**

(☎01681-700334; www.argyllhoteliona.co.uk; s £79, d £99-119; ☺mid-Mar–mid-Oct; 🛜🐾) 🍽
This lovable, higgledy-piggledy warren of a hotel has great service and appealing snug rooms (those with sea views cost more – £174 for a double), including good-value family options. The rooms offer simple comfort and relaxation rather than luxury. Most look out to the rear, where a huge organic garden supplies the restaurant. This is a relaxing and amiably run Iona haven.

Iona Pods
CABIN **££**

(☎01681-700233; www.ionapods.com; pods £80; 🅿🛜) Sleeping up to four, these pods on a working croft have a simple kitchen. There's power, but washing and toilet facilities are separate.

ℹ Getting There & Away

The ferry from Fionnphort to Iona (£3.40 adult return, five minutes, hourly) runs daily. Cars can only be taken with a permit. There are also various day trips available to Iona from Tobermory and Oban.

Tiree
POP 700

Low-lying Tiree (tye-*ree;* from the Gaelic *tiriodh,* meaning 'land of corn') is a fertile sward of lush, green machair liberally sprinkled with yellow buttercups, much of it so flat that, from a distance, the houses seem to rise out of the sea. It's one of the sunniest places in Scotland, but also one of the windiest – cyclists soon find that, although it's flat, heading west usually feels like going uphill. One major benefit – the constant breeze keeps away the midges.

The surf-lashed coastline here is scalloped with broad, sweeping beaches of white sand, hugely popular with windsurfers and kite-surfers. Most visitors, however, come for the birdwatching, beachcombing and lonely coastal walks.

In the 19th century Tiree had a population of 4500, but poverty, food shortages and overcrowding led the Duke of Argyll to introduce a policy of assisted emigration. Between 1841 and 1881, more than 3600 left, many emigrating to Canada, the USA, Australia and New Zealand.

◎ Sights & Activities

Look out for the Tyree gin distillery, due to open on the island in around 2020. The gin is already produced on the mainland using local botanicals.

Skerryvore Lighthouse Museum
MUSEUM

(☎01879-220045; www.hebrideantrust.org; Hynish; ☺9am-5pm May-Sep) FREE The picturesque harbour and hamlet of Hynish, near Tiree's southern tip, was built in the 19th century to house workers and supplies for the construction of lonely Skerryvore Lighthouse, 10 miles offshore. This museum occupies the old workshops by the sand-filled but flushable harbour; up the hill is the signal tower once used to communicate by semaphore with the lighthouse.

An Iodhlann
LIBRARY

(☎01879-220793; www.aniodhlann.org.uk; Scarinish; ☺9am-1pm Mon & Wed-Thu Sep-Jun, 11am-5pm Mon-Fri Jul & Aug) FREE An Iodhlann is a historical and genealogical library and archive, where some of the tens of thousands of descendants of Tiree emigrants come to trace their ancestry. The centre stages summer exhibitions on island life and history. Check the website for winter opening times as it varies by volunteer availability.

Wild Diamond
WATER SPORTS

(☎07712 159205; www.wilddiamond.co.uk; Cornaig; ☺Apr-Oct) Professional and friendly, this outfit runs courses in windsurfing (£35/100 per session/day), kitesurfing (£70/120 per half-/full day), surfing, sand-yachting and stand-up paddleboarding, and rents out equipment including surfboards.

Blackhouse Watersports
WATER SPORTS

(☎07711 807976; www.blackhouse-watersports.co.uk; Gott Bay; ☺Mar-Nov) Operating out of a beach hut at the far end of Gott Bay, this welcoming set-up runs kitesurfing (£100) and surf (£35) lessons, hires kayaks (£25 for three hours, including wetsuit), lends out fishing tackle and rents bikes (£10 per day).

🎪 Festivals & Events

Tiree Music Festival
MUSIC

(www.tireemusicfestival.co.uk; ☺mid-Jul) Held over a weekend in mid-July, this is a very likeable festival with a range of folksy, bluesy and rootsy music. They like to keep it small so limit the capacity; book ahead. Campsites are set up around the festival area in Crossapol.

Tiree Wave Classic SPORTS
(www.tireewaveclassic.co.uk; ⊘Oct) Reliable wind and big waves have made Tiree one of Scotland's top windsurfing venues. The annual Tiree Wave Classic competition has been held here since 1986, making it one of the world's longest-standing windsurfing championships.

🛏 Sleeping & Eating

Millhouse Hostel HOSTEL £
(☑01879-220802; www.tireemillhouse.co.uk; Cornaig; dm/s/tw £24/42/56; P🖘) Housed in a converted barn next to an old ruined water mill, this small but comfortable hostel is 5 miles west of the Tiree ferry pier. The dorms have beds rather than bunks, there's a common area and it's cheaper if you stay more than one night.

Balinoe Campsite CAMPSITE £
(☑07712 159205; www.tireecampsite.co.uk; Balinoe; tent sites adult/child £12/6, dm £23, pods £30; ⊘Apr-Oct; P🖘🐾) Balinoe is a sheltered campsite with full facilities in the southwest of Tiree island, near Balemartine, with great views of Mull. There are campsites with optional electric hook-up, pods and a very basic bothy. It's cheaper for multinight stays. A self-catering cottage is available year-round.

★Rockvale Guest House B&B ££
(☑01879-220675; www.rockvaletiree.co.uk; Balephetrish; s £68, d £88-98; P🖘🐾) Smart, comfortable, modern accommodation and a genuine welcome make this easily Tiree's best midrange accommodation choice. It's situated in the north of the island and does things with real panache. Breakfast is way above average, and features smoothies, fruit skewers, poached egg with spinach and pesto or banana mash.

Ceàbhar SCOTTISH ££
(☑01879-220684; www.ceabhar.com; Sandaig; mains £8-15; ⊘7-8.30pm Wed-Sat Easter-Oct, plus Tue Jul & Aug; 🖘🍴🐾) 🍽 At Tiree's western end, this attractive restaurant looks out over the Atlantic towards the sunset. The cordial owners have the right attitude; they grow their own salads, eschew chips, and brew craft beer. The menu includes handmade pizzas, soups, fish of the day and local lamb, with lots of vegetarian options. Book ahead.

A snug cottage sleeps up to eight people in five bedrooms.

ℹ Information

There's a bank (without an ATM), post office and supermarket in Scarinish, the main village on Tiree, half a mile south of the ferry pier. You can get cash back with debit-card purchases at the Co-op.

Some tourist information is available at the ferry terminal. A useful website is www.isleof tiree.com.

ℹ Getting There & Away

AIR

Loganair flies from Glasgow to Tiree daily. **Hebridean Air Services** (www.hebrideanair.co.uk) operates from Oban to Tiree via Coll (one way from Oban/Coll £65/10, twice daily Monday and Wednesday).

BOAT

CalMac (www.calmac.co.uk) has a ferry from Oban to Tiree (adult/car £10.60/57.65, four hours, one daily) via Coll, except on Friday when the boat calls at Tiree first (three hours 20 minutes). The one-way fare from Coll to Tiree (one hour) is £3.45/15.60 per adult/car.

On Wednesdays, the ferry continues to Barra in the Outer Hebrides (from Tiree adult/car £9.05/46.85 one way, three hours), and stops again on the way back to Oban, allowing a long day trip to Tiree from the mainland. In high summer, a day trip is also possible on Saturdays.

ℹ Getting Around

Rent bicycles and cars from **MacLennan Motors** (☑01879-220555; www.maclennanmotors. com; Pierhead, Scarinish; per day car £45, bicycle £10; ⊘9am-5pm Mon-Fri, to 1pm Sat) at the ferry pier. **Tiree Fitness** (☑07867 304640; www.tireefitness.co.uk; Sandaig; per day/week from £15/65) has better bikes and will deliver them to the ferry (£5 extra).

There's a transport-on-demand service on Tiree; phone 01879-220419.

Coll

POP 200

Coll is more rugged and less populous than Tiree, its neighbour. The northern part of the island is a mix of bare rock, bog and lochans (small lochs), while the south is swathed in golden shell-sand beaches and machair dunes up to 30m high. It's a gloriously relaxing place.

The island's main attraction is the peace and quiet – empty beaches, bird-haunted coastlines, and long walks along the shore. The biggest and most beautiful sandy beaches are at Crossapol in the south, and Hogh Bay and Cliad on the west coast.

In summer the corncrake's 'krek-krek' is heard at the RSPB Coll (☏01879-230301; www.rspb.org.uk; ⏰24hr) at Totronald in the southwest of the island. From Totronald a sandy 4WD track runs north past the dunes backing Hogh Bay to the road at Totamore, allowing walkers and cyclists to make a circuit back to Arinagour rather than backtracking.

🛏 Sleeping & Eating

There's a handful of places to stay, several of them excellent. You can wild camp for free on the hill above the Coll Hotel; ask at the hotel first.

★ **Coll Bunkhouse**   HOSTEL £

(☏01879-230217; www.collbunkhouse.com; Arinagour; dm/tw £22/50; 🅿🛜🐾) This gorgeous modern bunkhouse is in Coll's main settlement, just a 10- to 15-minute walk from the ferry pier. It's a great facility, with a kitchen, good showers and access for travellers with disabilities.

Island Café   CAFE ££

(☏01879-230262; www.visitcoll.co.uk; Arinagour; mains £6-13; ⏰11am-2pm & 5-9pm Wed-Sat, noon-6pm Sun; 🛜) This cheerful spot serves hearty, homemade meals such as sausage and mash, haddock and chips, and vegetarian cottage pie, accompanied by organic beer, wine and cider. Sunday roasts are legendary on Coll island.

❶ Information

For information on Coll, visit www.visitcoll.co.uk. Arinagour, half a mile from the ferry pier, is Coll's only village, home to a shop, post office (with ATM), craft shops and aged petrol station. Pride of the island is the phone mast; there was virtually no signal until 2015.

❶ Getting There & Away

AIR

Hebridean Air Services (www.hebrideanair.co.uk) operates from Oban to Coll (one way £65, twice daily Monday and Wednesday) and on to Tiree (£10).

BOAT

Ferries with **CalMac** (www.calmac.co.uk) run from Oban to Coll (adult/car £10.60/57.65, 2¾ hours, one daily) and on to Tiree, except on Friday when the ferry calls at Tiree first. The one-way fare between Coll and Tiree (one hour) is £3.45/15.60 per adult/car.

On Wednesdays, the ferry continues to Barra in the Outer Hebrides (from Coll adult/car £9.05/46.85 one way, four hours), and stops again on the way back to Oban, allowing a long day trip to Coll from the mainland. In high summer, a day trip is also possible on Saturdays.

❶ Getting Around

There is no public transport. Mountain bikes can be hired from the **post office** (☏01879-230395; fionaangus233@btinternet.com; per day £20; ⏰9am-1pm Mon-Sat) in Arinagour, while walking is another good option. Locals always offer lifts.

NORTH ARGYLL

The northern parts of Argyll harbour a diverse range of attractions, including two of Scotland's most photogenic castles and an island made for exploration by bike. Though it's often traversed rapidly by folk heading for the northern Highlands, it's worth slowing down to appreciate its many charms.

Loch Awe

Loch Awe is one of Scotland's most beautiful lochs, with rolling forested hills around its southern end and spectacular mountains in the north. It lies between Oban and Inveraray and is the longest loch in Scotland – about 24 miles – but is less than 1 mile wide for most of its length. At its northern end, it escapes to the sea through the narrow Pass of Brander, where Robert the Bruce defeated the MacDougalls in 1309.

★ **Kilchurn Castle**   CASTLE

(www.historicenvironment.scot; Dalmally; ⏰9.30am-5.30pm Apr-Sep, 10am-4pm Oct) **FREE** At the northern end of Loch Awe are the scenic ruins of the strategically situated and much-photographed Kilchurn Castle. Built in 1440, it enjoys one of Scotland's finest settings. Even when it's not open, it's worth visiting for the scenic stroll to it. It's a half-mile walk from an unmarked car park on the A85, just west of the Inveraray turnoff between Dalmally and Lochawe.

Cruachan Power Station   NOTABLE BUILDING

(☏01416-149105; www.visitcruachan.co.uk; A85; adult/child £7.50/2.50; ⏰9.30am-4.45pm Apr-Oct, 10am-3.45pm Mon-Fri Nov-Dec & Feb-Mar) In the Pass of Brander, by the A85, you can visit this power station. Electric buses take you more than half a mile inside Ben Cruachan,

WORTH A TRIP

CASTLE STALKER

One of Scotland's most spectacularly sited castles, **Castle Stalker** (☑ 01631-730354; www.castlestalker.com; Portnacroish; adult/child/family £20/10/50; ☺ tours Apr–Oct) perches on a tiny offshore island – Monty Python buffs will recognise it as the castle that appears in the final scenes of the film *Monty Python and the Holy Grail*. Visits are by two-hour guided tour by a family member (book by email or phone), and leave from a boat dock just off the A828. There's a maximum of one a day, so arrange your visit in advance.

allowing you to see the pump-storage hydro-electric scheme, which occupies a vast cavern hollowed out of the mountain. The tour takes half an hour. Falls of Cruachan railway station (seasonal) is very close by.

ℹ Getting There & Away

Trains from Glasgow to Oban stop at Dalmally and Lochawe villages.

In summer three daily buses with **Scottish Citylink** (www.citylink.co.uk) from Glasgow to Oban go via Dalmally, Lochawe village and Cruachan Power Station.

Connel & Taynuilt

Hemmed in by dramatic mountain scenery, **Loch Etive** stretches 17 miles from Connel to Kinlochetive (accessible by road from Glencoe). Some very different but worthwhile sights complement the beautiful scenery around here.

★ **Bonawe Iron Furnace**   HISTORIC SITE
(☑ 01866-822432; www.historicenvironment.scot; Taynuilt; adult/child £5/3; ☺ 9.30am–5.30pm Apr–Sep) Bonawe Iron Furnace is one of the region's most unusual historical sights. Near Taynuilt (not Bonawe), and dating from 1753, it was built by an iron-smelting company from Cumbria because of the abundance of birch and oak in the area. The coppiced wood was made into the charcoal that was needed for smelting the iron. It's now a tranquil, beautiful place, with the old

buildings picturesquely arranged around a green hillside, and there's great background information on the iron industry. Take a picnic!

Falls of Lora   WATERFALL
(Connel) At Connel Bridge, 5 miles north of Oban, the loch joins the sea via a narrow channel partly blocked by an underwater rock ledge. When the tide flows in and out, water pours through this bottleneck, creating spectacular white-water rapids known as the Falls of Lora. Park near the north end of the bridge and walk back into the middle to have a look.

Dunstaffnage Castle   CASTLE
(☑ 01631-562465; www.historicenvironment.scot; adult/child £6/3.60; ☺ 9.30am–5.30pm Apr–Sep, 10am–4pm Oct, 10am–4pm Sat–Wed Nov–Mar) Dunstaffnage, 2 miles west of Connel, looks like a child's drawing of what a castle should be – square and massive, with towers at the corners, and perched on top of a rocky outcrop. It was built around 1260 and was captured by Robert the Bruce during the Wars of Independence in 1309. The haunted ruins of the nearby 13th-century **chapel** contain lots of Campbell tombs decorated with skull-and-crossbone carvings.

Inverawe Smokehouse & Fishery   FOOD & DRINKS
(☑ Easter–Dec 01866-822808, Jan–Easter 01866-822777; www.inverawe-fisheries.co.uk; Inverawe, near Taynuilt; ☺ 9am–5pm mid-Mar–Oct; ☏ ♿) Aficionados of smoked salmon should pay a visit to Inverawe Smokehouse and Fishery, 2 miles east of Taynuilt, where local salmon (and trout, herring and venison) is smoked over split oak logs. There's also an angling school and trout fishery where you can learn to fly-fish, lots of family-friendly features, and a tearoom where you can sample the smokery's mouthwatering produce.

ℹ Getting There & Away

Trains from Glasgow to Oban stop at Taynuilt and Connel.

In summer one daily bus with **Scottish Citylink** (www.citylink.co.uk) bus from Glasgow to Oban goes via Taynuilt and Connel. Citylink services between Oban and Fort William also stop in Connel.

Inverness & the Central Highlands

Includes ➡

Best Places to Eat

➡ Lime Tree (p335)

➡ Café 1 (p299)

➡ Restaurant at the Cross (p315)

➡ Lochleven Seafood Cafe (p333)

➡ Old Forge (p343)

Best Places to Stay

➡ Rocpool Reserve (p299)

➡ Grange (p335)

➡ Lovat (p308)

➡ Milton Eonan (p328)

➡ Trafford Bank (p298)

Why Go?

From the sub-Arctic plateau of the Cairngorms to the hills of Highland Perthshire and the rocky peaks of Glen Coe, the central mountain ranges of the Scottish Highlands are testimony to the sculpting power of ice and weather. Here the landscape is at its grandest, with soaring hills of rock and heather bounded by wooded glens and waterfalls.

Not surprisingly, this part of the country is an adventure playground for outdoor-sports enthusiasts. Aviemore, Glen Coe and Fort William draw hill walkers and climbers in summer, and skiers, snowboarders and ice climbers in winter. Inverness, the Highland capital, provides urban rest and relaxation, while nearby Loch Ness and its elusive monster add a hint of mystery.

From Fort William, base camp for climbing Ben Nevis, the Road to the Isles leads past the beaches of Arisaig and Morar to Mallaig, jumping-off point for the isles of Eigg, Rum, Muck and Canna.

When to Go
Inverness

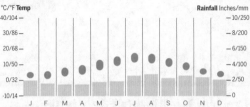

Apr–May Mountain scenery is at its most spectacular, with snow lingering on the higher peaks.

Jun Fort William hosts the UCI Mountain Bike World Cup, pulling huge crowds.

Sep Ideal for hiking and hill walking: midges are dying off, but weather is still reasonably good.

Central Highlands Highlights

① **Glen Affric** (p302) Hiking among the hills, lochs and forests of Scotland's most beautiful glen.

② **Rothiemurchus Estate** (p309) Wandering through

ancient Caledonian forest in the heart of the Cairngorms.

③ **Ben Nevis** (p338) Making it to the summit of the UK's highest mountain – and being able to see the view.

④ **Glen Lyon** (p328) Exploring the woods and mountains around this gorgeous and romantic glen.

⑤ **Rannoch Moor** (p325) Keeping right on to the end

of the road at this bleak but beautiful moor.

6 Nevis Range (p337) Rattling your teeth loose on this championship downhill mountain-bike course.

7 Sgurr of Eigg (p345) Taking in the stunning panorama from the summit of this dramatic island peak.

8 Glen Coe (p329) Soaking up the moody but magnificent scenery (when you can see it!).

9 Knoydart Peninsula (p342) Venturing into the country's most remote and rugged wilderness.

ⓘ Getting There & Around

For timetable information, call **Traveline Scotland** (www.travelinescotland.com).

BUS

Scottish Citylink (☑ 0871 266 3333; www.citylink.co.uk) Runs buses from Perth and Glasgow to Inverness and Fort William, and links Inverness to Fort William along the Great Glen.

Stagecoach (☑ 01463-233371; www.stagecoachbus.com) The main regional bus company, with offices in Aviemore, Inverness and Fort William. Dayrider tickets are valid for a day's unlimited travel on Stagecoach buses in various regions, including Inverness (£6.80), Aviemore (£7.30) and Fort William (£9.10).

TRAIN

Two railway lines serve the region: the Perth–Aviemore–Inverness line in the east, and the Glasgow–Fort William–Mallaig line in the west.

INVERNESS & THE GREAT GLEN

Inverness, one of Britain's fastest growing cities, is the capital of the Highlands. It's a transport hub and jumping-off point for the central, western and northern Highlands, the Moray Firth coast and the Great Glen.

The Great Glen is a geological fault running in a line across Scotland from Fort William to Inverness. The glaciers of the last ice age eroded a deep trough along the fault line, which is now filled by four lochs – Linnhe, Lochy, Oich and Ness. The glen has always been an important communication route – General George Wade built a military road along the southern side of Loch Ness in the early 18th century, and in 1822 the various lochs were linked by the Caledonian Canal (p334) to create a cross-country waterway. The A82 road along the glen was completed in 1933 – a date that coincides neatly with the first modern sightings of the Loch Ness Monster.

Inverness

POP 61,235

Inverness has a great location astride the River Ness at the northern end of the Great Glen. In summer it overflows with visitors intent on monster hunting at nearby Loch Ness, but it's worth a visit in its own right for a stroll along the picturesque River Ness,

a cruise on Loch Ness, and a meal in one of the city's excellent restaurants.

Inverness was probably founded by King David in the 12th century, but thanks to its often violent history few buildings of real age or historical significance have survived – much of the older part of the city dates from the period following the completion of the Caledonian Canal in 1822. The broad and shallow River Ness, famed for its salmon fishing, runs through the heart of the city.

◉ Sights & Activities

★ **Ness Islands**   PARK

The main attraction in Inverness is a leisurely stroll along the river to the Ness Islands. Planted with mature Scots pine, fir, beech and sycamore, and linked to the river banks and each other by elegant Victorian footbridges, the islands make an appealing picnic spot. They're a 20-minute walk south of the castle – head upstream on either side of the river (the start of the Great Glen Way), and return on the opposite bank.

On the way you'll pass the red-sandstone towers of **St Andrew's Cathedral** (11 Ardross St), dating from 1869, and the modern Eden Court Theatre (p300), which hosts regular art exhibits, both on the west bank.

Inverness Museum & Art Gallery   MUSEUM

(☑ 01463-237114; www.inverness.highland.museum; Castle Wynd; ◉ 10am-5pm Tue-Sat Apr-Oct, noon-4pm Thu-Sat Nov-Mar) **FREE** Inverness Museum & Art Gallery has wildlife dioramas, geological displays, period rooms with historic weapons, Pictish stones and exhibitions of contemporary Highland arts and crafts.

Dolphin Spirit   WILDLIFE WATCHING

(☑ 07544 800620; www.dolphinspirit.co.uk; Inverness Marina, Stadium Rd; adult/child £18.50/12; ◉ Easter-Oct) Four times a day in season, this outfit runs cruises from Inverness into the Moray Firth to spot the UK's largest pod of bottlenose dolphins – around 130 animals. The dolphins feed on salmon heading for the rivers at the head of the firth, and can often be seen leaping and bow-surfing.

☞ Tours

Loch Ness by Jacobite   BOATING

(☑ 01463-233999; www.jacobite.co.uk; Glenurquhart Rd; adult/child £23/15; ◉ Jun-Sep;) Boats depart from Tomnahurich Bridge twice daily for a three-hour cruise along

Inverness

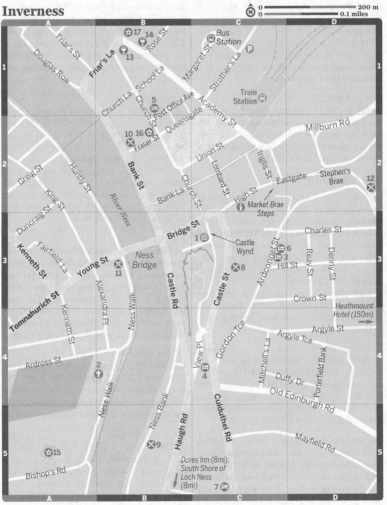

INVERNESS & THE CENTRAL HIGHLANDS INVERNESS

Inverness

⊙ Sights
1 Inverness Museum & Art Gallery	C3
2 St Andrew's Cathedral	B4

⊜ Sleeping
3 Ardconnel House	C3
4 Bazpackers Backpackers Hotel	C4
5 Black Isle Bar & Rooms	B1
6 Crown Hotel Guest House	C3
7 Rocpool Reserve	C5

⊗ Eating
8 Café 1	C3

9 Contrast Brasserie	B5
10 Mustard Seed	B2
11 Rocpool	B3
12 Velocity Cafe	D2

⊙ Drinking & Nightlife
13 MacGregor's	B1
14 Phoenix	B1

⊙ Entertainment
15 Eden Court Theatre	A5
16 Hootananny	B2
17 Ironworks	B1

the Caledonian Canal to Loch Ness and back, with a live commentary on local history and wildlife. Buy tickets at the tourist office (p300) and catch a free minibus to the boat. Other cruises and combined cruise and coach tours, from one to 6½ hours, are also available, some year-round.

Happy Tours BUS
(📞 07828 154683; www.happy-tours.biz; per person £70) Provides entertaining guided day trips by minibus around Inverness, taking in various sights including Loch Ness, Urquhart Castle and Culloden.

🛌 Sleeping

Inverness has a good range of backpacker accommodation, and also some excellent boutique hotels. There are lots of guesthouses and B&Bs along Old Edinburgh Rd and Ardconnel St on the east side of the river, and on Kenneth St and Fairfield Rd on the west bank; all are within 10 minutes' walk of the city centre.

The city fills up quickly in July and August, so you should either book your accommodation or else start looking early in the day.

Black Isle Bar & Rooms HOSTEL £
(📞 01463-229920; www.blackislebar.com; 68 Church St; dm/s/d £25/55/100; 📶) It's a beer drinker's dream come true – top-quality hostel accommodation in a central location, upstairs from a bar that serves real ales from the local Black Isle Brewery.

Bazpackers Backpackers Hotel HOSTEL £
(📞 01463-717663; www.bazpackershostel.co.uk; 4 Culduthel Rd; dm/d £18/60; @📶) 🍃 This may be Inverness' smallest hostel (34 beds), but it's hugely popular. It's a friendly, quiet place – the main building has a convivial lounge centred on a wood-burning stove, and a small garden and great views (some rooms are in a separate building with no garden). The dorms and kitchen can be a bit cramped, but the showers are great.

Inverness SYHA HOSTEL £
(SYHA; 📞 01463-231771; www.syha.org.uk; Victoria Dr; dm/tr £19/77; P@📶) Inverness' modern 166-bed hostel is 10 minutes' walk northeast of the city centre. Clean and well-equipped, with comfy beds and a flashy stainless-steel kitchen. Booking is essential, especially at Easter and in July and August.

Bught Caravan Park & Campsite CAMPSITE £
(📞 01463-236920; www.invernesscaravanpark.com; Bught Lane; tent sites per person £10, campervans £20; ☀Easter-Sep; 📶) A mile southwest of the city centre near Tomnahurich Bridge, this camping ground is hugely popular with backpackers.

Ardconnel House B&B ££
(📞 01463-240455; www.ardconnel-inverness.co.uk; 21 Ardconnel St; r per person £45-50; 📶) The six-room Ardconnel is one of our favourites (advance booking is essential, especially in July and August) – a terraced Victorian house with comfortable en suite rooms, a dining room with crisp white table linen, and a breakfast menu that includes Vegemite for homesick Antipodeans. Kids under 10 years not allowed.

Ach Aluinn B&B ££
(📞 01463-230127; www.achaluinn.com; 27 Fairfield Rd; r per person £40-45; P📶) This large, detached Victorian house is bright and homely, and offers all you might want from a B&B – a private bathroom, TV, reading lights, comfy beds with two pillows each, and an excellent breakfast. Less than 10 minutes' walk west from the city centre.

Crown Hotel Guest House B&B ££
(📞 01463-231135; www.crownhotel-inverness.co.uk; 19 Ardconnel St; s/d from £60/70; P@) Two of the six bedrooms here are family rooms, and there's a spacious lounge equipped with games consoles, DVDs and board games.

★Trafford Bank B&B £££
(📞 01463-241414; www.traffordbankguesthouse.co.uk; 96 Fairfield Rd; d £130-150; P📶) Lots of rave reviews for this elegant Victorian villa, which was once home to a bishop, just a mitre's-toss from the Caledonian Canal and 10 minutes' walk west from the city centre. The luxurious rooms include fresh flowers and fruit, bathrobes and fluffy towels – ask for the Tartan Room, which has a wrought-iron king-size bed and Victorian roll-top bath.

★Heathmount Hotel BOUTIQUE HOTEL £££
(📞 01463-235877; www.heathmounthotel.com; Kingsmills Rd; r from £160; P📶) Small and friendly, the Heathmount combines a popular local bar and restaurant with eight designer hotel rooms, each one different, ranging from a boldly coloured family room in purple and gold to a slinky black velvet four-poster double. Five minutes' walk east of the city centre.

★ **Rocpool Reserve** BOUTIQUE HOTEL **£££**
(☎01463-240089; www.rocpool.com; Culduthel Rd; r from £270; P☎) Boutique chic meets the Highlands in this slick and sophisticated little hotel, where an elegant Georgian exterior conceals an oasis of contemporary cool. A gleaming white entrance hall lined with red carpet and contemporary art leads to designer rooms in shades of chocolate, cream and gold; a restaurant by Albert Roux completes the luxury package.

Expect lots of decadent extras in the more expensive rooms, ranging from two-person showers to balcony hot tubs with aquavision TV.

✕ Eating

Velocity Cafe CAFE **£**
(☎01463-419956; www.velocitylove.co.uk; 1 Crown Ave; mains £4-7; ☺8am-5pm Mon-Wed & Fri, to 9pm Thu, 9am-5pm Sat, 10am-5pm Sun; ☎☎☎) This cyclists cafe serves soups, sandwiches and salads prepared with organic, locally sourced produce, as well as yummy cakes and coffee. There's also a workshop where you can repair your bike or book a session with a mechanic.

★ **Café 1** BISTRO **££**
(☎01463-226200; www.cafe1.net; 75 Castle St; mains £12-28; ☺noon-2.30pm & 5-9.30pm Mon-Fri, 12.30-3pm & 6-9.30pm Sat; ☎☎) ☎ Café 1 is a friendly, appealing bistro with candle-lit tables amid elegant blonde-wood and wrought-iron decor. There is an international menu based on quality Scottish produce, from Aberdeen Angus steaks to crisp pan-fried sea bass and meltingly tender pork belly. There's a separate vegan menu.

Contrast Brasserie BRASSERIE **££**
(☎01463-223777; www.glenmoristontownhouse.com/restaurant; 20 Ness Bank; mains £16-24; ☺noon-10pm) Book early for one of the best-value restaurants in Inverness – a dining room that drips designer style, with smiling professional staff and truly delicious food prepared using fresh Scottish produce. The two-/three-course lunch menu (£13/16) and three-course early bird menu (£18, 5pm to 6.30pm) are bargains.

Mustard Seed BISTRO **££**
(☎01463-220220; www.mustardseedrestaurant.co.uk; 16 Fraser St; mains £13-23; ☺noon-3pm & 5.30-10pm) ☎ The menu at this bright and bustling bistro changes weekly, but focuses on Scottish and French cuisine with a mod-

ern twist. Grab a table on the upstairs balcony if you can – it's the best outdoor lunch spot in Inverness, with a great view across the river. And a two-course lunch for £10 – yes, that's right – is hard to beat.

Rocpool MEDITERRANEAN **£££**
(☎01463-717274; www.rocpoolrestaurant.com; 1 Ness Walk; mains £14-31; ☺noon-2.30pm & 5.45-10pm Mon-Sat) ☎ Lots of polished wood, crisp white linen and leather booths and banquettes lend a sophisticated nautical air to this relaxed bistro, which offers a Mediterranean-influenced menu that makes the most of quality Scottish produce, especially seafood. The two-course lunch is £17.

☕ Drinking & Nightlife

MacGregor's BAR
(www.macgregorsbars.com; 113 Academy St; beer set menu for 2 from £21; ☺11am-midnight Mon-Thu, 11am-1am Fri & Sat, noon-midnight Sun) Decked out in timber and tweed, this bar strikes a distinctly modern chord. There's a huge selection of Scottish craft beers on tap, and even a beer 'set menu' described as 'a journey through the basics of craft beer'. The beer nerdiness extends to the gents' toilets, where urinals and washbasins have been fashioned out of beer kegs.

Clachnaharry Inn PUB
(☎01463-239806; www.clachnaharryinn.co.uk; 17-19 High St, Clachnaharry; ☺11am-11pm Mon-Thu, 11am-1am Fri & Sat, noon-11pm Sun; ☎) Just over a mile northwest of the city centre, on the bank of the Caledonian Canal just off the A862, this is a delightful old coaching inn (with beer garden out the back) serving an excellent range of real ales and good pub grub.

Phoenix PUB
(☎01463-233685;www.phoenixalehouse.co.uk;108 Academy St; ☺11am-1am Mon-Sat, noon-midnight Sun) Beautifully refurbished, this is the most traditional of the pubs in the city centre, with a mahogany horseshoe bar and several real ales on tap, including beers from the Cairngorm, Cromarty and Isle of Skye breweries.

☆ Entertainment

Hootananny LIVE MUSIC
(☎01463-233651; www.hootananyinverness.co.uk; 67 Church St; ☺noon-1am Mon-Thu, to 3am Fri & Sat, 4pm-midnight Sun) Hootananny is the

city's best live-music venue, with traditional folk- and/or rock-music sessions nightly, including big-name bands from all over Scotland (and, indeed, the world). The bar is well stocked with a range of beers from the local Black Isle Brewery.

Ironworks LIVE MUSIC, COMEDY
(✆0871 789 4173; www.ironworksvenue.com; 122 Academy St) With live bands (rock, pop, tribute) and comedy shows two or three times a week, the Ironworks is the town's main venue for big-name acts.

Eden Court Theatre THEATRE
(✆01463-234234; www.eden-court.co.uk; Bishop's Rd; ⊙ box office from 10am Mon-Sat, from 11am Sun, until show time; 🛜) The Highlands' main cultural venue – with theatre, art-house cinema and a conference centre – Eden Court stages a busy program of drama, dance, comedy, music, film and children's events, and has a good bar and restaurant. Pick up a program from the foyer or check the website.

❶ Information

Inverness Tourist Office (✆01463-252401; www.visithighlands.com; 36 High St; ⊙9am-5pm Mon & Wed-Sat, from 10am Tue, 10am-3pm Sun, longer hours Mar-Oct; 🛜) Accommodation booking service; also sells tickets for tours and cruises.

❶ Getting There & Away

AIR

Inverness Airport (INV; ✆01667-464000; www.invernessairport.co.uk) is at Dalcross, 10 miles east of the city, off the A96 towards Aberdeen. There are scheduled flights to Amsterdam, London, Manchester, Dublin, Orkney, Shetland and the Outer Hebrides, as well as other places in the UK.

Stagecoach (www.stagecoachbus.com) bus 11/11A runs from the airport to Inverness bus station (£4.40, 25 minutes, every 30 minutes).

BUS

Services depart from **Inverness bus station** (Margaret St). Most intercity routes are served by **Scottish Citylink** (www.citylink.co.uk) and **Stagecoach**. **National Express** (✆08717 818181; www.nationalexpress.com) has services to London (from £30, 13½ hours, one daily – more frequent services require changing at Glasgow).

Aberdeen (Stagecoach) £13.45, four hours, hourly

Aviemore £10.80, 45 minutes, eight daily
Edinburgh £32.20, 3½ to 4½ hours, seven daily
Fort William £12.20, two hours, six daily
Glasgow £32.20, 3½ to 4½ hours, hourly
Portree £26.40, 3¼ hours, two daily
Thurso (Stagecoach) £21, 3½ hours, three daily
Ullapool £14, 1½ hours, two daily except Sunday

If you book far enough in advance, **Megabus** (✆0141-352 4444; www.megabus.com) offers fares from as little as £1 for buses from Inverness to Glasgow and Edinburgh, and £10 to London.

TRAIN

Aberdeen £29.70, 2¼ hours, eight daily
Edinburgh £40, 3½ hours, eight daily
Glasgow £40, 3½ hours, eight daily
Kyle of Lochalsh £20, 2½ hours, four daily Monday to Saturday, two Sunday; one of Britain's great scenic train journeys
London £180, eight to nine hours, one daily direct; others require a change at Edinburgh
Wick £18, 4½ hours, four daily Monday to Saturday, one or two on Sunday; via Thurso

❶ Getting Around

BICYCLE

Ticket to Ride (✆01463-419160; www.tickettoridehighlands.co.uk; Bellfield Park; per day from £30; ⊙9am-6pm Apr-Aug, Wed-Mon Sep & Oct) Hires out mountain bikes, hybrids and tandems; can be dropped off in Fort William. Will deliver bikes free to local hotels and B&Bs.

BUS

City services and buses to places around Inverness, including Nairn, Forres, the Culloden battlefield, Beauly, Dingwall and Lairg, are operated by **Stagecoach**. An Inverness Zone 2 Dayrider ticket costs £6.80 and gives unlimited travel for a day on buses as far afield as Culloden, Fortrose and Drumnadrochit.

CAR

Focus Vehicle Rental (✆01463-709517; www.focusvehiclerental.co.uk; 6 Harbour Rd) The big boys charge from around £55 to £75 per day, but Focus has cheaper rates starting at £45 per day.

TAXI

Inverness Taxis (✆01463-222222; www.inverness-taxis.com) There's a taxi rank outside the train station.

Around Inverness

Culloden Battlefield

The Battle of Culloden in 1746 – the last pitched battle ever fought on British soil – saw the defeat of Bonnie Prince Charlie and the end of the Jacobite dream when 1200 Highlanders were slaughtered by government forces in a 68-minute rout. The Duke of Cumberland, son of the reigning King George II and leader of the Hanoverian army, earned the nickname 'Butcher' for his brutal treatment of the defeated Jacobite forces. The battle sounded the death knell for the old clan system, and the horrors of the Clearances soon followed. The sombre moor where the conflict took place has scarcely changed in the ensuing 260 years.

Culloden Visitor Centre   MUSEUM
(NTS; www.nts.org.uk/culloden; adult/child £11/9.50; ⊙9am-7pm Jun-Aug, to 6pm Mar-May, Sep & Oct, 10am-4pm Nov-Feb; P) This impressive visitor centre has everything you need to know about the Battle of Culloden in 1746, including the lead-up and the aftermath, with perspectives from both sides. An innovative film puts you on the battlefield in the middle of the mayhem, and a wealth of other audio presentations must have kept Inverness' entire acting community in business for weeks. The admission fee includes an audio guide for a self-guided tour of the battlefield itself.

ℹ Getting There & Away

Culloden is 6 miles east of Inverness. Bus 5 runs from Eastgate shopping centre in Inverness to Culloden battlefield (£3.15, 30 minutes, hourly except Sunday).

Fort George

The headland guarding the narrows in the Moray Firth opposite Fortrose is occupied by the magnificent and virtually unaltered 18th-century artillery fortification of Fort George.

Fort George   FORTRESS
(HES; ☑01667-462777; www.historicenvironment. scot; adult/child £9/5.40; ⊙9.30am-5.30pm Apr-Sep, 10am-4pm Oct-Mar; P) One of the finest artillery fortifications in Europe, Fort George was established in 1748 in the aftermath of the Battle of Culloden, as a base for George II's army of occupation in the Highlands. By the time of its completion in 1769 it had cost the equivalent of around £1 billion in today's money. It still functions as a military barracks; public areas have exhibitions on 18th-century soldiery, and the mile-plus walk around the ramparts offers fine views.

Given its size, you'll need at least two hours to do the place justice. The fort is off the A96 about 11 miles northeast of Inverness; there is no public transport.

Nairn

POP 9775

Nairn is a popular golfing and seaside resort with good sandy beaches. You can spend many pleasant hours wandering along the **East Beach**, one of the finest in Scotland.

The most interesting part of town is the old fishing village of **Fishertown**, down by the harbour, a maze of narrow streets lined with picturesque cottages.

The big events in the town's calendar are the **Nairn Highland Games** (www.nairn highlandgames.co.uk; ⊙mid-Aug) and the **Nairn Book & Arts Festival** (www.nairnfestival. co.uk; ⊙Sep).

Nairn Museum   MUSEUM
(☑01667-456791; www.nairnmuseum.co.uk; Viewfield House; adult/child £4/3; ⊙10am-4.30pm Mon-Fri, to 1pm Sat Apr-Oct) Nairn Museum, a few minutes' walk from the tourist office, has displays on the history of the harbour community of Fishertown, as well as on local archaeology, geology and natural history.

Sunny Brae Hotel   HOTEL ££
(☑01667-452309; www.sunnybraehotel.com; Marine Rd; s/d from £90/115; P🖙) Beautifully decked out with fresh flowers and potted plants, the Sunny Brae enjoys an enviable location with great views across the Moray Firth. The hotel restaurant specialises in Scottish produce cooked with Continental flair.

Boath House Hotel   HOTEL £££
(☑01667-454896; www.boath-house.com; Auldearn; s/d from £190/295; P🖙) This beautifully restored Regency mansion, set in private woodland gardens 2 miles east of Nairn on the A96, is one of Scotland's most luxurious country-house hotels. It includes a spa offering holistic treatments and a highly regarded restaurant (three-/six-course dinner £45/70).

Classroom GASTROPUB ££
(☑01667-455999; www.theclassroombistro.com;
1 Cawdor St; mains £14-26; ⊙noon-4.30pm &
5-9pm; 🕾🖥) ⏸ Done up in an appealing
mixture of modern and traditional styles –
lots of richly glowing wood with designer
detailing – Classroom doubles as cocktail
bar and gastropub, with a tempting menu
that ranges from Cullen skink (soup made
with smoked haddock, potato, onion and
milk) to Highland steak with pepper-
corn sauce.

ⓘ Getting There & Away

Buses run hourly (less frequently on Sunday)
from Inverness to Nairn (£6.05, 30 minutes) and
on to Aberdeen. The bus station is just west of
the town centre.

The town also lies on the Inverness–Aberdeen
railway line, with five to seven trains a day from
Inverness (£6.30, 15 minutes).

Cawdor Castle

This castle (☑01667-404615; www.cawdorcastle.
com; Cawdor; adult/child £11.50/7.20; ⊙10am-
5.30pm May-Sep; 🅿), 5 miles southwest of
Nairn, was once the seat of the Thane of
Cawdor, one of the titles bestowed on Shakespeare's *Macbeth*. The real Macbeth – an
ancient Scottish king – couldn't have lived
here though, since he died in 1057, 300 years
before the castle was begun. Nevertheless
the tour gives a fascinating insight into the
lives of the Scottish aristocracy.

Cawdor Tavern (www.cawdortavern.co.uk;
mains £12-25; ⊙food served noon-9pm Mon-Sat,
12.30-9pm Sun; 🅿🕾🖥), in the village close
to Cawdor Castle, is worth a visit, though
it can be difficult deciding what to drink as
it stocks more than 100 varieties of whisky.
There's also excellent pub food, with tempting daily specials.

West of Inverness

Beauly

POP 1365

Mary, Queen of Scots is said to have given
this village its name in 1564 when she visited, exclaiming: '*Quel beau lieu!*' (What
a beautiful place!). Founded in 1230, the
red-sandstone Beauly Priory is now an
impressive ruin, haunted by the cries of
rooks nesting in a magnificent centuries-old
sycamore tree.

Priory Hotel HOTEL ££
(☑01463-782309; www.priory-hotel.com; The
Square; s/d from £58/89; 🅿🕾) The Priory
Hotel, on Beauly's central square, has bright,
modern rooms and serves good bar meals.

★ **Corner on the Square** CAFE £
(☑01463-783000; www.corneronthesquare.co.uk;
1 High St; mains £7-13; ⊙8.30am-5.30pm Mon-Fri,
8.30am-5pm Sat, 9.30am-5pm Sun) Beauly's best
lunch spot is this superb little delicatessen
and cafe that serves breakfast (till 11.30am),
daily lunch specials (11.30am to 4.30pm)
and excellent coffee.

ⓘ Getting There & Away

Buses 28 and 28A from Inverness run to Beauly
(£5.30, 30 to 45 minutes, hourly Monday to
Saturday, five on Sunday), and the town lies on
the Inverness–Thurso railway line.

Strathglass & Glen Affric

The broad valley of Strathglass extends
about 18 miles inland from Beauly, followed
by the A831 to Cannich (the only village in
the area), where there's a grocery store and
a post office.

Glen Affric (www.glenaffric.org), one of
the most beautiful glens in Scotland, extends
deep into the hills beyond Cannich. The
upper reaches of the glen are designated as
the Glen Affric National Nature Reserve
(www.nnr.scot).

About 4 miles southwest of Cannich is
Dog Falls, a scenic spot where the River
Affric squeezes through a narrow, rocky
gorge. A circular walking trail (red waymarks) leads from Dog Falls car park to a
footbridge below the falls and back on the
far side of the river (2 miles, allow one hour).

The road continues beyond Dog Falls to
a parking area and picnic site at the eastern
end of Loch Affric, where there are several
short walks along the river and the loch
shore. The circuit of Loch Affric (10 miles,
allow five hours walking, two hours by
mountain bike) follows good paths right
around the loch and takes you deep into the
heart of some very wild scenery.

It's possible to walk all the way from
Cannich to Glen Shiel on the west coast
(35 miles) in two days, spending the night
at the remote Glen Affric SYHA. The route
is now part of the waymarked Affric-Kintail
Way (www.affrickintailway.com), a 56-mile
walking or mountain-biking trail leading
from Drumnadrochit to Kintail via Cannich.

A minor road on the east side of the River Glass leads to the pretty little conservation village of Tomich, 3 miles southwest of Cannich, built in Victorian times as accommodation for estate workers. The road continues (unsurfaced for the last 2 miles) to a forestry car park, the starting point for a short (800m) walk to Plodda Falls.

Sleeping & Eating

Glen Affric SYHA HOSTEL £
(SYHA; ☑ bookings 0845 293 7373; www.syha.org.uk; Allt Beithe; dm £24.50; ☺ Apr–mid-Sep) This remote and rustic hostel is set amid magnificent scenery at the halfway point of the cross-country walk from Cannich to Glen Shiel, 8 miles from the nearest road. Facilities are basic and you'll need to take all supplies with you (and all litter away). Book in advance. There is no phone, internet or mobile phone signal at the hostel.

Cannich Caravan & Camping Park CAMPSITE £
(☑ 01456-415364; www.highlandcamping.co.uk; sites per adult/child £9/5, pods s/d £26/36; ☎) Good, sheltered spot, with on-site cafe and the option of wooden camping 'pods'. Mountain bikes for hire from £17 a day.

★ **Kerrow House** B&B ££
(☑ 01456-415243; www.kerrow-house.co.uk; Cannich; r per person £45-50; P ☎) ⋒ This wonderful Georgian hunting lodge has bags of old-fashioned character – it was once the home of Highland author Neil M Gunn – and has spacious grounds with cosy self-catering cottages (from £510 per week) and 3.5 miles of private trout fishing. It's a mile south of Cannich on the minor road along the east side of the River Glass.

Tomich Hotel HOTEL ££
(☑ 01456-415399; www.tomichhotel.co.uk; Tomich; s/d from £75/120; ☺ closed Dec & Jan; P ☎ ☎) About 3 miles southwest of Cannich on the southern side of the River Glass, this Victorian hunting lodge has a dog-friendly bar with blazing log fire that serves food from noon to 9pm; an intimate, candlelit restaurant; and eight comfortable en suite rooms. It can organise trout fishing on local waters.

★ **Struy Inn** SCOTTISH £££
(☑ 01463-761308; www.thestruy.co.uk; Struy Village; mains £18-27; ☺ 5.30-9.30pm Wed-Sun Apr-Oct, Thu-Sat Nov-Mar; P ☎) Set in the heart of lovely Strathglass, on the road between Cannich and Beauly, this fine Victorian inn is a haven of old-fashioned charm. It houses a top-quality restaurant serving the finest Scottish cuisine; with just 18 seats, booking is essential.

ⓘ Getting There & Away

Stagecoach (www.stagecoachbus.com) buses 17 and 117 run from Inverness to Cannich (£5.90, one hour, two daily Monday to Friday) via Drumnadrochit. D&E Coaches (www.decoaches.co.uk) runs a service from Inverness to Cannich that continues to Tomich (£6.50, 1¼ hours, three daily, weekdays only).

Black Isle

The Black Isle – a peninsula rather than an island – is linked to Inverness by the Kessock Bridge. Bypassed by the main A9 road, it's a peaceful backwater of wooded hills, picturesque villages and dramatic coastlines, with the added attraction of Scotland's best mainland dolphin-watching spot.

Black Isle Brewery BREWERY
(☑ 01463-811871; www.blackislebrewery.com; Old Allangrange; ☺ 10am-6pm Mon-Sat year-round, 11am-5pm Sun Easter-Sep) ⓕ FREE One of Britain's best artisan breweries, Black Isle Brewery has won many awards for its organically produced ales. Enjoy a free tour then try a glass of Yellowhammer, a light, hoppy and refreshing bitter, or the strong, flowery Heather Honey Beer. It's a few miles north of the Kessock Bridge.

Fortrose & Rosemarkie

At **Fortrose Cathedral** (HES; Cathedral Sq; ☺ 9.30am-5.30pm Apr-Sep, to 4.30pm Oct-Mar) FREE you'll find the vaulted crypt of a 13th-century chapter house and sacristy, and the ruinous 14th-century south aisle and chapel. Chanonry Point, 1.5 miles to the east, is a favourite dolphin-spotting vantage point; there are one-hour dolphin-watching cruises (☑ 01381-622383; www.dolphintripsavoch.co.uk; adult/child £18/12) departing from the harbour at Avoch (pronounced 'auch'), 3 miles southwest.

In Rosemarkie, the Groam House Museum (☑ 01381-620961; www.groamhouse.org.uk; High St, Rosemarkie; ☺ 11am-4.30pm Mon-Fri, 2-4.30pm Sat & Sun Apr-Oct) FREE has a superb collection of Pictish stones engraved with designs similar to those on Celtic Irish stones.

From the northern end of Rosemarkie's High St, a short but pleasant signposted walk leads you through the gorges and waterfalls of the **Fairy Glen**.

Once you've worked up a thirst, retire to the bar at the **Anderson** (☑ 01381-620236; www.theanderson.co.uk; Union St, Fortrose; ⊙ 4-11pm, closed Sun-Tue Nov-Mar) to sample its range of real ales (including Belgian beers and Somerset cider) and more than 200 single malt whiskies.

Cromarty

POP 725

The pretty village of Cromarty at the northeastern tip of the Black Isle has lots of 18th-century red-sandstone houses, and a lovely green park beside the sea for picnics and games. An excellent walk, known as the **100 Steps**, leads from the north end of the village to the headland viewpoint of South Sutor (4 miles round trip).

Hugh Miller's Cottage
& Museum
MUSEUM

(NTS; www.nts.org.uk; Church St; adult/child £6.50/5.50; ⊙ 1-5pm Apr-Sep) This thatch-roofed cottage is the birthplace of Hugh Miller (1802–56), a local stonemason and amateur geologist who pioneered the study of fossil fishes in Scotland; he later moved to Edinburgh and became a famous journalist and newspaper editor. The Georgian villa next door is home to a museum celebrating his life and achievements.

Ecoventures
WILDLIFE WATCHING

(☑ 01381-600323; www.ecoventures.co.uk; Cromarty Harbour; adult/child £30/23) Ecoventures runs two-hour boat trips from Cromarty harbour into the Moray Firth to see bottlenose dolphins and other wildlife.

Sutor Creek
CAFE ££

(☑ 01381-600855; www.sutorcreek.co.uk; 21 Bank St; mains £13-18; ⊙ noon-9pm May-Sep, Thu-Sun Oct-Apr; ⓐ) 🌿 This excellent little cafe-restaurant serves wood-fired pizzas and fresh local seafood including Shetland scallops, Lewis mussels, and Cromarty langoustines with garlic and lemon butter.

Couper's Creek
CAFE £

(☑ 01381-600729; www.couperscreek.co.uk; 20 Church St; mains £6-11; ⊙ 10am-5pm; ⓐ) This lively cafe serves cake, coffee, ice-cream sundaes and superb, doorstep-size open sandwiches with salad.

Getting There & Away

Stagecoach (www.stagecoachbus.com) buses 26 and 26A run from Inverness to Cromarty (£5.30, one hour, hourly Monday to Saturday).

Loch Ness

Deep, dark and narrow, Loch Ness stretches for 23 miles between Inverness and Fort Augustus. Its bitterly cold waters have been extensively explored in search of Nessie, the elusive Loch Ness monster, but most visitors see her only in the form of a cardboard cut-out at Drumnadrochit's monster exhibitions. The busy A82 road runs along the northwestern shore, while the more tranquil and picturesque B862 follows the southeastern shore. A complete circuit of the loch is about 70 miles – travel anticlockwise for the better views.

🏃 Activities

The 79-mile **Great Glen Way** (www.highland. gov.uk/ggw) long-distance footpath stretches from Inverness to Fort William, where walkers can connect with the **West Highland Way**. It is described in detail in *The Great Glen Way*, a guide by Jacquetta Megarry and Sandra Bardwell.

The Great Glen Way can also be ridden (strenuous!) by mountain bike, while the **Great Glen Mountain Bike Trails** at Nevis Range and Abriachan Forest offer challenging cross-country and downhill trails. You can hire a mountain bike in Fort William (p336) and drop it off in Inverness (p300), and vice versa.

The **South Loch Ness Trail** (www.visit invernesslochness.com) links a series of footpaths and minor roads along the less-frequented southern side of the loch. The 28 miles from Loch Tarff near Fort Augustus to Torbreck on the fringes of Inverness can be done on foot, by bike or on horseback.

The climb to the summit of **Meallfuarvonie** (699m), on the northwestern shore of Loch Ness, makes an excellent short hill walk: the views along the Great Glen from the top are superb. It's a 6-mile round trip, so allow about three hours. Start from the car park at the end of the minor road leading south from Drumnadrochit to Bunloit.

The **Great Glen Canoe Trail** (www. greatglencanoetrail.info), a series of access points, waymarks and informal campsites, allows you to travel the length of the glen by canoe or kayak.

WORTH A TRIP

DORES INN

While crowded tour coaches pour down the west side of Loch Ness to the hot spots of Drumnadrochit and Urquhart Castle, the narrow B862 road along the eastern shore is relatively peaceful. It leads to the village of Foyers, where you can enjoy a pleasant hike to the **Falls of Foyers**.

But it's worth making the trip just for the **Dores Inn** (☏01463-751203; www.thedoresinn. co.uk; Dores; mains £10-27; ⊙pub 10am-11pm, food served noon-2pm & 6-9pm; P🖰), a beautifully restored country pub furnished with recycled furniture, local landscape paintings and fresh flowers. The menu specialises in quality Scottish produce, from haggis, turnips and tatties (potatoes), and haddock and chips, to steaks, scallops and seafood platters.

The garden enjoys a stunning view along Loch Ness, and even has a dedicated monster-spotting vantage point. The nearby campervan, emblazoned with Nessie-Serry Independent Research, has been home to dedicated Nessie hunter Steve Feltham (www.nessie hunter.co.uk) since 1991; in 2015 he finally concluded that Nessie was in fact a giant catfish!

🎇 Festivals & Events

Groove Loch Ness   MUSIC
(www.groovefestival.co.uk; ⊙Aug) A vast lochside field at the village of Dores hosts this successor to the now-defunct Rock Ness Festival, a one-day smorgasbord of the best in Scottish and international DJs.

Drumnadrochit

POP 1100

Seized by Loch Ness Monster madness, its gift shops bulging with Nessie cuddly toys, Drumnadrochit is a hotbed of beastie fever, with two monster exhibitions battling it out for the tourist dollar.

◉ Sights & Activities

Urquhart Castle   CASTLE
(HES; ☏01456-450551; adult/child £9/5.40; ⊙9.30am-8pm Jun-Aug, to 6pm Apr, May & Sep, to 5pm Oct, to 4.30pm Nov-Mar; P) Commanding a superb location 1.5 miles east of Drumnadrochit, with outstanding views (on a clear day), Urquhart Castle is a popular Nessie-hunting hot spot. A huge visitor centre (most of which is beneath ground level) includes a video theatre (with a dramatic 'reveal' of the castle at the end of the film) and displays of medieval items discovered in the castle. The site includes a huge gift shop and a restaurant, and is often very crowded in summer.

The castle was repeatedly sacked and rebuilt (and sacked and rebuilt) over the centuries; in 1692 it was blown up to prevent the Jacobites from using it. The five-storey tower house at the northern point is the most impressive remaining fragment and offers wonderful views across the water.

Loch Ness Centre & Exhibition   MUSEUM
(☏01456-450573; www.lochness.com; adult/child £7.95/4.95; ⊙9.30am-6pm Jul & Aug, to 5pm Easter-Jun, Sep & Oct, 10am-4pm Nov-Easter; P🖰) This Nessie-themed attraction adopts a scientific approach that allows you to weigh the evidence for yourself. Exhibits include original equipment – sonar survey vessels, miniature submarines, cameras and sediment coring tools – used in various monster hunts, plus original photographs and film footage of sightings. You'll find out about hoaxes and optical illusions, as well as learning a lot about the ecology of Loch Ness – is there enough food in the loch to support even one 'monster', let alone a breeding population?

Nessie Hunter   BOATING
(☏01456-450395; www.lochness-cruises.com; adult/child £16/10; ⊙Easter-Oct) One-hour monster-hunting cruises, complete with sonar and underwater cameras. Cruises depart from Drumnadrochit hourly (except 1pm) from 10am to 6pm daily.

🛏 Sleeping

BCC Loch Ness Hostel   HOSTEL £
(☏07780 603045; www.bcclochnesshostel.co.uk; Glen Urquhart; tr/q from £60/75, tent sites per person £5, 2-person pods £70; P🖰) Clean, modern, high-quality budget accommodation located 6.5 miles west of Drumnadrochit, halfway between Cannich and Loch Ness; booking well in advance is recommended. There's also a good campsite with the option of luxury glamping pods.

Loch Ness Backpackers Lodge   HOSTEL £
(☏01456-450807; www.lochness-backpackers. com; Coiltie Farmhouse, East Lewiston; dm/d from

£20/50; P) This snug, friendly hostel housed in a cottage and barn has six-bed dorms, one double and a large barbecue area. It's almost a mile from Drumnadrochit, along the A82 towards Fort William; turn left where you see the sign for Loch Ness Inn, just before the bridge.

Borlum Farm Camping   CAMPSITE £
(01456-450220; www.borlum.co.uk; sites per adult/child £10.50/5.50; Mar-Oct;) An attractive farm-based campsite with a mix of grass pitches and hard standings, beside the main road half a mile southeast of Drumnadrochit.

★ **Loch Ness Inn**   INN ££
(01456-450991; www.staylochness.co.uk; Lewiston; s/d/f £99/120/140; P) Loch Ness Inn ticks all the weary traveller's boxes, with comfortable bedrooms (the family suite sleeps two adults and two children), a cosy bar pouring real ales from the Cairngorm and Isle of Skye breweries, and a rustic restaurant (mains £10 to £20) serving wholesome fare. It's conveniently located in the quiet hamlet of Lewiston, between Drumnadrochit and Urquhart Castle.

Drumbuie Farm   B&B ££
(01456-450634; www.loch-ness-farm.co.uk; s/d from £54/68; P) A B&B in a modern house on a working farm surrounded by fields full of sheep and highland cattle, with views over Urquhart Castle and Loch Ness. Walkers and cyclists are welcome.

✕ Eating & Drinking

Fiddler's Coffee Shop & Restaurant   CAFE ££
(www.fiddledrum.co.uk; mains £12-20; 11am-11pm;) The coffee shop here serves cappuccino and croissants, while the restaurant dishes up traditional Highland fare, such as venison and haggis, and a wide range of bottled Scottish beers. There's also a whisky bar with a huge range of single malts.

Benleva Hotel   MICROBREWERY
(01456-450080; www.benleva.co.uk; Kilmore Rd; noon-midnight Mon-Thu, to 1am Fri, to 12.45am Sat, 12.30-11pm Sun;) Set in an 18th-century manse a half-mile east of the main road, the Benleva is a rough diamond of a pub – a bit frayed around the edges but with a heart of gold. The beer is the main event, with a selection of real ales from around the country, including those from their own Loch Ness Brewery, located nearby.

ℹ Getting There & Away

Stagecoach (www.stagecoachbus.com) buses run from Inverness to Drumnadrochit (£3.70, 30 minutes, six to eight daily, five on Sunday) and Urquhart Castle car park (£4, 35 minutes).

Fort Augustus
POP 620

Fort Augustus, at the junction of four old military roads, was originally a government garrison and the headquarters of General George Wade's road-building operations in the early 18th century. Today it's a neat and picturesque little place bisected by the Caledonian Canal, and often overrun by coach-tour crowds in summer.

◉ Sights & Activities

Caledonian Canal   CANAL
(www.scottishcanals.co.uk) At Fort Augustus, boats using the Caledonian Canal are raised and lowered 13m by a 'ladder' of five consecutive locks. It's fun to watch, and the neatly landscaped canal banks are a great place to soak up the sun or compare accents with fellow tourists. The **Caledonian Canal Centre** (Ardchattan House, Canalside; 9am-6pm) FREE, beside the lowest lock, has information on the history of the canal.

Clansman Centre   MUSEUM
(www.scottish-swords.com; 10am-6pm Apr-Oct) FREE This exhibition of 17th-century Highland life has live demonstrations of how to put on a plaid (the forerunner of the kilt) and how the claymore (Highland sword) was made and used. There is also a workshop where you can purchase handcrafted reproduction swords, dirks and shields.

Cruise Loch Ness   BOATING
(01320-366277; www.cruiselochness.com; adult/child £14.50/8.50; hourly 10am-4pm Apr-Oct, 1pm & 2pm Nov-Mar) One-hour cruises on Loch Ness are accompanied by the latest high-tech sonar equipment so you can keep an underwater eye open for Nessie. There are also one-hour evening cruises, departing 8pm daily (except Friday) April to August, and 90-minute speedboat tours.

🛏 Sleeping & Eating

Morag's Lodge   HOSTEL £
(01320-366289; www.moragslodge.com; Bunoich Brae; dm/tw from £24.50/62; P @) This large, well-run hostel is based in a big Victorian house with great views of Fort

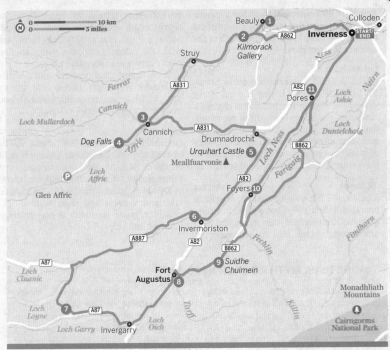

Driving Tour
A Loch Ness Circuit

START INVERNESS
END INVERNESS
LENGTH 130 MILES; SIX TO SEVEN HOURS

Head out of Inverness on the A862 to Beauly, arriving in time for breakfast at ❶ **Corner on the Square** (p302). Backtrack a mile and turn right on the A831 to Cannich, passing ❷ **Kilmorack Gallery**, which exhibits contemporary art in a converted church. The scenery gets wilder as you approach ❸ **Cannich**; turn right and follow the single-track road to the car park at ❹ **Dog Falls**. Take a stroll along the rushing river, or hike to the viewpoint (about one-hour round trip; 2.5 miles) for a glimpse of remote Glen Affric.

Return to Cannich and turn right on the A831 to Drumnadrochit, then right on the A82 past picturesque ❺ **Urquhart Castle** (p305) and along the shores of Loch Ness. At ❻ **Invermoriston**, pause to look at the old bridge, built by Telford in 1813, then head west on the A887 towards Kyle of Lochalsh; after 16 miles go left on the A87 towards

Invergarry. You are now among some of the finest mountain scenery in the Highlands; as the road turns east above Loch Garry, stop at the famous ❼ **viewpoint** (layby on right, signposted Glengarry Viewpoint). Through a quirk of perspective, the lochs to the west appear to form the map outline of Scotland.

At Invergarry, turn left on the A82 to reach ❽ **Fort Augustus** and a late lunch at the Lovat or Lock Inn. Take the B862 out of town, following the line of General Wade's 18th-century military road, to another viewpoint at ❾ **Suidhe Chuimein**. A short (800m) walk up the well-worn path to the summit affords an even better panorama.

Ahead, you can choose the low road via the impressive ❿ **Falls of Foyers**, or stay on the high road (B862) for more views; both converge on Loch Ness at the ⓫ **Dores Inn** (p305), where you can sip a pint with a view along Loch Ness, and even stay for dinner before returning to Inverness.

Augustus' hilly surrounds, and has a convivial bar with open fire. It's hidden away in the trees up the steep side road just north of the tourist office car park.

Lorien House
B&B ££

(☎01320-366576; www.lorien-house.co.uk; Station Rd; s/d £70/80; P☎) Lorien is a cut above your usual B&B – the bedrooms are spick and span, the house is set up to accommodate walkers and cyclists, the breakfasts include smoked salmon, and there's a library of walking, cycling and climbing guides in the lounge. No children under 10 years.

★ Lovat
HOTEL £££

(☎01456-459250; www.thelovat.com; Main Rd; d from £173; P☎☎) 🖉 A boutique-style makeover has transformed this former huntin'-and-shootin' hotel into a luxurious but eco-conscious retreat set apart from the tourist crush around the canal. The bedrooms are spacious and stylishly furnished, while the lounge is equipped with a log fire, comfy armchairs and grand piano.

It has an informal brasserie and a highly acclaimed restaurant (five-course dinner £55), which serves top-quality cuisine (open noon to 2.30pm and 6pm to 9pm).

Lock Inn
PUB FOOD ££

(☎01320-366302; Canal Side; mains £10-15; ☉meals noon-8pm) A superb little pub right on the canal bank, the Lock Inn has a vast range of malt whiskies and a tempting menu of bar meals, which includes Orkney salmon, Highland venison and daily seafood specials; the house speciality is beer-battered haddock and chips.

MONSTERS, MYTHS & LOCH NESS

Highland folklore is filled with tales of strange creatures living in lochs and rivers, notably the kelpie (water horse) that lures unwary travellers to their doom. The use of the term 'monster', however, is a relatively recent phenomenon, whose origins lie in an article published in the *Inverness Courier* on 2 May 1933, entitled 'Strange Spectacle on Loch Ness'.

The article recounted the sighting of a disturbance in the loch by Mrs Aldie Mackay and her husband: 'There the creature disported itself, rolling and plunging for fully a minute, its body resembling that of a whale, and the water cascading and churning like a simmering cauldron.'

The story was taken up by the London press and sparked a flurry of sightings that year, including a notorious on-land encounter with London tourists Mr and Mrs Spicer on 22 July 1933, again reported in the *Inverness Courier*:

'It was horrible, an abomination. About 50 yards ahead, we saw an undulating sort of neck, and quickly followed by a large, ponderous body. I estimated the length to be 25ft to 30ft, its colour was dark elephant grey. It crossed the road in a series of jerks, but because of the slope we could not see its limbs. Although I accelerated quickly towards it, it had disappeared into the loch by the time I reached the spot. There was no sign of it in the water. I am a temperate man, but I am willing to take any oath that we saw this Loch Ness beast. I am certain that this creature was of a prehistoric species.'

The London newspapers couldn't resist. In December 1933 the *Daily Mail* sent Marmaduke Wetherell, a film director and big-game hunter, to Loch Ness to track down the beast. Within days he found 'reptilian' footprints in the shoreline mud (soon revealed to have been made with a stuffed hippopotamus foot). Then in April 1934 came the famous long-necked monster photograph taken by the seemingly reputable Harley St surgeon Robert Kenneth Wilson. The press went mad and the rest, as they say, is history.

In 1994, however, Christian Spurling – Wetherell's stepson, by then 90 years old – revealed that the most famous photo of Nessie ever taken was in fact a hoax, perpetrated by his stepfather with Wilson's help. Today, of course, there are those who claim that Spurling's confession is itself a hoax. And, ironically, the researcher who exposed the surgeon's photo as a fake still believes wholeheartedly in the monster's existence.

There have been regular sightings of the monster through the years (see www.lochnesssightings.com), with a peak in 1996–97 (the Hollywood movie *Loch Ness* was released in 1996), but reports have tailed off in recent years.

Hoax or not, the bizarre mini-industry that has grown up around Loch Ness and its mysterious monster since that eventful summer last century is a spectacle in itself.

ⓘ Getting There & Away

Scottish Citylink (www.citylink.co.uk) and **Stagecoach** (www.stagecoachbus.com) buses from Inverness to Fort William stop at Fort Augustus (£8 to £11.20, one hour, five to eight daily Monday to Saturday, five on Sunday).

THE CAIRNGORMS

The Cairngorms National Park (www.cairn gorms.co.uk) is the largest national park in the UK, more than twice the size of the Lake District. It stretches from Aviemore in the north to the Angus Glens in the south, and from Dalwhinnie in the west to Ballater and Royal Deeside in the east.

The park encompasses the highest landmass in Britain – a broad mountain plateau, riven only by the deep valleys of the Lairig Ghru and Loch Avon, with an average altitude of more than 1000m and including five of the six highest summits in the UK. This wild mountain landscape of granite and heather has a sub-Arctic climate and supports rare alpine tundra vegetation and high-altitude bird species, such as snow bunting, ptarmigan and dotterel.

This is prime hill-walking territory, but even couch potatoes can enjoy a taste of the high life by riding the Cairngorm Mountain Railway (p312).

Aviemore

POP 3150

The gateway to the Cairngorms, Aviemore is the region's main centre for transport, accommodation, restaurants and shops. It's not the prettiest town in Scotland by a long stretch – the main attractions are in the surrounding area – but when bad weather puts the hills off-limits, Aviemore fills up with hikers, cyclists and climbers (plus skiers and snowboarders in winter) cruising the outdoor-equipment shops or recounting their latest adventures in the cafes and bars. Add in tourists and locals and the eclectic mix makes for a lively little town.

Aviemore is on a loop off the A9 Perth–Inverness road. Almost everything of note is to be found along the main drag, Grampian Rd; the train station and bus stop are towards its southern end.

The Cairngorm Mountain funicular railway and ski area lie 10 miles southeast of Aviemore along the B970 (Ski Rd) and its continuation, past Coylumbridge and Glenmore.

◉ Sights

★ **Rothiemurchus Estate**   FOREST
(www.rothiemurchus.net) The Rothiemurchus Estate, which extends from the River Spey at Aviemore to the Cairngorm summit plateau, is famous for having one of Scotland's largest remnants of **Caledonian forest**, the ancient forest of Scots pine that once covered most of the country. The forest is home to a large population of red squirrels, and is one of the last bastions of the capercaillie and the Scottish wildcat.

The **Rothiemurchus Centre** (☑01479-812345; www.rothiemurchus.net; Ski Rd, Inverdruie; ☺9.30am-5.30pm; 🅿) FREE, a mile southeast of Aviemore along the B970, sells an *Explorer Map* detailing more than 50 miles of footpaths and cycling trails, including the wheelchair-accessible 4-mile trail around **Loch an Eilein**, with its ruined castle and peaceful pine woods.

Strathspey Steam Railway   HERITAGE RAILWAY
(☑01479-810725;   www.strathspeyrailway.co.uk; Station Sq; return ticket adult/child £15/11.80; 🅿) The Strathspey railway runs steam trains on a section of restored line between Aviemore and Broomhill, 10 miles to the northeast, via Boat of Garten. There are four or five trains daily from June to August, and a more limited service in April, May, September, October and December, with the option of enjoying afternoon tea, Sunday lunch or a five-course dinner on board.

An extension to Grantown-on-Spey is under construction, but will not be complete for several years.

Craigellachie Nature Reserve   NATURE RESERVE
(www.nnr.scot; Grampian Rd) FREE This reserve is a great place for short hikes across steep hillsides covered in natural birch forest where you can spot wildlife such as the peregrine falcons that nest on the crags from April to July. A trail leads west from Aviemore SYHA (p310) and passes under the A9 into the reserve.

🏃 Activities

Bothy Bikes   MOUNTAIN BIKING
(☑01479-810111; www.bothybikes.co.uk; 5 Granish Way, Dalfaber; per half-/full day from £16/20; ☺9am-5.30pm) Located in northern Aviemore, this place rents out mountain bikes and can also

advise on routes and trails; a good choice for beginners is the Old Logging Way, which runs from Aviemore to Glenmore, where you can make a circuit of Loch Morlich before returning. For experienced bikers, the whole of the Cairngorms is your playground. Booking recommended.

Rothiemurchus Fishery FISHING
(☑ 01479-812915; www.rothiemurchus.net; Rothiemurchus Estate; ⊙ 9.30am-5pm Sep-May, to dusk Jun-Aug; ♠) Cast for rainbow trout at this loch at the southern end of the village; buy permits (from £10 for one hour, plus £7 for tackle hire) at the Fish Farm Shop. If you're new to fly-fishing, there's a beginner's package, including tackle hire, one hour's instruction and one hour's fishing, for £49 per person.

For experienced anglers, there's also salmon and sea-trout fishing on the River Spey – a day permit costs around £30. Numbers are limited, so it's best to book in advance.

Cairngorm Sled-Dog Centre DOG SLEDDING
(☑ 07767-270526; www.sled-dogs.co.uk; Ski Rd; ♠) This outfit offers 45-minute dog-sledding training sessions (adult/child £60/40) on local forest trails with a team of huskies, or a three-hour sled-dog safari (£175 per person) into the hills (children must be at least 12 years old). The sleds have wheels, so snow's not necessary. The centre is 3 miles east of Aviemore, signposted off the road to Loch Morlich.

There are also one-hour guided tours of the kennels (adult/child £8/4) and sled-dog museum.

Cairngorm Brewery BREWERY
(☑ 01479-813303; www.cairngormbrewery.com; Dalfaber Industrial Estate; tours per person £5; ⊙ 10am-5.30pm Mon-Sat year-round, 12.30-4pm Sun May-Sep) Creator of multi-award-winning Trade Winds ale; tours of the brewery begin at 11.30am and 2.30pm on weekdays.

🛏 Sleeping

Aviemore SYHA HOSTEL £
(SYHA; ☑ 01479-810345; www.syha.org.uk; 25 Grampian Rd; dm £23; P @ 🛜) Upmarket hostelling in a spacious, well-equipped modern building, five minutes' walk south of the village centre. There are four- and six-bed rooms, and a comfortable lounge with views of the mountains.

Rothiemurchus Camp & Caravan Park CAMPSITE £
(☑ 01479-812800; www.rothiemurchus.net; Coylumbridge; tent sites per adult/child £12/3) The nearest campsite to Aviemore is this year-round park, beautifully sited among Scots pines at Coylumbridge, 1.5 miles along the B970.

Aviemore Bunkhouse HOSTEL £
(☑ 01479-811181; www.aviemore-bunkhouse.com; Dalfaber Rd; dm/d/f from £23/55/75; P @ 🛜) This independent hostel provides accommodation in bright, modern six- or eight-bed dorms, each with private bathroom, and one twin/family room. It has a drying room, secure bike storage and wheelchair-accessible dorms. From the train station, cross the pedestrian bridge over the tracks, turn right and walk south on Dalfaber Rd.

Cairngorm Hotel HOTEL ££
(☑ 01479-810233; www.cairngorm.com; Grampian Rd; s/d from £84/118; P 🛜) Better known as 'the Cairn', this long-established hotel is set in the fine old granite building with the pointy turret opposite the train station. It's a welcoming place with comfortable rooms and a determinedly Scottish atmosphere, with tartan carpets and stags' antlers. There's live music on weekends, so it can get a bit noisy – not for early-to-bedders.

Ardlogie Guest House B&B ££
(☑ 01479-810747; www.ardlogie.co.uk; Dalfaber Rd; s/d £80/100, bothy per 3 nights £360; P 🛜) Handy to the train station, the welcoming five-room Ardlogie has great views over the River Spey towards the Cairngorms, and the chance of spotting red squirrels from your bedroom window. There's also self-catering accommodation in the Bothy, a cosy, two-person timber cabin. Facilities include a boules pitch in the garden. Two-night minimum stay.

Ravenscraig Guest House B&B ££
(☑ 01479-810278; www.aviemoreonline.com; Grampian Rd; s/d from £65/90; 🛜) Ravenscraig is a large, flower-bedecked Victorian villa with seven spacious en suite rooms, plus another six in a modern chalet at the back (one wheelchair accessible). It serves traditional and veggie breakfasts in an attractive conservatory dining room.

Old Minister's House B&B £££
(☑ 01479-812181; www.theoldministershouse.co.uk; Ski Rd, Inverdruie; s/d £160/170; P 🛜) This

The Cairngorms

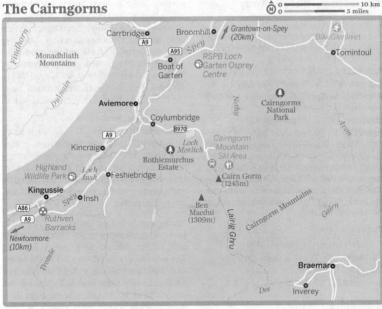

former manse dates from 1906 and has five rooms with a luxurious, country-house atmosphere. It's in a lovely setting amid Scots pines on the banks of the River Druie, southeast of Aviemore.

✗ Eating & Drinking

★ Route 7 Cafe
CAFE £

(☎01479-812433; http://highlandhomecentre.com/route-7-cafe.html; 18 Dalfaber Industrial Estate; mains £6-10; ☺9am-4pm; P ⏰ 🖶) This place, named for the cycle route that passes the door, takes a bit of finding (at the end of the side road that passes Cairngorm Brewery), but is well worth seeking out for its hearty menu of burgers, grilled sandwiches and salads; also wood-fired pizzas (noon to 3pm weekends only). Cyclists can use the power washer and tools outside.

Mountain Cafe
CAFE ££

(www.mountaincafe-aviemore.co.uk; 111 Grampian Rd; mains £10-15; ☺8.30am-5pm Mon-Fri, to 5.30pm Sat & Sun; P 🖊 🖶) The Mountain Cafe offers freshly prepared local produce with a Kiwi twist (the owner is from New Zealand): healthy breakfasts of muesli, porridge and fresh fruit (till 11.30am); hearty lunches of seafood chowder, burgers and imaginative salads; and home-baked breads, cakes and

biscuits. Caters for vegan, coeliac and nut-allergic diets.

Roo's Leap
AMERICAN ££

(☎01479-811161; www.roosleap.com; Station Sq; mains £8-15, steaks £22-25; ☺noon-2.30pm & 5-9pm Mon-Fri, noon-9pm Sat & Sun; 🛜 🖶) Friendly service, cold bottled beer and great barbecue contribute to the antipodean atmosphere at this lively restaurant set in the old railway station building. However, the menu is more like classic American and Tex Mex – sizzling steaks, juicy burgers, fajitas and nachos.

Winking Owl
PUB

(www.thewinkingowl.co; Grampian Rd; ☺noon-11pm Mon-Thu, 11am-1am Fri & Sat, 12.30-11pm Sun; 🛜) Lively local pub that operates under the wing of the Cairngorm Brewery. It's popular with hikers and climbers, and serves a good range of real ales and malt whiskies.

ℹ Information

There are ATMs outside the Tesco supermarket, and currency exchange at the post office and the **tourist office** (☎01479-810930; www.visitaviemore.com; The Mall, Grampian Rd; ☺9am-5pm Mon-Sat, 10am-4pm Sun year-round, longer hours Jul & Aug), all located on Grampian Rd.

❶ Getting There & Away

BUS

Buses stop on Grampian Rd opposite the train station; buy tickets at the tourist office (p311). Services include the following:

Edinburgh £28.50, four hours, five daily

Glasgow £28.50, 2¾ hours, five daily

Grantown-on-Spey £4, 35 minutes, five daily weekdays, two Saturday

Inverness £10.80, 45 minutes, eight daily

Perth £20.90, 2¼ hours, five daily

Bus 31 links Aviemore to Cairngorm Mountain car park (£2.90, 30 minutes, hourly) via Coylumbridge and Glenmore. A Strathspey Dayrider/Megarider ticket (£7.30/18.40) gives one/seven days unlimited bus travel from Aviemore as far as Cairngorm, Carrbridge and Kingussie; buy it from the bus driver.

TRAIN

The train station is on Grampian Rd.

Edinburgh £41, three hours, six daily

Glasgow £41, three hours, six daily

Inverness £12.80, 40 minutes, 12 daily

❶ Getting Around

Several places in Aviemore, Rothiemurchus Estate (p309) and Glenmore have mountain bikes for hire. Easy off-road cycle tracks link Aviemore with Glenmore and Loch Morlich to the east, and Boat of Garten to the north.

Bothy Bikes (p309) charges from £20 a day for a quality bike with front suspension and disc brakes.

Around Aviemore

Loch Morlich

Six miles east of Aviemore, Loch Morlich is surrounded by some 8 sq miles of pine and spruce forest that make up the Glenmore Forest Park. Its attractions include a sandy beach (at the east end) and a watersports centre.

The visitor centre at Glenmore has a small exhibition on the Caledonian forest and sells the *Glenmore Forest Park Map*, detailing local walks. The **circuit of Loch Morlich** (one hour) makes a pleasant outing; the trail is pram- and wheelchair-friendly.

🏃 Activities

★**Glenmore Lodge**   ADVENTURE SPORTS
(🖉 01479-861256; www.glenmorelodge.org.uk; Glenmore; 1-day courses from £65) One of Brit-

ain's leading adventure-sports training centres, offering courses in hill walking, rock climbing, ice climbing, canoeing, mountain biking and mountaineering. The centre's comfortable **B&B accommodation** (🖉 01479-861256; www.glenmorelodge.org.uk; Glenmore; s/tw £60/83; 🅿 🛜 🏊) is available to all, even if you're not taking a course, as is the indoor climbing wall, gym and sauna.

Loch Morlich
Watersports Centre   WATER SPORTS
(🖉 01479-861221; www.lochmorlich.com; ⏰ 9am-5pm Easter-Oct) This popular outfit rents out Canadian canoes (£23 an hour), kayaks (£9), sailboards (£18), sailing dinghies (£25) and stand-up paddle boards (£15), and also offers instruction.

Cairngorm Reindeer Centre   TOURS
(www.cairngormreindeer.co.uk; Glenmore; adult/child £15/9; ⏰ closed early Jan–mid-Feb; 🚼) The warden here leads guided walks to see and feed Britain's only herd of reindeer, which are very tame and will even eat out of your hand. Walks take place at 11am daily (weather-dependent), plus there's another at 2.30pm from May to September, and a third at 3.30pm Monday to Friday in July and August.

🛌 Sleeping

Glenmore Campsite   CAMPSITE £
(🖉 01479-861271; www.campingintheforest.co.uk; tent & campervan sites £18-27; ⏰ year-round; 🚼) Campers can set up base at this attractive lochside site with pitches amid the Scots pines; rates include up to four people per tent/campervan.

Cairngorm Lodge SYHA   HOSTEL £
(🖉 01479-861238; www.syha.org.uk; Glenmore; dm £19.50; ⏰ closed Nov & Dec; 🅿 @ 🛜 🏊) Set in a former shooting lodge that enjoys a great location at the east end of Loch Morlich; booking ahead is essential.

❶ Getting There & Away

Bus 31 links Aviemore with Loch Morlich and Glenmore (£2.90, 20 minutes, hourly) .

Cairngorm Mountain

Cairngorm Mountain Railway   FUNICULAR
(🖉 01479-861261; www.cairngormmountain.org; adult/child return £13.90/9.30; ⏰ every 20min 10am-4pm May-Nov, 9am-4.30pm Dec-Apr; 🅿) The national park's most popular attrac-

tion is this funicular railway that will whisk you to the edge of the Cairngorm plateau (altitude 1085m) in just eight minutes. The bottom station is at the Coire Cas car park at the end of Ski Rd; at the top is an exhibition, a shop (of course) and a restaurant. Unfortunately, for environmental and safety reasons, you're not allowed out of the top station in summer unless you book a guided walk.

From May to October, a 90-minute guided walk to the summit of Cairn Gorm (£21.60 per person) departs twice a day, while a four-hour guided hill walk runs four days a week. Check the website for details.

Cairngorm Mountain Ski Area SNOW SPORTS (www.cairngormmountain.org; 1-day ski pass per adult/child £35/21) Aspen or Val d'Isère it ain't, but with 19 runs and 23 miles of piste, Cairngorm is Scotland's most popular ski area. When the snow is at its best and the sun is shining you can close your eyes and imagine you're in the Alps; sadly, low cloud, high winds and horizontal sleet are more likely.

Ski or snowboard hire is around £26/19 per adult/child per day; there are lots of hire outlets at Coire Cas, Glenmore and Aviemore.

The season usually runs from December until the snow melts, which may be as late as the end of April, but snowfall here is unpredictable – in some years the slopes can be open in November, but closed for lack of snow in February. During the season the tourist office (p311) in Aviemore displays snow conditions and avalanche warnings. You can check the latest snow conditions at www.cairngormmountain.org/lifts-pistes and www.winterhighland.info.

Kincraig & Glen Feshie

At Kincraig, 6 miles southwest of Aviemore, the Spey widens into Loch Insh, home of the **Loch Insh Outdoor Centre** (☑ 01540-651272; www.lochinsh.com; Kincraig; day ticket incl all activities adult/child £35/25; ☻ 8.30am-5.30pm; ♠), which offers canoeing, windsurfing, sailing, mountain biking and fishing, as well as B&B accommodation.

Beautiful, tranquil Glen Feshie extends south from Kincraig, deep into the Cairngorms, with Scots pine woods in its upper reaches surrounded by big, heathery hills. The 4WD track to the head of the glen makes a great mountain-bike excursion (25-mile round trip).

★ **Highland Wildlife Park** ZOO (☑ 01540-651270; www.highlandwildlifepark.org; Kincraig; adult/child £17/9.95; ☻ 10am-6pm Jul & Aug, to 5pm Apr-Oct, to 4pm Nov-Mar; P) This place features a drive-through safari park as well as animal enclosures offering the chance to view rarely seen native wildlife, such as wildcats, capercaillies, pine martens, white-tailed sea eagles and red squirrels, as well as species that once roamed the Scottish hills but have long since disappeared, including wolf, lynx, wild boar, beaver and European bison.

There are also iconic species from around the world – snow leopard, red panda, Amur tiger and polar bear (a polar bear cub was born in 2018, the first to be born in the UK for 25 years).

Visitors without cars get driven around by staff (at no extra cost). Last entry is two hours before closing.

Carrbridge

POP 700

Carrbridge, 7 miles north of Aviemore, is a good alternative base for exploring the region. It takes its name from the graceful **old bridge** (spotlit at night), built in 1717, over the thundering rapids of the River Dulnain.

Landmark Forest Adventure Park AMUSEMENT PARK (☑ 0800 731 3446; www.landmarkpark.co.uk; adult/child £20.70/18.60; ☻ 10am-7pm mid-Jul–mid-Aug, to 6pm early Jul & late Aug, to 5pm Sep-Jun; ♠) Set in a forest of Scots pines, this is a theme park with a difference: the theme is timber. The main attractions are the Ropeworx high-wire adventure course, the Red Squirrel Nature Trail (a raised walkway through the forest canopy that allows you to view red squirrels, crossbills and crested tits), and the view from the Fire Lookout Tower.

❶ Getting There & Away

Bus 34 runs from Inverness to Carrbridge (£5.35, 45 minutes, six daily Monday to Friday, three on Saturday) and onwards to Grantown-on-Spey (£2.90, 20 minutes). Bus 32 links with Aviemore (£2.90, 15 minutes, five daily except Sunday).

Boat of Garten

Boat of Garten is known as the Osprey Village because these rare and beautiful birds of prey nest nearby at the **RSPB Loch Garten Osprey Centre** (☑ 01479-831694; www.

rspb.org.uk/lochgarten; Tulloch; osprey hide adult/child £5/2; ⊙osprey hide 10am-6pm Apr-Aug). The ospreys migrate here each spring from Africa and nest in a tall pine tree.

There is flexible, good-quality homestay accommodation at Fraoch Lodge (☎01479-831331; www.scotmountainholidays.com; Deshar Rd; per person £25-30; P🐾), along with a wide range of outdoor activities, while the Boat Hotel (☎01479-831258; www.boathotel.co.uk; s/d from £75/95; P🐾🍴) offers country-style accommodation.

❶ Getting There & Away

Boat of Garten is 5 miles northeast of Aviemore. The most interesting way to get here is on the Strathspey Steam Railway (p309) from Aviemore, or you can ride or walk along National Cycle Network Route 7 (allow 30 to 40 minutes by bike, two hours on foot).

Grantown-on-Spey

POP 2430

Grantown (*gran*-ton) is an elegant Georgian town with a grid of streets and a broad, tree-lined main square. It is a fine example of a planned settlement, founded by Sir Ludovic Grant in 1766 as a centre for the linen industry, and later becoming a tourist town after Queen Victoria's visit in 1860.

THE SNOW ROADS

The Snow Roads (https://visitcairn gorms.com/snowroads) is a 90-mile scenic driving route between Blairgowrie in Perthshire and Grantown-on-Spey, by way of Braemar and Ballater. It takes in two high mountain passes that are often snow-covered in winter – Glenshee and the Lecht (both are ski centres) – and is marked by a series of landscape artworks at particularly picturesque viewpoints:

Connecting Contours A gracefully sinuous bench beside the A93 on the southern approach to Glenshee.

The Watchers A series of eerie steel shapes reminiscent of standing stones, near Corgarff Castle.

Still A polished steel sculpture that frames the view near Tomintoul.

The route is not signposted, but described online and in a leaflet available from local tourist offices.

A favoured haunt of anglers and the tweed-cap-and-green-wellies brigade, Grantown is thronged with visitors in summer, but it reverts to a quiet backwater in winter. Most hotels can kit you out for a day of fly-fishing on the Spey, or put you in touch with someone who can.

Grantown Museum   MUSEUM
(☎01479-872478; www.grantownmuseum.co.uk; Burnfield Ave; adult/child £4/free; ⊙10am-5pm Mon-Sat Apr-Oct; P🚻) A small museum that chronicles the history of the town and its relationship with Clan Grant; also houses a tourist information point (☎01479-870477; Burnfield Ave; ⊙10am-5pm Mon-Sat Apr-Oct).

Brooklynn   B&B ££
(☎01479-873113; www.woodier.com; Grant Rd; s/d £48/96; P🐾) 🍴 This beautiful Victorian villa features original stained glass and wood panelling, and seven spacious, luxurious rooms (all doubles have en suites). The food – dinner is available (£28 per person), as well as breakfast – is superb, too.

★Muckrach Country
House Hotel   HOTEL £££
(☎01479-851227; www.muckrach.com; Dulnain Bridge; r from £209; P🐾🍴) Built as a Victorian shooting lodge in 1860, Muckrach has been tastefully converted into a luxurious country house hotel with a relaxed and informal atmosphere. The lounge, complete with grand piano, serves coffee, cake and snacks through the day, and the restaurant (mains £13 to £21) serves a brasserie-style menu at lunch and dinner weekdays, and all day Saturday.

❶ Getting There & Away

Bus 34X runs from Inverness to Grantown-on-Spey (£6.70, 1¼ hours, six daily Monday to Friday, three Saturday) and on to Aviemore (£4, 35 minutes).

Kingussie & Newtonmore

The old Speyside towns of Kingussie (kin-*yew*-see) and Newtonmore sit at the foot of the great heather-clad humps known as the Monadhliath Mountains. Newtonmore is best known as the home of the excellent Highland Folk Museum, Kingussie for one of the Highlands' best restaurants.

The road west from Newtonmore to Spean Bridge passes Ardverikie Estate and Loch Laggan, famous as the setting for the BBC TV series *Monarch of the Glen*.

◉ Sights & Activities

Ruthven Barracks
RUINS

(HES; ⊙24hr; [P]) FREE Ruthven Barracks was one of four garrisons built by the British government after the first Jacobite rebellion of 1715, as part of a Hanoverian scheme to take control of the Highlands. Ironically the barracks were last occupied by Jacobite troops awaiting the return of Bonnie Prince Charlie after the Battle of Culloden. Perched dramatically on a river terrace and clearly visible from the main A9 road near Kingussie, the ruins are spectacularly floodlit at night.

Highland Folk Museum
MUSEUM

(☑01540-673551; www.highlandfolk.museum; Kingussie Rd, Newtonmore; ⊙10.30am-5.30pm Apr-Aug, 11am-4.30pm Sep & Oct; [P]) FREE This open-air museum comprises a collection of historical buildings and artefacts revealing many aspects of Highland culture and lifestyle. Laid out like a farming township, it has a community of traditional thatch-roofed cottages, a sawmill, a schoolhouse, a shepherd's bothy (hut) and a rural post office. Actors in period costume give demonstrations of woodcarving, wool-spinning and peat-fire baking. You'll need at least two to three hours to make the most of a visit here.

Laggan Wolftrax
MOUNTAIN BIKING

(http://scotland.forestry.gov.uk/visit/laggan-wolftrax; Strathmashie Forest; trails free, parking per day £3; ⊙10am-6pm Mon, 9.30am-5pm Tue, Thu & Fri, 9.30am-6pm Sat & Sun) Ten miles southwest of Newtonmore, on the A86 road towards Spean Bridge, this is one of Scotland's top mountain-biking centres with purpose-built trails ranging from open-country riding to black-diamond downhills with rock slabs and drop-offs. Includes bike hire outlet and a good cafe (open 10am to 5pm April to October).

Highland All Terrain
ADVENTURE

(☑01528-544358; www.quadbiketours.co.uk; Old Filling Station, Kinloch Laggan; per person from £50) Join an off-road quad-bike tour of Ardverikie Estate, which appears as Glen Bogle in the TV series *Monarch of the Glen*. Tours range from one hour to 3½ hours, and take in many of the TV locations. Located 15 miles southwest of Newtonmore.

🛏 Sleeping & Eating

★ Eagleview Guest House
B&B ££

(☑01540-673675; Perth Rd, Newtonmore; r £78-85; [P][🛜][🐾]) Welcoming Eagleview is one of the most pleasant places to stay in the area, with beautifully decorated bedrooms, super-king-size beds, spacious bathrooms with power showers (except room 4, which has a Victorian slipper bath!), and nice little touches such as cafetières (coffee plungers) with real coffee – and fresh milk – on your hospitality tray.

★ Restaurant at the Cross
SCOTTISH £££

(☑01540-661166; www.thecross.co.uk; Tweed Mill Brae, off Ardbroilach Rd, Kingussie; 3-course lunch/dinner £30/55; ⊙noon-2pm & 7-8.30pm; [P][🛜]) 🍴 Housed in a converted watermill, the Cross is one of the finest restaurants in the Highlands. The intimate, low-raftered dining room has an open fire and a patio overlooking the stream, and serves a daily changing menu of fresh Scottish produce accompanied by a superb wine list (booking essential).

If you want to stay the night, there are eight stylish rooms (double or twin £110 to £200) to choose from.

ℹ Getting There & Away

BUS

Kingussie and Newtonmore are served by **Scottish Citylink** (www.citylink.co.uk) coaches on the main Perth-to-Inverness bus route, as well as local Stagecoach buses.

Aviemore £3.70, 20 minutes, hourly

Inverness £10.70, 1½ hours, three daily, change at Carrbridge

Perth £17.10, 1¾ hours, one daily

TRAIN

Kingussie and Newtonmore are on the Edinburgh/Glasgow-to-Inverness railway line.

Edinburgh £37.50, 2¾ hours, seven daily Monday to Saturday, two Sunday

Inverness £12.80, one hour, eight daily Monday to Saturday, four Sunday

Tomintoul & Around

POP 320

Tomintoul (tom-in-towel) is a pretty, stone-built village with a grassy, tree-lined main square. It was built by the Duke of Gordon in 1775 on the old military road that leads over the Lecht pass from Corgarff, a route now followed by the A939 (usually the first road in Scotland to be blocked by snow when winter closes in). The duke hoped that settling the dispersed population of his estates in a proper village would help to stamp out cattle stealing and illegal distilling.

The Glenlivet Estate (now the property of the Crown) has lots of walking and cycling trails – the estate's **tourist office** (☑ 01479-870070; www.glenlivetestate.co.uk; Main St; ☉ 9am-5pm Mon-Fri) distributes free maps of the area – and a spur of the Speyside Way long-distance footpath runs between Tomintoul and Ballindalloch, 15 miles to the north.

Accommodation for walkers includes the **Smugglers Hostel** (☑ 01807-580364; www. thesmugglershostel.co.uk; Main St; dm/tw £20/85; 🗣), housed in the old village school. The highly recommended **Argyle Guest House** (☑ 01807-580766; www.argyletomintoul.co.uk; 7 Main St; d/f from £70/120; 🗣🐾) is a more comfortable alternative (best porridge in the Cairngorms!).

For something to eat in town, try **Clockhouse Restaurant** (☑ 01807-580378; The Square; mains £10-21; ☉ 11am-9pm Tue-Sun); the best food in the area is out of town at **Coffee Still** (☑ 07599 973845; www.coffeestillcafe.co.uk; BikeGlenlivet Trail Centre; mains £6-9; ☉ 10am-5pm Thu-Mon; 🅿🐾).

Tomintoul & Glenlivet Discovery Centre

MUSEUM

(☑ 01807-580760; discovery@tgdt.org.uk; The Square; ☉ 10am-5pm Apr-Oct) **FREE** This visitor centre and rural museum celebrates local history, with reconstructions of a crofter's kitchen and a blacksmith's forge.

BikeGlenlivet

MOUNTAIN BIKING

(www.glenlivetestate.co.uk; trails free, parking £3) There's excellent mountain-biking at this trail centre, 4.5 miles north of Tomintoul, off the B9136 road. Custom-built trails range from the 9km blue run for beginners to the 22km red route for more experienced riders. Cafe and bike hire on site.

Cockbridge to Tomintoul Road

The A939, known as the Cockbridge-Tomintoul road – a magnificent roller-coaster of a route much loved by motorcyclists – crosses the Lecht pass (637m), where there's a small skiing area with lots of short easy and intermediate runs.

Corgarff Castle

CASTLE

(HES; ☑ 01975-651460; www.historicenvironment. scot; adult/child £6/3.60; ☉ 9.30am-5.30pm Apr-Sep; 🅿) In the wild hills of the eastern Cairngorms, near the A939 road from Cockbridge to Tomintoul, is the impressive fortress of Corgarff Castle. The tower house dates from the 16th century, but the star-shaped defensive curtain wall was added in 1748 when the castle was converted to a military barracks in the wake of the Jacobite rebellion.

Lecht 2090

SNOW SPORTS

(www.lecht.co.uk) The Lecht is Scotland's smallest snow-sports centre. In winter, you can hire skis, boots and poles for £22 a day; a one-day lift pass is £30. In summer (weekends only), the chairlift serves mountain-biking trails (day ticket £30); there are no bike-hire facilities, though, so you'll need to bring your own.

Royal Deeside

The upper valley of the River Dee stretches west from Aboyne and Ballater to Braemar, closely paralleled by the A93 road. Made famous by its long association with the monarchy – today's Royal Family still holiday at Balmoral Castle, built for Queen Victoria in 1855 – the region is often called Royal Deeside.

The River Dee, renowned world-over for its salmon fishing, has its source in the Cairngorm Mountains west of Braemar, the starting point for long walks into the hills. The FishDee website (www.fishdee.co.uk) has all you need to know about fishing on the river.

Ballater

POP 1530

The attractive little village of Ballater owes its 18th-century origins to the curative waters of nearby Pannanich Springs (now bottled commercially as Deeside Natural Mineral Water), and its prosperity to nearby Balmoral Castle.

The village received a double dose of misfortune when the Old Royal Station (its main tourist attraction) burned down in May 2015, followed by the worst flooding in living memory in January 2016. The restored station building reopened in 2018 with a museum, restaurant and tourist office.

Note the crests on the shop fronts along the main street proclaiming 'By Royal Appointment' – the village is a major supplier of provisions to Balmoral Castle.

Activities

As you approach Ballater from the east the hills start to close in, and there are many pleasant walks in the surrounding area. The steep woodland walk up **Craigendarroch** (400m) takes just over one hour. **Morven** (871m) is a more serious prospect, taking about six hours return, but offers good views from the top.

You can hire bikes from **CycleHighlands** (🌐 01339-755864; www.cyclehighlands.com; The Pavilion, Victoria Rd; bicycle hire per half-/full day £15/20; ☺ 9am-6pm) and **Bike Station** (🌐 01339-754004; www.bikestationballater.co.uk; Station Sq; bicycle hire per 3hr/day £12/18; ☺ 9am-6pm), which also offer guided bike rides and advice on local trails.

🛏 Sleeping & Eating

Ballater Hostel HOSTEL £
(🌐 01339-753752; www.ballater-hostel.com; Bridge Sq; dm/tw from £22/50; ☎) ✐ Tucked up a lane near the bridge over the River Dee, this is an attractive, ecofriendly hostel with six en suite private rooms (sleeping two to eight). Rooms have personal lockers and reading lamps, and there's a comfortable lounge with big, soft sofas and a wood-burning stove.

★ Auld Kirk HOTEL ££
(🌐 01339-755762; www.theauldkirk.com; Braemar Rd; r from £85; 🅿🛜🐾) Here's something a little out of the ordinary – a seven-bedroom hotel housed in a converted 19th-century church. The interior blends original features with sleek modern decor – the pulpit now serves as the reception desk, while the lounge is bathed in light from leaded Gothic windows. Breakfast not included, but guests can buy it at the hotel's coffee shop.

Rock Salt & Snails CAFE £
(🌐 07834 452583; www.facebook.com/rocksalt andsnailsballater; 2 Bridge St; mains £4-9; ☺10am-5pm Mon-Fri, to 9pm Sat, to 6pm Sun May-Sep, 10am-5pm Mon-Sat, 11am-5pm Sun Oct-Apr; 🛜♿🐾) A great little cafe serving excellent coffee and tempting lunch platters featuring locally sourced deli products

(cheese, ham, salads etc), including a kids' platter.

Getting There & Away

Bus 201 runs from Aberdeen to Ballater (£12.10, 1¾ hours, hourly Monday to Saturday, six on Sunday) via Crathes Castle, and continues to Braemar (£6.25, 35 minutes) every two hours.

Balmoral Castle

Built for Queen Victoria in 1855 as a private residence for the Royal Family, **Balmoral Castle** (🌐 01339-742534; www.balmoralcastle. com; Crathie; adult/child £11.50/6; ☺ 10am-5pm Apr-Jul, last admission 4.30pm; 🅿) kicked off the revival of the Scottish Baronial style of architecture that characterises so many of Scotland's 19th-century country houses. The admission fee includes an interesting and well-thought-out audio guide, but the tour is very much an outdoor one through garden and grounds.

As for the castle itself, only the ballroom, which displays a collection of Landseer paintings and royal silver, is open to the public. Don't expect to see the Queen's private quarters! The main attraction is learning about Highland estate management, rather than royal revelations.

You can buy a booklet that details several waymarked walks within Balmoral Estate; the best is the climb to **Prince Albert's Cairn**, a huge granite pyramid that bears the inscription 'To the beloved memory of Albert the great and good, Prince Consort. Erected by his broken hearted widow Victoria R. 21st August 1862'.

The massive pointy-topped mountain that looms to the south of Balmoral is **Lochnagar** (1155m), immortalised in verse by Lord Byron, who spent his childhood years in Aberdeenshire:

England, thy beauties are tame and domestic
To one who has roamed o'er the mountains afar.
Oh! for the crags that are wild and majestic,
The steep frowning glories of dark Lochnagar.

Lord Byron, 'Lochnagar'

Balmoral is eight miles west of Ballater, and can be reached on the Aberdeen–Braemar bus.

Braemar

POP 450

Braemar is a pretty little village with a grand location on a broad plain ringed by mountains where the Dee valley and Glen Clunie meet. In winter this is one of the coldest places in the country – temperatures as low as -29°C have been recorded – and during spells of severe cold, hungry deer wander the streets looking for a bite to eat. Braemar is an excellent base for hill walking, and there's also skiing at nearby Glenshee.

◉ Sights & Activities

An easy walk from Braemar is up Creag Choinnich (538m), a hill to the east of the village above the A93. The 1-mile route is waymarked and takes about 1½ hours return. For a longer walk (4 miles; about three hours return) and superb views of the Cairngorms, head for the summit of Morrone (859m), southwest of Braemar. Ask at the tourist office for details of these and other walks.

Braemar Castle CASTLE
(www.braemarcastle.co.uk; adult/child £8/4; ⊙10am-5pm Jul & Aug, Wed-Sun Apr-Jun, Sep & Oct; P) Just north of Braemar village, turreted Braemar Castle dates from 1628 and served as a government garrison after the 1745 Jacobite rebellion. It was taken over by the local community in 2007, which now offers guided tours of the historic castle apartments. There's a short walk from the car park to the castle.

Braemar Mountain Sports CYCLING
(✆01339-741242; www.braemarmountainsports.com; 5 Invercauld Rd; bike hire per 4hr/day £15/20; ⊙9am-6pm) You can hire bikes from Braemar Mountain Sports. It also rents skiing and mountaineering equipment.

⚜ Festivals & Events

Braemar Gathering SPORTS
(✆01339-755377; www.braemargathering.org; adult/child from £12/2; ⊙Sep) There are Highland games in many towns and villages throughout the summer, but the best known is the Braemar Gathering, which takes place on the first Saturday in September. It's a major occasion, organised every year since 1817 by the Braemar Royal Highland Society.

Events include Highland dancing, pipers, tug-of-war, a hill race up Morrone, tossing the caber, hammer- and stone-throwing and the long jump. International athletes are among those who take part.

These kinds of events took place informally in the Highlands for many centuries as tests of skill and strength, but they were formalised around 1820 as part of the rise of Highland romanticism initiated by Sir Walter Scott and King George IV. Queen Victoria attended the Braemar Gathering in 1848, starting a tradition of royal patronage that continues to this day.

🛏 Sleeping

Rucksacks Bunkhouse HOSTEL £
(✆01339-741517; 15 Mar Rd; bothy £7, dm £12-15, tw £36; P) This appealing cottage has a comfy dorm, and cheaper beds in an alpine-style bothy (shared sleeping platform for 10 people; bring your own sleeping bag). Extras include a drying room (for wet-weather gear), a laundry and even a sauna (£10 an hour). The friendly owner is a fount of knowledge about the local area.

Braemar SYHA HOSTEL £
(✆01339-741659; www.syha.org.uk; 21 Glenshee Rd; dm/tw £21/49; ⊙Feb-Oct; P@☎☀) This hostel is housed in a grand former shooting lodge just south of Braemar village centre on the A93 to Perth. It has a comfy lounge with pool table, and a barbecue in the garden.

Braemar Caravan Park CAMPSITE £
(✆01339-741373; www.braemarcaravanpark.co.uk; tent sites incl 2 people £22.50; ⊙closed mid-Oct–mid-Dec; ☎) There is good camping here, in a sheltered spot surrounded by mountains, with hot showers, a laundry and a small shop selling caravan and camping essentials.

Braemar Cabins CABIN ££
(✆01339-741242; http://braemarcabins.com; 7-9 Invercauld Rd; 3 nights from £285; P☎☀) These attractive larch-clad cabins at the entrance to the village can sleep up to four people in two double or twin bedrooms (some wheelchair accessible). They have underfloor heating, well-equipped kitchens and outdoor decks. In high season the minimum stay is one week (£695).

Braemar Lodge Hotel HOTEL ££
(✆01339-741627; www.braemarlodge.co.uk; Glenshee Rd; dm/s/d from £15/80/120; P☎) This Victorian shooting lodge on the southern outskirts of Braemar has bags of character, not least in the wood-panelled Malt Room

bar, which is as well stocked with mounted deer heads as it is with single malt whiskies. There's a good restaurant with views of the hills, plus a 12-berth hikers' bunkhouse (book in advance) in the hotel grounds.

Craiglea   B&B **££**
(☑ 01339-741641; www.craigleabraemar.com; Hillside Rd; d/f from £72/107; P 🖂) Craiglea is a homely B&B set in a pretty stone cottage with three en suite bedrooms. Vegetarian breakfasts are available and the owners can rent you a bike and give advice on local walks.

✖ Eating

Bothy   CAFE **£**
(Invercauld Rd; mains £4-7; ⊙ 9am-5.30pm Sun-Thu, to 6pm Fri & Sat; 🖂) An appealing little cafe tucked behind the Mountain Sports shop, with a sunny terrace out front and a balcony at the back overhanging the river.

Taste   CAFE **£**
(☑ 01339-741425; www.taste-braemar.co.uk; Airlie House, Mar Rd; mains £5-9; ⊙ 10am-5pm Tue-Sat; 🖂) ✐ Taste is a relaxed little cafe which has armchairs in the window bays, and serves homemade soups, sandwiches, coffee and cakes.

ⓘ Information

The **tourist office** (☑ 01399-741600; The Mews, Mar Rd; ⊙ 9am-6pm Aug, to 5pm Jun, Jul, Sep & Oct, shorter hours Nov-May), opposite the Fife Arms Hotel, has lots of useful info on walks in the area.

ⓘ Getting There & Away

Bus 201 runs from Aberdeen to Braemar (£12.10, 2¼ hours, every two hours Monday to Saturday, five on Sunday). The 50-mile drive from Perth to Braemar is beautiful, but there's no public transport on this route.

The Angus Glens

Five scenic glens – Isla, Prosen, Clova, Lethnot and Esk – cut into the hills along the southern fringes of the Cairngorms National Park, accessible from Kirriemuir in Angus. All have attractive scenery, though each glen has its own distinct personality: Glen Clova and Glenesk are the most beautiful, while Glen Lethnot is the least frequented. You can get detailed information on walks

The route along the A93 from Braemar to Blairgowrie through the ski area of Glenshee is one of the most scenic drives in the country. It's fantastic **walking** country in summer, and has some of Scotland's best **skiing** in winter.

Although this is Scotland's biggest ski area, there's only a car park, ticket office, cafe and uplift – no services or accommodation.

With 22 lifts and 36 runs **Glenshee Ski Resort** (☑ 01339-741320; www.ski-glenshee.co.uk; 1-day ski pass per adult/child £30/20) is Scotland's largest skiing area. When the sun burns through the clouds after a good fall of snow, you'll be in a unique position to drink in the beauty of the country; the skiing isn't half bad either.

The chairlift, which also opens in July and August for walkers and mountain bikers, can whisk you up to 910m, near the top of the Cairnwell (933m).

in the Angus Glens from the **Gateway to the Glens Museum** (kirriemuirmuseum@angusalive.scot; 32 High St; ⊙ 10am-5pm Tue-Sat) **FREE** in Kirriemuir and from the Glen Clova Hotel (p320) in Glen Clova.

ⓘ Getting There & Away

There is no public transport to the Angus Glens other than a limited school-bus service along Glen Clova; ask at the Gateway to the Glens Museum in Kirriemuir for details.

Glen Clova

The longest and loveliest of the Angus Glens stretches north from Kirriemuir for 20 miles, broad and pastoral in its lower reaches but growing narrower and craggier as the steep, heather-clad Highland hills close in around its head.

The minor road beyond the Glen Clova Hotel (p320) ends at a Forestry Commission car park at Glen Doll with a **ranger centre** (☑ 01575-550233; Glen Doll; parking £2; ⊙ 9am-6pm Apr-Sep, to 4.30pm Oct-Mar) and picnic area, which is the trailhead for a number of strenuous walks through the hills to the north.

Jock's Road is an ancient footpath that was much used by cattle drovers, soldiers, smugglers and shepherds in the 18th and 19th centuries; 700 Jacobite soldiers passed this way during their retreat in 1746, en route to defeat at Culloden. From the car park the path strikes west along Glen Doll, then north across a high plateau (900m) before descending steeply into Glen Callater and on to Braemar (15 miles; allow five to seven hours). The route is hard going and should not be attempted in winter; you'll need OS 1:50,000 maps numbers 43 and 44.

An easier walk leads from Glen Doll car park to **Corrie Fee**, a spectacular glacial hollow in the edge of the mountain plateau (4.5-mile round trip, waymarked).

Glen Clova Hotel   HOTEL **££**
(☑ 01575-550350; www.clova.com; s/d from £85/120; ℗ 🐾) The Glen Clova Hotel is a lovely old drover's inn near the head of the glen, and a great place to get away from it all. As well as 18 comfortable, country-style, en suite rooms (one with a four-poster bed), it has a rustic, stone-floored climbers' bar with a roaring log fire, and a **restaurant** (☑ 01575-550350; mains £9-25; ⊙ noon-7.45pm Sun-Thu, to 8.45pm Fri & Sat, shorter hours Nov-Mar; ℗ 🐾). No mobile phone reception.

Glenesk

The most easterly of the Angus Glens, Glenesk runs for 15 miles from Edzell to lovely **Loch Lee**, surrounded by beetling cliffs and waterfalls.

Fifteen miles up the glen from Edzell, the public road ends near **Invermark Castle**, an impressive ruined tower. From the car park, good hiking trails lead to a 17th-century kirkyard beside Loch Lee (1 mile), the monument at **Queen's Well** (a spring once visited by Queen Victoria; 2 miles), and the summit of **Mt Keen** (939m; 5 miles).

Glenesk Retreat & Folk Museum   MUSEUM
(www.gleneskretreat.scot; admission by donation; ⊙ 10am-5pm Mon-Fri, to 6pm Sat & Sun Apr-Oct; ℗ 🐾) 🏛 Ten miles up Glenesk from Edzell is a former shooting lodge that houses a fascinating collection of antiques and artefacts documenting everyday life in the glen from the 17th to the early 20th centuries – 860 people once lived here; today the population is less than 100.

There's also internet access, a gift shop and a restaurant (mains £5 to £10) serving superb fish and chips.

HIGHLAND PERTHSHIRE

The Highland border cuts diagonally across Scotland from Dumbarton to Stonehaven, dividing the county of Perthshire into two distinctive regions. Highland Perthshire, spreading north of a line from Comrie to Blairgowrie, is a land of mountains, forest and lochs, with some of the finest scenery in the UK. The ancient city of Dunkeld, on the main A9 road from Perth to Inverness, is the main gateway to the region.

❶ Getting There & Around

Citylink (p296) buses from Edinburgh or Glasgow to Inverness stop at Birnam and Pitlochry. There are regular buses from Perth to most of the towns in the area. Trains running between Perth and Inverness stop at Blair Atholl and Pitlochry.

Away from the main A9 Perth-to-Inverness road, public transport is thin on the ground, and often geared to the needs of local schools.

Dunkeld & Birnam
POP 1005

The Tay runs like a storybook river through the heart of Perthshire's Big Tree Country, where the twin towns of Dunkeld and Birnam are linked by Thomas Telford's graceful bridge of 1808. As well as Dunkeld's ancient cathedral, there's much walking to be done in this area of magnificent forested hills. These same walks were one of the inspirations for Beatrix Potter to create her children's tales.

There's less to see in Birnam, a name made famous by Macbeth. There's not much left of Birnam Wood, but a riverside path leads to the **Birnam Oak**, a venerable 500-year-old survivor from Shakespeare's time, its ageing boughs propped up with timber supports. Nearby is the 300-year-old Birnam Sycamore.

◉ Sights & Activities

Dunkeld Cathedral   CHURCH
(HS; www.dunkeldcathedral.org.uk; High St; ⊙ 9.30am-5.30pm Apr-Sep, 10am-4pm Oct-Mar) 🆓 Situated on the grassy banks of the River Tay, Dunkeld Cathedral is one of the most beautifully sited churches in Scotland; don't miss it on a sunny day, when there are few lovelier places to be. Half the cathedral is still in use as a church; the rest is a romantic ruin. It partly dates from the 14th century, having suffered damage during

the Reformation and the battle of Dunkeld (Jacobites versus the government) in 1689.

The Wolf of Badenoch, a fierce 14th-century noble who burned towns and abbeys to the ground in protest at his excommunication, is buried here – undeservedly – in a fine medieval tomb behind the wooden screen in the church.

Dunkeld House Grounds
GARDENS

(⊘24hr) **FREE** Waymarked walks lead upstream from Dunkeld Cathedral through the gorgeous grounds of Dunkeld House Hotel, formerly a seat of the dukes of Atholl. In the 18th and early 19th centuries the 'planting dukes', as they became known, planted more than 27 million conifers on their estates 'for beauty and profit', introducing species such as larch, Douglas fir and sequoia, and sowing the seeds of Scottish forestry.

The abundance of vast, ancient trees here has given rise to the nickname Big Tree Country (www.perthshirebigtreecountry. co.uk). Just west of the cathedral is the 280-year-old '**parent larch**', the lone survivor of several planted in 1738, and said to have provided the seed stock for all Scottish larch trees. On the far side of the river is **Niel Gow's Oak**, another ancient tree, said to have provided inspiration for legendary local fiddler Niel Gow (1727–1807).

Loch of the Lowes
Wildlife Centre
WILDLIFE RESERVE

(☑01350-727337; www.swt.org.uk; adult/child £4/50p; ⊘10am-5pm Mar-Oct, 10.30am-4pm Fri-Sun Nov-Feb; P) Loch of the Lowes, 2 miles east of Dunkeld off the A923, has a visitor centre devoted to red squirrels and the majestic osprey. There's a birdwatching hide (with binoculars provided), where you can see the birds nesting during breeding season (late April to August), complete with a live video link to the nest.

Beatrix Potter Exhibition & Garden
MUSEUM

(www.birnaminstitute.com; Station Rd; £3; ⊘10am-4.30pm; P) In the middle of Birnam village is the small, leafy Beatrix Potter Garden; the children's author, who wrote the evergreen story of *Peter Rabbit,* spent her childhood holidays in the area. Next to the park, in the Birnam Arts Centre, is a small exhibition on Potter and her characters.

Hermitage
WALKING

One of the most popular walks near Dunkeld is the Hermitage, where a well-marked trail follows the River Braan to Ossian's Hall, a quaint folly built by the Duke of Atholl in 1758 overlooking the spectacular Falls of Braan (salmon can be seen leaping here, especially in September and October). It's signposted off the A9 just west of the village.

🛏 Sleeping & Eating

⭐ **Jessie Mac's**
HOSTEL, B&B £

(☑01350-727324; www.jessiemacs.co.uk; Murthly Tce, Birnam; dm/d from £20/59; 🛜🐾) ✎ Set in a Victorian manse complete with baronial turret, Jessie Mac's is a glorious cross between B&B and luxury hostel, with three gorgeous doubles and four shared or family rooms with bunks. Guests make good use of the country-style lounge, sunny dining room and well-equipped kitchen, and breakfasts are composed of local produce, from organic eggs to Dunkeld smoked salmon.

Erigmore Estate
LODGE ££

(☑01350-727236; www.erigmore.co.uk; Birnam; d 3 nights from £273; P🐾) Scattered around the wooded, riverside grounds of Erigmore House, the former country retreat of a

---

FISHING & RAFTING ON THE TAY

The Tay is Scotland's longest river (117 miles) and the most powerful in Britain, with a flow rate greater than the Thames and the Severn combined. It's also Europe's most famous salmon river, attracting anglers from all over the world (the season runs from 15 January to 15 October). The British record rod-caught salmon, weighing in at a whopping 64lb (29kg) was hooked in the Tay near Dunkeld in 1922 by local woman Georgina Ballantine.

Salmon fishing has an air of exclusivity and can be expensive, but anyone – even complete beginners – can have a go. There's lots of information on the FishTay website (www.fishtay. co.uk), but novices would be best to hire a guide – check out Fishinguide Scotland (p263).

The Tay is also famous for its canoeing, kayaking and white-water rafting; the latter is best around Grandtully rapids near Aberfeldy, where Splash (p326) runs rafting trips.

INVERNESS & THE CENTRAL HIGHLANDS DUNKELD & BIRNAM

wealthy clipper ship's captain, these luxury timber lodges provide cosseted comfort complete with outdoor deck and – at the more expensive end of the range – a private hot tub. The house itself contains shared facilities, including a bar, restaurant and swimming pool. There's a three-night minimum stay.

★ **Taybank**　　　　　　　　　　PUB FOOD **££**
(☑ 01350-727340; www.thetaybank.co.uk; Tay Tce, Dunkeld; mains £9-13; ⊙ food served noon-9pm; P) ✎ Top choice for a sun-kissed pub lunch by the river is the Taybank, a regular meeting place and performance space for folk musicians and a wonderfully welcoming bar serving ales from the local Strathbraan Brewery. There's live music several nights per week, and the menu features local produce with dishes such as smoked venison or grilled sea trout.

ℹ Information

Dunkeld Tourist Office (☑ 01350-727688; www.dunkeldandbirnam.org.uk; The Cross; ⊙ 10.30am-4.30pm Mon-Sat, 11am-4pm Sun Apr-Oct, longer hours Jul & Aug, Fri-Sun only Nov-Mar) Has information on local hiking and biking trails.

ℹ Getting There & Away

Citylink (p300) buses running between Glasgow/Edinburgh and Inverness stop at the Birnam Hotel (£18.10, two hours, two or three daily). **Stagecoach** (www.stagecoachbus.com) runs hourly buses (only five on Sunday) between Perth and Dunkeld (£2.80, 45 minutes), continuing to Aberfeldy.

Pitlochry

POP 2780

Pitlochry, with the scent of the Highlands already in the air, is a popular stop on the way north. In summer the main street can be a conga line of tour groups, but linger a while and it can still charm – on a quiet spring evening it's a pretty place with salmon leaping in the Tummel and good things brewing at the Moulin Hotel.

◉ Sights & Activities

One of Pitlochry's attractions is its beautiful riverside; the River Tummel is dammed here, and if you're lucky you might see salmon swimming up the fish ladder to Loch Faskally above (May to November; best month is October).

★ **Pitlochry Dam**
Visitor Centre　　　　　　　VISITOR CENTRE
(www.pitlochrydam.com; Armoury Rd; ⊙ 9.30am-5.30pm; P) FREE Opened in 2017, this architecturally stunning visitor centre is perched above the dam on the River Tummel, and houses an exhibition that details the history of hydroelectricity in Scotland, alongside the life cycle of the Atlantic salmon (all hydro stations need a fish ladder to allow salmon to migrate upstream past the dams). Includes an excellent cafe.

★ **Edradour Distillery**　　　　　DISTILLERY
(☑ 01796-472095; www.edradour.co.uk; Moulin Rd; tour adult/child £10/5; ⊙ 10am-5pm Mon-Sat Apr-Oct, to 4.30pm Mon-Fri Nov-Mar; P ✿) This is proudly Scotland's smallest and most picturesque distillery and one of the best to visit: you can see the whole process, easily explained, in one building. It's 2.5 miles east of Pitlochry by car, along the Moulin road, or a pleasant 1-mile walk.

Blair Athol Distillery　　　　　DISTILLERY
(☑ 01796-482003; www.malts.com; Perth Rd; standard tour £8; ⊙ 10am-5pm Apr-Oct, to 4pm Nov-Mar) Tours here focus on whisky making and the blending of this well-known dram. More detailed private tours give you greater insights and superior tastings.

Explorers Garden　　　　　　　GARDENS
(☑ 01796-484600; www.explorersgarden.com; Foss Rd; adult/child £4/1; ⊙ 10am-5pm Apr-Oct; P) This gem of a garden is based around plants brought to Scotland by 18th- and 19th-century Scottish botanists and explorers such as David Douglas (after whom the Douglas fir is named), and celebrates 300 years of collecting and the 'plant hunters' who tracked down these exotic species.

Pass of Killiecrankie　　　　HISTORIC SITE
(NTS; parking £2; ⊙ 24hr; P ✿) FREE The beautiful, rugged Pass of Killiecrankie, 3.5 miles north of Pitlochry, where the River Garry tumbles through a narrow gorge, was the site of the 1689 **Battle of Killiecrankie** that ignited the Jacobite rebellion. The visitor centre (NTS; ☑ 01796-473233; www.nts.org.uk; ⊙ 10am-5pm Apr-Sep, 11am-4pm Oct; P ✿) FREE has great interactive displays on Jacobite history and local flora and fauna. There's plenty to touch, pull and open – great for kids. There are some stunning walks along the wooded gorge, too; keep an eye out for red squirrels.

Highland Fling Bungee ADVENTURE SPORTS
(📞 0845 366 5844; www.bungeejumpscotland.
co.uk; per person £79, repeat jumps £30) Based
at Killiecrankie, 3.5 miles north of Pitlochry,
Highland Fling offers breathtaking 130ft
bungee jumps off the bridge over the River
Garry gorge on weekends year-round, plus
selected weekdays from March to October.

🎎 Festivals & Events

Enchanted Forest LIGHT SHOW
(www.enchantedforest.org.uk; adult/child £20/10;
☺ Oct) This spectacular three-week sound-
and-light show staged in Faskally Wood near
Pitlochry is a major family hit.

Winter Words LITERATURE
(www.pitlochry.org/events; ☺ Feb) A 10-day literary festival, with a packed program of talks
by authors, poets and broadcasters. Past
guests have ranged from novelist Louis de
Bernières to mountaineer and author Sir
Chris Bonington.

🛏 Sleeping

Pitlochry Backpackers Hotel HOSTEL £
(📞 01796-470044; www.scotlands-top-hostels.
com; 134 Atholl Rd; dm/tw £20/53; ☺ Apr–mid-
Nov; P@🤶) Friendly, laid-back and very
comfortable, this is a cracking hostel smack
bang in the middle of town, with three- to
eight-bed dorms that are in mint condition.
There are also good-value en suite twins and
doubles, with beds, not bunks. Cheap breakfast and a pool table add to the convivial
party atmosphere. No extra charge for linen.

Ashleigh B&B £
(📞 01796-470316; www.ashleighbedandbreakfast.
com; 120 Atholl Rd; s/d £30/57; 🤶) Genuine
welcomes don't come much better than
Nancy's, and her place on the main street
makes a top Pitlochry pit stop. Two comfortable doubles share an excellent bathroom, and there's an open kitchen stocked
with goodies where you make your own
breakfast in the morning. A home away
from home and a standout budget choice.
Cash only; no kids. She also has a good self-
catering apartment with great views, available by the night.

★ Craigatin House B&B ££
(📞 01796-472478; www.craigatinhouse.co.uk; 165
Atholl Rd; d from £107, ste £134; P@🤶) Several
times more tasteful than the average Scottish B&B, this elegant house and garden is
set back from the main road. Chic contem-

THE 'THEATRE IN THE HILLS'

Founded in 1951 (in a tent!), the famous
and much-loved **Pitlochry Festival
Theatre** (📞 01796-484626; www.
pitlochryfestivaltheatre.com; Port-na-Craig;
tickets £6-35) is the focus of Highland
Perthshire's cultural life. The summer
season, from May to mid-October,
stages a different production each night
of the week except Sunday.

porary fabrics covering expansive beds offer
a standard of comfort above and beyond the
reasonable price; the rooms in the converted
stable block are particularly inviting. A fabulous breakfast and lounge area gives views
over the lush garden.

Breakfast choices include whisky-laced
porridge, smoked-fish omelettes and apple
pancakes. No children under 13 years.

★ Fonab Castle Hotel HISTORIC HOTEL £££
(📞 01796-470140; www.fonabcastlehotel.com; Foss
Rd; r from £225; P🤶) This Scottish Baronial
fantasy in red sandstone was built in 1892 as
the country house of Lt Col George Sande-
man, a scion of the famous port and sherry
merchants. Now a luxury hotel and spa, it
has a tasteful modern extension with commanding views over Loch Faskally, and a
superb restaurant serving the finest Scottish
venison, beef and seafood.

Knockendarroch House HOTEL £££
(📞 01796-473473; www.knockendarroch.co.uk;
Higher Oakfield Rd; d incl dinner from £245;
P🤶🎎) Top of the town and boasting the
best views, this genteel, well-run hotel has
a range of luxurious rooms with huge windows that take advantage of the Highland
light. The standard rooms have better views
than the larger, slightly pricier superior
ones; a couple have great little balconies,
perfect for a sundowner. Meals are highly
commended.

🍴 Eating & Drinking

★ Moulin Hotel PUB FOOD ££
(📞 01796-472196; www.moulinhotel.co.uk; Kirk-
michael Rd; mains £9-16; ☺ food served noon-
9.30pm; P🤶🎎) A mile away from town but
a world apart, this atmospheric inn has low
ceilings, ageing wood and snug booths. It's
a wonderfully romantic spot for a home-
brewed ale (there's a microbrewery out

back) and some Highland comfort food: try the mince and tatties, or game casserole. It's a pleasant uphill stroll from Pitlochry, and an easy roll down afterwards.

Port-na-Craig Inn   BISTRO **££**
(✆ 01796-472777; www.portnacraig.com; Port-na-Craig; mains £8-17; ⊙ 11am-8.30pm; P ♿) Across the river from the town centre, this cute little cottage sits in what was once a separate hamlet. Top-quality main meals are prepared with confidence and panache; there are also simpler sandwiches, kids' meals and light lunches. Or you could just sit outdoors by the river with a pint and watch the salmon anglers.

🔒 Shopping

Melt Gallery   ARTS & CRAFTS
(✆ 01796-472358; www.meltgallery.com; 14 Bonnethill Rd; ⊙ 10am-5pm Thu-Tue) This gallery is a treasure trove of quality Scottish arts and crafts, including polished aluminium jewellery that is handmade in the owner's workshop at the back. Potential purchases include paintings, photography, bronzes, ceramics and more unusual items – ever seen a Harris Tweed cafetière cosy? You have now...

ℹ️ Information

Pitlochry Tourist Office (✆ 01796-472215; www.perthshire.co.uk; 22 Atholl Rd; ⊙ 9.30am-5.30pm Mon-Sat, 10am-4pm Sun Mar-Oct, longer hours Jul & Aug, shorter hours Nov-Feb) Good information on local walks.

ℹ️ Getting There & Away

BUS

Scottish Citylink (www.citylink.co.uk) Buses run two to four times daily to Inverness (£18.10, 1¾ hours), Perth (£11.50, 50 minutes), Edinburgh (£18.10, two to 2½ hours) and Glasgow (£18.10, 2¼ hours).

Megabus (✆ 0871 266 3333; www.megabus.com) Offers discounted fares to Inverness, Perth, Edinburgh and Glasgow.

Stagecoach (www.stagecoachbus.com) Buses run to Aberfeldy (£3, 40 minutes, hourly Monday to Saturday, three Sunday), Dunkeld (£2.60, 40 minutes, hourly Monday to Saturday) and Perth (£4.10, 1¼ hours, hourly Monday to Saturday).

TRAIN

Pitlochry is on the main railway line from Perth (£14.40, 30 minutes, nine daily Monday to Saturday, five on Sunday) to Inverness (£23.40, 1¾ hours, same frequency).

ℹ️ Getting Around

Local buses between Pitlochry and Blair Atholl stop at Killiecrankie (£1.75, 10 minutes, three to seven daily).

Escape Route (✆ 01796-473859; www.escape-route.co.uk; 3 Atholl Rd; bike hire per half-/full day from £16/24; ⊙ 9am-5.30pm Mon-Sat, 10am-5pm Sun) Rents out bikes and provides advice on local trails; it's worth booking ahead at weekends.

Blair Atholl

The village of Blair Atholl dates only from the early 19th century, springing up along the main road to the north after a new bridge was thrown across the River Tilt in 1822 (the original 16th-century Black Bridge, upgraded by General Wade in 1730, still stands just under a mile upstream at Old Bridge of Tilt).

Blair Castle is the main attraction here, but there's also the Atholl Country Life Museum, the old watermill, and many superb walks in the surrounding countryside, from short strolls through the castle grounds and longer walks to various viewpoints, to day-long hikes along Glen Tilt and up into the surrounding mountains (details from the information point in the museum).

⭐ **Blair Castle**   CASTLE
(✆ 01796-481207; www.blair-castle.co.uk; adult/child £12/7.70; ⊙ 9.30am-5.30pm Easter-Oct, 10am-4pm Sat & Sun Nov-Mar; P ♿) One of the most popular tourist attractions in Scotland, magnificent Blair Castle – and its surrounding estates – is the seat of the Duke of Atholl, head of the Murray clan. (The current duke visits every May to review the **Atholl Highlanders**, Britain's only private army.) It's an impressive white heap set beneath forested slopes above the River Garry. Thirty rooms are open to the public and they present a wonderful picture of upper-class Highland life from the 16th century on.

The original tower was built in 1269, but the castle underwent significant remodelling in the 18th and 19th centuries. Highlights include the 2nd-floor **Drawing Room** with its ornate Georgian plasterwork and Zoffany portrait of the fourth duke's family, complete with a pet lemur (yes, you read that correctly) called Tommy; and the **Tapestry Room** draped with 17th-century wall hangings created for Charles I. The **dining room** is sumptuous – check out the 9-pint wine glasses – and the **ballroom** is a vast oak-panelled chamber hung with hundreds of stag antlers.

Blair Atholl Watermill CAFE £
(☑ 01796-481321; www.facebook.com/blairatholl watermill; Ford Rd; mains £4-8; ☉ 9.30am-5pm late Mar-Oct; [P][☎][♿]) 🥐 This working water-mill grinds its own flour and bakes its own bread, and serves it up in this atmospheric cafe as deliciously fresh sandwiches and toasties. You can watch the mill at work, and even sign up for bakery courses.

Lochs Tummel & Rannoch

The scenic route along Lochs Tummel and Rannoch (www.rannochandtummel.co.uk) is worth doing any way you can – by foot, bicycle or car. Hillsides shrouded with ancient birchwoods and forests of spruce, pine and larch make up the fabulous **Tay Forest Park**, whose wooded hills roll into the glittering waters of the lochs; a visit in autumn, when the birch leaves are at their finest, is recommended.

Eighteen miles west of Kinloch Rannoch the road ends at romantic and isolated **Rannoch Station**, which lies on the Glasgow–Fort William railway line. Beyond sprawls the desolate expanse of Rannoch Moor. There's an excellent tearoom on the station platform, and a welcoming small hotel alongside. Be aware that Rannoch Station is a dead-end, and the nearest service station is at Aberfeldy.

The Queen's View at the eastern end of Loch Tummel is a magnificent viewpoint with a vista along the loch to the prominent mountain of Schiehallion. The nearby **visitor centre** (www.forestry.gov.uk; admission free, parking £2; ☉ 9am-6pm Apr-Oct, 10am-4pm Nov-Mar; [P]) provides parking and houses a cafe and gift shop.

Kinloch Rannoch is a great base for walks and cycle trips, or for fishing on Loch Rannoch for brown trout, Arctic char and pike; you can get permits (£8 per day) at the Country Store in the village. Walking trails lead into the wildlife-rich Black Wood of Rannoch, a remnant of Caledonian pine forest on the south shore of the loch.

Schiehallion (1083m), whose conical peak dominates views from Loch Rannoch, is a relatively straightforward climb from Braes of Foss car park (6.5 miles return), and is rewarded by spectacular views. See www.john muirtrust.org/trust-land/east-schiehallion for more information.

🛏️ Sleeping & Eating

There are useful accommodation listings at www.rannochandtummel.co.uk.

Places to eat are widely scattered – think about bringing a picnic lunch just in case.

Kilvrecht Campsite CAMPSITE £
(☑ 01350-727284; https://scotland.forestry.gov.uk; Kilvrecht; tent sites with/without car £10/5; ☉ Apr-mid-Oct) This basic but beautiful campsite (toilet block, but no electricity or hot water) is 2 miles west of Kinloch Rannoch on the south shore of the loch. Hiking and mountain-biking trails begin from the site.

RANNOCH MOOR

Beyond Rannoch Station, civilisation fades away and Rannoch Moor begins. This is the largest area of moorland in Britain, stretching west for eight barren, bleak and uninhabited miles to the A82 Glasgow–Fort William road. A triangular plateau of blanket bog occupying more than 50 sq miles, the moor is ringed by high mountains and puddled with countless lochs, ponds and peat hags. Water covers 10% of the surface, and it has been canoed across, swum across, and even skated across in winter.

Despite the appearance of desolation, the moor is rich in wildlife, with curlew, golden plover and snipe darting among the tussocks, black-throated diver, goosander and merganser on the lochs, and – if you're lucky – osprey and golden eagle overhead. Herds of red deer forage alongside the railway, and otters patrol the loch shores. Keep an eye out for the sundew, a tiny, insect-eating plant with sticky-fingered leaves.

A couple of excellent (and challenging) walks start from Rannoch Station – north to Corrour Station (11 miles, four to five hours) from where you can return by train; and west along the northern edge of the moor to the Kings House Hotel (p332) at the eastern end of Glen Coe (11 miles, four hours).

Moor of Rannoch Restaurant & Rooms
HOTEL £££

(☑ 01882-633238; www.moorofrannoch.co.uk; Rannoch Station; s/d £125/180; ⊙ mid-Feb–Oct; P 🐾) At the end of the road beside Rannoch train station, this is one of Scotland's most isolated places (no internet, no TV, only fleeting mobile-phone reception), but luckily this beautifully renovated hotel is here to keep your spirits up – a magical getaway. It does excellent dinners (three courses £35, 6.30pm to 8pm), and can prepare a packed lunch.

Rannoch Station Tea Room
CAFE £

(☑ 01882-633247; www.rannochstationtearoom. co.uk; Rannoch Station; mains £4-6; ⊙ 8.30am-4.30pm Mon-Thu & Sat, 10am-4.30pm Sun; P 🐾) This superb little tearoom sits on the platform at remote Rannoch Station, serving coffee, sandwiches and cake to visiting hikers, mountain bikers and railway excursionists. Next door, in the former waiting room, is a fascinating exhibition on Rannoch Moor and the history of the railway.

ℹ Getting There & Around

A demand-responsive minibus service (www.pkc.gov.uk) – ie you have to phone and book it at least 24 hours in advance – runs between Kinloch Rannoch and Rannoch Station (£3, 35 minutes).

Elizabeth Yule Coaches (☑ 01796-472290; www.elizabethyulecoaches.co.uk) operates a bus service from Pitlochry to Kinloch Rannoch (£4.10, 50 minutes, three to five daily Monday to Saturday April to October) via Queen's View and the Inn at Loch Tummel.

There are two to four trains daily from Rannoch Station north to Fort William (£11.10, one hour) and Mallaig, and south to Glasgow (£25.30, 2¾ hours).

Aberfeldy
POP 1895

Aberfeldy is the gateway to Breadalbane (the historic region surrounding Loch Tay), and a good base: adventure sports, angling, art and castles all feature on the menu here. It's a peaceful, pretty place on the banks of the Tay, but if it's moody lochs and glens that steal your heart, you may want to push a little further west.

The B846 road towards Fortingall crosses the Tay via the elegant Wade's Bridge, built in 1733 as part of the network of military roads designed to tame the Highlands.

◉ Sights & Activities

The Birks of Aberfeldy, made famous by a Robert Burns poem, offer a great short walk from the centre of town, following a vigorous burn upstream past several picturesque cascades.

Aberfeldy Distillery
DISTILLERY

(www.dewarsaberfeldydistillery.com; tour per person from £10.50; ⊙ 10am-6pm Mon-Sat, noon-4pm Sun Apr-Oct, 10am-4pm Mon-Sat Nov-Mar; P) At the eastern end of Aberfeldy, the home of the famous Dewar's blend offers a good 90-minute tour. After the usual overblown film, there's a museum section with audio guide, and an entertaining interactive blending session, as well as the tour of the whisky-making process. More expensive tours allow you to try venerable Aberfeldy single malts and others.

Castle Menzies
CASTLE

(www.castlemenzies.org; adult/child £6.50/3; ⊙ 10.30am-5pm Mon-Sat, 2-5pm Sun Easter-Oct; P) Castle Menzies is the 16th-century seat of the chief of clan Menzies (*ming*-iss), magnificently set against a forest backdrop. Inside it reeks of authenticity, despite extensive restoration work. Check out the fireplace in the dungeon-like kitchens, and the gaudy Great Hall with windows revealing a ribbon of lush, green countryside extending into wooded hills beyond the estate. It's about 1.5 miles west of Aberfeldy, off the B846.

Watermill
GALLERY

(www.aberfeldywatermill.com; Mill St; ⊙ 10am-5pm Mon-Sat, 11am-5pm Sun Oct-Apr, to 5.30pm May-Sep) FREE You could while away several hours at this converted watermill, which houses a cafe (☑ 01887-822896; mains £5-8; 🐾) 🖉 , bookshop and art gallery exhibiting contemporary works of art. The shop has the biggest range of titles in the Highlands, with a great selection of books on Scottish history, landscape and wildlife.

Splash
RAFTING

(☑ 01887-829706; www.rafting.co.uk; Dunkeld Rd; ⊙ 9am-9pm; 🖝) Splash offers family friendly white-water rafting on the River Tay (adult/child £40/30, Wednesday to Sunday year-round) and more advanced adult trips on the Tummel (Grade III/IV, June to September) and the Orchy (Grade III/V, October to March). It also offers pulse-racing descents on river bugs (£60), canyoning (£55) and mountain-bike hire (per half-/full day £15/20).

Highland Safaris   TOURS
(☎01887-820071;www.highlandsafaris.net;☺9am-5pm, closed Mon Nov-Feb; ⚐) This outfit offers an ideal way to spot some wildlife or simply enjoy Perthshire's magnificent countryside. Standard trips include the 2½-hour Mountain Safari (adult/child £40/25), which includes whisky and shortbread in a mountain bothy; and the four-hour Safari Trek (adult/child £75/45), culminating in a walk in the mountains and a picnic.

You may spot wildlife such as golden eagles, osprey and red deer. There's also gold panning for kids (£5) and mountain-bike hire (£20 per day).

🛏 Sleeping & Eating

Tigh'n Eilean Guest House   B&B **££**
(☎01887-820109; www.tighneilean.co.uk; Taybridge Dr; s/d from £48/80; P🅿🛜🐾) Everything about this property screams comfort. It's a gorgeous place overlooking the Tay, with individually designed rooms – one has a jacuzzi, while another is set on its own in a cheery yellow summer house in the garden, giving you a bit of privacy. The garden itself is fabulous, with hammocks for lazing in, and the riverbank setting is delightful.

Balnearn Guest House   B&B **££**
(☎01887-820431; www.balnearnhouse.com; Crieff Rd; s/d/f from £55/75/120; P🅿🛜🗺) Balnearn is a sedate and luxurious mansion near the centre of town, with space to spare. Most rooms have great natural light, and there's a particularly good family room downstairs. Breakfast has been lavishly praised by guests, and the attentive, cordial hosts are helpful while respecting your privacy.

★ Inn on the Tay   PUB FOOD **££**
(☎01887-840760; www.theinnonthetay.co.uk; Grandtully; mains £10-22; ☺food served noon-2.45pm & 5-8.45pm; P🅿🛜⚐) This convivial pub, with its modern bistro-style dining room, makes a great pit stop on the way west to Loch Tay. The menu is simple – salads, burgers, fish and chips – but top quality, and there's an outdoor deck above the river, where you can enjoy a drink while watching rafters and canoeists descend the Grandtully rapids.

❶ Getting There & Away

Stagecoach (www.stagecoachbus.com) bus 23 runs from Perth to Aberfeldy (£4.10, 1½ hours, hourly Monday to Saturday, fewer on Sunday)

via Dunkeld; from Pitlochry (£3.80, 40 minutes), you'll need to change buses at Ballinluig. There's no bus link west to Killin.

Local buses run a circular route from Aberfeldy through Kenmore, Fortingall and back to Aberfeldy once each way on school days only.

Kenmore

The picturesque village of Kenmore lies at Loch Tay's eastern end, 6 miles west of Aberfeldy. Dominated by a striking archway leading to Taymouth Castle (not open to the public), it was built by the 3rd Earl of Breadalbane in 1760 to house his estate workers.

★ Scottish Crannog Centre   MUSEUM
(☎01887-830583; www.crannog.co.uk; tours adult/child £10/7; ☺10am-5.30pm Apr-Oct; P🅿⚐) Less than a mile south of Kenmore on the banks of Loch Tay is the fascinating Scottish Crannog Centre, perched on stilts above the loch. Crannogs – effectively artificial islands – were a favoured form of defensive dwelling from the 3rd millennium BC onwards. This superb re-creation (based on studies of Oakbank crannog, one of 18 discovered in Loch Tay) offers a guided tour that includes an impressive demonstration of fire making and Iron Age crafts.

Taymouth Marina   SCOTTISH **££**
(☎01887-830450;http://taymouthmarinarestaurant.co.uk; mains £14-25; ☺11am-9.30pm; P🅿🛜⚐) This appealing modern restaurant has a prime position on the banks of Loch Tay, with window tables making the most of the gorgeous views. Service is friendly and the menu runs from Scottish mussels and Cullen skink to seafood platters and sirloin steaks.

❶ Getting There & Away

Local buses run from Aberfeldy to Kenmore (£2.80, 15 minutes) twice a day on school days only.

Loch Tay & Ben Lawers

Loch Tay is the heart of the ancient region known as Breadalbane (from the Gaelic Bràghad Albainn, 'the heights of Scotland') – mighty **Ben Lawers** (1214m), looming over the loch, is the highest peak outside the Ben Nevis and Cairngorms regions. Much of the land to the north of Loch Tay falls within the **Ben Lawers National Nature**

Reserve (www.nnr.scot), known for its rare alpine flora.

The main access point for the ascent of Ben Lawers is the car park 1.5 miles north of the A827, on the minor road from Loch Tay to Bridge of Balgie. The climb is 6.5 miles and can take up to five hours (return): pack wet-weather gear, water and food, and a map and compass. There's also an easier nature trail here.

Loch Tay is famous for its fishing – salmon, trout and pike are all caught here. Fish 'n' Trips (p253) can kit you out for a day's fishing with boat, tackle and guide for £120 for two people, or rent you a boat for £60 a day.

The main road from Kenmore to Killin runs along the north shore of Loch Tay. The minor road along the south shore is narrow and twisting (unsuitable for large vehicles), but offers great views of the hills to the north.

Fortingall

Fortingall is one of the prettiest villages in Scotland, with 19th-century thatched cottages in a tranquil setting beside an ancient church with impressive wooden beams and a 7th-century monk's bell.

The famous **Fortingall Yew Tree** in the churchyard is estimated to be between 2000 and 3000 years old, one of the oldest living organisms in Europe. Its girth was measured at 16m in 1769, but since then souvenir hunters and natural decay have reduced it to a few gnarly but thriving boughs – in 2015 it produced berries for the first time on record. It was almost certainly around when the Romans camped in the meadows by the River Lyon in the 1st century AD; popular, if unlikely, tradition says that Pontius Pilate was born here.

Glen Lyon

The 'longest, loneliest and loveliest glen in Scotland', according to Sir Walter Scott, stretches for 32 unforgettable miles of rickety stone bridges, native woodland and heather-clad hills, becoming wilder and less populated as it snakes its way west. The ancients believed it to be a gateway to Faerieland, and even the most sceptical of visitors will be entranced by the valley's magic.

From Fortingall, a narrow road winds up the glen, while another steep and spectacular route from Loch Tay crosses the hills to meet it at **Bridge of Balgie**. The road continues west as far as the dam on Loch Lyon, passing a memorial to Robert Campbell (1808–94; a Canadian explorer and fur trader, born in the glen).

There are no villages in the glen – the majestic scenery is the main reason to be here – just a cluster of houses and a **tearoom** (☑01887-866221; Bridge of Balgie; snacks £3-6; ☉10am-5pm Apr-Oct; 🅿🛜🎮) 🍴 at Bridge of Balgie.

There are several waymarked **woodland walks** beginning from a car park a short distance beyond Bridge of Balgie, and more challenging hill walks into the surrounding mountains (see www.walkhighlands.co.uk/perthshire). **Cycling** is an ideal way to explore the glen, and fit riders can complete a loop over to Glen Lochay via a potholed road (motor vehicles not permitted) leading south from the Loch Lyon dam.

⭐**Milton Eonan** B&B ££
(☑01887-866337; www.miltoneonan.com; Bridge of Balgie; per person £39-43; 🅿🛜🎮) 🍴 Milton Eonan is a must for those seeking tranquillity. On a bubbling stream where a watermill once stood, it's a working rare-breed croft with a romantic one-bedroom cottage at the bottom of the garden (available as B&B or self-catering). It can sleep three at a pinch.

The helpful owners offer packed lunches and evening meals using local and home-grown produce. After crossing the bridge at Bridge of Balgie, you'll see Milton Eonan signposted to the right.

WEST HIGHLANDS

This region extends from the bleak blanket-bog of the Moor of Rannoch to the west coast beyond Glen Coe and Fort William, and includes the southern reaches of the Great Glen. The scenery is grand throughout, with high, rocky mountains rising above wild glens. Great expanses of moor alternate with lochs and patches of commercial forest. Fort William, at the inner end of Loch Linnhe, is the only sizeable town in the area.

Since 2007 the region has been promoted as Lochaber Geopark (www.lochabergeopark.org.uk), an area of outstanding geology and scenery.

Glen Coe

Scotland's most famous glen is also one of its grandest and – in bad weather – its grimmest. The approach to the glen from the east is guarded by the rocky pyramid of **Buachaille Etive Mor** – the Great Shepherd of Etive – and the lonely **Kings House Hotel** (closed for renovation until 2019). After the Battle of Culloden in 1745 it was used as a Hanoverian garrison – hence the name.

The A82 road leads over the Pass of Glencoe and into the narrow upper glen. The southern side is dominated by three massive, brooding spurs, known as the **Three Sisters**, while the northern side is enclosed by the continuous steep wall of the knife-edged **Aonach Eagach** ridge, a classic mountaineering challenge. The road threads its way past deep gorges and crashing waterfalls to the more pastoral lower reaches of the glen around Loch Achtriochtan and the only settlement here, **Glencoe village**.

◎ Sights

Glencoe Visitor Centre   MUSEUM
(NTS; ☑ 01855-811307; www.nts.org.uk; adult/child £6.50/5; ☺ 9.30am-5.30pm Mar-Oct, 10am-4pm Nov-Feb; ℗) ✿ The centre provides comprehensive information on the geological, environmental and cultural history of Glen Coe via high-tech interactive and audiovisual displays, charts the history of mountaineering in the glen, and tells the story of the Glencoe Massacre in all its gory detail. It's 1.5 miles southeast of Glencoe village.

Glencoe Folk Museum   MUSEUM
(☑ 01855-811664; www.glencoemuseum.com; adult/child £3/free; ☺ 10am-4.30pm Tue-Sat Easter-Oct) This small, thatched cottage houses a varied collection of farm equipment, tools of the woodworking, blacksmithing and slate-quarrying trades, and military memorabilia, including a riding boot that once belonged to Robert Campbell of Glenlyon, who took part in the Glencoe Massacre.

🏃 Activities

There are several short, pleasant walks around **Glencoe Lochan**, near the village. To get there, turn left off the minor road to the SYHA hostel, just beyond the bridge over the River Coe. There are three walks (40 minutes to an hour), all detailed on a signboard at the car park. The artificial lochan was created by Lord Strathcona

in 1895 for his homesick Canadian wife, Isabella, and is surrounded by a North American-style forest.

A more strenuous hike, but well worth the effort on a fine day, is the climb to the **Lost Valley**, a magical mountain sanctuary still haunted by the ghosts of MacDonalds who died here while escaping the Glencoe Massacre in 1692 (only 2.5 miles round trip, but allow three hours). A rough path from the car park at Allt na Reigh (on the A82, 6 miles east of Glencoe village) bears left down to a footbridge over the river, then climbs up the wooded valley between Beinn Fhada and Gearr Aonach. The route leads steeply up through a maze of giant, jumbled, moss-coated boulders before emerging – quite unexpectedly – into a broad, open valley with a half-mile-long meadow as flat as a football pitch. Back in the days of clan warfare, the valley – invisible from below – was used for hiding stolen cattle; its Gaelic name, Coire Gabhail, means 'corrie of capture'.

The summits of Glen Coe's mountains are for experienced mountaineers only. The Cicerone guidebook *Ben Nevis & Glen Coe*, by Ronald Turnbull, available in most bookshops and outdoor equipment stores, details everything from short easy walks to challenging mountain climbs.

Steven Fallon Mountain Guides   OUTDOORS
(☑ 0131-466 8152; www.stevenfallon.co.uk; per person from £69) If you lack the experience or confidence to tackle Scotland's challenging mountains alone, then you can join a guided hill walk or hire a private guide from this outfit.

Glencoe Mountain Resort   OUTDOORS
(☑ 01855-851226; www.glencoemountain.com; Kingshouse; chairlift adult/child £12/6; ☺ 9am-4.30pm) Scotland's oldest ski area (eight lifts and 20 runs), established in the 1950s, is also one of the best, with grand views across the wild expanse of Rannoch Moor. The lower chairlift continues to operate in summer providing access to mountain-biking trails. In winter a lift pass costs £32 a day; equipment hire is £25.

The Lodge Café-Bar (open 9am to 8.30pm) at the base station has comfy sofas where you can soak up the view through floor-to-ceiling windows.

There are tent pitches (£6 per person), camping pods (£50 a night) and campervan hookups (£15 a night) beside the car park.

1. Loch Awe (p291) 2. Caledonian Canal (p334) and Ben
Nevis (p338) 3. Loch Ness (p304) 4. Schiehallion (p325)

SIMON BUTTERWORTH/GETTY IMAGES ©

Lochs & Mountains

Since the 19th century, when the first tourists started to arrive, the Scottish Highlands have been famed for their wild nature and majestic scenery, and today the country's biggest draw remains its magnificent landscape. At almost every turn is a vista that will stop you in your tracks – keep your camera close at hand.

Ben Nevis

Scotland's highest peak is a perennial magnet for hillwalkers and ice climbers, but it's also one of the country's most photographed mountains. The classic viewpoints for the Ben include Corpach Basin at the entrance to the Caledonian Canal, and the B8004 road between Banavie and Gairlochy, from where you can see the precipitous north face.

Loch Ness

Scotland's largest loch by volume (it contains more water than all the lakes in England and Wales added together) may be most famous for its legendary monster, but it is also one of Scotland's most scenic. The minor road along the southeastern shore reveals a series of classic views.

Schiehallion

From the Gaelic *Sìdh Chailleann* (Fairy Hill of the Caledonians), this is one of Scotland's most distinctive mountains, its conical peak a prominent feature of views along Loch Tummel and Loch Rannoch. It's also one of the easier Munros, and a hike to the summit is rewarded with a superb panorama of hills and lochs.

Loch Awe

Loch Awe is a little off the beaten track, but is well worth seeking out for its gorgeous scenery. Dotted with islands and draped with native woodlands of oak, birch and alder, its northern end is dominated by the evocative ruins of Kilchurn Castle, with the pointed peaks of mighty Ben Cruachan reflected in its shifting waters.

📖 Sleeping

There are several campsites, B&Bs and hotels in and around Glencoe village at the western end of the glen, plus camping at Glencoe Mountain Resort (p329) at the eastern end.

Invercoe Caravan & Camping Park
CAMPSITE £

(📞01855-811210; www.invercoe.co.uk; Invercoe; tent sites without car per person £11, campervan sites £25; 🐾) This place has great views of the surrounding mountains and is equipped with anti-midge machines. There's a covered cooking area for campers.

Glencoe Independent Hostel
HOSTEL £

(📞01855-811906; www.glencoehostel.co.uk; farmhouse/bunkhouse dm £17/15; P@🐾) This handily located hostel, just 1.5 miles southeast of Glencoe village, is set in an old farmhouse with six- and eight-bed dorms, and a bunkhouse with another 16 bed spaces in communal, alpine-style bunks. There's also a cute little wooden cabin that sleeps up to three (£80 per night).

Glencoe SYHA
HOSTEL £

(📞08155-811219; www.syha.org.uk; dm/tr £19/83; P@🐾) Very popular with hikers, though the atmosphere can be a little institutional. It's a 1.5-mile walk from Glencoe village along the minor road on the northern side of the river.

Clachaig Inn
HOTEL ££

(📞01855-811252; www.clachaig.com; s/d £57/114; P🐾) The Clachaig, 2 miles east of Glencoe village, has long been a favourite haunt of hill walkers and climbers. As well as comfortable en suite accommodation, there's a smart, modern lounge bar with snug booths and high refectory tables, mountaineering photos and bric-a-brac, and climbing magazines to leaf through.

Climbers usually head for the lively Boots Bar on the other side of the hotel – it has log fires, serves real ale and good pub grub (mains £10 to £21, served noon to 9pm), and has live Scottish music on Saturday nights.

Kings House Hotel
HOTEL ££

(📞01855-851259; www.kingshousehotel.co.uk; Kingshouse; s/d £45/100; P) This remote hotel claims to be one of Scotland's oldest licensed inns, dating from the 17th century. It has long been a favourite meeting place for climbers, skiers and walkers (it's on the West Highland Way). It closed in 2017 for a major redevelopment, which includes a hikers' bunkhouse, and is scheduled to reopen in January 2019.

🍴 Eating

★ Glencoe Café
CAFE £

(📞01855-811168; www.glencoecafe.co.uk; Glencoe village; mains £4-8; ⏰10am-4pm, to 5pm May-Sep, closed Nov; P🐾) This friendly cafe is the social hub of Glencoe village, serving breakfast fry-ups till 11.30am (including vegetarian versions), light lunches based on local produce (think Cullen skink, smoked salmon quiche, venison burgers), and the best cappuccino in the glen.

Crafts & Things
CAFE £

(📞01855-811325; www.craftsandthings.co.uk; Annat; mains £4-8; ⏰9.30am-5pm Mon-Thu, to 5.30pm Fri-Sun Apr-Oct, shorter hours Nov-Mar; P🐾♿) Just off the main road between Glencoe village and Ballachulish, the tearoom in this craft shop is a good spot for a lunch of homemade lentil soup with crusty rolls, ciabatta sandwiches, or just coffee and carrot cake. There are tables outdoors and a box of toys to keep little ones occupied.

ℹ️ Getting There & Away

Scottish Citylink (www.citylink.co.uk) buses run between Fort William and Glencoe (£8.50, 30 minutes, four to eight daily) and from Glencoe to Glasgow (£22.70, 2¾ hours, four to eight daily). Buses stop at Glencoe village, Glencoe Visitor Centre and Glencoe Mountain Resort.

Stagecoach (www.stagecoachbus.com) bus 44 links Glencoe village with Fort William (£4.10, 40 minutes, hourly Monday to Saturday, three on Sunday) and Kinlochleven (£2.20, 15 minutes).

Kinlochleven

POP 900

Kinlochleven is hemmed in by high mountains at the head of beautiful Loch Leven, about 7 miles east of Glencoe village. The aluminium smelter that led to the town's development in the early 20th century has long since closed, and the opening of the Ballachulish Bridge in the 1970s allowed the main road to bypass it completely. Decline was halted by the opening of the **West Highland Way**, which now brings a steady stream of hikers through the village.

The final section of the West Highland Way stretches for 14 miles from Kinlochleven to Fort William. The village is also the starting point for easier walks up the glen of the River Leven, through pleasant woods to the Grey Mare's Tail waterfall, and harder mountain hikes into the Mamores.

Activities

Via Ferrata
ADVENTURE SPORTS
(☑ 01397-747111; http://verticaldescents.com/via-ferrata/via-ferrata.html; Unit 3, Kinlochleven Business Park; per person/family £65/240) Scotland's first via ferrata – a 500m climbing route equipped with steel ladders, cables and bridges – snakes through the crags around the Grey Mare's Tail waterfall, allowing non-climbers to experience the thrill of climbing (you'll need a head for heights, though!).

Ice Factor
ADVENTURE SPORTS
(☑ 01855-831100; www.ice-factor.co.uk; Leven Rd; ⊙ 9am-10pm Tue & Thu, to 6pm Mon, Wed & Fri-Sun; 🛋) If you fancy trying your hand at ice-climbing, even in the middle of summer, the world's biggest indoor ice-climbing wall offers a one-hour beginner's 'taster' session for £30. You'll also find a rock-climbing wall, an aerial adventure course, a soft-play area for kids, and a cafe (open 9am to 5pm) and bar-bistro (food served 6pm to 9pm).

Sleeping & Eating

Blackwater Hostel
& Campsite
HOSTEL, CAMPSITE £
(☑ 01855-831253; www.blackwaterhostel.co.uk; Lab Rd; tr/q from £63/84, tent sites per person £10, pods from £45; P 🛜) This 39-bed hostel (preference given to groups – individual travellers should check availability in advance) has spotless dorms with en suite bathrooms and TV, and a well-sheltered campsite with the option of wooden 'glamping' pods for two or four persons.

★ Lochleven Seafood Cafe
SEAFOOD ££
(☑ 01855-821048; www.lochlevenseafoodcafe.co.uk; mains £11-23, whole lobster £40; ⊙ meals noon-3pm & 6-9pm, coffee & cake 10am-noon & 3-5pm mid-Mar–Oct; P 🛋) This outstanding place serves superb shellfish freshly plucked from live tanks – oysters, razor clams, scallops, lobster and crab – plus a daily fish special and some non-seafood dishes. For warm days, there's an outdoor terrace with a view across the loch to the Pap of Glencoe. The cafe is 5 miles west of Kinlochleven, on the north shore of the loch.

ℹ Getting There & Away

Stagecoach bus 44 runs from Fort William to Kinlochleven (£5.30, one hour, hourly Monday to Saturday, three on Sunday) via Ballachulish and Glencoe village.

Fort William
POP 9910

Basking on Loch Linnhe's shores amid magnificent mountain scenery, Fort William has one of the most enviable settings in all of Scotland. If it weren't for the busy dual carriageway crammed between the less-than-attractive town centre and the loch, and one of the highest rainfall records in the country, it would be almost idyllic. Even so, the Fort has carved out a reputation as the 'Outdoor Capital of the UK' (www.outdoorcapital.co.uk), and easy access by rail and bus makes it a good base for exploring the surrounding mountains and glens.

Magical Glen Nevis begins near the northern end of the town and wraps itself around the southern flanks of Ben Nevis (1345m) – Britain's highest mountain and a magnet for hikers and climbers. The glen is also popular with movie makers – parts of *Braveheart* (1995), *Pokemon: Detective Pikachu* (2018), the Harry Potter movies and the *Outlander* TV series were filmed here.

◎ Sights

★ Jacobite Steam Train
HERITAGE RAILWAY
(☑ 0844 850 4685; www.westcoastrailways.co.uk; day return adult/child from £35/20; ⊙ daily mid-Jun–Aug, Mon-Fri mid-May–mid-Jun, Sep & Oct) The Jacobite Steam Train, hauled by a former LNER K1 or LMS Class 5MT locomotive, travels the scenic two-hour run between Fort William and Mallaig. Classed as one of the great railway journeys of the world, the route crosses the historic Glenfinnan Viaduct, made famous in the Harry Potter films – the Jacobite's owners supplied the steam locomotive and rolling stock used in the film.

Trains depart from Fort William train station in the morning and return from Mallaig in the afternoon. There's a brief stop at Glenfinnan station, and you get 1½ hours in Mallaig.

West Highland Museum
MUSEUM
(☑ 01397-702169; www.westhighlandmuseum.org.uk; Cameron Sq; ⊙ 10am-5pm Mon-Sat May-Sep, to 4pm Oct-Apr, 11am-3pm Sun Jul & Aug)

FREE This small but fascinating museum is packed with all manner of Highland memorabilia. Look out for the secret portrait of Bonnie Prince Charlie – after the Jacobite rebellions, all things Highland were banned, including pictures of the exiled leader, and this tiny painting looks like nothing more than a smear of paint until viewed in a cylindrical mirror, which reflects a credible likeness of the prince.

Activities

3 Wise Monkeys Climbing   CLIMBING
(☑01397-600200;www.threewisemonkeysclimbing.com; Fassifern Rd; adult/child £9/6; ☺10am-10pm Mon-Fri, to 8pm Sat & Sun; ☺) When the weather on the mountains keeps you off the crags, you can keep your fingers in trim at this popular indoor climbing wall. There's a cafe too, and you can book a sports massage. Hire of rock shoes and harness is £5, and instruction is available.

Crannog Cruises   WILDLIFE
(☑01397-700714; www.crannog.net/cruises; adult/child £15/7.50; ☺11am, 1pm & 3pm Easter-Oct) Operates 1½-hour wildlife cruises on Loch Linnhe, visiting a seal colony and a salmon farm.

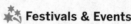 Festivals & Events

UCI Mountain Bike World Cup   SPORTS
(www.fortwilliamworldcup.co.uk) In June, Fort William pulls in crowds of more than 18,000 spectators for this World Cup downhill mountain-biking event. The gruelling downhill course is at nearby Nevis Range ski area.

Sleeping

It's best to book well ahead in summer, especially for hostels.

Calluna   APARTMENT £
(☑01397-700451;   www.fortwilliamholiday.co.uk; Heathercroft, Connochie Rd; dm/tw £20/44, 6-person apt per 3 nights £124; P ☼) Run by well-known mountain guide Alan Kimber and wife Sue, the Calluna offers self-catering apartments geared to groups of hikers and climbers, but also takes individual travellers prepared to share. There's a fully equipped kitchen and an excellent drying room for your soggy hiking gear.

Fort William Backpackers   HOSTEL £
(☑01397-700711; www.scotlands-top-hostels.com; Alma Rd; dm/tw £21/50; P @ ☼) A 10-minute walk from the bus and train stations, this lively and welcoming hostel is set in a grand

---

THE CALEDONIAN CANAL

Running for 59 miles from Corpach, near Fort William, to Inverness via lochs Lochy, Oich and Ness, the Caledonian Canal (www.scottishcanals.co.uk) links the east and west coasts of Scotland, avoiding the long and dangerous sea passage around Cape Wrath and through the turbulent Pentland Firth. Designed by Thomas Telford and completed in 1822 at a cost of £900,000 – a staggering sum then – the canal took 20 years to build, including 29 locks, four aqueducts and 10 bridges.

Conceived as a project to ease unemployment and bring prosperity to the Highlands in the aftermath of the Jacobite rebellions and the Clearances, the canal proved to be a commercial failure – the locks were too small for the new breed of steamships that came into use soon after its completion. But it proved to be a success in terms of tourism, especially after it was popularised by Queen Victoria's cruise along the canal in 1873. Today the canal is used mainly by yachts and pleasure cruisers, though since 2010 it has also been used to transport timber from west-coast forestry plantations to Inverness.

Much of the Great Glen Way follows the line of the canal; it can be followed on foot, by mountain bike or on horseback, and 80% of the route has even been done on mobility scooters. An easy half-day hike or bike ride is to follow the canal towpath from Corpach to Gairlochy (10 miles), which takes you past the impressive flight of eight locks known as **Neptune's Staircase**, and through beautiful countryside with grand views to the north face of Ben Nevis.

If you're cycling the length of the Great Glen Way, you can hire mountain bikes from Nevis Cycles (p336) in Fort William and drop them off at Ticket to Ride (p300) in Inverness, or vice versa.

The glen can also be explored by water, by following the **Great Glen Canoe Trail** (www.greatglencanoetrail.info).

Victorian villa, perched on a hillside with great views over Loch Linnhe.

6 Caberfeidh
B&B ££

(☎01397-703756; www.6caberfeidh.com; 6 Caberfeidh, Fassifern Rd; d/f £78/108; 🛜) Friendly owners and comfortable accommodation make a great combination; add a good central location and you're all set. Choose from one of two family rooms (one double and one single bed) or a romantic double with four-poster. Freshly prepared breakfasts include scrambled eggs with smoked salmon.

St Andrew's Guest House
B&B ££

(☎01397-703038; www.standrewsguesthouse. co.uk; Fassifern Rd; s/d £75/85; ⊙Mar-Oct; P🛜) Set in a lovely 19th-century building that was once a rectory and choir school, St Andrew's retains period features such as carved masonry, wood panelling and stained-glass windows. It has six spacious bedrooms; those at the front have stunning views.

★Grange
B&B £££

(☎01397-705516; www.grangefortwilliam.com; Grange Rd; d from £180; P🛜) An exceptional 19th-century villa set in its own landscaped grounds, the Grange is crammed with antiques and warmed by log fires, and has two luxury suites fitted with leather sofas, handcrafted furniture and rolltop baths, one situated in a charming self-contained cottage in the sprawling gardens, all with a view over Loch Linnhe. No children.

Lime Tree
HOTEL £££

(☎01397-701806; www.limetreefortwilliam.co.uk; Achintore Rd; r from £140; P🛜🐾) Much more interesting than your average guesthouse, this former Victorian manse overlooking Loch Linnhe is an 'art gallery with rooms', decorated throughout with the artist-owner's atmospheric Highland landscapes. Foodies rave about the restaurant, and the gallery space – a triumph of sensitive design – stages everything from serious exhibitions (works by David Hockney and Andy Goldsworthy have appeared) to folk concerts.

✖ Eating & Drinking

DeliCraft
DELI £

(☎01397-698100; www.delicraft.co.uk; 61 High St; mains £3-10; ⊙8am-6.30pm Mon-Sat, 10am-4pm Sun; 🖉) This deli serves great coffee, excellent pizza and delicious sandwiches, including deli classics such as pastrami on rye, to eat in or take away, as well as a range of Scottish cheeses, craft beers and gins.

★Lime Tree
SCOTTISH ££

(☎01397-701806; www.limetreefortwilliam.co.uk; Achintore Rd; mains £16-20; ⊙6.30-9.30pm; P🛜) 🖉 Fort William is not over-endowed with great places to eat, but the restaurant at this small hotel and art gallery has put the UK's Outdoor Capital on the gastronomic map. The chef turns out delicious dishes built around fresh Scottish produce, ranging from Loch Fyne oysters to Loch Awe trout and Ardnamurchan venison.

★Crannog Seafood Restaurant
SEAFOOD ££

(☎01397-705589; www.crannog.net; Town Pier; mains £15-24; ⊙noon-2.30pm & 6-9pm) 🖉 The Crannog wins the prize for the best location in town – perched on the Town Pier, giving window-table diners an uninterrupted view down Loch Linnhe. Informal and unfussy, it specialises in fresh local fish – there are three or four daily fish specials plus the main menu – though there are lamb, venison and vegetarian dishes, too. Two-/three-course lunch costs £16/19.

Geographer
INTERNATIONAL ££

(☎01397-705011; www.geographerrestaurant. co.uk; 88 High St; mains £10-15; ⊙noon-2pm & 5-9.30pm; 🛜🖉🖿) Bright and modern in atmosphere, this restaurant takes its inspiration from the owner's travels with a menu that mixes standards, such as burgers and fish and chips, with a selection of dishes from around the globe, including Middle Eastern falafel and flatbread, Mexican vegetable chilli and Burmese lamb curry. There's also a selection of Scottish gins and bottled craft beers.

Grog & Gruel
PUB

(☎01397-705078; www.grogandgruel.co.uk; 66 High St; ⊙noon-midnight; 🛜) The Grog & Gruel is a traditional-style, wood-panelled pub with an excellent range of cask ales from regional Scottish and English microbreweries.

🛍 Shopping

★Highland Bookshop
BOOKS

(www.highlandbookshop.com; 60 High St; ⊙9.30am-6pm Mon-Sat, 11am-4pm Sun) As well as a good selection of fiction and children's books, this shop stocks a superb range of outdoor-related books and maps covering climbing, walking, cycling, canoeing and other subjects. The upstairs lounge offers coffee and tea, and hosts regular literary events.

DON'T MISS

COMMANDO MEMORIAL

Near Spean Bridge, at the junction of the B8004 and A82, 2.5 miles east of Gairlochy, stands the **Commando Memorial**, which commemorates the WWII special forces soldiers who trained in this area.

The Commandos were an elite unit of the British armed forces, formed in 1940 to carry out raids behind enemy lines in German-occupied Europe. In 1942, a centre was set up at Achnacarry, 6 miles west of Spean Bridge, where Commando units were trained in secrecy. This memorial was erected in 1952, in a glorious setting with superb views of Ben Nevis and its neighbouring mountains.

ℹ Information

Fort William Tourist Office (☏ 01397-701801; www.visithighlands.com; 15 High St; internet per 20min £1; ☺ 9am-5pm Mon-Sat, 10am-3pm Sun, longer hours Jun-Aug; ☏)

ℹ Getting There & Away

BUS

Scottish Citylink (www.citylink.co.uk) buses link Fort William with other major towns and cities.

Edinburgh £37, 5¼ hours, four daily with a change at Glasgow; via Glencoe and Crianlarich

Glasgow £25, three hours, four daily

Inverness £12.20, two hours, six daily

Oban £9.40, 1½ hours, two daily

Portree £32.20, three hours, three daily

Shiel Buses (☏01397-700700; www.shielbuses.co.uk) service 500 runs to Mallaig (£6.10, 1½ hours, four daily Monday to Friday, plus one daily Saturday and Sunday) via Glenfinnan and Arisaig (£5.60, one hour).

TRAIN

The spectacular West Highland line runs from Glasgow to Mallaig via Fort William. The overnight **Caledonian Sleeper** (www.sleeper.scot) service connects Fort William and London Euston (from £135 sharing a twin-berth cabin, 13 hours).

There's no direct rail connection between Oban and Fort William – you have to change at Crianlarich, so it's faster to use the bus.

Edinburgh £40, five hours; change at Glasgow's Queen St station, three daily, two on Sunday

Glasgow £30, 3¾ hours, three daily, two on Sunday

Mallaig £13, 1½ hours, four daily, three on Sunday

ℹ Getting Around

BICYCLE

Nevis Cycles (☏ 01397-705555; www.neviscycles.com; cnr Montrose Ave & Locheil Rd, Inverlochy; per day from £25; ☺ 9am-5.30pm) Located a half-mile northeast of the town centre, this place rents everything from hybrid bikes and mountain bikes to full-suspension downhill racers. Bikes can be hired here and dropped off in Inverness.

BUS

A Zone 2 Dayrider ticket (£9.10) gives unlimited travel for one day on Stagecoach bus services in the Fort William area, as far as Glencoe and Fort Augustus. Buy from the bus driver.

CAR

Fort William is 146 miles from Edinburgh, 104 miles from Glasgow and 66 miles from Inverness. The tourist office has listings of car-hire companies.

Easydrive Car Hire (☏ 01397-701616; www.easydrivescotland.co.uk; North Rd; ☺ 8am-5.30pm Mon-Fri, to 5pm Sat, to 4pm Sun) Hires out small cars from £40/175 a day/week, including tax and unlimited mileage, but not Collision Damage Waiver (CDW).

TAXI

There's a taxi rank on the corner of High St and the Parade.

Around Fort William

Glen Nevis

Scenic Glen Nevis – used as a filming location for *Braveheart* and the Harry Potter movies – lies just an hour's walk from Fort William town centre. The **Glen Nevis Visitor Centre** (☏ 01397-705922; www.bennevisweather.co.uk; ☺ 8.30am-6pm Jul & Aug, 9am-5pm Apr-Jun, Sep & Oct, 9am-3pm Nov-Mar) is situated 1.5 miles up the glen, and provides information on hiking, weather forecasts, and specific advice on climbing Ben Nevis.

From the car park at the far end of the road along Glen Nevis, there is an excellent 1.5-mile walk through the spectacular Nevis Gorge to Steall Meadows, a verdant valley dominated by a 100m-high bridal-veil waterfall. You can reach the foot of the falls by crossing the river on a wobbly, three-cable wire bridge – one cable for your feet and one for each hand – which is a real test of balance!

🛏 Sleeping & Eating

Glen Nevis SYHA
HOSTEL £

(SYHA; 📞 01397-702336; www.syha.org.uk; dm £24; 🅿 @ 🛜) Benefitting from a complete overhaul in early 2018, this hostel is 3 miles from Fort William, right beside one of the starting points for the tourist track up Ben Nevis. Cooked breakfasts (£7) and packed lunches (£6) are available.

Glen Nevis Caravan & Camping Park
CAMPSITE £

(📞 01397-702191; www.glen-nevis.co.uk; tent sites per person £9.50, campervan £26; 🌣 mid-Mar–early Nov; 🛜) This big, well-equipped site is a popular base camp for Ben Nevis and the surrounding mountains. The site is 2.5 miles from Fort William, along the Glen Nevis road.

Achintee Farm
B&B, HOSTEL ££

(📞 01397-702240; www.achinteefarm.com; Achintee; B&B d £110, hostel tw/tr £54/81; 🌣 B&B May-Sep, hostel year-round; 🅿 🛜) This attractive farmhouse offers excellent B&B accommodation and also has a small hostel attached. It's at the start of the path up Ben Nevis.

★ Ben Nevis Inn
SCOTTISH ££

(📞 01397-701227; www.ben-nevis-inn.co.uk; Achintee; mains £10-15; 🌣 noon-11pm Apr-Oct, Thu-Sun Dec-Mar, closed Nov; 🅿) This great barn of a pub serves real ale and tasty bar meals (till 9pm), and has a comfy 24-bed bunkhouse downstairs (beds £17 per person). It's at the start of the path from Achintee up Ben Nevis, and only a mile from the end of the West Highland Way.

ⓘ Getting There & Away

Bus 41 runs from Fort William bus station to the Glen Nevis SYHA hostel (£2.30, 15 or 20 minutes, two daily year-round, five daily Monday to Saturday June to September). Check at the tourist office for the latest timetable, which is liable to alteration.

Nevis Range

Six miles to the north of Fort William lies Nevis Range ski area, where a gondola gives access to the upper part of Aonach Mor mountain. The facility operates year-round, allowing visitors to access mountain paths and downhill mountain-biking trails outside of the ski season.

🏃 Activities

Nevis Range Downhill & Witch's Trails
MOUNTAIN BIKING

(📞 01397-705825; www.nevisrange.co.uk/bike; single/multitrip ticket £18.50/34.50; 🌣 downhill course 10.15am-3.45pm Apr-Oct, forest trails 24hr year-round) Nevis Range ski area has a world championship downhill mountain-bike trail – for experienced riders only; bikes are carried up on the gondola cabin. There's also a 4-mile XC red trail that begins at the ski area's Snowgoose restaurant, and the Witch's Trails – 25 miles of waymarked forest road and singletrack in the nearby forest, including a 5-mile world championship loop.

A multitrip ticket gives unlimited uplift for a day; full-suspension bike hire costs from £65 per day.

Nevis Range
OUTDOORS

(📞 01397-705825; www.nevisrange.co.uk; day ticket per adult/child £21/12; 🌣 10am-6pm Jul & Aug, to 5pm Apr-Jun, Sep & Oct, 9.30am-dusk Nov-Mar) The Nevis Range ski area, 6 miles north of Fort William, spreads across the northern slopes of Aonach Mor (1221m). The gondola that gives access to the bottom of the ski area at 655m operates year-round. At the top there's a restaurant and a couple of hiking trails through nearby Leanachan Forest, as well as excellent mountain-biking trails.

The gondola takes 15 minutes each way; tickets are valid for multiple trips.

During the ski season a one-day lift pass costs £34.50/22.50 per adult/child; a one-day package, including equipment hire, lift pass and two hours' instruction, costs £78.50.

INVERNESS & THE CENTRAL HIGHLANDS AROUND FORT WILLIAM

NEPTUNE'S STAIRCASE

Three miles north of Fort William, at Banavie, is **Neptune's Staircase**, an impressive flight of eight locks that allows boats to climb 20m to the main reach of the **Caledonian Canal**. The B8004 road runs along the west side of the canal to Gairlochy at the south end of Loch Lochy, offering superb views of Ben Nevis; the **canal towpath** on the east side makes a great walk or bike ride (6.5 miles).

CLIMBING BEN NEVIS

As the highest peak in the British Isles, Ben Nevis (1345m) attracts many would-be ascensionists who would not normally think of climbing a Scottish mountain – a staggering (often literally) 100,000 people reach the summit each year.

Although anyone who is reasonably fit should have no problem climbing Ben Nevis on a fine summer's day, an ascent should not be undertaken lightly; every year people have to be rescued from the mountain. You will need proper walking boots (the path is rough and stony, and there may be snow on the summit), warm clothing, waterproofs, a map and compass, and plenty of food and water. And don't forget to check the weather forecast (www.bennevisweather.co.uk).

Here are a few facts to mull over before you go racing up the tourist track: the summit plateau is bounded by 700m-high cliffs and has a sub-Arctic climate; at the summit it can snow on any day of the year; the summit is wrapped in cloud nine days out of 10; in thick cloud, visibility at the summit can be 10m or less; and in such conditions the only safe way off the mountain requires careful use of a map and compass to avoid walking over those 700m cliffs.

The tourist track (the easiest route to the top) was originally called the Pony Track. It was built in the 19th century for the pack ponies that carried supplies to a meteorological observatory on the summit (now in ruins), which was in use continuously from 1883 to 1904.

There are three possible starting points for the tourist track ascent – Achintee Farm (p337); the footbridge at Glen Nevis SYHA (p337) hostel; and, if you have a car, the car park at Glen Nevis Visitor Centre (p336). The path climbs gradually to the shoulder at Lochan Meall an t-Suidhe (known as the Halfway Lochan), then zigzags steeply up beside the Red Burn to the summit plateau. The highest point is marked by a trig point on top of a huge cairn beside the ruins of the old observatory; the plateau is scattered with countless smaller cairns, stones arranged in the shape of people's names and, sadly, a fair bit of litter.

The total distance to the summit and back is 8 miles; allow at least four or five hours to reach the top, and another 2½ to three hours for the descent. Afterwards, as you celebrate in the pub with a pint, consider the fact that the record time for the annual Ben Nevis Hill Race is just under 1½ hours – up and down. Then have another pint.

❶ Getting There & Away

Bus 41 runs from Fort William bus station to Nevis Range (£2.30, 25 minutes, three daily Monday to Saturday, limited service October to April). Check at Fort William's tourist office (p336) for the latest timetable, which is liable to alteration.

Ardnamurchan

Ten miles south of Fort William, a car ferry makes the short crossing to Corran Ferry. The drive from here to Ardnamurchan Point (www.ardnamurchan.com), the most westerly point on the British mainland, is one of the most beautiful in the western Highlands, especially in late spring and early summer when much of the narrow, twisting road is lined with the bright pink and purple blooms of rhododendrons.

The road clings to the northern shore of Loch Sunart, going through the pretty villages of Strontian – which gave its name to the element strontium, first discovered in ore from nearby lead mines in 1790 – and Salen.

The mostly single-track road from Salen to Ardnamurchan Point is only 25 miles long, but it'll take you 1½ hours each way. It's a dipping, twisting, low-speed roller coaster of a ride through sun-dappled native woodlands draped with lichen and fern. Just when you're getting used to the views of Morvern and Mull to the south, it makes a quick detour to the north for a panorama over the islands of Rum and Eigg.

◉ Sights

Ardnamurchan Lighthouse LIGHTHOUSE
(☎01972-510210; www.ardnamurchanlighthouse. com; Ardnamurchan Point; visitor centre adult/ child £3/2, guided tour £6/4; ◷10am-5pm Apr-

Oct; P☕) The final 6 miles of road from Kilchoan to Ardnamurchan Point end at this 36m-high, grey granite tower, built in 1849 by the 'Lighthouse Stevensons' – family of Robert Louis – on the westernmost point of the British mainland. There's a tearoom, and the visitor centre will tell you more than you'll ever need to know about lighthouses, with lots of hands-on stuff for kids.

The guided tour (every half-hour 11am to 4pm) includes a trip to the top of the lighthouse. But the main attraction here is the expansive view over the ocean – this is a superb sunset viewpoint, provided you don't mind driving back in the dark.

Ardnamurchan Natural History & Visitor Centre
MUSEUM

(☎01972-500209; www.ardnamurchannaturalhistorycentre.com; Glenmore; ⊙8.30am-5pm Sun-Fri; ☕) FREE This fascinating centre – midway between Salen and Kilchoan – was originally devised by a wildlife photographer and tries to bring you face to face with the flora and fauna of the Ardnamurchan peninsula. The Living Building exhibit is designed to attract local wildlife, with a mammal den that is occasionally occupied by hedgehogs or pine martens, an owl nest-box, a mouse nest and a pond.

If the beasties are not in residence, you can watch recorded video footage of the animals. There's also seasonal live CCTV coverage of local wildlife, ranging from nesting herons to a golden eagle feeding site.

Ardnamurchan Distillery
DISTILLERY

(Map p282; ☎01972-500285; www.adelphidistillery.com; Glenbeg; tours per person from £7; ⊙10am-6pm Mon-Fri, 11am-5pm Sun Easter-Oct, phone for winter hours) This whisky distillery went into production in 2014, complete with visitor centre and tasting room. Although you will be able to see the whisky-making process, the finished product will be matured in casks until 2022 before being bottled as a single malt.

🛏️ Sleeping & Eating

Ardnamurchan Campsite
CAMPSITE £

(☎01972-510766; www.ardnamurchanstudycentre.co.uk; Kilchoan; sites per adult/child £9/4; ⊙May-Sep; 🛜) Basic but beautifully situated campsite, with the chance of seeing otters from your tent. It's along the Ormsaig road, 2 miles west of Kilchoan village.

★ Ard Daraich
COTTAGE ££

(☎01855-841384; www.ardgour-selfcatering.co.uk; Sallachan, Ardgour; studio per week from £645; P🛜❄) 🍴 About 3 miles southwest of Corran Ferry, this handsome West Highland house once belonged to florist Constance Spry (who arranged flowers for Queen Elizabeth II's coronation), and is set in beautiful gardens filled with rhododendrons, azaleas and heathers; there's a chance of seeing otters and pine martens nearby. Let as a two-person garden studio, and five-person cottage.

Salen Hotel
INN ££

(☎01967-431661; www.salenhotel.co.uk; Salen; r £100-120; P🛜❄) A traditional Highland inn with views over Loch Sunart, the Salen Hotel has three rooms in the pub (two with sea views) and another three rooms (all en suite) in a modern chalet out the back. The cosy lounge has a roaring fire and comfy sofa, and the bar meals, including seafood, venison and other game dishes, are very good.

Lochview Tearoom
CAFE £

(Ardnamurchan Natural History & Visitor Centre, Glenmore; mains £5-8; ⊙8.30am-4.30pm Sun-Fri; P🛜☕) The cafe at the wildlife centre serves coffee, home-baked goods and lunch dishes, including fresh salads and sandwiches and homemade soup.

ℹ️ Information

Kilchoan Village Hall (☎01972-510222; Pier Rd, Kilchoan; ⊙9am-5pm Mon-Sat Easter-Nov), on the road to the pier, has information and leaflets on walking and wildlife.

ℹ️ Getting There & Away

Shiel Buses (www.shielbuses.co.uk) service 506 runs from Fort William to Acharacle, Salen and Kilchoan (£9.90, 2½ hours, one daily Monday to Saturday) via **Corran Ferry** (car £8.20, bicycle & foot passenger free; ⊙every 30min). There's a car ferry between Kilchoan and Tobermory on the Isle of Mull.

Road to the Isles

The 46-mile A830 road from Fort William to Mallaig is traditionally known as the Road to the Isles, as it leads to the jumping-off point for ferries to the Small Isles and Skye, itself a stepping stone to the Outer Hebrides. This is a region steeped in Jacobite history, having witnessed both the beginning and the end of Bonnie Prince Charlie's doomed attempt to regain the British throne in 1745–46.

The final section of this scenic route, between Arisaig and Mallaig, has been upgraded to a fast straight road. Unless you're in a hurry, opt instead for the more scenic old road (signposted Alternative Coastal Route).

Between the A830 and the A87 far to the north lie Knoydart and Glenelg – Scotland's 'Empty Quarter'.

❶ Getting There & Around

Shiel Buses service 500 runs from Fort William to Mallaig (£6.10, 1½ hours, four daily Monday to Friday, one on Saturday and Sunday) via Glenfinnan (30 minutes), Arisaig (one hour) and Morar (1¼ hours).

The Fort William–Mallaig railway line has four trains a day (three on Sunday), with stops at many points along the way, including Corpach, Glenfinnan, Lochailort, Arisaig and Morar.

Glenfinnan

POP 100

Glenfinnan is hallowed ground for fans of Bonnie Prince Charlie; the monument here marks where he raised his Highland army. It is also a place of pilgrimage for steam train enthusiasts and Harry Potter fans – the famous railway viaduct features in the Potter films, and is regularly traversed by the Jacobite Steam Train (p333).

◉ Sights & Activities

Glenfinnan Monument MONUMENT

FREE This tall column, topped by a statue of a kilted Highlander, was erected in 1815 on the spot where Bonnie Prince Charlie first raised his standard and rallied the Jacobite clans on 19 August 1745, marking the start of his ill-fated campaign, which would end in disaster at Culloden 14 months later. The setting, at the north end of Loch Shiel, is hauntingly beautiful.

Glenfinnan Visitor Centre MUSEUM

(NTS; www.nts.org.uk; adult/child £3.50/2.50; ◷9am-7pm Jul & Aug, to 6pm Mar-Jun, Sep & Oct, 10am-4pm Nov-Feb; ℗) This centre recounts the story of the '45, as the Jacobite rebellion of 1745 is known, when Bonnie Prince Charlie's loyal clansmen marched and fought their way from Glenfinnan south via Edinburgh to Derby, then back north to final defeat at Culloden.

Glenfinnan Station Museum MUSEUM

(www.glenfinnanstationmuseum.co.uk; admission by donation, suggested £1; ◷9am-5pm Easter-Oct; ℗) This fascinating little museum records the epic tale of building the West Highland railway line. The famous 21-arch **Glenfinnan viaduct**, just east of the station, was built in 1901, and featured in several Harry Potter movies. A pleasant walk of around 0.75 miles east from the station (signposted) leads to a viewpoint for the viaduct and for Loch Shiel.

Loch Shiel Cruises CRUISE

(☑07801 537617; www.highlandcruises.co.uk; per person £12-22; ◷Apr-Sep) Boat trips along Loch Shiel, with the opportunity of spotting golden eagles and other wildlife. There are one- to 2½-hour cruises on Tuesday and Thursday. On Wednesday the boat goes the full length of the loch to Acharacle (one way/return £20/30), calling at Polloch and Dalilea, allowing for walks and bike rides using the forestry track on the eastern shore.

The boat departs from a jetty near Glenfinnan House Hotel.

▭ Sleeping & Eating

Sleeping Car Bunkhouse HOSTEL £

(☑01397-722295; www.glenfinnanstationmuseum.co.uk; Glenfinnan Station; per person £15, entire coach £130; ◷May-Oct; ℗) Two converted railway carriages at Glenfinnan Station house this unusual 10-berth bunkhouse and the atmospheric **Dining Car Tearoom** (☑01397-722300; mains £6-10; ◷9am-4.30pm; ℗).

★**Prince's House Hotel** INN £££

(☑01397-722246; www.glenfinnan.co.uk; s/d from £95/160; ℗) A delightful old coaching inn dating from 1658, the Prince's House is a great place to pamper yourself – ask for the spacious, tartan-draped Stuart Room (£225), complete with four-poster bed, if you want to stay in the oldest part of the hotel. The relaxed but well-regarded restaurant specialises in Scottish produce (four-course dinner £46).

There's no documented evidence that Bonnie Prince Charlie actually stayed here in 1745, but it was the only sizeable house in Glenfinnan at that time, so…

Arisaig & Morar

The 5 miles of coast between the tiny villages of Arisaig and Morar is a fretwork of rocky islets, inlets and gorgeous silver-sand beaches backed by dunes and machair, with stunning sunset views across the sea to the silhouetted peaks of Eigg and Rum. The **Silver Sands of Morar**, as they are known, draw crowds of bucket-and-spade holiday-makers in July and August, when the many campsites scattered along the coast are filled to overflowing.

◉ Sights & Activities

Camusdarach Beach   BEACH
(P) Fans of the movie *Local Hero* still make pilgrimages to Camusdarach Beach, just south of Morar, which starred in the film as Ben's beach. To find it, look for the car park half a mile north of Camusdarach Camp-site; from here, a wooden footbridge and a quarter-mile walk through the dunes lead to the beach. (The village that featured in the film is on the other side of the country, at Pennan.)

Land, Sea & Islands
Visitor Centre   MUSEUM
(www.arisaigcommunitytrust.org.uk; Arisaig; ⊙10am-6pm Mon-Sat, noon-5pm Sun Apr-Oct, shorter hours Sat-Mon Nov-Mar; P) **FREE** This centre in Arisaig village houses exhibits on the cultural and natural history of the region. A small but fascinating exhibition explains the part played by the local area as a base for training spies for the Special Operations Executive (SOE, forerunner of MI6) during WWII, including famous names such as Violette Szabo (made famous by the 1958 film *Carve Her Name with Pride*) and the Czech paratroopers who assassinated Nazi leader Reinhard Heydrich in Prague in 1942.

Arisaig Marine   WILDLIFE WATCHING
(☑01687-450224; www.arisaig.co.uk; Arisaig Harbour; ⊙late Apr-Sep) In summer Arisaig Marine operates wildlife-watching cruises (minke whales, basking sharks, porpoises, dolphins) from Arisaig harbour to Eigg (£18 return, one hour, six weekly), Rum (£25 return, 2½ hours, two or three weekly) and Muck (£20 return, two hours, three weekly). Sailing times allow four or five hours ashore on Eigg, and two or three hours on Muck or Rum.

🛏 Sleeping & Eating

There are at least a half-dozen campsites between Arisaig and Morar; all are open in summer only, and are often full in July and August, so book ahead.

GLENUIG INN

Set on a peaceful bay, halfway between Lochailort and Acharacle on the A830, the **Glenuig Inn** (☑01687-470219; www.glenuig.com; Glenuig; B&B s/d/q from £80/120/170, bunkhouse per person £35; P🖥) is a great place to get away from it all. As well as offering comfortable accommodation, good food (mains £10 to £25, served noon to 9pm) and real ale on tap, it's a great base for exploring Arisaig, Morar and the Loch Shiel area.

Rockhopper Sea Kayaking (☑07739 837344; www.rockhopperscotland.co.uk; half-/full day £50/80) can take you on a guided kayak tour along the wild and beautiful coastline, starting and finishing at the inn.

Camusdarach Campsite   CAMPSITE £
(☑01687-450221; www.camusdarach.co.uk; Arisaig; tent/campervan sites £10/17.50, plus per person £5; ⊙Apr-Sep; 🖥🐾) 🍃 A small and nicely landscaped site with good facilities, only three minutes' walk from the *Local Hero* beach via a gate in the northwest corner.

Leven House   B&B £
(☑01687-450238; www.thelevenhouse.co.uk; Arisaig; s/d from £45/60; P🖥) Set back from the main road, three miles east of Arisaig village, this peaceful farmhouse offers a warm welcome and gorgeous views over the sea towards the Small Isles. Breakfasts include homemade bread and marmalade, and the friendly host is a mine of information about local history and wildlife. There's also a lovely two-bedroom, self-catering cottage (£400 a week).

Old Library Lodge
& Restaurant   SCOTTISH ££
(☑01687-450651; www.oldlibrary.co.uk; Arisaig; mains £10-21; ⊙noon-2pm & 6-8.30pm; P🖥) 🍃 The Old Library is a charming restaurant with rooms (singles/doubles £75/120) set in converted 200-year-old stables overlooking the waterfront in Arisaig village. The lunch menu concentrates on soups, burgers and smoked fish or meat platters, while dinner is a more sophisticated affair offering local seafood, beef and lamb.

Mallaig

POP 800

If you're travelling between Fort William and Skye, you may find yourself overnighting in the bustling fishing and ferry port of Mallaig (*mahl*-ig). Indeed, it makes a good base for a series of day trips by ferry to the Small Isles and Knoydart.

Mallaig has a post office, a bank with ATM and a co-op supermarket.

◉ Sights & Activities

Mallaig Heritage Centre MUSEUM
(☑01687-462085; www.mallaigheritage.org.uk; Station Rd; adult/child £2.50/free; ⊘11am-4pm Mon-Sat Apr-Oct, longer hours Jul & Aug, shorter hours Nov-Mar) The village's rainy-day attractions are limited to this heritage centre, which covers the archaeology and history of the region, including the heart-rending tale of the Highland Clearances in Knoydart.

Seafari Adventures Skye BOATING
(☑01471-833316; Harbour Pontoons; adult/child £42/34; ⊘Easter-Sep) Seafari runs three-hour whale-watching cruises around Skye and the Small Isles aboard the single-hulled *Amelia* and the 36-seat catamaran *Orion*. These trips have a high success rate for spotting minke whales in summer (an average of 180 sightings a year), with rarer sightings of bottlenose dolphins and basking sharks.

⿻ Sleeping & Eating

Springbank Guest House B&B ££
(☑01687-462459; www.springbank-mallaig.co.uk; East Bay; s/d from £45/75; 🛜) The Springbank is a traditional West Highland house with six homely guest bedrooms, with superb views across the harbour to the Cuillin of Skye.

Seaview Guest House B&B ££
(☑01687-462059; www.seaviewguesthousemallaig. com; Main St; s/d £65/90, cottage per week £600; 🅿🛜) This comfortable B&B has grand views over the harbour, not only from the upstairs bedrooms but from the breakfast room too. There's also a cute little cottage next door that offers self-catering accommodation (www.selfcateringmallaig.com; one double and one twin room).

Jaffy's FISH & CHIPS £
(www.jaffys.co.uk; Station Rd; mains £4-7; ⊘noon-3pm & 5-8pm Mon-Sat Apr-Nov, 5-8pm Thu-Sat Dec-Mar) 🍴 Owned by a third-generation fish merchant's family, Mallaig's chippy serves superbly fresh fish and chips, as well as kippers, prawns and other seafood.

Fish Market Restaurant SEAFOOD ££
(☑01687-462299; www.thefishmarketrestaurant. co.uk; Station Rd; mains £12-28; ⊘noon-3pm & 6-9pm) 🍴 At least half-a-dozen signs in Mallaig advertise 'seafood restaurant', but this bright, modern, bistro-style place next to the harbour is our favourite, serving simply prepared scallops, smoked salmon, mussels, and fresh Mallaig haddock fried in breadcrumbs, as well as the tastiest Cullen skink on the west coast.

Upstairs is a **coffee shop** (Station Rd; mains £4-8; ⊘11am-4pm, to 6pm Jun-Aug).

❶ Getting There & Away

BOAT

A passenger ferry operated by Western Isles Cruises links Mallaig to Inverie on the Knoydart Peninsula (25 to 40 minutes) four times daily Monday to Saturday (three on Sunday) from April to October.

CalMac (☑0800 066 5000; www.calmac. co.uk) operates the passenger-only ferry from Mallaig to the following destinations in the Small Isles:

Canna £10.90 return, two hours, six weekly
Eigg £8 return, 1¼ hours, five weekly
Muck £9.20 return, 1½ hours, five weekly
Rum £8.60 return, 1¼ hours, five weekly

There are CalMac car ferry services to Armadale in Skye (car/passenger £9.70/2.90, 30 minutes, eight daily Monday to Saturday, five to seven on Sunday), and Lochboisdale in South Uist (car/passenger £57.65/10.45, 3½ hours, one daily).

BUS

Shiel Buses (www.shielbuses.co.uk) service 500 runs from Fort William to Mallaig (£6.10, 1½ hours, four daily Monday to Friday, plus one daily Saturday and Sunday) via Glenfinnan (£3.30, 30 minutes) and Arisaig (£5.60, one hour).

TRAIN

The West Highland line runs between Fort William and Mallaig (£13, 1½ hours, four daily, three on Sunday).

Knoydart

POP 180

The Knoydart peninsula – a rugged landscape of wild mountains and lonely sea lochs – is the only sizeable area in Britain that remains inaccessible to the motor car, cut off by miles of rough country and the embracing arms of Lochs Nevis and Hourn (Gaelic for the lochs of Heaven and Hell). The main reasons for visiting are to climb the 1020m peak of **Ladhar Bheinn** (laarven), or just to enjoy the feeling of remoteness. There's no TV and no mobile-phone reception; electricity is provided by a private hydroelectric scheme.

No road penetrates this wilderness of rugged hills – **Inverie**, its sole village, can only be reached by ferry from Mallaig, or on foot from the remote road's end at Kinloch Hourn (a tough 16-mile hike). A 4WD track leads northwest from Inverie for 7 miles to the outposts of **Doune** and **Airor**, which offer even more remote accommodation options.

🛏 Sleeping & Eating

Inverie has a pub and tearoom, and there's a small community shop (www.knoydart shop.org) stocked with canned and dry goods.

Knoydart Foundation Bunkhouse   HOSTEL £
(📞01687-462163;   www.knoydart-foundation. com; Inverie; dm adult/child £18/10; @🤝) 🏃 A 15-minute walk east of Inverie ferry pier, this is a cosy hostel with wood-burning stove, kitchen and drying room.

Long Beach Campsite   CAMPSITE £
(📞01687-462242; www.knoydart-foundation.com; Inverie; per tent & 1 person £4, per extra person £3) A basic but beautiful campsite, a 10-minute walk east of the ferry; there's a water supply, fire pits and composting toilet, but no showers. The ranger comes around to collect fees; firewood available for £4.50 a bundle.

Knoydart Lodge   HOSTEL ££
(📞01687-460129;   www.knoydartlodge.co.uk; Inverie; r per person from £30; 🤝🍽) 🏃 This must be some of the most spacious and luxurious accommodation on the whole west coast, let alone in Knoydart. The fantastic, modern timber-built lodge – reminiscent of an Alpine chalet – has large, stylish two- to six-person bedrooms just a short stroll from the beach. You can order breakfast packs (from £5 per person) in advance.

⭐ **Old Forge**   PUB FOOD ££
(📞01687-462267; www.theoldforge.co.uk; Inverie; mains £16-24; ⏱12.30-11.30pm Thu-Tue mid-Mar–Oct, 4-11pm Thu-Tue Nov–mid-Mar; 🤝🍴) 🏃 The Old Forge is listed in the *Guinness Book of Records* as Britain's most remote pub. It's

surprisingly sophisticated – as well as having real ale on tap, there's an Italian coffee machine. Food is served 12.30pm to 2.30pm and 6.30pm to 9.30pm; the house special is a seafood platter (£38); all ingredients are sourced within 7 miles of the pub.

In the evening you can sit by the fire, pint of beer in hand and join the impromptu *ceilidh* (an evening of traditional Scottish entertainment including music, song and dance) that seems to take place just about nightly.

❶ Getting There & Away

Western Isles Cruises (📞01687-462233; https://westernislescruises.co.uk; one-way/ day return £10/20, bike £3) Passenger ferry linking Mallaig to Inverie (25 to 40 minutes) four times daily Monday to Saturday and three on Sunday from April to October. Taking the morning boat gives you up to 10 hours ashore in Knoydart before the return trip (first and last boats of the day should be booked in advance). There's also an afternoon sailing between Inverie and Tarbet on the south side of Loch Nevis, allowing walkers to hike along the northern shore of Loch Morar to Tarbet and return by boat (£15 Tarbet–Inverie–Mallaig).

It's also possible to join the boat just for the cruise, without going ashore (£22 for Mallaig–Inverie–Tarbet–Inverie–Mallaig).

SMALL ISLES

The scattered jewels of the Small Isles – Rum, Eigg, Muck and Canna – lie strewn across the silvery-blue Cuillin Sound to the south of Skye. Their distinctive outlines enliven the glorious views from the beaches of Arisaig and Morar.

Rum is the biggest and boldest of the four, a miniature Skye of pointed peaks and dramatic sunset silhouettes. Eigg is the most pastoral and populous, dominated by the miniature sugarloaf mountain of the Sgurr. Muck is a botanist's delight with its wildflowers and unusual alpine plants, and Canna is a craggy bird sanctuary made of magnetic rocks.

If your time is limited and you can only visit one island, choose Eigg or Rum; they have the most to offer on a day trip.

❶ Getting There & Away

The main ferry operator is **CalMac** (www.calmac. co.uk), which runs the passenger-only ferry from Mallaig.

Canna £10.90 return, two hours, six weekly

Eigg £8 return, 1¼ hours, five weekly

Muck £9.20 return, 1½ hours, five weekly

Rum £8.60 return, 1¼ hours, five weekly

You can also hop between the islands without returning to Mallaig, but the timetable is complicated and it requires a bit of planning – you would need at least five days to visit all four islands. Bicycles are carried for free.

Rum

POP 22

The Isle of Rum (www.isleofrum.com) – the biggest and most spectacular of the Small Isles – was once known as the Forbidden Island. Cleared of its crofters in the early 19th century to make way for sheep, from 1888 to 1957 it was the private sporting estate of the Bulloughs, a Lancashire family who made their fortune in the textile industry. Curious outsiders who ventured too close were liable to find themselves staring down the wrong end of a gamekeeper's shotgun.

The island was sold to the Nature Conservancy in 1957 and has since been a wildlife reserve with deer, wild goats, ponies, golden and white-tailed eagles, and a 120,000-strong colony of Manx shearwaters. Its dramatic, rocky mountains, known as the Rum Cuillin for their similarity to the peaks on neighbouring Skye, draw hill walkers and climbers.

Kinloch, with ferry landing, shop, post office and public telephone, is the island's only settlement.

◉ Sights & Activities

There's some great coastal and mountain walking on the island, including a couple of easy, waymarked nature trails in the woods around Kinloch. The first path on the left after leaving the pier leads to an **otter hide** (signposted).

The climb to the island's highest point, **Askival** (812m), is a strenuous hike and involves a bit of rock scrambling (allow six hours for the round trip from Kinloch).

Glen Harris is a 10-mile round trip from Kinloch, on a rough 4WD track – allow four to five hours' walking, or two hours by bike. You can hire bikes from **Rum Bike Hire** (☑ 01687-462744; fliss@isleofrum.com; Rum Crafts; per day £15; ⊙ 10am-6pm) at the craft shop near Kinloch Castle.

★**Kinloch Castle** CASTLE

(☑ 01687-462037; www.isleofrum.com; adult/child £9/4.50; ⊙ guided tours Mon-Sat Apr-Oct, to coincide with ferry times) When George Bullough, a dashing, Harrow-educated cavalry officer, inherited Rum along with half his father's fortune in 1891, he became one of the wealthiest bachelors in Britain. Bullough blew half his inheritance on building his dream bachelor pad – the ostentatious Kinloch Castle. Since the Bulloughs left, the castle has survived as a perfect time capsule of upper-class Edwardian eccentricity – the guided tour should not be missed.

Bullough shipped in pink sandstone from Dumfriesshire and 250,000 tonnes of Ayrshire topsoil for the gardens, and paid his workers a shilling extra a day to wear tweed kilts – just so they'd look more picturesque. Hummingbirds were kept in the greenhouses and alligators in the garden, and guests were entertained with an orchestrion, the Edwardian equivalent of a Bose hi-fi system (one of only six that were ever made).

🛏 Sleeping & Eating

Bring plenty of food supplies, as there is only one **tearoom** (www.isleofrumteashop.co.uk; Kinloch; mains £3-6; ⊙ 10am-4pm Mon-Fri, to 3pm Sat Apr-Sep; ☎), and the grocery **shop** (☑ 01687-460328; ⊙ 5-8pm, also 10am-noon on ferry days) opening times are limited.

Kinloch Village Campsite CAMPSITE £

(www.isleofrum.com; sites per adult/child £6/3, cabins £35; ☻) Situated between the pier and Kinloch Castle, this basic campsite has toilets, a water supply and hot showers. There are also two wooden camping cabins (sleeping two persons), which must be booked in advance at rumkabins@gmail.com.

Rum Bunkhouse HOSTEL £

(☑ 01687-460318; www.isleofrum.com; Kinloch; dm/tw £23/50; ☎) This beautiful, Scandinavian-style timber building was purpose-built as a hostel in 2014, and now provides the island's main accommodation, complete with hot showers, a wood-burning stove and picture windows overlooking the sea.

❶ Information

Kinloch has a **visitor centre** (⊙ 8.30am-5pm Apr-Oct) near the pier where you can get information and leaflets on walking and wildlife. For more information see www.isleofrum.com.

Eigg

POP 90

The island of Eigg (www.isleofeigg.org) made history in 1997 when it became the first Highland estate to be bought out by its inhabitants. The island is now owned and managed by the Isle of Eigg Heritage Trust, a partnership among the islanders, Highland Council and the Scottish Wildlife Trust.

It takes its name from the Old Norse *egg* (meaning 'edge'), a reference to the **Sgurr of Eigg** (393m), an impressive mini-mountain that towers over **Galmisdale**, the main settlement. Ringed by vertical cliffs on three sides, it's composed of pitchstone lava with columnar jointing similar to that seen on the Isle of Staffa and at the Giant's Causeway in Northern Ireland.

🏃 Activities

The climb to the summit of the **Sgurr of Eigg** (4.5 miles round trip; allow three to four hours) begins on the road that leads steeply uphill from the pier, which continues through the woods to a red-roofed cottage. Go through the gate to the right of the cottage and turn left; just 20m along the road a cairn on the right marks the start of a boggy footpath that leads over the eastern shoulder of the Sgurr, then traverses beneath the northern cliffs until it makes its way up onto the summit ridge.

On a fine day the views from the top are magnificent – Rum and Skye to the north, Muck and Coll to the south, Ardnamurchan Lighthouse to the southeast and Ben Nevis shouldering above the eastern horizon. Take binoculars – on a calm summer's day there's a good chance of seeing minke whales feeding down below in the Sound of Muck.

A shorter walk (2 miles; allow 1½ hours round trip, and bring a torch) leads west from the pier to the spooky and claustrophobic **Uamh Fraing** (Massacre Cave). Start as for the Sgurr of Eigg, but 800m from the pier turn left through a gate and into a field. Follow the 4WD track and fork left before a white cottage to pass below it. A footpath continues across the fields to reach a small gate in a fence; go through it and descend a ridge towards the shore.

The cave entrance is tucked inconspicuously down to the left of the ridge. The entrance is tiny – almost a hands-and-knees job – but the cave opens out inside and runs a long way back. Go right to the back, turn off your torch, and imagine the cave packed shoulder to shoulder with terrified men, women and children. Then imagine the panic as your enemies start piling firewood into the entrance. Almost the entire population of Eigg – around 400 people – sought refuge in this cave when the MacLeods of Skye raided the island in 1577. In an act of inhuman cruelty, the raiders lit a fire in the narrow entrance and everyone inside died of asphyxiation. There are more than a few ghosts floating around in here.

🛏 Sleeping & Eating

All accommodation should be booked in advance; wild camping is allowed. For a full listing of accommodation, see www.isleof eigg.org.

Eigg Organics   CAMPSITE £
(☏01687-482480; www.eiggorganics.co.uk; Cleadale; tent sites per person £5, yurt £50-55; 🖂) This organic croft in the north of the island has a campsite with basic facilities, and also offers accommodation for two in a Mongolian yurt.

Glebe Barn   HOSTEL £
(☏01687-315099; www.glebebarn.co.uk; Galmisdale; dm/tw £20/45; 🖂) Excellent bunkhouse accommodation in the middle of the island, with a smart, maple-floored lounge with a central fireplace, a modern kitchen, a laundry, a drying room, and bright, clean dorms and bedrooms.

★Lageorna   B&B ££
(☏01687-460081; www.lageorna.com; Cleadale; s/d £85/110; 🖂) 🍽 This converted croft house and lodge in the island's northwest is Eigg's most luxurious accommodation. Rooms are fitted with beautiful, locally made, 'driftwood-style' timber beds, and even have iPod docks (but no mobile-phone reception). Evening meals are available (£25 a head), with the menu heavy on locally grown vegetables, seafood and venison.

Galmisdale Bay   CAFE £
(☏01687-482487; www.galmisdale-bay.com; The Pier, Galmisdale; mains £6-11; ⊘check website, closed Wed & Sun) 🍽 The cafe-bar above the ferry pier is the social hub of the community, and serves tasty, great-value soups, salads and sandwiches, plus hot lunch specials. Opening hours differ from day to day; in winter they coincide with ferry arrivals and departures.

❶ Information

Above the pier, the **Isle of Eigg Shop** (☑ 01687-482432; https://isleofeiggshop.com; The Pier, Galmisdale; ⊙ 10am-5pm Mon, Wed & Fri, 11am-3pm Thu, noon-5pm Sat May–mid-Oct, shorter hours winter) serves as an information centre; it also has a post office, craft shop and cafe. You can hire **bikes** (☑ 01687-347007; www.eigg adventures.co.uk; The Pier, Galmisdale; per day £15) here, too.

Canna

POP 15

The island of Canna (www.theisleofcanna. com) is a moorland plateau of black basalt rock, just 5 miles long and 1.25 miles wide; it was gifted to the National Trust for Scotland in 1981 by its owner, the Gaelic scholar and author John Lorne Campbell.

The ferry arrives at the hamlet of **A'Chill** at the eastern end of the island, where visiting sailors have left extensive graffiti on the rock face south of the harbour. There's a tearoom and craft shop by the harbour, and a tiny post office in a hut. There is no mobile-phone reception.

You can walk to **An Coroghon**, just east of the ferry pier, a medieval stone tower perched atop a sea cliff, and continue to **Compass Hill** (143m), which contains enough magnetite (an iron oxide mineral) to deflect the navigation compasses in passing yachts, or take a longer hike along the southern shore past **Canna House** (the former home of John Lorne Campbell) and an ornately decorated **early Christian stone cross**. In 2012 a *bullaun* ('cursing stone'), with an inscribed cross was discovered nearby; these are common in Ireland, but this was the first to be found in Scotland.

Facilities are limited. **Tighard** (☑ 01687-462474; www.tighard.com; r £85-100; 🛜 🐾) is the only B&B, while **Canna Campsite** (☑ 01687-462477; www.cannacampsite.com; tent sites £10, pods £25-30, caravans £45; 🐾) provides tent, caravan and glamping pod accommodation.

Cafe Canna   BISTRO, CAFE ££

(☑ 01687-482488; www.cafecanna.co.uk; mains £10-20; ⊙ 11am-10pm Wed-Mon May-Aug, 1-9pm Wed-Mon early Sep; 🛜) 🍃 The only eating place on the island, this cafe serves meals such as haddock and chips (fish freshly landed at Mallaig) and Canna rabbit stew, in a lovely setting beside the harbour. Best to book for evening meals.

Muck

POP 38

The tiny island of Muck (www.isleofmuck. com), measuring just 2 miles by 1 mile, has exceptionally fertile soil, and the island is carpeted with wildflowers in spring and early summer. It takes its name from the Gaelic *muc* (pig), and pigs are still raised here.

Ferries call at the southern settlement of **Port Mor**. There's a tearoom and craft shop above the pier, which also acts as a tourist office.

It's an easy 15-minute walk along the island's only road from the pier to the sandy beach at **Gallanach** on the northern side of the island. A longer and rougher hike (3.5 miles; 1½ hours round trip) goes to the top of **Beinn Airein** (137m) for the best views. Puffins nest on the cliffs at the western end of Camas Mor, the bay to the south of the hill.

Northern Highlands & Islands

Best Places to Eat

➡ Three Chimneys (p383)

➡ Côte du Nord (p359)

➡ Captain's Galley (p358)

➡ Waterside (p373)

➡ Langass Lodge Restaurant (p393)

Best Places to Stay

➡ Torridon (p370)

➡ Pennyland House (p357)

➡ Mey House (p357)

➡ Craigvar (p350)

➡ Hillstone Lodge (p382)

➡ Tigh an Dochais (p377)

Why Go?

Scotland's vast and melancholy soul is here: an epic land with a stark beauty that indelibly imprints the hearts of those who journey through the mist and mountains, rock and heather. Long, sun-blessed summer evenings are the pay-off for so many days of horizontal rain. It's simply magical.

Stone tells stories throughout. The chambered cairns of Caithness and structures of the Western Isles are testament to the skills of prehistoric builders; cragtop castles and broken walls of abandoned crofts tell of the Highlands' turbulent history.

Outdoors is the place to be, whatever the weather; there's nothing like comparing windburn or mud-ruined boots over a well-deserved dram by the crackling fire of a Highland pub. The landscape lends itself to activity, from woodland strolls to thrilling mountain-bike descents, from sea kayaking to Munro bagging, from beachcombing to birdwatching. Best are the locals, big-hearted and straight-talking; make it your business to get to know them.

When to Go
Portree

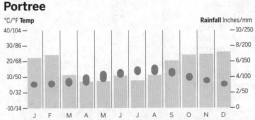

Jun Long evenings bathe achingly sublime landscapes in dreamy light.

Jul The Hebridean Celtic Festival is a top time to experience the culture of the Outer Hebrides.

Sep Less busy than summer, the midges have gone and temperatures are (maybe!) still OK.

Northern Highlands & Islands Highlights

1 North Coast 500 (p359) Driving one of Europe's most spectacularly scenic road trips.

2 Ullapool (p365) Gorging on fresh, succulent seafood in this delightful town with its picture-perfect harbour.

3 Harris (p389) Dipping your toes in the water at some of the world's most beautiful beaches in the Western Isles.

4 Cuillin Hills (p379) Shouldering the challenge of these hills, with their rugged silhouettes brooding over the skyscape of Skye.

5 Far Northwest (p361) Picking your jaw up off the ground as you marvel at the epic Highland scenery.

6 Cape Wrath (p363) Taking the trip out to Britain's gloriously remote northwestern shoulder.

7 Plockton (p371) Relaxing in a postcard-pretty village where the Highlands meet the Caribbean.

8 Skye (p374) Launching yourself in a sea kayak to explore the otter-rich waters around the Isle of Skye.

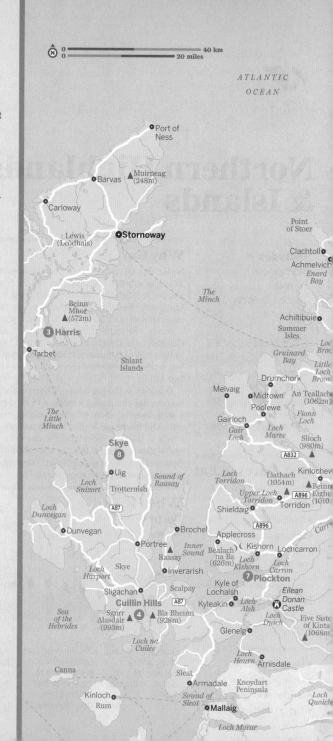

EAST COAST

In both landscape and character, the east coast is where the real barrenness of the Highlands begins to unfold. A gentle splendour and a sense of escapism mark the route along the twisting A9, as it heads north for the last of Scotland's far-flung, mainland population outposts. With only a few exceptions the tourism frenzy is left behind once the road traverses Cromarty Firth and snakes its way along wild and pristine coastline.

While the interior is dominated by the vast and mournful Sutherland mountain range, along the coast great heather-covered hills heave themselves out of the wild North Sea. Rolling farmland drops suddenly into the icy waters, and small, historic towns are moored precariously on the coast's edge.

Strathpeffer

POP 1100

Strathpeffer is a charming old Highland spa town, with creaking pavilions and grandiose hotels dripping with faded grandeur. It rose to prominence during Victorian times, when the fashionable flocked here in huge numbers to bathe in, wash with and drink the sulphurous waters. The tourist influx led to the construction of grand buildings and architectural follies.

◉ Sights & Activities

There are many good signposted walking trails around Strathpeffer.

Highland Museum of Childhood MUSEUM
(☑01997-421031; www.highlandmuseumofchildhood.org.uk; Old Train Station; adult/child £3/1.75; ⊙10am-5pm Mon-Sat Apr-Oct; 🖐) Strathpeffer's former train station houses a wide range of social-history displays about childhood and also has activities for children, including a dressing-up box and toy train. In the complex there's also a gift shop to buy presents for a little somebody and a peaceful cafe. Call for hours during winter, as it does open on some days.

**Spa Pavilion &
Upper Pump Room** HISTORIC BUILDING
(☑01997-420124; www.strathpefferpavilion.org; Golf Course Rd; ⊙Pump Room 10am-5pm Jun-Aug, 10am-5pm Tue-Thu & Sat, 1-5pm Mon, Fri & Sun Sep-Dec & Mar-May) **FREE** In Strathpeffer's heyday, the Pavilion was the social centre and venue for dances, lectures and concerts. These days it's a renovated performing-arts venue. The neighbouring Upper Pump Room has some splendid displays showing the bizarre lengths Victorians went to for a healthy glow. There are also local art exhibitions, as well as artisanal sweets and tourist information in the friendly shop. Opening hours vary.

Eagle Stone ARCHAEOLOGICAL SITE
The Eagle Stone is well worth a look. It's a pre-7th-century Pictish stone connected to a figure from local history – the Brahan Seer, who predicted many future events. The impressive carved eagle is topped by an arc dotted with symbols. It's a short, well-signposted stroll from the centre of town.

🛏 Sleeping & Eating

★ Craigvar B&B ££
(☑01997-421622; www.craigvar.com; The Square; r £105; 🅿🛜) Luxury living with a refined touch is what you'll find in this delightful Georgian house in Strathpeffer's heart. Classy little extras are all here, including a welcome drink, Highland-Belgian chocolates, bathrobes, mini-fridges and fresh fruit. The owners offer wonderfully genuine hospitality with guest comfort paramount. The two light, elegant rooms are great, with fabulous modern bathrooms and thoughtful extras.

Beds are extremely comfortable and the downstairs lounge area is very elegant and commodious. The gourmet breakfasts, with lots of fish options, are a real highlight. It's hard to conceive how this place could improve, yet every time we visit it has done just that. A standout.

Coul House Hotel HOTEL £££
(☑01997-421487; www.coulhousehotel.com; Contin; s £172-236, d £215-295; 🅿@🛜🐾) 🐾 At Contin, south of Strathpeffer on the A835, Coul House dates from 1821 but has a light, airy feel in contrast to many country houses of this vintage. It's family run, and very cordial. Beautiful dining and lounge areas are complemented by elegant rooms with views over the lovely gardens; superiors look up the glen to the mountains beyond.

There's a fairy trail in the garden, forest paths for walking or mountain biking right on the doorstep, and a good restaurant. You can often find lower prices or multiday offers on the website.

Red Poppy
BISTRO ££

(☑ 01997-423332; www.redpoppyrestaurant.co.uk; Main Rd; mains £12-19; ⊙ 11.30am-9pm Tue-Sat, 12.30-4pm Sun; 🛜) On the main road opposite the spa buildings, this is comfortably Strathpeffer's best eating establishment. The casual modern interior with its bright red chairs is the venue for confident, well-presented dishes covering game and other classic British ingredients. It's a little cheaper at lunchtime, when set-price menus are available, and for traditional hot-meal high teas from 5pm.

❶ Getting There & Away

Stagecoach (☑ 01463-233371; www.stage coachbus.com) operates from Inverness to Strathpeffer (£5.45, 45 minutes, hourly Monday to Saturday, five on Sunday) via Dingwall (£2, 15 minutes). Services from Inverness to Gairloch and Durness, plus some buses from Inverness to Ullapool, also drop in.

Tain
POP 3700

Scotland's oldest royal burgh, Tain is a proud sandstone town that rose to prominence as pilgrims descended to venerate the relics of St Duthac, who is commemorated by the 12th-century ruins of St Duthac's Chapel, and St Duthus Church. It makes a fine stop on the way north.

Glenmorangie
DISTILLERY

(☑ 01862-892477; www.glenmorangie.com; tours £7.50; ⊙ tours 10am-4pm Jun-Aug, 10am-3pm Mon-Sat Apr-May & Sep-Oct, 10am & 2pm Mon-Fri Nov-Mar) Located on Tain's northern outskirts, Glenmorangie (emphasis on the second syllable) produces a fine lightish malt, subjected to a number of different cask finishes for variation. The tour is less in-depth than some but finishes with a free dram. There's a more comprehensive Signet tour (£35) and, for real whisky geeks, a full-day Heritage Tour (£130, April to October).

Tain Through Time
MUSEUM

(☑ 01862-894089; www.tainmuseum.org.uk; Tower St; adult/child £3.50/2.50, museum only £1.50/50p; ⊙ 10am-5pm Mon-Fri Apr-Oct, plus Sat Jun-Aug) Set in the grounds of St Duthus Church is Tain Through Time, an entertaining heritage centre with a colourful and educational display on St Duthac, King James IV and key moments in Scottish history. Another building focuses on the town's fine

---

THE RIGHT SIDE OF THE TRACKS

Sleeperzzz (☑ 01408-641343; www.sleeperzzz.com; Rogart; dm £18-20, s/tw £30/54, d with bathroom £69; ⊙ Mar-Oct; 🅿🛜) is an unusual hostel is set in three caringly converted railway carriages, an old bus and a beautiful wooden caravan parked in a siding by Rogart station. The carriages contain cute two-person bedrooms, kitchenettes and tiny lounges. There's also a B&B in the former waiting room, now an en suite chamber with kitchen; light breakfast is supplied. The hostel is run on sustainable lines.

It's on the A839, 11 miles east of Lairg, but is also easily reached by train on the Inverness–Wick line (£1 discount if you arrive this way or by bike). There's beautifully lonely Highland scenery in the vicinity and a local pub doing food (whose future was in some doubt at the time of research).

---

silversmithing tradition and this is also a centre for Clan Ross. Admission includes an audio-guided walk around town.

Platform 1864
BISTRO ££

(☑ 01862-894181; 1 Station Rd; mains £11-16; ⊙ food noon-3pm & 5-9.30pm, to 8pm Nov-Feb; 🛜🍴) ❂ Real love has gone into this excellent restoration of Tain's train station building, which has become a handsome wood-clad bar and restaurant, open all day. The menu features hearty, bar-style fare with a few flourishes. The enthusiastic owner and a beer garden make it a fine place to drop by for a drink or coffee at any time, too.

Bonar Bridge & Around

While the main road north crosses Dornoch Firth near Tain, an alternative scenic route brings you to the almost-joined villages of Ardgay and Bonar Bridge. This is an area worth exploring, with reminders of the Clearances, fine old-growth forest and good scope for outdoor activities. The A836 to Lairg branches west at Bonar Bridge.

Croick
VILLAGE

From Ardgay, a single-track road leads 10 miles up Strathcarron to Croick, the scene of notorious evictions during the

1845 Clearances. You can still see the evocative messages scratched by refugee crofters from Glencalvie on the eastern windows of Croick Church.

Kyle of Sutherland Trails   MOUNTAIN BIKING
(0300-067-6850; www.scotland.forestry.gov.uk/visit/balblair) At Balblair, a mile from Bonar Bridge off the Lairg road, there are two mountain-biking trails. A two-mile blue trail winds through the forest, while a 4.5-mile black track will test expert bikers with a stiff climb and an adrenalin-surging rock-slab descent.

Alladale Wilderness Reserve   LODGE £££
(01863-755338; www.alladale.com; Ardgay; self-catering per week from £1200, r with full board Oct-May £213-340; P) In deep wilderness near Croick, this lodge is part of a notable rewilding project. The main lodge (which includes meals) is, in summer, for entire hire only (it sleeps 12 to 14). Individual rooms are available in low season. Smaller buildings – a farmhouse and cottages – accommodate up to four on a self-catering basis. The scope for outdoor activity here is superb.

Crannag   BISTRO ££
(01863-766111; www.crannag.com; Bonar Bridge; mains £12-19; 6-8.30pm Tue-Sat;) This likeable Highland bistro in Bonar Bridge is our favourite eating establishment in the area.

Lairg & Around
POP 900

Lairg is an attractive village, although the tranquillity can be rudely interrupted by the sound of military jets roaring overhead (the valley is frequently used by the RAF for low-flying exercises). Located at the southern end of Loch Shin, it's a remote but important Highlands crossroad, gateway to central Sutherland's remote mountains and loch-speckled bogs.

Falls of Shin   WATERFALL
(www.facebook.com/fallsofshin; visitor centre approx 10am-3pm late Oct-Feb, 9am-8pm Mar-late Oct;) FREE Four miles south of Lairg, the picturesque Falls of Shin provide one of the best places in the Highlands to see salmon leaping on their way upstream to spawn (June to September). A short, easy footpath leads to a viewing terrace overlooking the waterfall; there are waymarked forest trails here. There's also a gift shop and a pleasant community-run cafe in a salmon-shaped structure, with information panels on the fish.

★ Pier Café   CAFE, BISTRO £
(01549-402971; www.pier-cafe-co.uk; Lochside, Lairg; lunch mains £8-11; 10am-4pm Mon-Sat, plus 5.30-9pm Fri & Sat, 10am-6pm Sun;) A very worthwhile stop, this bustling cafe by the loch has pleasant views, art exhibitions on the walls and real flair. Great chalkboard specials augment a Mediterranean-influenced bistro menu that draws on local produce. The coffee is the best for some distance around and the cafe is licensed. There's a little craft shop too.

Dornoch
POP 1200

On the northern shore of Dornoch Firth, 2 miles off the A9, this attractive old market town, all elegant sandstone, is one of the east coast's most pleasant settlements. Dornoch is best known for its championship golf course, but there's a fine cathedral among other noble buildings. Other historical oddities: the last witch to be executed in Scotland was boiled alive in hot tar here in 1722 and Madonna married Guy Ritchie here in 2000.

◉ Sights & Activities

Have a walk along Dornoch's golden-sand beach, which stretches for miles. South of Dornoch, seals are often visible on the sandbars of Dornoch Firth.

Dornoch Cathedral   CHURCH
(www.dornoch-cathedral.com; St Gilbert St; 9am-7pm or later) FREE Consecrated in the 13th century, beautiful Dornoch Cathedral, one of the Highlands' loveliest churches, is an elegant Gothic edifice with an interior softly illuminated through modern stained-glass windows. The controversial first Duke of Sutherland, whose wife restored the church in the 1830s, lies in a sealed burial vault beneath the chancel.

By the western door is the sarcophagus of Sir Richard de Moravia, who died fighting the Danes at the battle of Embo in the 1260s. Until then, the battle had been going rather well for him; he'd managed to slay the Danish commander with the unattached leg of a horse that was to hand.

Royal Dornoch GOLF

(☑ 01862-810219; www.royaldornoch.com; Golf Rd; summer green fee £160) Royal Dornoch is one of Scotland's most famous links, described by Tom Watson as 'the most fun I ever had playing golf'. It's public, and you can book a slot online. Twilight rates are the most economical. A golf pass (www.dornochfirthgolf. co.uk) lets you play several courses in the area at a good discount.

🛏 Sleeping & Eating

★2 Quail B&B ££

(☑ 01862-811811; www.2quail.com; Castle St; r £120-130; 🐾) Intimate and upmarket, 2 Quail offers a warm main-street welcome. Tasteful, spacious chambers are full of old-world comfort, with sturdy metal bed frames, plenty of books and plump duvets. The downstairs guest lounge is an absolute delight, while the guest dinners (two/three courses £22/27) are a treat, as one of the owners is a noted chef. It's best to book ahead.

Dornoch Castle Hotel HOTEL £££

(☑ 01862-810216; www.dornochcastlehotel.com; Castle St; s/d £75/135, superior/deluxe d £185/260; 🅿🐾) This 16th-century former bishop's palace makes a wonderful place to stay. Standard rooms are compact but comfortable, although this is a spot to splash out on an upgrade. Spacious castle rooms come with a rustic Scottish feel, views, sherry and chocolates on the welcome tray; the two Deluxe rooms are unforgettable: you'll feel like a monarch in your own castle.

Add to this the convivial bar and restaurant and helpful staff and you have a very impressive package.

Courthouse Cafe CAFE £

(☑ 01862-811632; www.thecarnegiecourthouse. co.uk; Castle St; mains £7-11; 🕘 9am-5pm Apr-Oct, 10am-4pm Nov-Mar; 🐾) Beautifully set in the former town courtroom, this is an atmospheric upstairs spot for a coffee or lunch, with a range of attractive wooden tables, comfortable armchairs and other places to perch.

Luigi ITALIAN, CAFE ££

(☑ 01862-810893; www.luigidornoch.com; Castle St; lunch £7-12, dinner mains £16-21; 🕘 10am-5pm daily, plus 6.45-9pm Fri & Sat Mar-Oct, daily Jul & Aug; 🐾) The clean lines of this contemporary Italian-American cafe make a break from the omnipresent heritage and history of the coastline. Ciabattas and salads stuffed with tasty deli ingredients make it a good lunch stop; more elaborate dinners usually include fine seafood choices. The coffee is the best in town.

❶ Information

Carnegie Courthouse (☑ 01862-811632; www.thecarnegiecourthouse.co.uk; Castle St; 🕘 9am-5pm) There's visitor information downstairs in the old courthouse. Winter opening times are restricted.

❶ Getting There & Away

There are buses roughly hourly from Inverness (£12.05, 1¼ hours), with some services continuing north to Wick or Thurso.

Golspie

POP 1400

Golspie is a pretty little village most visited for nearby Dunrobin Castle. It's a congenial place to stop for a night or two, with good facilities and a pleasant beach.

There are several good local walks, including the classic 3.75-mile (return) hike that climbs steeply to the summit of Ben Bhraggie (394m), crowned by a massive monument to the Duke of Sutherland, notorious for his leading role in the Highland Clearances.

On the same slopes, Highland Wildcat (www.highlandwildcat.com; per day £3; 🕘 dawn-dusk) offers excellent mountain biking.

★ Dunrobin Castle CASTLE

(☑ 01408-633177; www.dunrobincastle.co.uk; A9; adult/child £11.50/7; 🕘 10.30am-4.30pm Apr, May & Oct, 10am-5pm Jun-Sep) Magnificent Dunrobin Castle, a mile past Golspie, is the Highlands' largest house. Although it dates to 1275, most of what you see was built in French style between 1845 and 1850. A home of the dukes of Sutherland, it's richly furnished and offers an intriguing insight into the aristocratic lifestyle. The beautiful castle inspires mixed feelings locally; it was once the seat of the first Duke of Sutherland, notorious for some of the cruellest episodes of the Highland Clearances.

The duke's estate was, at over 6000 sq km, the largest privately owned area of land in Europe. He evicted around 15,000 people from their homes to make way for sheep.

The classic fairy-tale castle is adorned with towers and turrets, but only 22 of its 187 rooms are on display, with hunting trophies much to the fore. Beautiful formal gardens, where impressive falconry displays take place two or three times a day, extend down to the sea. In the gardens is a museum with an eclectic mix of archaeological finds, natural-history exhibits, more non-PC animal remains and an excellent collection of Pictish stones.

⊙ Getting There & Away

Trains (£19.90, 2¼ hours) and buses (£12.05, 1½ hours) from Inverness towards Wick/Thurso stop in Golspie and at Dunrobin Castle.

Helmsdale

POP 700

Surrounded by hills whose gorse explodes mad yellow in springtime, this sheltered fishing town, like many spots on the east coast, was a major emigration point during the Clearances and also a booming herring port. It's surrounded by stunning, undulating coastline, and the River Helmsdale is one of the best salmon rivers in the Highlands.

Timespan MUSEUM

(☑ 01431-821327; www.timespan.org.uk; Dunrobin St; adult/child £4/2; ⊙ 10am-5pm Easter-Oct, 2-4pm Tue, 10am-3pm Sat & Sun Nov-Easter) In the heart of Helmsdale, this heritage centre has an impressive display covering local history, including a Pictish stone, the Clearances, the fishing industry and the 1869 gold rush; look out also for the impressive audiovisual content. Up the back are recreations of a traditional croft house, smithy, shop and byre. There are also local art exhibitions upstairs, a geology garden and a cafe.

CAITHNESS

Once you pass Helmsdale, you are entering Caithness, a place of jagged gorse-and-grass-topped cliffs hiding tiny fishing harbours. Scotland's top corner was once Viking territory, historically more connected to Orkney and Shetland than the rest of the mainland. It's a mystical, ancient land dotted with old monuments and peopled by folk who are proud of their Norse heritage.

CROFTING & THE CLEARANCES

The wild empty spaces of the northern Highlands are among Europe's least populated regions, but this wasn't always so. Ruins of cottages in desolate areas are mute witnesses to one of the most heartless episodes of Scottish history: the Highland Clearances.

Until the 19th century the most common form of farming settlement here was the *baile*, a group of a dozen or so families who farmed the land granted to them by the local chieftain in return for military service and a portion of the harvest. The arable land was divided into strips called *rigs*, which were allocated to different families by annual ballot so that each took turns at getting the poorer soils; this system was known as *runrig*. The families worked the land communally and their cattle shared grazing land.

After the Battle of Culloden, however, the king banned private armies and new laws made the clan chiefs actual owners of their traditional lands, often vast tracts of territory. With the prospect of unimagined riches allied to a depressing failure of imagination, the lairds decided that sheep were more profitable than agriculture and proceeded to evict tens of thousands of farmers. These desperate folk were forced to head for the cities in the hope of finding work or to emigrate to the Americas or the southern hemisphere. Those who stayed were forced to eke out a living from narrow plots of marginal agricultural land, often close to the coast. This form of smallholding became known as crofting. The small patch of land barely provided a living and had to be supplemented by other work such as fishing and kelp-gathering. It was always precarious, as rights were granted on a year-by-year basis, so at any moment a crofter could lose not only the farm but also the house they'd built on it.

The late 19th-century economic depression meant many couldn't pay their rent. This time, however, they resisted expulsion, instead forming the Highland Land Reform Association and their own political party. Their resistance led the government to accede to several demands, including security of tenure, fair rents and eventually the supply of land for new crofts. Crofters now have the right to purchase their farmland and 2004 laws finally abolished the feudal system, which created so much misery.

Helmsdale to Lybster

This spectacular stretch of coast follows the folds of the undulating landscape through villages established on the shoreline when communities were evicted from the interior in the Highland Clearances in the early 19th century.

The village of Dunbeath is spectacularly set in a deep glen. Lybster is a purpose-built fishing village dating from 1810, with a stunning harbour area surrounded by grassy cliffs. In its heyday, it was Scotland's third-busiest port. Things have changed – now there are only a couple of boats – but there are several interesting prehistoric sites in the area.

Grey Cairns of Camster   ARCHAEOLOGICAL SITE
(⊘24hr) FREE Dating from between 4000 BC and 2500 BC, these burial chambers are hidden in long, low mounds rising from an evocatively lonely moor. The Long Cairn measures 60m by 21m. You can enter the main chamber, but must first crawl into the well-preserved Round Cairn, which has a corbelled ceiling. From a turn-off a mile east of Lybster on the A99, the cairns are 4 miles north. You can continue 7 further miles to approach Wick on the A882.

Whaligoe Steps   HISTORIC SITE
(⊘24hr) FREE At Ulbster, 5 miles north of Lybster, this staircase cut into the cliff provides access to a tiny natural harbour, with an ideal grassy picnic spot, ringed by vertical cliffs and echoing with the cackle of nesting fulmars. The path begins at the end of the minor road opposite the road signposted 'Cairn of Get'. There's a cafe (☑01955-651702; www.whaligoesteps.co.uk; Ulbster; light meals £6-12; ⊘10.30am-5.30pm Thu-Sun mid-Mar–Sep, 11am-5pm Sat & Sun Oct-Dec) at the top.

Wick

POP 7100

Wick is worth a visit, particularly for its excellent museum and attractive, spruced-up harbour area, and it has some very good places to stay. More gritty than pretty, however, it's been a little down on its luck since the collapse of the herring industry. It was once the world's largest fishing port for the 'silver darlings', but when the market dropped off after WWII, job losses were huge and the town hasn't ever totally recovered.

◉ Sights & Activities

★**Wick Heritage Centre**   MUSEUM
(☑01955-605393; www.wickheritage.org; 20 Bank Row; adult/child £4/50p; ⊘10am-5pm Apr-Oct, last entry 3.45pm) Tracking the rise and fall of the herring industry, this great town museum displays everything from fishing equipment to complete herring boats. It's absolutely huge inside, and is crammed with memorabilia and extensive displays describing Wick's heyday in the mid-19th century. The Johnston collection is the star exhibit. From 1863 to 1977, three generations photographed everything that happened around Wick and the 70,000 photographs are an amazing record.

Old Pulteney   DISTILLERY
(☑01955-602371; www.oldpulteney.com; Huddart St; tours £10; ⊘10am-4pm Mon-Fri Oct-Apr, 10am-5pm Mon-Fri, 10am-4pm Sat May-Sep) Though it can no longer claim to be the most northerly whisky distillery on mainland Scotland (that goes to the upstart Wolfburn in Thurso), friendly Pulteney still runs excellent tours twice or more daily (normally at 11am and 2pm), with more expensive visits available for aficionados. Their Stroma whisky liqueur is dangerously more-ish.

Caithness Seacoast   BOATING
(☑01955-609200; www.caithness-seacoast.co.uk; South Quay; ⊘Apr-Oct) This outfit will take you out to sea to inspect the rugged coastline of the northeast. Various options include a half-hour jaunt (adult/child £19/12), a 1½-hour tour (£30/22) and a three-hour return trip down to Lybster (£50/39).

🛏 Sleeping & Eating

Bank Guesthouse   B&B ££
(☑01955-604001; www.guesthousewick.co.uk; 28 Bridge St; s £50-60, d £75-85; P ✿) In the very centre of Wick, this striking Victorian building contains a warmly welcoming B&B run by a local family. Rooms have plenty of space and feature attractive carpets, wallpaper and fabrics along with modern bathrooms with great showers. Breakfast is well above average. Stairs might be a problem for the less mobile.

Mackays Hotel   HOTEL ££
(☑01955-602323; www.mackayshotel.co.uk; Union St; s/d £93/129; ✿) Hospitable Mackays is Wick's best hotel by a long stretch. Attractive, mostly refurbished rooms vary in layout and size, so ask to see a few;

NORTHERN HIGHLANDS & ISLANDS HELMSDALE TO LYBSTER

prices are usually lower than the rack rates. On-site **No 1 Bistro** (mains £17-24; ⊙ noon-2pm & 5-9pm; 🔊) is a fine option for lunch or dinner. The world's shortest street, 2.06m-long Ebenezer Place, is one side of the hotel.

Guests get free use of a local gym and pool. The hotel also has some self-catering apartments and town houses nearby.

Bord de l'Eau FRENCH ££

(📮 01955-604400; 2 Market St; mains £16-24; ⊙ noon-2pm & 6-9pm Tue-Sat, 6-9pm Sun) This serene, relaxed French restaurant is Wick's best place to eat. It overlooks the river and serves a changing menu of mostly meat and game French classics, backed up by daily fish specials. Starters are great value, and mains include a huge assortment of vegetables. The conservatory dining room with water views is lovely on a sunny evening.

ℹ️ Information

Wick Tourist Office (📮 01955-602547; 66 High St; ⊙ 9am-5.30pm Mon-Sat) Upstairs in McAllans Clothing Store. Has a good selection of information.

ℹ️ Getting There & Away

AIR

Wick is a Caithness transport gateway. Loganair flies to Edinburgh and Flybe/Eastern Airways to Aberdeen (three daily, Monday to Friday).

BUS

Stagecoach and Citylink operate to/from Inverness (£20.15, three hours, six daily) and Stagecoach to Thurso (£3.90, 40 minutes, hourly). There's also connecting service to John O'Groats and Gills Bay (£3.60, 30 minutes, four to five Monday to Saturday) for the passenger and car ferries to Orkney.

TRAIN

Trains service Wick from Inverness (£21.10, 4¼ hours, four daily Monday to Saturday, one on Sunday).

John O'Groats

POP 300

Though not the northernmost point of the British mainland (that's Dunnet Head), John O'Groats still serves as the end point of the 874-mile trek from Land's End in Cornwall, a popular if arduous route for cyclists and walkers, many of whom raise money for charitable causes. Most of the settlement is taken up by a stylish modern self-catering complex. There's a passenger ferry from here to Orkney.

Duncansby Head VIEWPOINT

Two miles east of John O'Groats, Duncansby Head has a small lighthouse and 60m-high cliffs sheltering nesting fulmars. A 15-minute walk through a sheep paddock yields spectacular views of the sea-surrounded monoliths known as Duncansby Stacks.

Wildlife Cruises BOATING

(📮 01955-611353; www.jogferry.co.uk; adult/child £18/9; ⊙ mid-Jun–Aug) The friendly folk who run the Orkney ferry also have 1½-hour wildlife cruises to the island of Stroma or Duncansby Head. There are also **day tours** (⊙ May-Sep) of Orkney available.

ℹ️ Information

John O'Groats Tourist Office (📮 01955-611373; joginfor@btconnect.com; ⊙ 10am-4pm Nov-Apr, to 5pm May & Sep-Oct, 9am-6pm Jun-Aug) This locally run tourist office at the John O'Groats car park is helpful and, as well as information and souvenirs, has a fine selection of local novels and nonfiction titles.

ℹ️ Getting There & Away

Stagecoach (www.stagecoachbus.com) runs between John O'Groats and Wick (£3.60, 30 minutes, four to five Monday to Saturday) or Thurso (£4.25, 40 minutes, five to eight Monday to Saturday).

From May to September, a passenger ferry (p400) shuttles across to Burwick in Orkney. Three miles west, a car ferry (p400) runs all year from Gills Bay to St Margaret's Hope in Orkney.

Mey

POP 200

West of John O'Groats, the small village of Mey has a major drawcard for lovers of the Royal Family in its pretty castle, formerly a residence of the Queen Mother.

Castle of Mey CASTLE

(📮 01847-851473; www.castleofmey.org.uk; adult/child £11.75/6.50; ⊙ 10.20am-5pm May-Sep, last entry 4pm) The Castle of Mey, a big crowd-puller for its Queen Mother connections, is 6 miles west of John O'Groats. The exterior is grand but inside it feels domestic and everything is imbued with the Queen Mum's character. The highlight is the genteel guided tour, with various anecdotes recounted by staff who once worked for her. In the grounds there's a farm zoo, an unusual walled garden that's worth a stroll and lovely views over the Pentland Firth.

The castle normally closes for a couple of weeks at the end of July for royal visits; Prince Charles often comes here in summer. There may also be limited April openings; check the website.

★**Mey House**   B&B £££
(☑ 01847-851852; www.meyhouse.co.uk; East Mey; r £139; ☺ Easter–mid-Oct; P ☎) Beautifully situated among green fields running down to water and with majestic views of Orkney, Dunnet Head and the nearby Castle of Mey, this modern top-drawer sleep is a welcoming, sumptuous place to stay. They've thought it all through: the huge, luxurious rooms have arty designer decor, excellent custom-made beds, Nespresso machines, flatscreen TVs, sound bar and stunning modern bathrooms.

Breakfast comes with a view. The friendly owners offer free transfers to the Gills Bay ferry and can set you up with tours on Orkney. No toddlers are allowed, as there's an interior balcony. There's a minimum two-night stay.

Thurso & Scrabster

POP 7600

Britain's most northerly mainland town, Thurso makes a handy overnight stop if you're heading west or across to Orkney. There's a pretty town beach, riverside strolls and a good museum. Ferries for Orkney leave from Scrabster, 2.5 miles away.

◉ Sights & Activities

Thurso is an unlikely surfing centre but the nearby coast has arguably the best and most regular surf on mainland Britain. There's an excellent right-hand reef break on the eastern side of town, directly in front of the castle (closed to the public), and another shallow reef break 5 miles west at Brimms Ness. You'll want to wear 6mm cover outside the summer season. Conditions are best in autumn.

Caithness Horizons   MUSEUM
(☑ 01847-896508; www.caithnesshorizons.co.uk; High St; adult/child £4/2; ☺10am-4pm Tue-Sat Nov-Mar, 10am-5pm Tue-Sat Apr-Oct) This museum brings Caithness history and lore to life through excellent displays. Fine Pictish cross-slabs greet visitors downstairs; the main exhibition is a wide-ranging look

---

WORTH A TRIP

DUNNET HEAD

Eight miles east of Thurso a minor road leads to dramatic **Dunnet Head**, the most northerly point on the British mainland. There are majestic cliffs dropping into the turbulent Pentland Firth, inspiring views of Orkney, basking seals and nesting seabirds below (it's an RSPB reserve), and a lighthouse built by Robert Louis Stevenson's grandad. Two cottages are available for rent (see www.dunnetheadlighthouse.com).

at local history using plenty of audiovisuals. There's also a gallery space, an exhibition on the Dounreay nuclear reactor, tourist information and a cafe.

🛏 Sleeping & Eating

Sandra's Backpackers   HOSTEL £
(☑ 01847-894575; www.sandras-backpackers. co.uk; 24 Princes St; dm/d/f £18/42/65; P @ ☎) In the heart of town, this budget backpacker option has en suite dorms, mostly four-berthers with aged mattresses, a spacious kitchen and traveller-friendly facilities such as help-yourself cereals and toast. It's not luxurious but it's a reliable cheap sleep.

★**Pennyland House**   B&B ££
(☑ 01847-891194; www.pennylandhouse.co.uk; A9; s £80, d £90-100; P ☎ ✹) A super conversion of a historic house, this is a standout B&B choice. It offers phenomenal value for this level of accommodation, with huge oak-furnished rooms named after golf courses: we especially loved St Andrews – super-spacious, with a great chessboard-tiled bathroom. Hospitality is enthusiastic and helpful, and there's an inviting breakfast space, garden and terraced area with views across to Hoy.

Two-night minimum stay in summer.

Camfield House   B&B ££
(☑ 01847-891118; www.riversideaccommodation. co.uk; Janet St; r £125-145; P ☎) A Narnia-style portal leads from central Thurso through a gate and you're suddenly in what feels like an opulent rural estate. The garden is sumptuous and extravagantly features a manicured par-3 golf hole, complete with bunker and water hazard. The interior lacks nothing by comparison, with spacious rooms with huge TVs, quality linen and excellent bathrooms. There's even a full-sized billiard table.

NORTHERN HIGHLANDS & ISLANDS THURSO & SCRABSTER

Marine B&B ££
(📞 01847-890676; www.themarinethurso.co.uk; 38 Shore St; s £75-90, d £85-100; 🅿🛜) Tucked away in Thurso's most appealing corner you'll find a top spot right by the pretty town beach, offering spectacular vistas over it and across to Orkney. Rooms are just fabulous, with a designer's touch and a subtle maritime feel, and surfers can study the breakers from the stunning conservatory lounge. Two rooms in the adjacent house make a great family option.

Forss House Hotel HOTEL £££
(📞 01847-861201; www.forsshousehotel.co.uk; s/d £125/175; 🅿🛜🐾) Tucked into trees 5 miles west of Thurso is this Georgian mansion offering elegant accommodation with both character and style. Sumptuous upstairs rooms are preferable to basement rooms as they have lovely garden views. There are also beautifully appointed suites in the garden itself, providing both privacy and tranquillity. Thoughtful extras like CDs and books in every room add appeal.

It's right alongside a beautiful salmon river and if you've had a chilly day in the waders, some 300 malt whiskies await in the hotel bar. There are some cheaper rooms available (d £135) also.

★ **Captain's Galley** SEAFOOD £££
(📞 01847-894999; www.captainsgalley.co.uk; Scrabster; 5-course dinner £53.50, with wine flight £77; ⏲ 6.30-9pm Thu-Sat) 🍴 Classy but friendly Captain's Galley, by the Scrabster ferry, offers a short, seafood-based menu featuring local and sustainably sourced produce prepared in delicious ways that let the natural flavours shine through. The chef picks the best fish off the local boats, and the menu describes exactly which fishing grounds your morsel came from. It's worth scheduling a night in Thurso to eat here.

ⓘ Information

The Caithness Horizons museum (p357) provides helpful local tourist information.

ⓘ Getting There & Away

BUS
Stagecoach/Citylink buses link Thurso/Scrabster with Inverness (£20.15, three hours, five daily). There are also buses roughly every hour to Wick (£3.90, 40 minutes), as well as every couple of hours to John O'Groats (£4.25, 40 minutes, five to eight Monday to Saturday).

TRAIN
There are four daily trains (one on Sunday) from Inverness (£21.10, 3¾ hours), with a connecting bus to Scrabster.

It's a 2-mile walk from Thurso train station to the ferry at Scrabster; there are buses from Olrig St.

NORTH & WEST COAST

Quintessential Highland country such as this, with breathtaking emptiness, a wild, fragile beauty and single-track roads, is a rarity on the modern, crowded, highly urbanised island of Britain. You could get lost up here for weeks – and that still wouldn't be enough time.

Carving its way from Thurso to Glencoul, the north and northwest coastline is a feast of deep inlets, forgotten beaches and surging peninsulas. Within the rugged confines, the interior is home to vast, empty spaces, enormous lochs and some of Scotland's highest peaks.

Whether in blazing sunshine or murky greyness, the character of the land is totally unique and constantly changing – for that window of time in which you can glimpse it, you'll capture an exclusive snapshot of this ancient area in your mind. Park the car and gaze. This northernmost slab of the Highlands is the stuff of coastal-drive dreams.

Thurso to Durness

It's 80 winding – and utterly spectacular – coastal miles from Thurso to Durness.

Ten miles west of Thurso, the Dounreay nuclear power station was the first in the world to supply mains electricity; it's currently being decommissioned. The clean-up is planned to be finished by 2025; it's still a major source of employment for the region.

Beyond, Melvich overlooks a fine beach and there are great views from Strathy Point (a 2-mile drive from the coast road, then a 15-minute walk).

Bettyhill is a pretty village that overlooks a magnificent stretch of coastline, and the scenery just improves as you head west through Coldbackie and Tongue, with a succession of gorgeous sea lochs, stunning beaches and striking rock formations backed by imposing hills and mountains.

Bettyhill

POP 500

Bettyhill is a crofting community of resettled tenant farmers kicked off their land during the Clearances. The spectacular panorama of a sweeping, sandy beach backed by velvety green hills with rocky outcrops makes a sharp contrast to that sad history.

Strathnaver Museum   MUSEUM
(✎ 01641-521418; www.strathnavermuseum.org.uk; adult/child £2/1; ⊙ 10am-5pm Mon-Sat Apr-Oct) Housed in an old church, this museum tells the sad story of the Strathnaver Clearances through posters created by local kids. The museum contains memorabilia of Clan Mackay, various items of crofting equipment and a 'St Kilda mailboat', a small wooden boat-shaped container bearing a letter that was used by St Kildans to send messages to the mainland.

Outside the back door of the church is the **Farr Stone**, a fine carved Pictish cross-slab.

Bettyhill Hotel   INN **££**
(✎ 01641-521202; www.bettyhillhotel.com; s/d without bathroom £60/90, d with bathroom £140; ⊙ Apr-Oct, check for winter opening; P🛜🐾) This historic hotel has a fabulous position overlooking the marvellous perspective of the sandy beach fringing Torrisdale Bay. The owners have been doing a great renovation and the excellent updated rooms are bright, with top-grade mattresses. Rooms come in many different types (some have super views), with lots of singles as well as a cottage. Bar and restaurant meals are available.

★ **Côte du Nord**   MODERN SCOTTISH **£££**
(✎ 01641-521773; www.cotedunord.co.uk; The School House, Kirtomy; degustation £35-45; ⊙ 7.30pm Wed, Fri & Sat Apr-Sep; ✎) 🐾 Brilliantly innovative cuisine, wonderfully whimsical presentation and an emphasis on local ingredients are the highlights of the excellent gastronomic degustation menu here. It's an unlikely spot to find such a gourmet experience; the chef is none other than the local GP who forages for wild herbs and flavours in between surgery hours. Top value. It's tiny, so reserve well ahead.

Kirtomy is signposted off the main road about 2.5 miles east of Bettyhill; the restaurant is about a mile down this road.

NORTH COAST 500

The drive along Scotland's far northern coastline is one of Europe's finest road trips. Words fail to describe the sheer variety of the scenic splendour, which unfolds before you as you cross this empty landscape that combines desolate moorlands, brooding mountains, fertile coastal meadows and stunning white-sand beaches.

In a clever piece of recent marketing, it's been dubbed the **North Coast 500**, as the round-trip from Inverness is roughly that many miles, though you'll surely clock up a few more if you follow your heart down narrow byroads and seek perfect coastal vistas at the end of dead-end tracks.

In our opinion, the scenery is best viewed by taking the route anticlockwise, heading north from Inverness up the east coast to Caithness, then turning west across the top of Scotland before descending down the west coast. This way, you'll make the most of the coastal vistas, the light and the awesome backdrop of the Assynt mountains.

Much of the drive is along single-track road, so it's important to pull over to let both oncoming vehicles and faster traffic behind you pass. Though Inverness companies hire out prestige sports cars for the journey, these really aren't roads where you want to open the throttle; a lazy pace with plenty of photo stops makes for the best journey. It's worth taking several days to do it; in fact you could easily spend a week between Inverness and Ullapool, stopping off for leisurely seafood lunches, tackling some emblematic hills, detouring down valleys to explore the legacy of the Clearances or daring a dip in the North Sea.

While the drive hasn't actually changed, the new name has caught the imagination of tourists, so visitor numbers are well up. The villages along the way aren't overstocked with accommodation, so it's well worth reserving everything in advance if you're travelling the route in the spring or summer months. In winter lots of accommodation is closed so it's a good idea to book then too.

FORSINARD & STRATHNAVER

Though it's tough to tear yourself away from the coast, we recommend plunging down the A897 just east of Melvich. After 14 miles you reach the railway at **Forsinard**. On the platform is **Forsinard Flows Visitor Centre** (☎ 01641-571225; www.rspb.org.uk; Forsinard; ☺ visitor centre 9am-5pm Apr-Oct, trails open all year) FREE, a small nature exhibition. There's a live hen-harrier cam, plus guided walks and 4WD excursions available – phone for dates. A 1-mile trail and an impressive viewing tower introduce you to the Flows peatland; 4 miles north is a 4-mile trail crossing golden plover and dunlin nesting grounds. The deep peat blanket bog is a rare and important habitat, at risk from climate change.

Past here, the epic peaty moorscapes stir the heart with their desolate beauty. Take a right at Kinbrace onto the B871, which covers more jaw-dropping scenery before arriving at Syre. Turn right to follow the Strathnaver (valley) back to the coast near Bettyhill. **Strathnaver** saw some of the worst of the Clearances; the **Strathnaver Trail** is a series of numbered points of interest along the valley relating to both this and various prehistoric sites.

Accommodation options on this lonely detour include **Cornmill Bunkhouse** (☎ 01641-571219; www.achumore.co.uk; A897; dm £15; ℗), a comfortable, modern hostel occupying a picturesque old mill on a working croft in the middle of nowhere; it's on the A897 4 miles south of the coast road. Turning left instead of right at Syre, you'll eventually reach the remote **Altnaharra Hotel** (☎ 01549-411222; www.altnaharra.com; Altnaharra; s £70, d £109-120, superior d £140-160; ☺ Mar-Dec; ℗ ⊚ ⊛).

ℹ Getting There & Away

From Monday to Friday, there's one daily bus from Bettyhill to Dounreay, which feeds services to Thurso (£3.40, 1¼ hours total). You can also get to Wick.

There are also one to two services with Far North Bus (p361) from Monday to Saturday to Tongue (£3.30, 35 minutes).

Durness

POP 400

Scattered Durness (www.durness.org) is wonderfully located, strung out along cliffs rising from a series of pristine beaches. When the sun shines, the effects of blinding white sand, the cry of seabirds and the spring-green-coloured seas combine in a magical way.

⊙ Sights & Activities

Walking the sensational sandy coastline is a highlight, as is a visit to **Cape Wrath**. Durness' beautiful beaches include **Rispond** to the east, **Sango Sands** below town and **Balnakeil** to the west. At Balnakeil, a craft village occupies a one-time early-warning radar station. A northerly beach walk leads to **Faraid Head**, where there are puffins in early summer.

Bikes can be hired from a shed on the square.

Smoo Cave   CAVE
(www.smoocave.org) FREE A mile east of the centre of Durness is a path down to Smoo Cave. From the vast main chamber, you can head through to a smaller flooded cavern where a waterfall sometimes cascades from the roof. There's evidence the cave was inhabited about 6000 years ago. You can take a **tour** (☎ 01971-511704; www.smoocavetours. weebly.com; adult/child £5/2; ☺ 11am-4pm Apr-May & Sep, 10am-5pm Jun-Aug) to explore a little further into the interior.

🛏 Sleeping

Sango Sands Oasis   CAMPSITE £
(☎ 07838 381065; www.sangosands.com; sites per adult/child £9/6, second child £3, others free; ℗ ⊚ ⊛) You couldn't imagine a better location for a campsite: great grassy areas on the edge of cliffs, descending to two lovely sandy beaches. Facilities are good and very clean and there's a pub next door. Electric hook-up is an extra £4. You can camp for £9 per site from November to March, but don't complain about the cold.

Lazy Crofter Bunkhouse   HOSTEL £
(☎ 01971-511202; www.visitdurness.com/bunkhouse; dm £20; ⊚) Durness' best budget accommodation is here, opposite the supermarket. A bothy vibe gives it a very Highland feel. Inviting dorms have plenty of room and lockers, and there's also a sociable shared table for

meals and board games, and a great wooden deck with sea views, perfect for midge-free evenings.

★**Mackays Rooms**　　　　　HOTEL **££**
(☑ 01971-511202; www.visitdurness.com; d standard £129, deluxe £149-159; ⊙ May-Oct; P 🛜 🐾) You really feel you're at the furthest corner of Scotland here, where the road turns through 90 degrees. But whether heading south or east, you'll go far before you find a better place to stay than this haven of Highland hospitality. With its big beds, soft fabrics and contemporary colours, it's a romantic spot with top service and numerous boutique details.

There's also a self-contained cabin here, which can be rented on a self-catering or B&B basis. With two rooms, it sleeps up to four.

Morven　　　　　　　　　B&B **££**
(☑ 01971-511252; morven69@hotmail.com; s/d £50/70; P 🛜 🐾) Cheery owners, a handy next-to-pub location and a serious border-collie theme are key features of this ultra-cosy place. Rooms, which are upstairs and share a downstairs bathroom, have been renovated and feel new and super-comfortable. One is especially spacious and has a top coastal vista.

Smoo Lodge　　　　　　　B&B **£££**
(☑ 01971-511423; www.smoolodge.co.uk; r £135-155; P 🛜) A sizeable former shooting lodge on ample grounds has been lovingly restored to a very high standard. Excellent rooms feature high-quality mattresses and bedding as well as great modern bathrooms. Asian-inflected evening meals are available, and breakfast features an excellent Korean option – a nice change from bacon and eggs. No under-12s.

✕ **Eating**

★**Cocoa Mountain**　　　　　CAFE **£**
(☑ 01971-511233; www.cocoamountain.co.uk; Balnakeil; hot chocolate £4, 10 truffles £10; ⊙ 9am-6pm Easter-Oct) 🅿 At the Balnakeil craft village, this upbeat cafe and chocolate maker offers handmade treats including a chilli, lemongrass and coconut white-chocolate truffle, plus many more unique flavours. Tasty espresso and hot chocolate warm the cockles on those blowy horizontal-drizzle days. It offers light lunches and home-baking too, plus chocolate-making workshops.

Smoo Cave Hotel　　　　PUB FOOD **££**
(☑ 01971-511227;　　　www.smoocavehotel.co.uk; mains £9-15; ⊙ kitchen 11.30am-9.30pm; 🛜) Signposted off the main road at the eastern end of Durness, this amiable local has quality bar food in hefty portions. Haddock or daily seafood specials – plump scallops are a highlight – are an obvious and worthwhile choice; there's also a restaurant area with clifftop views.

ℹ️ **Information**

Durness has full services, including an ATM, shops and petrol.

ℹ️ **Getting There & Away**

A year-round service with **Far North Bus** (☑ 07782 110007; www.thedurnessbus.com) heads to Lairg (£9, 2½ hours, Monday to Friday), where there is a train station. On Saturday buses head to Inverness (£13.40, three hours) and Thurso (£10.30, 2½ hours). In summer school holidays, there's also an Ullapool service (£10, 2½ hours). All these services should be booked; some have bicycle capacity.

There are also two Tuesday services with **Transport for Tongue** (☑ 01847-611766; www.transportfortongue.co.uk) between Tongue and Durness (£7, one hour).

Durness to Ullapool

Perhaps Scotland's most spectacular road, the 69 miles connecting Durness to Ullapool is a smorgasbord of dramatic scenery, almost too much to take in. From Durness you pass through a broad heathered valley with the looming grey bulk of Foinaven and Arkle to the southeast. Heather gives way to a rockier

WORTH A TRIP

SANDWOOD BAY

South of Cape Wrath, **Sandwood Bay** boasts one of Scotland's best and most isolated beaches, guarded at one end by the spectacular rock pinnacle Am Buachaille. Sandwood Bay is about 2 miles north of the end of a track from Blairmore (approach from Kinlochbervie), or you could walk south from the cape (allow eight hours) and on to Blairmore. Sandwood House is a creepy ruin reputedly haunted by the ghost of a 16th-century shipwrecked sailor from the Spanish Armada.

landscape of Lewisian gneiss pockmarked with hundreds of small lochans. This is the most interesting zone geologically in the UK, with Britain's oldest rock. Next come gorse-covered hills prefacing the magnificent Torridonian sandstone mountains of Assynt and Coigach, including Suilven's distinctive sugarloaf, ziggurat-like Quinag and pinnacled Stac Pollaidh. The area has been named as the **Northwest Highlands Geopark** (www.nwhgeopark.com).

Scourie & Handa Island

Scourie is a pretty crofting community with decent services, halfway between Durness and Ullapool. A few miles north lies Handa Island, a nature reserve run by the Scottish Wildlife Trust.

Handa Island
Nature Reserve   NATURE RESERVE

(www.scottishwildlifetrust.org.uk) A few miles north of Scourie Bay lies this nature reserve run by the Scottish Wildlife Trust. The island's western sea cliffs provide nesting sites for important breeding populations of great skuas, arctic skuas, puffins, kittiwakes, razorbills and guillemots. Reach the island from Tarbet, 6 miles north of Scourie, via the **Handa Island Ferry** ([☑] 07780 967800; www.handa-ferry.com; Tarbet Pier; adult/child return £15/5; ☺ outbound 9am-2pm Mon-Sat Apr-Aug, last ferry back 5pm); call for times and to book your spot.

★ Shorehouse Seafood
Restaurant   SEAFOOD **££**

([☑] 01971-502251; www.shorehousetarbet.co.uk; Tarbet Pier; mains £10-19; ☺ noon-7pm Mon-Sat Easter-Sep) By the ferry pier for Handa Island Nature Reserve, Shorehouse is a restaurant and cafe in a lovely setting, looking across the sound to the sandy beach on Handa Island. There's a conservatory and outdoor terrace that make the most of the view, and a menu that concentrates on local seafood including crab and prawn salads and Achiltibuie smoked salmon.

Kylesku & Loch Glencoul

Hidden away on the shores of Loch Glencoul, tiny Kylesku served as a ferry crossing on the route north until it was made redundant by beautiful Kylesku Bridge in 1984. It's a good base for walks; you can hire bikes too.

Eas a'Chual Aluinn   WATERFALL

Five miles southeast of Kylesku, in wild, remote country, lies 213m-high Eas a'Chual Aluinn, Britain's highest waterfall. You can hike to the top of the falls from a parking area at a sharp bend in the main road 3 miles south of Kylesku; allow five hours for the 6-mile return trip. It can also be seen on **boat trips** ([☑] 01971-502231; www.kyleskuboattours.com; adult/child £30/20; ☺ Apr-Sep) from Kylesku.

★ Kylesku Hotel   SEAFOOD **££**

([☑] 01971-502231; www.kyleskuhotel.co.uk; mains £12-23; ☺ noon-2.30pm & 6-9pm mid-Feb–Apr & Oct-Nov, noon-9pm May-Sep; ☎) ✎ In this remote lochside location, it's a real pleasure to gorge yourself on delicious sustainable seafood. Local langoustines, squat lobsters and mussels are the specialties at this convivial restaurant, that has a new extension offering extra waterview seating. There's a good atmosphere of mingling locals and visitors at the bar.

Lochinver & Assynt

With its otherworldly scenery of isolated peaks rising above a sea of crumpled, lochan-spattered gneiss, Assynt epitomises the northwest's wild magnificence. Glaciers have sculpted the hills of Suilven (731m), Canisp (846m), Quinag (808m) and Ben More Assynt (998m) into strange, wonderful silhouettes.

Lochinver is the main settlement, a busy little fishing port that's a popular port of call with its laid-back atmosphere, good facilities and striking scenery. Just north of Lochinver (or if coming from the north, not far south of Kylesku), a 23-mile detour on the narrow B869 rewards with spectacular views and fine beaches. From the lighthouse at Point of Stoer, a one-hour cliff walk leads to the Old Man of Stoer, a spectacular sea stack.

🏃 Activities

The limestone hills around Inchnadamph are famous for their caves. There's some excellent walking in the area.

NorWest Sea Kayaking   KAYAKING

([☑] 07900 641860; www.norwestseakayaking.com; half/full-day trip £55/85) This outfit offers introductory sea-kayaking courses and guided kayaking tours around the Summer Isles and in the Lochinver and Ullapool area. It also hires kayaks and will do pick-ups and drop-offs.

CAPE WRATH

Though its name actually comes from the Norse word *hvarf* ('turning point'), there is something daunting and primal about Cape Wrath, the remote northwesternmost point of the British mainland.

The danger of the hazardous, stormy seas led to the building of the lighthouse at the cape by Robert and Alan Stevenson in 1828. The last keepers had left by 1998, when people were replaced by automation. Three miles to the east are the seabird colonies of Clo Mor, the British mainland's highest vertical sea cliffs (195m).

Part of the moorland has served for decades as a bombing range. The island of An Garbh-Eilean, 5 miles from the cape, has the misfortune to be around the same size as an aircraft carrier and is regularly ripped up by RAF bombs and missiles. There is no public access when the range is in use; times are displayed on www.visitcapewrath.com.

A cafe at the lighthouse serves soup and sandwiches. It's open year-round and John, the owner, will never turn anyone away whatever the time of day.

Getting to Cape Wrath involves taking a **ferry** (07719 678729; www.capewrathferry. co.uk; single/return trip £5/7; ⊙ Easter–mid-Oct) – passengers and bikes only – across the Kyle of Durness (10 minutes). It connects with the **Cape Wrath Minibus** (01971-511284; www.visitcapewrath.com; single/return trip £7/12; ⊙ Easter–mid-Oct), which runs the very slow and bumpy 11 miles to the cape (50 minutes).

This combination is a friendly but eccentric and sometimes shambolic service with limited capacity, so plan on waiting in high season, and call ahead to make sure the ferry is running. The ferry leaves from 2 miles southwest of Durness, and runs twice or more daily from Easter to mid-October. If you eschew the minibus, it's a spectacular 11-mile ride or hike from boat to cape over bleak scenery.

An increasingly popular but challenging walking route, the **Cape Wrath Trail** (www. capewrathtrail.org.uk) runs from Fort William up to Cape Wrath (230 miles). It's unmarked so buy the *Cape Wrath Trail* guidebook (www.cicerone.co.uk) or go with a guide – **C-n-Do** (01786-445703; www.cndoscotland.com) is one operator.

🛏 Sleeping & Eating

Clachtoll Beach Campsite CAMPSITE **£**
(01571-855377; www.clachtollbeachcampsite. co.uk; B869, Clachtoll; site £6-12, plus per adult/ child £5/2; ⊙ Apr–mid-Oct; P 🛜 🐾) Set among the machair beside a lovely white-sand beach and emerald seas, Clachtoll is a divine coastal camping spot, though somewhat overwhelmed by the adjacent self-catering development. It's 6 miles northwest of Lochinver by road.

Achmelvich Beach SYHA HOSTEL **£**
(01571-844480; www.syha.org.uk; dm/tw £21/53; ⊙ Apr–Sep) Off the B869, this white-washed cottage is set beside a great beach at the end of a side road. Dorms are simple, and there's a sociable common kitchen and eating area. Heat-up meals are available as is a basic shop in summer; otherwise, there's a chip van at the adjacent campsite, or you can take the 4-mile walk to Lochinver.

Davar B&B **££**
(01571-844501; www.davar-lochinver.co.uk; Baddidarroch, Lochinver; s £60, d £90-100; P 🛜) Run with a genuine welcome and enthusiasm, this is a beautiful house with a garden and a fabulous outlook across the bay to Suilven and the Assynt mountainscape. The four rooms are well appointed and have plenty of space; it's the ideal base for exploring the region. To find it, turn west at the northern end of Lochinver.

★**Albannach** HOTEL **£££**
(01571-844407; www.thealbannach.co.uk; Baddidarroch, Lochinver; s/d/ste £135/170/235; ⊙ mid-Feb–mid-Dec; P 🛜) 🍽 The Albannach combines old-fashioned country-house elements – steep creaky stairs, stuffed animals, fireplaces and noble antique furniture – with strikingly handsome rooms that range from a sumptuous four-poster to more modern spaces with underfloor heating and, in one case, a private deck with outdoor spa. Glorious views, spacious grounds and great walks in easy striking distance make this a perfect place to base yourself.

The renowned restaurant is closed but the welcoming owners do food at the **Caberfeidh** (01571-844321; www.thecaberfeidh.co.uk;

Main St, Lochinver; tapas £5-8, mains £12-18; ⊙kitchen 6-9pm Tue-Sat, 12.30-8pm Sun Easter-Oct, plus noon-2.30pm Tue-Sat in summer, 6-8pm Thu-Sat, 12.30-8pm Sun Nov-Mar; ☎) ✦ in town. The Albannach was for sale at the time of research so things may change.

Lochinver Larder & Riverside Bistro
CAFE, BISTRO ££

(☑ 01571-844356; www.lochinverlarder.co.uk; 3 Main St, Lochinver; pies £5-6, mains £12-16; ⊙10am-7.45pm Mon-Sat, to 5.30pm Sun Apr-Oct, 10am-4pm Mon-Sat Nov-Mar; ☎) An outstanding menu of inventive food made with local produce is on offer here. The bistro turns out delicious seafood dishes in the evening, while the takeaway counter sells tasty pies with a wide range of gourmet fillings (try the wild boar and apricot). It also does quality meals to take away and heat up: great for hostellers and campers.

❶ Getting There & Away

There are buses from Ullapool to Lochinver (£5.10, one hour, two to three Monday to Saturday) and a summer bus that goes on to Durness.

Coigach

The region south of Assynt, west of the main A835 road from Ullapool to Ledmore Junction, is known as Coigach (www.coigach.com). A lone, single-track road penetrates this wilderness, leading through gloriously wild scenery to remote settlements. At the western end of Loch Lurgainn, a branch leads north to Lochinver, a scenic backroad so narrow and twisting that it's nicknamed the Wee Mad Road.

Coigach is a wonderland for walkers and wildlife enthusiasts, with a patchwork of sinuous silver lochs dominated by the isolated peaks of Cul Mor (849m), Cul Beag (769m), Ben More Coigach (743m) and Stac Pollaidh (613m). The main settlement is the straggling township of Achiltibuie, 15 miles from the main road, with the gorgeous Summer Isles moored just off the coast, and silhouettes of mountains skirting the bay.

Stac Pollaidh
HIKING

Despite its diminutive size, Stac Pollaidh (613m) provides one of the most exciting hill walks in the Highlands, with some good scrambling on its narrow sandstone crest.

Begin at the car park overlooking Loch Lurgainn, 5 miles west of the A835, and follow a clearly marked and well-made footpath around the eastern end of the hill to ascend from the far side; return by the same route (3 miles return, two to four hours).

Summer Isles Seatours
CRUISE

(☑ 07927 920592; www.summerisles-seatours.co.uk; adult/child £30/15; ⊙Mon-Sat May-Sep) Cruises to the Summer Isles from Old Dornie pier, northwest of Achiltibuie. You get to spend some time ashore on Tanera Mòr.

Acheninver Hostel
HOSTEL £

(☑ 01854-622283; www.acheninverhostel.com; dm £20, d £50; ⊙Apr-Sep) A quarter-mile walk off the road a couple of miles southeast of Achiltibuie, this off-the-beaten-track hostel has a remote, serene location that's one of the country's best. It's a cosy spot, and has a female dorm with single beds, a male dorm with bunks and three en suite huts sleeping two to three. There's a kitchen, and some limited supplies are available.

★ Summer Isles Hotel
HOTEL £££

(☑ 01854-622282; www.summerisleshotel.com; Achiltibuie; s £110-190, d £150-250; ⊙Easter-Oct; ℗ ☎ 🐾) This is a special place, with cracking views and wonderfully romantic rooms (one themed on Charlie Chaplin, who stayed here), plus other suites in separate cottages and a snug bar with outdoor seating. 'Courtyard view' rooms are darkish; it's worth upgrading to one with vistas. It's the perfect spot for a romantic getaway or some quality time off life's treadmill.

The restaurant (noon to 3pm and 6pm to 9pm; dinner £49) is of high quality, with local lobster usually featuring in addition to renowned cheese and dessert trolleys. There's also a great wine list considering you're in the middle of nowhere.

Salt Seafood Kitchen
SEAFOOD ££

(☑ 01854-622380; www.saltseafood.com; 140 Badenscaillie; mains £11-16; ⊙5-9.15pm Mon-Sat Apr-Oct) ✦ A mile south of Achiltibuie, this sweet chalet offers views to the Summer Isles and fresh local seafood served with a smile. What's on offer varies, but expect to find mussels, langoustines and squat lobster among other denizens of the sea, as well as burgers, sandwiches and soups. Prices are very reasonable, and the seafood platter is an absolute feast for two.

❶ Getting There & Away

There are buses from Ullapool to Achiltibuie (£6.20, 1¼ hours, one to three daily Monday to Saturday).

Ullapool

POP 1500

This pretty port on the shores of Loch Broom is the largest settlement in Wester Ross and one of the most alluring spots in the Highlands, a wonderful destination in itself as well as a gateway to the Western Isles. Offering a row of whitewashed cottages arrayed along the harbour and special views of the loch and its flanking hills, the town has a very distinctive appeal. The harbour served as an emigration point during the Clearances, with thousands of Scots watching Ullapool recede behind as they began a journey to a new continent.

⊙ Sights & Activities

Ullapool is a great centre for hill walking. A good path up Gleann na Sguaib heads for the top of Beinn Dearg from Inverlael, at the inner end of Loch Broom. Ridge-walking on the Fannichs is relatively straightforward and many different routes are possible.

The Ullapool Tourist Office (p366) can supply you with all the information and maps you need. Good walking books are also sold there, and at **Ullapool Bookshop** (☑ 01854-612918; www.ullapoolbookshop.co.uk; Quay St; ☺ 9am-5.30pm Mon-Sat, 11am-5pm Sun Nov-Mar, to 9pm Mon-Sat Apr-Oct), or you can pick up a copy of the freebie guide to local woodland walks.

Ullapool Museum MUSEUM
(☑ 01854-612987; www.ullapoolmuseum.co.uk; 7 West Argyle St; adult/child £4/free; ☺ 11am-4pm Mon-Sat Apr-Oct) Housed in a converted Telford church, this museum relates the prehistoric, natural and social history of the town and Lochbroom area, with a particular focus on the emigration to Nova Scotia and other places. There's also a genealogy section if you want to trace your Scottish roots.

Shearwater Cruises BOATING
(☑ 01854-612472; www.summerqueen.co.uk; ☺ Mon-Sat May-Sep) Weather permitting, the catamaran *Shearwater* takes you out to the Summer Isles for a 2¼-hour cruise (adult/child £35/30). They leave twice a day.

🛏 Sleeping

There's a good selection of B&Bs, with some standout options. Note that during summer Ullapool is very busy and finding accommodation can be tricky – book ahead. Several places don't accept single-night stays.

Ullapool SYHA HOSTEL £
(☑ 01854-612254; www.syha.org.uk; Shore St; dm/tw/q £21.50/55/96; ☺ Apr-Oct; ☏) You've got to hand it to the SYHA – it's chosen some very sweet locations for its hostels. This one is right in the heart of town on the pretty waterfront; some rooms have harbour views and the busy dining area and little lounge are also good spots for contemplating the water.

★ Tamarin Lodge B&B ££
(☑ 01854-612667; www.tamarinullapool.com; 9 The Braes; s/d £45/90; 🅿 ☏ 🐾) Effortlessly elegant modern architecture in this hilltop house is noteworthy in its own right, but the glorious vistas over the hills opposite and water far below are unforgettable. All rooms face the view; some have a balcony, and all are very spacious, quiet and utterly relaxing, with unexpected features and gadgets. The great lounge and benevolent hosts are a delight.

Follow signs for Braes from the Inverness road.

OFF THE BEATEN TRACK

THE SUMMER ISLES

The dozen islands scattered in the sea to the west of Achiltibuie are known as the Summer Isles. There's a superb view of the islands, with the hills of Wester Ross in the background, from the minor road between Altandhu and Achnahaird – look out for a layby with a bench and a signpost, where a short path leads to the viewpoint.

In the late 19th century the Summer Isles were home to 120 people working at the herring fishery, but now the permanent population is only half a dozen, augmented by holiday visitors. The largest island, Tanera Mòr, has self-catering cottages.

You can visit the Summer Isles on boat trips from Ullapool; tour operators include **Seascape** (☑ 07511 290081; www.sea-scape.co.uk; ☺ May-Sep) and Shearwater Cruises. Otherwise, there are cruises with Summer Isles Seatours (p364) and other boat transport from Old Dornie pier, northwest of Achiltibuie, available in summer by prior arrangement.

★ **West House** B&B ££
(📞 01854-613126; www.westhousebandb.co.uk; West Argyle St; d without breakfast £75-85; ☺ May-Sep; P 🐕 📶) 🐾 Slap bang in Ullapool's centre, this solid house, once a manse, has excellent rooms with contemporary style and great bathrooms. There's no breakfast, but you get a fridge, juice and decent coffee, plus there are two good cafes close by. Most rooms have great views, as well as lots of conveniences. The genial owners also have tempting self-catering options in the area.

There's a minimum two-night stay.

Waterside House B&B ££
(📞 01854-612140; www.waterside.uk.net; 6 West Shore St; d £85-95; ☺ Apr-Oct; P) This typical whitewashed home is right on the waterfront, so close to the ferry that you can watch it docking out of your window. Waterside House features three compact but beautifully appointed rooms with excellent modern bathrooms. The location and the friendly welcome are fabulous, and your hosts go the extra mile at breakfast time – delicious. Minimum two-night stay in summer.

★ **Ceilidh Place** HOTEL £££
(📞 01854-612103; www.theceilidhplace.com; 14 West Argyle St; s £70-96, d £140-170; P 📶 🐕) This hotel is a celebration of Scottish culture: we're talking literature and traditional music, not tartan and Nessie dolls. Rooms go for character over modernity; instead of TVs they come with a selection of books chosen by Scottish literati, plus eclectic artwork and cosy touches. The sumptuous lounge has sofas, chaise longues and an honesty bar. There's a bookshop here, too.

It's not luxurious but it's one of the Highlands' more unusual and delightful places to stay.

✕ Eating

West Coast Delicatessen CAFE £
(📞 01854-613450; www.westcoastdeli.co.uk; 5 Argyle St; light meals £3-7; ☺ 9am-5pm Mon-Sat; 📶) A likeable venue for a coffee or snack, this upbeat modern place has sub rolls, decent coffee and a variety of deli produce, including some very tasty cheeses. It also does a good soup, perfect for windier Ullapool days.

Seafood Shack SEAFOOD £
(📞 07876 142623; www.seafoodshack.co.uk; West Argyle St; takeaways £4-9; ☺ noon-6pm Apr-late Oct) High-quality fresh seafood is served out of a trailer in this vacant lot by two

cheery lasses. There's a wide range of tasty fare available, from hand-dived scallops to calamari to mussels, crab, oysters and fish.

Ceilidh Place SCOTTISH ££
(📞 01854-612103; www.theceilidhplace.com; 14 West Argyle St; mains £10-18; ☺ 8am-9pm Feb-Dec; 📶) The restaurant in this hub of culture and good cheer serves inventive dishes that focus on fresh local seafood backed up by stews, plus lighter meals like pies and burgers during the day. Quality depends a bit on staffing, but it's an atmospheric, cosy place with outdoor seating, good wines by the glass and regular live music and events.

ℹ️ Information

Ullapool Library (📞 01854-612543; www.highlifehighland.com; Mill St; ☺ 9am-5pm Mon-Fri, plus 6-8pm Tue & Thu, shorter hours & closed Mon & Wed during holidays; 📶) Free internet access.

Ullapool Tourist Office (📞 01854-612486; ullapool@visitscotland.com; 6 Argyle St; ☺ 9am-6pm Mon-Sat, 9.30am-4.30pm Sun Jul & Aug, 9.30am-5pm Mon-Sat, 10am-3pm Sun Jun & Sep, 9.30am-4.30pm Mon-Sat, 10am-3pm Sun Easter-May & Oct, 9am-2pm Mon, Fri & Sat, 10am-2pm Sun Nov-Easter) Can book ferries and buses.

ℹ️ Getting There & Away

Citylink has buses from Inverness to Ullapool (£14, 1½ hours, one to three daily), connecting with the Lewis ferry.

Two daily ferries (only one on winter Sundays) with **CalMac** (📞 0800 066 5000; www.calmac.co.uk) run from Ullapool to Stornoway on Lewis in the Outer Hebrides (adult/car £9.50/50.95, 2½ hours).

Ullapool to Kyle of Lochalsh

Although it's less than 50 miles as the crow flies from Ullapool to Kyle of Lochalsh, it's more like 150 miles along the circuitous coastal road – but don't let that put you off. It's a deliciously remote region and there are fine views of beaches and bays backed by mountains all the way along.

Twelve miles southeast of Ullapool at Braemore, the A832 doubles back towards the coast as it heads for Gairloch (the A835 continues southeast across the wild, sometimes snowbound, Dirrie More pass to Garve and Inverness). If you're hurrying to Skye, use the A835 and catch up with the A832 further south, near Garve.

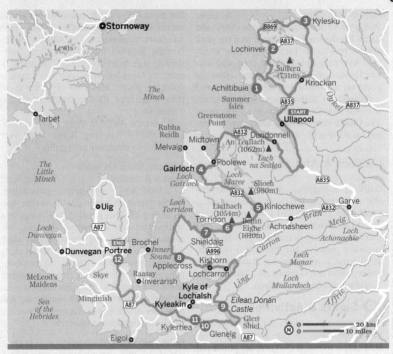

Driving Tour
Wee Roads & Mighty Mountains

START ULLAPOOL
END PORTREE
LENGTH 320 MILES; THREE TO FOUR DAYS

Starting in photogenic harbourside Ullapool, this drive takes in some of the lesser-known roads and the most majestic of Highland scenery, leaving you on the Isle of Skye.

Leave your bags in the hotel, because the first day is a long round trip from Ullapool. Head north on the A835, and turn left to ❶ **Achiltibuie** (p364), where, after gaping at impressive lochside Stac Pollaidh en route, you can admire the outlook over the Summer Isles. From here, backtrack 6 miles then turn left up the Wee Mad Road, a narrow, tortuous but scenic drive north to pretty ❷ **Lochinver** (p362). From here, the B869 winds north past spectacular beaches at Achmelvich and Clachtoll to ❸ **Kylesku** (p362), where the hotel makes a great lunch stop. Return south to Ullapool on the main road (A894–A837–A835), with classic northwestern scenery and things to see along the way, including the Inchnadamph Caves, Ardvreck Castle and Knockan Crag.

The next day head inland along the A835 before taking the A832 ❹ **Gairloch** (p368) turn-off, following the long, circuitous coast road with plenty of activity options, from whale-watching trips to a botanic garden and hill walking around scenic Loch Maree. At ❺ **Kinlochewe** (p369) turn back coastwards on the A896, descending a spectacular pass to ❻ **Torridon** (p370), where the rugged beauty is simply breathtaking. There are good overnight stops all along this route.

From ❼ **Shieldaig** (p370), take the coastal road to sublime little ❽ **Applecross** (p370), then brave the Bealach na Bà pass to get you back to the main road. A loop around Loch Carron will eventually bring you to the A87. Turn left, passing ❾ **Eilean Donan Castle** (p373) and, reaching Glen Shiel, take the right turn to ❿ **Glenelg** (p373), a scenic, out-of-the-way place with a wonderfully rustic summer ferry crossing to Skye. Disembark at ⓫ **Kylerhea** (p377) and enjoy the vistas on one of the island's least-trafficked roads before hitting the A87 again. From here, ⓬ **Portree** (p380) is an easy drive, but numerous picturesque detours – to Sleat or Elgol for example – mean you might take a while to reach it yet.

Falls of Measach
WATERFALL

Just west of the junction of the A835 and A832, 2 miles south of Braemore, a car park gives access to the Falls of Measach, which spill 45m into spectacularly deep and narrow Corrieshalloch Gorge. You can cross the gorge on a swaying suspension bridge, and walk west for 250m to a viewing platform that juts out dizzyingly above a sheer drop. The thundering falls and misty vapours rising from the gorge are very impressive.

Gairloch & Around
POP 1000

Gairloch is a group of villages (comprising Achtercairn, Strath and Charlestown) around the inner end of a loch of the same name. Gairloch is a good base for whale- and dolphin-watching excursions and the surrounding area has beautiful sandy beaches, good trout fishing and birdwatching. Hill walkers also use Gairloch as a base for the Torridon hills and An Teallach.

⊙ Sights & Activities

The B8056 runs along Loch Gairloch's southern shore, past the cute little harbour of Badachro, to end at the gorgeous pink-sand beach of Red Point – a perfect picnic spot. Another coastal road leads north from Gairloch 11 miles to the settlement of Melvaig. From here a private road (open to walkers and cyclists) continues 3 miles to Rua Reidh Lighthouse (building and grounds off-limits to nonguests).

★ Inverewe Garden
GARDENS

(NTS; ☑01445-712952; www.nts.org.uk; adult/concession £11/9.50; ☺9.30am-6pm Jun-Aug, to 5pm Mar, Apr & Sep, to 5.30pm May, to 4pm Oct, 10am-4pm Nov-Feb) Six miles north of Gairloch, this splendid place is a welcome splash of colour on this otherwise bleak coast. The climate here is warmed by the Gulf Stream, which allowed Osgood MacKenzie to create this exotic woodland garden in 1862. There are free guided tours on weekdays at 1.30pm from March to October. The licensed cafe-restaurant serves great cakes.

Parking for non-members is £2.

Russian Arctic Convoy Exhibition Centre
MUSEUM

(☑01445-731137;www.russianarcticconvoymuseum. org; Birchburn, Aultbea; adult/child £3.50/free; ☺10am-4pm Mon-Sat Apr–mid-Dec, 11am-3pm Fri-Sun Jan-Mar) The Arctic convoys were a vital supply line for Russia during WWII; these merchant ships escorted by Allied warships brought supplies into the northern ports through a gauntlet of German ships and submarines. Many left from Loch Ewe, and this volunteer project tells some of the stories of those tough trips. It's fascinating; there's also a small shop.

It's on the A832, 12 miles north of Gairloch. Winter opening hours may vary according to volunteer availability.

Gairloch Marine Wildlife Centre & Cruises
WILDLIFE, CRUISE

(☑01445-712636; www.porpoise-gairloch.co.uk; Pier Rd; cruises adult/child £20/15; ☺10am-4pm Easter-Oct) ✐ This small visitor centre has audiovisual and interactive displays, lots of charts, photos and knowledgable staff. From here, cruises run three times daily (weather permitting); during the two-hour trips you may see basking sharks, porpoises and minke whales. The crew collects data on water temperature and conditions, and monitors cetacean populations, so you are subsidising important research.

Hebridean Whale Cruises
WILDLIFE, CRUISE

(☑01445-712458; www.hebridean-whale-cruises. com; Pier Rd; cruises 2½/4hr £50/80; ☺Apr-Oct) Based at Gairloch's harbour, this set-up runs three trips: a standard 2½-hour whale-watching excursion (from May), a three-hour visit to the seabird-rich Shiant Islands and a four-hour excursion to further-flung feeding grounds in search of orca. Other wildlife it's possible to see include otters, dolphins and seals. Trips are in a zippy rigid inflatable.

⊨ Sleeping & Eating

Gairloch Sands Youth Hostel
HOSTEL £

(☑01445-712219; www.hostellingscotland.org. uk; Carn Dearg; dm/tw/q £22/55/96; ☺Apr-Sep; 🅿🛜🐾) Located 2.5 miles west of Gairloch in a stunning coastal position, this hostel is close to beaches and well set up fo walkers. Wood-panelled rooms and a large dining room/lounge offer comfort, but the real star is that view...magic!

Rua Reidh Lighthouse
LODGE ££

(☑01445-771263; www.stayatalighthouse.co.uk; Melvaig; s £75-90, d £100-120; ☺Easter-Oct; 🅿🐾) Three miles down a narrow private road beyond Melvaig (11 miles north of Gairloch), this simple yet excellent lodge gives a taste of a lighthouse keeper's life. It's a wild, lonely location great for walking and birdwatching. Breakfast is included and tasty evening meals are available. There's no mobile-phone signal or wi-fi and there's usually a two-night minimum stay: book well ahead.

There's a separate self-catering apartment that's available year-round.

Shieldaig Lodge
HOTEL £££

(☑ 01445-741333; www.shieldaiglodge.com; Badachro; s £150, d £200-300; P �<kbd>🖗</kbd>) This refurbished hunting lodge has a super waterside position on a sizeable estate offering good walking and fishing as well as falconry and archery. It's a cosy place – think drams and a log fire – with a good restaurant, a very well-stocked bar and tasteful rooms, the best of which have water views. There's also a snooker table and a lovely library.

Mountain Coffee Company
CAFE £

(☑ 01445-712316; www.facebook.com/mountain coffee.gairloch; Strath Sq, Strath; light meals £4-7; ⊙ 9am-5.30pm, shorter hours low season) ✐ More the sort of place you'd expect to find on the gringo trail in the Andes, this offbeat and cosy (if brusque) spot is a shrine to mountaineering and travelling. It serves tasty savoury bagels, home baking and sustainably sourced coffees. The conservatory is the place to lap up the sun, while the attached Hillbillies Bookshop is well worth a browse.

There are rather sweet rooms available, too.

Isle of Ewe Smokehouse
FOOD

(☑ 01445-731304; www.smokedbyewe.com; Ormiscaig, Aultbea; ⊙ 9am-5.30pm Mon-Fri) This excellent spot 14 miles north of Gairloch does really delicious hot- and cold-smoked salmon as well as other seafoody delicacies and a range of deli products. Addicted after your visit? Don't worry, they deliver by mail.

ⓘ Information

Gairloch Tourist Office (☑ 01445-712071; www.galeactionforum.co.uk; Achtercairn; ⊙ 9.30am-5.30pm Mon-Sat, 10.30am-5pm Sun Jun-Sep, 10am-5.30pm Mon-Sat, 10.30am-4.30pm Sun Oct-May) Community-run information centre in the wooden Gale Centre, on the road through town. Has good walking pamphlets; there's also a cafe here.

ⓘ Getting There & Away

Public transport to Gairloch is very limited. **Westerbus** (☑ 01445-712255) runs to/from Inverness (£10.30, 2¼ hours, Monday to Saturday) and Ullapool (£5.15, 1¾ hours, Thursday).

Loch Maree & Around

Stretching 12 miles between Poolewe and Kinlochewe, Loch Maree is considered one of Scotland's prettiest lochs, with the imposing bulk of Slioch on its northeastern side and Beinn Eighe on the southwestern. Look out for black-throated divers on the lake in summer. At its southern end, tiny Kinlochewe makes a good base for outdoor activities.

Beinn Eighe Mountain Trail
WALKING

This waymarked 4-mile loop walk to a plateau and cairn on the side of Beinn Eighe has magnificent views over Loch Maree. It's quite exposed up here, so take some warm clothing. The walk starts from a car park on the A832 about 1.5 miles northwest of the Beinn Eighe Visitor Centre.

From the same trailhead there's a shorter 1-mile trail through Scots pine forest.

Kinlochewe Hotel
INN, HOSTEL ££

(☑ 01445-760253; www.kinlochewehotel.co.uk; Kinlochewe; dm £17.50, s £60, d £100-110; P <kbd>🖗</kbd> <kbd>🐾</kbd>) ✐ This is a welcoming hotel that's very walker-friendly, with features such as a handsome lounge well stocked with books, a great bar with several real ales on tap and a menu of locally sourced food. There are 'economy' rooms that share a bath-only bathroom (£90) and also a bunkhouse with one no-frills 12-bed dorm, plus a decent kitchen and clean bathrooms.

★ Whistle Stop Cafe
CAFE, BISTRO ££

(☑ 01445-760423; www.facebook.com/Whistle-Stop-Cafe-Kinlochewe-223096744444313; Kinlochewe; meals £8-16; ⊙ 8am-8pm Mon-Sat, 10am-5pm Sun Apr-Sep, reduced hours mid-Feb–Mar & Oct–mid-Nov) A colourful presence in the former village hall, this is a tempting place to drop by for anything from a coffee to enticing bistro fare. There are great daily specials and delicious home baking, juices and smoothies. It's very friendly, and used to pumping life back into chilly walkers and cyclists. It's unlicensed, but you can take your own wine (£1 corkage).

Opening hours vary substantially season by season; check its Facebook page.

Torridon

The road southwest from Kinlochewe passes through Glen Torridon, amid some of Britain's most beautiful scenery. Carved by ice from massive layers of ancient sandstone that takes its name from the region, the mountains here are steep, shapely and imposing, whether flirting with autumn mists, draped in dazzling winter snows, or reflected in the calm blue waters of Loch Torridon on a summer day.

The road reaches the sea at spectacularly sited Torridon village, then continues westwards to lovely Shieldaig, which boasts an attractive main street of whitewashed houses right on the water.

Activities

The Torridon Munros – **Liathach** (1054m; pronounced '*lee*-agakh', Gaelic for 'the Grey One'), **Beinn Eighe** (1010m; 'ben *ay*', 'the File') and **Beinn Alligin** (986m; 'the Jewelled Mountain') – are big, serious mountains for experienced hill walkers only. Though not technically difficult, their ascents are long and committing, often over rough and rocky terrain. Further information is available at the **Torridon Countryside Centre** (NTS; ☑ 01445-791221; www.nts.org.uk; ☺ 10am-5pm Sun-Fri Easter-Sep).

Torridon Activities (☑ 01445-791242; www.thetorridon.com/activities; activities half-/full day £40/60) runs a number of outdoor pursuits, including sea kayaking and mountain biking.

Sleeping & Eating

Torridon SYHA HOSTEL £
(☑ 01445-791284; www.syha.org.uk; Torridon; dm/ tw £21.50/55; ☺ daily Mar-Oct, Fri & Sat nights Nov-Feb; P@🛜🛝) This spacious hostel has enthusiastic, can-do management and sits in a magnificent location, surrounded by spectacular mountains. Roomy dorms and privates (twins have single beds) are allied to a huge kitchen and convivial lounge area, with ales on sale. It's a very popular walking base, with great advice from the in-house mountain rescue team, so book ahead.

As well as breakfasts, there are packed lunches and heat-up dinners on offer.

Torridon Inn INN ££
(☑ 01445-791242; www.thetorridon.com; Torridon; s/d/q £110/140/215; ☺ daily Easter-Oct, Thu-Sun Nov & mid-Feb–Easter, closed Dec–mid-Feb;

P🛜🛝) This convivial but upmarket walkers hang-out has excellent modern rooms that vary substantially in size and layout. Rooms for groups (of up to six) offer more value than the commodious but overpriced doubles. The sociable bar serves all-day food and there are numerous activities on offer.

⭐ **Torridon** HOTEL £££
(☑ 01445-791242; www.thetorridon.com; Torridon; r standard/superior/deluxe/master £265/320/390/ 450; ☺ closed Jan, plus Mon & Tue Nov, Dec, Feb & Mar; P@🛜🛝) If you prefer the lap of luxury to the sound of rain beating on your tent, head for this lavish Victorian shooting lodge with a romantic lochside location. Sumptuous contemporary rooms with awe-inspiring views, top bathrooms and a cheery Highland cow atop the counterpane couldn't be more inviting. This is one of Scotland's top country hotels, always luxurious but never pretentious.

Tigh an Eilean HOTEL £££
(☑ 01520-755251; www.tighaneilean.co.uk; Shieldaig; s/d £72.50/145; ☺ Feb-Dec; 🛜) With a lovely waterfront position in the pretty village of Shieldaig, this is an appealing destination for a relaxing stay, offering old-style rooms that are comfortable, not luxurious. Loch-view rooms – with gloriously soothing vistas – are allocated on a first-booked basis, so it's worth reserving ahead. Service is very helpful, and there's a cosy lounge with an honesty bar.

Prices drop for stays of three or more nights.

Shieldaig Bar & Coastal Kitchen SEAFOOD ££
(☑ 01520-755251; www.shieldaigbarandcoastal kitchen.co.uk; Shieldaig; mains £10-21; ☺ food noon-2.30pm & 6-8.30pm or 9pm, closed some winter lunchtimes; 🛜) This attractive pub has real ales and waterside tables plus a great upstairs dining room and an outdoor deck. There's an emphasis on quality local seafood as well as wood-fired pizzas and bistro-style meat dishes such as steak-frites or sausages and mash. Blackboard specials feature the daily catch.

Applecross

POP 200

The delightfully remote seaside village of Applecross feels like an island retreat due to its isolation and the magnificent views of Raasay and the hills of Skye that set the pulse racing, particularly at sunset. On a clear day it's an unforgettable place. The campsite and pub fill to the brim in school holidays.

A road leads here 25 winding miles from Shieldaig, but more spectacular (accessed from further south on the A896) is the magnificent Bealach na Bà (626m; Pass of the Cattle), the third-highest motor road in the UK, and the longest continuous climb. Originally built in 1822, it climbs steeply and hair-raisingly via hairpin bends perched over sheer drops, with gradients of up to 25%, then drops dramatically to the village with views of Skye.

Hartfield House HOSTEL £
(📞 01520-744333; www.hartfieldhouse.org.uk; dm/s/tw/d £25/40/50/55; ⊙ Mar-Oct; 🅿 🛜) This former hunting lodge on the Applecross estate is about a mile off the road in a lovely rural location. With lots of beds across two separate buildings in both dorms and private rooms, plus good common areas, it offers plenty of space and comfort. Walkers and cyclists have decent facilities and a help-yourself continental breakfast is included.

Applecross Inn INN £££
(📞 01520-744262; www.applecross.uk.com; Shore St; s/d £90/140; 🅿 🛜 🐾) 🌱 The hub of the spread-out Applecross community, this inn is a great spot to hole up, but you'll need to book ahead. Seven snug bedrooms all have a view of the Skye hills and the sea. It's a magical spot and there's a cracking pub and **restaurant** (mains £10-18; ⊙ noon-9pm; 🛜) 🌱 too. It also has some cottage accommodation along the waterfront.

ℹ Getting There & Away

There are two buses a week (Wednesday and Saturday) with **Lochcarron Garage** (📞 01520-722997; www.facebook.com/BCSLochcarron Garage) from Inverness to Lochcarron that continue to Applecross (£11.10, 3½ hours) via Shieldaig on prior request.

Lochcarron
POP 900

Appealing, whitewashed Lochcarron is a veritable metropolis in this area of Scotland, with two supermarkets, a bank with an ATM and a petrol station. A long shoreline footpath at the loch's edge provides the perfect opportunity for a stroll to walk off breakfast.

Old Manse B&B ££
(📞 01520-722208; www.theoldmanselochcarron.com; Church St; s/d £45/75, tw with loch view £85; 🅿 🛜 🐾) The Old Manse is a top-notch Scottish guesthouse, beautifully appointed and in a prime, quiet lochside position. Rooms are traditional in style and simply gorgeous, with elegant furniture. Those overlooking the water are larger and well worth the extra tenner. Follow signs for the West End.

Pathend B&B B&B ££
(📞 01520-722109; www.pathend-lochcarron.co.uk; Main St; s/d £60/80; 🛜 🐾) This cottage on the waterfront road offers a genuine welcome and some charming features in its front-facing rooms, such as a heritage fireplace and great sunken bath. It's a lovely outlook, and patchwork quilts and plush red sofas add to the vintage appeal. Evening meals are available by prior arrangement.

★ **Kishorn Seafood Bar** SEAFOOD ££
(📞 01520-733240; www.kishornseafoodbar.co.uk; A896, Kishorn; mains £8-18; ⊙ 11am-5pm Mon-Sat, noon-4pm Sun, 6-9pm Thu-Sat Mar-Oct, plus 6-9pm Tue & Wed Jul-Aug, call for winter hours) 🌱 Four miles west of Lochcarron, the Kishorn Seafood Bar is a cute, pale blue bungalow that serves the freshest of local seafood simply and well, with very fair prices. The views are spectacular, and you've got the satisfaction of knowing that much of what you eat was caught in Loch Kishorn just below. Book for dinner.

Plockton
POP 400

Idyllic little Plockton, with its perfect cottages lining a perfect bay, looks like it was designed as a film set. And it has indeed served as just that – scenes from *The Wicker Man* (1973) were filmed here, and the village became famous as the location for the 1990s TV series *Hamish Macbeth*.

With all this picture-postcard perfection, it's hardly surprising that Plockton is a tourist hot spot, crammed with day trippers and holidaymakers in summer. But there's no denying its appeal, with 'palm trees' (actually hardy New Zealand cabbage palms) lining the waterfront, a thriving small-boat sailing scene and several good places to stay, eat and drink. The big event of the year is the **Plockton Regatta** (www.plockton-sailing.com; ⊙ Jul/Aug).

The website www.visitplockton.com is a useful source of local information.

NORTHERN HIGHLANDS & ISLANDS ULLAPOOL TO KYLE OF LOCHALSH

🏃 Activities

Hire canoes and rowboats on the waterfront to explore the bay.

Calum's Seal Trips BOATING

(📞 01599-544306; www.calums-sealtrips.com; adult/child £12/6; ☺ Apr-Oct) Seal-watching cruises visit swarms of the slippery suckers just outside the harbour. There's excellent commentary and you may even spot otters as well. Trips leave several times daily. There's also a longer dolphin-watching trip available.

Sea Kayak Plockton KAYAKING

(📞 01599-544422; www.seakayakplockton.co.uk; 1-day beginner course £85) Sea Kayak Plockton offers everything from beginner lessons to multiday trips around Skye and right out to St Kilda.

🛏️ Sleeping

Plockton Station Bunkhouse HOSTEL £

(📞 01599-544235; www.visitplockton.com/stay/bunkhouse; dm £18; 🅿🛜📶) Airily set in the former train station (the new one is opposite), this hostel has cosy four-bed dorms, a garden and kitchen-lounge with plenty of light and good perspectives over the frenetic comings-and-goings (OK, that last bit's a lie) of the platforms below. The owners also have good-value B&B accommodation (single/double £35/60) next door in the inaccurately named 'Nessun Dorma'.

⭐ Plockton Hotel INN ££

(📞 01599-544274; www.plocktonhotel.co.uk; 41 Harbour St; s/d £100/150, cottage s/d £65/100; 📶) 🍴 Black-painted Plockton Hotel is one of those classic Highland spots that manages to make everyone happy, whether it's thirst, hunger or fatigue that brings people knocking. Assiduously tended rooms are a real delight, with excellent facilities and thoughtful touches. Those without a water view are consoled with more space and a balcony with rock-garden perspectives. The cottage nearby offers simpler comfort.

⭐ Tigh Arran B&B ££

(📞 01599-544307; www.plocktonbedandbreakfast.com; Duirinish; s/d £70/80; 🅿🛜📶) It's hard to decide which is better at this sweet spot 2 miles from the Plockton shorefront – the warm personal welcome or the absolutely stunning views across to Skye. All three of the en suite rooms – with appealing family

options – enjoy the views, as does the comfy lounge. A top spot, far from stress and noise, it's great value as well.

Seabank B&B ££

(📞 01599-544221; www.seabank-plockton.co.uk; 6 Bank St; d £80-90; ☺ Easter-early Oct; 📶) On the water and centrally located, but still a little removed from the main-street bustle, this tranquil spot has two very sweet rooms with dormer windows overlooking the loch. There's a little garden by the water where you can sit and absorb the peace. The delightful host makes staying here a very pleasant experience. There's a separate self-catering apartment that's great, too.

One room has an en suite, the other a private bathroom outside the room.

🍴 Eating

⭐ Plockton Shores SEAFOOD ££

(📞 01599-544263; www.plocktonshoresrestaurant.com; 30 Harbour St; restaurant mains £14-19; ☺ cafe 9am-5.30pm Mon-Sat, noon-4pm Sun, restaurant 5-9pm Tue-Sat; 🍴) 🍴 This restaurant attached to a shop has a tempting menu of local seafood, including good-value platters with langoustines, mussels, crab, squat lobster and more, and succulent hand-dived tempura scallops. There's also a very tasty line in venison, steaks and a small selection of good vegetarian dishes that are more than an afterthought. The licensed cafe does home baking and light lunches.

Hours are reduced in winter but it's open year-round.

Plockton Inn SEAFOOD ££

(📞 01599-544222; www.plocktoninn.co.uk; Innes St; mains £10-18; ☺ noon-2.15pm & 6-9pm; 📶) Offering a wide range of anything from haggis to toothsome local langoustines (Plockton prawns) and daily seafood specials, Plockton Inn covers lots of bases and has genuinely welcoming service.

A range of rooms – some substantially more spacious than others, and some in an annexe – are also available at a decent price.

ℹ️ Getting There & Away

Trains running between Kyle of Lochalsh (£2.80, 15 minutes) and Inverness (£23.10, 2½ hours) stop in Plockton up to four times daily each way.

Kyle of Lochalsh

POP 700

Before the connecting bridge was opened in 1995, this was Skye's principal mainland ferry port. Visitors now tend to buzz through town, but Kyle has some good boat trips if you're interested in marine life, and there's some great seafood eating here. The railway trip from Inverness is spectacular.

Seaprobe Atlantis   BOATING
(⌨0800 980 4846; www.seaprobeatlantis.com; adult/child from £14/8; ☺Easter-Oct) A glass-hulled boat takes you on a spin around the kyle to spot seabirds, seals and maybe an otter. The basic trip includes entertaining commentary and plenty of beautiful jellyfish; longer trips also take in a WWII shipwreck. At the time of research pick-ups were from Kyleakin across on Skye but the ticket office was still in Kyle.

Buth Bheag   SEAFOOD £
(⌨01599-534002; www.buthbheag.co.uk; Old Ferry Slip; salads £3-6; ☺10am-5pm Tue-Fri, to 3pm Sat Easter-Oct, 10am-3pm Tue-Fri Nov–mid-Dec & mid-Jan–Easter) This tiny place by the water near the tourist office has great fresh seafood salads and rolls for a pittance. Get them to take away and munch on them while sitting by the harbour. They were hoping to move to slightly larger premises just across the road at our last visit.

★Waterside   SEAFOOD ££
(⌨01599-534813;www.watersideseafoodrestaurant. co.uk; Train Station; mains £17-21; ☺5.30-9pm mid-Mar–mid-Oct) ∅ In a former waiting room on Kyle's train station platform, this quaint little spot serves reliably delicious fresh fish and shellfish. A big effort is made to source sustainably from local producers, and the quality is sky-high. A great list of specials is chalked up nightly on the blackboard. In summer you nearly always have to book ahead.

❶ Information

Kyle of Lochalsh Tourist Office (⌨01471-822716; ☺9.30am-4.30pm Easter-Oct) Next to the main seafront car park, this tour booking office has tourist information on Skye and the Lochalsh region. Next to it is one of Scotland's most lavishly decorated public toilets.

❶ Getting There & Away

Citylink runs two to three daily buses from Inverness (£21.70, two hours) and three from Glasgow (£41.20, five to six hours).

The train route between Kyle of Lochalsh and Inverness (£24.10, 2¾ hours, up to four daily) is marvellously scenic.

Kyle to the Great Glen

It's 55 miles southeast via the A87 from Kyle to Invergarry, which lies between Fort William and Fort Augustus, on Loch Oich. The road passes one of Scotland's most famous castles and through picturesque Glen Shiel, while a detour leads to the off-the-beaten-track Glenelg area.

Eilean Donan Castle

Photogenically sited at the entrance to Loch Duich, Eilean Donan (⌨01599-555202; www.eileandonancastle.com; A87, Dornie; adult/child/family £7.50/4/20; ☺10am-6pm Apr-May & Oct, 9.30am-6pm Jun & Sep, 9am-6pm Jul & Aug, 10am-4pm Nov-Dec & Feb-Mar, closed Jan) is one of Scotland's most evocative castles and must now be represented in millions of photo albums. It's on an offshore islet, elegantly linked to the mainland by a stone-arched bridge. It's very much a recreation inside, with an excellent introductory exhibition. Citylink buses from Fort William and Inverness to Portree stop opposite the castle. The last entry is strictly one hour before closing.

Keep an eye out for the photos of castle scenes from the movie *Highlander;* there's also a sword used at the battle of Culloden in 1746. The castle was bombarded into ruins by government ships in 1719 when Jacobite forces were defeated at the Battle of Glenshiel; it was rebuilt between 1912 and 1932.

Glen Shiel & Glenelg

From Eilean Donan Castle, the A87 follows Loch Duich into spectacular Glen Shiel, with 1000m-high peaks soaring on either side of the road. Here, in 1719, a Jacobite army was defeated by Hanoverian government forces. Among those fighting on the rebel side were clansmen led by famous outlaw Rob Roy MacGregor and 300 soldiers loaned by the king of Spain; the mountain above the battlefield is still called Sgurr nan Spainteach (Peak of the Spaniard).

At Shiel Bridge, home to a famous wild-goat colony, a narrow side road goes over the Bealach Ratagain (pass), with great views of the Five Sisters of Kintail peaks, to Glenelg, where there's a community-run ferry to Skye. From palindromic Glenelg round to the road-end at Arnisdale, the scenery becomes even more spectacular, with great views across Loch Hourn to the remote Knoydart peninsula. Along this road are two fine ruined Iron Age brochs.

There are several good walks in the area, including the two-day, cross-country hike from Morvich to Cannich via scenic **Gleann Lichd** and Glen Affric SYHA (35 miles). The **Five Sisters of Kintail** hill-walking expedition is a classic but seriously challenging.

Glenelg Inn   GASTROPUB **££**
(☑ 01599-522273; www.glenelg-inn.com; Glenelg; mains £10-18; ☺ kitchen 12.30-3pm daily, plus 6.30-9pm Thu-Sun Easter-Oct; P 🛜 🐾) One of the Highlands' most picturesque places for a pint or a romantic away-from-it-all stay (doubles £120), the Glenelg Inn has tables in a lovely garden with cracking views of Skye. The elegant dining room and cosy bar area serve posh fare, with local langoustines, scallops and fish usually featuring. Winter opening is sporadic; check the website.

❶ Getting There & Away

BOAT

A picturesque community-owned **vehicle ferry** (www.facebook.com/glenelgskyeferry; foot passenger/bike/car with passengers £3/4/15; ☺ 10am-6pm Easter–mid-Oct) runs from Glenelg across to Kylerhea on Skye. This highly recommended way of reaching the island runs every 20 minutes and doesn't need booking.

BUS

Citylink buses between Fort William/Inverness and Skye travel along the A87.

One bus runs Monday, Tuesday and Friday from Kyle of Lochalsh to Arnisdale, via Shiel Bridge, Ratagan and Glenelg (£8, 1¼ hours).

SKYE

POP 10,000

The Isle of Skye (an t-Eilean Sgiathanach in Gaelic) takes its name from the old Norse *sky-a,* meaning 'cloud island', a Viking reference to the often-mist-enshrouded Cuillin Hills. It's the second-largest of Scotland's islands, a 50-mile-long patchwork of velvet moors, jagged mountains, sparkling lochs and towering sea cliffs.

The stunning scenery is the main attraction, but when the mist closes in there are plenty of castles, crofting museums and cosy pubs and restaurants; there are also dozens of art galleries and craft studios.

Along with Edinburgh and Loch Ness, Skye is one of Scotland's top-three tourist destinations. However, the crowds tend to stick to Portree, Dunvegan and Trotternish – it's almost always possible to find peace and quiet in the island's further-flung corners. Come prepared for changeable weather: when it's fine it's very fine indeed, but all too often it isn't.

🏃 Activities

Walking

Skye offers some of the finest – and in places, the roughest and most difficult – walking in Scotland. There are many detailed guidebooks available, including a series of four walking guides by Charles Rhodes, available from the Aros Centre (p380) and the tourist office (p381) in Portree. You'll need Ordnance Survey (OS) 1:50,000 maps 23 and 32, or Harvey's 1:25,000 *Superwalker – The Cuillin.* Don't attempt the longer walks in bad weather or in winter.

Easy, low-level routes include: through **Strath Mor** from Luib (on the Broadford–Sligachan road) and on to Torrin (on the Broadford–Elgol road; allow 1½ hours, 4 miles); from **Sligachan to Kilmarie** via Camasunary (four hours, 11 miles); and from **Elgol to Kilmarie** via Camasunary (2½ hours, 6.5 miles). The walk from **Kilmarie to Coruisk** and back via Camasunary and the 'Bad Step' is superb but slightly harder (11 miles round-trip; allow at least six hours). The **Bad Step** is a rocky slab poised above the sea that you have to scramble across; it's easy in fine, dry weather, but some walkers find it intimidating.

Skye Wilderness Safaris (p376) runs one-day guided hiking trips for small groups (four to six people) through the Cuillin Hills, into the Quiraing or along the Trotternish ridge; transport to/from Portree is included.

Climbing

The Cuillin Hills are a playground for rock climbers, and the two-day traverse of the

Skye & Outer Hebrides

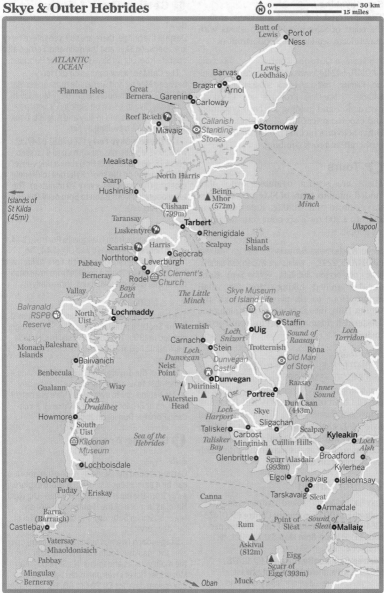

Cuillin Ridge is the finest mountaineering expedition in the British Isles. There are several mountain guides in the area who can provide instruction and safely introduce inexperienced climbers to the more difficult routes.

Skye Guides (p377) offers a one-day introduction-to-rock-climbing course for around £260; a private mountain guide can be hired for £280 a day (both rates are for two clients).

Sea Kayaking

The sheltered coves and sea lochs around the coast of Skye provide enthusiasts with magnificent sea-kayaking opportunities.

Whitewave Outdoor Centre   KAYAKING
(☑ 01470-542414; www.white-wave.co.uk; 19 Linicro, Kilmuir; half-day kayak session per person £40-50; ☺ Mar-Oct) Provides sea kayaking instruction and guiding for both beginners and experts; prices include equipment hire. Other activities include mountain-boarding, bushcraft and rock climbing.

☞ Tours

There are several operators who offer guided minibus tours of Skye, covering history, culture and wildlife. Rates are from £150 to £200 for a six-hour tour for up to six people.

Skye Wilderness Safaris   WALKING
(☑ 01470-552292; www.skye-wilderness-safaris.com; per person £95-120; ☺ May-Sep) Runs one-day guided hiking trips for small groups (four to six people) through the Cuillin Hills, into the Quiraing or along the Trotternish ridge; transport to/from Portree included.

Skye Tours   BUS
(☑ 01471-822716; www.skye-tours.co.uk; adult/child £40/30; ☺ Mon-Sat) Five-hour sightseeing tours of Skye in a minibus, taking in the Old Man of Storr (p383), Kilt Rock and Dunvegan Castle (p382). Tours depart from Kyle of Lochalsh train station at 11.30am (connects with 8.55am train from Inverness, returns to Kyle by 4.45pm in time to catch the return train at 5.13pm).

ℹ Information

Only Portree and Broadford have banks and ATMs.
Columba 1400 Community Centre (☑ 01478-611407; www.columba1400.com; Staffin; per hour £1; ☺ 10am-8pm Mon-Sat Apr-Oct; 🛜) Internet access.

Portree Community Hospital (☑ 01478-613200; www.nhshighland.scot.nhs.uk; Fancyhill) There's a minor injury unit and dental surgery here.

Portree Tourist Office (☑ 01478-612992; www.visitscotland.com; Bayfield Rd; ☺ 9am-6pm Mon-Sat, 10am-4pm Sun Jun-Aug, shorter hours Sep-May; 🛜) The only tourist office on the island; provides internet access and an accommodation booking service. Ask for the free *Art Skye – Gallery & Studio Trails* booklet.

ℹ Getting There & Away

BOAT

Despite the bridge, there are still a couple of ferry links between Skye and the mainland. Ferries also operate from Uig on Skye to the Outer Hebrides.

The **CalMac** (www.calmac.co.uk) ferry between Mallaig and Armadale (passenger/car £2.90/9.70, 30 minutes, eight daily Monday to Saturday, five to seven on Sunday) is very popular on weekends and in July and August. Book ahead if you're travelling by car.

The **Glenelg-Skye Ferry** (☑ 07881 634726; www.skyeferry.co.uk; car with up to 4 passengers £15; ☺ Easter-mid-Oct) runs a tiny vessel (six cars only) on the short Kylerhea to Glenelg crossing (five minutes, every 20 minutes). The ferry operates from 10am to 6pm daily (till 7pm June to August).

BUS

There are buses from Glasgow to Portree (£44, seven hours, three daily), and Uig (£44, 7½ hours, two daily) via Crianlarich, Fort William and Kyle of Lochalsh, plus a service from Inverness to Portree (£26.40, 3¼ hours, three daily).

CAR & MOTORCYCLE

The Isle of Skye became permanently tethered to the Scottish mainland when the Skye Bridge opened in 1995. The controversial bridge tolls were abolished in 2004 and the crossing is now free.

Much of the driving is on single-track roads – remember to use passing places to allow any traffic behind you to overtake. There are petrol stations at Broadford (open 24 hours), Armadale, Portree, Dunvegan and Uig.

ℹ Getting Around

BUS

Getting around the island by public transport can be a pain, especially if you want to explore away from the main Kyleakin–Portree–Uig road. Here, as in much of the Highlands, there are fewer buses on Saturday and only a handful of Sunday services.

Stagecoach (www.stagecoachbus.com) operates the main bus routes on the island, linking all the main villages and towns. Its Skye Dayrider/Megarider ticket gives unlimited bus travel for one/seven days for £9.20/34.60. For timetable info, call **Traveline** (☑ 0871 200 22 33; www.travelinescotland.com).

TAXI

You can order a taxi or hire a car (arrange for the car to be waiting at Kyle of Lochalsh train station) from **Kyle Taxi Company** (☑ 01599-534323; www.skyecarhire.co.uk; car hire per day/week from around £40/240).

Kyleakin (Caol Acain)

POP 100

Poor wee Kyleakin had the carpet pulled from under it when the Skye Bridge opened and it went from being the gateway to the island to a backwater bypassed by the main road. It's now a pleasant, peaceful little place, with a harbour used by yachts and fishing boats.

About 3 miles southwest of Kyleakin, a minor road leads southwards to Kylerhea, where there's a 1½-hour nature trail to a shore-front otter hide, where you stand a good chance of seeing these elusive creatures. A little further on is the jetty for the car ferry to Glenelg on the mainland.

Bright Water Visitor Centre VISITOR CENTRE (☑01599-530040; www.eileanban.org; The Pier; adult/child £1/free; ☉10am-4pm Mon-Fri Easter-Sep) The community-run visitor centre serves as a base for tours of Eilean Ban – the island used as a stepping stone by the Skye Bridge – where Gavin Maxwell (author of *Ring of Bright Water*) spent the last 18 months of his life in 1968–69, living in the lighthouse keeper's cottage. The island is now a nature reserve, and tours (£7 per person, departing 2pm weekdays) are available in summer; bookings are a must.

The visitor centre also houses a child-friendly exhibition on Maxwell, the lighthouse and the island's wildlife.

Broadford (An T-Ath Leathann)

POP 750

The long, straggling village of Broadford is a service centre for the scattered communities of southern Skye. It has a 24-hour petrol station, a bank and a large Co-op supermarket with an ATM.

There are lots of B&Bs in and around Broadford and the village is well placed for exploring southern Skye by car.

🛌 Sleeping

Skye Basecamp HOSTEL £ (☑01471-820044; www.skyebasecamp.co.uk; Lime Park; dm/q from £20/70; P☎) Run by the mountaineers at Skye Guides (☑01471-822116; www.skyeguides.co.uk), this well-equipped hostel is set in a converted residential house with great views across the sea towards the Crowlin Islands. Maps, guidebooks, weather forecasts and walking advice are all to hand.

★Tigh an Dochais B&B ££ (☑01471-820022; www.skyebedbreakfast.co.uk; 13 Harrapool; d £105; P☎) ✦ A cleverly designed modern building, Tigh an Dochais is one of Skye's best B&Bs – a little footbridge leads to the front door, which is on the 1st floor. Here you'll find the dining room (gorgeous breakfasts) and lounge offering a stunning view of sea and hills; the bedrooms (downstairs) open onto an outdoor deck with that same wonderful view.

Berabhaigh B&B ££ (☑01471-822372; www.isleofskye.net/berabhaigh; 3 Lime Park; r per person £42.50; ☉Mar-Oct; P☎) This lovely old croft house with bay views is located just off the main road at the eastern end of the village, not far from Creelers.

Skye Picture House B&B ££ (☑01471-822531; www.skyepicturehouse.com; Ard Dorch; s/d from £40/80; P☎) Perched just a stone's throw above the sea with a view across to the island of Scalpay, the setting of this welcoming B&B could hardly be better. No cooked breakfast, but the cold buffet is delicious.

🍴 Eating

★Creelers SEAFOOD ££ (☑01471-822281; www.skye-seafood-restaurant. co.uk; Lower Harrapool; mains £14-20; ☉noon-8.30pm Tue-Sat Mar-Nov; ⚑) ✦ Broadford has several places to eat but one really stands out: Creelers is a small, bustling restaurant (refurbished in 2018) that serves some of the best seafood on Skye. The house speciality is traditional Marseille bouillabaisse (a rich, spicy seafood stew). Best to book ahead.

★Cafe Sia CAFE, PIZZERIA ££ (☑01471-822616; www.cafesia.co.uk; Rathad na h-Atha; mains £7-17; ☉10am-9pm; ☎⚑) ✦ Serving everything from eggs Benedict and cappuccino to cocktails and seafood specials, this appealing cafe specialises in wood-fired pizzas (also available to take away) and superb artisan coffee. There's also an outdoor deck with great views of the Red Cuillin. Takeaway coffee from 8am.

Armadale & Sleat

If you cross over the sea to Skye on the ferry from Mallaig you arrive in Armadale, at the southern end of the long, low-lying peninsula known as Sleat (pronounced 'slate'). The landscape of Sleat itself is not exceptional, but it provides a grandstand for ogling the magnificent scenery on either side – take the steep and twisting minor road that loops through Tarskavaig and Tokavaig for stunning views of the Isle of Rum, the Cuillin Hills and Bla Bheinn.

Armadale is little more than a store, a post office, a cluster of craft shops and a scattering of houses.

Museum of the Isles   MUSEUM
(☑ 01471-844305; www.clandonald.com; adult/child £8.50/7; ☉ 10am-5.30pm Apr-Oct, occasionally shorter hours Oct; P ☺) Just along the road from Armadale pier is the part-ruined **Armadale Castle**, former seat of Lord MacDonald of Sleat. The neighbouring museum will tell you all you ever wanted to know about Clan Donald, and also provides an easily digestible history of the Lordship of the Isles. Prize exhibits include rare portraits of clan chiefs, and a wine glass that was once used by Bonnie Prince Charlie. The ticket also gives admission to the lovely castle gardens.

Shed   CAFE ££
(☑ 01471-844222; mains £6-15; ☉ 9am-6pm May-Sep, call to check Oct-Apr; P) A cute little wooden shed at Armadale pier has some outdoor tables and serves good seafood salads, pizzas, fish and chips, and coffee. You can sit in or take away.

❶ Getting There & Away

From late May to August there are three to five buses a day Monday to Saturday (three on Sunday) from Armadale to Broadford (£4.10, 30 minutes) and Portree (£7.70, 1¼ hours), timed to meet the arrival of ferries from Mallaig. Outside the summer season, services are less frequent and may not coincide with ferry times.

Isleornsay

This pretty bay, 8 miles north of Armadale, lies opposite Sandaig Bay on the mainland, where Gavin Maxwell lived and wrote his much-loved memoir *Ring of Bright Water*. It's home to an atmospheric old hotel and bar, and an arts and crafts gallery.

Torabhaig Distillery   DISTILLERY
(☑ 01471-833447; www.torabhaig.com; Teangue; tours per person £10; ☉ 10am-5pm Mon-Fri) A converted farm steading overlooking the sea houses Skye's second distillery, opened in 2017. There's a visitor centre and cafe; tours are best booked in advance.

★ **Toravaig House Hotel**   HOTEL ££
(☑ 01471-820200; www.toravaig.com; Toravaig; d £110-149; P ☞) This hotel, 3 miles south of Isleornsay, is one of those places where the owners know a thing or two about hospitality – as soon as you arrive you'll feel right at home, whether relaxing on the sofas by the log fire in the lounge or admiring the view across the Sound of Sleat from the lawn chairs in the garden.

The spacious bedrooms – ask for room 1 (Eriskay), with its enormous sleigh bed – are luxuriously equipped, from the crisp bed linen to the huge, high-pressure shower heads. The elegant restaurant serves the best of local fish, game and lamb. After dinner you can retire to the lounge with a single malt and flick through the yachting and angling magazines.

Hotel Eilean Iarmain   HOTEL £££
(☑ 01471-833332; www.eilean-iarmain.co.uk; d from £200; P ☞ ☺) A charming old Victorian hotel with log fires, chintzy traditional decor, a candlelit restaurant and 12 luxurious rooms (plus another six in the Garden House), many with sea views. The hotel's cosy, wood-panelled **Prában Bar** (mains £11-16; ☉ noon-2.30pm & 5.30-9pm) hosts live folk music and serves delicious, upmarket pub grub.

An Crùbh   CAFE £
(☑ 01471-833417; http://ancrubh.com; Duisdale Beag; mains £4-10; ☉ 10am-4.30pm Wed-Sun Apr-Sep; P ☞) This gorgeous modern community centre, opened in 2017, has a cafe with fantastic views over the sea to the mainland mountains, and sofas in front of a wood-burning stove. As well as coffee and cake, there are soups, salads and sandwiches that make the most of local produce.

Elgol (Ealaghol)

On a clear day, the journey along the road from Broadford to Elgol is one of the most scenic on Skye. It takes in two classic postcard panoramas – the view of Bla Bheinn across Loch Slapin (near Torrin), and the superb view of the entire Cuillin range from Elgol pier. Elgol itself is a tiny settlement at the end of a long, single-track road.

◉ Sights

Spar Cave
CAVE

Just east of Elgol is the Spar Cave, famously visited by Sir Walter Scott in 1814 and mentioned in his poem 'Lord of the Isles'. The 80m-deep cave is wild, remote and filled with beautiful flowstone formations. It is a short walk from the village of Glasnakille, but the approach is over seaweed-covered boulders and is only accessible for one hour either side of low water. Check tide times and route information at the tearoom in Elgol.

☞ Tours

Aquaxplore
BOATING

(☏0800 731 3089; www.aquaxplore.co.uk; Elgol Pier; ☺Apr-Oct) Runs 1½-hour high-speed boat trips from Elgol to an abandoned shark-hunting station on the island of Soay (adult/child £30/22), once owned by *Ring of Bright Water* author Gavin Maxwell. There are longer trips (£60/48, four hours) to Rum, Canna and Sanday to visit breeding colonies of puffins, with the chance of seeing minke whales on the way.

Misty Isle
BOATING

(☏01471-866288; www.mistyisleboattrips.co.uk; Elgol Pier; adult/child £25/12.50; ☺Apr-Oct) The pretty, traditional wooden launch *Misty Isle* offers cruises to Loch Coruisk with 1½ hours ashore (no Sunday service).

⌫ Sleeping & Eating

The only places to eat are the cafe above the car park halfway down the hill towards the pier, and the restaurant at Coruisk House (☏01471-866330; www.coruiskhouse.com; ☺Mar-Oct; P☺). You can buy groceries and get takeaway soup and sandwiches at the Elgol Shop (www.elgolshop.com; ☺10am-5pm Mon-Sat; P) nearby.

★Mary's Thatched Cottages COTTAGE £££
(☏01471-866275; www.isleofskyecottages.com; 4/7 nights from £700/945; ☺Apr-Sep; P☺☺) These thatch-roofed dwellings (each sleeping two to four people) by the roadside as you arrive in Elgol from Broadford must be the island's cutest accommodation. Four beautifully reconstructed stone cottages have been designed with modern comforts

in mind – the stone slab floors have underfloor heating. Minimum stay is three nights, Friday to Monday; book as far in advance as possible.

❶ Getting There & Away

Bus 55 runs from Broadford to Elgol (£4.30, 40 minutes, three daily Monday to Friday only).

Cuillin Hills

The Cuillin Hills are Britain's most spectacular mountain range (the name comes from the Old Norse *kjöllen,* meaning 'keel-shaped'). Though small in stature – Sgurr Alasdair, the highest summit, is only 993m – the peaks are near-alpine in character, with knife-edge ridges, jagged pinnacles, scree-filled gullies and hectares of naked rock.

While they are a paradise for experienced mountaineers, the higher reaches of the Cuillin are off limits to the majority of hikers. The good news is that there are also plenty of good low-level hikes within the ability of most walkers.

There are two main bases for exploring the Cuillin – Sligachan to the north (on the Kyle of Lochalsh–Portree bus route), and Glenbrittle to the south (no public transport).

One of the best hikes (on a fine day) is the steep climb from Glenbrittle campsite to Coire Lagan (6 miles round trip; allow at least three hours). The impressive upper corrie contains a lochan for bathing (for the hardy!), and the surrounding cliffs are a playground for rock climbers – bring your binoculars.

Even more spectacular, but much harder to reach on foot, is Loch Coruisk (from the Gaelic Coir'Uisg, the Water Corrie), a remote loch ringed by the highest peaks of the Cuillin. Accessible by boat trip (☏0800 731 3089; www.bellajane.co.uk; Elgol Pier; adult/child £28/16; ☺Apr-Oct) from Elgol, or via an arduous 5.5-mile hike from Kilmarie, Coruisk was popularised by Sir Walter Scott in his 1815 poem 'Lord of the Isles'. Crowds of Victorian tourists and landscape artists followed in Scott's footsteps, including JMW Turner, whose watercolours were used to illustrate Scott's works.

Glenbrittle Campsite
CAMPSITE £

(☏01478-640404; www.dunvegancastle.com; Glenbrittle; sites per adult/child incl car £10/6; ☺Apr-Sep) Excellent site, close to mountains and sea, with a shop selling food and outdoor kit. The midges can be diabolical, though.

Glenbrittle SYHA   HOSTEL £
(☎ 01478-640278; www.syha.org.uk; Glenbrittle; dm/tw £20/59; ☺ Apr-Sep; ℗) Scandinavian-style timber hostel that quickly fills up with climbers on holiday weekends.

Sligachan Campsite   CAMPSITE £
(www.sligachan.co.uk; Sligachan; sites per person £8; ☺ Apr-Oct) This basic campsite is across the road from the Sligachan Hotel. Be warned – this spot is a midge magnet. No bookings.

Sligachan Hotel   HOTEL £££
(☎01478-650204; www.sligachan.co.uk; Sligachan; r from £170; ℗🐾) The Slig, as it has been known to generations of climbers, is a near village in itself, encompassing a comfortable hotel, a microbrewery, self-catering cottages, a small mountaineering museum, a big barn of a pub – **Seamus Bar** (mains £9-18; ☺food served noon-9pm Apr-Oct, to 3pm Nov-Mar; 🐾🍴) – and an adventure playground.

Minginish

Loch Harport, to the north of the Cuillin, divides the Minginish peninsula from the rest of Skye. On its southern shore lies the village of **Carbost**, home to Talisker malt whisky, produced at Talisker Distillery.

Magnificent **Talisker Bay**, 5 miles west of Carbost, is framed by a sea stack and a waterfall.

As well as the excellent **Skyewalker** (☎01478-640250; www.skyewalkerhostel.com; Fiskavaig Rd, Portnalong; dm £20-22; ℗) hostel and the **Old Inn** (☎01478-640205; www.theoldinn skye.co.uk; Carbost; bunkhouse per person from £23, B&B s/d £75/100; ℗), there are several B&Bs and self-catering cottages. As ever, book ahead to avoid being caught without a bed.

Talisker Distillery   DISTILLERY
(☎01478-614308; www.malts.com; tours from £10; ☺9am-5.30pm Mon-Sat, 10am-5.30pm Sun Apr-Oct, shorter hours Nov-Mar; ℗) Skye's oldest distillery (established 1830) produces smooth, sweet and smoky Talisker single malt whisky. The guided tour includes a free dram.

Oyster Shed   SEAFOOD £
(www.facebook.com/oystershedskye; Carbost; mains £4-20; ☺noon-5pm Mon-Fri Apr-Oct, shorter hours Nov-Mar) 🌾 A farm shop selling fresh local seafood to take away, including oysters (£1.25 each), cooked mussels and scallops, lobster and chips, and seafood platters.

❶ Getting There & Away

There are two buses a day (school days only) from Portree to Carbost and Portnalong (£5.65, 55 minutes) via Sligachan.

Portree (Port Righ)
POP 2320

Portree is Skye's largest and liveliest town. It has a pretty harbour lined with brightly painted houses, and there are great views of the surrounding hills. Its name (from the Gaelic for King's Harbour) commemorates James V, who came here in 1540 to pacify the local clans.

◉ Sights & Activities

Aros Centre   CULTURAL CENTRE
(☎01478-613750; www.aros.co.uk; Viewfield Rd; exhibition £5; ☺9am-5pm; ℗🍴) **FREE** On the southern edge of Portree, the Aros Centre is a combined visitor centre, book and gift shop, restaurant, theatre and cinema. The St Kilda Exhibition details the history and culture of these remote rocky outcrops, and Xbox technology allows you to take a virtual tour of the islands.

The centre is a useful rainy-day retreat, with an indoor soft play area for children.

MV Stardust   BOATING
(☎07798 743858; www.skyeboat-trips.co.uk; Portree Harbour; adult/child £20/10) MV *Stardust* offers 1½-hour boat trips around Portree Bay, with the chance to see seals, porpoises and – if you're lucky – white-tailed sea eagles. There are longer two-hour cruises to the Sound of Raasay (£25/15). You can also arrange fishing trips, or to be dropped off for a hike on the Isle of Raasay and picked up again later.

🛏 Sleeping

Portree is well supplied with B&Bs, but accommodation fills up fast from April to October, so be sure to book ahead.

Portree SYHA   HOSTEL £
(☎01478-612231; www.syha.org.uk; Bayfield Rd; dm/tw £26/78; ℗🐾) This SYHA hostel (formerly Bayfield Backpackers) was completely renovated in 2015 and offers

brightly decorated dorms and private rooms, a stylish lounge with views over the bay, and outdoor seating areas. Its location in the town centre just 100m from the bus stop is ideal.

Torvaig Campsite   CAMPSITE £
(☑ 01478-611849; www.portreecampsite.co.uk; Torvaig; tent sites per person £9, campervan £21; ☺ Apr-Oct; ☎) An attractive, family-run campsite located 1.5 miles north of Portree, on the road to Staffin.

Ben Tianavaig B&B   B&B ££
(☑ 01478-612152; www.ben-tianavaig.co.uk; 5 Bosville Tce; r £80-98; Ⓟ☎) ✈ A warm welcome awaits from the Irish-Welsh couple who run this appealing B&B bang in the centre of town. All four bedrooms have a view across the harbour to the hill that gives the house its name, and breakfasts include free-range eggs and vegetables grown in the garden. Two-night minimum stay April to October; no credit cards.

Woodlands   B&B ££
(☑ 01478-612980; www.woodlands-portree.co.uk; Viewfield Rd; r £80; ☺ Mar-Oct; Ⓟ☎) A great location, with views across the bay, and unstinting hospitality make this modern B&B, a half-mile south of the town centre, an excellent choice.

Cuillin Hills Hotel   HOTEL £££
(☑ 01478-612003; www.cuillinhills-hotel-skye.co.uk; Scorrybreac Rd; r from £295; Ⓟ☎) Located on the eastern fringes of Portree, this luxury hotel enjoys a superb outlook across the harbour towards the Cuillin mountains. The more expensive rooms cosset guests with four-poster beds and panoramic views, but everyone can enjoy the scenery from the glass-fronted restaurant and well-stocked whisky bar.

✖ Eating

Café Arriba   CAFE £
(☑01478-611830; www.cafearriba.co.uk; Quay Brae; mains £6-12; ☺7am-6pm May-Sep, 8am-5pm Tue-Sat Oct-Apr; ☑) ✈ Arriba is a funky little cafe, brightly decked out in primary colours and offering delicious flatbread melts (bacon, leek and cheese is a favourite), as well as the best choice of vegetarian grub on the island, ranging from a veggie breakfast fry-up to felafel wraps with hummus and chilli sauce. Also serves excellent coffee.

Isle of Skye Baking Co   CAFE £
(www.isleofskyebakingco.co.uk; Old Woollen Mill, Dunvegan Rd; mains £4-9; ☺10am-5pm Mon-Sat; Ⓟ☖) ✈ Famous for its 'lunch bread' – a small loaf baked with a filling inside, like cheese and leek, or beef stew – and platters of Scottish cheese and charcuterie, this cafe is also an art gallery and craft shop.

★**Scorrybreac**   MODERN SCOTTISH ££
(☑ 01478-612069; www.scorrybreac.com; 7 Bosville Tce; 3-course dinner £42; ☺5-9pm Wed-Sun year-round, noon-2pm mid-May–mid-Sep) ✈ Set in the front rooms of what was once a private house, and with just eight tables, Scorrybreac is snug and intimate, offering fine dining without the faff. Chef Calum Munro (son of Donnie Munro, of Gaelic rock band Runrig fame) sources as much produce as possible from Skye, including foraged herbs and mushrooms, and creates the most exquisite concoctions.

Dulse & Brose   MODERN SCOTTISH ££
(☑ 01478-612846; www.bosvillehotel.co.uk; Bosville Hotel, 7 Bosville Tce; mains £17-23; ☺noon-3pm & 6-10pm May-Sep, 6-8.15pm Oct-Apr; ☎) ✈ This hotel restaurant sports a relaxed atmosphere, an award-winning chef and a menu that makes the most of Skye produce – including lamb, game, seafood, cheese, organic vegetables and berries – and adds a French twist to traditional dishes. The neighbouring Merchant Bar (food served noon to 5pm), also part of the Bosville Hotel, serves tapas-style bar snacks through the afternoon.

ⓘ Information

Portree Tourist Office (p376).

ⓘ Getting There & Around

BUS

The main bus stop is at Somerled Sq. There are five or six Scottish Citylink buses every day from Kyle of Lochalsh to Portree (£7.10, one hour) continuing to Uig.

Local buses (mostly six to eight Monday to Saturday, three on Sunday) run from Portree to:

Armadale (£7.70, 1¼ hours) Connecting with the ferry to Mallaig late May to August.

Broadford (£6, 45 minutes) Four or five daily.

Dunvegan Castle (£5.35, 50 minutes) Four daily on Saturday year-round; also four daily Monday to Friday from May to September.

There are also three buses a day on a circular route around Trotternish (in both directions), taking in Flodigarry (£4.10, 35 minutes), Kilmuir (£4.80, 45 minutes) and Uig (£3.60, 30 minutes).

BICYCLE

Island Cycles (☑ 01478-613121; www.island cycles-skye.co.uk; The Green; bike hire per 24hr £20; ⊘ 9am-5pm Mon-Sat) You can hire bikes here.

Dunvegan (Dun Bheagain)

Dunvegan, an unremarkable village on the western side of Skye, is famous for its historic namesake castle which has links to Sir Walter Scott and Bonnie Prince Charlie.

Dunvegan Castle   CASTLE
(☑ 01470-521206;   www.dunvegancastle.com; adult/child £14/9;   ⊘ 10am-5.30pm Easter–mid-Oct;   P) Skye's most famous historic building, and one of its most popular tourist attractions, Dunvegan Castle is the seat of the chief of Clan MacLeod. In addition to the usual castle stuff – swords, silver and family portraits – there are some interesting artefacts, including the Fairy Flag, a diaphanous silk banner that dates from some time between the 4th and 7th centuries, and Bonnie Prince Charlie's waistcoat and a lock of his hair, donated by Flora MacDonald's granddaughter.

Coral Beaches   BEACH
From the end of the minor road beyond Dunvegan Castle entrance, an easy 1-mile walk leads to the Coral Beaches – a pair of blindingly white beaches composed of the bleached exoskeletons of coralline algae known as *maerl*.

Edinbane Pottery   ARTS & CRAFTS
(☑ 01470-582234;   www.edinbane-pottery.co.uk; Edinbane;   ⊘ 9am-6pm   Easter-Oct,   Mon-Fri Nov-Easter) On the way to Dunvegan from Portree you'll pass Edinbane Pottery, one of the island's original craft workshops, established in 1971, where you can watch potters at work creating beautiful and colourful stoneware.

🛈 Getting There & Away

Stagecoach bus 56 runs from Portree to Dunvegan (£5.35, 50 minutes), four times on Saturday year-round, and also Monday to Friday from May to September.

Duirinish & Waternish

The Duirinish peninsula to the west of Dunvegan, and Waternish to the north, boast some of Skye's most atmospheric hotels and restaurants, plus an eclectic range of artists' studios and crafts workshops.

The sparsely populated Duirinish peninsula is dominated by the distinctive flat-topped peaks of Helabhal Mhor (469m) and Helabhal Bheag (488m), known locally as MacLeod's Tables. There are some fine walks from Orbost, including the summit of Helabhal Bheag (allow 3½ hours return) and the 5-mile trail from Orbost to MacLeod's Maidens, a series of pointed sea stacks at the southern tip of the peninsula.

It's worth making the long drive beyond Dunvegan to the western side of the Duirinish peninsula to see the spectacular sea cliffs of Waterstein Head and to walk down to Neist Point lighthouse with its views to the Outer Hebrides.

🛏 Sleeping

Eco Bells Glamping   CAMPSITE £
(☑ 01470-521461; www.facebook.com/skyeecobells; Orbost, Duirinish; per tent £86;   ⊘ Apr-Sep;   P)
Tucked away in a remote corner, on a minor road about 3 miles south of Dunvegan, this place offers accommodation in three large bell tents in a rural setting. Each tent sleeps up to three adults (or two adults and two children) and has beds, heating, a fire pit and barbecue. There's also a smaller tent and two wooden cabins.

★ Hillstone Lodge   B&B £££
(☑ 01470-511434;   www.hillstonelodge.com;   12 Colbost; r from £140;   P 🛜) You can't help notice the many new houses on Skye that bear the hallmarks of award-winning local architects Rural Design – weathered timber walls and modern materials used with traditional shapes and forms. Hillstone is one of the best, with tasteful modern styling and stunning views across Loch Dunvegan. It's about 1km north of the Three Chimneys, above the pier.

🍴 Eating

Cafe Lephin   CAFE £
(☑ 01470-511465; www.cafelephin.co.uk; 2 Lephin, Glendale;   ⊘ 11am-4.30pm Tue-Sat; 🛜 ♿ 🐾) A mixture of modern and rustic with touches of tweed and sheepskin, this wee cafe cap-

tures the spirit of enterprise that's bringing life back to areas of Skye that were deserted during the Highland Clearances. Great coffee, comfy sofas and a menu of cake and quiche.

Stein Inn PUB FOOD **££**
(☎01470-592362; www.stein-inn.co.uk; Stein, Waternish; mains £8-16; ⊘kitchen noon-4pm & 6.30-9pm Easter-Oct, 12.30-2.30pm & 5.30-8pm Nov-Easter; 🅿) This old country inn dates from 1790 and has a lively little bar and a delightful beer garden beside the loch – a real suntrap on summer afternoons. The bar serves real ales from the Isle of Skye Brewery and excellent bar meals. Food is served in winter too, but call ahead to confirm hours.

There's also a handful of bedrooms here (£83 to £125 per room), all with sea views.

★Loch Bay SEAFOOD **£££**
(☎01470-592235; www.lochbay-restaurant.co.uk; Stein, Waternish; 3-course dinner £43.50; ⊘12.15-1.45pm Wed-Sun, 6.15-9pm Tue-Sat Apr-early Oct; 🅿) 🍽 One of Skye's most romantic restaurants, a cosy farmhouse kitchen of a place with terracotta tiles and a wood-burning stove, Loch Bay was awarded a Michelin star in 2018. The menu includes most things that swim in the sea or live in a shell, but there are non-seafood choices too. Best to book ahead.

★Three Chimneys MODERN SCOTTISH **£££**
(☎01470-511258; www.threechimneys.co.uk; Colbost; 3-course lunch/dinner £40/68; ⊘12.15-1.45pm Mon-Sat mid-Mar–Oct, plus Sun Easter-Sep, 6.30-9.15pm daily year-round; 🅿🛜) 🍽 Halfway between Dunvegan and Waterstein, the Three Chimneys is a superb romantic retreat combining a gourmet restaurant in a candlelit crofter's cottage with sumptuous five-star rooms (double £345) in the modern house next door. Book well in advance, and note that children are not welcome in the restaurant in the evenings.

Red Roof SCOTTISH **£££**
(☎01470-511766; www.redroofskye.co.uk; Glendale, Duirinish; 3-course dinner £35; ⊘7-9pm Tue-Thu Apr-Oct; 🅿🛜📶🐾) 🍽 Tucked away up a glen, a mile off the main road, this restored 250-year-old byre is a wee haven of home-grown grub. The dinner-only menu, served at 7.30pm, specialises in Skye seafood, game and cheeses served with salad leaves and edible flowers grown just along the road. Must be booked in advance.

Trotternish

The Trotternish peninsula to the north of Portree has some of Skye's most beautiful – and bizarre – scenery. A loop road allows a circular driving tour of the peninsula from Portree, passing through the village of Uig, where the ferry to the Outer Hebrides departs.

◉ Sights

★Quiraing NATURAL FEATURE
Staffin Bay is dominated by the dramatic basalt escarpment of the Quiraing: its impressive land-slipped cliffs and pinnacles constitute one of Skye's most remarkable landscapes. From a parking area at the highest point of the minor road between Staffin and Uig you can walk north to the Quiraing in half an hour.

Old Man of Storr NATURAL FEATURE
(🅿) The 50m-high, pot-bellied pinnacle of crumbling basalt known as the Old Man of Storr is prominent above the road 6 miles north of Portree. Walk up to its foot from the car park at the northern end of Loch Leathan (2-mile round trip). This seemingly unclimbable pinnacle was first scaled in 1955 by English mountaineer Don Whillans, a feat that has been repeated only a handful of times since.

Fairy Glen AREA
Just south of Uig, a minor road (signposted 'Sheader and Balnaknock') leads a mile or so to the Fairy Glen, a strange and enchanting natural landscape of miniature conical hills, rocky towers, ruined cottages and a tiny roadside lochan.

Skye Museum of Island Life MUSEUM
(☎01470-552206; www.skyemuseum.co.uk; Kilmuir; adult/child £2.50/50p; ⊘9.30am-5pm Mon-Sat Easter-late Sep; 🅿) The peat-reek of crofting life in the 18th and 19th centuries is preserved in the thatched cottages, croft houses, barns and farm implements of the Skye Museum of Island Life. Behind the museum is Kilmuir Cemetery, where a tall Celtic cross marks the grave of Flora MacDonald; the cross was erected in 1955 to replace the original monument, of which 'every fragment was removed by tourists'.

Isle of Skye Brewery FOOD & DRINKS
(☎01470-542477; www.skyeale.com; The Pier, Uig; ⊘10am-6pm Mon-Fri, to 4pm Sat, noon-4pm Sun

DINOSAUR FOOTPRINTS ON SKYE

The occasional dinosaur bone has been turning up in the Jurassic rocks of the Trotternish peninsula since 1982 – intriguing, but nothing very exciting. Then, following a storm in 2002, a set of fossilised dinosaur footprints was exposed at An Corran in Staffin Bay. Their interest piqued, geologists began taking a closer interest in the Trotternish rocks and, in 2015, a major discovery was made near Duntulm Castle – a 170-million-year-old trackway of footprints left by a group of sauropods. Skye is now a major focus for research into dinosaur evolution.

A collection of Jurassic fossils and further information on dinosaur sites in Skye can be found at the **Staffin Dinosaur Museum** (www.staffindinosaur museum.com; 3 Ellishadder, Staffin; adult/child £2/1; ◉9.30am-5pm; ℗).

Apr-Oct) If you've time to kill while waiting for a ferry at Uig, the Isle of Skye Brewery shop sells locally brewed ales by the bottle, as well as gifts and souvenirs.

🛏 Sleeping & Eating

★**Cowshed Boutique Bunkhouse** HOSTEL £

(☏07917 536820; www.skyecowshed.co.uk; Uig; dm/tw £20/80, pod £70; ℗🐕🛏) This hostel enjoys a glorious setting overlooking Uig Bay, with superb views from its ultra-stylish lounge. The dorms have custom-built wooden bunks that offer comfort and privacy, while the camping pods (sleeping up to four, but more comfortable with two) have heating and en suite shower rooms; there are even mini 'dog pods' for your canine companions.

Shulista Croft CAMPSITE £

(☏01470-552314; www.shulistacroft.co.uk; North Duntulm, Shulista; 2-/4-person pod per night £50/90; ◉Mar-Nov) 🌱 Set on a working croft amid sheep, lambs and chickens, Shulista has luxury timber camping pods with great views (two-night minimum stay; sleeps up to four, kids stay free). Each one is heated and insulated, and has an en suite shower room, basic kitchenette and even a TV. There are also more basic, two-person pods.

Dun Flodigarry Hostel & Camping HOSTEL, CAMPSITE £

(☏01470-552212; www.hostelflodigarry.co.uk; Flodigarry; dm/tw £20/47, tent sites per person £10; ℗@🛏) A bright and welcoming hostel that enjoys a stunning location overlooking the sea, with views across Raasay to the mainland mountains. A nearby hiking trail leads to the Quiraing (p383) rock formation (2.5 miles away), and there's a hotel bar barely 100m from the door. You can also camp nearby and use all the hostel facilities.

Single Track CAFE £

(www.facebook.com/singletrackskye; Kilmaluag; snacks £3-4; ◉10.30am-5pm Sun-Thu mid-May–late Oct; ℗🛏) This turf-roofed, timber-clad art gallery and espresso bar will be familiar to fans of British TV's *Grand Designs* – it was featured on the Channel 4 series in 2012. The owners are serious about their coffee, and it's seriously good, as are the accompanying cakes and scones. Art by the owners and other Skye artists is on display, and for sale.

Raasay

POP 160

Raasay is the rugged, 10-mile-long island that lies off Skye's east coast. The island's fascinating history is recounted in the book *Calum's Road* by Roger Hutchinson.

There are several good walks here, including one to the flat-topped conical hill of **Dun Caan** (443m), and another to the extraordinary ruin of **Brochel Castle**, perched on a pinnacle at the northern end of Raasay. The Forestry Commission publishes a free leaflet (available in the ferry waiting room) with suggested walking trails.

Accommodation is very limited – don't turn up without a reservation unless you are planning to wild camp (there are plenty of places to do so in the east and north of the island).

Raasay Distillery DISTILLERY

(☏01478-470178; https://raasaydistillery.com; Borodale House; tours £10; ◉9.30am-5.30pm Mon-Sat; ℗) Raasay's first ever (legal!) distillery opened in 2017, and comes with a twist – you can stay the night here, in one of the six designer bedrooms in the Victorian hotel that has been incorporated into the modern building.

★ **Raasay House** HOSTEL, B&B £££
(☎01478-660266; www.raasay-house.co.uk; dm
£25, d £175; ℗🛜) 🞇 Beautifully renovated
Raasay House (originally the laird's residence), just a short walk from the ferry pier,
provides outdoor activity courses and accommodation ranging from hostel bunks to luxury B&B. The bar and restaurant (mains £10
to £23) serves good-quality seafood, beef
and game, and locally brewed beers.

❶ Getting There & Away

CalMac (www.calmac.co.uk; return passenger/
car £3.90/12.60) ferries run from Sconser, on
the road from Portree to Broadford, to Raasay
(25 minutes, nine daily Monday to Saturday,
twice daily Sunday). There are no petrol stations
on the island, nor is there any public transport.

OUTER HEBRIDES

POP 27,670

The Western Isles, or Na h-Eileanan an Iar
in Gaelic – also known as the Outer Hebrides – are a 130-mile-long string of islands
lying off the northwest coast of Scotland.
There are 119 islands in total, of which the
five main inhabited islands are Lewis and
Harris (two parts of a single island, although
often described as if they are separate
islands), North Uist, Benbecula, South Uist
and Barra. The middle three (often referred
to simply as 'the Uists') are connected by
road-bearing causeways.

The ferry crossing from Ullapool or Uig to
the Western Isles marks an important cultural divide – more than a third of Scotland's
registered crofts are in the Outer Hebrides,
and no less than 60% of the population are
Gaelic speakers.

If your time is limited, head straight for
the west coast of Lewis with its prehistoric
sites, preserved blackhouses and beautiful
beaches.

❶ Information

The only tourist offices are in Stornoway and
Tarbert. See www.visitouterhebrides.co.uk for
tourist information.

❶ Getting There & Away

AIR

There are airports at Stornoway (Lewis), Benbecula and Barra. Flights operate to Stornoway
from Edinburgh, Inverness, Glasgow, Aberdeen
and Manchester. There are also two flights a day

(Tuesday to Thursday only) between Stornoway
and Benbecula.

There are daily flights from Glasgow to Barra,
and from Tuesday to Thursday to Benbecula. At
Barra, the planes land on the hard-sand beach at
low tide, so the schedule depends on the tides.
Eastern Airways (☎ 0870 366 9100; www.
easternairways.com)
Loganair (☎ 0344 800 2855; www.loganair.
co.uk)

BOAT
Standard one-way fares on CalMac ferries:

Crossing	Duration (hours)	Car (£)	Driver/ Passenger (£)
Ullapool– Stornoway	2¾	51	9.50
Uig– Lochmaddy	1¾	31	6.30
Uig–Tarbert	1½	31	6.30
Oban– Castlebay	4¾	68	14.75
Mallaig– Lochboisdale	3½	58	10.45

There are two or three ferries a day to Stornoway, one or two a day to Tarbert and Lochmaddy,
and one a day to Castlebay and Lochboisdale.
See www.calmac.co.uk for ferry timetables.

Advance booking for cars is recommended
(essential in July and August); foot and bicycle
passengers should have no problems. Bicycles
are carried free.

❶ Getting Around

Despite their separate names, Lewis and Harris
are actually one island. Berneray, North Uist,
Benbecula, South Uist and Eriskay are all linked
by road bridges and causeways. There are car
ferries between Leverburgh (Harris) and Berneray and between Eriskay and Castlebay (Barra).

The local council publishes timetables of
all bus and ferry services within the Outer
Hebrides, which are available at tourist offices.
Timetables can also be found online at www.
cne-siar.gov.uk.

BICYCLE
Bikes can be hired for around £10 to £20 a day
in Stornoway (Lewis), Leverburgh (Harris),
Howmore (South Uist) and Castlebay (Barra).

BUS
The bus network covers almost every village in
the islands, with around four to six buses a day on
all the main routes; however, there are no buses
at all on Sunday. You can pick up timetables from
Stornoway tourist office (p387), or call Stornoway bus station (p387) for information.

CAR & MOTORCYCLE

Apart from the fast, two-lane road between Tarbert and Stornoway, most roads are single track (p466). The main hazard is posed by sheep wandering about or sleeping on the road. Petrol stations are far apart (almost all of those on Lewis and Harris are closed on Sunday), and fuel is about 10% more expensive than on the mainland.

There are petrol stations at Stornoway, Barvas, Borve, Uig, Breacleit (Great Bernera), Ness, Tarbert and Leverburgh on Lewis and Harris; Lochmaddy and Cladach on North Uist; Balivanich on Benbecula; Howmore, Lochboisdale and Daliburgh on South Uist; and Castlebay on Barra.

Cars can be hired from around £35/170 per day/week from **Car Hire Hebrides** (☑ 01851-706500; www.carhire-hebrides.co.uk; Ferry Terminal, Shell St).

Lewis (Leodhais)

POP 21,000 (INCLUDING HARRIS)

The northern part of Lewis is dominated by the desolate expanse of the Black Moor, a vast, undulating peat bog dimpled with glittering lochans, seen clearly from the Stornoway–Barvas road. But Lewis' finest scenery is on the west coast, from Barvas southwest to Mealista, where the rugged landscape of hill, loch and sandy strand is reminiscent of the northwestern Highlands. The Outer Hebrides' most evocative historic sites – Callanish Standing Stones (p388), **Dun Carloway** and Arnol Blackhouse (p388) – are also to be found here.

Stornoway (Steornabhagh)

POP 5715

Stornoway is the bustling 'capital' of the Outer Hebrides and the only real town in the whole archipelago. It's a surprisingly busy little place, with cars and people swamping the centre on weekdays. Though set on a beautiful natural harbour, the town isn't going to win any prizes for beauty or atmosphere, but it's a pleasant enough introduction to this remote corner of the country.

◎ Sights & Activities

Museum nan Eilean　　　　MUSEUM
(www.lews-castle.co.uk; Lews Castle; ◎10am-5pm Mon-Wed, Fri & Sat Apr-Sep, 1-4pm same days Oct-Mar; ℗) FREE The 'Museum of the Isles' opened in 2017, occupying a modern extension built onto the side of Lews Castle.

Artefacts, photos and videos celebrate the culture and history of the Outer Hebrides and explore traditional island life. The highlights of the collection are six of the famous **Lewis chess pieces**, discovered at Uig in west Lewis in 1831. Carved from whale and walrus ivory, they are thought to have been made in Norway more than 800 years ago.

Lews Castle　　　　CASTLE
(☑ 01851-822750; www.lews-castle.co.uk; ◎8am-5pm; ℗) FREE The Baronial mansion across the harbour from Stornoway town centre was built in the 1840s for the Matheson family, then owners of Lewis; it was gifted to the community by Lord Leverhulme in 1923. A major redevelopment completed in 2017 saw it converted to luxury self-catering accommodation, but the grand public rooms on the ground floor are free to visit when not in use. There's also an excellent **cafe** (mains £7-15; ◎8am-4pm; 🛜🖩), one of the few local eateries to open on Sundays.

The beautiful wooded grounds, crisscrossed with walking trails, are open to the public and host the Hebridean Celtic Festival (p386) in July.

An Lanntair Arts Centre　　　ARTS CENTRE
(☑ 01851-708480; www.lanntair.com; Kenneth St; ◎10am-9pm Mon-Wed, to midnight Thu-Sat) FREE The modern, purpose-built An Lanntair (Gaelic for 'lighthouse'), complete with art gallery, theatre, cinema and restaurant, is the centre of the town's cultural life. It hosts changing exhibitions of contemporary art and is a good source of information on cultural events.

Hebridean Adventures　　WILDLIFE WATCHING
(☑ 07871 463755; www.hebrideanadventures.co.uk; Stornoway Harbour; per person £95; ◎Apr-Sep) Seven-hour whale-watching trips (Wednesdays only) out of Stornoway harbour in a converted fishing boat with a cosy saloon to shelter from any wild weather.

✯ Festivals & Events

Hebridean Celtic Festival　　　MUSIC
(www.hebceltfest.com; ◎Jul) A four-day extravaganza of folk, rock and Celtic music held in the second half of July.

🛏 Sleeping

★ Heb Hostel　　　　HOSTEL £
(☑ 01851-709889; www.hebhostel.com; 25 Kenneth St; dm/f £19/75; @🛜) The Heb is an easy-

going hostel close to the ferry, with comfy wooden bunks, a convivial living room with peat fire and a welcoming owner who can provide all kinds of advice on what to do and where to go.

29 Kenneth St
B&B ££

(☑ 07917 035295; www.stornowaybedandbreakfast. co.uk; 29 Kenneth St; s/d £65/105; ☜) Nine smartly fitted out bedrooms spread between two houses (the other is across the street at No 32) offer great-value accommodation, just five minutes' walk from the ferry terminal.

Hal o' the Wynd
B&B ££

(☑ 01851-706073; www.halothewynd.com; 2 Newton St; r from £108; ☜) Touches of tartan and Harris Tweed lend a traditional air to this welcoming B&B, conveniently located directly opposite the ferry pier. Most rooms have views over the harbour to Lews Castle.

Park Guest House
B&B ££

(☑ 01851-702485; www.the-parkguesthouse.com; 30 James St; s/d from £79/110; ☜) A charming Victorian villa with a conservatory and six luxurious rooms (mostly en suite), the Park Guest House is comfortable and central and has the advantage of an excellent restaurant specialising in Scottish seafood, beef and game plus one or two vegetarian dishes (three-course dinner £38). Rooms overlooking the main road can be noisy on weekday mornings.

Eating

Artizan Cafe
CAFE £

(☑ 01851-706538; www.facebook.com/artizan stornoway; 12-14 Church St; mains £4-7; ☺ 10am-6pm Mon-Fri, 9am-6pm Sat; ☜⊞) Recycled timber and cool colours mark out this cafe-gallery as one of Stornoway's hip hang-outs, serving great coffee and cake and tapas-style lunches (noon to 2.30pm). Hosts cultural events, including poetry nights on Saturday.

An Lanntair Arts Centre
BISTRO ££

(www.lanntair.com; Kenneth St; mains £11-17; ☺ kitchen 10am-8pm Mon-Sat; ☜☑⊞) The stylish and family-friendly cafe-bar at the arts centre serves a broad range of freshly prepared dishes, from tasty bacon rolls at breakfast to burgers, salads or fish and chips for lunch and chargrilled steaks or local scallops for dinner.

OFF THE BEATEN TRACK

BUTT OF LEWIS

The **Butt of Lewis** (Ⓟ) – the extreme northern tip of the Hebrides – is windswept and rugged, with a very imposing lighthouse, pounding surf and large colonies of nesting fulmars on the high cliffs. There's a bleak sense of isolation here, with nothing but the grey Atlantic between you and Canada. The main settlement is **Port of Ness** (Port Nis), which has an attractive harbour. To the west is the sandy beach of **Traigh**, which is popular with surfers.

Lido
INTERNATIONAL ££

(☑ 01851-703354; 5 Cromwell St; mains £8-13; ☺ noon-3pm & 5-9pm Mon-Sat; ☜⊞) Black-and-chrome decor and grey-granite tabletops lend an art-deco air to this busy diner, whose menu covers all bases from gourmet burgers to smoked-salmon salads to Italian meatballs. Speciality of the house is pizza, though, and these are excellent – thin, crispy and well-fired.

★ Digby Chick
BISTRO £££

(☑ 01851-700026; www.digbychick.co.uk; 5 Bank St; mains £19-26, 2-course lunch £15; ☺ noon-2pm & 5.30-9pm Mon-Sat; ☑) ✔ A modern restaurant that dishes up bistro cuisine such as haddock and chips, slow-roast pork belly or roast vegetable panini at lunchtime, the Digby Chick metamorphoses into a candlelit gourmet restaurant in the evening, serving dishes such as grilled langoustines, seared scallops, venison and steak. Three-course early bird menu (5.30pm to 6.30pm) for £24.

ℹ Information

Sandwick Rd Petrol Station (Engebret Ltd; ☑ 01851-702304; www.engebret.co.uk; Sandwick Rd; ☺ 6am-11pm Mon-Sat, 10am-4pm Sun) The only shop in town that's open on a Sunday, selling groceries, alcohol, hardware, fishing tackle and outdoor kits. The Sunday papers arrive around 2pm.

Stornoway Tourist Office (☑ 01851-703088; www.visitouterhebrides.co.uk; 26 Cromwell St; ☺ 9am-6pm Mon-Sat Apr-Oct, to 5pm Mon-Fri Nov-Mar)

ℹ Getting There & Away

The **bus station** (☑ 01851-704327; South Beach) is on the waterfront next to the ferry terminal (left luggage 25p to £1.30 per piece).

NORTHERN HIGHLANDS & ISLANDS LEWIS (LEODHAIS)

Bus W10 runs from Stornoway to Tarbert (£4.80, one hour, four or five daily Monday to Saturday) and Leverburgh (£6.80, two hours).

The Westside Circular bus W2 runs a circular route from Stornoway through Callanish (£2.70, 30 minutes), Carloway, Garenin and Arnol; the timetable allows you to visit one or two of the sites in a day.

The bus network covers almost every village in the islands, with around four to six buses a day on all the main routes; however, there are no buses at all on Sunday. You can pick up time-tables from the tourist offices, or call Stornoway bus station for information.

Arnol

One of Scotland's most evocative historic buildings, the **Arnol Blackhouse** (HES; ☑ 01851-710395; www.historicenvironment.scot; adult/child £5/3; ⏱ 9.30am-5.30pm Mon-Sat Apr-Sep, 10am-4pm Mon, Tue & Thu-Sat Oct-Mar; ℗) is not so much a museum as a perfectly preserved fragment of a lost world. Built in 1885, this traditional blackhouse – a combined byre, barn and home – was inhabited until 1964 and has not been changed since the last inhabitant moved out. The museum is about 3 miles west of Barvas.

The staff faithfully rekindle the central peat fire every morning so you can experience the distinctive peat-reek; there's no chimney, and the smoke finds its own way out through the turf roof, windows and door – spend too long inside and you might feel like you've been kippered!

At nearby Bragar, a pair of whalebones forms an arch by the road, with the rusting harpoon that killed the whale dangling from the centre.

Garenin (Na Gearrannan)

The picturesque and fascinating Gearrannan Blackhouse Village is a cluster of nine restored thatch-roofed blackhouses perched above the exposed Atlantic coast. One of the cottages is home to the **Blackhouse Museum** (☑ 01851-643416; www.gearrannan. com; adult/child £3.60/1.20; ⏱ 9.30am-5.30pm Mon-Sat Apr-Sep; ℗), a traditional 1955 blackhouse with displays on the village's history, while another houses a **cafe** (mains £3-6; ⏱ 9.30am-5.30pm Mon-Sat).

Some of the blackhouses in the village are let out as self-catering **holiday cottages** (☑ 01851-643416; www.gearrannan.com; 2-person cottage for 3 nights £275; ℗).

Callanish (Calanais)

Callanish, on the western side of Lewis, is famous for its prehistoric standing stones. One of the most atmospheric prehistoric sites in the whole of Scotland, its ageless mystery, impressive scale and undeniable beauty leave a lasting impression.

Callanish Standing Stones   HISTORIC SITE
(HES; www.historicenvironment.scot; ⏱ 24hr) **FREE** The Callanish Standing Stones, 15 miles west of Stornoway on the A858 road, form one of the most complete stone circles in Britain. It is one of the most atmospheric prehistoric sites anywhere. Sited on a wild and secluded promontory overlooking Loch Roag, 13 large stones of beautifully banded gneiss are arranged, as if in worship, around a 4.5m-tall central monolith.

Some 40 smaller stones radiate from the circle in the shape of a cross, with the remains of a chambered tomb at the centre. Dating from 3800 to 5000 years ago, the stones are roughly contemporary with the pyramids of Egypt.

Calanais Visitor Centre   MUSEUM
(☑ 01851-621422; www.callanishvisitorcentre. co.uk; admission free, exhibition £2.50; ⏱ 9.30am-8pm Mon-Sat Jun-Aug, 10am-6pm Mon-Sat Apr, May, Sep & Oct, 10am-4pm Tue-Sat Nov-Mar; ℗) This visitor centre near the Callanish Standing Stones is a tour de force of discreet design. Inside is a small exhibition that speculates on the origins and purpose of the stones, and an excellent **cafe** (mains £4-7).

Great Bernera

This rocky island is connected to Lewis by a bridge built by the local council in 1953 – the islanders had originally planned to blow up a small hill with explosives and use the material to build their own causeway. Great Bernera's attractions include fine coastal walks, a remote sandy beach, and a fascinating reconstruction of an Iron Age house.

Bosta   BEACH
(Bostadh) On a sunny day, it's worth making the long detour to Great Bernera's northern tip for a picnic at the perfect little sandy beach of Bosta. As an alternative to driving, there's a signposted 5-mile coastal walk from Breacleit, the island's only village, to Bosta.

Iron Age House   HISTORIC SITE
(📞01851-612314; Bosta; adult/child £3/1; ⊙noon-4pm Mon-Fri May–mid-Sep; 🅿) In 1996 archaeologists excavated an entire Iron Age village at the head of Bosta beach. Afterwards, the village was reburied for protection, but a reconstruction of an Iron Age house now stands nearby. Gather round the peat fire, above which strips of mutton are being smoked, while the custodian explains the domestic arrangements – fascinating, and well worth the trip. Opening hours are provisional, so call ahead to check.

Western Lewis

The B8011 road (signposted Uig, on the A858 Stornoway–Callanish road) from Garrynahine to Timsgarry (Timsgearraidh) meanders through scenic wilderness to some of Scotland's most stunning beaches. At **Miavaig**, a loop road detours north through the Bhaltos Estate to the pretty, mile-long white strand of **Reef Beach**; there's a basic but spectacular **campsite** (Cnip; Traigh na Beirigh; tent sites £10; ⊙May-Sep) in the machair behind the beach.

From Miavaig, the road continues west through a rocky defile to Timsgarry and the vast, sandy expanse of **Traigh Uige** (Uig Sands). The famous 12th-century **Lewis chess pieces**, made of walrus ivory, were discovered in the sand dunes here in 1831.

The minor road that continues south from Timsgarry to **Mealista** passes a few smaller, but still spectacular, white-sand and boulder beaches on the way to a remote dead end; on a clear day you can see St Kilda on the horizon.

🅾 Sights & Activities

Uig Museum   MUSEUM
(www.ceuig.co.uk; Timsgarry; adult/child £2/free; ⊙noon-5pm Mon-Sat May–mid-Sep) This small community museum, housed in the local school, has lots of info on the **Lewis chess pieces** (discovered nearby in 1831) and on other historic sites in western Lewis.

Gallan Head   LANDMARK
(www.gallanhead.org.uk) Gallan Head, 3 miles north of Uig, was once an RAF radar station and surveillance post until it was abandoned in the 1960s. The old military camp, ringed by spectacular sea cliffs, has undergone several incarnations as a hotel and restaurant, but was finally taken over in 2016 by a local community trust that plans to clean

up the site and create a visitor centre, cafe, wildlife-watching viewpoint and all-abilities hiking trail.

Meanwhile, the headland remains a strange hybrid of alternative community and ugly dereliction. You can drive through the gate beyond the settlement to reach the former radar base; there are views west to the Flannan Isles in clear weather.

SeaTrek   BOATING
(📞01851-672469; www.seatrek.co.uk; Miavaig Pier) From April to September, SeaTrek runs two-hour boat trips (adult/child £38/28, Monday to Saturday) in a high-speed RIB to spot seals and nesting seabirds. There are also three-hour trips (£48/38) to deserted islands in Loch Roag, with time ashore to go exploring.

🛏 Sleeping & Eating

There are precious few places to eat out here, so check that your accommodation offers evening meals if you don't want to go hungry.

★Port Carnish   COTTAGE £££
(📞07855 843375; www.portcarnishlewis.co.uk; Carnais, Uig; per week £995) A beautifully designed timber building set on an old croft with a stunning outlook across the sands of Uig Bay, this romantic cottage offers luxury self-catering accommodation for two people.

Baile-na-Cille   B&B £££
(📞01851-672242; www.bailenacille.co.uk; Timsgarry; per person £75; 🅿📶) This lovely old house hidden away at the northern end of Uig Bay is well worth seeking out for its friendly, old-fashioned hospitality, comfortable rooms and stunning location; there's even a tennis court and croquet lawn. Evening meals are available most nights (book in advance) for £35 per person.

Harris (Na Hearadh)

POP 2000

Harris, to the south of Lewis, is the scenic jewel in the necklace of islands that comprise the Outer Hebrides. It has a spectacular blend of rugged mountains, pristine beaches, flower-speckled machair and barren rocky landscapes. The isthmus at Tarbert splits Harris neatly in two: North Harris is dominated by mountains that rise forbiddingly above the peat moors to the south of Stornoway – Clisham (799m) is the highest point. South Harris is lower-lying, fringed by beautiful white-sand beaches in the west and a convoluted rocky coastline to the east.

Harris is famous for Harris Tweed, a high-quality woollen cloth still hand-woven in islanders' homes. The industry employs around 400 weavers; staff at Tarbert tourist office can tell you about weavers and workshops you can visit.

Tarbert (An Tairbeart)

POP 480

Tarbert is a harbour village with a spectacular location, tucked into the narrow neck of land that links North and South Harris. It is one of the main ferry ports for the Outer Hebrides, and home to the Isle of Harris Distillery.

Village facilities include two petrol stations, a bank, an ATM, two general stores and a tourist office.

Isle of Harris Distillery   DISTILLERY

(☑01859-502212; www.harrisdistillery.com; Main St; tours £10; ⊙10am-5pm Mon-Sat; 🅿) This distillery started production in 2015, so its first batch of single malt whisky will be ready in 2019; meanwhile, it's producing Isle of Harris gin too. The modern building is very stylish – the lobby feels like a luxury hotel – and 75-minute tours depart two or three times daily (weekdays only) in summer; they're popular, so book in advance. There's a cafe here too.

🛏 Sleeping & Eating

Tigh na Mara   B&B £

(☑01859-502270; flora@tigh-na-mara.co.uk; East Tarbert; per person £30-35; 🅿) Excellent-value B&B (though the single room is a bit cramped) just five minutes' walk from the ferry – head up the hill above the tourist office and turn right. The owner bakes fresh cakes every day, which you can enjoy in the conservatory with a view over the bay.

Harris Hotel   HOTEL ££

(☑01859-502154; www.harrishotel.com; s/d from £90/115; 🅿🛜) Run since 1903 by four generations of the Cameron family, Harris Hotel is a 19th-century sporting hotel, built in 1865 for visiting anglers and deer stalkers, and retains a distinctly old-fashioned atmosphere. It has spacious, comfy rooms and a decent restaurant; look out for JM Barrie's initials on the dining-room window (the author of *Peter Pan* visited in the 1920s).

Hotel Hebrides   HOTEL £££

(☑01859-502364; www.hotel-hebrides.com; Pier Rd; s/d/f £80/160/190; 🛜) The location and setting don't look promising – a nondescript building squeezed between the ferry pier and car park – but this modern establishment brings a dash of urban glamour to Harris, with flashy fabrics and wall coverings, luxurious towels and toiletries, and a stylish restaurant and lounge bar. There are also luxury suites (from £215 per night) in a separate building.

Distillery Canteen   CAFE £

(Harris Distillery, Main St; mains £6-9; ⊙10am-4pm Mon-Sat) The cafe at the Isle of Harris Distillery, with its communal, scrubbed-timber tables and chunky benches, is bright and convivial. The menu is not extensive – a choice of soups, cakes, home-baked bread, smoked salmon and crowdie (Scottish cream cheese) – but the quality of the food shines brightly, most of it sourced directly from Harris.

Hebscape   CAFE £

(www.hebscapegallery.co.uk; Ardhasaig; mains £3-7; ⊙10.30am-4.30pm Tue-Sat Apr-Oct; 🅿🛜) 🍽 This stylish cafe and art gallery, a couple of miles outside Tarbert on the road north towards Stornoway, occupies a hilltop site with breathtaking views over Loch A Siar. Enjoy home-baked cakes or scones with Suki tea or freshly brewed espresso, or a hearty bowl of homemade soup, while admiring the gorgeous landscape photography of co-owner Darren Cole.

ℹ Information

Tarbert Tourist Office (☑01859-502011; www.visithebrides.com; Pier Rd; ⊙9am-5pm Mon-Sat Apr-Oct)

ℹ Getting There & Away

There are four or five daily buses, Monday to Saturday, from Tarbert to Stornoway (£4.80, one hour) and Leverburgh (£3.20, 50 minutes) via the west coast road.

Tarbert also has ferry connections to Uig (car/pedestrian £31/6.30, 1½ hours, one or two daily) on Skye.

North Harris

Magnificent North Harris is the most mountainous region of the Outer Hebrides. There are few roads here, but many opportunities for climbing, walking and birdwatching.

The B887 leads west, from a point 3 miles north of Tarbert, to Hushinish, where there's a lovely silver-sand beach. Along the way the road passes an old whaling station, one of Lord Leverhulme's failed development schemes, and the impressive shooting lodge of Amhuinnsuidhe Castle (www.amhuinnsuidhe.com), now exclusive holiday accommodation.

Golden Eagle Observatory   BIRDWATCHING
Between the old whaling station and Amhuinnsuidhe Castle, at Miavaig, a parking area and gated track gives hikers access to a golden eagle observatory, a 1.3-mile walk north from the road. On Wednesday from April to September, local rangers lead a 3½-hour guided walk (£5 per person) in search of eagles; details from Tarbert tourist office or www.north-harris.org.

South Harris
South Harris' west coast has some of the most beautiful beaches in Scotland. The blinding white sands and turquoise waters of Luskentyre and Scarasta would be major holiday resorts if they were transported to somewhere with a warm climate; as it is, they're usually deserted.

The east coast is a complete contrast to the west – a strange, rocky moonscape of naked gneiss pocked with tiny lochans, the bleakness lightened by the occasional splash of green around the few crofting communities. Film buffs will know that the psychedelic sequences depicting an alien landscape in *2001: A Space Odyssey* were shot from an aircraft flying over Harris' east coast.

The narrow, twisting road that winds along this coast is known locally as the Golden Road because of the vast amount of money it cost per mile. It was built in the 1930s to link all the tiny communities known as 'The Bays'.

◉ Sights & Activities

★ Luskentyre   BEACH
(Losgaintir) Luskentyre is one of the biggest and most beautiful beaches in Scotland, famed for its acres of low-tide white sands and turquoise waters. A minor road leads along the northern side of the bay to a parking area beside an ancient graveyard; from here you can walk west along the beach or through the grassy dunes with gorgeous views across the sea to the island of Taransay.

Clò Mòr   MUSEUM
(☏01859-502040; Old School, Drinishader; ◷9am-5.30pm Mon-Sat Mar-Oct; P) FREE The Campbell family has been making Harris tweed for 90 years, and this exhibition (behind the family shop) celebrates the history of the fabric known in Gaelic as *clò mòr* (the 'big cloth'); ask about live demonstrations of tweed weaving on the 70-year-old Hattersley loom. Drinishader is 5 miles south of Tarbert on the east coast road.

St Clement's Church   HISTORIC BUILDING
(Rodel; ◷9am-5pm Mon-Sat) FREE At the southernmost tip of the east coast of Harris stands the impressive 16th-century St Clement's Church, built by Alexander MacLeod of Dunvegan between the 1520s and 1550s, only to be abandoned after the Reformation. There are several fine tombs inside, including the cenotaph of Alexander MacLeod, finely carved with hunting scenes, a castle, a *birlinn* (the traditional longboat of the islands) and various saints, including St Clement clutching a skull.

Talla na Mara   ARTS CENTRE
(☏01859-503900; www.tallanamara.co.uk; Pairc Niseaboist; ◷9am-5pm Mon-Sat; P) FREE Opened in 2017 as a community enterprise, this beautiful modern building houses several artists' studios and an exhibition space that displays works celebrating the landscapes and culture of Scotland's Western Isles.

Sea Harris   BOATING
(☏01859-502007; www.seaharris.com; Leverburgh Pier; ◷Apr-Sep) Operates private-hire boat trips to spot wildlife around the Sound of Harris (from £40 per person), and also runs 10-hour day trips to St Kilda (£185 per person) with four to five hours ashore.

Kilda Cruises   BOATING
(☏01859-502060; www.kildacruises.co.uk; Leverburgh Pier; per person £215) Operates 12-hour day trips to the remote and spectacular island group of St Kilda. Daily from mid-April to mid-September.

🛏 Sleeping

Lickisto Blackhouse Camping   CAMPSITE £
(☏01859-530485; www.freewebs.com/vanvon; Liceasto; tent sites per adult/child £12/6, yurt £70; 🐾) ✿ Remote and rustic campsite on an old croft, with pitches set among heather and outcrops and chickens running wild. Campers can use a communal kitchen-lounge in a converted blackhouse,

and there are two yurts with wood-burning stove and gas cooker (no electricity). Bus W13 from Tarbert to Leverburgh stops at the entrance.

Am Bothan
HOSTEL £

(☑ 01859-520251; www.ambothan.com; Ferry Rd, Leverburgh; dm £25; P 🔿) An attractive, chalet-style hostel, Am Bothan has small, neat dorms and a great porch where you can enjoy morning coffee with views over the bay. The hostel has bike hire and can arrange wildlife-watching boat trips.

Carminish House
B&B ££

(☑ 01859-520400; www.carminish.com; 1a Strond, Leverburgh; s/d £75/95; ☺ Apr-Oct; P 🔿) The welcoming Carminish is a modern house with three comfy bedrooms. There's a view of the ferry from the dining room, and lots of nice little touches such as handmade soaps, a carafe of drinking water in the bedroom and tea and cake on arrival.

Sorrel Cottage
B&B ££

(☑ 01859-520319; www.sorrelcottage.co.uk; 2 Glen, Leverburgh; s/d from £70/90; P 🔿🐾) Sorrel Cottage is a pretty crofter's house with beautifully modernised rooms, about 1.5 miles west of the ferry at Leverburgh. Vegetarians and vegans are happily catered for. Bike hire available.

★ Borve Lodge Estate
COTTAGE £££

(☑ 01859-550358; www.borvelodge.com; per 3/7 nights £900/1850; P 🔿) This estate on the west side of South Harris has developed some of the most spectacular self-catering accommodation in the Outer Hebrides, including the Rock House, a turf-roofed nook built into the hillside with sweeping views over the sea, and the stunning Broch, a three-storey rock tower based on Iron Age designs (both sleep two persons).

✕ Eating

★ Skoon Art Café
CAFE £

(☑ 01859-530268; www.skoon.com; Geocrab; mains £5-9; ☺ 10am-4.30pm Tue-Sat Apr-Sep, shorter hours Oct-Mar; P) ✐ Set halfway along the Golden Road, this neat little art gallery doubles as an excellent cafe serving delicious homemade soups, sandwiches, cakes and desserts (try the gin-and-tonic cake).

Temple Cafe
CAFE £

(☑ 07876 340416; www.facebook.com/thetemplecafe; Northton; mains £5-12; ☺ 10.30am-5pm Tue-Sun Apr-Sep, shorter hours Oct-Mar; P 🖰) Set in a cute stone-and-timber 'hobbit house' that was originally a visitor centre, and strewn with cushions covered in Harris tweed, this rustic cafe serves homemade scones, soups, salads and hot lunch specials to a soundtrack of '70s tunes. Evening meals 6.30pm to 8pm Friday to Sunday in summer (must be booked in advance).

★ Machair Kitchen
SCOTTISH ££

(☑ 01859-550333; www.tallanamara.co.uk; Talla na Mara; mains £7-15; ☺ noon-4pm & 6-9pm) The restaurant in this community centre (p391) and art gallery enjoys a stunning location, with views across the sea to the island of Taransay, and an outdoor deck that makes the most of any sunny weather. The menu includes local mussels, crab and smoked salmon, plus sandwiches, fish and chips and burgers. Open for coffee and cake from 10am to 5pm.

❶ Getting There & Away

A **CalMac** (www.calmac.co.uk) car ferry zig-zags through the reefs of the Sound of Harris from Leverburgh to Berneray (pedestrian/car £3.60/13.55, one hour, three or four daily Monday to Saturday, two or three Sunday).

There are two to four buses a day (except Sunday) from Tarbert to Leverburgh; W10 takes the main road along the west coast (£3.20, 40 minutes), while W13 winds along the Golden Road on the east coast (£3.20, one hour).

Berneray (Bearnaraigh)
POP 138

Berneray was linked to North Uist by a causeway in October 1998, but that hasn't altered the peace and beauty of the island. The beaches on its west coast are some of the most beautiful and unspoilt in Britain, and seals and otters can be seen in Bays Loch on the east coast.

Accommodation on the island is limited to the **Gatliff Hostel** (www.gatliff.org.uk; dm adult/child £16/8, camping per person £11), a bunkhouse, two B&Bs and half a dozen self-catering cottages (see the full listing at www.isleofberneray.com), so be sure to book ahead.

Bus W19 runs from Berneray (Gatliff Hostel and Harris ferry) to Lochmaddy (£2.30, 20 to 30 minutes, eight daily Monday to Saturday). There are daily ferries to Leverburgh (Harris).

North Uist (Uibhist A Tuath)

POP 1255

North Uist, an island half-drowned by lochs, is famed for its trout fishing (www.nuac.co.uk) but also has some magnificent beaches on its north and west coasts. For birdwatchers this is an earthly paradise, with regular sightings of waders and wildfowl ranging from redshank to red-throated diver to red-necked phalarope. The landscape is less wild and mountainous than Harris but it has a sleepy, subtle appeal.

Little **Lochmaddy** is the first village you hit after arriving on the ferry from Skye. It has a couple of stores, a bank with an ATM, a petrol station, a post office and a pub.

◉ Sights

Balranald RSPB Reserve   WILDLIFE RESERVE
(www.rspb.org.uk; P) FREE Birdwatchers flock to this Royal Society for the Protection of Birds (RSPB) nature reserve, 18 miles west of Lochmaddy, in the hope of spotting the rare red-necked phalarope or hearing the distinctive call of the corncrake. There's a visitor centre with a resident warden who offers 1½-hour guided walks (£6), departing at 10am Tuesday from May to September.

St Kilda Viewpoint   VIEWPOINT
(P) From the westernmost point of the road that runs around North Uist, a minor, drivable track leads for 1.5 miles to the summit of Clettraval hill where a lookout point with telescope affords superb views west to the distant peaks of St Kilda and the Monach Isles.

Taigh Chearsabhagh   ARTS CENTRE, MUSEUM
(☑01870-603970; www.taigh-chearsabhagh.org; Lochmaddy; arts centre free, museum £3; ☉10am-5pm Mon-Sat Apr-Oct, to 4pm Nov-Mar; P) Taigh Chearsabhagh is a museum and arts centre that preserves and displays the history and culture of the Uists, and is also a thriving community centre, post office and meeting place. The centre's cafe (mains £4 to £6, closes at 3pm) dishes up homemade soups, sandwiches and cakes.

🛏 Sleeping & Eating

Balranald Campsite   CAMPSITE £
(☑01876-510304; www.balranaldhebrideanholidays.com; Balranald Nature Reserve, Hougharry; tent sites £8-10, plus per person £2; ☎) You can birdwatch from your tent at this lovely campsite set on the machair alongside the RSPB's Balranald nature reserve, and listen to rare corncrakes calling as the sun goes down beyond the neighbouring white-sand beach.

★Langass Lodge   HOTEL ££
(☑01876-580285;   www.langasslodge.co.uk; Locheport; s/d from £95/115; P☎) The delightful Langass Lodge hotel is a former shooting lodge set in splendid isolation overlooking Loch Langais. Refurbished and extended, it now offers a dozen appealing rooms, many with sea views, as well as one of the Hebrides' best **restaurants** (mains £15-25, 3-course dinner £38; ☉6-8.30pm), noted for its fine seafood and game.

Rushlee House   B&B ££
(☑01876-500274; www.rushleehouse.co.uk; Lochmaddy; s/d £60/78; P☎) A lovely modern bungalow with three luxuriously appointed bedrooms and great views of the hills to the south. No evening meals, but it's just a short walk to the restaurant at Hamersay House. The B&B is 0.75 miles from the ferry pier; take the first road on the right, then first left.

Hamersay House   HOTEL £££
(☑01876-500700;   www.hamersayhouse.co.uk; Lochmaddy; s/d £95/135; P☎) Hamersay is Lochmaddy's most luxurious accommodation, with eight designer bedrooms, a lounge with leather sofas set around an open fire, and a good restaurant (mains £13 to £21, open 6pm to 8.30pm) with sea views from the terrace.

Hebridean Smokehouse   FOOD & DRINKS
(☑01876-580209;   www.hebrideansmokehouse.com; Clachan; ☉8am-5.30pm Mon-Fri, plus 9am-5pm Sat Easter-Oct) Smokehouse shop selling locally sourced, peat-smoked salmon, sea trout, scallops, lobster and mackerel.

Benbecula (Beinn Na Faoghla)

POP 1305

Benbecula, which sits between North Uist and South Uist, and is connected to both by causeways, is a low-lying island with a flat, lochan-studded landscape that's best appreciated from the summit of **Rueval** (124m), the island's highest point. There's a path around the southern side of the hill (signposted from the main road; park beside

NORTHERN HIGHLANDS & ISLANDS NORTH UIST (UIBHIST A TUATH)

the landfill site) that is said to be the route taken to the coast by Bonnie Prince Charlie and Flora MacDonald during the prince's escape in 1746.

The main village is Balivanich, which has a bank with an ATM, a post office, a couple of supermarkets and a petrol station (open on Sunday). It is also the location of Benbecula airport.

South Uist (Uibhist A Deas)

POP 1755

South Uist is the second-largest island in the Outer Hebrides and saves its choicest corners for those who explore away from the main north–south road. The low-lying west coast is an almost unbroken stretch of white-sand beach and flower-flecked machair – a waymarked hiking trail, the Hebridean Way, follows the coast – while the multitude of inland lochs provide excellent trout fishing (www.southuistfishing.com). The east coast, riven by four large sea lochs, is hilly and remote, with spectacular Beinn Mhor (620m) the highest point.

Driving south from Benbecula you cross from the predominantly Protestant northern half of the Outer Hebrides into the mostly Roman Catholic south, a religious transition marked by the granite statue of Our Lady of the Isles on the slopes of Rueval and the presence of many roadside shrines.

The ferry port of Lochboisdale is the island's largest settlement, with a bank, ATM, grocery store and petrol station.

Sights & Activities

Kildonan Museum   MUSEUM

(☑ 01878-710343; www.kildonanmuseum.co.uk; Kildonan; adult/child £3/free; ⊙10am-5pm Apr-Oct; ℙ) Six miles north of Lochboisdale, Kildonan Museum explores the lives of local crofters through its collection of artefacts, an absorbing exhibition of B&W photography and firsthand accounts of harsh Hebridean conditions. There's also an excellent tearoom (mains £4 to £8, open 11am to 4pm) and craft shop.

Amid Milton's ruined blackhouses, half a mile south of the museum, a cairn marks the site of Flora MacDonald's birthplace.

Eriskay   ISLAND

There's not much to see on Eriskay, but you'll pass through it on the way to the car ferry that crosses to Ardmhor at the northern end of Barra; Eriskay itself is connected to South Uist by a causeway that was constructed in 2001.

In 1745 Bonnie Prince Charlie first set foot in Scotland on the west coast of Eriskay, on the sandy beach (immediately north of the ferry terminal) still known as Prince's Strand (Coilleag a'Phrionnsa).

More recently the SS Politician sank just off the island in 1941. The islanders salvaged much of its cargo of around 250,000 bottles of whisky and, after a binge of dramatic proportions, the police intervened and a number of the islanders landed in jail. The story was immortalised by Sir Compton Mackenzie in his comic novel Whisky Galore, made into a famous film in 1949 and remade in 2016.

Uist Sea Tours   BOATING

(☑ 07810 238752; www.uistseatours.com; The Pier, Lochboisdale) From mid-April to mid-September this outfit runs two-hour boat trips (£40 per person) from Lochboisdale to spot bottlenose dolphins in the Sound of Barra (Monday, Wednesday and Friday evenings), and six-hour trips from Eriskay harbour (£85 per person) to see nesting puffins on the island of Mingulay (Friday). There are also seven-hour day trips to St Kilda (£175 per person).

Sleeping & Eating

Uist Storm Pods   CAMPSITE £

(☑ 01878-700845; www.uiststormpods.co.uk; Lochboisdale; per pod £70; ℙ☀) This place has two Scandinavian-style timber camping pods set on a hillside on a working farm. Each has an outdoor deck and barbecue overlooking the sea; a mini-kitchen, fridge and chemical toilet; and can sleep up to four people. The pods are a short walk from the ferry; take the second road on the left, immediately before the RBS bank.

Tobha Mor Crofters' Hostel   HOSTEL £

(www.gatliff.org.uk; Howmore; dm adult/child £16/8, camping per person £10) An atmospheric hostel housed in a restored thatched blackhouse, about 12 miles north of Lochboisdale.

★ Polochar Inn   INN ££

(☑ 01878-700215; www.polocharinn.com; Polochar; s/d from £80/95; ℙ☎) This 18th-century inn has been transformed into a stylish, welcoming hotel with a stunning location looking out across the sea to Barra. The excellent

ST KILDA

St Kilda is a collection of spectacular sea stacks and cliff-bound islands about 45 miles west of North Uist. The largest island, Hirta, measures only 2 miles by 1 mile, with huge cliffs along most of its coastline. Owned by the NTS, the islands are a Unesco World Heritage Site and are the biggest seabird nesting site in the North Atlantic, home to more than a million birds.

There is no accommodation on St Kilda other than a tiny campsite at Village Bay on Hirta (£12 per person, no more than six people) with toilets, showers and a drinking-water supply; the maximum permitted stay is five nights. Must be arranged in advance through the NTS (details at www.kilda.org.uk).

Boat tours to St Kilda are a major undertaking – day trips are at least seven-hour affairs, involving a minimum 2½-hour crossing each way, often in rough seas; all must be booked in advance and are weather-dependent (April to September only).

Tour operators include the following:

Go To St Kilda (07789 914144; www.gotostkilda.co.uk; Stein Jetty; per person £260)

Kilda Cruises (p391)

Uist Sea Tours (p394)

Sea Harris (p391)

restaurant and bar menu (mains £11 to £20; booking recommended) includes seafood chowder, venison casserole, local salmon and scallops, and Uist lamb. Polochar is 7 miles southwest of Lochboisdale, on the way to Eriskay.

Lochside Cottage B&B ££
(01878-700472; www.lochside-cottage.co.uk; Lochboisdale; s/d/f £50/70/90; P) Lochside Cottage is a friendly B&B, 1.5 miles west of the ferry, and has rooms with views and a sun lounge barely a fishing-rod's length from its own trout loch.

ⓘ Getting There & Around

Bus W17 runs about four times a day (except Sunday) between Berneray and Eriskay via Lochmaddy, Balivanich and Lochboisdale. The trip from Lochboisdale to Lochmaddy (£5.30) takes 1¾ hours.

CalMac (www.calmac.co.uk) ferries run between Lochboisdale and Mallaig.

Rothan Cycles (07740 364093; www.rothan. scot; Howmore; per day from £10; 9am-5pm) offers bike hire, and a delivery and pick-up service (extra charge on top of rental) at various points between Eriskay and Stornoway.

Barra (Barraigh)

POP 1175

With its beautiful beaches, wildflower-clad dunes, rugged little hills and strong sense of community, diminutive Barra – just 14 miles

in circumference – is the Outer Hebrides in miniature. For a great view of the island, walk up to the top of Heaval (383m), a mile northeast of Castlebay (Bagh a'Chaisteil), the largest village.

You can hire bikes from **Barra Bike Hire** (07876 402842; www.barrabikehire.co.uk; Vatersay Rd, Castlebay; per half-/full day £10/16; 9am-5pm Mon-Sat).

⊙ Sights & Activities

The uninhabited islands of Pabbay, Mingulay and Berneray, gifted to the National Trust for Scotland (NTS) in 2000, are important breeding sites for seabird species such as fulmar, black guillemot, common and Arctic tern, great skua, puffin and storm petrel.

Uist Sea Tours runs boat trips to the islands from Lochboisdale in South Uist in settled weather. The puffin season lasts from June to early August.

Kisimul Castle CASTLE
(HES; 01871-810313; www.historicenvironment. scot; Castlebay; adult/child incl ferry £6/3.60; 9.30am-5.30pm Apr-Sep) Castlebay takes its name from the island fortress of Kisimul Castle, first built by the MacNeil clan in the 11th century. A short boat trip (weather permitting) takes you out to the island, where you can explore the fortifications and soak up the view from the battlements.

The castle was restored in the 20th century by American architect Robert MacNeil, who became the 45th clan chief; he gifted the castle to Historic Scotland in 2000 for an annual rent of £1 and a bottle of whisky (Talisker single malt, if you're interested).

Traigh Mor
BEACH

This vast expanse of firm golden sand (the name means 'Big Strand') serves as Barra's airport (a mile across at low tide, and big enough for three 'runways'), the only beach airport in the world that handles scheduled flights. Watching the little Twin Otter aircraft come and go is a popular spectator sport. In between flights, locals gather cockles, a local seafood speciality, from the sands.

🛏 Sleeping & Eating

Accommodation on Barra is limited, so make a reservation before committing to a night on the island. Wild camping (on foot or by bike) is allowed almost anywhere; campervans and car campers are restricted to official sites – check www.isleofbarra.com for details.

Dunard Hostel
HOSTEL £

(☑ 01871-810443; www.dunardhostel.co.uk; Castlebay; dm/tw from £20/48; P 🛜) Dunard is a friendly, family-run hostel just a five-minute walk from the ferry terminal. The owners can help to organise sea-kayaking trips.

Tigh na Mara
B&B ££

(☑ 01871-810304; www.tighnamara-barra.co.uk; Castlebay; s/d £45/75; ⊙ Apr-Oct; P 🛜) A lovely cottage B&B with a brilliant location just above the ferry pier, looking out over the bay and Kisimul Castle (p395). Ask for the en suite double bedroom with bay view.

Castlebay Hotel
HOTEL ££

(☑ 01871-810223; www.castlebayhotel.com; Castlebay; s/d from £70/125; P 🛜) The Castlebay Hotel has spacious bedrooms decorated with a subtle tartan motif – it's worth paying a bit extra for a sea view – and there's a comfy lounge and conservatory with grand views across the harbour to the islands south of Barra. The hotel bar is the hub of island social life, with regular sessions of traditional music.

The restaurant specialises in local seafood and game (often rabbit).

Deck
CAFE £

(www.hebrideantoffeecompany.com; Castlebay; mains £4-7; ⊙ 9am-5pm Mon-Thu, to 7pm Fri & Sat, noon-4pm Sun Apr-Sep) There are only outdoor seats at this cafe (attached to the Hebridean Toffee factory), on a wooden deck overlooking the bay, but it's worth waiting for a fine day to sample the freshly baked scones and homemade cakes.

ℹ Getting There & Away

There are two daily flights from Glasgow to Barra airport.

CalMac (www.calmac.co.uk) ferries link Eriskay with Ardmhor (pedestrian/car £3.05/10.55, 40 minutes, three to five daily) at the northern end of Barra. Ferries also run from Castlebay to Oban.

A bus service links ferry arrivals and departures at Ardmhor with Castlebay (£1.80, 20 minutes). Bus W32 makes a circuit of the island up to five times daily (except Sunday), and also connects with flights at the airport.

Orkney & Shetland

Best Places to Eat

➡ Scalloway Hotel (p423)

➡ Foveran (p404)

➡ Fjarå (p420)

➡ Hay's Dock (p421)

➡ Hamnavoe
Restaurant (p411)

Best Places to Stay

➡ Brinkies Guest
House (p410)

➡ Scalloway Hotel (p423)

➡ Almara (p425)

➡ West Manse (p413)

➡ Albert Hotel (p404)

➡ Busta House Hotel (p425)

Why Go?

Up here at Britain's top end it can feel more Scandinavian than Scottish, and no wonder. For the Vikings, the jaunt across the North Sea from Norway was as easy as a stroll down to the local mead hall and they soon controlled these windswept, treeless archipelagos, laying down longhouses alongside the stony remains of ancient prehistoric settlements.

An ancient magic hovers in the air above Orkney and Shetland, endowing them with an allure that lodges firmly in the soul. It's in the misty seas, where seals, whales and porpoises patrol lonely coastlines; it's in the air, where squadrons of seabirds wheel above huge nesting colonies; and it's on land, where standing stones catch late summer sunsets and strains of folk music disperse in the air before the wind gusts shut the pub door. These islands reward the journey.

When to Go
Lerwick

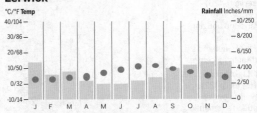

Jan Shetland's Up Helly Aa: horned helmets and burning Viking ships on the beach.

Jun Orkney rocks to the St Magnus Festival: book accommodation ahead.

Jul Summer sunlight and Scotland's longest daylight hours.

Orkney & Shetland Highlights

1 Skara Brae (p408) Shaking your head in astonishment at extraordinary prehistoric perfection that predates the pyramids.

2 Maeshowe (p407) Sensing the gulf of years in this ancient tomb enlivened by later Viking graffiti.

3 Hoy (p411) Soaking up the glorious scenery and making the hike to the spectacular Old Man of Hoy.

4 Northern Islands (p413) Island-hopping through Orkney, where crystal azure waters lap against glittering white-sand beaches.

5 Scapa Flow (p412) Submerging yourself among the sunken warships of Scapa Flow.

6 Lerwick (p418) Discovering your inner Viking at the Up Helly Aa festival.

7 Hermaness National Nature Reserve (p426) Capering with puffins and dodging dive-bombing skuas at Shetland's birdwatching centre.

8 Lighthouse Cottages (p422) Staying in one of Shetland's romantic lighthouse cottages; one of the best is at spectacular Sumburgh.

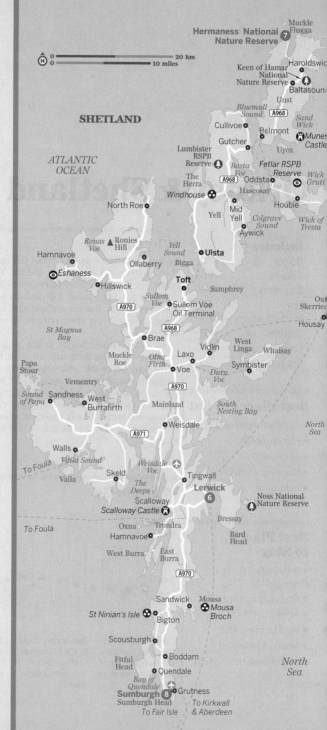

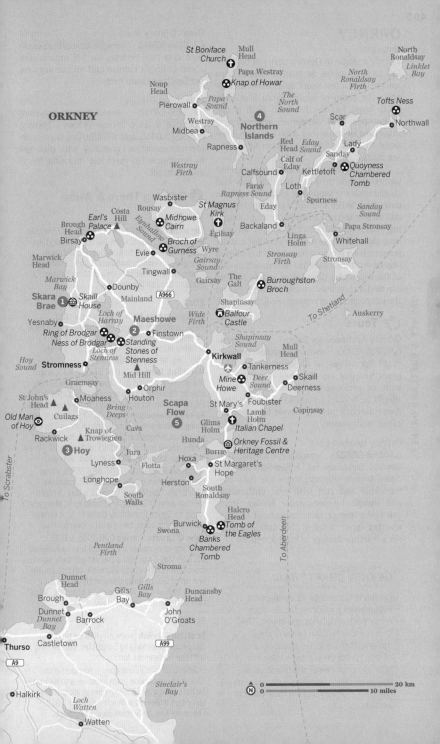

ORKNEY

St Boniface Church

Mull Head

Papa Westray

Knap of Howar

Noup Head

Pierowall

Papa Sound

North Ronaldsay

Linklet Bay

④ Northern Islands

The North Sound

Scar

Tofts Ness

Northwall

North Ronaldsay Firth

Westray

Midbea

Rapness

Red Head

Eday Sound

Lady

Sanday

Sanday Sound

Westray Firth

Calfsound

Calf of Eday

Kettletoft

Quoyness Chambered Tomb

Faray

Rapness Sound

Loth

Spurness

Wasbister

Rousay

St Magnus Kirk

Eday

Papa Stronsay

Brough Head

Earl's Palace

Costa Hill

Midhowe Cairn

Egilsay

Backaland

Linga Holm

Whitehall

Birsay

Evie

Broch of Gurness

Wyre

Stronsay Firth

Stronsay

Marwick Head

Tingwall

Gairsay Sound

Marwick Bay

Dounby

Gairsay

The Galt

Wide Firth

Burroughston Broch

Skara Brae ① ⊞ Skaill House

Mainland

A966

Shapinsay

Yesnaby

Loch of Harray

Maeshowe

Balfour Castle

Ring of Brodgar

② Finstown

Shapinsay Sound

Mull Head

Ness of Brodgar

Standing Stones of Stenness

Loch of Stenness

Kirkwall

Tankerness

Skaill

Stromness

Mid Hill

Mine Howe

Deer Sound

Deerness

Hoy Sound

Graemsay

Orphir

Houton

Scapa Flow

St Mary's

Foubister

Copinsay

St John's Head

Moaness

⑤

Lamb Holm

Old Man of Hoy

Cuilags

Bring Deeps

Cava

Glims Holm

Italian Chapel

Rackwick

Knap of Trowiegien

Fara

Hunda

Orkney Fossil & Heritage Centre

③ **Hoy**

Lyness

Flotta

Hoxa

Burray

Longhope

Herston

St Margaret's Hope

South Walls

South Ronaldsay

Halcro Head

Burwick

Tomb of the Eagles

Swona

Banks Chambered Tomb

Pentland Firth

Stroma

Dunnet Head

Gills Bay

Duncansby Head

Brough

Gills Bay

Dunnet

Barrock

John O'Groats

Dunnet Bay

Thurso

Castletown

A99

A9

Halkirk

Loch Watten

Sinclair's Bay

Watten

0 20 km

0 10 miles

To Shetland

Auskerry

To Scrabster

To Aberdeen

ORKNEY

POP 21,670

There's a magic to Orkney that you begin to feel as soon as the Scottish mainland slips astern. Only a few short miles of ocean separate the chain of islands from Scotland's north coast, but the Pentland Firth is one of Europe's most dangerous waterways, a graveyard of ships that adds an extra mystique to these islands shimmering in the sea mists.

An archipelago of mostly flat, green-topped islands stripped bare of trees and ringed with red sandstone cliffs, its heritage dates back to the Vikings, whose influence is still strong today. Famed for ancient standing stones and prehistoric villages, for sublime sandy beaches and spectacular coastal scenery, it's a region whose ports tell of lives shared with the blessings and rough moods of the sea, and a destination where seekers can find melancholy wrecks of warships and the salty clamour of remote seabird colonies.

Tours

Orkney Archaeology Tours TOURS
(☎01856-721450; www.orkneyarchaeologytours.co.uk) Specialises in all-inclusive multiday tours focusing on Orkney's ancient sites, with an archaeologist guide. These tours should be booked far ahead (a year or two). Also runs customisable private tours outside of the main season.

Orkney Uncovered TOURS
(☎01856-878822; www.orkneyuncovered.co.uk; Viewfield, Sunnybank Rd; ☺8am-8pm Mon-Sat) These private minivan tours are fully customisable and run with real enthusiasm and insight by personable Kinlay. Tours can cover one or more aspects of Orkney, whether your interest be archaeological sites, wartime history or craft jewellery.

ORKNEY CRAFT TRAIL

Orkney is famous for its handicrafts, with makers producing fabulous jewellery, pottery, fabrics and chairs. The Orkney Craft Trail (www.orkney designercrafts.com) is an association of small producers, mostly based in little communities or the countryside, that produces a booklet you can use to navigate your way around their various workshops.

Great Orkney Tours TOURS
(☎01856-861443; www.greatorkneytours.co.uk) Jean gets rave reviews for her enthusiasm about Orkney's culture and archaeology on her flexible private tours.

Wildabout Orkney BUS
(☎01856-877737; www.wildaboutorkney.com) Operates tours covering Orkney's history, ecology, folklore and wildlife. Day trips operate year-round and cost £59, with pick-ups in Stromness (to meet the morning ferry) and Kirkwall.

⚐ Getting There & Away

AIR

Loganair (☎outside UK 0141-642 9407, within UK 0344 800 2855; www.loganair.co.uk) flies daily from Kirkwall to Aberdeen, Edinburgh, Glasgow, Inverness and Sumburgh (Shetland). There are summer services to Manchester, Fair Isle and Bergen (Norway).

BOAT

During summer, book car spaces ahead. Peak-season fares are quoted here. At the time of research, the road-equivalent tariff (RET) scheme was due to be rolled out on Orkney services, so prices should drop.

Northlink Ferries (☎0845 6000 449; www.northlinkferries.co.uk) Operates from Scrabster to Stromness (passenger/car £19.40/59, 1½ hours, two to three daily), from Aberdeen to Kirkwall (passenger/car £31.50/111, six hours, three or four weekly) and from Kirkwall to Lerwick (passenger/car £24.65/103, six to eight hours, three or four weekly) on Shetland. Fares are up to 35% cheaper in the low season.

Pentland Ferries (☎0800 688 8998; www.pentlandferries.co.uk; adult/child/car/bike £16/8/38/free) Leave from Gills Bay, 3 miles west of John O'Groats, and head to St Margaret's Hope on South Ronaldsay three to four times daily. The crossing takes a little over an hour.

John O'Groats Ferries (☎01955-611353; www.jogferry.co.uk; s £19, incl bus to Kirkwall £20; ☺May-Sep) Has a passenger-only service from John O'Groats to Burwick, on the southern tip of South Ronaldsay, with connecting buses to Kirkwall. A 40-minute crossing, with two to three departures daily.

BUS

Scottish Citylink (www.citylink.co.uk) runs daily from Inverness to Scrabster, connecting with the Stromness ferries.

John O'Groats Ferries has a summer-only 'Orkney bus' service from Inverness to Kirkwall. Tickets (one way £25, five hours) include bus-ferry-bus travel from Inverness to Kirkwall. There are two daily from June to August.

ⓘ Getting Around

The *Orkney Transport Guide* details all island transport and is free from tourist offices. There's a winter and summer version; ferry sailings, flights and some bus services are reduced from October to April.

The largest Orkney island, Mainland, is linked by causeways to four southern islands; others are reached by air and ferry.

AIR

Loganair Inter-Isles Air Service (☏ 01856-873457; www.loganair.co.uk) operates inter-island flights from Kirkwall to Eday, Stronsay, Sanday, Westray, Papa Westray and North Ronaldsay. Fares are reasonable, with some special discounted tickets if you stay a night on the outer islands. You have to book by email or phone.

BICYCLE

Various locations on Mainland hire out bikes, including **Cycle Orkney** (☏ 01856-875777; www.cycleorkney.com; Tankerness Lane, Kirkwall; per day/3 days/week £20/40/80; ☺ 9am-5.30pm Mon-Sat) and Orkney Cycle Hire (p411). Both offer out-of-hours pick-ups and options for kids.

BOAT

Orkney Ferries (☏ 01856-872044; www.orkneyferries.co.uk) operates car ferries from Mainland to the islands. An Island Explorer pass costs £42 for a week's passenger travel in summer. Bikes are carried free.

BUS

Stagecoach (☏ 01856-870555; www.stagecoachbus.com) runs buses on Mainland and connecting islands. Most don't operate on Sunday. Dayrider (£8.65) and 7-Day Megarider (£19.25) tickets allow unlimited travel.

CAR

Small-car hire rates are around £45/240 per day/week, although there are sometimes specials for as low as £30 per day. **Orkney Car Hire** (James D Peace & Co; ☏ 01856-872866; www.orkneycarhire.co.uk; Junction Rd, Kirkwall; per day/week £45/240; ☺ 8am-5pm Mon-Fri, 9am-1pm Sat) and **WR Tullock** (☏ 01856-875500; www.orkneycarrental.co.uk; Castle St; per day/week £45/240; ☺ 8.30am-6pm Mon-Fri, to 5pm Sat) are both close to the bus station in Kirkwall.

Kirkwall

POP 7000

Orkney's main town is the islands' commercial centre and there's a comparatively busy feel to its main shopping street and ferry dock. It's set back from a wide bay, and its

ⓘ EXPLORING ORKNEY

There's an excellent range of tourist information on Orkney, including a useful annual guide, as well as a separate guide to the smaller islands. The Kirkwall Tourist Office (p405) has a good range of info and very helpful staff.

The **Orkney Explorer Pass** (www.historicenvironment.scot; adult/child/family £19/11.40/38) covers all Historic Environment Scotland sites in Orkney, including Maeshowe, Skara Brae, the Broch of Gurness, the Brough of Birsay, the Bishop's Palace and Earl's Palace in Kirkwall and the Hackness Martello Tower on Hoy, as well as Jarlshof on Shetland. It lasts for 30 consecutive days and is only available from April to October.

vigour, combined with the atmospheric paved streets and twisting wynds (lanes), give Orkney's capital a distinctive character. Magnificent St Magnus Cathedral takes pride of place in the centre of town, and the nearby Earl's and Bishop's Palaces are also worth a ramble. Founded in the early 11th century, the original part of Kirkwall is one of the best examples of an ancient Norse town.

⊙ Sights

★ **St Magnus Cathedral** CATHEDRAL
(☏ 01856-874894; www.stmagnus.org; Broad St; ☺ 9am-6pm Mon-Sat, 1-6pm Sun Apr-Sep, 9am-1pm & 2-5pm Mon-Sat Oct-Mar) **FREE** Constructed from local red sandstone, Kirkwall's centrepiece, dating from the early 12th century, is among Scotland's most interesting cathedrals. The powerful atmosphere of an ancient faith pervades the impressive interior. Lyrical and melodramatic epitaphs of the dead line the walls and emphasise the serious business of 17th- and 18th-century bereavement. Tours of the upper level (£8) run on Tuesday and Thursday; phone to book.

Earl Rognvald Brusason commissioned the cathedral in 1137 in the name of his martyred uncle, Magnus Erlendsson, who was killed by Earl Hakon Paulsson on Egilsay in 1117. Magnus' remains are entombed in an interior pillar. Another notable interment is that of the Arctic explorer John Rae.

ORKNEY & SHETLAND KIRKWALL

Kirkwall

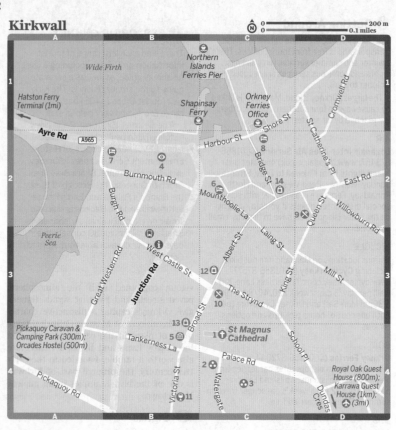

ORKNEY & SHETLAND KIRKWALL

Kirkwall

★ **Highland Park Distillery** DISTILLERY
(☎01856-874619; www.highlandpark.co.uk; Holm Rd; tours adult/child £10/free; ☉tours 10am-4pm Apr-Oct, 2pm & 3pm Mon-Fri Nov-Mar) South of Kirkwall's centre, this distillery is great to visit. Despite a dodgy Viking rebrand, it's a serious distillery that malts its own barley; see it and the peat kiln used to dry it on the excellent, well-informed hour-long tour (book ahead). The standard 12-year-old is a soft, balanced malt, great for novices and aficionados alike; the 18-year-old is among the

world's finest drams. This and older whiskies can be tasted on more specialised tours (£20 to £75), which you can prearrange.

Kirkjuvagr Orkney Gin DISTILLERY
(☑ 01856-875338; www.orkneydistilling.com; Ayre Rd; tours adult/child £15/8; ⊙ tours 11am & 2pm Mon-Sat) Opened in 2018, this distillery and visitor centre on the waterfront is a new showcase for this tasty Orkney spirit. Tours run for an hour and include an audiovisual display and a tasting; it's wise to prebook online. There's also a cafe-bar here. At the time of research, they were about to roll out an in-depth day-long tour that would let you create your own gin.

Earl's Palace RUINS
(☑ 01856-871918; www.historicenvironment.scot; Watergate; adult/child £5/3; ⊙ 9.30am-5.30pm Apr-Sep) The intriguing Earl's Palace was once known as the finest example of French Renaissance architecture in Scotland. One room features an interesting history of its builder, Earl Patrick Stewart, a bastard in every sense of the word, who was beheaded in Edinburgh for treason. He started construction in about 1600, but ran out of money and never completed it. When it's closed you can still get a good look at it from the garden. Admission includes the adjacent **Bishop's Palace**.

Orkney Museum MUSEUM
(☑ 01856-873191; www.orkney.gov.uk; Broad St; ⊙ 10.30am-5pm Mon-Sat year-round, closed 12.30-1.30pm Oct-Apr) FREE This labyrinthine display in a former merchant's house gives an overview of Orcadian history and prehistory, including Pictish carvings and a display on the ba' (p404). Most engaging are the last rooms, covering 19th- and 20th-century social history.

🎭 Festivals & Events

St Magnus Festival PERFORMING ARTS, MUSIC
(☑ 01856-871445; www.stmagnusfestival.com; ⊙ late Jun) Running for a week over midsummer, this festival is a colourful celebration of music and the arts, with high-quality orchestral performances at the heart of it. It's held in various venues around Kirkwall.

🛏️ Sleeping

Orcades Hostel HOSTEL £
(☑ 01856-873745; www.orcadeshostel.com; Muddisdale Rd; dm/s/d £20/40/52; P@🛜) Book ahead to get a bed in this cracking hos-

tel on the western edge of Kirkwall. It's a guesthouse conversion, so there's a very smart kitchen and lounge, and great-value doubles. Comfortable, spacious en suite dorms with just four bunks make for sound sleeping; enthusiastic owners give the place spark. There are lockers for valuables at reception.

Peedie Hostel HOSTEL £
(☑ 01856-877177; www.stayinkirkwall.co.uk; Ayre Rd; dm/s/tw £15/20/35; P🛜) Nestling into a corner at the end of the Kirkwall waterfront, this marvellously located hostel set in former fisherfolk's cottages has a cute, tiny downstairs section and a more sizeable upper area. Most of the dorms have just two beds, and there are three separate kitchen areas. It's normally unstaffed, but the keen new owner is giving it a gradual facelift.

Laundry facilities are available.

Pickaquoy Caravan & Camping Park CAMPSITE £
(Orkney Caravan Park; ☑ 01856-879900; www.orkneycaravanpark.co.uk; Muddisdale Rd; sites per adult/child £10/2.50, pod d £49; ⊙ Mar–mid-Dec; P🛜🏊🐕) There's no view, but plenty of grass and excellent modern facilities at this campsite, which is handily close to the centre of Kirkwall. There are also two camping pods sleeping up to six. If unattended, check in at the adjacent leisure centre.

Royal Oak Guest House B&B ££
(☑ 01856-877177; www.royaloakhouse.co.uk; Holm Rd; s £55-64, d £80; P🛜) This likeable spot south of Kirkwall's centre has eight bright rooms, all with modern en suite bathrooms. Photos of Orkney decorate the guesthouse, which features a luminous dining room and guest access to fridge, microwave and lounge. Best is having a great chat with owner Liz.

Shore HOTEL ££
(☑ 01856-872200; www.theshore.co.uk; Shore St; d £100-140; 🛜) Right on the harbour, the Shore has a can-do attitude and a friendly vibe. The rooms vary widely, from compact upstairs chambers to excellent, spacious premier doubles with water views (well worth the upgrade), but all are modern. Breakfast is also above average.

Karrawa Guest House GUESTHOUSE ££
(☑ 01856-871100; www.karrawaguesthouseorkney.co.uk; Inganess Rd; s £65-70, d £85-90; P🛜) In

a peaceful location on the southeastern edge of Kirkwall, this enthusiastically run guesthouse offers significant value for well-kept modern double rooms with comfortable mattresses. Breakfast is generously proportioned and bikes are available for hire.

★ **Albert Hotel** HOTEL £££
(☑01856-876000; www.alberthotel.co.uk; Mounthoolie Lane; s £97, d £146-181; 🛜) Stylishly refurbished in plum and grey, this central but peaceful hotel is Kirkwall's finest address. Comfortable contemporary rooms in a variety of categories sport superinviting beds and smart bathrooms. Staff are helpful, and will pack you a breakfast box if you've got an early ferry. A great Orkney base, with the more-than-decent **Bothy Bar** (mains £7-12; ⊙noon-2pm & 5-9pm; 🛜) downstairs. Walk-in prices are often cheaper.

🍴 Eating & Drinking

Reel CAFE £
(www.facebook.com/thereelkirkwall; Albert St; sandwiches £3-6; ⊙9am-6pm Mon-Sat; 🛜) Part music shop, part cafe, the Reel is Kirkwall's best coffee stop and sits alongside St Magnus Cathedral (p401), bravely putting tables outside at the slightest threat of sunshine. It's a relaxed spot, good for a morning-after debriefing, a quiet Orkney ale, or lunchtime panini and musically named sandwiches (plus the cheese-and-mushroom Skara Brie).

It's a local folk-musicians' centre, with three evening sessions a week; check the Facebook page.

THE BA'
....

Every Christmas Day and New Year's Day, Kirkwall holds a staggering spectacle: a crazy ball game known as the ba'. Two enormous teams, the Uppies and the Doonies, fight their way, no holds barred, through the streets, trying to get a leather ball to the other end of town. The ball is thrown from the Mercat Cross to the waiting teams; the Uppies have to get the ba' to the corner of Main St and Junction Rd, the Doonies must get it to the water. Violence, skulduggery and other stunts are common, and the event, fuelled by plenty of strong drink, can last hours.

Judith Glue Real Food Cafe CAFE £
(☑01856-874225; www.judithglue.com; 25 Broad St; light meals £8-16; ⊙9am-6pm Mon-Sat, 10am-6pm Sun mid-Sep–May, 9am-9pm Mon-Sat, 10am-6pm Sun Jun–mid-Sep; 🛜) 🍴 At the back of a lively craft shop opposite St Magnus Cathedral, this licensed cafe-bistro serves tasty sandwiches and salads, as well as daily specials and succulent seafood platters. There's a strong emphasis on sustainable and organic ingredients, but put the feelgood factor aside for a moment when fighting for a table at lunchtime. Check Facebook for regular events.

★ **The Shore** SCOTTISH ££
(☑01856-872200; www.theshore.co.uk; 6 Shore St; bar meals £9-11, restaurant mains £17-22; ⊙food noon-2pm & 6-9pm Mon-Fri, 10am-9pm Sat & Sun, reduced hours winter; 🛜) This popular harbourside place is a convivial spot with a helpful attitude. It offers highstandard bar meals and excellent evening meals in the restaurant section, which features local seafood and beautifully prepared meat dishes. Upstairs are some very decent rooms.

★ **Foveran** SCOTTISH ££
(☑01856-872389; www.thefoveran.com; St Ola; mains £15-26; ⊙6.30-8.30pm mid-May–mid-Sep, Fri & Sat only plus other days by arrangement low season; 🛜) 🍴 Three miles down the Orphir road, one of Orkney's best dining options is surprisingly affordable for its quality. Tranquilly located, with a cosy eating area overlooking the sea, it shines with its classic Orcadian ingredients – the steak with haggis and whisky sauce is feted, while North Ronaldsay lamb comes in four different, deliciously tender cuts.

A medley of toothsome vegetables accompanies the mains, and interesting wines complement the dishes. If you like the spot – and why wouldn't you? – there are compact, comfortable, Laura Ashley–decorated rooms available (singles/doubles £85/125).

Old Storehouse SCOTTISH ££
(☑01856-252250; www.thestorehouserestaurant withrooms.co.uk; Bridge St Wynd; mains lunch £9-12, dinner £14-22; ⊙noon-11pm; 🛜) This exciting project that was just about to open as we last passed by has seen a transformation of a listed 19th-century herring warehouse into an Orcadian restaurant. There are also eight luxurious, individu-

ally designed rooms upstairs (doubles £150 to £190).

Royal Cask
PUB

(☑ 01856-873477; www.orkneyhotel.co.uk; 40 Victoria St; ⊙ 11am-midnight Mon-Wed, to 1am Thu-Sat, noon-midnight Sun; 🛜) Tucked away in the Orkney Hotel, this refurbished bar is best visited for its fabulous selection of single malt whisky, with over 800 different bottlings and lots of knowledge about them. There are also bar meals available to soak it all up.

🛍 Shopping

Kirkwall has some gorgeous jewellery and crafts along Albert St, as well as shops selling quality Orcadian food and drink.

Sheila Fleet
JEWELLERY

(☑ 01856-861203; www.sheilafleet.com; 30 Bridge St; ⊙ 9am-5pm Mon-Sat year-round, plus 11am-4pm Sun Jun-Aug) Orkney's best-known jewellery designer creates some exquisite pieces seemingly lit from within. She draws on local traditions and storytelling for her creations. If you want to see them being made you can visit her workshop, located past the airport in Tankerness.

Judith Glue
ARTS & CRAFTS

(☑ 01856-874225; www.judithglue.com; 25 Broad St; ⊙ 9am-6pm Mon-Sat, 10am-6pm Sun mid-Sep–May, 9am-9pm Mon-Sat, 10am-6pm Sun Jun–mid-Sep) This absorbing shop has some fine handmade knitwear as well as an eclectic range of Orkney crafts and souvenirs.

Aurora
JEWELLERY

(☑ 01856-871521; www.aurora-jewellery.com; 69 Albert St; ⊙ 9.30am-5.15pm Mon-Sat) This jewellery store features the work of three Orcadian designers, with their beautiful earrings, brooches and necklaces inspired by local landscapes and history.

ℹ Information

Balfour Hospital (☑ 01856-888000; www.ohb. scot.nhs.uk; New Scapa Rd) Follow Junction Rd south out of town and you'll see it on your right. It's scheduled to be replaced by **Orkney Hospital** (www.ohb.scot.nhs.uk; Foreland Rd) in 2019.

Kirkwall Tourist Office (☑ 01856-872856; www.visitorkney.com; West Castle St; ⊙ 9am-5pm Mon-Sat Nov-Mar, to 6pm Mon-Sat Apr & Sep-Oct, to 6pm daily May-Aug) Has a good range of Orkney info and helpful staff. Shares a building with the bus station.

ℹ Getting There & Away

AIR

Kirkwall Airport (☑ 01856-872421; www.hial. co.uk) is located 2.5 miles southeast of town and is served regularly by bus 4 (15 minutes).

BOAT

Ferries to Orkney's northern islands depart from the **pier** (www.orkneyferries.co.uk; Shore St) in the centre of town. Here too is the **Orkney Ferries Office** (☑ 01856-872044; www.orkney ferries.co.uk; Shore St; ⊙ 7am-5pm Mon-Fri, 7am-noon & 1-3pm Sat) for bookings. **Ferries to Shapinsay** (www.orkneyferries.co.uk; Shore St) depart from the next pier to the west.

Ferries to Aberdeen and Shetland use the **Hatston Ferry Terminal** (www.northlinkferries. co.uk; Grainshore Rd; 🛜), 2 miles northwest. Bus X10 heads there to coincide with departures.

BUS

All services leave from the **bus station** (West Castle St):

Bus X1 Stromness (£3.20, 30 minutes, hourly Monday to Saturday, seven on Sunday); in the other direction to St Margaret's Hope (£3).

Bus 2 Orphir and Houton (£2.35, 20 minutes, four or five daily Monday to Saturday, five on Sunday from mid-June to mid-August).

Bus 6 Evie (£3.50, 30 minutes, three to five daily Monday to Saturday) and Tingwall (Rousay ferry). Runs Sunday in summer to Tingwall only.

East Mainland to South Ronaldsay

After a German U-boat sank battleship HMS *Royal Oak* in 1939, Winston Churchill had causeways of concrete blocks erected across the channels on the eastern side of Scapa Flow, linking Mainland to the islands of Lamb Holm, Glims Holm, Burray and South Ronaldsay. The Churchill Barriers, flanked by rusting wrecks of blockships, now support the main road from Kirkwall to Burwick.

East Mainland

On a farm at Tankerness, the mysterious Iron Age site of **Mine Howe** is an eerie underground chamber, about 1.5m in diameter and 4m high. Its function is unknown; archaeologists from the TV series *Time Team* carried out a dig here and concluded that it may have had some ritual significance, perhaps as an oracle or shrine. At the time of research it was closed to the public.

Lamb Holm

Italian Chapel
CHURCH

(☑01865-781268; adult/child £3/free; ⊙9am-6.30pm Jun-Aug, to 5pm May & Sep, 10am-4pm Mon-Sat, to 3pm Sun Apr & Oct, 10am-1pm Nov-Mar) The Italian Chapel is all that remains of a POW camp that housed the Italian soldiers who worked on the Churchill Barriers. They built the chapel in their spare time, using two Nissen huts, scrap metal and their considerable artistic skills. It's quite extraordinary inside and the charming back story makes it an Orkney highlight. One of the artists returned in 1960 to restore the paintwork.

Orkney Wine Company
DRINKS

(☑01856-781736; www.orkneywine.co.uk; ⊙10am-5pm Mon-Sat May-Sep, plus noon-4pm Sun Jul & Aug, reduced hours Mar-Apr & Oct-Dec) The Orkney Wine Company has handmade wines produced with berries, flowers and vegetables, all naturally fermented. Get stuck into some strawberry-rhubarb wine or blackcurrant port – unusual flavours but surprisingly delicious.

Burray

POP 400

This small island, a link in the chain joined by the Churchill Barriers, has a fine beach at Northtown on the east coast, where you may see seals. The village has a shop and places to stay, and there's a worthwhile museum on the island.

★ Fossil & Heritage Centre
MUSEUM

(☑01865-731255; www.orkneyfossilcentre.co.uk; adult/child £4.50/3; ⊙10am-5pm mid-Apr–Sep) This eclectic museum is a great visit, combining some excellent 360-million-year-old Devonian fish fossils found locally with a well-designed exhibition on the World Wars and Churchill Barriers. Upstairs is a selection of household and farming implements. There's a good little gift shop and an enjoyable coffee shop. Coming from Kirkwall it's on the left half a mile after crossing onto Burray.

South Ronaldsay

POP 900

South Ronaldsay's main village, pristine St Margaret's Hope, was named after the Maid of Norway, who died here in 1290 on her way to marry Edward II of England (strictly a political affair: Margaret was only seven years old). The island has some intriguing prehistoric tombs and fine places to stay and eat, and is also the docking point of two of the three mainland ferries.

⊙ Sights

★ Tomb of the Eagles
ARCHAEOLOGICAL SITE

(☑01856-831339; www.tomboftheeagles.co.uk; Cleat; adult/child £7.50/3.50; ⊙9.30am-5.30pm Apr-Sep, 10am-noon Mar, 9.30am-12.30pm Oct) Two significant archaeological sites were found here by a farmer on his land. The first is a Bronze Age stone building with a firepit, indoor well and plenty of seating (a communal cooking site or the original Orkney pub?). Beyond, in a spectacular clifftop position, the neolithic tomb (wheel yourself in prone on a trolley) is an elaborate stone construction that held the remains of up to 340 people who died some five millennia ago.

An excellent personal explanation is given at the visitor centre; you meet a few spooky skulls and can handle some of the artefacts found, plus absorb information on the mesolithic period. It's about a mile's airy walk to the tomb from the centre, which is near Burwick.

Banks Chambered Tomb
ARCHAEOLOGICAL SITE

(Tomb of the Otters; ☑01856-831605; www.bankschamberedtomb.co.uk; Cleat; adult/child £6/3; ⊙11am-5pm Apr-Sep) Discovered while digging was under way for a car park, this 5000-year-old chambered tomb has yielded a vast quantity of human bones, well preserved thanks to the saturation of the earth. The tomb, dug into bedrock, is an atmospheric if claustrophobic visit. The guided tour mixes homespun archaeological theories with astute observations. Within the adjacent bistro, you can handle discoveries of stones and bones, including the remains of otters, who presumably used this as a den. Follow signs for Tomb of the Eagles.

🛏 Sleeping & Eating

★ Bankburn House
B&B ££

(☑01856-831310; www.bankburnhouse.co.uk; A961, St Margaret's Hope; s/d £60/90, without bathroom £47.50/75; P @ 🕏 🐕) 🍃 This large rustic house does everything right, with smashing good-sized rooms and engaging owners who put on quality breakfasts and take pride in constantly innovating to improve guests' comfort levels. The huge lawn overlooks St Margaret's Hope and the bay – perfect for sunbathing on shimmering Orkney summer days. Prices drop substantially for multinight stays. Evening meals are available by request.

They also have Tesla chargers and an electric car available for hire.

Robertsons CAFE £
(📞01856-831889; www.facebook.com/coffee hoosebar; Church Rd, St Margaret's Hope; light meals £3-9; ⏱food 10am-9pm Mon-Sat, 11am-9pm Sun; 📶) Tastefully renovated, this characterful high-ceilinged former general store with chessboard tiles makes an atmospheric venue for a morning coffee and filled roll, or light meals such as soups and cheeseboards with local varieties (available for purchase). It also does cocktails and opens as a bar until midnight or later.

Skerries Bistro SEAFOOD ££
(📞01856-831605; www.skerriesbistro.co.uk; Cleat; lunch £6-10, dinner mains £14-18; ⏱noon-4pm & 6-9pm Mon, Wed, Fri & Sat, noon-4pm Tue, Thu & Sun Apr-Sep) This cafe-bistro occupies a spectacular setting at the southern end of South Ronaldsay. It's a smart, modern glass-walled building with a deck and great clifftop views. Meals range from soups and sandwiches to daily fish and shellfish specials. Dinner should be booked ahead. A romantic little separate pod is available for private dining.

West & North Mainland

This part of Mainland island is sprinkled with outstanding prehistoric monuments: the journey to Orkney is worth it for these alone and they stand proud as some of the world's most important neolithic sites. It would take a day to see all of them – if pushed for time, visit Skara Brae then Maeshowe, but book your visit to the latter in advance.

◉ Sights

The Heart of Neolithic Orkney is Unesco-listed and consists of four standout archaeological sites: Skara Brae (p408), Maeshowe, the Standing Stones of Stenness (p408) and the Ring of Brodgar (p408). These and other associated sites are not to be missed. It's important to prebook your entry slot to Maeshowe ahead of time.

★**Maeshowe** ARCHAEOLOGICAL SITE
(📞01856-761606; www.historicenvironment. scot; adult/child £5.50/3.30; ⏱9.30am-5pm Apr-

Sep, 10am-4pm Oct-Mar, tours hourly 10am-4pm, plus 6pm & 7pm Jul & Aug) Constructed about 5000 years ago, Maeshowe is an extraordinary place, a Stone Age tomb built from enormous sandstone blocks, some of which weighed many tons and were brought from several miles away. Creeping down the long stone passageway to the central chamber, you feel the indescribable gulf of years that separate us from the architects of this mysterious tomb.

Entry is by 45-minute guided tours (prebooking online is strongly advised) that leave by bus from the visitor centre at nearby Stenness.

Though nothing is known about who and what was interred here, the scope of the project suggests it was a structure of great significance.

In the 12th century, the tomb was broken into by Vikings searching for treasure. A couple of years later, another group sought shelter in the chamber from a three-day blizzard. Waiting out the storm, they carved runic graffiti on the walls. As well as the some-things-never-change 'Olaf was 'ere' and 'Thorni bedded Helga', there are also more intricate carvings, including a particularly fine dragon and a knotted serpent.

Prebook tickets online as recommended, or buy them at the visitor centre in Stenness, from where the tour buses depart. Guides tend to only show a couple of the Viking inscriptions, but they'll happily show more if asked. Check out the virtual-reality tour in the visitor centre while you wait.

For a few weeks around the winter solstice the setting sun shafts up the entrance passage, and strikes the back wall of the tomb in

> ### NESS OF BRODGAR
>
> Ongoing excavations on the **Ness of Brodgar** (www.nessofbrodgar.co.uk; ⏱tours 2-3 times Mon-Fri early Jul-late Aug) FREE, between the Standing Stones of Stenness and the Ring of Brodgar, are rapidly revealing that this was a neolithic site of huge importance. Probably a major power and religious centre and used for over a millennium, the settlement had a mighty wall, a large building (a temple or palace?) and as many as 100 other structures, some painted. Each dig season reveals new, intriguing finds.

DON'T MISS

SKARA BRAE

Idyllically situated by a sandy bay 8 miles north of Stromness, and predating Stonehenge and the pyramids of Giza, extraordinary **Skara Brae** (www.historicenvironment.scot; Sandwick; adult/child Nov-Mar £6.50/3.90, Apr-Oct incl Skaill House £7.50/4.50; ⊙9.30am-5.30pm Apr-Sep, 10am-4pm Oct-Mar), one of the world's most evocative prehistoric sites, is northern Europe's best-preserved neolithic village. Even the stone furniture – beds, boxes and dressers – has survived the 5000 years since a community lived and breathed here. It was hidden until 1850, when waves whipped up by a severe storm eroded the sand and grass above the beach, exposing the houses underneath.

There's an excellent interactive exhibit and short video, arming visitors with facts and theory, which will enhance the impact of the site. You then enter a reconstructed house, giving the excavation (which you head to next) more meaning. The official guidebook, available from the visitor centre, includes a good self-guided tour.

In the summer months, your ticket also gets you into **Skaill House** (☑01856-841501; www.skaillhouse.co.uk; Sandwick; incl Skara Brae adult/child £7.50/4.50; ⊙9.30am-5.30pm Apr-Sep, 10am-4pm Oct), an important step-gabled Orcadian mansion built for the bishop in 1620. It may feel a bit anticlimactic catapulting straight from the neolithic to the 1950s decor, but it's an interesting sight in its own right. You can see a smart hidden compartment in the library as well as the bishop's original 17th-century four-poster bed.

At the time of research, a trial bus route (8S) was running to Skara Brae from Kirkwall and Stromness a few times weekly, but not all were useful to visit the site. It's possible to walk along the coast from Stromness to Skara Brae (9 miles), or it's an easy taxi (£15), hitch or cycle from Stromness. Mobility scooters are available at the visitor centre to cut out the walk to the site.

spooky alignment. If you can't be here then, check the webcams on www.maeshowe. co.uk.

Ring of Brodgar
ARCHAEOLOGICAL SITE
(www.historicenvironment.scot; ⊙24hr) **FREE**
A mile northwest of Stenness is this wide circle of standing stones, some over 5m tall. The last of the three Stenness monuments to be built (2500–2000 BC), it remains a most atmospheric location. Twenty-one of the original 60 stones still stand among the heather. On a grey day with dark clouds thudding low across the sky, the stones are a spine-tingling sight.

Standing Stones of Stenness
ARCHAEOLOGICAL SITE
(www.historicenvironment.scot; ⊙24hr) **FREE**
Part of this Mainland area's concentration of neolithic monuments, four mighty stones remain of what was once a circle of 12. Recent research suggests they were perhaps erected as long ago as 3300 BC, and they impose by their sheer size; the tallest measures 5.7m in height. The narrow strip of land they're on, the Ness of Brodgar, separates the Harray and Stenness lochs and was the site of a large settlement inhabited throughout the neolithic period (3500–1800 BC).

Unstan Chambered Cairn
ARCHAEOLOGICAL SITE
(www.historicenvironment.scot; A965; ⊙24hr)
FREE This atmospheric neolithic tomb, on a smaller scale than nearby Maeshowe, is a site that you may well get to yourself. It's a very tight squeeze down the entrance passage; once inside you can appreciate several different burial compartments divided by vertical stone slabs. The modern roof protects the structure.

Barnhouse Neolithic Village
ARCHAEOLOGICAL SITE
(www.historicenvironment.scot; ⊙24hr) **FREE**
Alongside the Standing Stones of Stenness are the excavated remains of a village thought to have been inhabited by the builders of Maeshowe. Don't skip this: it brings the area to life. The houses are well preserved and similar to Skara Brae with their stone furnishings. One of the buildings was entered by crossing a fireplace: possibly an act of ritual significance.

Orkney Brewery
BREWERY
(☑01856-841777; www.orkneybrewery.co.uk; Quoyloo; tours adult/child £6.50/3.50; ⊙10am-4.30pm Mon-Sat, 11am-4.30pm Sun mid-Mar–Dec) The folk here have been producing their brilliant Orcadian beers – Dark Island is a standout, while Skullsplitter lives up to its

name – for years now, and this brewery's visitor centre is a great place to come and try them. Tours run regularly from noon to 3pm and explain the brewing process, while, fashionably decked out in local stone, the cafe-bar is atmospheric.

Birsay

The small village of Birsay is 6 miles north of Skara Brae, set amid peaceful countryside. It has some excellent attractions, including the Brough of Birsay, which makes a tempting picnic destination if you plan the tides right.

Brough of Birsay   ARCHAEOLOGICAL SITE
(www.historicenvironment.scot; adult/child £5/3; ☉9.30am-5.30pm mid-Jun–Sep) At low tide – check tide times at any Historic Environment Scotland site – you can walk out to this windswept island, the site of extensive Norse ruins, including a number of longhouses and the 12th-century **St Peter's Church**. There's also a replica of a Pictish stone found here. This is where St Magnus was buried after his murder on Egilsay in 1117, and the island became a pilgrimage place. The attractive lighthouse has fantastic views. Take a picnic, but don't get stranded...

The Brough features heavily in George Mackay Brown's excellent novel, *Magnus*.

Earl's Palace   RUINS
(☉24hr) **FREE** The ruins of this palace, built in the 16th century by the despotic Robert Stewart, Earl of Orkney, dominate the village of Birsay. Today it's a mass of half walls and crumbling columns; the size of the palace is impressive, matching the reputed ego and tyranny of its former inhabitant.

Birsay Hostel   HOSTEL, CAMPSITE **£**
(☏after hours 01856-721470, office hours 01856-873535; https://orkney.campstead.com; junction of B9056 & A967; tent sites 1/2 people £8.25/12.70, dm/tw £19/37.90; ☉Apr-Sep; **P**🐾) A former activity centre and school now has dorms that vary substantially in spaciousness – go for the two- or four-bedded ones. There's a big kitchen and a grassy camping area; kids and families sleep substantially cheaper. Book online to avoid an admin fee (private rooms only). It will open for bookings of four or more in the low season.

Birsay Bay Tearoom   CAFE **£**
(☏01856-721399; www.birsaybaytearoom.co.uk; light meals £3-8; ☉11am-4.30pm Thu-Mon Apr, to 6pm Wed-Mon May-Sep, 10.30am-3.30pm Fri-Sun

Oct-Dec & Feb-Mar; ☏) A pleasant spot with sweeping views over green grass, black cows and blue-grey sea, this cafe serves tea, coffee, home baking and light meals. It's a good place to wait for the tide to go out before crossing to the Brough of Birsay (in plain sight). Check the website for latest winter opening times as these vary substantially.

Broch of Gurness

Broch of Gurness (www.historicenvironment. scot; Evie; adult/child £6/3.60; ☉9.30am-5.30pm Apr-Sep, 10am-4pm Oct) is a fine example of the drystone fortified towers that were both a status symbol for powerful farmers and useful protection from raiders some 2200 years ago. The imposing entranceway and sturdy stone walls – originally 10m high – are impressive; inside you can see the hearth and where a mezzanine floor would have fitted. Around the broch are a number of well-preserved outbuildings, including a curious shamrock-shaped house. The visitor centre has some interesting displays on the culture that built these remarkable fortifications.

The broch is on an exposed headland at Aikerness, a 1.5-mile walk northeast from the strung-out village of Evie.

Stromness

POP 1800

This appealing grey-stone port has a narrow, elongated, flagstone-paved main street and tiny alleys leading down to the waterfront between tall houses. It lacks the size of Kirkwall, Orkney's main town, but makes up for that with bucketloads of character, having changed little since its heyday in the 18th century, when it was a busy staging post for ships avoiding the troublesome English Channel during European wars. Stromness is ideally located for trips to Orkney's major prehistoric sites.

◎ Sights

Stromness, formerly a slightly rough-edged maritime town, has gone all arty, with a string of quirky craft shops, galleries and boutiques along the picturesque main shopping street. It's great for browsing.

★**Stromness Museum**   MUSEUM
(☏01856-850025; www.stromnessmuseum.co.uk; 52 Alfred St; adult/child £5/1; ☉10am-5pm daily Apr-Sep, 10am-5pm Mon-Sat Oct, 11am-3.30pm

Mon-Sat Nov-Mar) This superb museum, run with great passion, is full of knick-knacks from maritime and natural-history exhibitions covering whaling, the Hudson's Bay Company and the German fleet sunk after WWI. Recent finds from the jaw-dropping excavations at the Ness of Brodgar are on display and there's always an excellent summer exhibition, too. You can happily nose around for a couple of hours. Across the street is the house where local poet and novelist George Mackay Brown lived.

Pier Arts Centre
GALLERY

(📞 01856-850209; www.pierartscentre.com; 30 Victoria St; ⊙ 10.30am-5pm Tue-Sat year-round, plus Mon Jun-Sep) FREE This gallery has really rejuvenated the Orkney modern-art scene with its sleek lines and upbeat attitude. It's worth a look as much for the architecture as for its high-quality collection of 20th-century British art and changing exhibitions.

★✦ Festivals & Events

Orkney Folk Festival
MUSIC

(www.orkneyfolkfestival.com; ⊙ late May) A four-day event in late May, with folk concerts, *ceilidhs* (evenings of traditional Scottish entertainment) and casual pub sessions. Stromness packs out, and late-night buses from Kirkwall are laid on. Book tickets and accommodation ahead.

🛏 Sleeping

Hamnavoe Hostel
HOSTEL £

(📞 01856-851202; www.hamnavoehostel.co.uk; 10a North End Rd; dm/s/tw £22/24/48; 📶) This well-equipped hostel is efficiently run and has excellent facilities, including a fine kitchen and a lounge room with great perspectives over the water. The dorms are very spacious, with duvets, decent mattresses and reading lamps (bring a pound coin for the heating), and the showers are good. Ring ahead as the owner lives off-site.

Brown's Hostel
HOSTEL £

(📞 01856-850661; www.brownsorkney.com; 45 Victoria St; s/d £22.50/40, d with bathroom £50; @📶) On Stromness' main street, this handy, sociable place has cosy private rooms – no dorms, no bunks – at a good price. There's an inviting common area, where you can browse the free internet or swap pasta recipes in the open kitchen. There are en suite rooms in a house up the street, with self-catering options available.

Point of Ness Caravan & Camping Park
CAMPSITE £

(📞 office hours 01856-873535, site 01856-850532; https://orkney.campstead.com; Ness Rd; tent sites 1/2 people £8.25/12.70; ⊙ Apr-Sep; P📶🏠) This breezy, fenced-in campsite has a super location overlooking the bay at the southern end of Stromness and is as neat as a pin.

★ Brinkies Guest House
B&B ££

(📞 01856-851881; www.brinkiesguesthouse.co.uk; Brownstown Rd; s £65, d £80-90; P📶) Just a short walk from the centre of Stromness, but with a lonely, king-of-the-castle position overlooking the town and bay, this exceptional place offers five-star islander hospitality. Compact, modern rooms are handsome, stylish and comfortable, and the public areas are done out attractively in wood, but above all it's the charming owner's flexibility and can-do attitude that makes this place so special.

Breakfast is 'continental Orcadian' – a stupendous array of quality local cheese, smoked fish and homemade bere bannocks (a wheat-barley bread). Want a lie-in? No problem, saunter down at 10am. Don't want breakfast? How about a packed lunch instead? To get here, take Outertown Rd off Back Rd, turn right on to Brownstown Rd, and keep going.

Burnside Farm
B&B ££

(📞 01856-850723; www.burnside-farm.com; North End Rd/A965; s £60, d £80-90; P📶) On a working dairy farm on the edge of Stromness, this place has lovely views over green fields, town and harbour. Rooms are elegant and maintain the style from when the house was built in the late 1940s, with attractive period furnishings. The top-notch bathrooms, however, are sparklingly contemporary. Breakfast comes with views, and the kindly owner couldn't be more welcoming.

Anderson's Harbour Cottages
COTTAGE ££

(📞 +27 79 492 9789; www.andersoncottage.co.uk; high season per week £595-995; P📶) Within a few paces of the Stromness Museum are these traditional stone cottages for rent, ranging from one to four bedrooms each. All are right on the water and some have a private jetty. They are well furnished with modern amenities, while still conserving the cosiness and romance of these former fishermen's dwellings.

✕ Eating

Bayleaf Delicatessen   DELI £
(☑ 01856-851605; www.bayleafdelicatessen.co.uk;
103 Victoria St; snacks £2-6; ⊙10am-5pm Mon-
Sat year-round, plus 10am-4pm Sun Jun-Aug) 🍴
On the meandering main street through
Stromness you'll find this very likeable little deli. Local cheeses and yoghurts are a
highlight, alongside smoked fish, takeaway
seafood salads and other tasty Orkney produce. There's good coffee too and a friendly
attitude.

★ Hamnavoe Restaurant   SEAFOOD ££
(☑ 01856-851226, 01856-850606; 35 Graham Pl;
mains £15-24; ⊙7-9pm Tue-Sun Jun-Aug) Tucked
away off the main street, this Stromness
favourite specialises in excellent local seafood in an intimate, cordial atmosphere.
There's always something good off the boats,
and the chef prides himself on his lobster.
Booking is a must. It opens some weekends in low season; it's worth calling ahead
to check.

Ferry Inn   PUB FOOD ££
(☑ 01856-850280; www.ferryinn.com; 10 John
St; mains £10-19; ⊙food 7am-9pm Apr-Oct; 🛜)
Every port has its pub, and in Stromness it's
the Ferry. Convivial and central, it warms
the cockles with folk music, local beers
and characters, and all-day food that offers
decent value in a dining area done out like
the deck of a ship. The fish and chips are
excellent, and a few blackboard specials fill
things out.

❶ Getting There & Around

BICYCLE

Orkney Cycle Hire (☑ 01856-850255; www.
orkneycyclehire.co.uk; 54 Dundas St; per day
£10-15; ⊙8am-5pm) Family options include
kids' bikes and child trailers.

BOAT

Northlink Ferries (www.northlinkferries.co.uk)
Runs services from Stromness to Scrabster
on the mainland (passenger/car £19.40/59,
1½ hours, two to three daily). At the time of
research, the road-equivalent tariff scheme
was due to be rolled out on Orkney services, so
prices should drop.

BUS

Bus X1 runs regularly to Kirkwall (£3.20, 30
minutes, hourly Monday to Saturday, seven
Sunday), with some going on to St Margaret's
Hope (£5.90, 1¼ hours).

Hoy
POP 400

Orkney's second-largest island, Hoy (meaning 'High Island'), got the lion's share of
the archipelago's scenic beauty. Shallow
turquoise bays lace the east coast and massive seacliffs guard the west, while peat
and moorland cover Orkney's highest hills.
Much of the north is a reserve for breeding
seabirds. The Scrabster–Stromness ferry
gives you a decent perspective of the island's
wild good looks.

◎ Sights

Old Man of Hoy   NATURAL FEATURE
Hoy's best-known sight is this 137m-high
rock stack jutting from the ocean off the tip
of an eroded headland. It's a tough ascent
and for experienced climbers only, but the
walk to see it is a Hoy highlight, revealing
much of the island's most spectacular scenery. You can also spot the Old Man from the
Scrabster–Stromness ferry.

The easiest approach to the Old Man is
from Rackwick Bay, a 5-mile walk by road
from Moaness Pier (in Hoy village on the
east coast, where the ferries dock) through
the beautiful Rackwick Glen. You'll pass
the 5000-year-old **Dwarfie Stane**, the
only example of a rock-cut tomb in Scotland. On your return you can take the path
via the Glens of Kinnaird and Berriedale
Wood, Scotland's most northerly tuft of
native forest.

From Rackwick Bay, where there's a
hostel, the most popular path climbs
steeply westwards then curves northwards,
descending gradually to the edge of the cliffs
opposite the Old Man of Hoy. Allow seven
hours for the return trip from Moaness Pier,
or three hours from Rackwick Bay.

Scapa Flow Visitor
Centre & Museum   MUSEUM
(☑ 01856-791300; www.orkney.gov.uk; Lyness;
⊙10am-4.30pm Mon-Sat Mar, Apr & Oct, 9am-
4.30pm Mon-Sat, 1st to last ferry Sun May-Sep)
FREE Lyness was an important naval base
during both World Wars, when the British
Grand Fleet was based in Scapa Flow. This
fascinating museum and photographic display, located in an old pumphouse that once
fed fuel to the ships, is a must-see for anyone interested in Orkney's military history.
Take your time to browse the exhibits and
have a look at the folders of supplementary

information: letters home from a seaman lost when the *Royal Oak* was torpedoed are particularly moving.

It's easily visited just by the ferry slip at Lyness, and there's a decent cafe here. The museum was being renovated at time of research and due to reopen in spring 2019.

Hackness Martello Tower & Battery FORT (www.historicenvironment.scot; Hackness; adult/child £5/3; ⊙9.30am-5.30pm Apr-Sep, 10am-4pm Mon-Sat Oct) Built during the Napoleonic Wars, when French ships passed through the Pentland Firth to prey on North Sea merchant vessels, this battery, accompanied by two towers (one across the water), never saw action but is an impressive piece of military architecture. The custodian gives an excellent tour of the barracks and tower – there's a lovely view from the gun platform on top – that really evokes the period.

🛏 Sleeping & Eating

Hoy Centre HOSTEL £ (☑office hours 01856-873535, warden 01856-791315; https://orkney.campstead.com; dm/tw £20/57.70; P🛜) This clean, bright, modern hostel has an enviable location, around 15 minutes' walk from Moaness Pier, at the base of the rugged Cuilags. Rooms are all en suite and include good-value family options; it also has a spacious kitchen and DVD lounge. It's open year-round: book via the website to avoid an admin fee (private rooms only).

Stromabank Hotel INN ££ (☑01856-701494; www.stromabank.co.uk; Longhope; s/d £55/90; P🛜) Perched on the hill above Longhope, the small atmospheric Stromabank Hotel has very acceptable, refurbished en suite rooms, as well as tasty home-cooked meals, including seafood and steaks (£8 to £14) using lots of local produce. (Served 6pm to 8pm Friday to Wednesday, plus noon to 2pm Sunday. They do meals for residents only on Thursday and takeaways on Saturday evenings.)

Beneth'ill Cafe CAFE £ (☑01856-791119; www.benethillcafe.co.uk; Hoy Village; light meals £7-9; ⊙10am-6pm Apr-Sep) Handy for the Moaness ferry, this cafe has a spectacular location by the water with great views of the brooding Hoy hills. It offers home baking and light meals such as salads and quiches. There's also a daily hot dish, often something hearty like stew, which is great after a walk. The food is pleasingly fresh, tasty and well presented.

ℹ Getting There & Away

Orkney Ferries (www.orkneyferries.co.uk) runs a passenger/bike ferry (adult £4.25, 30 minutes, two to six daily) between Stromness and Moa-

---

DIVING SCAPA FLOW

One of the world's largest natural harbours, Scapa Flow has been in near constant use by fleets from the time of the Vikings onwards. After WWI, 74 German ships were interned here; when the armistice dictated a severely reduced German navy, Admiral von Reuter, in charge of the fleet, took matters into his own hands. A secret signal was passed around and the British watched incredulously as every German ship began to sink. Fifty-two of them went to the bottom, with the rest left aground in shallow water.

Most were salvaged, but seven vessels remain to attract divers. There are three battleships – the *König*, the *Kronprinz Wilhelm* and the *Markgraf*. The first two were partially blasted for scrap, but the *Markgraf* is undamaged and considered one of Scotland's best dives.

Numerous other ships rest on the sea bed. HMS *Royal Oak*, sunk by a German U-boat in October 1939 with the loss of 833 crew, is a war grave and diving is prohibited.

It's worth prebooking diving excursions far in advance. **Scapa Scuba** (☑01856-851218; www.scapascuba.co.uk; Lifeboat House, Dundas St; beginner dive £85, 2 guided dives £160-185; ⊙noon-7pm Mon-Fri & 3-6pm Sat & Sun May-Sep) is an excellent operator that caters for both beginners – with 'try dives' around the Churchill barriers – and tried-and-tested divers. You'll need plenty of experience to dive the wrecks, some of which are 47m deep, plus have recent drysuit experience: this can be organised for you. Other boats that you can charter for dives include **MV Karin** (www.scapaflow.com) and **MV Jean Elaine** (www.jeanelaine.co.uk).

ness at Hoy's northern end, and a car ferry to Lyness (with one service to/from Longhope) from Houton on Mainland (passenger/car £4.25/13.60, 40 minutes, up to seven daily Monday to Friday, two or three Saturday and Sunday); book cars well in advance. Sunday service is from May to September only.

The Moaness ferry also stops at Graemsay. The Houton service also links to Flotta.

Northern Islands

The group of windswept islands north of Mainland is a haven for birds, rich in archaeological sites and blessed with wonderful white-sand beaches and azure seas. Though some are hillier than others, all offer a broadly similar landscape of flattish green farmland running down to scenic coastline. Some give a real sense of what Orkney was like before the modern world impinged upon island life.

Accessible by reasonably priced ferry or plane, the islands are well worth exploring. Though you can see 'the sights' in a matter of hours, the key is to stay a day or two and relax into the pace of island life.

Note that the 'ay' at the end of island names (from the Old Norse for 'island') is pronounced closer to 'ee'.

Orkney Ferries and Loganair Inter-Isles Air Service enable you to make day trips to many of the islands from Kirkwall.

Most islands offer a bus service that meets ferries: you may have to call to book this. The same operator often offers island tours.

Westray

POP 600

If you've time to visit only one of Orkney's Northern Islands, make Westray (www.westraypapawestray.co.uk) the one. The largest of the group, it has rolling farmland, handsome sandy beaches, great coastal walks and several appealing places to stay.

◉ Sights & Activities

★Noltland Castle   CASTLE
(www.historicenvironment.scot;   ⊙8am-8pm)
FREE A half-mile west of Pierowall stands this sturdy ruined towerhouse, built in the 16th century by Gilbert Balfour, aide to Mary, Queen of Scots. The castle is super-atmospheric and bristles with shot holes, part of the defences of the deceitful Balfour, who plotted to murder Cardinal Beaton and,

after being exiled, the king of Sweden. Like a pantomime villain, he met a sticky end.

At the nearby Links of Noltland, archaeological investigation is regularly unearthing interesting neolithic finds. Most intriguing has been a chamber built over a spring, which was possibly used as a sauna.

Noup Head   NATURE RESERVE
FREE This bird reserve at Westray's northwestern tip is a dramatic area of sea cliffs, with vast numbers of breeding seabirds from April to July. You can walk here along the clifftops from a car park, passing the impressive chasm of **Ramni Geo**, and return via the lighthouse access road (4 miles).

Westray Heritage Centre   MUSEUM
(☎01857-677414;   www.westrayheritage.co.uk;
Pierowall;   adult/child £3/50p;   ⊙11.30am-5pm
Mon, 9am-noon & 2-5pm Tue-Sat, 1.30-5pm Sun May-Sep, 2-4pm Wed or by arrangement Oct-Apr) This heritage centre has displays on local history, nature dioramas and archaeological finds, with some famous neolithic carvings (including the 5000-year-old 'Westray Wife'). These small sandstone figurines are the oldest known depictions of the human form so far found in the British Isles.

Westraak   TOURS
(☎01857-677777; www.westraak.co.uk; Pierowall; adult half-/full day £42/60) This husband-and-wife outfit runs informative and engaging trips around Westray, covering everything from Viking history to puffin mating habits. It also runs the island's taxi service.

🛏️ Sleeping

★West Manse   B&B £
(☎01857-677482; www.westmanse.co.uk; Westside; r per person £25; P🐾🛜💻) 🐾 No timetables reign at this imposing house with arcing coastal vistas; make your own breakfast when you feel like it. Your welcoming hosts have introduced a raft of green solutions for heating, fuel and more. Kids will love this unconventional place, with its play nooks and hobbit house, while art exhibitions, eclectic workshops, venerably comfortable furniture and clean air are drawcards for parents.

There's also a self-catering apartment, Brotchie (£300 per week). The owners also let out a fabulous little waterside cottage in Pierowall that's totally designed for the needs of a visitor with a disability, accompanied by a carer.

Chalmersquoy & the Barn
B&B, HOSTEL £

(☏ 01857-677214; www.chalmersquoywestray.
co.uk; Pierowall; dm/s/q £24/32/72, B&B s/d
£58/80, apt for 4/6 £60/100, tent sites £9-12 plus
per adult/child £2/1; P ⏦) This excellent, intimate, modern hostel is an Orcadian gem. It's
heated throughout and has pristine kitchen
facilities and an inviting lounge; rooms sleep
two or three in comfort. Out front, the lovely
owners have top self-catering apartments
with great views, and spacious en suite B&B
rooms. There's also a campsite and a fabulous byre that hosts atmospheric concerts. A
recommended all-round choice.

Bis Geos
COTTAGE ££

(☏ 01857-677420; www.bisgeos.com; per week from
£370; P) There are stunning views at this
spectacular, quirky and cosy self-catering
option between Pierowall and Noup Head.
There are three separate units here, with
the largest sleeping eight and offering the
finest vistas. Shorter stays are sometimes
available.

Braehead Manse
B&B ££

(Reid Hall; ☏ 01857-677861; www.braeheadmanse.
co.uk; Braehead; s/d £50/65; P ⏦) ∅ A top-
notch conversion of a former village hall
behind the church in the middle of Westray,
this place has two luminous, high-ceilinged
rooms with modern en suite bathrooms and
a swish open-plan kitchen/living/dining
area with excellent facilities. You can choose
either self-catering – perfect for a family of
four – or the B&B option, with your hosts
making breakfast.

Pierowall Hotel
PUB FOOD £

(☏ 01857-677472; www.pierowallhotel.co.uk; Pierowall; mains £9-14; ☺ food noon-2pm & 5-9pm May-
Sep, noon-1.30pm & 6-8pm Oct-Apr; ⏦) The heart
of the Westray community, this refurbished
local pub is famous throughout Orkney for
its popular fish and chips – whatever has
turned up in the day's catch from the hotel's
boats is displayed on the blackboard. There
are also some curries available, but the sea
is the way to go here. It also has rooms, and
hires out bikes (£10 per day).

❶ Getting There & Away

There are daily flights with Loganair (p401) from
Kirkwall to Westray (one way £37, 20 minutes).

Orkney Ferries (www.orkneyferries.co.uk)
links Kirkwall with Rapness (passenger/car
£8.35/19.70, 1½ hours, daily). A bus to the main
town, Pierowall, meets the ferry.

Papa Westray

Known locally as Papay, this exquisitely
peaceful, tiny island (4 miles by 1 mile) is
home to possibly Europe's oldest domestic
building, the 5500-year-old **Knap of Howar**
(☺ 24hr) FREE, and largest Arctic tern colony.
Plus the two-minute hop from Westray is the
world's shortest scheduled air service. It's a
charming island with seals easily spotted
while walking its coast.

Papay Ranger
TOURS

(☏ 07931 235213; www.papawestray.co.uk) The
Papay ranger runs excellent day-long tours
of Papay in summer that include lunch
and afternoon tea (£50/25 per adult/child),
guided visits to **Holm of Papay** (£25/12.50),
bike hire on the island and bespoke tours.

Beltane House
GUESTHOUSE, HOSTEL £

(☏ 01857-644224; www.papawestray.co.uk; Beltane; dm/s/d £20/28/44; P ⏦ ☺) Owned by
the local community, this is Papa Westray's
hub. It has the only shop, and functions as
a makeshift pub on Saturday nights. One
wing is a hostel with bunks, the other a
guesthouse with immaculate rooms with
en suites. There are two kitchens, zippy
wi-fi (when it works), a big lounge/eating
area and views over grassy fields to the
sea beyond.

It's just over a mile north of the ferry.
You can also camp here (£8/4 per adult/
child) and there are camping pods available
that sleep two (£20 per person plus £5 for
bedding).

❶ Getting There & Away

AIR

There are two or three daily flights with Loganair
(p401) to Papa Westray (£18, 20 minutes) from
Kirkwall. The £21 return offer (you must stay
overnight) is great value. Some of the Kirkwall
flights go via Westray (£17, two minutes, the
world's shortest scheduled flight) or North
Ronaldsay (£17, 10 minutes).

BOAT

A passenger-only ferry with **Orkney Ferries**
(www.orkneyferries.co.uk) runs from Pierowall
on Westray to Papa Westray (£4.15, 25 minutes,
three to six daily in summer); the crossing is
free if you've come straight from the Kirkwall–
Westray ferry. From October to April the boat
sails by arrangement (call 01857-677216). On
Tuesday and Friday a car ferry from Kirkwall
makes the journey to Papa Westray.

Rousay

POP 200

Just off the north coast of Mainland, hilly Rousay merits exploration for its fine assembly of prehistoric sites, great views and relaxing away-from-it-all ambience. Connected by regular ferry from Tingwall, it makes a great little day trip, but you may well feel a pull to stay longer. A popular option is to hire a bike from Trumland Farm near the ferry and take on the 14-mile circuit of the island.

★Midhowe Cairn & Broch
ARCHAEOLOGICAL SITE

(www.historicenvironment.scot; ⊘24hr) FREE Six miles from the ferry on Rousay, mighty Midhowe Cairn has been dubbed the 'Great Ship of Death'. Built around 3500 BC and enormous, it's divided into compartments, in which the remains of 25 people were found. Covered by a protective stone building, it's nevertheless memorable. Adjacent Midhowe Broch, whose sturdy stone lines echo the rocky shoreline's striations, is a muscular Iron Age fortified compound with a mezzanine floor. The sites are on the water, a 10-minute walk downhill from the main road.

Prehistoric Sites
ARCHAEOLOGICAL SITE

(www.historicenvironment.scot; ⊘24hr) FREE Rousay's major archaeological sites are clearly labelled from the road ringing the island. Heading west from the ferry, you soon come to Taversoe Tuick, an intriguing burial cairn constructed on two levels, with separate entrances – perhaps a joint tomb for different families; a semidetached solution in posthumous housing. Not far beyond are two other significant cairns: Blackhammer, then Knowe of Yarso, the latter a fair walk up the hill but with majestic views.

Trumland Farm
HOSTEL £

(☑01856-821252; trumland@btopenworld.com; sites £7, dm £15-16; P🐾) 🅿 An easy stroll from the ferry (turn left at the main road), this organic farm has a wee hostel with two dorms and a pretty little kitchen and common area. You can pitch tents and use the facilities; there's also well-equipped self-catering in a cottage and various farm buildings. Linen is £2 extra. Bikes can be hired here.

Taversoe
INN ££

(☑ 01856-821325; www.taversoehotel.co.uk; s £40-50, d £80-95; P🛜) Two miles west from the ferry pier, Rousay's only hotel is an attrac-

tively low-key place, with renovated rooms offering excellent bathrooms – one suitable for people with disabilities – and beautiful water vistas. The best views are from the dining room, which serves good-value meals. The friendly owners will collect you from the ferry.

Food is served from noon to 5pm Monday, to 9pm Tuesday to Saturday and to 7.30pm Sunday from May to September, with shorter hours in winter.

ⓘ Getting There & Around

A small ferry connects Tingwall on Mainland with Rousay (passenger/bicycle/car £4.25/free/13.60, 30 minutes, up to six daily) and the nearby islands of Egilsay and Wyre.

Rousay Tours (☑ 01856-821234; www. rousaytours.co.uk; adult/child £35/12) offers taxi service and recommended guided tours of the island, including wildlife-spotting (seals and otters), visits to the prehistoric sites and an optional tasty packed lunch.

Sanday

POP 500

Aptly named, blissfully quiet and flat, Sanday is ringed by Orkney's best beaches – with dazzling-white sand of the sort you'd expect in the Caribbean. It's a peaceful, green, pastoral landscape with the sea revealed at every turn.

Quoyness Chambered Tomb
ARCHAEOLOGICAL SITE

(⊘24hr) FREE There are several archaeological sites on Sanday, the most impressive being this chambered tomb, similar to

Maeshowe and dating from the 3rd millennium BC. It has triple walls, a main chamber and six smaller cells.

Sanday Heritage Centre   MUSEUM

(www.sanday.co.uk; Lady; donations appreciated; ⏰9.30am-5pm May-Oct, weekends only Nov-Apr) FREE This museum in the former temperance hall has intriguing displays on various aspects of island history, including fishing, WWI, archaeology and shipwrecks. In an adjacent field a typical croft house is preserved.

Ayre's Rock Hostel & Campsite   HOSTEL, CAMPSITE £

(☑01857-600410; www.ayres-rock-hostel-orkney. com; tent sites £8-10, pods £35, dm/s/tw £19.50/ 23.50/39; P🖥📶🐕) This super-friendly spot by a beach 6 miles north of the Sanday ferry offers a cosy three-room hostel sleeping two or four in beds, and a sweet, grassy campsite by the water. As well as tent pitches, there are heated two-person pods and a static caravan. Evening meals are available. It has a craft shop and Saturday chip shop; hosts are extremely helpful.

Backaskaill   B&B ££

(☑01857-600305; www.bedandbreakfastsanday orkney.com; s/d £50/80; P📶) Set on a working cattle farm by the sea, this place offers comfortable accommodation in a noble stone farmhouse. The polished interior features an eclectic collection of art and curios. The hospitality is cordial and professional. Rooms feel light and modern, and there's a fabulous guest lounge. The island's best meals (mains £9 to £16) are here and can be booked by non-guests.

❶ Getting There & Away

There are flights with Loganair (p401) from Kirkwall to Sanday (one way £37, 20 minutes, once or twice daily).

Orkney Ferries (www.orkneyferries.co.uk) runs from Kirkwall (passenger/car £8.35/19.70, 1½ hours), with a link to Eday. A bus meets the boat (book on 01857-600438).

North Ronaldsay

POP 70

North Ronaldsay is a real outpost surrounded by rolling seas and big skies. Delicious peace and quiet and the island's excellent birdwatching lure visitors. There are enough semi-feral sheep to seize power, but a 13-mile drystone wall running around the island keeps them off the grass; they make do with seaweed, which gives their meat a distinctive flavour.

North Ronaldsay Lighthouse   LIGHTHOUSE

(www.northronaldsay.co.uk; ⏰10am-5pm May-Aug or by arrangement) At the northern end of the island, this lighthouse is over 100ft high and one of many built across Scotland by the Stevenson family. A visitor centre and licensed cafe are here, as are bikes for hire and a gift shop selling the woollens made from yarn supplied by the local seaweed-eating sheep. You can climb the lighthouse itself and/or visit the woollen mill on a tour (☑01857-633257, 07703-112224; www.north ronaldsay.co.uk; lighthouse or mill adult/child £6/4, combined £9/7).

On the shore to the south of the lighthouse is an earlier model, an 18th-century beacon tower some 70ft high.

Observatory Guest House   B&B, HOSTEL ££

(☑01857-633200; www.nrbo.co.uk; campsites £5, dm/s/d £18.50/42.50/85; P@📶) 🐾 Powered by wind and solar energy, this place offers first-rate accommodation and ornithological activities next to the ferry pier. There's a cafe-bar with lovely coastal views and convivial communal dinners (£15) in a (sometimes) sun-kissed conservatory; if you're lucky, local lamb might be on the menu. You can also camp here.

❶ Getting There & Away

There are two or three daily flights with Loganair (p401) to North Ronaldsay (£18, 20 minutes) from Kirkwall. The £21 return offer (you must stay overnight) is great value.

Orkney Ferries runs from Kirkwall on Friday (passenger/car £8.35/19.70, 2½ hours), plus Tuesday in summer.

SHETLAND

Close enough to Norway geographically and historically to make nationality an ambiguous concept, the Shetland Islands are Britain's most northerly outpost. There's a Scandinavian lilt to the local accent, and streets named King Haakon or St Olaf are reminders that Shetland was under Norse rule until 1469, when it was gifted to Scotland in lieu of the dowry of a Danish princess.

The stirringly bleak setting – it's a Unesco geopark – still feels uniquely Scottish, though, with deep, naked glens flanked by steep hills, twinkling, sky-blue lochs and, of course, sheep on the roads.

Despite the famous ponies and woollens, it's no agricultural backwater. Offshore oil makes it quite a busy, comparatively well-heeled place, despite drops in barrel prices. Nevertheless nature still rules the seas and islands, and the birdlife (p428) is spectacular: pack binoculars.

☞ Tours

Discover Shetland TOURS
(☑ 07387-167205; www.discovershetland.net) Customisable tours of Shetland with a knowledgable guide, who's strong on the natural world and the ecology of the archipelago.

Shetland Nature WILDLIFE
(☑01595-760333; www.shetlandnature.net) This operator specialises in otter-watching excursions but also runs birdwatching trips all around the archipelago as well as scenic tours.

❶ Information

Visit www.shetland.org, an excellent website with good info on accommodation, activities and more.

The archipelago is replete with handicraft workshops, many working to produce artisanal jewellery and Shetland's famous woollens. The **Shetland Craft Trail** (☑ 07447-377856; www.shetlandartsandcrafts.co.uk) publishes a useful brochure of makers across the islands; the info is also available on their website.

Lerwick Tourist Office (p422) In the centre of the Shetland's main town, with comprehensive information on the islands.

Sumburgh Airport Tourist Office (☑01950-460905; www.shetland.org; Sumburgh Airport; ☺8.45am-4.45pm Mon-Fri, 10.15am-4pm Sat, 10.30am-5.30pm Sun, closed Sat Nov-Mar) Brochures are available even when this office is shut.

❶ Getting There & Away

AIR

Sumburgh Airport (☑ 01950-460905; www.hial.co.uk) is Shetland's main airport, 25 miles south of Lerwick. **Loganair** (☑ 0344 800 2855; www.loganair.co.uk) runs daily services to Aberdeen, Kirkwall, Inverness, Edinburgh and Glasgow, and summer services to Manchester and Bergen (Norway).

BOAT

Northlink Ferries (www.northlinkferries.co.uk) runs daily overnight car ferries between Aberdeen and Lerwick (high-season one way passenger/car £41/146, 12 to 15 hours), some stopping at Kirkwall, Orkney. With a basic ticket

you can sleep in recliner chairs or the bar area. It's £36.50 for a berth in a shared cabin and from £84 to £137 for a comparatively luxurious double cabin. Sleeping pods (£18) are comfortable, reclinable seats. Ferries have a cafe, bar, paid lounge and cinema on board, plus slow wi-fi. Road-equivalent tariffs were set to be rolled out on this route, so fares could drop.

❶ Getting Around

Public transport within and between the islands of Shetland is managed by **ZetTrans** (www.zettrans.org.uk). Timetable information for all air, bus and ferry services can be obtained at http://travel.shetland.org, from the ZetTrans website and from Lerwick's Viking Bus Station (p422).

AIR

The **Shetland Inter-Island Air Service** (Airtask; ☑ 01595-840246; www.airtask.com) is operated by Airtask from Tingwall airport, 6.5 miles northwest of Lerwick. There are big discounts for under-25s. Flights run to Papa Stour, Foula and Fair Isle.

BICYCLE

If it's fine, cycling on the islands' excellent roads can be an exhilarating way to experience the stark beauty of Shetland. It can, however, be very windy and there are few spots to shelter. You can hire bikes from several places, including Grantfield Garage in Lerwick.

BOAT

Ferry services run by Shetland Islands Council (www.shetland.gov.uk/ferries) link Mainland to other islands from various points.

BUS

An extensive bus network, coordinated by **ZetTrans** (www.zettrans.org.uk), radiates from Lerwick to all corners of Mainland, with connecting services to the islands of Yell, Fetlar and Unst. The schedules aren't generally great for day tripping from Lerwick as they're suited to people coming in to the capital for the day.

CAR

Shetland has broad, well-made roads (due to oil money). Car hire is fuss-free, and vehicles can be delivered to transport terminals. Prices are usually around £40/200 for a day/week.

Bolts Car Hire (☑01595-693636; www.boltscarhire.co.uk; 26 North Rd; ☺9am-5.30pm Mon-Fri year-round, plus to 1pm Sat Nov-Mar, to 4pm Sat Apr-Oct) Has an office in Lerwick and by the airport; delivers to Lerwick's ferry terminal.

Grantfield Garage (☑ 01595-692709; www.grantfieldgarage.co.uk; North Rd; ☺9am-5.30pm Mon-Fri, to 5pm Sat) Generally the cheapest. A short walk towards Lerwick from the Northlink ferry terminal.

Star Rent-a-Car (☑ 01595-692075; www.star rentacar.co.uk; 22 Commercial Rd; ⊙ 8am-7pm Mon-Fri, to 6pm Sat, noon-5pm Sun) Opposite Lerwick's Viking Bus Station. Has an office at Sumburgh Airport as well.

Lerwick

POP 7000

Built on the herring trade and modernised by the oil trade, Lerwick is Shetland's only real town, home to a third of the islands' population. It has a solidly maritime feel, with aquiline oilboats competing for space in the superb natural harbour with the dwindling fishing fleet. Wandering along atmospheric Commercial St is a delight, and the excellent Shetland Museum provides cultural background.

⊙ Sights & Activities

★ **Shetland Museum**   MUSEUM
(☑ 01595-695057;   www.shetlandmuseumand archives.org.uk; Hay's Dock; ⊙ 10am-4pm Mon-Sat, noon-5pm Sun Sep-Apr) FREE This museum houses an impressive recollection of 5000 years' worth of culture, people and their interaction with this ancient landscape. Comprehensive but never dull, it covers everything from the archipelago's geology to its fishing industry, via local mythology – find out about scary *nyuggles* (ghostly horses), or detect *trows* (fairies). Pictish carvings and replica jewellery are among the finest pieces. The museum also includes a working lighthouse mechanism, a small gallery, a boat-building workshop and an archive for tracing Shetland ancestry.

Shetland Textile Museum   MUSEUM
(Böd of Gremista; ☑ 01595-694386; www.shetland textilemuseum.com; Gremista Rd; adult/child £3/free; ⊙ noon-5pm Tue-Sat, to 7pm Thu late-Apr–early Oct) A mile north of the centre of Lerwick, this four-square stone house, birthplace of P&O founder Arthur Anderson, was also once a fish-curing station. It now holds a good display on the knitted and woven textiles and patterns that Shetland is famous for.

Clickimin Broch   RUINS
(Clickimin Rd; ⊙ 24hr) FREE This fortified site, just under a mile southwest of Lerwick's town centre, was occupied from the 7th century BC to the 6th century AD. It's impressively large, and its setting on a tongue of land in a small loch gives it a feeling of being removed from the present day.

Knab   VIEWPOINT
(Knab Rd) This headland gives a marvellous perspective of the entrance to Lerwick's harbour, as well as Breiwick (bay) and Bressay. There's a golf course, parkland, a cemetery and fortifications to ramble around.

Shetland Wildlife Boat Tours   BOATING
(☑ 07876-522292; www.thule-charters.co.uk; adult/child £45/35; ⊙ Apr-Sep) This outfit runs two daily trips to Noss in summer in a small catamaran. An underwater camera offers glimpses of the birds diving in the depths.

Shetland Seabird Tours   BIRDWATCHING
(☑ 07767 872260; www.shetlandseabirdtours.com; adult/child £45/25; ⊙ Apr-Oct) With two daily departures, these three-hour cruises head out to watch gannets feeding, observe the raucous seabird colonies of Bressay and Noss, and do a bit of seal-spotting. You can book at the Lerwick Tourist Office (p422).

⚒ Festivals & Events

Shetland Folk Festival   MUSIC
(www.shetlandfolkfestival.com; ⊙ late Apr or early May) This four-day festival sees local and international folk musicians playing in various venues across Lerwick and beyond.

⨈ Sleeping

Lerwick has very average hotels but excellent B&Bs. Accommodation fills up year-round, so book ahead. There are no campsites within 15 miles.

Woosung   B&B £
(☑ 01595-693687; conroywoosung@hotmail.com; 43 St Olaf St; d £70, s/d without bathroom £40/65; 🖥 🏠) A budget gem in the heart of Lerwick B&B-land, this place has a wise and welcoming host, and comfortable, clean, good-value rooms with fridge and microwave. Two of them share a compact but spotless bathroom. The solid stone house dates from the 19th century, built by a clipper captain who traded tea out of the Chinese port it's named after.

Islesburgh House Hostel   HOSTEL £
(☑ 01595-745100;   www.islesburgh.org.uk;   King Harald St; dm/s/tw/q £21.50/39/43/61; 🅿 @ 🛜) This typically grand Lerwick mansion houses an excellent hostel, with comfortable dorms, a shop, a laundry, a cafe and an industrial kitchen. Electronic keys offer reliable security and no curfew. It's wise to book ahead in summer. If nobody's about you can check in at the nearby community centre.

★ Fort Charlotte Guesthouse
B&B **££**

(☎01595-692140; www.fortcharlotte.co.uk; 1 Charlotte St; s/d £40/80; 🛜🐾) Sheltering under Fort Charlotte's walls, this friendly place offers summery en suite rooms, including great singles. Views down the pedestrian street are on offer in some; sloping ceilings and Asian touches add charm to others. It has local salmon for breakfast and a bike shed. Very popular; book ahead. There's also a self-catering option available.

Aald Harbour
B&B **££**

(☎01595-840689; www.aaldharbourbedandbreakfast.com; 7 Church Rd; s/d £55/80; 🛜) With a handy location just off the pedestrian street, this upbeat spot has four cute rooms decked out in IKEA furniture with Shetland fabrics and toiletries creating a cosy Nordic fusion. Rooms have fridges and good showers and wi-fi; there are good public areas downstairs. Breakfast includes fresh fruit and smoked fish options; an on-site tearoom operates some days.

Rockvilla Guest House
B&B **££**

(☎01595-695804; www.rockvillaguesthouse.com; 88 St Olaf St; s/d £65/90; 🛜🐾) Some of Shetland's B&Bs are aimed more at oil workers than visitors, but this is quite the reverse: a relaxing, welcoming spot in a fine house behind a pretty garden. The three rooms are colour themed: Blue is bright, with a front-and-back outlook, Red is sultry, with a sofa in the window, and smaller Green is shyer, under the eaves.

Your hosts are friendly, and Jeff runs airport transfers (£35) plus day tours to Sumburgh, Eshaness or Unst, among other places.

Breiview Guest House
B&B **££**

(☎01595-695956; www.breiviewguesthouse.co.uk; 43 Kantersted Rd; s/d £50/80; 🅿🛜) On a hill a little removed from Lerwick's centre, this is a fine option with some water views. Rooms – some in the house next door – are spacious, light and furnished with blonde wood and have good bathrooms. Dieter is a lifeboat volunteer but guarantees to get your morning eggs perfect before dashing off to rescue a stricken ship.

Coming from the centre, turn left after passing the big Tesco supermarket and follow the signs.

Alder Lodge Guesthouse
B&B **££**

(☎01595-695705; www.alderlodge-guesthouse.com; 6 Clairmont Pl; s/d £45/85; 🅿🛜) A friendly young family run this likeable place in a

UP HELLY AA

Shetland's long Viking history has rubbed off in more ways than just street names and square-shouldered locals. Most villages have a **fire festival** (www.uphellyaa.org; ⊘ Jan), a continuation of Viking midwinter celebrations of the rebirth of the sun, with the most spectacular happening in Lerwick, on the last Tuesday in January.

Squads of *guizers* dress in Viking costume and march through the streets with blazing torches, dragging a replica longship, which they then surround and burn, bellowing out Viking songs from behind bushy beards.

former bank building handily located close to Lerwick's centre. Imbued with a sense of space and light, the rooms are large and very well furnished, with good en suites and fridges. The top-floor rooms are worth the climb with their cosy sloping ceilings. Breakfast is a filling affair.

Kveldsro House Hotel
HOTEL **£££**

(☎01595-692195; www.shetlandhotels.com; Greenfield Pl; s/d £118/145; 🅿🛜) Lerwick's best hotel overlooks the harbour and has a quiet but central setting. It's a dignified small set-up that will appeal to older visitors or couples. All doubles cost the same, but some are markedly better than others, with four-poster beds or water views. All boast new stylish bathrooms. The bar area is elegant and has fine perspectives.

✖ Eating

Mareel Cafe
CAFE **£**

(☎01595-745500; www.mareel.org; Hay's Dock; light meals £3-5; ⊘9am-11pm Sun-Thu, 9am-1am Fri & Sat, food to 9pm; 🛜) Buzzy, arty and colourful, this cheery venue in Mareel overlooks the water and does sandwiches and snacks by day, and shared platters, burgers and nachos in the evenings. The coffee is decent, too, and it's a nice place for a drink. Cocktail mixing at weekends, DJs and other events spice it up.

Peerie Shop Cafe
CAFE **£**

(☎01595-692816; www.peerieshop.co.uk; Esplanade; light meals £3-8; ⊘8am-6pm Mon-Sat; 🛜) If you've been craving proper espresso since leaving the mainland, head to this gem, with

Lerwick

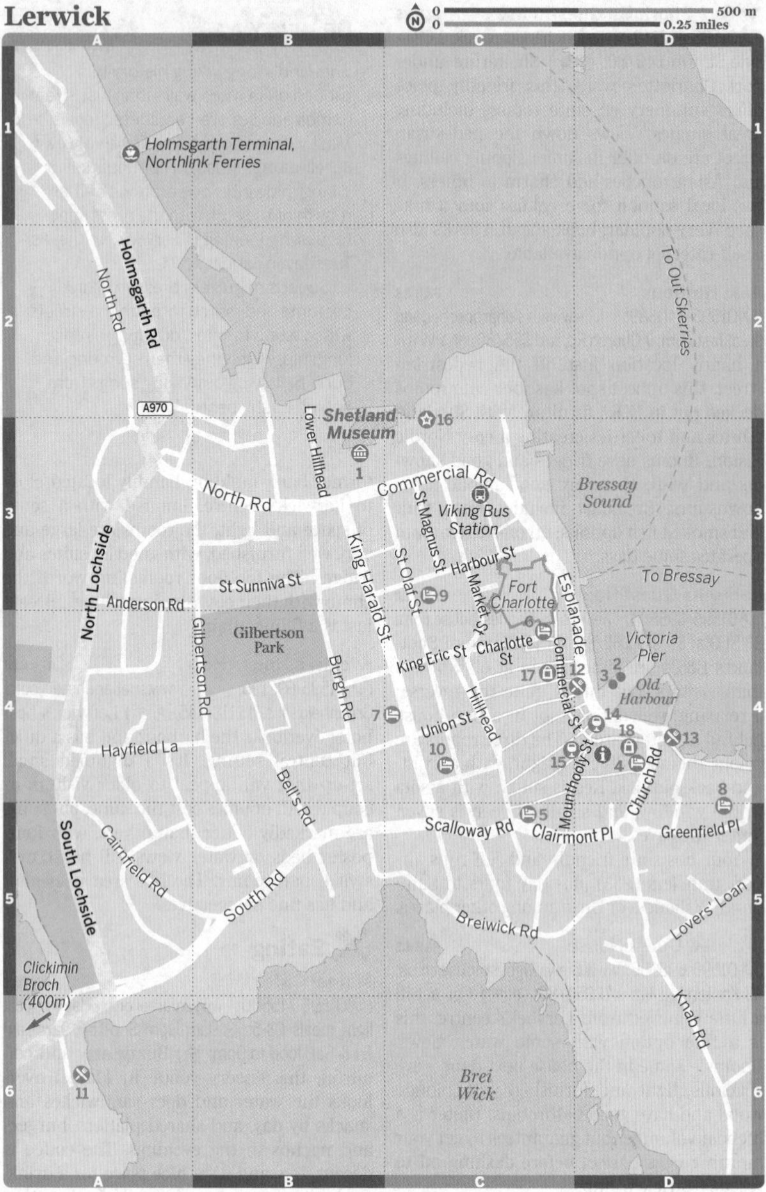

art exhibitions, wire-mounted halogens and industrial-gantry chic. Newspapers, scrumptious cakes and sandwiches, hot chocolate that you deserve after that blasting wind outside, and – less often – outdoor seating give everyone a reason to be here.

★ **Fjarå** CAFE, BISTRO ££

(☎01595-697388; www.fjaracoffee.com; Sea Rd; mains £8-22; ⏱8am-10pm Tue-Sat, 10am-6pm Sun, food until 8pm; 📶) A cute wooden building in a super location, Fjarå is perched above a rocky shore and takes full advantage, with

Lerwick

big picture windows looking out over the water and occasionally some basking seals. It does a bit of everything, with breakfasts, sandwiches, salads and bagels, plus beers, cocktails and some excellent dinner offerings, including creative burgers, game and local seafood.

It's across the road from the Tesco supermarket at the southern entrance to town.

★ **Hay's Dock** SCOTTISH, CAFE ££
(☎01595-741569; www.haysdock.co.uk; Hay's Dock, Shetland Museum; mains lunch £8-13, dinner £17-24; ⊘10am-3pm Mon-Thu, 10am-3pm & 5-9pm Fri & Sat; ☎️) ✿ Upstairs in the Shetland Museum, this place sports a wall of picture windows and a fairweather balcony that overlooks the harbour. Clean lines and pale wood recall Scandinavia, but the menu relies on carefully selected local and Scottish produce, with a substantial dash of international influence. Lunch ranges from delicious fish and chips to chowder, while evening menus concentrate on seafood and steak.

Queen's Hotel SCOTTISH ££
(☎01595-692826; www.kgqhotels.co.uk; Commercial St; mains £11-22; ⊘noon-2pm & 6-9.30pm; ☎) The dining room in this slightly run-down hotel wins marks for its harbour views – book one of the window tables. It's best visited for beautifully presented, classy local seafood dishes.

▼ **Drinking & Entertainment**

The Lounge PUB
(☎01595-692231; 4 Mounthooly St; ⊘11am-1am; ☎) Tucked away behind Lerwick's tourist office, the Lounge features an earthy down-

stairs bar populated by friendly local characters. The attractive upstairs space features live music several times a week and informal jam sessions at other times. It's well worth checking out.

Captain Flint's PUB
(☎01595-692249; 2 Commercial St; ⊘11am-1am; ☎) This upstairs port-side bar has a distinctly nautical, creaky-wooden feel. There's a cross-section of young 'uns, tourists, boat folk and older locals. It has live music some nights and a pool table tucked away on another level. Try a G&T with the seaweed-infused version of the local Reel gin.

Mareel ARTS CENTRE
(☎01595-745500; www.mareel.org; Hay's Dock) Modern Mareel is a thriving arts centre, with a cinema, concert hall and cafe in a great waterside location.

🛍 **Shopping**

Best buys are the woollen cardigans and sweaters for which Shetland is world-famous. For info on handicraft outlets around the islands grab the brochure for the Shetland Craft Trail (p417) from the Lerwick Tourist Office. It's also available from the trail website.

Shetland Times Bookshop BOOKS
(☎01595-695531; www.shetlandtimes.co.uk; 71 Commercial St; ⊘9am-5pm Mon-Sat) On Lerwick's picturesque main shopping street, this place has every book you could possibly want to read about Shetland, plus a good children's section.

Mirrie Dancers CHOCOLATE
(☏ 01595-690592; www.mirriedancers.co.uk; 161 Commercial St; ⊙ 10am-5pm Mon, Tue & Thu-Sat) The amazing chocolate creations of this little high-street shop bring a touch of colour and sparkle to even the bleakest Shetland day. The name is a local term for the aurora borealis.

❶ Information

There are several free wi-fi networks around the centre, and the **Shetland Library** (☏ 01595-743868; www.shetland-library.gov.uk; Lower Hillhead; ⊙ 10am-8pm Mon & Thu, to 5pm Tue, Wed, Fri & Sat; 🛜) has both terminals and wireless access.

Gilbert Bain Hospital (☏ 01595-743000; www.shb.scot.nhs.uk; South Rd)

Lerwick Tourist Office (☏ 01595-693434; www.shetland.org; cnr Commercial & Mounthooly Sts; ⊙ 9am-5pm Mon-Sat & 10am-4pm Sun Apr-Sep, 10am-4pm Mon-Sat Oct-Mar) Helpful, with a good range of books and maps.

❶ Getting There & Away

Northlink Ferries (www.northlinkferries.co.uk; 🛜) from Aberdeen and Kirkwall dock at **Holmsgarth Terminal** (Holmsgarth Rd), a 15-minute walk northwest from the town centre.

From **Viking Bus Station** (☏ 01595-744868; Commercial Rd), buses service various corners of the archipelago, including regular services to/from Sumburgh Airport.

OFFBEAT ACCOMMODATION

Shetland offers intriguing options for getting off the beaten accommodation track. There's a great network of *böds* – simple rustic cottages or huts with peat fires. They cost £12 per person, or £10 for the ones without electricity, and are available March to October. Contact and book via **Shetland Amenity Trust** (☏ 01595-694688; www.camping-bods.com; ⊙ 9am-5pm Mon-Thu, to 4pm Fri).

The same organisation runs three **Shetland Lighthouse Cottages** (☏ 01595-694688; www.shetlandlighthouse.com; per 3 days high season £300-372, per week £700-868), all commanding dramatic views of rugged coastline: one, renovated and classy, at Sumburgh; one on the island of Bressay near Lerwick; and one at Eshaness. They sleep six to seven, and prices drop substantially in the low season.

Bressay & Noss
POP 400

These islands lie across Bressay Sound just east of Lerwick. Bressay (*bress*-ah) has interesting walks, especially along the cliffs and up **Ward Hill** (226m), which has good views of the islands. Much smaller Noss is a nature reserve, notable for its seabird life. As well as the crossing to Noss from Bressay, there are boat trips around the island from Lerwick.

★**Isle of Noss** NATURE RESERVE
(☏ 0800 107 7818; www.nnr-scotland.org.uk/noss; boat adult/child £3/1.50; ⊙ 10am-5pm Tue, Wed & Fri-Sun mid-Apr–Aug) Little Noss, 1.5 miles wide, lies just east of Bressay. High seacliffs harbour over 100,000 pairs of breeding seabirds, while inland heath supports hundreds of pairs of great skua. Access is by dinghy from Bressay; phone in advance to check that it's running. Walking anticlockwise around Noss is easier, with better cliff-viewing. There's a small visitor centre by the dock.

Maryfield House Hotel INN ££
(☏ 01595-820203; www.maryfieldhousehotel.co.uk; Maryfield, Bressay; r £120; P 🛜) By the Bressay ferry slip, this solid old hotel has reopened and makes a fine alternative to staying in Lerwick. Comfortable rooms with good, large beds and refurbished bathrooms are complemented by friendly hosts. Decent bar meals are on offer, as well as items such as seafood platters, by preordering.

❶ Getting There & Away

Ferries (passenger/car and driver return £5.50/13.60, seven minutes, frequent) link Lerwick and Bressay. The Noss crossing is 2.5 miles across the island.

Scalloway
POP 1200

Surrounded by bare, rolling hills, Scalloway (*scall*-o-wah) – Shetland's former capital – is a busy fishing and yachting harbour with a thriving seafood-processing industry. It's 6 miles from Lerwick.

There are pretty beaches and pleasant walks on the nearby islands (linked by bridges) of Trondra and East and West Burra.

Scalloway Museum MUSEUM
(☏ 01595-880734; www.scallowaymuseum.org; Castle St; adult/child £3/1; ⊙ 11am-4pm Mon-Sat,

2-4pm Sun mid-Apr–Sep; 🎨) This enthusiastic modern museum by Scalloway Castle has an excellent display on Scalloway life and history, with prehistoric finds, witch-burnings and local lore all featuring. It has a detailed section on the Shetland Bus and a fun area for kids, as well as a cafe.

Shetland Bus Memorial   MONUMENT
(Main St) During WWII, the Norwegian resistance movement operated the 'Shetland Bus' from here. The trips were very successful, carrying agents, wireless operators and military supplies to Norway for the resistance movement and returning with refugees, recruits for the Free Norwegian Forces and, in December, Christmas trees for the treeless Shetlands. This is a moving tribute on the waterfront, built with stones from both countries. The Norwegian stones are from the home areas of 44 Norwegians who died running the gauntlet between Norway and Scalloway.

Scalloway Castle   CASTLE
(www.historicenvironment.scot; Castle St; ⊙24hr) FREE Scalloway's most prominent landmark is its castle, built around 1600 by Earl Patrick Stewart. The turreted and corbelled tower house is fairly well preserved. If you happen to find it locked, get keys from the Scalloway Museum or Scalloway Hotel.

★**Scalloway Hotel**   HOTEL **£££**
(📱01595-880444; www.scallowayhotel.com; Main St; s/d £100/140; 🅿🛜) One of Shetland's best hotels, this energetically run waterfront place has very stylish rooms featuring sheepskins, local tweeds and other fabrics, and views over the harbour. Some rooms are larger than others; the best is the fabulous superior, with handmade furniture, artworks and a top-of-the-line mattress on a four-poster bed. The **restaurant** (restaurant mains £18-25; ⊙restaurant 5-9pm Mon-Sat, noon-9pm Sun, bar food also noon-3pm Mon-Sat; 🛜) is also excellent.

Da Haaf   SEAFOOD **££**
(📱01595-772480; www.nafc.uhi.ac.uk; NAFC Marine Centre; lunches £6-10, dinner mains £12-20; ⊙8.30am-4pm Mon-Thu, 8.30am-4pm & 5.30-9pm Fri, 5.30-9pm Sat; 🛜) In a fisheries college, this place has a slightly canteeny feel but great water views out of big windows. It does simple but tasty snacks all day and lunches from noon to 2.30pm. The kitchen comes into its own at weekend dinnertime (must be booked), when haddock, monkfish and other seafood specials are served.

ℹ Getting There & Away

Buses run from Lerwick (£1.80, 25 minutes, roughly hourly Monday to Saturday, four Sunday) to Scalloway.

South Mainland

From Lerwick, it's 25 miles down this narrow, hilly tail of land to Sumburgh Head. Important prehistoric sights, fabulous birdwatching and glorious white-sand beaches make it one of Shetland's most interesting areas. The lapping waters are an inviting turquoise – if it weren't for the raging Arctic gales, you'd be tempted to have a dip.

Sandwick & Mousa

Opposite the scattered village of Sandwick, where you pass the 60-degree latitude line, is the small isle of Mousa, an RSPB reserve protecting some 7000 breeding pairs of nocturnal storm petrels. Mousa is also home to rock-basking seals as well as impressive Mousa Broch, the best preserved of these northern Iron Age fortifications.

Mousa Broch   HISTORIC BUILDING
(⊙24hr) FREE On the island of Mousa, off Sandwick, this prehistoric fortified house, dating from some 2000 years ago, is an impressive sight. Rising to 13m, it's an imposing double-walled structure with a spiral staircase to access a 2nd floor. It has featured in Viking sagas as a hideout for eloping couples. In its walls nest hundreds of storm petrels, whose return to the nest at dusk is a stirring sight.

Mousa Boat   BOATING
(📱07901-872339; www.mousa.co.uk; Sandwick; ⊙Apr-Sep) This operator runs boat trips to Mousa (adult/child return £16/7, cash only, 15 minutes, daily except Saturday) from Sandwick, allowing three hours ashore on the island. It also offers night petrel-viewing trips (£25/10, dates on website) and short cruises. There's a small interpretation centre at the dock.

Mackenzies Farm Shop & Café   CAFE **£**
(📱01950-477790; www.mackenziesfarmshop.co.uk; A970, Cunningsburgh; mains £6-15; ⊙8.30am-6pm Mon-Thu, 7am-6pm Fri, 9am-5pm Sat, 11am-5pm

Sun, extended hours summer; 🐾) 🍴 Local farmers supply the produce for this excellent shop and cafe, which stocks cheeses, quality meats and more, and presents dishes that range from quiches and sandwiches to fuller offerings with Shetland lamb.

Bigton & Boddam

On the western side of the narrow southern end of Mainland, Bigton sits near the largest shell-and-sand tombolo (sand or gravel isthmus) in Britain, St Ninian's Isle.

South of here, Shetland's best beach is gloriously white Scousburgh Sands (Spiggie Beach). Back on the main road, from small Boddam a side road leads to the Shetland Crofthouse Museum (🖉01950-460557; www.shetlandmuseumandarchives.org.uk/ crofthouse-museum; ⊙10am-1pm & 2-4pm May-Sep) FREE.

South of Boddam, a minor road runs southwest to Quendale. Here you'll find the small but excellent, restored and fully operational 19th-century Quendale Water Mill (🖉01950-460969; www.quendalemill.co.uk; adult/child £4/1; ⊙10am-5pm mid-Apr–mid-Oct). The village overlooks a long, sandy beach to the south in the Bay of Quendale. West of the bay there's dramatic cliff scenery and diving in the waters between Garth's Ness and Fitful Head, and to the wreck of the oil tanker *Braer* off Garth's Ness.

Spiggie   INN ££

(🖉01950-460409; www.spiggie.co.uk; s/d/superior d £70/120/140; 🅿🐾🍽) An enthusiastic family has taken over this old Shetland stalwart near Scousburgh and guarantee a warm welcome. The Spiggie has compact, pretty rooms as well as larger chambers that can fit a family; there's also a self-catering lodge. Good dinners are available and the whole place boasts great views down over the local loch, a birdwatching haven.

Sumburgh

With sea cliffs, and grassy headlands jutting out into sparkling blue waters, Sumburgh is one of the most scenic places on Mainland, with a far greener landscape than the peaty north. It has a handful of excellent attractions clustered near Shetland's major airport.

★Sumburgh Head   BIRDWATCHING

(www.rspb.org.uk) At Mainland's southern tip, these spectacular cliffs offer a good

chance to get up close to puffins, and huge nesting colonies of fulmars, guillemots and razorbills. If you're lucky, you might spot dolphins, minke whales or orcas. Also here is the excellent Sumburgh Head Visitor Centre, in the lighthouse buildings.

★Sumburgh Head
Visitor Centre   LIGHTHOUSE, MUSEUM

(🖉01595-694688; www.sumburghhead.com; adult/ child £6/2; ⊙11am-5.30pm Apr-Sep) High on the cliffs at Sumburgh Head, this excellent attraction is set across several buildings. Displays explain about the lighthouse, foghorn and radar station that operated here, and there's a good exhibition on the local marine creatures and birds. You can visit the lighthouse itself on a guided tour for an extra charge.

Jarlshof   ARCHAEOLOGICAL SITE

(🖉01950-460112; www.historicenvironment.scot; adult/child £6/3.60; ⊙9.30am-5.30pm Apr-Sep, to 4.30pm Oct-Mar) Old and new collide here, with Sumburgh airport right by this picturesque, instructive archaeological site. Various periods of occupation from 2500 BC to AD 1500 can be seen; the complete change upon the Vikings' arrival is obvious: their rectangular longhouses present a marked contrast to the preceding brochs, roundhouses and wheelhouses. Atop the site is 16th-century Old House, named 'Jarlshof' in a novel by Sir Walter Scott. There's an informative audio tour included with admission.

Old Scatness   ARCHAEOLOGICAL SITE

(🖉01595-694688; www.shetland-heritage.co.uk/ old-scatness; adult/child £5/4; ⊙10.15am-4.30pm Fri mid-May–Aug; 🐾) This dig brings Shetland's prehistory vividly to life; it's a mustsee for archaeology buffs, but fun for kids, too. Clued-up guides in Iron Age clothes show you the site, which has provided important clues on the Viking takeover and dating of Shetland material. It has an impressive broch from around 300 BC, roundhouses and later wheelhouses. Best of all is the reconstruction with peat fire and working loom. At the time of research, a lack of funding had badly restricted the opening hours.

🛈 Getting There & Away

Bus 6 runs to Sumburgh and Sumburgh Airport from Lerwick (£2.90 to Sumburgh, £3.30 to the airport; one hour, five to seven daily).

North Mainland

The north of Mainland is very photogenic – jumbles of cracked, peaty, brown hills blend with grassy pastureland and extend like bony fingers into numerous lochs and out into the wider, icy, grey waters of the North Sea. Different shades of light give it a variety of characters.

Around Hillswick, there's stunning scenery and several good places to stay; this makes it one of the best places to base yourself in the Shetland Islands.

Brae

The crossroads settlement of Brae has several accommodation options and is an important service centre for the whole of northern Shetland. It's no beauty, despite its bayside location, but there's fine walking on the peninsula west of Brae and to the south on the red-granite island of Muckle Roe, which is connected to the peninsula by a bridge. Muckle Roe also offers good diving off its west and north coasts.

South of Brae, Voe (Lower) is a pretty collection of buildings beside a tranquil bay on Olna Firth. With a cheap sleep and pub meals opposite, it can make a good stop.

★ Busta House Hotel HOTEL ££

(01806-522506; www.bustahouse.com; Busta; s/d £99/125;) This genteel, characterful hotel near Brae has a long, sad history and inevitable rumours of a (friendly) ghost. Built in the late 18th century (though the oldest part dates from 1588), it has creaks and quirks and likeable rooms that are compact and retain a cosy charm. Sea views and/or a four-poster bed cost a bit more.

There's also a fine restaurant, a lovely guest lounge and very helpful staff.

Frankie's Fish & Chips FISH & CHIPS £

(01806-522700; www.frankiesfishandchips.com; Brae; mains £6-12; 9.30am-8pm Mon-Sat, noon-8pm Sun;) This famous Shetland chippie uses only locally sourced and sustainable seafood. As well as chip-shop standards, the menu runs to tasty Shetland mussels in garlicky sauces and, when available, plump juicy scallops. It also does breakfast rolls, baked potatoes and fry-ups. Eat in, out on the deck with views over the bay, or take away.

DON'T MISS

SEA KAYAKING

Paddling is a great way to explore Shetland's tortuous coastline, and allows you to get up close to seals and bird life. **Sea Kayak Shetland** (01595-840272; www.seakayakshetland.co.uk; beginner session £27, half-/full day £45/80) is a reliable operator catering for beginners and experts alike, and offering various guided trips.

Getting There & Away

Buses from Lerwick to Brae (£2.90, 45 minutes, eight daily Monday to Saturday) run via Tingwall and Voe. Some continue to Hillswick.

Eshaness & Hillswick

Eleven miles northwest of Brae the road ends at the red basalt cliffs of Eshaness, site of some of Shetland's most impressive coastal scenery. When the wind subsides there's superb walking and panoramic views from the headland lighthouse. On the way, the village of Hillswick is set on a pretty bay.

Tangwick Haa Museum MUSEUM

(01806-503389; 11am-5pm mid-Apr–Sep) FREE A mile east of Eshaness, a side road leads south to the Tangwick Haa Museum, housed in a restored 17th-century house. The wonderful collection of old B&W photos captures the sense of community in this area.

★ Almara B&B ££

(01806-503261; www.almara.shetland.co.uk; s/d £40/80; Apr-Oct;) Follow the puffin signpost a mile short of Hillswick to find Shetland's finest welcome. With sweeping views over the bay, this house has a great lounge, unusual features in the excellent rooms and bathrooms (including thoughtful extras such as USB chargers), and a good eye on the environment. You'll feel completely at home and appreciated; this is a B&B at its best.

St Magnus Bay Hotel HOTEL ££

(01806-503372; www.stmagnusbayhotel.co.uk; Hillswick; d £95, superior d £120;) This wonderful wooden mansion was built in 1896. The owners are involved in an ongoing renovation – a major project – to return it to former glories, and are doing a great job. Try for a renovated room, but all are winningly wood-clad, and half also boast big windows taking full advantage of the fine water views. The bar serves food all day until 9pm.

ℹ️ Getting There & Away

Three buses from Lerwick run to Hillswick (£3.50, 1¼ hours, Monday to Saturday), with a feeder bus on to Eshaness. Two buses run the return route. There are other connections at Brae.

The North Isles

Yell, Unst and Fetlar make up the North Isles of the Shetlands, which are connected to each other by ferry, as is Yell to Mainland. All are great for nature-watching; Unst has the most to offer overall.

Yell

POP 1000

Yell if you like but nobody will hear; the desolate peat moors here are typical Shetland scenery. The bleak landscape has an appeal though. Yell is all about colours: the browns and vivid, lush greens of the bogland, grey clouds thudding through the skies and the steely blue waters of the North Atlantic, which are never far away. The peat makes the ground look cracked and parched, although it's swimming most of the year. Though many folk fire on through to Unst, Yell offers several good hill walks, especially around the Herra peninsula, about halfway up the west coast.

Old Haa Museum   MUSEUM

(📞01957-722339; www.shetlandheritageassociation. com; Burravoe; ⊙10am-4pm Mon-Thu & Sat, 2-5pm Sun mid-Apr–Sep) **FREE** This museum has a medley of curious objects (pipes, piano, a doll in cradle, tiny bibles, ships in bottles and a sperm-whale jaw), as well as an archive of local history and a tearoom. It's in Burravoe, 4 miles east of the southern ferry terminal in Ulsta.

Lumbister   BIRDWATCHING

Red-throated divers, merlins, skuas and other bird species breed at this birdwatching hot spot on the Shetland moorland. The area is home to a large otter population, too, best viewed around Whale Firth, where you may also spot common and grey seals.

Quam B&B   B&B ££

(📞01957-766256; www.quambandbyellshetland. co.uk; Westsandwick; d £80; P🅿️🛜) Just off the main road through Yell island, this farm B&B has friendly owners and three good rooms. Breakfast features eggs from the farm, which also has cute ponies that you can meet. Dinners (£15 per person) can be arranged.

ℹ️ Getting There & Away

Yell is connected with Mainland by **ferries** (📞01595-745804; www.shetland.gov.uk/ ferries) between Toft and Ulsta (adult/car and driver return £5.50/13.60, 20 minutes, frequent). It's wise to book car space in summer.

An integrated bus and ferry connection runs once daily Monday to Saturday from Lerwick to Yell (£3.80, 1¼ hours), connecting with ferries to Fetlar and Unst; connecting services cover other parts of the island.

Unst

POP 600

You're fast running out of Scotland once you cross to rugged Unst (www.unst.org). Scotland's most northerly inhabited island is prettier than nearby Yell, with bare, velvety-smooth hills and settlements clinging to waterside locations, fiercely resisting the buffeting winds.

◎ Sights

⭐**Hermaness National Nature Reserve**   NATURE RESERVE

(www.nnr-scotland.org.uk) At marvellous Hermaness headland, a 4.5-mile round walk takes you to cliffs where gannets, fulmars and guillemots nest, and numerous puffins frolic. You can also see Scotland's most northerly point, the rocks of **Out Stack**, and **Muckle Flugga**, with its lighthouse built by Robert Louis Stevenson's uncle. Duck into the **Hermaness Visitor Centre** (📞01595-711278; ⊙9am-5pm Apr-early Sep) **FREE**, with its poignant story about one-time resident Albert Ross.

The path to the cliffs is guarded by a squadron of great skuas who nest in the nearby heather, and dive-bomb at will if they feel threatened. They're damn solid birds too, but don't usually make contact.

⭐**Unst Bus Shelter**   LANDMARK

(Bobby's Bus Shelter; www.unstbusshelter.shetland. co.uk; Baltasound) At the turn-off to Little-hamar, just past Baltasound, is Britain's most impressive bus stop. Enterprising locals,

FAIR ISLE
....

Fair Isle has stunning cliff scenery, isolation and squadrons of winged creatures. It's worth making the stomach-churning ferry ride here, to one of Scotland's most remote inhabited islands. About halfway to Orkney, it's only 3 miles by 1.5 miles in size and is probably best known for its patterned knitwear, still produced in three workshops on the island.

It's also a paradise for birdwatchers, who form the bulk of the island's visitors. Fair Isle is in the flight path of migrating birds, and thousands breed here. They're monitored by the bird observatory, which collects and analyses information year-round; visitors are more than welcome to participate.

Fair Isle Lodge & Bird Observatory (📞 01595-760258; www.fairislebirdobs.co.uk; s/d incl full board £80/150; ⊘ Apr-Oct; P @ 🛜) offers good accommodation in en suite rooms. Rates include full board, and there are free guided walks and other bird-related displays and activities. Under-25s get a big discount, paying £40 per person.

From Tingwall, Shetland Inter-Island Air Service (p417) operates flights to Fair Isle (£84 return, 25 minutes). There's also a weekly service from Sumburgh in summer.

Ferries sail from Grutness (near Sumburgh) and some from Lerwick (one way passenger/car and driver £5.50/7.20, three hours) two to three times weekly.

---

tired of waiting in discomfort, decided to do a job on it, and it now boasts posh seating, novels, numerous decorative features and a visitors' book to sign. The theme and colour scheme changes yearly.

Unst Boat Haven MUSEUM
(📞 01957-711809; Haroldswick; adult/child £3/free, combined ticket with Unst Heritage Centre £5; ⊘ 11am-4pm Mon-Sat, 2-4pm Sun May-Sep) This large shed is a boatie's delight, packed with a beautifully cared for collection of Shetland rowing and sailing boats, all with a backstory. Old photos and maritime artefacts speak of the glory days of Unst fishing. There's a seasonal tearoom out front.

Unst Heritage Centre MUSEUM
(📞 01957-711528; www.unstheritage.com; Haroldswick; adult/child £3/free, combined ticket with Unst Boat Haven £5; ⊘ 11am-4pm Mon-Sat, 2-4pm Sun May-Sep) This heritage centre houses a modern museum with a history of the Shetland pony and a recreation of a croft house.

🛏 Sleeping & Eating

The only restaurants are at the Baltasound Hotel and Saxa Vord, though there are several cafes.

Self-caterers can stock up at Baltasound's Skibhoul Stores, which has a bakery and cafe, and the Final Checkout, between Baltasound and Haroldswick. Known locally as 'the garage', the Final Checkout has an ATM, and sells petrol and diesel.

★ **Gardiesfauld Hostel** HOSTEL, CAMPSITE £
(📞 01957-755279; www.gardiesfauld.shetland.co.uk; 2 East Rd, Uyeasound; per adult/child tent sites £8/4, dm £16/9; ⊘ Apr-Sep; P 🛜) This spotless hostel has very spacious dorms with lockers, family rooms, a garden, an elegant lounge and a wee conservatory dining area with great bay views. You can camp here, too; there are separate areas for tents and vans. The bus stops right outside. Bring 20p coins for the showers. They'll open in winter if you prebook.

Saxa Vord HOSTEL £
(📞 01957-711711; www.saxavord.com; Haroldswick; s/d £22.50/45; ⊘ mid-May-mid-Sep; P 🛜 🍽) This old RAF base (though the radar station it served reopened in 2018) is not the most atmospheric lodging, though the tired barracks-style rooms offer great value for singles, and there's something nice about watching the weather through the skylight-style windows. The restaurant dishes out surprisingly decent food, and there's a cafe, a bar – Britain's northernmost, by our reckoning – and a friendly, helpful atmosphere.

Wi-fi is only in public areas. Part of the same complex, self-catering houses (£788 per week) are good for families and are available year-round.

Baltasound Hotel HOTEL ££
(📞 01957-711334; www.baltasoundhotel.co.uk; Baltasound; s £68-75, d £125-135; ⊘ Apr-mid-Oct; P 🛜) Brightly decorated rooms – some bigger than others – are complemented by wooden

WILDLIFE WATCHING IN SHETLAND

For birdwatchers, Shetland is paradise – a stopover for migrating Arctic species and host to vast seabird breeding colonies. June is the height of the season.

Every bird has its own name here: rain geese are red-throated divers, bonxies are great skuas, and alamooties are storm petrels. Clownish puffin antics are a highlight. The **Royal Society for the Protection of Birds** (RSPB; www.rspb.org.uk) maintains several reserves, plus there are National Nature Reserves at **Hermaness**, **Keen of Hamar** and **Noss**. **Foula** and **Fair Isle** also support large seabird populations.

Keep an eye on the sea: sea otters, orcas and other cetaceans are regularly sighted. Latest sightings are logged at useful www.nature-shetland.co.uk.

Shetland Nature Festival (www.shetlandnaturefestival.co.uk; ⊙ early Jul) has guided walks, talks, boat trips, open days and workshops.

chalets arrayed around the lawn here. Rooms feel a little overpriced so it's worth the small upgrade to the 'large doubles', which sport modern bathrooms. There's a lovely country outlook, and evening bar meals in a dining room dappled by the setting sun. Contact them for winter opening details.

ⓘ Getting There & Around

Unst is connected with Yell and Fetlar by ferries (p426) between Gutcher and Belmont (free if coming from Mainland that day, otherwise adult/car and driver £5.50/13.60 return, 10 minutes, frequent).

An integrated bus and ferry connection runs once daily Monday to Saturday from Lerwick to Baltasound and other Unst villages (£4.40, 2¼ hours). There are connecting services around Unst itself.

Unst Cycle Hire (☏ 01957-711254; www.unst cyclehire.co.uk; Saxa Vord, Haroldswick; per day/week £10/50; ⊙ 11am-5pm) at the Saxa Vord complex in Haroldswick has bikes for hire.

Fetlar

POP 60

Fetlar, a notable birdwatching destination, is the smallest but most fertile of the North Isles. Its name is derived from the Viking term for 'fat land'.

Fetlar Interpretive Centre   VISITOR CENTRE
(☏ 01957-733206; www.fetlar.com; Houbie; adult/ child £3/free; ⊙ 11am-4pm Mon-Sat, 12.30-4pm Sun May-Sep) The excellent Fetlar Interpretive Centre has photos, audio recordings and videos on the island and its history. You'll find it 4.5 miles from the ferry, by the water in the hamlet of Houbie.

ⓘ Getting There & Away

Four to nine daily ferries (p426; free if coming from Mainland that day, otherwise adult/car and driver £5.50/13.60 return, 25 minutes) connect Fetlar with Gutcher on Yell and Belmont on Unst.

Understand Scotland

Scotland Today

Although an integral part of Great Britain since 1707, Scotland has maintained a separate and distinct identity throughout the last 300 years, which was strengthened by the return of a devolved Scottish parliament to Edinburgh in 1999. Since then Scottish politics have diverged significantly from those of the rest of the UK, culminating in 2016 when 62% of Scots voters chose to remain in the EU, while the UK as a whole voted to leave.

Best in Print

Raw Spirit (Iain Banks; 2003) An enjoyable jaunt around Scotland in search of the perfect whisky.

Mountaineering in Scotland (WH Murray; 1947) Classic account of climbing in Scotland in the 1930s, when just getting to Glen Coe was an adventure in itself.

Adrift in Caledonia (Nick Thorpe; 2006) An insightful tale of hitchhiking around Scotland on a variety of vessels.

The Poor Had No Lawyers (Andy Wightman; 2010) A penetrating (and fascinating) analysis of who owns land in Scotland, and how they got it.

Best on Film

Whisky Galore! (1949) Classic Ealing comedy about wily Scottish islanders outfoxing the government when a cargo of whisky gets shipwrecked; remade in 2016.

Local Hero (1983) Gentle Bill Forsyth comedy-drama sees American oil executive beguiled by the Highland landscape and eccentric locals.

Trainspotting (1996) 'Who needs reasons when you've got heroin?' Danny Boyle's second film (based on the novel by Irvine Welsh) dives into the gritty underbelly of life among Edinburgh drug addicts. The 2017 sequel **T2** is worth a look too.

Political Equations: Does Brexit Equal Indyref2?

Since the return of the Scottish Parliament to Edinburgh in 1999, politics north of the border have been heading in a different direction from those of England, with the Scottish National Party (SNP) holding power in Holyrood since 2007. Key policy differences include university education (students in England must pay their own tuition fees; in Scotland the state pays); health care (prescription medicines are free in Scotland, but not in England); and income tax (Scotland sets higher rates than England for middle and high earners).

This separatist trend climaxed in a 2014 referendum posing the question: 'Should Scotland be an independent country?' The result was that a majority (55% to 45%) voted 'No'. Despite maintaining the status quo, the referendum campaign re-energised Scottish politics and led to a huge increase in membership of political parties and a flourishing of debate, not only in the mainstream media but also online and among local interest groups.

But the 2016 referendum on whether the UK should remain part of the EU heralded a new era of uncertainty. While the UK as a whole voted to exit the EU (a process nicknamed 'Brexit') by a margin of 52% to 48%, Scotland voted to remain by 62% to 38%. Within days of the result, Scotland's first minister, Nicola Sturgeon, declared that Scotland should not be pulled out of the EU against its will.

Since then, the Scottish and UK governments have been at loggerheads over Brexit, with the SNP leadership arguing that Britain should remain in the EU Customs Union, while Theresa May, the UK prime minister, and Brexit hardliners in her party (the Conservatives) are, as of April 2018, committed to leaving the customs union.

A major feature of the 2014 'No to Independence' referendum campaign was the warning that a newly independent Scotland would be expelled from the EU and would have to reapply for membership. Now that Scotland appears to be getting forced out of the EU because of the UK's Brexit decision, the question of a second independence referendum (often referred to in the media as 'Indyref2') has raised its head.

Renewable Energy

One of the central planks of the SNP's vision for the future of Scotland is its energy policy. The Scottish Energy Strategy, published in December 2017, sets an objective of 50% of the country's total energy consumption to be supplied from renewable sources by 2030. A target to produce 100% of electricity consumption from renewables by 2020 is well on track, with a figure of 68% achieved in 2017, making Scotland a world leader in eco-friendly electricity.

Of course, all this has an effect on the landscape. There has been a proliferation of wind turbines, even in some of the wilder parts of the country, and new hydroelectric power plants are being built, ranging in size from small local projects to the massive pumped-storage scheme (with new dam and reservoir) planned for Coire Glas in the Great Glen. Most visually intrusive of all is the controversial 137-mile-long, high-voltage overhead power line from Beauly (near Inverness) to Denny in Stirlingshire that was completed in 2016, with 615 giant pylons marching through some of the Highlands' most scenic areas (notably along the A9 Perth–Inverness road near Drumochter).

However, the future of Scotland's energy industry arguably lies not on land but in the sea: Scotland has access to 25% of Europe's available tidal energy and 10% of its wave power. The country is at the leading edge of developing wave, tidal and offshore wind power; in 2012 the waters around Orkney and the Pentland Firth were designated a Marine Energy Park, with a second one planned for southwest Islay in 2018.

Tourist Numbers Hit the Headlines

Scotland has always been a popular tourist destination, but summer 2017 saw the number of visitors make the news. Headlines proclaimed that Edinburgh had become an overcrowded theme park, that vehicle pressures on the North Coast 500 route were causing road damage and parking problems, and that police were advising people to book accommodation before visiting Skye because the island was 'full'.

Many of these stories can be dismissed as media hype, but there has definitely been a marked rise in the popularity of certain areas, notably Edinburgh, the northwest Highlands and Skye. However, the total number of visitors to Scotland as a whole has not shown a significant increase, and Scots remain very much pro-tourist – after all, tourism accounts for around 8% of all jobs in the country. Most see increased visitor numbers as an opportunity rather than a problem.

POPULATION: **5.45 MILLION**

AREA: **78,722 SQ KM**

UNEMPLOYMENT: **4.3% (2018)**

ANNUAL WHISKY EXPORTS: **1.23 BILLION BOTTLES (2017)**

if Scotland were 100 people

96 would be white
3 would be Asian
1 would be African, Afro-Caribbean or other

belief systems
(% of population)

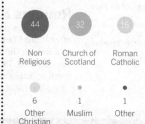

44 Non Religious
32 Church of Scotland
16 Roman Catholic
6 Other Christian
1 Muslim
1 Other

population per sq km

EDINBURGH   SCOTLAND   UK

👤 ≈ 70 people

History

Scotland was forged from the melting pot of several cultures and grew to wield great cultural, scientific and manufacturing influence globally. From the Vikings' decline onwards, Scottish history has been intertwined, often violently, with that of its southern neighbour, England. Battles and border raids were commonplace until shared kingship, then political union, drew the two together. Even then, Jacobite risings reflected divisions in Scottish and British society. More recently a trend towards self-determination led to devolved parliament in 1999, and 2014's independence referendum.

Early Days

Hunters and gatherers have left fragments of evidence of Scotland's earliest human habitation. These people came in waves from northern Europe and Ireland as glaciers retreated in the wake of the last ice age around 10,000 BC.

The Neolithic period was similarly launched by arrivals from mainland Europe. Scotland's Stone Age has left behind an astonishing diary of human development, unforgettable memories in stone of a distant past. Caithness, Orkney and Shetland have some of the world's best-preserved prehistoric villages, burial cairns and standing stones. Further south, crannogs (round structures built on stilts over a loch) were a favoured form of defensible dwelling through the Bronze Age.

The Iron Age saw the construction of a remarkable series of defence-minded structures of a different sort. Brochs (again a northeastern island development) were complex, muscular stone fortresses, some of which still stand well over 10m high.

Top Prehistoric Sites

Jarlshof (Shetland)

Skara Brae (Orkney)

Maeshowe (Orkney)

Kilmartin Glen (Argyll)

Callanish (Lewis)

Tomb of the Eagles (Orkney)

Scottish Crannog Centre (Kenmore)

Romans & Picts

The Roman occupation of Britain began in AD 43, almost a century after Julius Caesar first invaded. However, the Roman onslaught ground to a halt in the north, not far beyond the present-day Scottish border. Between AD 78 and 84, governor Agricola marched northwards and spent several years trying to subdue tribes the Romans called the Picts (from the Latin *pictus*, meaning 'painted'). By the 2nd century Emperor

TIMELINE	4000 BC	2200 BC	AD 43
	Neolithic farmers move to Scotland from mainland Europe; sites from these ancient days dot Scotland, with the best concentrated in Orkney.	Beaker culture arrives in Scotland. The Bronze Age produces swords and shields. Construction of hill forts, crannogs and mystifying stone circles.	Claudius begins the Roman conquest of Britain, almost a century after Julius Caesar first invaded. By AD 80 a string of forts is built from the Clyde to the Forth.

Hadrian, tired of fighting in the north, decided to cut his losses and built the wall (AD 122–28) that bears his name across northern England. Two decades later Hadrian's successor, Antoninus Pius, invaded Scotland again and built a turf rampart, the Antonine Wall, between the Firth of Forth and the River Clyde. In northern Britain, the Romans had met their match.

Little is known about the Picts, who inhabited northern and eastern Scotland. The Roman presence probably helped forge disparate Celtic tribes into a unified group; we can assume they were fierce fighters given the trouble the hardy Roman army had with them. The main material evidence of their culture is their fabulous carved symbol stones, found across eastern Scotland.

Eventually the Romans left Britain, and at this time there were at least two indigenous peoples in the northern region of the British Isles: the Picts in the north and east, and the Britons in the southwest. A new group, the Celtic Scots, probably arrived around AD 500, crossing from Ireland and establishing a kingdom called Dalriada in Argyll. St Ninian was the earliest recorded bringer of Christianity to the region, establishing a mission in Whithorn in Scotland's southwest. In the 6th century, St Columba, Scotland's most famous missionary, resumed St Ninian's work. Columba was a scholar and monk who was exiled, tradition has it, after involvement in a bloody battle. After fleeing Ireland in 563, he established a monastery on Iona – an island that retains an ancient, mystical aura – and also travelled northeast to take his message to the Picts. By the late 8th century most of Scotland had converted.

The First Kings of Scotland

The Picts and Scots were drawn together by the threat of a Norse invasion and by political and spiritual power from their common Christianity. Kenneth MacAlpin, first king of a united Scotland, achieved power using a mixture of blood ties and diplomacy. He set his capital in Pictland at Scone and brought to it the sacred Stone of Destiny, used in the coronation of Scottish kings.

Nearly two centuries later, MacAlpin's descendant Malcolm II (r 1005–18) defeated the Northumbrian Angles, a Germanic tribe who had settled in eastern England, at the Battle of Carham (1018), bringing Edinburgh and Lothian under Scottish control and extending Scottish territory as far south as the Tweed.

But the Highland clans, inaccessible in their glens, remained a law unto themselves for another 700 years. A cultural and linguistic divide grew up between the Gaelic-speaking Highlanders and the Lowlanders who spoke the Scots tongue.

Columba was a man of fixed ideas. On Iona he promptly set about banishing women and cows, as he believed that 'where there is a cow there is a woman, and where there is a woman there is mischief'. He wasn't a memory-foam-bed kind of person – he slept on the bare floor with a stone for a pillow.

Pictish Stones

St Vigeans Museum (Arbroath)

Aberlemno Stones (Angus)

Dupplin Cross (Dunning)

Groam House Museum (Rosemarkie)

Meigle Museum (Meigle)

Inverness Museum (Inverness)

Tarbat Discovery Centre (Portmahomack)

142	397	Early 500s	685
Building of Antonine Wall marks the northern limit of the Roman Empire. It is patrolled for about 40 years, but after this the Romans decide northern Britain is too difficult to conquer.	The first Christian mission beyond Hadrian's Wall, in Whithorn, is initiated by St Ninian. The earliest recorded church in Scotland is built to house his remains.	A Celtic tribe, the Scots, crosses the sea from northern Ireland and establishes a kingdom in Argyll called Dalriada.	The Pictish king Bridei defeats the Northumbrians at Nechtansmere in Angus, an against-the-odds victory that sets the foundations for Scotland as a separate entity.

Robert the Bruce & William Wallace

When Alexander III fell to his death in Fife in 1286, the succession was disputed by no fewer than 13 claimants, but in the end it came down to two: Robert Bruce, lord of Annandale, and John Balliol, lord of Galloway. Edward I of England was asked to arbitrate. He chose Balliol, whom he thought he could manipulate more easily.

Seeking to tighten his feudal grip on Scotland, Edward – known as the 'Hammer of the Scots' – treated the Scots king as vassal rather than equal. The humiliated Balliol finally turned against him and allied Scotland with France in 1295, thus beginning the enduring 'Auld Alliance' and ushering in the Wars of Independence.

Edward's response was bloody. In 1296 he invaded Scotland and Balliol was incarcerated in the Tower of London; in another blow to Scots pride, Edward removed the Stone of Destiny from Scone and took it back to London.

Enter William Wallace. Bands of rebels were attacking the English occupiers and Wallace led one such band to defeat the English at Stirling Bridge in 1297. After Wallace's betrayal and execution, Robert the Bruce, grandson of the former claimant, saw his chance, defied Edward (whom he had previously aligned himself with), murdered his rival John Comyn and had himself crowned King of Scotland at Scone in 1306. Bruce mounted a campaign to drive the English out of Scotland but suffered repeated defeats. Persistence paid off and he went on to secure an illustrious victory over the English at Bannockburn in 1314, enshrined in Scottish legend as one of the finest moments in the country's history.

Scottish independence was eventually won in 1328, though 'the Bruce' died the next year. Wars with England and civil strife continued, however. In 1371 Robert the Bruce's grandson, Robert II, acceded to the throne, founding the Stewart (later written as Stuart) dynasty, which was to rule Scotland and, in time, the rest of Britain, until 1714.

Robert the Bruce Trail

Melrose Abbey
(Melrose)

Scone Palace
(Perth)

Bannockburn
(Stirling)

Arbroath Abbey
(Arbroath)

Dunfermline Abbey
(Dunfermline)

THE DECLARATION OF ARBROATH

During the Wars of Independence, a group of Scottish nobles sent a letter to Pope John XXII requesting support for the cause of Scottish independence. Having railed against Edward I's tyranny and sung the praises of Robert the Bruce, the declaration famously stated: 'For so long as a hundred of us remain alive, we will yield in no least way to English dominion. For we fight, not for glory nor for riches nor for honours, but only and alone for freedom, which no good man surrenders but with his life'. The Pope initially supported the Scottish cause, but English lobbying changed his mind.

780	848	1040	1263
From the 780s onwards, Norsemen in longboats from Scandinavia begin to pillage the Scottish coast and islands, eventually taking control of Orkney, Shetland and the Western Isles.	Kenneth MacAlpin unites the Scottish and Pictish thrones, uniting Scotland north of the Firth of Forth into a single kingdom.	Macbeth takes the Scottish throne after defeating Duncan. This, and the fact that he was later killed by Duncan's son Malcolm, are the only parallels with Shakespeare's version of the story.	Norse power is finally broken at the Battle of Largs, which marks the retreat of Viking influence and eventually the handing back of the Western Isles to Scotland.

The Renaissance

James IV (r 1488–1513) married the daughter of Henry VII of England, the first of the Tudor monarchs, thereby linking the two royal families through 'the Marriage of the Thistle and the Rose'. This didn't prevent the French from persuading James to go to war against his in-laws, and he was killed at the Battle of Flodden in 1513, along with some 10,000 of his subjects. Renaissance ideas, in particular Scottish poetry and architecture, flourished during this time; some of the finest Scottish Renaissance buildings can be seen within the fortress of Stirling Castle.

Mary, Queen of Scots, & the Reformation

In 1542 James V, childless, lay on his deathbed – broken-hearted, it is said, after his defeat by the English at Solway Moss. Then news came that his wife had given birth to a baby girl. Fearing the end of the Stewart dynasty, and recalling its origin through Robert the Bruce's daughter, James sighed, 'It cam' wi' a lass, and it will gang wi' a lass'. He died shortly afterwards, leaving his week-old daughter, Mary, to inherit the throne as Queen of Scots.

She was sent to France young, and Scotland was ruled by regents, who rejected overtures from Henry VIII of England urging them to wed the infant queen to his son. Furious, Henry sent his armies to take vengeance on the Scots. The 'Rough Wooing', as it was called, failed to win hearts and minds and in 1558 Mary was married to the French dauphin. When he became king the next year, Mary was briefly queen of France as well as Scotland.

While Mary was in France, being raised Catholic, the Reformation tore through Scotland, to where, following the death of her sickly French husband, the 18-year-old returned in 1561. She was formally welcomed to her capital city and held a famous audience with John Knox. The great reformer harangued the young queen and she later agreed to protect the budding Protestant Church in Scotland while continuing to practise Catholicism in private.

She married Lord Darnley in the Chapel Royal at Holyrood and gave birth to a son (later James VI) in 1565. Any domestic bliss was short-lived and, in a scarcely believable train of events, Darnley was involved in the murder of Mary's Italian secretary Rizzio (rumoured to be her lover), before he himself was murdered, probably by Mary's new lover and third-husband-to-be, the Earl of Bothwell.

The Scots had had enough; Mary's enemies – an alliance of powerful nobles – finally confronted her at Carberry Hill, east of Edinburgh, and Mary was forced to abdicate in 1567 and thrown into prison at Castle Leven. She escaped and met her enemies in battle at Langside, but she was defeated and fled to England, where she was imprisoned for 19 years by Elizabeth I and finally executed in 1587.

Mary Queen of Scots (1969) by Antonia Fraser is the classic biography of Scotland's ill-starred queen, digging deep behind the myths to discover the real woman caught up in the labyrinthine politics of the period.

1296	1298–1305	1314	1328
Edward I marches on Scotland with an army of 30,000 men, razing ports, butchering citizens and capturing the castles of Berwick, Edinburgh, Roxburgh and Stirling.	William Wallace is proclaimed Guardian of Scotland in March 1298. After Edward's force defeats the Scots at the Battle of Falkirk, Wallace resigns as guardian and goes into hiding, but he is fatally betrayed after his return in 1305.	Robert the Bruce wins a famous victory over the English at the Battle of Bannockburn, despite being outnumbered by his opponents.	Continuing raids on northern England force Edward III to sue for peace and the Treaty of Northampton confirms Scotland's independence, with Robert I, the Bruce, as king.

History, however, has a habit of providing a twist in the tale. Mary's son James VI (r 1567–1625) had meanwhile been crowned at Stirling, and a series of regents ruled in his place. In England, Elizabeth died childless, and the English, desperate for a male monarch, soon turned their attention north. James VI of Scotland became James I of England and moved his court to London. His plan to politically unite the two countries, however, failed. For the most part, the Stuarts ignored Scotland from then on.

> Jacobite, a term derived from the Latin for 'James', is used to describe the political movement committed to the return of the Catholic Stuart kings to the thrones of England and Scotland.

Union with England

Civil war and 17th-century religious conflict left the country and its economy ruined. Scotland couldn't compete in this new era of European colonialism and, to add to its woes, during the 1690s famine killed up to a third of the population in some areas. Anti-English feeling ran high: the Protestant king William, who had replaced the exiled Catholic James VII/II to the chagrin of many in Scotland, was at war with France and employing Scottish soldiers and taxes – many Scots, sympathetic to the French, disapproved. This feeling was exacerbated by the failure of the Darien Scheme, an investment plan designed to establish a Scottish colony in Panama, which resulted in widespread bankruptcy in Scotland.

The failure made it clear to wealthy Scottish merchants and stockholders that the only way they could gain access to the lucrative markets

THE LORDS OF THE ISLES

In medieval times, when overland Highland travel was slow, difficult and dangerous, the sea lochs, firths (estuaries), kyles (narrow sea channels) and sounds of the west coast were the motorways of their time. Cut off from the rest of Scotland, but united by these sea roads, the west coast and islands were a world unto themselves.

Descended from the legendary Somerled (a half-Gaelic, half-Norse warrior of the 12th century), the chiefs of Clan Donald claimed sovereignty over this watery kingdom. It was John MacDonald of Islay who first styled himself Dominus Insularum (Lord of the Isles) in 1353. He and his descendants ruled their vast territory from their headquarters at Finlaggan in Islay, backed up by fleets of swift *birlinns* and *nyvaigs* (Hebridean galleys), an intimate knowledge of the sea routes of the west and a network of coastal castles.

Clan Donald held sway over the isles, often in defiance of the Scottish kings, from 1350 to 1493. At its greatest extent, in the second half of the 15th century, the Lordship of the Isles included all the islands on the west coast of Scotland, the west-coast mainland from Kintyre to Ross-shire, and the Antrim coast of northern Ireland. But in a greedy grab for territory, Clan Donald finally pushed its luck too far. John MacDonald made a secret pact with the English king Edward IV to divide Scotland between them. When this treason was discovered 30 years later, the Lordship was forfeited to James IV of Scotland, and the title has remained in possession of the Scottish, and later British, royal family ever since. Lord of the Isles is one of the many titles held today by Prince Charles, heir to the British throne.

1468–69	1488–1513	1513	1567
Orkney and then Shetland are mortgaged to Scotland as part of a dowry from Danish king Christian I, whose daughter is to marry the future James III of Scotland.	The Scottish Renaissance produces an intellectual climate that encourages Protestantism, a reaction against the perceived wealth and corruption of the medieval Roman Catholic Church.	James IV invades northern England and is soundly defeated (and killed) in Northumberland at the Battle of Flodden. It marks a watershed in war history, with artillery on the upswing and archery on the way out.	Mary, Queen of Scots, is deposed and thrown into prison. Though her last stand is still to come, the days of wilful royal action in Scotland seem to be over.

of developing colonies was through union with England. The English parliament favoured union through fear of Jacobite sympathies in Scotland being exploited by its enemies, the French.

On receiving the Act of Union in 1707 in Edinburgh, the Chancellor of Scotland, Lord Seafield – leader of the parliament that the Act of Union abolished – is said to have murmured under his breath, 'Now there's an end to an auld sang'. Robert Burns later castigated the wealthy politicians who engineered the union in characteristically stronger language: 'We're bought and sold for English gold – such a parcel of rogues in a nation!'

The Jacobites

The Jacobite rebellions of the 18th century sought to displace the Hanoverian monarchy (chosen by the English parliament in 1701 to ensure a Protestant succession after the Stuart queens Mary II and Anne died without heirs) and restore a Catholic Stuart king to the British throne.

James Edward Stuart, known as the Old Pretender, was the son of James VII/II. With French support he arrived in the Firth of Forth with a fleet of ships in 1708 but was seen off by government men-of-war.

The Earl of Mar led another Jacobite rebellion in 1715 but proved an ineffectual leader; his campaign fizzled out soon after the inconclusive Battle of Sheriffmuir.

The Old Pretender's son, Charles Edward Stuart, better known as Bonnie Prince Charlie or the Young Pretender, landed in Scotland for the final uprising. He had little military experience, didn't speak Gaelic and had a shaky grasp of English. Nevertheless, supported by an army of Highlanders, he marched southwards and captured Edinburgh, except for the castle, in September 1745. He got as far south as Derby in England, but success was short-lived; a government army led by the Duke of Cumberland harried him all the way back to the Highlands, where Jacobite dreams were finally extinguished at the Battle of Culloden in 1746.

Although a heavily romanticised figure, Bonnie Prince Charlie was partly responsible for the annihilation of Highland culture, given the crackdown following his doomed attempt to recapture the crown. After returning to France he gained a reputation for drunkenness and mistreatment of mistresses. France had plans to invade Britain during the mid 18th century, but it eventually ceased to regard the prince as a serious character. When French ambitions were thwarted by British naval victories in 1759, the Bonnie Prince's last chance had gone. He died in Rome in 1788.

The Highland Clearances

In the aftermath of the Jacobite rebellions, Highland dress, the bearing of arms and the bagpipes were outlawed. The Highlands were put under military control and private armies were banned.

Charlie, Meg & Me by Gregor Ewing (2013) is an entertaining account of one man and his dog retracing Bonnie Prince Charlie's epic 500-mile trek through the Scottish Highlands in 1746.

HISTORY THE JACOBITES

Bonnie Prince Charlie's flight after the Battle of Culloden is legendary. He lived in hiding in the remote Highlands and islands for months before being rescued by a French frigate. His narrow escape from Uist to Skye, dressed as Flora MacDonald's maid, is the subject of the 'Skye Boat Song'.

1603	1692	1707	1745–46
James VI of Scotland inherits the English throne in the so-called Union of the Crowns, becoming James I of Great Britain.	The Massacre of Glencoe causes further rifts between those clans loyal to the Crown and those loyal to the old ways.	Despite popular opposition, the Act of Union – which brings England and Scotland under one parliament, one sovereign and one flag – takes effect on 1 May.	The culmination of the Jacobite rebellions: Bonnie Prince Charlie lands in Scotland, gathers an army and marches south. Though he gains English territory, he is eventually defeated at the Battle of Culloden.

The clansmen, no longer of any use as soldiers and uneconomical as tenants, were evicted from their homes and farms by the Highland chieftains to make way for flocks of sheep. A few stayed to work the sheep farms; many more were forced to seek work in the cities, or to eke a living from crofts (smallholdings) on poor coastal land. Men who had never seen the sea were forced to take to boats to try their luck at herring fishing, and many thousands emigrated – some willingly, some under duress – to the developing colonies of North America, Australia and New Zealand.

If you do much walking in the Highlands and islands, you are almost certain to come across a pile of stones among the bracken, all that remains of a house or cottage. Look around and you'll find another, and another, and soon you'll realise that this was once a crofting settlement.

John Prebble's wonderfully written book *The Highland Clearances* (1963) tells the terrible story of how the Highlanders were driven out of their homes and forced into emigration.

The Scottish Enlightenment

During the period known as the Scottish Enlightenment (roughly 1740–1830) Edinburgh became known as 'a hotbed of genius'. Philosophers David Hume and Adam Smith and sociologist Adam Ferguson emerged as influential thinkers, nourished on generations of theological debate. Medic William Cullen produced the first modern pharmacopoeia, chemist Joseph Black advanced the science of thermodynamics, and geologist James Hutton challenged long-held beliefs about the age of the Earth.

After centuries of bloodshed and religious fanaticism, people applied themselves with the same energy and piety to the making of money and the enjoyment of leisure. There was a revival in Scottish history and literature. The writings of Sir Walter Scott and the poetry of Robert Burns achieved lasting popularity. The cliched images that spring to mind when you say 'Scotland' – bagpipes, haggis, tartans, misty glens – owe much to the romantic depictions of the country developed at this time.

The Industrial Revolution

The development of the steam engine ushered in the Industrial Revolution. Glasgow, deprived of its lucrative tobacco trade following the American War of Independence (1776–83), developed into an industrial powerhouse, the 'second city' of the British Empire. Cotton mills, iron and steelworks, chemical plants, shipbuilding yards and heavy-engineering works proliferated along the River Clyde in the 19th century, powered by southern Scotland's abundant coal mines.

The Clearances and the Industrial Revolution had shattered the traditional rural way of life, and though manufacturing cities and ports thrived in these decades of Empire, wealth was generated for a select few by an impoverished many. Deep poverty forced many into emigration and others to their graves. The depopulation was exacerbated by WWI, which took a heavy toll on Scottish youth. The ensuing years were bleak and marked by labour disputes.

1740s–1830s	1890–1910	1914–32	1941–45
Cultural and intellectual life flourishes during the Scottish Enlightenment. Meanwhile, the Industrial Revolution brings preeminence in the production of textiles, iron, steel and coal – and above all in shipbuilding.	The 'Glasgow Boys' bring European influence and international recognition to Scottish art, breaking away from the Edinburgh mainstream.	Scottish industry slumps during WWI and collapses in its aftermath in the face of overseas competition and the Great Depression. About 400,000 Scots emigrate between 1921 and 1931.	Clydebank is blitzed by German bombers in 1941, with 1200 deaths; by 1945 one out of four males in the workforce is employed in heavy industries to support the war effort.

War & Peace

Scotland largely escaped the trauma and devastation wrought by WWII on the industrial cities of England (although Clydebank was bombed). Indeed, the war brought a measure of renewed prosperity to Scotland as the shipyards and engineering works geared up to supply material. But the postwar period saw the collapse of shipbuilding and heavy industry, on which Scotland had become overreliant.

After the discovery of North Sea oil off the Scottish coast, excitement turned to bitterness for many Scots, who felt that revenues were being siphoned off to England, though some parts of the country, such as Aberdeen, prospered. This issue, along with takeovers of Scottish companies by English ones (which then closed the Scots operation, asset-stripped and transferred jobs to England), fuelled increasing nationalist sentiment. The Scottish National Party (SNP) developed into a third force (then a second as it eclipsed the Conservatives, and then first as it won power from the Labour Party) in Scottish politics.

Devolution

In 1979 a referendum was held on whether to set up a directly elected Scottish Assembly. Fifty-two per cent of those who voted said yes to devolution, but Labour prime minister James Callaghan decided that everyone who didn't vote should be counted as a no, so the Scottish Assembly was rejected.

From 1979 to 1997 Scotland was ruled by a Conservative government in London, for which the majority of Scots hadn't voted. Separatist feelings, always present, grew stronger. Following the landslide victory of the Labour Party in 1997, another referendum was held on the creation of a Scottish parliament. This time the result was overwhelmingly and unambiguously in favour.

Elections were held and the Scottish parliament convened for the first time in 1999 in Edinburgh, with Labour's Donald Dewar, who died in office the very next year, becoming first minister. Labour held power until 2007, when the proindependence Scottish National Party formed government. It was overwhelmingly re-elected in 2011 and pushed for a referendum on independence. The campaign engaged the nation and resulted in a huge turnout, and in September 2014 the Scots voted against becoming an independent nation by 55% to 45%.

One of the major factors for many Scots who voted to remain part of the UK was the guarantee of continued EU membership, so when in June 2016 the UK population narrowly voted to leave the EU, this again brought the issue of Scottish independence into the spotlight.

Between 1904 and 1931 around one million people emigrated from Scotland to begin a new life in North America and Australasia.

1970s	1999–2004	2014	2016
The discovery of oil and gas in the North Sea brings new prosperity to Aberdeen and the surrounding area, and also to the Shetland Islands.	Scottish parliament is convened in May 1999 after a three-century hiatus. The new Parliament Building is opened in Edinburgh by Elizabeth II in 2004.	Scotland votes on and rejects becoming a fully independent nation by 55% to 45%, and so remains part of the UK.	Scots vote 62% to remain in the EU, but the UK as a whole votes to leave, raising further questions about Scotland's future path.

The Scottish Larder

Traditional Scottish cookery is all about basic comfort food: solid, nourishing fare, often high in fat, that will keep you warm on a winter's day spent in the fields or at sea. But Scotland has been a frontrunner in the recent British culinary revolution, and an inspiring array of local and sustainable produce is on offer. Scotland's traditional drinks – whisky and beer – have also found a new lease of life, with single malts being marketed like fine wines, and numerous new microbreweries.

Breakfast, Lunch & Dinner

The Full Scottish

Though it's making a comeback, surprisingly few Scots eat porridge for breakfast – these days a cappuccino and a croissant is just as likely – and even fewer eat it in the traditional way; that is, with salt to taste, but no sugar.

The typical 'full Scottish' breakfast offered in a B&B or hotel usually consists of fruit juice and cereal, toast and jam, a pot of coffee or tea, and a fry-up combination of any or all of bacon, sausage, black pudding (a type of sausage made from dried blood), grilled tomato, mushrooms, potato scones and a fried egg or two. Most B&Bs offer a vegetarian version these days. An increasing number are eliminating the fried plate in favour of a healthier option like fruit salad.

Fish for breakfast may sound strange but was not unusual in crofting (smallholding) and fishing communities where seafood was a staple; many hotels still offer grilled kippers (smoked herrings) or smoked haddock (poached in milk and served with a poached egg) for breakfast – delicious with lots of buttered toast.

Scottish food writer Sue Lawrence's book *A Cook's Tour of Scotland* contains 120 recipes based on the use of fresh, seasonal Scottish produce.

Traditional Soups

Scotch broth, made with mutton stock, barley, lentils and peas, is nutritious and tasty, while cock-a-leekie is a hearty soup made with chicken and leeks. Warming vegetable soups include leek and potato soup, and lentil soup (traditionally made using ham stock – vegetarians, beware!).

Seafood soups include the delicious Cullen skink, made with smoked haddock, potato, onion and milk, and *partan bree* (crab soup).

Seafood Specialities

Scottish seafood is among the world's best, and it's a major highlight of a visit to the country, particularly along the west coast. There's an increasing awareness of sustainability issues and most serious seafood places

EATING PRICE RANGES

The following price ranges refer to the average price of a main course from the dinner menu.

£ less than £10

££ £10–20

£££ more than £20

SSSSSMOKIN'!

Scotland is famous for its smoked salmon, but there are many other varieties of smoked fish – plus smoked meats and cheeses – to enjoy. Smoking food to preserve it is an ancient art that has recently undergone a revival, but this time it's more about flavour than preservation.

There are two parts to the process – first the cure, which involves covering the fish in a mixture of salt and molasses, or soaking it in brine; and then the smoke, which can be either cold smoking (at less than 34°C), which results in a raw product, or hot smoking (at more than 60°C), which cooks it. Cold-smoked products include traditional smoked salmon, kippers and Finnan haddies. Hot-smoked products include *bradan rost* ('flaky' smoked salmon) and Arbroath smokies.

Arbroath smokies are haddock that have been gutted, de-headed and cleaned, then salted and dried overnight, tied together at the tail in pairs, and hot-smoked over oak or beech chippings for 45 to 90 minutes. Finnan haddies (named after the fishing village of Findon in Aberdeenshire) are also haddock, but these are split down the middle like kippers, and cold smoked.

Kippers (smoked herring) were invented in Northumberland, in northern England, in the mid-19th century, but Scotland soon picked up the technique, and both Loch Fyne and Mallaig were famous for their kippers.

There are dozens of modern smokehouses scattered all over Scotland, many of which offer a mail-order service as well as an on-site shop. A few recommended ones include Hebridean Smokehouse (p393) for peat-smoked salmon and sea trout, and Inverawe Smokehouse & Fishery (p292) for delicate smoked salmon and plump, juicy kippers. **Marrbury Smokehouse** (☎01671-820476; www.marrbury.co.uk; Carsluith Castle, A75; ☺10am-5pm Feb-Dec), supplier to Gleneagles Hotel and other top restaurants, is another one to try.

will give information on provenance. Tucking into some local hand-dived scallops and creel-caught langoustines as the sun sets over a west-coast or island bay is one of Europe's great gastronomic pleasures.

And it's not all about crisp linen, claw crackers and finger bowls. A number of simple seafood shacks serve up delicious fresh fare in a very no-frills manner – a great way to eat straight from the boats without busting the budget.

Juicy langoustines (also known as Dublin Bay prawns, Norway lobsters or, in some places, simply 'prawns') are a highlight; crabs, squat lobsters, lobsters, oysters, mussels and scallops are also widely available.

Scottish salmon is famous worldwide, but there's a big difference between the now-ubiquitous farmed salmon and the leaner, more expensive, wild fish. Also, there are concerns over the environmental impact of salmon farms on the marine environment.

Smoked salmon is traditionally dressed with a squeeze of lemon juice and eaten with fresh brown bread and butter. Trout, salmon's smaller cousin – whether wild, rod-caught brown trout or farmed rainbow trout – is delicious fried in oatmeal.

As an alternative to kippers, you may be offered Arbroath smokies (lightly smoked fresh haddock), traditionally eaten cold. Herring fillets fried in oatmeal are good, if you don't mind picking out a few bones. Mackerel pâté and smoked or peppered mackerel (both served cold) are also popular.

Scottish Beef

Steak eaters will enjoy a thick fillet of world-famous Aberdeen Angus beef, and beef from Highland cattle is much sought after. Venison, from red deer, is leaner and appears on many menus, particularly in the Highlands. Scotland, particularly Ayrshire, has some quality pork that appears in various forms.

A variety of meat-based deli products is beginning to appear from smaller, often organic, producers, with pork, mutton and venison being used in a very tasty array of smoked and charcuterie products.

Puddings

Traditional Scottish puddings are irresistibly creamy, high-calorie concoctions. Cranachan is whipped cream flavoured with whisky, and mixed with toasted oatmeal and raspberries. Atholl brose is a mixture of cream, whisky and honey, flavoured with oatmeal. Clootie dumpling is a rich steamed pudding filled with currants and raisins; it's so named because it's wrapped in a 'cloot' (linen cloth) for steaming.

Vegetarian & Vegan

Scotland has the same proportion of vegetarians as the rest of the UK – around 8% to 10% of the population – and vegetarianism is now firmly in the mainstream. Even the most remote Highland pub usually has at least one vegetarian dish on the menu, and there are many dedicated vegetarian restaurants in the cities. If you get stuck, there's almost always an Italian or Indian restaurant where you can get meat-free pizza, pasta or curry. Vegans, though, may find the options a bit limited outside Edinburgh and Glasgow.

One thing to keep in mind is that lentil soup, a seemingly vegetarian staple of Scottish pub and restaurant menus, is traditionally made with ham stock.

Most B&Bs offer a vegetarian fry-up option these days, though vegans are advised to explain beforehand to their host exactly what the term means – just in case.

Eating with Kids

Following the introduction of the ban on smoking in public places in 2006, many Scottish pubs and restaurants have had to broaden their appeal by becoming more family friendly. As a result, especially in the cities and more popular tourist towns, many restaurants and pubs now have family rooms and/or play areas. Children's menus are common but not usually very imaginative.

You should be aware, though, that children under the age of 14 are not allowed into the majority of Scottish pubs, even those that serve bar meals; and in family-friendly pubs (those in possession of a Children's Certificate), under-14s are only allowed in between 11am and 8pm, and must be accompanied by an adult aged 18 or older.

HAGGIS – SCOTLAND'S NATIONAL DISH

Scotland's national dish is often avoided by visitors because of its ingredients, which admittedly don't sound promising – the finely chopped lungs, heart and liver of a sheep, mixed with oatmeal and onion and stuffed into a sheep's stomach bag. However, it actually tastes surprisingly good.

Haggis should be served with *champit tatties* and *bashed neeps* (mashed potatoes and turnips), with a generous dollop of butter and a good sprinkling of black pepper.

Although it's eaten year-round, haggis is central to the Burns Night celebrations of 25 January, in honour of Scotland's national poet, Robert Burns, when Scots worldwide unite to revel in their Scottishness. A piper announces the arrival of the haggis and Burns' poem *Address to a Haggis* is recited to this 'Great chieftan o' the puddin-race'. The bulging haggis is then lanced with a *dirk* (dagger) to reveal the steaming offal within, 'warm-reekin, rich'.

Vegetarians (and quite a few carnivores, no doubt) will be relieved to know that veggie haggis is available in some restaurants.

Takeaways serve deep-fried haggis with chips – tasty, but don't tell your cardiologist.

Top Macallan distillery (p238), Speyside

Bottom Scotland's national dish – haggis (p442)

NITSAWAN KATERATTANAKUL/SHUTTERSTOCK ©

Farmers Markets & Food Festivals

Many towns, city districts and villages, particularly in the south of Scotland, have a regular farmers market that showcases local produce. There's an inspiring variety of new, sustainably grown fare, with everything from chorizo to tea being brought from farm to table by small-scale producers. Local food festivals are another increasingly popular way to publicise regional delicacies.

Cookery Courses

More than a dozen places in Scotland offer courses in Scottish cookery. Two of the most famous:

Kinloch Lodge Hotel (☎01471-833333; www.kinloch-lodge.co.uk; Kinloch, Sleat) Courses in Scottish cookery and demonstrations using fresh, seasonal Scottish produce by Lady Claire Macdonald, author of *Scottish Highland Hospitality* and *Celebrations*. Fees range from £25 per person for a 45-minute express class, to £149 for a full-day workshop including breakfast and lunch.

Nick Nairn Cook School (Map p226; ☎01877-389900; www.nicknairn cookschool.com; 15 Back Wynd, Aberdeen; 1-day course per person £149) One-day courses in modern Scottish cooking at the school owned by Scotland's top TV chef, Nick Nairn, author of *Wild Harvest* and *Island Harvest*.

Beer

Scottish breweries produce a wide range of beers, with generic multinational lagers alongside traditional-style real ales and a huge and growing selection of craft-brewed beers from small regional brewing operations.

Traditional Scottish ales use old-fashioned 'shilling' categories to indicate strength (the number of shillings was originally the price per barrel; the stronger the beer, the higher the price). The usual range is from 60 to 80 shillings (written 80/-). You'll also see IPA, which stands for India Pale Ale, a strong, hoppy beer first brewed in the early 19th century for export to India (the extra alcohol meant that it kept better on the long sea voyage).

Draught beer is served in pints (568mL, usually costing from £2.60 to £4) or half pints; alcoholic content generally ranges from 3% to 6%. What the English call bitter, Scots call heavy, or export.

The craft-beer revolution of recent years has hit Scotland with full force, and a large number of small breweries are producing beers ranging from organic lagers to traditional Scottish ales, American-influenced pale ales and various styles of dark beer. An increasing number of pubs have given over one or more taps to local craft beers or real ales, immeasurably improving the Scottish beer scene.

Visit http://glasgowcamra.org.uk/breweries.php for a comprehensive list of Scottish breweries, both large and small.

In the last decade there has been a swing away from the big international brands in favour of beers made by small, local breweries –

Scotland's most famous soft drink is Barr's Irn-Bru: a sweet, fizzy drink, radioactive orange in colour, that smells like bubble gum and almost strips the enamel from your teeth. Many Scots swear by its restorative effects as a cure for a hangover.

TOP SEAFOOD RESTAURANTS

Ondine (p82), Edinburgh

Café Fish (p285), Tobermory

Ee-usk (p278), Oban

Kishorn Seafood Bar (p371), Lochcarron

Tolbooth Restaurant (p235), Stonehaven

Lochleven Seafood Cafe (p333), Kinlochleven

Starfish (p259), Tarbert

Silver Darling (p230), Aberdeen

TOP FIVE SINGLE MALTS – OUR CHOICE

After a great deal of diligent research (and not a few sore heads), Lonely Planet's *Scotland* authors have selected their five favourite single malts from across the country.

Ardbeg (p263; Islay) The 10-year-old from this noble distillery is a byword for excellence. Peaty but well balanced. Hits the spot after a hill walk.

Highland Park (p402; Orkney) Full and rounded, with heather, honey, malt and peat. Award-winning distillery tour.

Isle of Arran (p272; Arran) One of Scotland's newer distilleries, offering a lightish, flavoursome malt with flowery, fruity notes.

Macallan (p238; Speyside) The king of Speyside malts, with sherry and bourbon finishes. The distillery is set amid waving fields of Golden Promise barley.

Talisker (p380; Skye) Brooding, heavily peated nose balanced by a satisfying sweetness from this lord of the isles. Great postdinner dram.

so-called craft beers. Many of these have their own pubs, or even combine pub and brewery in one place, like Pitlochry's Moulin Hotel (p323), Dundee's **Beer Kitchen** (Map p116; ☎0141-334 6688; www.innisandgunn.com; 44 Ashton Lane; ⊙10am-midnight; ☎) and Edinburgh's **Royal Dick** (Map p52; ☎0131-560 1572; www.summerhall.co.uk/the-royal-dick; 1 Summerhall; ⊙noon-1am Mon-Sat, 12.30pm-midnight Sun; ☎; ☐41, 42, 67).

Traditional Pubs

The traditional Scottish pub ranges from the grandiose, purpose-built, Victorian pubs typical of Edinburgh and Glasgow through former coaching inns dotted along ancient highways to cottage drinking dens hidden away in Highland glens and island villages.

What they have in common today is that they have preserved much of their original 18th- or 19th-century decor – timber-beamed ceilings, glowing mahogany bar tops, polished brass rails and stained-glass windows – and generally serve cask-conditioned real ales and a range of malt whiskies.

Pubs like these are often the social hub of rural communities, a meeting place and venue for live music, quiz nights and ceilidhs (p449).

Whisky

Scotch whisky (always spelt without an 'e' – whiskey with an 'e' is Irish or American) is Scotland's best-known product and biggest export. The spirit has been distilled in Scotland at least since the 15th century and probably for much longer.

At a bar, older Scots may order a 'half' or 'nip' of whisky as a chaser to a pint or half pint of beer (a 'hauf and a hauf'). Only tourists ask for 'Scotch' – what else would you be served in Scotland? The standard measure in pubs is either 25mL or 35mL.

As well as whiskies, there are whisky-based liqueurs such as Drambuie. If you must mix your whisky with anything other than water, try a whisky mac (whisky with ginger wine). After a long walk in the rain there's nothing better for putting a warm glow in your belly.

Whisky Bars

Some pubs, especially in the whisky-distilling region of Speyside, have become known as whisky bars because of their staggering range of single-malt whiskies – the famous Quaich Bar in the Craigellachie Hotel (p239), established in 1894, offers more than 900 varieties.

The revival of interest in single malts since the late 1990s has seen a new wave of whisky bars open across the country, mainly in the cities. Places like Glasgow's Òran Mór (p130) have more than 300 malts stacked behind the bar.

Scottish Culture

The notion of 'the Scottish arts' often conjures up cliched images of bagpipe music, incomprehensible poetry and romanticised paintings of Highland landscapes. But Scottish artists have given the world a wealth of unforgettable treasures, from the songs and poems of Robert Burns and the novels of Sir Walter Scott to the architecture of Charles Rennie Mackintosh.

Literature

Scotland has a long and distinguished literary history, from the era of the medieval makars ('makers' of verses; ie poets) to the present-day crime novels of Val McDermid, Christopher Brookmyre, Louise Welsh and Ian Rankin.

Burns & Scott

Scotland's most famous literary figure is, of course, Robert Burns (1759–96). His works have been translated into dozens of languages and are known the world over. Burns wrote in Lowland Scots (Lallans); in fact, his poetry was instrumental in keeping Lallans alive to the present day. He was also very much a man of the people, satirising the upper classes and the church for their hypocrisy. Although he is best known for the comical tale of *Tam O'Shanter* and for penning the words to 'Auld Lang Syne', his more political poems – including 'Such a Parcel of Rogues in a Nation' (about the 1707 Act of Union) and 'A Man's a Man for a' That' (about class and solidarity) – reveal his socialist leanings.

The son of an Edinburgh lawyer, Sir Walter Scott (1771–1832) was Scotland's greatest and most prolific novelist. Scott was born in Edinburgh and lived at various New Town addresses before moving to his country house at Abbotsford. His early works were rhyming ballads, such as *The Lady of the Lake*, and his first historical novels – Scott effectively invented the genre – were published anonymously. Plagued by debt in later life, he wrote obsessively in order to make money but will always be best remembered for classic tales such as *Waverley, The Heart of Midlothian, Ivanhoe, Redgauntlet* and *Castle Dangerous*.

RLS & Sherlock Holmes

Along with Sir Walter Scott, Robert Louis Stevenson (RLS; 1850–94) ranks as Scotland's best-known novelist. Born at 8 Howard Pl in Edinburgh into a family of famous lighthouse engineers, Stevenson studied law at Edinburgh University but was always intent on pursuing the life of a writer. An inveterate traveller, but dogged by ill health, he finally settled in Samoa in 1889, where he was revered by the local people and known as 'Tusitala' – the teller of tales. Stevenson is known and loved around the world for those tales: *Kidnapped, Catriona, Treasure Island, The Master of Ballantrae* and *The Strange Case of Dr Jekyll and Mr Hyde*.

Sir Arthur Conan Doyle (1859–1930), the creator of Sherlock Holmes, was born in Edinburgh and studied medicine at Edinburgh University. He based the character of Holmes on one of his lecturers, the surgeon

Essential Scottish Novels

....

Sunset Song (Lewis Grassic Gibbon, 1932)

....

The Prime of Miss Jean Brodie (Muriel Spark, 1961)

....

Greenvoe (George Mackay Brown, 1972)

....

Trainspotting (Irvine Welsh, 1993)

Dr Joseph Bell, who had employed his forensic skills and powers of deduction on several murder cases in Edinburgh.

MacDiarmid to Muriel Spark

Scotland's finest modern poet was Hugh MacDiarmid (born Christopher Murray Grieve; 1892–1978). Originally from Dumfriesshire, he moved to Edinburgh in 1908, where he trained as a teacher and a journalist, but he spent most of his life in Montrose, Shetland, Glasgow and Biggar. His masterpiece is 'A Drunk Man Looks at the Thistle', a 2685-line Joycean monologue.

The poet and storyteller George Mackay Brown (1921–96) was born in Stromness in Orkney, and lived there almost all his life. Although his poems and novels are rooted in Orkney, his work, like that of Burns, transcends local and national boundaries. His best-known novel, *Greenvoe* (1972), is a poetic evocation of an Orkney community threatened by the coming of modernity.

Dame Muriel Spark (1918–2006) was born in Edinburgh and educated at James Gillespie's High School for Girls, an experience that provided material for perhaps her best-known novel, *The Prime of Miss Jean Brodie*, a shrewd portrait of 1930s Edinburgh.

The Contemporary Scene

The most widely known Scots writers today include Iain Banks (1954–2013; *The Crow Road*), Irvine Welsh (b 1961; *Trainspotting*), Janice Galloway (b 1955; *The Trick Is to Keep Breathing*) and Ali Smith (b 1962; *How to Be Both*). The grim realities of modern Glasgow are vividly conjured in the short-story collection *Not Not While the Giro* by James Kelman (b 1946), whose controversial novel *How Late It Was, How Late* won the 1994 Booker Prize.

The Scottish crime-writing charts are topped by Val McDermid (b 1955) and Ian Rankin (b 1960). McDermid's novels feature private

SCOTTISH LANGUAGES

From the 8th to the 19th centuries the common language of central and southern Scotland was Lowland Scots (sometimes called Lallans), which evolved from Old English and has Dutch, French, Gaelic, German and Scandinavian influences. As distinct from English as Norwegian is from Danish, it was the official language of state in Scotland until the Act of Union in 1707.

Following the Union, English rose to predominance as the language of government, church and polite society. The spread of education and literacy in the 19th century eventually led to Lowland Scots being perceived as backward and unsophisticated – children were often beaten for speaking Scots in school instead of English.

The Scots tongue persisted, however, and has undergone a revival – there are now Scots language dictionaries, university degree courses in Scots language and literature, and Scots is studied as part of the school curriculum.

Scottish Gaelic (*Gàidhlig* – pronounced 'gaa-lik') is spoken by about 60,000 people in Scotland, mainly in the Highlands and islands. It is a member of the Celtic family of languages, which includes Irish Gaelic, Manx, Welsh, Cornish and Breton.

Gaelic culture flourished in the Highlands until the Jacobite rebellions of the 18th century. After the Battle of Culloden in 1746 many Gaelic speakers were forced from their ancestral lands, and Gaelic was regarded as little more than a 'peasant' language of no modern significance.

It was only in the 1970s that Gaelic began to make a comeback. After two centuries of decline, the language has been encouraged through financial help from government agencies and the EU, and Gaelic education is flourishing at every level from playgroups to tertiary institutions.

investigator Kate Brannigan and psychologist Tony Hill; *Wire in the Blood* became a successful TV series. Rankin's Edinburgh-based crime novels, featuring the hard-drinking, introspective Detective Inspector John Rebus, are sinister, engrossing mysteries that explore the darker side of Scotland's capital city. He has a growing international following (his books have been translated into 22 languages).

Music

Traditional Music

Scotland has always had a strong folk tradition. In the 1960s and 1970s Robin Hall and Jimmy MacGregor, the Corries and the hugely talented Ewan McColl worked the pubs and clubs up and down the country. The Boys of the Lough, headed by Shetland fiddler Aly Bain, was one of the first professional bands to promote the traditional Celtic music of Scotland and Ireland. It was followed by the Battlefield Band, Alba, Capercaillie and others.

The Scots folk songs that you will often hear sung in pubs and at *ceilidhs* (evenings of traditional Scottish entertainment, including music, song and dance) draw on Scotland's rich history. A huge number of them relate to the Jacobite rebellions in the 18th century and, in particular, to Bonnie Prince Charlie – 'Hey Johnnie Cope', the 'Skye Boat Song' and 'Will Ye No Come Back Again', for example – while others relate to the Covenanters and the Highland Clearances.

In recent years there has been a revival in traditional music, often adapted and updated for the modern age. Bands such as Runrig pioneered with their own brand of Gaelic rock, while Shooglenifty blend Scottish folk music with anything from indie rock to electronica, producing a hybrid that has been called 'acid croft'.

But perhaps the finest modern renderings of traditional Scottish songs come from singer-songwriter Eddi Reader, who rose to fame with the band Fairground Attraction and their 1988 hit 'Perfect'. Her album *Eddi Reader Sings the Songs of Robert Burns* (2003, re-released with extra tracks in 2009) is widely regarded as one of the best interpretations of Burns' works.

Bagpipes

The bagpipe is one of the oldest musical instruments still in use today. Although no piece of film footage on Scotland is complete without the drone of the pipes, their origin probably lies in the Middle East; when they first arrived in Scotland is unknown, but it was certainly premedieval.

The traditional Highland bagpipe consists of a leather bag held under the arm, kept inflated by blowing through the blowstick; the piper forces air through the pipes by squeezing the bag with the forearm. Three of the pipes, known as drones, play a constant note (one bass, two tenor) in the background; the fourth pipe, the chanter, plays the melody.

Highland soldiers were traditionally accompanied into battle by the skirl of the pipes, and the Scottish Highland bagpipe is unique in being the only musical instrument ever to be classed as a weapon. The playing of the pipes was banned – under pain of death – by the British government in 1747 as part of a scheme to suppress Highland culture in the wake of the Jacobite uprising of 1745. The pipes were revived when the Highland regiments were drafted into the British Army towards the end of the 18th century.

Bagpipe music may not be to everyone's taste, but Scotland's most famous instrument has been reinvented by bands like the Red Hot Chilli Pipers (https://rhcp.scot), who use pipes, drums, guitars and keyboards to create rock versions of trad tunes. They feature regularly at festivals throughout the country.

The Traditional Music & Song Association (www.tmsa.org.uk) website has listings of music, dance and cultural festivals around Scotland.

The Living Tradition (www.livingtradition.co.uk) is a bimonthly magazine covering the folk and traditional music of Scotland and the British Isles, as well as Celtic music, with features and reviews of albums and live gigs.

Ceilidhs

The Gaelic word *ceilidh* (*kay*-lay) means 'visit'. A *ceilidh* was originally a social gathering in the house after the day's work was over, enlivened with storytelling, music and song. These days, a *ceilidh* means an evening of traditional Scottish entertainment including music, song and dance. To find one, check the village noticeboard, or just ask at the local pub; visitors are always welcome to join in.

Rock & Pop

It would take an entire book to list all the Scottish artists and bands that have made it big in the world of rock and pop. From Glasgow-born King of Skiffle, Lonnie Donegan, in the 1950s, to the chart-topping Dumfries DJ Calvin Harris today, the roll-call is long and impressive, and only a few can be mentioned here.

The '90s saw the emergence of three bands that took the top three places in a 2005 vote for the best Scottish band of all time – melodic indie-pop songsters Belle and Sebastian, Brit-rock band Travis, and indie rockers Idlewild, who opened for the Rolling Stones in 2003. Scottish artists who have made an international impression in more recent times include Ayrshire rockers Biffy Clyro, indie rock group Frightened Rabbit, Glasgow synth-pop band Chvrches, and Edinburgh hip-hop trio Young Fathers.

The airwaves are awash with female singer-songwriters, but few are as gutsy and versatile as Edinburgh-born, St Andrews–raised KT Tunstall. Although she's been writing and singing since the late 1990s, it was her 2005 debut album *Eye to the Telescope* that introduced her to a wider audience. Others include Glasgow-born Amy Macdonald, who was only 20 years old when her first album *This Is the Life* (2007) sold three million copies; and Karine Polwart, whose songs combine folk influences with modern themes and subjects.

As far as male singer-songwriters are concerned, few are more popular than bespectacled twin brothers Craig and Charlie Reid, better known as The Proclaimers. Nine studio albums from 1987 to 2012 provided ample material for the hugely successful movie based on their music, *Sunshine on Leith* (2013); their 10th album, *Let's Hear It for the Dogs* (2015), reached number 26 in the UK album charts.

Scottish Pop Playlist
'Suddenly I See' by KT Tunstall

'Letter from America' by The Proclaimers

'This Is the Life' by Amy Macdonald

'Top of the Pops' by The Rezillos

Painting

Perhaps the most famous Scottish painting is the portrait of *Reverend Robert Walker Skating on Duddingston Loch* by Sir Henry Raeburn (1756–1823), held in the National Gallery of Scotland. This image of a Presbyterian minister at play beneath Arthur's Seat, with all the poise of a ballerina and the hint of a smile on his lips, is a symbol of Enlightenment Edinburgh, the triumph of reason over wild nature. However, recent research has suggested it may not be the work of Raeburn after all but may have been painted by French artist Henri-Pierre Danloux.

Scottish portraiture reached its peak during the Scottish Enlightenment in the second half of the 18th century with the paintings of Raeburn and his contemporary Allan Ramsay (1713–84), while Sir David Wilkie (1785–1841), whose genre paintings depicted scenes of rural Highland life, was one of the greatest artists of the 19th century.

In the early 20th century the Scottish painters most widely acclaimed outside the country were the group known as the Scottish Colourists – SJ Peploe (1871–1935), Francis Cadell (1883–1937), Leslie Hunter (1877–1931) and JD Fergusson (1874–1961) – whose striking paintings drew on French post-Impressionist and Fauvist influences. Peploe and Cadell, active in the 1920s and 1930s, often spent the summer painting together on the Isle of Iona, and reproductions of their beautiful landscapes and seascapes appear on many a print and postcard.

Cinema

Perthshire-born John Grierson (1898–1972) is acknowledged around the world as the father of the documentary film. His legacy includes the classic *Drifters* (1929; about the Scottish herring fishery) and the Oscar-winning *Seawards the Great Ships* (1961; about Clyde shipbuilding). Writer-director Bill Forsyth (b 1946) is best known for *Local Hero* (1983), a gentle comedy about an oil magnate seduced by the beauty of the High-lands, and *Gregory's Girl* (1980), about an awkward teenage schoolboy's romantic exploits.

In the 1990s the rise of the director-producer-writer team of Danny Boyle (English), Andrew Macdonald and John Hodge (both Scottish) – who wrote the scripts for *Shallow Grave* (1994), *Trainspotting* (1996) and *A Life Less Ordinary* (1997) – marked the beginnings of what might be described as a home-grown Scottish film industry; a *Trainspotting* sequel, *T2: Trainspotting*, was released in 2017.

Other Scottish directorial talent includes Kevin Macdonald, who made *Touching the Void* (2003), *State of Play* (2009) and the TV series of Stephen King's *11.22.63* (2016); and Lynne Ramsay, who directed *Morvern Callar* (2002), the BAFTA-nominated *We Need To Talk About Kevin* (2011), and *You Were Never Really Here* (2017), which won Best Screenplay at Cannes.

> For a guide to Scottish film locations, check out www.scotland themovie.com.

> *Rob Roy* (1995) is a witty and moving cinematic version of Sir Walter Scott's tale of the outlaw MacGregor – despite dodgy Scottish accents from Liam Neeson and Jessica Lange.

Architecture

The leading Scottish architects of the 18th century were William Adam (1684–1748) and his son Robert Adam (1728–92), whose revival of classical Greek and Roman forms influenced architects throughout Europe. Among the many neoclassical buildings they designed are Hopetoun House, Culzean Castle and Edinburgh's Charlotte Sq, possibly the finest example of Georgian architecture anywhere.

Alexander 'Greek' Thomson (1817–75) changed the face of 19th-century Glasgow with his neoclassical designs, while in Edinburgh, William Henry Playfair (1790–1857) continued Adam's tradition in the Greek temples of the National Monument on Calton Hill, the Royal Scottish Academy and the National Gallery of Scotland.

The 19th-century resurgence of interest in Scottish history and identity, led by writers such as Sir Walter Scott, saw architects turn to the towers, pointed turrets and crow-stepped gables of ancient castles for inspiration. The Victorian revival of the Scottish Baronial style, which first made an appearance in 16th-century buildings such as Craigievar Castle, produced many fanciful abodes such as Balmoral Castle, Scone Palace and Abbotsford.

Scotland's best known 20th-century architect and designer was Charles Rennie Mackintosh (1868–1928), one of the most influential exponents of the art-nouveau style. His finest building is the Glasgow School of Art (1896), which still looks modern more than a century after it was built.

> *Scotland's Castles* (1997) by Chris Tabraham is an excellent companion for anyone touring Scottish castles – a readable, illustrated history detailing how and why they were built.

Sport

Many Scots are sports-mad and follow football or rugby with fierce dedication, identifying closely with local teams and individuals. The most popular games are football (soccer), rugby union, shinty, curling and golf, the last two of which the Scots claim to have invented.

Football

Football (soccer) in Scotland is not so much a sport as a religion, with thousands turning out to worship their local teams on Wednesday and weekends throughout the season (August to May). Sacred rites include standing in the freezing cold of a February day, drinking hot Bovril and eating a Scotch pie as you watch your team getting gubbed.

Scotland's top 12 clubs play in the Scottish Premiership (www.spfl.co.uk), but two teams – Glasgow Rangers and Glasgow Celtic – have dominated the competition. On only 18 occasions since 1890 has a team other than Rangers or Celtic won the league; the last time was when Aberdeen won in 1985.

Rugby Union

Traditionally, football was the sport of Scotland's urban working classes, while rugby union (www.scottishrugby.org) was the preserve of middle-class university graduates and farmers from the Borders. Although this distinction is breaking down – rugby's popularity soared after the 1999 World Cup was staged in the UK, and the middle classes have invaded the football terraces – it persists to some extent.

Each year, from January to March, Scotland takes part in the Six Nations Rugby Championship. The most important fixture is the clash against England for the Calcutta Cup – it's always an emotive event; Scotland has won twice and drawn once since 2006.

At club level, the season runs from September to May, and among the better teams are those from the Borders such as Hawick, Kelso and Melrose. At the end of the season, teams play a rugby sevens (seven-a-side) variation of the 15-player competition.

Golf

Scotland is the home of golf. The game was probably invented here in the 12th century, and the world's oldest documentary evidence of a game being played (dating from 1456) was on Bruntsfield Links in Edinburgh.

Today there are more than 550 golf courses in Scotland – that's more per capita than in any other country (see www.scottishgolfcourses.com). The sport is hugely popular and much more egalitarian than in other countries, with lots of affordable, publicly owned courses. There are many world-famous championship courses, too, including Muirfield in East Lothian, Turnberry and Troon in Ayrshire, Carnoustie in Angus and St Andrews' Old Course in Fife.

Highland Games

Highland games are held in Scotland throughout the summer, and not just in the Highlands. You can find dates and details of Highland games held all over the country on the Scottish Highland Games Association website (www.shga.co.uk).

The traditional sporting events are accompanied by piping and dancing competitions and attract locals and tourists alike. Some events are peculiarly Scottish, particularly those that involve trials of strength: tossing the caber (heaving a tree trunk into the air), throwing the hammer and putting the stone. The biggest Highland games are staged at Dunoon, Oban and Braemar.

SCOTTISH CULTURE SPORT

Curling, a winter sport that involves propelling a 19kg granite stone along the ice towards a target, was probably invented in Scotland in medieval times. For more information, see www.scottishcurling.org.

Shinty (*camanachd* in Gaelic) is a fast and physical ball-and-stick sport similar to Ireland's hurling, with more than a little resemblance to clan warfare. It's an indigenous Scottish game played mainly in the Highlands, and the most prized trophy is the Camanachd Cup. For more information, see www.shinty.com.

Natural Scotland

Visitors revel in rural Scotland's solitude and dramatic scenery. Soaring peaks, steely lochs, deep inlets, forgotten beaches and surging peninsulas evince astonishing geographic diversity. Scotland's wild places harbour Britain's most majestic wildlife, from the emblematic osprey to the red deer, its bellow reverberating among stands of native forest. Seals, dolphins and whales patrol the seas, islands moored in the Atlantic are havens for species long hunted to extinction further south, while the northeastern archipelagos clamour with seabird colonies of extraordinary magnitude.

The Land

Scotland accounts for one-third of the British mainland's surface area, but it has a massive 80% of Britain's coastline and only 10% of its population.

Scotland's mainland divides neatly into thirds. The Southern Uplands, ranges of grassy rounded hills bounded by fertile coastal plains, occupy the south, divided from the Lowlands by the Southern Uplands Fault.

The central Lowlands lie in a broad band stretching from Glasgow and Ayr in the west to Edinburgh and Dundee in the east. This area is underlain by sedimentary rocks, including beds of coal that fuelled Scotland's Industrial Revolution. It's only a fifth of the nation by land area, but it has most of the country's industry, its two largest cities and 80% of the population.

Another geological divide – the Highland Boundary Fault – marks the southern edge of the Scottish Highlands. These hills – with most of their summits around 900m to 1000m – were scoured by ice-age glaciers, creating a series of deep, U-shaped valleys, some now flooded by the long, narrow sea lochs that today are such a feature of west Highland scenery. The Highlands form 60% of the Scottish mainland, and are cut in two by the Great Glen, a long, glacier-gouged valley running southwest to northeast.

Despite their pristine beauty, the wild, empty landscapes of the western and northern Highlands are artificial wildernesses. Before the Highland Clearances (p437) many of these empty corners of Scotland supported sizeable rural populations.

Offshore, some 790 islands are concentrated in four main groups: the Shetland Islands, the Orkney Islands, the Outer Hebrides and the Inner Hebrides.

The Water

Some 90% of Britain's surface fresh water is found in Scotland, and Loch Lomond is Britain's largest body of fresh water (by area).

It rains a lot in Scotland – some parts of the western Highlands get over 4m of rainfall a year, compared to 2.3m in the Amazon Basin – so it's not surprising that there's plenty of water about. Around 3% of Scotland's land surface is fresh water. The numerous lochs, rivers and burns (streams) form the majority of this, but about a third is in the form of wetlands: the peat bogs and marshes that form a characteristic Highland and island landscape.

But it's salt water that really shapes the country. Including the islands, there's over 10,000 miles of tortuous, complex Scottish shoreline.

Mammals

While the Loch Ness monster still hogs headlines, Scotland's wild places harbour a wide variety of animals, including red deer, otters and 75% of Britain's red squirrels.

> ## WILDLIFE SAFARIS
>
> If you're pushed for time, you can improve your chances of spotting wildlife by joining a 'wildlife safari'. Many operators around the country run full- or half-day 4x4 safaris searching for eagles, deer and other species, or operate boat trips to spot seals, dolphins, whales and seabirds.
>
> **Ecoventures** (p304)
>
> **Hebridean Whale Cruises** (p368)
>
> **Highland Safaris** (p327)
>
> **Mull Wildlife Expeditions** (p282)
>
> **Hebridean Adventures** (p386)

Other small mammals include the Orkney vole and various bats, as well as stoats and weasels. The mountain hare swaps a grey-brown summer coat for a pure-white winter one.

Rarer beasts slaughtered to the point of near-extinction in the 19th century include pine martens, polecats and Scottish wildcats. Populations of these are small and remote but are slowly recovering.

Of course, most animals you'll see will be in fields or obstructing you on single-track roads. Several indigenous sheep varieties are still around, smaller and stragglier than the purpose-bred supermodels to which we're accustomed. Other emblematic domestic animals include the Shetland pony and the gentle Highland cow, with its broad horns and shaggy reddish-brown coat and fringe.

The waters are rich in marine mammals. Dolphins and porpoises are fairly common, and in summer minke whales are regular visitors. Orcas are regularly sighted around Shetland and Orkney. Seals are widespread. Both the Atlantic grey and common seal are easily seen on coasts and islands.

One of the best-loved pieces of Scottish wildlife writing is *Ring of Bright Water* (1960) by Gavin Maxwell, in which the author describes life on the remote Glenelg peninsula with his two pet otters in the 1950s.

Birds

Scotland has an immense variety of birds. For birdwatchers, the Shetland Islands are paradise. Twenty-one of the British Isles' 24 seabird species are found here, breeding in huge colonies. Being entertained by the puffins' clownish antics is a highlight for visitors.

Large numbers of red grouse – a popular game bird – graze the heather on the moors. The ptarmigan plays the Arctic trick of changing its plumage from mottled brown in summer to dazzling white in winter. In heavily forested areas you may see the capercaillie, a black, turkey-like bird that is the largest member of the grouse family. Millions of greylag geese winter on Lowland stubble fields.

The Royal Society for the Protection of Birds (RSPB; www.rspb.org.uk) is very active in Scotland. Several species have been successfully reintroduced, and the populations of other precariously placed species have stabilised, including those of ospreys (absent for most of the 20th century), golden eagles, white-tailed eagles, peregrine falcons and hen harriers.

Scottish Natural Heritage (www.nature.scot) is the government agency responsible for the conservation of Scotland's wildlife, habitats and landscapes. A key initiative is to reverse biodiversity loss.

National Parks

Scotland has two national parks – Loch Lomond & the Trossachs and the Cairngorms. There's a huge range of other protected areas: 43 national nature reserves (www.nnr.scot) span the country, and there are also marine areas under various levels of protection.

Environmental Issues

Scotland's abundance of wind and water means the government hasn't had to look far for sources of renewable energy. The ambitious grand plan is to generate 100% of the country's electricity needs from renewable

FIVE ICONIC SCOTTISH SPECIES

Red Deer

The red deer, Britain's largest land animal, is present in large numbers in Scotland. You're bound to see them if you spend any time in the Highlands; in winter especially, harsh weather will force them down into the glens to crop the roadside verges. But the most spectacular time to spot them is during the rutting season (late September and October), when stags roar and clash antlers in competition for females.

Best places to spot Jura, Rum, Torridon, Galloway

Golden Eagle

Perhaps the most majestic wildlife sight on moor and mountain is the golden eagle, which uses its 2m wingspan to soar on rising thermals as it hunts for its favourite prey, the mountain hare. Almost all of the 400 or so pairs known to nest in the UK are to be found in the Scottish Highlands and islands, as they prefer remote glens and open moorland well away from human habitation.

Best places to spot Harris, Skye, Rum, Mull

Red Squirrel

Scotland's woods are home to 75% of Britain's red-squirrel population; in most of the rest of the UK they've been pushed out by the dominant grey squirrel, introduced from North America. The greys often carry a virus that's lethal to the reds, so measures are in place to try to prevent their further encroachment.

Best places to spot Galloway Forest Park, Glen Affric, Landmark Forest Adventure Park, Rothiemurchus

Otter

From a low point in the late 20th century, when the population was decimated by hunting, pollution and habitat loss, otters have made a comeback and are now widespread in Scotland. They frequent fresh and salt water but are easiest to spot along the coast, where they time their foraging to coincide with an ebbing tide (river otters tend to be nocturnal).

Best places to spot Orkney, Shetland, Skye, Outer Hebrides; the piers at Kyle of Lochalsh and Portree are otter 'hot spots', as they have learned to scavenge from fishing boats

Scottish Wildcat

Trapping, hunting, habitat loss and interbreeding with feral domestic cats have made the Scottish wildcat Britain's most endangered mammal; it's thought that fewer than 400 purebred individuals survive. It hunts around the edges of woodland at dawn and dusk and is very wary of humans; seeing one in the wild is extremely rare.

Best places to spot Angus Glens, Strathpeffer area, Highland Wildlife Park (in captivity)

sources by 2020 (and total energy needs by 2030). And things are going to plan, with a level of 68% achieved by 2016, and a solid commitment to reject fracking and nuclear power.

Though a major goal is to halt a worrying decline in biodiversity, climate change is a huge threat to existing species. Temperature rises would leave plenty of mountain plants and creatures with no place to go; a steady decline in Scotland's seabird population is also surmised to have been partly caused by a temperature-induced decrease in plankton.

The main cause, however, of the worrying level of fish stocks is clear: we've eaten them all. In 2010 the *Marine (Scotland) Act* was passed. It's a compromise solution that tries to both protect vulnerable marine stocks and sustain the flagging fishing industry, which is pinning its hopes on Brexit freeing it from the EU's Common Fisheries Policy.

Survival Guide

Directory A–Z

Accessible Travel

Travellers with disabilities will find a strange mix of accessibility and inaccessibility in Scotland. Most new buildings are accessible to wheelchair users, so modern hotels and tourist attractions are fine. However, most B&Bs and guesthouses are in hard-to-adapt older buildings, which means that travellers with mobility problems may pay more for accommodation. Things are constantly improving, though.

It's a similar story with public transport. Newer buses have steps that lower for easier access, as do trains, but it's wise to check before setting out. Tourist attractions usually reserve parking spaces near the entrance for drivers with disabilities.

Many places such as ticket offices and banks are fitted with hearing loops to assist the hearing-impaired; look for a posted symbol of a large ear.

An increasing number of tourist attractions have audio guides. Some have Braille guides or scented gardens for the visually impaired.

Download Lonely Planet's free Accessible Travel guides from http://lptravel.to/AccessibleTravel.

VisitScotland (www.visitscotland.com/accommodation) Details accessible accommodation; many tourist offices have leaflets with accessibility details for their area. Also produces the guide *Accessible Scotland* for travellers using wheelchairs. Many regions have organisations that hire out wheelchairs; contact the local tourist office for details. Many nature trails have been adapted for wheelchair use.

Disability Rights UK (☎020-7250 8181; www.disabilityrightsuk.org) This is an umbrella organisation for voluntary groups for people with disabilities. Many wheelchair-accessible toilets can be opened only with a special Royal Association of Disability & Rehabilitation (Radar) key, which can be obtained via the website or from tourist offices for £5.40.

Disabled Persons Railcard (www.disabledpersons-railcard.co.uk) Discounted train travel. Costs £20.

Tourism for All (☎0845 124 9971; www.tourismforall.org.uk) Publishes regional information guides for travellers with disabilities and can offer general advice.

Accommodation

For budget travel, the options are campsites, hostels and cheap B&Bs. Above this price level is a plethora of comfortable B&Bs, pubs and guesthouses (£35 to £60 per person per night). Midrange hotels are present in most places, while in the higher price bracket (£65-plus per person per night) there are some superb hotels, the most interesting being converted castles and country houses, or chic designer options in cities.

If you're travelling solo, expect to pay a supplement in hotels and B&Bs, meaning you'll often be forking out over 75% of the price of a double for your single room.

Rates at almost all B&Bs, guesthouses and hotels (and even some hostels) include breakfast, either full Scottish or continental style. If you don't want it, you may be able to negotiate a lower price, but this is rare.

Prices increase over the peak tourist season (June to September) and are at their highest in July and August. Outside these months, and particularly in winter, special deals are often available at guesthouses and hotels.

BOOK YOUR STAY ONLINE

For more accommodation reviews by Lonely Planet authors, check out http://lonelyplanet.com/hotels/. You'll find independent reviews, as well as recommendations on the best places to stay. Best of all, you can book online.

Booking Services

VisitScotland tourist offices offer an accommodation-booking service, which can be handy, but note that they can only book places that are registered with VisitScotland. There are many other fine options that, mostly due to the hefty registration fee, choose not to register with the tourist board.

VisitScotland (www.visitscotland.com/accommodation) Accommodation approved by the official tourist board.

Scottish Cottages (www.scottish-cottages.co.uk) Booking service for self-catering cottages.

Lonely Planet (www.lonelyplanet.com/scotland/hotels) Recommendations and bookings.

B&Bs & Guesthouses

B&Bs – bed and breakfasts – are an institution in Scotland. At the bottom end you get a bedroom in a private house, a shared bathroom and the 'full Scottish' (fruit juice, coffee or tea, cereal and cooked breakfast – bacon, eggs, sausage, baked beans and toast). Midrange B&Bs have en suite bathrooms, TVs in each room and more variety (and healthier options) for breakfast. Almost all B&Bs provide hospitality trays (tea- and coffee-making facilities) in bedrooms. Common B&B options range from urban houses to pubs and farmhouses.

Guesthouses, often large converted private houses, are an extension of the B&B concept. They are normally bigger and less personal than B&Bs.

Bothies, Barns & Bunkhouses

Bothies are simple shelters, often in remote places; many are maintained by the Mountain Bothies Association (www.mountainbothies.org.uk). They're not locked, there's no charge and usually no toilets – and you can't book. Take your own cooking equipment, sleeping bag and mat. Users should stay one

night only, and leave the place as they find it.

Camping barns – usually converted farm buildings – offer shared sleeping space for around £5 to £10 per night. Take your own cooking equipment, sleeping bag and mat.

Bunkhouses, a grade or two up from camping barns, have stoves for heating and cooking and may supply utensils. They may have mattresses, but you'll still need a sleeping bag. There will be toilets but probably no showers. Most charge from £10 to £15 per person.

In Shetland, the Shetland Amenity Trust (www.camping-bods.com) has created a number of **böds** – converted croft houses or fishing huts with bunks, and washing and cooking facilities, but often no electricity or heating – many in remote and dramatic locations. Beds cost £10 to £12, but you'll need to prebook through the trust in Lerwick, which will give you the keys.

Camping & Caravan Sites

Free wild camping (p34) became a legal right under the Land Reform Bill of 2003. However, campers are obliged to camp on unenclosed land, in small numbers, and away from buildings and roads.

Most commercial campsites offer a variety of pitches for touring campers – hard-standing and grass, with or without electricity – and accept tents, campervans and caravans; some are caravan only.

VisitScotland (www.visitscotland.com/accommodation) Book

registered campsites; listings also available on a free map available at tourist offices.

Cool Camping (www.coolcamping.com) Booking service for offbeat, remote and interesting campsites, including 'glamping' options.

Camping & Caravanning Club (www.campingandcaravanningclub.co.uk) Listings of sites across the country.

Hostels

Backpacker hostels offer cheap, sociable accommodation, and in Scotland the standard of facilities is generally very good. The more upmarket hostels have en suite bathrooms in their dorms, and all manner of luxuries that give them the feel of hotels, if it weren't for the bunk beds.

Hostels nearly always have facilities for self-catering, and, apart from very remote ones, internet access of some kind. Many can arrange activities and tours.

INDEPENDENT HOSTELS

There is a large number of independent hostels, most with prices around £16 to £25 per person. Facilities vary considerably. Scottish Independent Hostels (www.hostel-scotland.co.uk) is an affiliation of over 100 hostels in Scotland, mostly in the north. You can browse them online or pick up the free *Scottish Independent Hostels* map-guide from tourist offices.

SYHA HOSTELS

The **Scottish Youth Hostels Association** (SYHA; ☎01786-891400;

www.syha.org.uk; annual membership 26yr & over/25yr & under £15/6, life membership £150) has a network of decent, reasonably priced hostels and produces a free booklet that's available from SYHA hostels and tourist offices. There are dozens of hostels to choose from around Scotland, ranging from basic walkers' digs to mansions and castles. You must be an HI member to stay, but nonmembers can pay a £3 supplement per night that goes towards the annual membership fee. Prices vary according to the month but average around £18 to £25 per adult in high season.

Most SYHA hostels close from around mid-October to early March, but they can be rented out by groups.

Hotels

There are some wonderfully luxurious places, including elegant country-house hotels in fabulous settings, and castles complete with crenellated battlements, grand staircases and the obligatory rows of stag heads. Expect all the perks at these places, often including gym, sauna, pool and first-class service. Even if you're on a budget, it's worth splashing out for a night at one of the classic Highland hotels.

In the cities, dullish chain options dominate the mid-range category, though there are some quirkier places to be found in Glasgow and Edinburgh.

Increasingly, hotels use an airline-style pricing system, so it's worth booking well ahead to take advantage of the cheapest rates.

Rental Accommodation

Self-catering accommodation is very popular in Scotland, and staying in an apartment in a city or a cottage in the country gives you the opportunity to get a feel for a place and its community. The minimum stay is usually one week in the summer peak season, and three days or less at other times.

Accommodation of this type varies widely, from rustic one-bedroom cottages with basic facilities and sheep cropping the grass outside to castles, historic houses and purpose-built designer retreats with every mod con.

The best place to start looking for this kind of accommodation is the VisitScotland (www.visitscotland.com/accommodation) website, which lists numerous options all over the country. These also appear in the regional accommodation guides available from tourist offices. A quick internet search will reveal many websites listing thousands of self-catering places across Scotland.

Expect a week's rent for a two-bedroom cottage to cost from £250 in winter, and up to £600 or more July to September.

University Accommodation

Many Scottish universities offer their student accommodation to visitors during the summer holidays (late June to August). Most rooms are comfy, functional single bedrooms, some with shared bathroom, but there are also twin and family units, self-contained flats and shared houses. Full-board, half-board, B&B and self-catering options are often available. Rooms are usually let out from late June to mid-September.

Children

Scotland offers a range of child-friendly accommodation and activities suitable for families.

It's worth asking in tourist offices for local family-focused publications. *The List* magazine (available at newsagents and bookshops) has a section on children's activities and events in and around Glasgow and Edinburgh.

The **National Trust for Scotland** (☑0131-458 0200; www.nts.org.uk; annual membership adult/family £57/102) and **Historic Environment Scotland** (HES; ☑0131-668 8999; www.historicenvironment. scot; annual membership adult/family £55/101) organise family-friendly activities at their properties throughout summer.

Children are generally well received around Scotland, and every area has some child-friendly attractions and B&Bs. Even dryish local museums usually make an effort with an activity sheet or child-focused information panels.

A lot of pubs are family-friendly and some have great beer gardens where kids can run around and exhaust themselves while you have a quiet pint. However, be aware that many Scottish pubs, even those that serve bar meals, are forbidden by law to admit children under 14. In family-friendly pubs (ie those in possession of a Children's Certificate), accompanied under-14s are admitted between 11am and 8pm. There's no clear indication on which is which: just ask the bartender.

Children under a certain age can often stay free with their parents in hotels, but be prepared for hotels and B&Bs (normally upmarket ones) that won't accept children; call ahead to get the low-down. More hotels and guesthouses these days provide child-friendly facilities, including cots. Many restaurants (especially the larger ones) have highchairs and decent children's menus.

Breastfeeding in public is accepted and breastfeeding is actively encouraged by government campaigns.

The larger car-hire companies can provide safety seats for children, but they're worth booking well ahead.

See also Lonely Planet's *Travel with Children*.

Customs Regulations

Travellers arriving in the UK from EU countries don't have to pay tax or duty on goods for personal use, and can bring in as much EU duty-paid alcohol and tobacco as they like. However, if you bring in more than the following, you'll probably be asked some questions:

➡ 800 cigarettes
➡ 1kg of tobacco
➡ 10L of spirits
➡ 90L of wine
➡ 110L of beer

Travellers from outside the EU can bring in, duty free:

➡ 200 cigarettes *or* 100 cigarillos *or* 50 cigars *or* 250g of tobacco
➡ 16L of beer
➡ 4L of nonsparkling wine
➡ 1L of spirits *or* 2L of fortified wine or sparkling wine
➡ £390 worth of all other goods, including perfume, gifts and souvenirs

Anything over this limit must be declared to customs officers on arrival. Check www.gov.uk/duty-free-goods for further details, and for information on reclaiming VAT on items purchased in the UK by non-EU residents.

Discount Cards
Historic Sites

Membership of Historic Environment Scotland (HES) and/or the National Trust for Scotland (NTS) is worth considering, especially if you're going to be in Scotland for a while. Both are

organisations dedicated to the preservation of the environment, and both care for hundreds of spectacular sites. You can join at any of their properties.

Historic Environment Scotland (HES; ☑0131-668 8999; www.historicenvironment.scot; annual membership adult/family £55/101) This organisation cares for hundreds of sites of historical importance. An annual membership costs £55/101 and gives free entry to HES sites (half-price entry to sites in England and Wales). Also offers a short-term Explorer Pass – three days out of five for £31, or seven days out of 14 for £42. It can be great value, particularly if you visit both Edinburgh and Stirling Castles.

National Trust for Scotland (☑0131-458 0200; www.nts.org.uk; annual membership adult/family £57/102) NTS looks after hundreds of sites of historical, architectural or environmental importance. An annual membership, costing £57/102 per adult/family, offers free access to all NTS and National Trust properties (in the rest of the UK). If you're 25 or under, it's a great deal at only £26.

Hostel Cards

If travelling on a budget, membership of the **Scottish Youth Hostels Association** (SYHA; ☑01786-891400; www.syha.org.uk; annual membership 26yr & over/25yr & under £15/6, life membership £150) is a must.

Senior Cards

Discount cards for those over 60 years are available for train travel (p468).

Student & Youth Cards

The most useful card is the International Student Identity Card (www.isic.org), which displays your photo. It gives you discounted entry to many attractions and on many forms of transport.

Electricity

230V, 50Hz; UK-type plug with three flat pins.

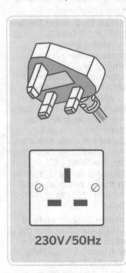

230V/50Hz

Health

→ If you're an EU citizen, a European Health Insurance Card (EHIC) – available from health centres or, in the UK, post offices – covers you for most medical care. An EHIC will not cover you for non-urgent cases or emergency repatriation. The status of EHIC after Brexit (March 2019) is uncertain.

→ Citizens from non-EU countries should find out if there is a reciprocal arrangement for free medical care between their country and the UK. Australian travellers are eligible for free essential health care, for example.

→ If you do need health insurance, make sure you get a policy that covers you for the worst possible scenarios, including emergency flights home.

→ No jabs (vaccinations) are required to travel to Scotland.

Ticks & Lyme Disease

Ticks are tiny invertebrates (barely 1mm or 2mm across) that feed on the blood of sheep, deer and, occasionally, humans. They lurk amid vegetation and clamber on as you brush past; then they find a spot of bare flesh and tuck in. Their bites are painless and, for the most part, harmless (they will drop off once full). But a small percentage of ticks are known to transmit Lyme disease, a potentially serious infection.

Ticks occur all over Scotland in woodlands, moorlands and long grass, but mainly in the wetter areas of the western Highlands. They are active mainly between March and October. Tips for avoiding ticks include sticking to paths, wearing long trousers tucked into socks, and using insect repellent. Check yourself (and your children and pets) for ticks after hiking, especially around the hairline, in the navel, groin and armpits, and between the toes, behind the ears and behind the knees. Outdoor shops sell plastic tick-removal tools.

More information: https://www.mountaineering.scot/safety-and-skills/health-and-hygiene/ticks.

Insurance

Insurance covers you not only for medical expenses, theft or loss but also for cancellation of, or delays in, any of your travel arrangements.

Lots of bank accounts give their holders automatic travel insurance – check if this is the case for you.

Always read the small print carefully. Some policies specifically exclude 'dangerous activities', such as scuba-diving, motorcycling, skiing, mountaineering and even trekking.

There's a variety of policies, and your travel agent can give recommendations. Make sure the policy includes healthcare and medication in the countries you may visit on your way to/from Scotland.

You may prefer a policy that pays doctors or hospitals directly rather than forcing you to pay on the spot and claim the money back later. If you have to claim later, make sure you keep all documentation. Some policies ask you to call back (reverse charges) to a centre in your home country, where an immediate assessment of your problem will be made.

Not all policies cover ambulances, helicopter rescue or emergency flights home. Most policies exclude cover for pre-existing illnesses.

Worldwide travel insurance is available at www.lonelyplanet.com/travel-insurance. You can buy, extend and claim online anytime – even if you're already on the road.

Internet Access

→ If you're travelling with a laptop or smartphone, you'll find a wide range of places offering a wi-fi connection. These range from cafes to B&Bs and public spaces. Nearly all accommodation offers it.

→ Wi-fi is often free, but some places (typically, upmarket hotels and SYHA hostels) charge.

→ There are good deals on pay-as-you-go mobile data from mobile-network providers.

→ If you don't have a laptop or smartphone, the best places to check email and surf the internet are public libraries – nearly all of them have at least a couple of computer terminals, and they are free to use, though there's often a time limit.

→ Internet cafes also still exist in the cities and larger towns and are generally good value, charging approximately £2 to £3 per hour.

Language Courses

Scotland is a popular place to learn English, and there are numerous places to do it. Dedicated language academies offer intensive tuition at a price and can also arrange accommodation in residences or with local families. Much cheaper are colleges, some of which even offer free English classes for foreigners.

A good resource to start you off is the English UK Scotland (www.englishuk scotland.com) website, which has details of many colleges and language schools, mostly in Edinburgh and Glasgow.

Legal Matters

➡ The 1707 Act of Union preserved the Scottish legal system as separate from the law in England and Wales.

➡ Police have the power to detain, for up to 24 hours, anyone suspected of having committed an offence punishable by imprisonment (including drug offences).

➡ If you need legal assistance, contact the **Scottish Legal Aid Board** (☑ 0131-226 7061; www.slab.org.uk; 91 Haymarket Tce, Edinburgh).

➡ Possession of cannabis is illegal, with a spoken warning for first offenders with small amounts. Fines and prison sentences apply for repeat offences and larger quantities. Possession of harder drugs is much more serious. Police have the right to search anyone they suspect of possessing drugs.

LGBTIQ+ Travellers

Although most Scots are tolerant of homosexuality, couples overtly displaying affection away from acknowledged 'gay' venues

---

MIDGES

If you've never been to the Scottish Highlands and islands before, be prepared for an encounter with the dreaded midge. These tiny, 2mm-long blood-sucking flies appear in huge swarms in summer, and can completely ruin a holiday if you're not prepared to deal with them.

They proliferate from late May to mid-September, but especially mid-June to mid-August – which unfortunately coincides with the main tourist season – and are most common in the western and northern Highlands. Midges are at their worst during the twilight hours, and on still, overcast days – strong winds and bright sunshine tend to discourage them.

The only way to combat them is to cover up, particularly in the evening. Wear long-sleeved, light-coloured clothing (midges are attracted to dark colours) and, most importantly, use a reliable insect repellent.

---

or districts may encounter disapproval.

Edinburgh and Glasgow have small but flourishing gay scenes. The website and monthly magazine *Scotsgay* (www.facebook.com/ ScotsGayMag) keeps folk informed about LGBTIQ-scene issues.

Maps

If you're going to do some hill walking, you'll require maps with far greater detail than the free maps supplied by tourist offices. The Ordnance Survey (OS) caters to walkers, with a wide variety of maps at 1:50,000 and 1:25,000 scales. Alternatively, look out for the excellent walkers maps published by Harvey; they're at scales of 1:40,000 and 1:25,000.

Money
ATMs

ATMs (called cashpoints in Scotland) are widespread and you'll usually find at least one in small towns and villages. You can use Visa, MasterCard, Amex, Cirrus, Plus and Maestro to withdraw cash from ATMs belonging to most banks

and building societies in Scotland.

Cash withdrawals from some ATMs may be subject to a small charge, but most are free. If you're not from the UK, your home bank will likely charge you for withdrawing money overseas; it pays to be aware of how much, as it may be much better to withdraw larger amounts less often.

If there's no ATM, it's often possible to get 'cash back' at a hotel or shop in remote areas – ie make a payment by debit card and get some cash back (the cash amount is added to the transaction).

Credit & Debit Cards

Credit and debit cards can be used almost everywhere except for some B&Bs that only accept cash. Make sure bars or restaurants will accept cards before you order, as some don't. The most popular cards are Visa and MasterCard; American Express is only accepted by the major chains, and virtually no one will accept Diners or JCB. Chip-and-PIN is the norm for card transactions; only a few places will accept a signature. Contactless card payments (up to £30) are increasingly accepted.

Moneychangers

Be careful using bureaux de change; they may offer good exchange rates but frequently levy outrageous commissions and fees. The best-value places to change money in the UK tend to be travel agents. A handy tool for finding the best rates is the website http://travelmoney. moneysavingexpert.com/ buy-back.

You'll normally find better rates in London than in Scotland, so do your changing there if you're visiting that city first.

Banks, post offices and some of the larger hotels will change cash and travellers cheques.

Tipping

Hotels One pound per bag is standard; gratuities for cleaning staff are completely at your discretion.

Pubs Not expected unless table service is provided, then £1 for a round of drinks.

Restaurants For decent service 10%; up to 15% at more expensive places. Check to see if service has been added to the bill already (most likely for large groups).

Taxis Fares are generally rounded up to the nearest pound.

Opening Hours

Hours may vary throughout the year; in rural areas many places have shorter hours from around October to April. In the Highlands and islands Sunday opening is restricted.

Banks 9.30am–4pm Monday to Friday, some to 1pm Saturday.

Post offices 9am–6pm Monday to Friday, to 12.30pm Saturday.

Nightclubs 9pm–1am Thursday to Saturday.

Pubs 11am–11pm Monday to Thursday, to 1am Friday and Saturday, 12.30pm–11pm Sunday; lunch noon–2.30pm, dinner 6pm–9pm daily.

Shops 9am–5.30pm Monday to Saturday, often 11am–5pm Sunday.

Restaurants Lunch noon–2.30pm, dinner 6pm–9pm.

Post

The **UK Post Office** (www. postoffice.co.uk) is a reliable service with a network of dedicated mail centres as well as shops with post-office facilities. Mail sent within the UK can go either 1st or 2nd class. First-class mail is faster (there's normally next-day delivery) and slightly more expensive.

Public Holidays

Although bank holidays are general public holidays in the rest of the UK, in Scotland they only apply to banks and some other commercial offices.

Scottish towns normally have four days of public holiday, which they allocate themselves; dates vary from year to year and from town to town. Most places celebrate St Andrew's Day (30 November) as a public holiday.

General public holidays:

New Year 1 and 2 January

Good Friday March or April

Christmas Day 25 December

Boxing Day 26 December

Telephone

You'll mainly see two types of phone booth in Scotland: one takes money (and doesn't give change), while the other uses prepaid phonecards and credit cards. Some phones accept both coins and cards. Payphone cards are widely available.

The cheapest way of calling internationally is via the internet, or by buying a discount-call card; you'll see these in newsagents, along with tables of countries and the number of minutes you'll get for your money.

Mobile Phones

The UK uses the GSM 900/1800 network, which covers the rest of Europe, Australia and New Zealand but isn't compatible with the North American GSM 1900 network. Most modern mobiles can function on both networks, but check before you leave home just in case.

Roaming charges within the EU have been eliminated (though charges may re-appear when the UK leaves the EU in 2019). Other international roaming charges can be prohibitively high, and you'll probably find it cheaper to get a UK number. This is easily done by buying a SIM card (around £1) and sticking it into your phone. Your phone may be locked to your home network, however, so you'll have to either get it unlocked or buy a cheap phone to use.

Operators offer a variety of packages that include UK calls, messages and data; a month's worth will typically cost around £20.

Though things are improving, coverage in Highland and island areas can be sketchy; don't rely on mobile data.

Pay-as-you-go phones can be recharged online or by buying vouchers from shops.

Phone Codes & Useful Numbers

Dialling the UK Dial your country's international access code, then 44 (the UK country code), then the area code (dropping the first 0) followed by the telephone number.

Dialling out of the UK The international access code is 00; dial this, then add the code of the country you wish to dial.

Making a reverse-charges (collect) international call Dial 155 for the operator. It's an expensive option, but not for the caller.

Area codes in Scotland Begin with 01; eg Edinburgh 0131, Wick 01955.

Directory assistance There are several numbers; 118500 is one.

Mobile phones Codes usually begin with 07.

Free calls Numbers starting with 0800 are free; calls to 0845 numbers are charged at local rates.

Time

Scotland is on UTC/GMT +1 hour during summer daylight-saving time (late March to late October) and UTC/GMT +0 the rest of the year.

Toilets

➡ Public toilets increasingly uncommon but still found in larger cities.

➡ Usually free, but some public toilets charge a small fee.

Tourist Information

The Scottish Tourist Board is known as **VisitScotland** (www.visitscotland.com). You can request regional brochures to be posted out to you, or download them from the website.

Most larger towns have tourist offices ('information centres') that open from 9am or 10am to 5pm Monday to Friday, and at weekends in summer. In small places, particularly in the Highlands, tourist offices only open from Easter to September.

If you want to email a tourist office, it's [insert townname]@visitscotland. com.

Visas

➡ If you're a citizen of the EEA (European Economic Area) nations or Switzerland, you don't need a visa to enter or work in Britain – you can enter using your national identity card.

➡ Visa regulations are always subject to change, which is especially likely after Britain's exit from the EU on 29 March 2019, so it's essential to check before leaving home.

➡ Currently, if you're a citizen of Australia, Canada, New Zealand, Japan, Israel, the US and several other countries, you can stay for up to six months (no visa required) but are not allowed to work.

➡ Nationals of many countries, including South Africa, will need to obtain a visa: for more info, see www. gov.uk/browse/visas -immigration.

➡ The Youth Mobility Scheme, for Australian, Canadian, Japanese, Hong Kong, Monégasque, New Zealand, South Korean and Taiwanese citizens aged 18 to 31, allows working visits of up to two years but must be applied for in advance.

➡ Commonwealth citizens with a UK-born parent may be eligible for a Certificate of Entitlement to the Right of Abode, which entitles them to live and work in the UK.

➡ Commonwealth citizens with a UK-born grandparent could qualify for a UK Ancestry Employment Certificate, allowing them to work full time for up to five years in the UK.

➡ British immigration authorities have always been tough; dress neatly and carry proof that you have sufficient funds with which to support yourself. A credit card and/ or an onward ticket will help.

Volunteering

Various organisations offer volunteering opportunities in Scotland, with conservation, organic-farming and animal-welfare projects to the fore.

Women Travellers

Solo women travellers are likely to feel safe in Scotland.

The contraceptive pill is available only on prescription; however, the 'morning-after' pill (effective against conception for up to 72 hours after unprotected sexual intercourse) is available over the counter at chemists.

Work

Whatever your skills, it's worth registering with a number of temporary employment agencies; there are plenty in the cities.

Low-paid seasonal work is available in the tourist industry, usually in restaurants and pubs.

At the time of research, EU citizens didn't need a work permit, but this may change as a result of Britain's planned exit from the EU on 29 March 2019.

The Youth Mobility Scheme allows working visits for some foreign nationals.

Transport

GETTING THERE & AWAY

Flights, cars and tours can be booked online at www.lonelyplanet.com/bookings.

Entering the Country

The UK's withdrawal from the EU on 29 March 2019 means that information in this section is liable to change; it's important to check the current regulations before travel.

Air

There are direct flights to Scottish airports from Britain, lots of European countries, the Middle East, the US and Canada. From elsewhere, you'll probably have to fly into a European or Middle Eastern hub and get a connecting flight to a Scottish airport – London has the most connections. This will often be a cheaper option anyway if flying in from North America.

Airports

Scotland has four main international airports: Aberdeen, Edinburgh, Glasgow and Glasgow Prestwick, with a few short-haul international flights landing at Inverness. London is the main UK gateway for long-haul flights. Sumburgh on Shetland has summer service from Norway.

Aberdeen Airport (ABZ; ☑0844 481 6666; www.aberdeenairport.com) Located at Dyce, 6 miles northwest of the city centre. There are regular flights to numerous Scottish and UK destinations, including Orkney and Shetland, and international flights to several European countries.

Edinburgh Airport (EDI; ☑0844 448 8833; www.edinburghairport.com) Eight miles west of the city, this airport has numerous flights to other parts of Scotland and the UK, Ireland and mainland Europe, as well as long-haul flights to the US, Canada, the UAE and Qatar.

Glasgow Airport (GLA; ☑0344 481 5555; www.glasgowairport.com; ☎) Glasgow's principal airport offers connections all over Scotland, Britain and Europe. Long-haul destinations include the US, Canada and Dubai.

Glasgow Prestwick Airport (PIK; ☑0871 223 0700; www.glasgowprestwick.com) Southwest of Glasgow near Ayr, this airport is a Ryanair hub serving mainly holiday destinations in southern Europe.

Inverness Airport (INV; ☑01667-464000; www.invernessairport.co.uk) At Dalcross, east of the city, this airport has direct flights to several British and western-European destinations.

London Gatwick (www.gatwickairport.com) London's second airport, with numerous flights to Scotland.

London Heathrow (www.heathrow.com) Britain's principal international airport.

CLIMATE CHANGE & TRAVEL

Every form of transport that relies on carbon-based fuel generates CO_2, the main cause of human-induced climate change. Modern travel is dependent on aeroplanes, which might use less fuel per kilometre per person than most cars but travel much greater distances. The altitude at which aircraft emit gases (including CO_2) and particles also contributes to their climate change impact. Many websites offer 'carbon calculators' that allow people to estimate the carbon emissions generated by their journey and, for those who wish to do so, to offset the impact of the greenhouse gases emitted with contributions to portfolios of climate-friendly initiatives throughout the world. Lonely Planet offsets the carbon footprint of all staff and author travel.

Land

Bus

Buses are usually the cheapest way to get to Scotland from other parts of the UK.

Megabus (☎0141-352 4444; www.megabus.com) One-way fares from London to Glasgow from as little as £1 if you book well in advance. Has some fully reclinable sleeper services.

National Express (☎0871 781 8181; www.nationalexpress. com) Regular services from London and other cities in England and Wales to Glasgow and Edinburgh.

Scottish Citylink (☎0871 266 3333; www.citylink.co.uk) Daily service between Belfast and Glasgow and Edinburgh via Cairnryan ferry.

Car & Motorcycle

Drivers of EU-registered vehicles will find bringing a car or motorcycle into Scotland fairly easy. Note: this may change following the UK's exit from the EU on 29 March 2019; check the latest situation before travelling.

The vehicle must have registration papers and a nationality plate, and you must have insurance. The International Insurance Certificate (Green Card) isn't compulsory, but it's excellent proof that you're covered.

If driving from mainland Europe via the Channel Tunnel or ferry ports, head for London and follow the M25 orbital road to the M1 motorway, then follow the M1 and M6 north.

Train

Travelling to Scotland by train is faster and usually more comfortable than the bus, but it's more expensive. Taking into account check-in and travel time between city centre and airport, the train is a competitive alternative to air travel from London. The **National Rail Enquiry Service** (☎03457 48 49 50;

www.nationalrail.co.uk) has timetable and fare info for all trains in Britain.

Virgin Trains East Coast (www. virgintrainseastcoast.com) Trains between London Kings Cross and Edinburgh (4½ hours, every half-hour).

Eurostar (www.eurostar.com) You can travel from Paris or Brussels to London in around two hours on the Eurostar service. From St Pancras, it's a quick and easy change to Kings Cross or Euston for trains to Edinburgh or Glasgow.

Caledonian Sleeper (www. sleeper.scot) This is an overnight service connecting London Euston with Edinburgh, Glasgow, Stirling, Perth, Dundee, Aberdeen, Fort William and Inverness. There are two departures nightly from Sunday to Friday.

Virgin Trains (www.virgintrains. co.uk) Trains between London Euston and Glasgow (4½ hours, hourly).

Crosscountry (☎0844 811 0124; www.crosscountrytrains. co.uk) Trains between Wales, central and southwest England to Glasgow, Edinburgh and Aberdeen.

TransPennine Express (www. tpexpress.co.uk) Trains from Manchester to Glasgow and Edinburgh.

Sea

Car-ferry links between Northern Ireland and Scotland are operated by **Stena Line** (☎08447 70 70 70; www.stenaline.co.uk) and **P&O** (☎01304-448888; www. poferries.com). Stena Line travels the Belfast–Cairnryan route and P&O Irish Sea the Larne–Cairnryan route.

GETTING AROUND

Air

Most domestic air services are geared to business needs, or are lifelines for remote island communities. Flying is a pricey way to cover relatively short distances, but it's certainly worth considering if you're short of time and want to visit the Outer Hebrides, Orkney or Shetland.

Airlines in Scotland

Eastern Airways (☎0870 366 9100; www.easternairways. com) Flies from Aberdeen to Stornoway and Wick.

Loganair (☎0344 800 2855; www.loganair.co.uk) The main domestic airline in Scotland, with flights from Glasgow to Barra, Benbecula, Campbeltown, Kirkwall, Stornoway, Sumburgh and Tiree; from Edinburgh to Kirkwall, Stornoway, Sumburgh and Wick; from Aberdeen to Kirkwall, Sumburgh and Tiree; from Inverness to Benbecula, Kirkwall, Stornoway and Sumburgh; and from Stornoway to Benbecula. It also operates interisland flights in Orkney.

Hebridean Air (☎0845 805 7465; www.hebrideanair.co.uk; Oban Airport, North Connel) Flies from Connel airfield near Oban to the islands of Coll, Tiree, Colonsay and Islay.

Bicycle

Scotland is a compact country, and travelling around by bicycle is a perfectly feasible proposition if you have the time. Indeed, for touring the islands a bicycle is both cheaper than driving (for ferry fares) and more suited to the islands' small sizes and leisurely pace of life. For more information, see www.visitscotland.com/see-do/active and the Sustrans (www.sustrans.org.uk/scotland/national-cycle-network) pages about the National Cycle Network.

Boat

The Scottish government has introduced a scheme called the Road Equivalent Tariff (RET) on most ferry crossings. This reduces the price of ferry transport to what it would cost to drive the same distance by road, in the hope of attracting more tourists and reducing business costs on the islands. Fares on many crossings have been cut by as much as 60%, and signs are that the scheme has been successful, with visitor numbers well up.

Caledonian MacBrayne (CalMac; ☎0800 066 5000; www.calmac.co.uk) Serves the west coast and islands. A comprehensive timetable booklet is available from tourist offices and online. There's a summer timetable and one for winter, when services are reduced. CalMac offers 28 Island Hopscotch tickets, giving reduced fares for various combinations of crossings; these are listed online and in the timetable booklet. Bicycles travel free with foot-passenger tickets.

Northlink Ferries (☎0845 600 0449; www.northlinkferries.co.uk) Ferries from Aberdeen and Scrabster (near Thurso) to Orkney, from Orkney to Shetland and from Aberdeen to Shetland.

Bus

Scotland is served by an extensive bus network that covers most of the country. In remote rural areas, however, services are geared to the needs of locals (getting to school or the shops in the nearest large town) and may not be conveniently timed for visitors.

First (www.firstgroup.com) Operates local bus routes in several parts of Scotland.

Scottish Citylink (www.citylink.co.uk) National network of comfy, reliable buses serving main towns. Away from main roads, you'll need to switch to local services.

Stagecoach (www.stagecoachbus.com) Operates local bus routes in many parts of Scotland.

Bus Passes

National Entitlement Card (www.entitlementcard.org.uk) Available to seniors and people with disabilities who are Scottish citizens; allows free bus travel throughout the country. The youth version, for 11- to 26-year-olds, gives discounted travel, and SYHA members receive a 20% discount on Scottish Citylink services. Students do, too, by registering online.

Scottish Citylink Explorer Pass Offers unlimited travel on Scottish Citylink services (and selected other bus routes) within Scotland for any three days out of five (£49), any five days out of 10 (£74) or any eight days out of 16 (£99). Also gives discounts on various regional bus services, on Northlink and CalMac ferries,

and in SYHA hostels. Can be bought in the UK by both UK and overseas citizens.

Car & Motorcycle

Scotland's roads are generally good and are far less busy than those in England, making driving more enjoyable.

Motorways (designated 'M') are toll-free dual carriageways, limited mainly to central Scotland. Main roads ('A') are dual or single carriageways and are sometimes clogged with slow-moving trucks or caravans; the A9 from Perth to Inverness is notoriously busy.

Life on the road is more relaxed and interesting on the secondary roads (designated 'B') and minor roads (undesignated), although in the Highlands and islands there's the added hazard of sheep wandering onto the road (be particularly wary of lambs in spring).

Petrol is more expensive than in countries like the US or Australia but roughly in line with the rest of western Europe. Prices tend to rise as you get further from the main centres and are more than 10% higher in the Outer Hebrides. In remote areas petrol stations are widely spaced and sometimes closed on Sunday.

Car Hire

Car hire in the UK is competitively priced by European standards, and shopping around online can unearth some great deals, which can drop to as low as £23 per day for an extended hire period. Hit comparison sites like Kayak to find some of the best prices.

The minimum legal age for driving is 17, but to rent a car, drivers must usually be aged 23 to 65 – outside these limits special conditions or insurance requirements may apply.

If planning to visit the Outer Hebrides or Shetland,

it'll often prove cheaper to hire a car on the islands rather than paying to take a hire car across on the ferry.

Avis (www.avis.co.uk)

Budget (www.budget.co.uk)

Europcar (www.europcar.co.uk)

Hertz (www.hertz.co.uk)

Sixt (www.sixt.co.uk)

Driving Licences

A non-EU licence is valid in Britain for up to 12 months from time of entry into the country. If bringing a car from Europe, make sure you're adequately insured.

Road Rules

The *Highway Code,* widely available in bookshops, and also online and downloadable at www.gov.uk/highway-code, details all UK road regulations.

➡ Vehicles drive on the left. Seatbelts are compulsory if fitted; this technically applies to buses, too.

➡ The speed limit is 30mph (48km/h) in built-up areas, 60mph (96km/h) on single carriageways and 70mph (112km/h) on dual carriageways.

➡ Give way to your right at roundabouts (traffic already on the roundabout has right of way).

➡ Motorcyclists must wear helmets. They are not compulsory for cyclists.

➡ It is illegal to use a hand-held mobile phone or similar device while driving.

➡ The maximum permitted blood-alcohol level when driving is 50mg/100mL (22mg per 100mL of breath); this is lower than in the rest of the UK but equivalent to the limit in many other countries.

➡ Traffic offences (illegal parking, speeding etc) usually incur a fine for which you're given 30 to 60 days to pay. In Glasgow and Edinburgh the parking inspectors are numerous

and without mercy – never leave your car around the city centres without a valid parking ticket, as you risk a hefty fine.

Hitching

Hitching is fairly easy in Scotland, except around big cities and in built-up areas, where you'll need to use public transport. Although the northwest is more difficult because there's less traffic, long waits are unusual (except on Sunday in 'Sabbath' areas). On some islands, where public transport is infrequent, hitching is so much a part of getting around that local drivers may stop and offer you lifts without your even asking.

It's against the law to hitch on motorways or their immediate slip roads; make a sign and use approach roads, nearby roundabouts or service stations.

Hitching is never entirely safe, however, and Lonely Planet doesn't recommend it. Travellers who hitch should understand that they are taking a small but potentially serious risk.

Tours

There are numerous companies in Scotland offering all kinds of tours, including historical, activity-based and backpacker tours. It's a question of picking the tour that suits your requirements and budget.

Discreet Scotland (☑07989 416990; www. discreetscotland.com) Luxurious private tours in an upmarket 4WD that range from day trips from Edinburgh to full weeks staying in some of Scotland's finest hotels.

Timberbush Tours (☑0131-226 6066; www.timberbush-tours.co.uk) Comfortable small-group minibus tours around Scotland, with Glasgow and Edinburgh departures.

Train

Scotland's train network extends to all major cities and towns, but the railway map has a lot of large, blank areas in the Highlands and the Southern Uplands where you'll need to switch to road transport. The West Highland line from Glasgow to Fort William and Mallaig, and the Inverness to Kyle of Lochalsh line, offer two of the world's most scenic rail journeys.

National Rail Enquiry Service (www.nationalrail.co.uk) Lists timetables and fares for all trains in Britain.

ScotRail (www.scotrail.co.uk) Operates most train services in Scotland; its website has downloadable timetables.

Costs & Reservations

Train travel is more expensive than the bus, but it's usually more comfortable.

Reservations are recommended for intercity trips, especially on Friday and public holidays. For shorter journeys, just buy a ticket at the station before you go. On certain routes, including the Glasgow–Edinburgh express, and in places where there's no ticket office at the station, you can buy tickets on the train.

Children under five travel free; those five to 15 years usually pay half-fare.

Bikes are carried free on all ScotRail trains, but space is sometimes limited. Bike reservations are compulsory on certain routes, including the Glasgow–Oban–Fort William–Mallaig line and the Inverness–Kyle of Lochalsh line; they're recommended on many others. You can make reservations for your bicycle from eight weeks to two hours in advance at main stations, or when booking tickets by phone or online.

There's a bewilderingly complex labyrinth of ticket types. In general, the further ahead you book, the cheaper your ticket will be.

TRAIN FARES

The complex British train-ticketing system rewards advance planning, particularly on long routes. A one-way fare from London to Edinburgh, for example, can cost over £150, but a fare purchased well in advance, at off-peak times, can be as low as £30. Regional fares in Scotland have a lot less variation.

Advance Purchase Book by 6pm on the day before travel; cheaper than Anytime tickets.

Anytime Buy any time and travel any time, with no restrictions.

Off Peak There are time restrictions (you're not usually allowed to travel on a train that leaves before 9.15am); relatively cheap.

It's always worth checking the ScotRail website for current family or senior offers.

Discount Cards

Discount railcards are available for people aged 60 and over, for people aged 16 to 25 (or mature full-time students), for two over-16s travelling together, and for those with a disability.

The **Senior Railcard** (www.senior-railcard.co.uk; per year £30), **16-25 Railcard** (Young Persons Railcard; www.16-25railcard.co.uk; per year £30), **Two Together Railcard** (www.twotogether -railcard.co.uk; per year £30) and **Disabled Persons Railcard** (www.disabledpersons -railcard.co.uk; per year £20) are each valid for a year and give one-third off most train fares in Scotland, England and Wales.

You'll find they pay for themselves pretty quickly if you plan to take a couple of long-distance journeys or a handful of short-distance ones. Fill in an application at any major station. You'll need proof of age (birth certificate, passport or driving licence) for the Young Persons and Senior Railcards (proof of enrolment for mature-age students) and proof of entitlement for the Disabled Persons Railcard. You'll need a passport photo for all of them. You can also buy railcards online, but you'll need a UK address to have them sent to.

Train Passes

ScotRail (☑0344 811 0141; www.scotrail.co.uk) has a range of good-value passes for train travel. You can buy them online, by phone or at stations throughout Britain. Note that Travelpass and Rover tickets are not valid for travel on certain (eg commuter) services before 9.15am weekdays.

Central Scotland Rover Covers train travel between Glasgow, Edinburgh, North Berwick, Stirling and Fife; costs £39 for three days' travel out of seven.

Spirit of Scotland Travelpass Gives unlimited travel on all Scottish train services (with some restrictions), all CalMac ferry services and on certain Scottish Citylink coach services (on routes not covered by rail). It's available for four days' travel out of eight (£139) or eight days' out of 15 (£179).

Highland Rover Allows unlimited train travel from Glasgow to Oban, Fort William and Mallaig, and from Inverness to Kyle of Lochalsh, Aviemore, Aberdeen and Thurso. It also gives free travel on the Oban/Fort William–Inverness bus, on the Oban–Mull and Mallaig–Skye ferries, and on buses on Mull and Skye. It's valid for four days' travel out of eight (£85).

Glossary

bag – reach the top of (as in to 'bag a couple of peaks' or 'Munro bagging')

bailey – the space enclosed by castle walls

birlinn – Hebridean galley

blackhouse – low-walled stone cottage with thatch or turf roof and earth floors; shared by both humans and cattle and typical of the Outer Hebrides until the early 20th century

böd – once a simple trading booth used by fishing communities, today it refers to basic accommodation for walkers etc

bothy – hut or mountain shelter

brae – hill

broch – defensive tower

burgh – town

burn – stream

cairn – pile of stones to mark path or junction; also peak

camanachd – Gaelic for *shinty*

ceilidh (*kay*-li) – evening of traditional Scottish entertainment including music, song and dance

Celtic high cross – a large, elaborately carved stone cross decorated with biblical scenes and Celtic interlace designs dating from the 8th to 10th centuries

chippy – fish-and-chip shop

Clearances – eviction of Highland farmers from their land by *lairds* wanting to use it for grazing sheep

Clootie dumpling – rich steamed pudding filled with currants and raisins

close – entrance to an alley

corrie – circular hollow on a hillside

craic – lively conversation

craig – exposed rock

crannog – an artificial island in a *loch* built for defensive purposes

crofting – smallholding in marginal agricultural areas following the Clearances

Cullen skink – soup made with smoked haddock, potato, onion and milk

dene – valley

dirk – dagger

dram – a measure of whisky

firth – estuary

gloup – natural arch

Hogmanay – Scottish celebration of New Year's Eve

howff – pub or shelter

HS – Historic Scotland

laird – estate owner

linn – waterfall

loch – lake

lochan – small *loch*

machair – grass- and wildflower-covered dunes

makar – maker of verses

Mercat Cross – a symbol of the trading rights of a market town or village, usually found in the centre of town and usually a focal point for the community

motte – early Norman fortification consisting of a raised, flattened mound with a keep on top; when attached to a *bailey* it is known as a motte-and-bailey

Munro – mountain of 3000ft (914m) or higher

Munro bagger – a hill walker who tries to climb all the *Munros* in Scotland

NNR – National Nature Reserve, managed by the *SNH*

NTS – National Trust for Scotland

nyvaig – Hebridean galley

OS – Ordnance Survey

Picts – early inhabitants of north and east Scotland (from Latin *pictus*, or 'painted', after their body paint decorations)

provost – mayor

RIB – rigid inflatable boat

rood – an old Scots word for a cross

RSPB – Royal Society for the Protection of Birds

Sassenach – from Gaelic 'Sasannach': anyone who is not a Highlander (including Lowland Scots)

shinty – fast and physical ball-and-stick sport similar to Ireland's hurling

SMC – Scottish Mountaineering Club

SNH – Scottish Natural Heritage, a government organisation directly responsible for safeguarding and improving Scotland's natural heritage

sporran – purse worn around waist with the kilt

SYHA – Scottish Youth Hostel Association

wynd – lane

GAELIC & NORSE PLACE NAMES

The Gaelic language has left a rich legacy of place names, often intermixed with Old Norse names brought by the Vikings who occupied the western and northern islands. The spellings may be Anglicised, but the meaning is usually still clear.

Gaelic Place Names

ach, auch	from *achadh* (field)
ard	from *ard* or *aird* (height, hill)
avon	from *abhainn* (river or stream)
bal	from *baile* (village or homestead)
ban	from *ban* (white, fair)
beg	from *beag* (small)
ben	from *beinn* (mountain)
buie	from *buidhe* (yellow)
dal	from *dail* (field or dale)
dow, dhu	from *dubh* (black)
drum	from *druim* (ridge or back)
dun	from *dun* or *duin* (fort or castle)
glen	from *gleann* (narrow valley)
gorm	from *gorm* (blue)
gower, gour	from *gabhar* (goat), eg Ardgour (height of the goats)
inch, insh	from *inis* (island, water-meadow or resting place for cattle)
inver	from *inbhir* (rivermouth or meeting of two rivers)
kil	from *cille* (church), eg Kilmartin (Church of St Martin)
kin, ken	from *ceann* (head), eg Kinlochleven (head of Loch Leven)
kyle, kyles	from *caol* or *caolas* (narrow sea channel)
more, vore	from *mor* or *mhor* (big), eg Ardmore (big height), Skerryvore (big reef)
strath	from *srath* (broad valley)
tarbert, tarbet	from *tairbeart* (portage), meaning a narrow neck of land between two bodies of water, across which a boat can be dragged
tay, ty	from *tigh* (house), eg Tyndrum (house on the ridge)
tober	from *tobar* (well), eg Tobermory (Mary's well)
tom	small hill

Norse Place Names

a, ay, ey	from *ey* (island)
bister, buster, bster	from *bolstaor* (dwelling place, homestead)
geo	from *gja* (chasm)
holm	from *holmr* (small island)
kirk	from *kirkja* (church)
pol, poll, bol	from *bol* (farm)
quoy	from *kvi* (sheep fold, cattle enclosure)
sker, skier, skerry	from *sker* (rocky reef)
ster, sett	from *setr* (house)
vig, vaig, wick	from *vik* (bay, creek)
voe, way	from *vagr* (bay, creek)

Behind the Scenes

SEND US YOUR FEEDBACK

We love to hear from travellers – your comments keep us on our toes and help make our books better. Our well-travelled team reads every word on what you loved or loathed about this book. Although we cannot reply individually to your submissions, we always guarantee that your feedback goes straight to the appropriate authors. Each person who sends us information is thanked in the next edition – the most useful submissions are rewarded with a selection of digital PDF chapters. Visit **lonelyplanet.com/contact** to submit your updates and suggestions or to ask for help. Our award-winning website also features inspirational travel stories, news and discussions.

Note: We may edit, reproduce and incorporate your comments in Lonely Planet products such as guidebooks, websites and digital products, so let us know if you don't want your comments reproduced or your name acknowledged. For a copy of our privacy policy visit lonelyplanet.com/privacy.

OUR READERS

Many thanks to the travellers who used the last edition and wrote to us with helpful hints and useful advice: Adrienne Murray Nielsen, Andreas Schoenherr, Babette van Dongen, Carrie Evje, Danielle Menzies, Ferdinand Sander, Hui Syn Chan, Ian Stafford, Ivan McMorris, Joseph Stevens, Marta Pelle, Molly Hoyt, Ruth Jenkins, Scott Thornton

WRITER THANKS

Neil Wilson

Thanks to the friendly and helpful tourist office staff all over the Highlands; to Steven Fallon, Keith Jeffrey, Fiona Garven, Derek McCrindle, Brendan Bolland, Jenny Neil, Tom and Christine Duffin, Steve Hall, Elaine Simpson, Peter Fallon and Duncan Pepper; and, as ever, to Carol Downie. Thanks also to James Smart and the editorial team at Lonely Planet.

Andy Symington

It's always a huge pleasure to enjoy the very generous hospitality of Jenny Neil and Brendan Bolland, and to work with Neil Wilson, Cliff Wilkinson and the excellent LP team. Numerous other people have been very generous with time and information. I'd particularly like to thank Robin Mitchell, Maggie Maguire,

Graeme Campbell, Jen Stewart and the staff at many tourist information offices, especially Judith and Janice at Bowmore, Sheona at John O'Groats, Susan at Callander and Neil at Kirkwall.

Sophie McGrath

Thanks to Elaine Carmichael, Claire Dutton, Caroline Wight and Anna Young of the Lothians' tourist boards for your helpful suggestions, and to Cliff Wilkinson for entrusting me with my first content update and graciously answering all my questions. Thank you Sean McMahon and Diana Marosi for getting my trip off to the nicest possible start, and my wonderful brother for keeping me company at the end (altogether now: 'Inspector...'). To my whole family, thank you for your love and support.

ACKNOWLEDGEMENTS

Climate map data adapted from Peel MC, Finlayson BL & McMahon TA (2007) 'Updated World Map of the Köppen-Geiger Climate Classification', Hydrology and Earth System Sciences, 11, 163344.

Illustrations p56-7, p102-3 and p182-3 by Javier Zarracina.

Cover photograph: Davidson in old colours tartan, cloth woven and kilt made by Geoffrey (Tailor) Kiltmakers; Matteo Carassale/4Corners ©

THIS BOOK

This 10th edition of Lonely Planet's *Scotland* guidebook was curated by Neil Wilson, and researched and written by Neil, Andy Symington and Sophie McGrath. The previous two editions were written by Neil Wilson and Andy Symington.

Destination Editors James Smart, Clifton Wilkinson
Senior Product Editor Genna Patterson
Product Editor Will Allen
Senior Cartographer Mark Griffiths
Book Designer Clara Monitto
Assisting Editors Sarah Bailey, Michelle Bennett, Katie Connolly, Nigel Chin, Michelle Coxall, Victoria Harrison, Kellie Langdon, Kristin Odijk, Maja Vatrić
Assisting Cartographer Rachel Imeson
Cover Researcher Naomi Parker
Thanks to Imogen Bannister, Andi Jones, Anne Mason

Index

Map Pages **000**
Photo Pages **000**

Map Legend

Sights

- Beach
- Bird Sanctuary
- Buddhist
- Castle/Palace
- Christian
- Confucian
- Hindu
- Islamic
- Jain
- Jewish
- Monument
- Museum/Gallery/Historic Building
- Ruin
- Shinto
- Sikh
- Taoist
- Winery/Vineyard
- Zoo/Wildlife Sanctuary
- Other Sight

Activities, Courses & Tours

- Bodysurfing
- Diving
- Canoeing/Kayaking
- Course/Tour
- Sento Hot Baths/Onsen
- Skiing
- Snorkelling
- Surfing
- Swimming/Pool
- Walking
- Windsurfing
- Other Activity

Sleeping

- Sleeping
- Camping
- Hut/Shelter

Eating

- Eating

Drinking & Nightlife

- Drinking & Nightlife
- Cafe

Entertainment

- Entertainment

Shopping

- Shopping

Information

- Bank
- Embassy/Consulate
- Hospital/Medical
- Internet
- Police
- Post Office
- Telephone
- Toilet
- Tourist Information
- Other Information

Geographic

- Beach
- Gate
- Hut/Shelter
- Lighthouse
- Lookout
- Mountain/Volcano
- Oasis
- Park
- Pass
- Picnic Area
- Waterfall

Population

- Capital (National)
- Capital (State/Province)
- City/Large Town
- Town/Village

Transport

- Airport
- Border crossing
- Bus
- Cable car/Funicular
- Cycling
- Ferry
- Metro station
- Monorail
- Parking
- Petrol station
- S-Bahn/Subway station
- Taxi
- T-bane/Tunnelbana station
- Train station/Railway
- Tram
- Tube station
- U-Bahn/Underground station
- Other Transport

Routes

- Tollway
- Freeway
- Primary
- Secondary
- Tertiary
- Lane
- Unsealed road
- Road under construction
- Plaza/Mall
- Steps
- Tunnel
- Pedestrian overpass
- Walking Tour
- Walking Tour detour
- Path/Walking Trail

Boundaries

- International
- State/Province
- Disputed
- Regional/Suburb
- Marine Park
- Cliff
- Wall

Hydrography

- River, Creek
- Intermittent River
- Canal
- Water
- Dry/Salt/Intermittent Lake
- Reef

Areas

- Airport/Runway
- Beach/Desert
- Cemetery (Christian)
- Cemetery (Other)
- Glacier
- Mudflat
- Park/Forest
- Sight (Building)
- Sportsground
- Swamp/Mangrove

Note: Not all symbols displayed above appear on the maps in this book

OUR STORY

A beat-up old car, a few dollars in the pocket and a sense of adventure. In 1972 that's all Tony and Maureen Wheeler needed for the trip of a lifetime – across Europe and Asia overland to Australia. It took several months, and at the end – broke but inspired – they sat at their kitchen table writing and stapling together their first travel guide, *Across Asia on the Cheap*. Within a week they'd sold 1500 copies. Lonely Planet was born.

Today, Lonely Planet has offices in Franklin, London, Melbourne, Oakland, Dublin, Beijing and Delhi, with more than 600 staff and writers. We share Tony's belief that 'a great guidebook should do three things: inform, educate and amuse'.

OUR WRITERS

Neil Wilson

Edinburgh, Central Scotland, Northeast Scotland, Inverness & the Central Highlands, Northern Highlands & Islands Neil was born in Scotland and has lived there most of his life. Based in Perthshire, he has been a full-time writer since 1988, working on more than 80 guidebooks for various publishers, including the Lonely Planet guides to Scotland, England, Ireland and Prague. An outdoors enthusiast since childhood, Neil is an active hill-walker, mountain-biker, sailor, snowboarder, fly-fisher and rock-climber, and has climbed and tramped in four continents, including ascents of Jebel Toubkal in Morocco, Mount Kinabalu in Borneo, the Old Man of Hoy in Scotland's Orkney Islands and the Regular Northwest Face of Half Dome in California's Yosemite Valley.

Andy Symington

Glasgow, Southern Scotland, Southern Highlands & Islands, Northern Highlands & Islands, Orkney & Shetland Andy has written or worked on over a hundred books and other updates for Lonely Planet (especially in Europe and Latin America) and other publishing companies, and has published articles on numerous subjects for a variety of newspapers, magazines, and websites. He part-owns and operates a rock bar, has written a novel and is currently working on several fiction and non-fiction writing projects. Originally from Australia, Andy moved to northern Spain many years ago.

Sophie McGrath

Around Edinburgh Sophie is a London-based travel writer who has written for many UK publications. Formerly on staff at Lonely Planet magazine, she was named 2017 AITO Young Travel Writer of the Year. Her most memorable adventures include chasing the Northern Lights in Norway, getting stranded on a mountain in China and falling head over heels for Addis Ababa, Ethiopia. This is her first destination update for Lonely Planet.

Published by Lonely Planet Global Limited
CRN 554153
10th edition – April 2019
ISBN 978 1 78657 803 7
© Lonely Planet 2019   Photographs © as indicated 2019
10 9 8 7 6 5 4 3 2 1
Printed in China